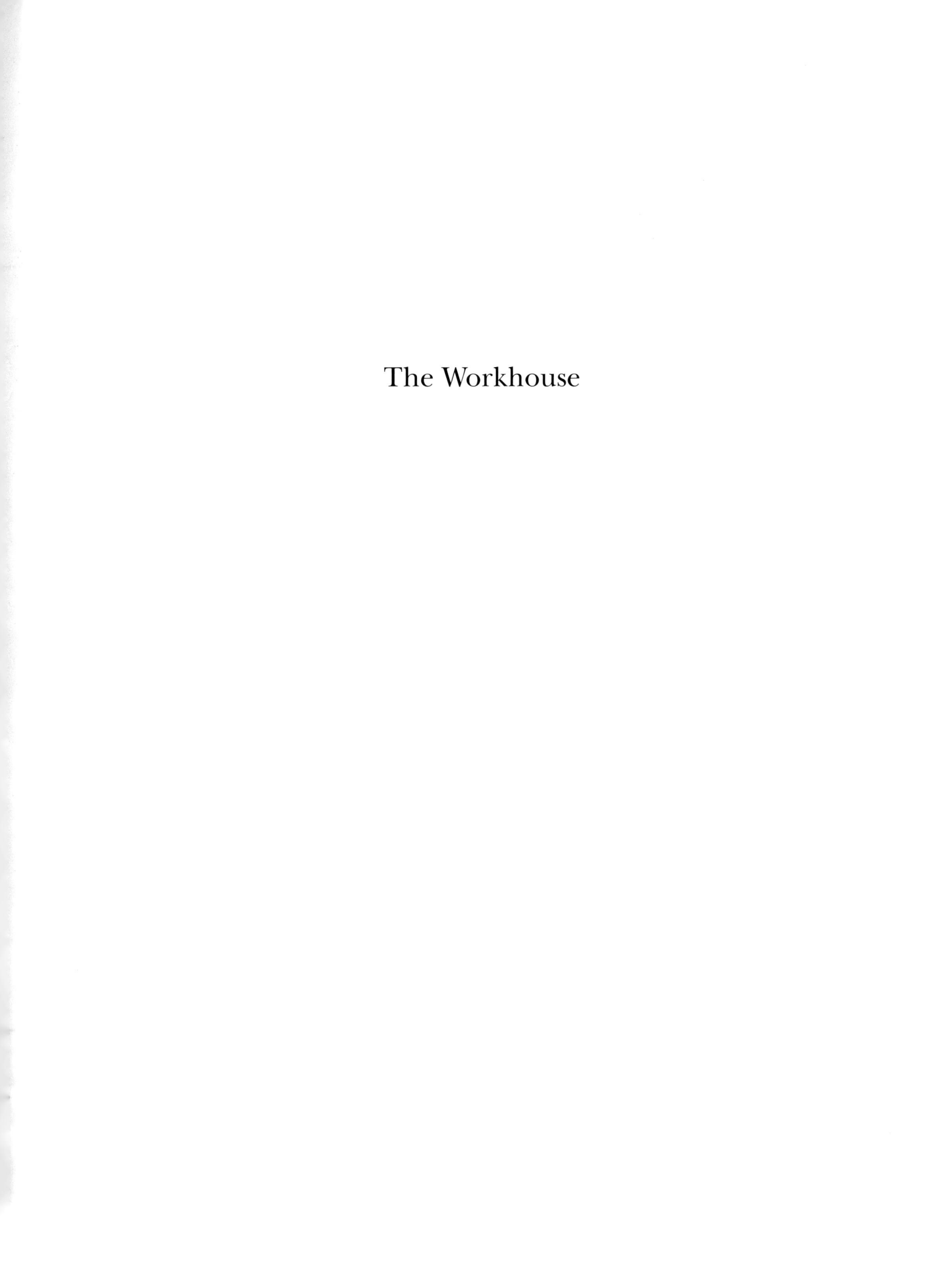

The Workhouse

Female paupers at Leeds Union Workhouse [St James's Hospital, Leeds]

ENGLISH HERITAGE

The Workhouse

A STUDY OF POOR-LAW BUILDINGS IN ENGLAND

by
Kathryn Morrison

ROYAL COMMISSION ON THE HISTORICAL MONUMENTS OF ENGLAND

Published by English Heritage at the National Monuments Record Centre,
Kemble Drive, Swindon SN2 2GZ

© English Heritage 1999
Images (except as otherwise shown) © Crown copyright 1999

Applications for the reproduction of images should be made to the
National Monuments Record

The Royal Commission on the Historical Monuments of England and
English Heritage merged on 1 April 1999

First published 1999

ISBN 1 873592 36 1

British Library Cataloguing in Publication Data
A CIP catalogue record for this book is available from the British Library

All rights reserved
No part of this publication may be reproduced or transmitted in any form
or by any means, electronic or mechanical, including photocopying,
recording or any information storage and retrieval system, without
permission in writing from the publisher.

Designed by Chuck Goodwin, 27 Artesian Road, London W2 5DA

Printed in Great Britain by BAS Printers, Over Wallop, Hampshire

Contents

	Foreword	vii
	Acknowledgements	viii
	Illustration Credits	ix
	Glossary of Terms	x
	Introduction	xi
1	The Building Evidence	1
2	Old Poor Law Institutions, *c* 1550–1750	3
3	Old Poor Law Institutions, *c* 1750–1834	21
4	The New Poor Law of 1834	43
5	New Poor Law Workhouses, 1835–1840	53
6	Corridor-Plan Workhouses, 1840–1870	85
7	Separate-Block Workhouses, 1870–1914	103
8	Poor-Law Buildings for Children	131
9	Poor-Law Buildings for the Sick, the Mentally Ill and the Mentally Handicapped	155
10	Poor-Law Buildings for Vagrants and the 'Houseless Poor'	179
11	The Workhouse after 1914	189
12	Conclusion: The Changing Role of the Poor-Law Institution in English Society	192
	Appendix 1 The Study of Poor-Law Buildings	197
	Appendix 2	
	Catalogue A: Poor-Law Institutions Outside Metropolitan London (post-1834)	201
	Catalogue B: Poor-Law Institutions for Metropolitan London (post-1834)	214
	Appendix 3 Model Plans issued by the Central Poor-Law Authority	221
	Notes and References	230
	Bibliography	240
	Index	244

Foreword

The English poor law is receding from living memory, yet many of its buildings still stand, bearing testament to the grim power the system once wielded over generations of destitute men, women and children. After 1930, most workhouses and infirmaries were transformed into municipal hospitals, or homes for the elderly and mentally handicapped, while children's homes and schools continued to function much as before. The threat of wholesale closure only confronted these institutions in the 1980s, with the reorganisation of National Health Service provision for the sick and elderly, and the widespread adoption of 'care in the community' policies for children and the mentally handicapped. Closure was inevitably followed by decay or redevelopment and, in many cases, by demolition.

By the early 1990s it had become clear to the Royal Commission that these neglected buildings merited a national survey, and that the task would have to be completed with some urgency. Investigation and research were carried out in parallel to a national survey of hospitals and asylums, and resulted in the creation of over 700 site files.

It is difficult to present a case for the preservation of the majority of poor-law buildings: they are not examples of great or *avant garde* architecture and, by the 1980s, few could meet modern standards of comfort. They have, nevertheless, made an important contribution to the built environment of communities throughout England, and are crucial to the history of the poor. Their appearance and planning reflect contemporary attitudes and policies towards the needy and affected many thousands of pauper inmates.

This book explains how poor-law buildings developed from the small 'hospitals' and 'working-houses' of the 16th and 17th centuries to the parish workhouses and houses of industry of the 18th century, to the huge union workhouses and industrial schools of the Victorian era and to the more specialised institutions of the early 20th century. We believe that this book will throw additional light on one aspect of the lives of the poorest members of society, and will help those working with historic buildings to assess the significance of individual examples in a national context, ensuring that the most important are recognised and dealt with appropriately.

Commissioners are grateful to all who permitted access to former poor-law buildings in their care, especially to private owners and to NHS managers and staff. They also wish to acknowledge the work of RCHME staff involved in the survey, especially that of Kathryn Morrison, who was responsible for conceiving the project and for writing the book, and that of other members of the Hospitals Project team who undertook much of the fieldwork. They, and other members of staff involved in the project, are credited in the Acknowledgements.

FARINGDON
Former Chairman of the RCHME

Acknowledgements

The groundwork for this survey of poor-law buildings was carried out in the course of the Royal Commission Hospitals Project (1991–4), and particular thanks are due to my colleagues Ian Goodall, Jaqueline Hall, Ian Pattison, Harriet Richardson, Robert Taylor and Colin Thom, all of whom researched and recorded numerous workhouses and poor-law infirmaries at that time. Thanks are also due to Tina Garratt, who assisted with fieldwork and research, to Nick Hammond and Tony Berry for preparing publication drawings, and to the field photographers who contributed to the project (Sid Barker, Alun Bull, Steve Cole, James Davies, Len Furbank, Derek Kendall, Pat Payne, Tony Perry, Mike Hesketh-Roberts, Dank Silva, Bob Skingle, and Peter Williams). I am also grateful to two Commissioners, Dr Marilyn Palmer and Anne Riches, for reading the text and offering useful advice.

The project has greatly benefited from the co-operation of owners and occupiers of former poor-law buildings who gave us generous access to their property and imparted useful information about the history of the buildings. The staff of libraries and record offices throughout the country were invariably helpful and patient, especially those at the British Library, Cambridge University Library, London Metropolitan Archives and the Public Record Office.

The book has been brought to publication by Rachel Brown and Dr Robin Taylor. The text was edited and proof read by Susan Whimster. The design was by Chuck Goodwin and the index was prepared by Ann Hudson.

Illustration Credits

Unless otherwise specified below, illustrations are Crown copyright. The negative numbers are given in brackets at the end of the captions to assist reference and the ordering of prints from the National Monuments Record.

We gratefully acknowledge permission from the following institutions and individuals to reproduce illustrations:

The British Library: Figs 16, 47; The British Museum: Fig 12; Buckinghamshire Record Office: App 3 figs 14, 15; The Syndics of Cambridge University Library: Figs 4, 6, 7, 11, 17, 26, 29, 30, 44, 45, 63, 90, 99, 104, 110, 121, 122, 123, 131, 147, 152, 156, 158, 171, 185, 203, 210, 212, 234, 238, 240, App 3 figs 1–13, 16, 17; Guildhall Library, Corporation of London: Fig 2; Hulton Getty: Figs 112, 235, 236; Liverpool Record Office, Liverpool Libraries and Information Services: Fig 28; London Metropolitan Archives: Figs 15, 125, 130, 144, 150, 159, 175, 177, 189, 191, 194, 205, 206, 230; Metropolitan Borough of Rochdale Community Services Department: Fig 43; The Board of Trustees of the National Museums and Galleries on Merseyside (Walker Art Gallery, Liverpool): Fig 143; The Public Record Office: Figs 153, 157; Reading Museum: Fig 3; St James's Hospital, Leeds: frontis; Dorothy Thelwall: Figs 243, 244; Westcountry Studies Library, Devon Library Services: Fig 8; Wisbech and Fenland Museum: Fig 10; Witt Library, Courtauld Institute of Art: Fig 86.

Every effort has been made to trace copyright holders; we wish to apologise to any who may have been inadvertently omitted from the above list.

Notes on Drawings

Royal Commission draughtsmen used existing drawings to produce floor plans, sections, elevations and perspective views to illustrate this publication. While imperial measurements are used in the text, the drawings have scales in feet and metres.

Conversion Table
1 in. = 25.4 mm
1 ft (12 in.) = 304.8 mm
1 mile = 1.6 km
1 acre = 0.4 ha
1 cu ft = 0.0283 cu m

Glossary of Terms

Able-bodied pauper Rather than simply describing a pauper capable of work, this term was applied to all adults under 60 who did not suffer from a serious ailment, and included pregnant women, those suffering from temporary sickness, imbeciles and those with minor disabilities. The term, however, was never clearly defined by the central poor-law authority and was interpreted in a variety of ways.

Associate(d) ward Dormitory for vagrants.

Casual One in temporary need of relief, usually a vagrant or tramp but also the temporarily homeless and those travelling in search of work.

Cellular wards Cells for vagrants.

Deterrent workhouse A term current in the first half of the 19th century, describing a strict workhouse run by an authority which banned outdoor relief, thus deterring all but the genuinely destitute from seeking relief.

Fever A term embracing a number of different infectious diseases, including typhus, typhoid, scarlet fever and diphtheria, but generally excluding smallpox.

General mixed workhouse A workhouse housing all the different classes of pauper, including the aged and infirm, the able-bodied and children.

Guardians of the poor Name generally given to the body of men – and later women – elected or appointed to look after poor-law affairs in a parish, poor-law incorporation or union. Under an incorporation or union, one or more guardians were elected to represent each parish within the authority.

House of correction County or borough reformatory for petty criminals.

House of Industry A common term for 18th and early 19th-century workhouses, generally including 'manufactories' of woollens or cloths.

Idiot A term used to describe a mentally handicapped person.

Imbecile A term used to describe a mentally handicapped person.

Impotent pauper/poor A pauper incapable of work, including the aged and infirm, the permanently sick, infants, the mentally ill and some imbeciles.

Indoor relief Relief in an institution.

Ins and Outs A term applied to those who used the workhouse sporadically, often reflecting seasonal employment patterns.

Insane An umbrella term for lunatics and imbeciles, used by the central poor-law authority throughout the late 19th century.

Lavatory This term is used throughout the book to describe a washing place, not a toilet.

Less-eligibility This was one of the chief principles contained in the *Poor Law Report* of 1834. It meant that conditions inside the workhouse were to be made less comfortable, or 'eligible', than conditions outside.

Lunatic A term applied to those suffering from madness or mental illness.

Lying-in room/ward Room or ward for maternity or labour cases.

Mental defective This term replaced 'idiot' and 'imbecile' in the early 20th century.

Outdoor relief Relief, in the form of money, food, fuel or rent, given outside the workhouse.

Overseer of the poor This position existed from the late 16th century until 1834. The overseer of the poor was an unpaid poor-law officer, appointed to collect and distribute poor rates within a parish for the period of one year.

Pauper A person in receipt of relief financed from the poor rate, involving automatic disfranchisement.

Poorhouse A common term for workhouses at all times, implying an institution in which sheltering the poor was more important than setting them to work. Often with a high proportion of 'impotent' paupers.

Privy This term is generally applied to an earth closet, as opposed to a water closet.

Roundsman system A labourer in need of parish relief, who was sent round from one farmer to another for employment, partly at the expense of the farmer and partly at the cost of the parish.

Test workhouse Generally current in the late 19th and early 20th century. A workhouse with a harsh regime, usually involving long hours of solitary, tedious labour, to deter the able-bodied from seeking relief.

Vagrant wards Rooms at a workhouse where tramps or travellers were accommodated for short periods of time.

Workhouse test The use of the workhouse to test a person's destitution, by offering admission to the workhouse as the sole means of relief.

Introduction

This study of workhouses, and other buildings erected under the English poor-law system, emerged from an earlier RCHME project on hospitals and asylums which was carried out between 1991 and 1995. In the course of the Hospitals Project, staff based in Cambridge, London and York visited and recorded numerous poor-law sites, but concentrated on their infirmary elements. The realisation that all types of former poor-law institutions – not just infirmaries – were threatened by the rationalisation of the National Health Service and the adoption of 'care in the community' policies, and evidence that they formed a poorly understood category of buildings, prompted the Royal Commission to undertake a programme of further fieldwork and research from the Cambridge Office between 1995 and 1997. The result is this book, and an archive of over 700 files.

The range of institutions embraced by the poor-law buildings project includes workhouses, infirmaries, industrial schools and children's homes. The first poor-law institutions were established soon after the Dissolution of the Monasteries, but few occupied purpose-built premises before the early 18th century. As a result, most of the sites investigated in the course of the project were founded between the 18th century and 1930, the year in which the poor law was abolished. One of the principal aims of the project was to create a written and photographic record of extant sites before the majority were demolished or redeveloped. It was impossible to create a comprehensive record, but a sample of well-preserved sites throughout England was selected for fieldwork and photography. Historical research was conducted for all sites, including those which had been demolished or rebuilt, permitting this book to consider the development of poor-law institutions and their buildings from the 16th century onward.

The catalogues at the end of this book list every poor-law authority set up in England following the passage of the Poor Law Amendment Act of 1834. As they are meant to function as tools for historical research, as well as indices to the archive, the catalogues are arranged according to old (pre-1974) counties, with the exception of Metropolitan London, which was always treated as a special entity by the central poor-law authority. The institutions set up by each authority are listed with information about their function, location, date and architect, whenever that is known. The archive files for these sites typically contain a short written report, notes and extracts from documentary sources, copies of first, second or third edition 1:2500 Ordnance Survey maps, ground and aerial photographs. Most of these files may be consulted in the National Monuments Record at the National Monuments Record Centre, Kemble Drive, Swindon SN2 2GZ (telephone 01793 414600), but those for Greater London are held in our London Office, at 55 Blandford Street, London W1H 3AF (telephone 0171 208 8200).

1
The Building Evidence

Our cities, towns, villages and countryside are still peppered with buildings which were erected to serve the English poor law. For generations these workhouses, infirmaries and children's homes accommodated people who, through destitution or an inability to care for themselves, had been forced to seek assistance from the poor rates. Amongst them were orphaned and abandoned children, the physically and mentally sick, the disabled, the elderly, the mentally handicapped, unmarried mothers, the unemployed and the plain disreputable. As inmates of a poor-law institution, or 'indoor paupers', people were segregated according to their sex, age, health and character. They were compelled to submit to the grinding monotony of institutional routine: their hours of waking and sleeping, their diet, their clothing and their work were subjected to close control. Theoretically, adults were free to quit the workhouse at short notice, but with no alternative means of subsistence many were only released by death. The system operated through shame and fear: the spectre of the workhouse was designed to spur men on to work hard to maintain their families and to save against the possibility of hard times to come. For those existing on the borderline of poverty, with no regular work and no hope of saving, that spectre was very substantial indeed. The stigma associated with workhouses is remembered to the present day although the administrative basis of the poor law was disbanded as long ago as 1930, when institutions were handed over to county and county borough councils. Eighteen years later many former workhouses and infirmaries passed into the hands of the newly created National Health Service. These key events in the transition from poor law to welfare state were marked by superficial changes in the names of institutions, and by more profound changes in the official attitude towards the destitute, yet day-to-day life in most institutions remained unaffected. In some cases the same staff continued to care for the same long-term inmates in the same buildings, while in others staff and patients were simply redistributed to create more specialised institutions. The best infirmaries, as well as workhouses with a substantial infirmary component, became general hospitals, while more old-fashioned workhouses became specialist 'hospitals' for geriatrics or the mentally handicapped. To a degree, the rehabilitation of former poor-law institutions was hampered by the retention of elements of the old workhouse system. In particular, some hospitals maintained vagrant wards and continued to provide a refuge for unmarried mothers well into the 1950s.

In recent years, all categories of former poor-law building have fallen victim to central and local government policies. The restructuring of the health service, including the removal of elderly patients from National Health Service geriatric hospitals into private nursing homes and the centralisation of general hospital provision, together with a policy of 'care in the community' for children and the mentally handicapped, has led to the closure of numerous local hospitals and children's homes. As a result, many former workhouse sites have been abandoned, and subsequently demolished or redeveloped, often as housing or, ironically, private nursing homes. The structural remnants of the poor law are fast disappearing from our urban and rural landscape, or being transformed beyond recognition.

In terms of architectural impact, few poor-law buildings can vie with contemporary institutions such as prisons, asylums, schools or voluntary hospitals. They were not given highly visible positions in urban centres, but lurked on the outskirts of towns, on back streets or in open countryside. The guardians of the poor were concerned with economy and decorum, and generally commissioned local architects to produce cheap, unpretentious buildings with no superfluous ornamentation. Even the most attractive buildings, including a few highly decorative mid-Victorian workhouses and stylish Arts & Crafts cottage-home villages, were scarcely in the *avant garde*. Moreover, generations of institutional users have wreaked havoc with their appearance: doors and windows have been cheaply and haphazardly replaced, intrusive sanitary towers and lift shafts have been added, machine-made tiles have replaced slates, and roofs have been denuded of chimneys and ventilators.

In most cases, the chief value and interest of these buildings resides in their expression of contemporary poor-law policy which, whether benign or censorious, informed their external appearance and internal planning. The fact that buildings are central to our understanding of the English poor law may be insufficient to ensure their preservation, but it justifies the process of recording them and analysing their historical development. That, however, has been neglected, and considering the wealth of published material on the poor law it is surprising that no comprehensive study of poor-law buildings already exists.

The present study aims to piece together the story of how poor-law buildings evolved throughout the 350 years of the English poor law, in response to changing social and economic conditions as much as to the changing policies of governments, philanthropists and local worthies. While narrating that story, the following chapters will demonstrate that even buildings which are cheaply constructed and devoid of ornamentation can make a great contribution to our understanding of past society.

2
Old Poor Law Institutions, *c* 1550–1750

The Old Poor Law, requiring individual parishes throughout England to relieve their own poor and set able-bodied paupers to work, evolved through a series of late-Tudor statutes, culminating in the definitive 'Act of Elizabeth' of 1601.[1] Parishes financed their new responsibilities by levying a poor rate, a local tax on householders, which was collected and distributed by unsalaried, and often unwilling, overseers of the poor. By 1640 many urban parishes were using the poor rate both to shelter children and the aged in 'hospitals' and to employ those capable in 'working-houses' or with local employers. As they were also obliged to punish those who refused to work, buildings adapted as hospitals or working-houses often included, or lay adjacent to, a house of correction or bridewell. Workhouses of the 17th century, however, never became places of residence for those unemployed poor who were willing to work.

At the beginning of the 18th century, the idea that poverty could be blamed on idle and indulgent habits, rather than on independent economic factors, hardened attitudes towards able-bodied paupers. That led the parishes of several towns to band together under expensive local acts and set up large residential workhouses. It also inspired Knatchbull's Act of 1723, which empowered individual parishes throughout the country to offer able-bodied applicants a place in a workhouse as a condition of receiving relief.[2] Although many parishes had recourse to a workhouse after 1723, few adopted totally inflexible relief practices, and various methods of indoor and outdoor relief generally coexisted. By the middle of the century, however, parish-based administration was being subjected to severe criticism, stimulating a rash of proposals for poor-law reform.

Most of the workhouse buildings which survive from the period covered in this chapter, *c* 1550 to 1750, were erected in the 18th century. Despite the dissemination of the designs of two 'model' workhouses in 1726, there was no standard form of institution. Indeed, the size and appearance of Old Poor Law workhouses were just as varied as the objectives which motivated their foundation and the regimes which operated inside them. While many parish workhouses were no more than adapted cottages or farmhouses, those serving larger areas could assume the formality, and pretension of grandeur, of contemporary civic architecture. Large or small, the design of the building seldom assisted the governor to supervise or control the inmates, merely permitting a basic separation of the sexes.

The condemnation of the 'general mixed workhouses' of the Old Poor Law in the *Poor Law Report* of 1834 was echoed by social commentators well into the 20th century.[3] According to the most influential of these, Sidney and Beatrice Webb, 'the overcrowding, insanitation, filth and gross indecency of workhouse life during the whole of the eighteenth, and even for the first thirty or forty years of the nineteenth century are simply indescribable'.[4] However, standards were not universally bad. Some Old Poor Law workhouses undoubtedly were overcrowded, dirty and ill-disciplined, but others provided their inmates – or 'family' – with a much cleaner and more comfortable environment, as well as a more nourishing diet, than many of the poor could afford through their own efforts.

Hospitals and Working-Houses in the 16th and 17th Centuries

The emergence of a poor law can be attributed to numerous socio-economic factors. In the mid-16th century poverty was exacerbated by population growth, the conversion of arable land to pasture, migration and inflation. The feudal ties of medieval society had loosened some time before and traditional sources of relief, such as the Church and private charity, were proving unable to meet the ever-expanding needs of the poor. Monasteries, significant distributors of alms throughout the medieval period, had been dissolved in the 1530s and 1540s. Many hospitals, almshouses and guilds with religious associations were also suppressed, and it was some time before secular benefactors took over their social responsibilities. In many cases, the destitute had no alternative but to quit their usual place of residence and resort to a life of wandering and begging. It was in an effort to curb persistent vagrancy, long considered a threat to the social and economic stability of the nation, that Parliament laid increasing responsibility for the poor on the shoulders of parochial authorities.

A compulsory parish poor rate was introduced only when persuasion failed. An Act of 1536 ordered churchwardens to collect voluntary alms 'towards relieving the said poor, needy, sick, sore, and indigent persons, and also towards setting in work the said sturdy and idle vagabonds and valiant beggars'.[5] Several parish churches throughout the country still possess the poor boxes (Fig 1) which were set up specifically for that purpose in the 16th and 17th centuries. Reluctance to offer alms made it necessary to introduce a compulsory poor rate in London in 1547, in Norwich in 1549 and in both Colchester and Ipswich in 1557, but for some time these remained isolated cases.[6] From 1563, recalcitrant alms-givers could be assessed for compulsory contributions,[7] and finally, in 1572, Justices were instructed to compile a register of 'all aged, poor, impotent and decayed persons' in their divisions and to tax and assess all householders for their relief.[8] The poor rate was now to be collected by specially appointed, but unpaid, overseers of the poor. By the end of the century, poor-law administration had been placed firmly on a parish footing, with overseers assuming full responsibility for the collection as well as the distribution of relief.

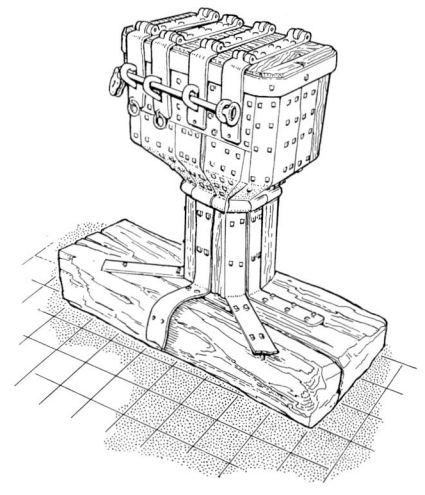

Figure 1
Boxes to collect alms for the poor were placed in many churches during the 16th and 17th centuries. This one is from Holy Trinity Church, Loddon, in Norfolk.

Before the 1550s there is little evidence that poor rates were invested in the institutionalisation or systematic employment of the poor. The first influential move in that direction was the establishment of four Royal Hospitals in the City of London. The sick and aged were cared for in St Bartholomew's Hospital (refounded 1546) and St Thomas's Hospital (refounded 1551), orphans over the age of 4 were maintained and educated in Christ's Hospital (refounded 1553), and vagrants and prostitutes were punished and set to work in Bridewell (founded 1555). In addition, Bethlehem Hospital, or 'Bedlam' served as a small lunatic asylum for the poor. These five hospitals were funded by charitable endowments, monthly parish collections, levies on the livery companies and the revenues of a suppressed hospital which had been based in the former Savoy Palace. None can be considered a template for future workhouses, but Bridewell became the institutional model for numerous houses of correction throughout the country.[9] Under the original scheme of its founders, part of Bridewell was to function as a training school for pauper children, but that did not develop for some years. The reformatory ambitions of the institution, rather than its corrective intent, allow it to be regarded as the forerunner of those 17th and early 18th-century English workhouses which concentrated on the moral and industrial training of poor children, yet existed in association with a house of correction for habitual idlers. In an architectural sense, however, Bridewell (Fig 2), a former royal palace, had little influence over later establishments.

The London hospitals inspired the foundation of several less specialised provincial establishments which combined the reformatory and training aspects of Bridewell and Christ's Hospital with the more benevolent functions of almshouses and orphanages. Christ's Hospital in Ipswich was set up in 1569, on the site of Blackfriars, as an asylum for the old, a training school for the young and a house of correction.[10] By 1578, the former house of Greyfriars in Reading was being used by the council as a 'hospital' for both children and old people.[11] Several other late 16th-century 'hospitals' for the old and young, including those in York and Norwich, also occupied confiscated church or guild property. With such buildings abounding throughout England, there was little need to erect expensive new structures.

Parishes were encouraged to spend some of their poor rates in setting the able-bodied unemployed to work. From 1576, Justices were permitted to buy or hire buildings and equip

Figure 2
The Tudor palace of Bridewell was burnt down by the Great Fire and rebuilt in 1676. This engraving of 1818 shows the palace as it might have appeared c 1660 and, in the vignette at the bottom, c 1540.
[Guildhall Library]

them with a stock of wool, hemp, flax, iron or other materials to set the poor to work so that they 'shall not for want of work go abroad either begging, or committing pilferings, or . . . living in idleness'.[12] The poor worked on these materials in a workshop or in their own homes; those refusing to work were sent to a house of correction, 'there to be straightly kept as well in diet as in work, and also punished from time to time'.[13]

Few examples of late 16th-century parish workshops are known. By 1577 Linton in Cambridgeshire had established a 'Taske House' as well as a 'Hospital', which occupied part of the guildhall.[14] In 1582 Cambridge proposed to build 'a house to set pore men on works in and of reformacion for Iddle persons', and a building with a similar purpose was set up in Bury St Edmunds in 1589.[15] In December 1591 the Corporation of Reading decreed that Greyfriars Hospital be 'converted to a house of correction, as well for the setting of the poore people to worke . . . for their reliefes . . . as also for the punishinge and correctinge of idle and vagrant persons'.[16] Parish workshops and houses of correction continued to be closely associated in this way, or even confused, throughout the 17th century. For example, the house of correction erected in 1622 at Tothill Fields, Westminster, also functioned as 'a house to set the poor of the parish on work'.[17]

One other class of poor-law building to emerge in this period was the paupers' cottage. From 1601 parishes could erect cottages on waste ground for the use of the poor.[18] Throughout the 17th and 18th centuries other properties were given to parishes by the friendless poor in exchange for meeting their wants during old age. Parishes frequently allowed paupers to live in such properties rent free, thus dealing with the problem of the houseless poor. Indeed, it is often difficult to know whether mention of a 'poor house' or 'house of the poor' in contemporary documents refers to cottages such as these, or to a workhouse.[19]

Despite the existence of permissive legislation,[20] few parishes had bothered to institute a poor rate or 'set their poor on work' by the early 17th century. *Greevous Grones for the Poore*, a pamphlet published in 1622, claimed that parishes merely 'turneth forth their poor . . . to beg, filch and steal for their maintenance so that the country is pitifully pestered by them'.[21] Prior to the Civil War, three initiatives encouraged the implementation of the poor laws: from 1608 Justices were obliged to establish a house of correction in every county and borough; in 1623 an Act was passed to encourage 'the erecting of Hospitals and Working-houses for the Poor' and, in 1630, Charles I instructed a select committee of the Privy Council, known as the

Figure 3
The Oracle in Reading was built in 1625–8 as a workhouse for unemployed textile workers. This engraving, based on a view by Grimm, shows the building in April 1778. Although it was later demolished, its carved wooden gates are displayed in the Museum of Reading, and the site has been excavated.
[Copyright Reading Museum (Reading Borough Council). All rights reserved]

Commissioners for the Poor, to investigate the execution of the poor laws throughout the country and to ensure their proper administration at every level of local government.[22]

The new legislation was effective, and by the eve of the Civil War the Elizabethan poor laws had been put into operation in many English towns.[23] One of the first was Dorchester which, in 1617, set up a 'hospital or working-house', bearing the grand title 'Hospital of the Bailiffs and Burgesses of the Borough of Dorchester in the County of Dorset', in which fifty poor children were taught a trade by a governor and matron, and the idle poor were set to work.[24] The site, formerly six burgages on the west side of the High Street, contained the 'mansion house' of John Coke, a fustian-weaver who was appointed first governor of the hospital.

The Act of 1623 encouraged charitable donations which allowed other towns to follow the example of Dorchester. Many of these new establishments, however, had no 'hospital' element and were little more than workshops, or workhouses. At that time the term 'workhouse' signified no more than 'a house, shop, or room in which work is regularly performed; a workshop or factory'.[25] In the 17th century, workhouses were generally concerned with textile manufacture, and were mostly set up in towns where there was no opportunity to send paupers to work for local farmers, tradesmen or manufacturers. As well as providing work for unemployed textile workers, they provided a means of training the unskilled, thus better equipping them to earn their own living. While vagrants and petty offenders were incarcerated in houses of correction for a set term, the ordinary pauper was free to set off home from the workhouse at the close of each day, like any independent labourer.

In 1623, the Lord Mayor and Aldermen of London unsuccessfully attempted to promote a scheme devised by the President of Bridewell, Sir Thomas Middleton, whereby parishes would group together to build hemp and flax houses to provide local employment.[26] A year later, a woollen draper, John Kendrick, bequeathed £7,500 to Reading and £4,000 to Newbury for similar purposes.[27] Each town was to use part of the money to provide a house 'fit and commodious for setting of the poor to work therein, with a fair garden adjoining'.[28] In 1625, Reading Corporation purchased a house for £2,000, and by 1628 it had been enlarged and converted into an establishment for poor clothiers (Fig 3). The amount of new building work undertaken is indicated by the number of bricks and tiles supplied by a local brickmaker, 200,000 and 20,000 respectively. The establishment, known as 'The Oracle', comprised a courtyard surrounded by ranges of workshops, through which ran the Holy Brook.[29] Its fine stone gateway was flanked by Corinthian columns and surmounted by a Dutch gable.

Soon similar schemes were established in other large textile towns. In 1628 Sheffield spent £200, a sizeable sum, on building a workhouse.[30] In the same year a carrier named Hobson conveyed a site in St Andrew's Street, Cambridge to twelve trustees, for the purpose of erecting a combined workhouse and house of correction; his will of 1630 stipulated that the building, 'in great part erected and built', be completed within four years.[31] By the mid-18th century it was 'chiefly used for the confinement of such lewd women as the Proctors apprehend in houses of ill-fame . . . and the crier of the town is often there to discipline the ladies of pleasure with his whip'.[32] Despite this, the building, known as the 'Spinning House' (Fig 4), provided employment for textile workers as well as correction for vagrants until 1807.

Towns continued to set up workhouses throughout the 1630s.[33] Taunton and Abingdon operated newly erected workhouses in 1631, and one was approved for Totnes in 1632.[34] In 1635, Halifax was given a large house by a gentleman, Nathaniel Waterhouse, to be used as a workhouse.[35] Others were set up in Salisbury (1638),[36] St Thomas, Exeter (1638)[37] and Plymouth (1640). But workhouses were not confined to towns: in 1635 the Justices of Little Holland in Lincolnshire reported that in 'all our severall parishes we have a Towne stocke with a workhouse, a master and utensills and that there hath been above 200 poore people set on worke and employed weekly by the officers'.[38]

The first workhouses in London were set up by the Corporation of the Poor, which was established by parliamentary ordinance of 1647 and 1649 and endured until the Restoration in 1660.[39] This move was heralded by a number of pamphlets, advocating workhouses in which the poor could be trained as well as employed. In 1646, a timely reprint of an earlier tract, *Staneye's Remedy*, complained about the absence of such institutions:

> The poor may be whipped to death and branded for rogues . . . before any private man will set them to work or provide houses for labour . . . I have heard the rogues and beggars curse the magistrate unto their faces for providing such a law to whip and brand them and not provide houses of labour for them; for surely many will go voluntarily to workhouses to work, if such houses were provided for them.[40]

Pamphleteers such as Samuel Hartlib and Rice Bush seem to have conceived these workhouses on the model of Dorchester. Only the impotent poor, such as children, would have been resident, and the buildings would have included a 'Generall Store-house' where those who worked at home would collect hemp and flax, deliver completed goods and receive payment.[41]

The Corporation of London set up workhouses in two confiscated royal properties, Heydon House in the Minories and the Wardrobe building in Vintry, but chose to send vagrants and prostitutes to Bridewell rather than run its own house of correction. Little is known about either workhouse, but eighty children were maintained and taught at the Wardrobe workhouse in 1655, and when the Corporation folded in 1660 over a hundred children were transferred to Christ's Hospital.[42] That the first class of pauper to take up residence in workhouses in any numbers should be orphaned or abandoned children is understandable, as they were the single social group considered capable of labour, yet incapable of caring for themselves.

Figure 4
The 'Spinning House' in Cambridge was built in 1628–34 and demolished in 1901. When this photograph was taken, c 1895–6, the building was in use as a police station.
[By permission of the Syndics of Cambridge University Library Views a. 53 (2) 92.1(5)]

*Figure 5
From 1681, Chichester Workhouse occupied these almshouses, which had been built by the MP William Cawley in 1625. A chapel with a crow-stepped gable and bell-turret occupies the centre of the building.
[BB97/1068]*

It is uncertain whether many of the workhouses known to have existed before 1640 survived the political upheavals of the 1640s and 1650s. The fate of Kendrick's foundation at Reading may have been typical: it became a garrison during the Civil War, then 'an Habitation for an idle sort of Poor, who lived in it Rent free'.[43] The late Stuarts largely neglected the problems posed by widespread poverty, leaving parish officers to their own devices, and it was undoubtedly easier for overseers to distribute outdoor relief than to inaugurate complex systems to set the poor to work.[44] One of the few new provincial workhouses known to have been set up between 1660 and 1697 was established by the Mayor of Chichester in a former almshouse (Fig 5), a building which continued in use as a workhouse from 1681 until the middle of the 20th century.[45] The Act of Settlement of 1662, however, launched further experiments in London.[46]

The Act of Settlement, properly known as the Act for the Better Relief of the Poor of this Kingdom, had a significant and long-lasting effect on the poor. The notion that everyone had a parish of settlement had been implicit in the vagrancy laws of the 16th century. The new Act authorised a parish to remove any newcomer who might become chargeable on the rates, provided they had arrived within the last 40 days and had not rented a house worth £10 a year or more. Qualifications for settlement were modified over the years, but the principle endured.

The Act of Settlement also provided for the formation of corporations in the City of London, Westminster and those parts of Middlesex and Surrey lying within the Bills of Mortality.[47] Each corporation would have the right to erect workhouses and houses of correction.[48] Middlesex and Westminster took advantage of this in 1664 and 1666 respectively, but neither workhouse was long-lived. The Middlesex County Workhouse stood on the corner of Corporation Lane and Bridewell Walk in Clerkenwell and cost £5,000 to establish. As well as supplying the poor with stock to work on at home, part of the building was set apart 'for the reception and Breeding up of poor Fatherless or Motherless Infants'.[49] Some years after the workhouse closed in 1672, the building housed Thomas Rowe's College of Infants, or 'Infantory', indicating some continuity of use.[50]

A few London parishes set up their own workhouses in the 1660s, but these appear to have met with as little success as the Middlesex and Westminster establishments. A workhouse was mentioned in the vestry minutes of St Margaret, Westminster for 1664.[51] Another, erected in the churchyard of St Martin-in-the-Fields in 1665, was so little used by 1683 that the building was let.[52]

These brief London experiments confirmed that workhouses were not a social panacea, and the last decades of the century are distinguished by a rash of pamphlets considering alternative ways of 'setting the poor on work'. Workhouses had proved particularly difficult to set up and administer in small, rural parishes and larger areas of administration were therefore proposed. Tracts written in the late 17th century reveal an increasingly harsh, and occasionally exploitative, attitude towards the poor. As the national economy prospered, poor rates continued to rise and poverty was blamed on the poor themselves, rather than on trade depression or low wages.

Chief Justice Sir Matthew Hale, writing shortly after the Restoration, was one of the first to realise that most parishes were too small to operate an efficient and economical workhouse. He suggested that up to six parishes unite and 'build or procure a convenient Work-House for imploying the Poor, if need be, in it, and for lodging Materials, and for instructing Children in the Trade or Work'.[53] It was still common for workhouses and houses of correction to form a combined establishment and, while Hale made no suggestion that workers should reside in a workhouse, he recommended that a person refusing to work be subjected to 'Imprisonment and moderate correction in such a Work-House'.[54] His ideas, largely inspired by the disbanded Corporation of London workhouses, came to nothing, but their influence lingered into the 18th century.

In 1669, the East India merchant Sir Josiah Child urged the replacement of the parochial poor-law system in London by a single union governed by 'Fathers of the Poor'.[55] They would have the power to purchase land, and erect and endow workhouses, hospitals and houses of correction in which:

> the Girls may be employed in mending the cloaths of the Aged, in Spinning, Carding and other Linnen Manufactures . . . the Boys in picking oakum, making Pins, rasping Wood, making Hangings, or any other Manufacture of any kind, which whether it turns to present Profit or not, is not much material, the great Business of the Nation being first but to keep the Poor from Begging and Starving, and enduring such as are able to Labour and Discipline, that they may be hereafter useful Members to the Kingdom.[56]

The merchant Thomas Firmin, who publicised his views through pamphlets in 1678 and 1681, was one of the few who disagreed with the practice of sending paupers to work in factories and set up a non-residential workhouse in Aldersgate, London. It served as a spinning school for young children and a storehouse for flax, which the poor took away to spin in their own homes.[57] Firmin believed that the home of the poor 'though never so mean and homely, is more desired than any other place; and the way which several Persons have proposed, of bringing them to a publick Work-house, will never affect the end intended . . . not one person of twenty will endure the thoughts of Working at a publick Work-house'.[58] Workhouses were necessary, nevertheless, for 'vagrants and sturdy beggars, who have no habitation, and must be held to their Labour, as Gally-slaves are tied to their oars'.[59]

Firmin's scheme never became self-supporting, yet other reformers began to suggest that the unemployed poor be set to work for profit. In 1678 Richard Haines suggested the erection of 'Working Alms Houses' by groups, or unions, of parishes. This would be the 'best expedient to perfect the trade and manufacture of linen cloth' and would, incidentally, provide a market for his newly invented spinning machine.[60] The idea of setting the unproductive poor to work for profit inspired many experiments at the end of the 17th century and throughout the 18th, but seldom with any lasting effect.

The Quaker community had relieved its own poor from the mid-17th century and its experiences prompted several recommendations. In 1677, the Six Weeks Meeting of London Quakers established a scheme similar to Firmin's, whereby flax was supplied for poor Friends to spin in their own homes.[61] The treasurer of that project from 1680 was the merchant John Bellers, who published his *Proposals for Raising a Colledge of Industry* in 1695 and 1696.[62] The 'Colledge' was to be an independent co-operative community, a mixed agricultural and manufacturing settlement of 300 persons, including 200 labourers and 100 impotent poor. In 1698, George Fox suggested that the Quakers set up a house 'wherein a hundred may have rooms to work in, and shops of all sorts of things to sell, and where widows and young women might work and live'.[63] At a later date Lawrence Braddon came up with a proposal outstripping Bellers's in scope and imagination: he suggested building three great hospitals for all the poor within the Bills of Mortality, one for the sick and lame, one for the aged, and one for infants.[64] The able-bodied would receive training in the 'Mechanical-Arts' in collegiate cities which could each hold 20,000 inhabitants. Ultimately, none of these grandiose schemes were adopted and, perhaps in reaction to them, some commentators were coming round to the idea that the poor should be compelled, by stricter relief practices, to find work for themselves.[65]

In addition to workhouses where children and able-bodied paupers were set to work, there were several late 17th-century parish establishments which were little more than poorhouses, or public almshouses, for the aged and infirm. In 1688, the parish of St James, Westminster, housed aged and impotent paupers in six small houses in Salter's Court. Women were employed to tend the inmates, and the place became known as 'the nurses' houses'.[66] St Anne's, Soho, rented twelve small houses in Symbell's Alley as a poorhouse from 1697 until 1711, and a small building on Oxford Street from 1711 to 1766.[67] Many such establishments may have existed throughout the country, but little is known about them. In England, the terms 'poorhouse' and 'workhouse' were interchangeable throughout the 18th century, and it is significant that 'workhouse' eventually gained precedence.[68]

The government stood aloof from the debate surrounding workhouse provision and organisation until 1696, when the newly established Board of Trade was instructed 'to consider of proper methods for setting on work and employing the poor, and making them useful to the public'.[69] Its report, drawn up by the philosopher John Locke in 1697, recommended that working schools be set up by each parish, but that their stock be supplied by the Hundred. As a result of the report several bills were presented to Parliament, all unsuccessfully.

Urban Corporation Workhouses, 1696–1722

A number of large urban workhouses were set up at the turn of the 18th century with the stated intention of training poor children while profiting from pauper labour. Functionally, they seem to have closely resembled certain earlier establishments, such as the Dorchester workhouse, but they achieved greater publicity and were more influential.

In 1696, the eighteen parishes of Bristol were incorporated by a local Act 'for the better employing and maintaining of the poor'.[70] This permitted the Corporation to set up one or more workhouses and appoint paid officers. Initially, plans were drawn up for a U-shaped workhouse and a site was purchased on the outskirts of the town, but for reasons of economy that scheme was abandoned and two existing buildings were converted instead.[71] One, the 'new workhouse', accommodated about 100 girls who were taught to read and spin worsted yarn. The other, a fine timber-framed building known as the 'Mint Workhouse' (Fig 6), housed boys, the aged, infants and, eventually, lunatics.[72] While little is known of the 'new workhouse', the 'Mint Workhouse' survived into the 20th century as St Peter's Hospital but, sadly, was destroyed by bombing in 1940.

An influential account of the Bristol experiment was published in 1700 by its instigator, the Whig merchant John Cary.[73] By then Bristol's example had already been followed by a number of other large towns, all of which

Figure 6
St Peter's Hospital in Bristol originated as a timber-framed house, built by Mayor Robert Aldworth in 1612. It was used as the Bristol Mint, then as a 'Sugar-House', before becoming a workhouse around 1700.
[From Seyer 1821, by permission of the Syndics of Cambridge University Library]

obtained costly local Acts enabling them to set up residential workhouses. The earliest were, in 1698, Crediton, Tiverton, Hereford, Colchester, Kingston-upon-Hull, Shaftesbury and Exeter; in 1699, King's Lynn and Sudbury; in 1702, Gloucester; in 1703, Worcester; in 1707, Plymouth and in 1712, Norwich.[74] In addition, in 1698, London finally set up a Corporation under the terms of the Act of Settlement. As at Bristol, in the early years of their existence many of these authorities concentrated on housing and training pauper children.

Little is known of the buildings which housed the workhouses of these early incorporations. Some were set up in former monastic buildings, houses or guildhalls, but at least three, Kingston-upon-Hull, Tiverton and Exeter, were built for the purpose.[75] Kingston-upon-Hull erected a large U-shaped building with hipped dormers, known as Charity Hall (Fig 7).[76] There are no records of the Tiverton workhouse, built in 1704 for 300 inmates, but Exeter Workhouse survived until, like St Peter's Hospital in Bristol, it was bombed during the 1940s.

Exeter Workhouse was designed by Ralph Mitchell and erected between 1699 and 1707.[77] A vignette on Rocque's map of Exeter (Fig 8), dated 1744, shows two-storey-and-attic ranges around three sides of a broad courtyard which was open to the south, with a central U-shaped

Figure 7
Kingston-upon-Hull Incorporation built 'Charity Hall' on Whitefriargate in 1698. Until 1726 the building was used as a training school and home for poor children rather than a general workhouse.
[From Hadley 1788, by permission of the Syndics of Cambridge University Library]

Figure 8
This view of Exeter Incorporation Workhouse is taken from Roque's Map of Exeter, 1744. The building was designed by Ralph Mitchell, and erected between 1699 and 1707. Like St Peter's Hospital in Bristol, it continued to be used as an institution until it was bombed during the Second World War.
[Devon Library Services (Westcountry Studies Library) SC 999]

THE WORKHOUSE

Figure 9
The parish of Witham in Essex set up this workhouse in 1714. The building, which has been divided into cottages, stands opposite the parish church, in the heart of the town.
[BB97/06205]

block set back from the centre of the north side. The building was in a restrained classical style, with a central pediment and cupola, and could hold about 200 inmates. The internal arrangements are not known in detail, but there was a chapel in the centre, a house for the master of the works in one wing and another for the master of the house in the other.

In 1698, the Corporation of London was re-established and in the following year it took a house in Half-Moon Alley off Bishopsgate Street, to which a house of correction and chapel were added.[78] The 'Steward's Side', for children aged between 7 and 14, opened in 1699 and the 'Keeper's Side', for vagabonds and sturdy beggars, in 1700. Its organisation resembled Bridewell, and at its height the institution could accommodate 450 children and 50 vagrants. The boys' workroom occupied the lowest floor, the girls' the second, and two lodgings for boys the third; the girls' dormitory was over the new chapel, which separated the workhouse from the house of correction. The children were employed in spinning, sewing and knitting, and were taught to 'read, write and cast Accompts'.[79] The vagabonds beat hemp and washed the children's linen.

Few other workhouses existed in early 18th-century London although, in 1702, the Quakers founded a workhouse for fifty-six 'decayed Friends and Orphans' on the site of the 17th-century Middlesex Workhouse in Clerkenwell.[80] It occupied three sides of a square, with the local house of correction on the fourth side.[81]

An ill-fated bill presented to Parliament by Sir Humphrey Mackworth on several occasions between 1703 and 1707 would have given parishes *carte blanche* to set up workhouses along the lines of the urban incorporations, but was unsuccessful as not everyone believed the new workhouses to be beneficial.[82] Daniel Defoe, in his pamphlet *Giving Alms no Charity, and Employing the Poor a Grievance to the Nation*, argued that the enforced employment of the poor was bound to interfere with natural market forces and put small independent masters out of business. He regarded workhouses as 'public nuisances, mischiefs to the nation, which serve to the ruin of families and the encrease of the poor'.[83]

Corporations certainly placed the economic interests of their own town before those of the kingdom at large. The Act establishing the Worcester Corporation in 1703 protected trade within the town by stipulating that any cloth manufactured in the workhouse or house of correction must be sold outside Worcester.[84] But in the end it was their own economic failure, rather than their disturbance of the national economy, that led to the demise or modification of several early incorporations of the poor.

Ironically, the first to flounder was the model incorporation, Bristol. In 1700, Cary had reported on the success of the scheme, but by 1714 it had set aside projects of labour. Indeed, the Gloucester Corporation had lapsed after only five years, in 1707.[85] The Corporation of London workhouse had encountered opposition from several parishes which withheld their portion of the poor rate and preferred to send their children to charity schools.[86] By 1713, the Corporation was in debt and its workhouse operated as little more than a house of correction.[87] The incorporations of Sudbury and Colchester may also have been troubled from an early date: in 1751, Charles Gray, MP for Colchester, published a pamphlet in which he complained that the incorporation of Sudbury had 'most grievously hurt the town, and been attended with all the inconveniences, expences, jobs, and law-suits, that might reasonably be expected from so improper a scheme'. The incorporation of parishes in Colchester itself had had similar consequences and was disunited in the middle of the century.[88]

The only new incorporations to be formed between 1712 and the middle of the century were Canterbury (1727) and Bury St Edmunds (1747). This lull can be ascribed partly to the economic failure of many existing incorporations and partly to the passage, in 1723, of an Act which enabled parishes to operate their own smaller, and potentially cheaper, workhouses, without having to resort to costly legislation.

Early 18th-Century Parish Workhouses

Faced with rising poor rates and inspired by the initial success of urban incorporation workhouses, several parishes in the South East decided to take action: from now on the idle poor who placed a permanent burden on the rates would be housed and employed in a workhouse managed by a private contractor.[89] The idea of contracting out the care of the poor was not particularly novel: in 1660, the Quaker Thomas Lawson had suggested that each parish appoint an 'undertaker' who would arrange the employment of paupers and the relief of those unable to work.[90] The idea of using the residential workhouse as a deterrent for healthy adults, however, was completely new.

Matthew Marriott of Olney in Buckinghamshire made a lucrative career from the management of parish workhouses, beginning with that of his home town in 1714, but eventually assuming control of numerous establishments, including those of Berkhampstead, Hemel Hempstead, Luton, Peterborough, Tring and several in the City of Westminster.[91] At Olney, the town purchased a piece of ground adjoining a building already 'belonging to the poor', so little capital expenditure was involved. If a long-term pauper refused to enter the workhouse as a condition of receiving relief, no relief was given; if a workhouse inmate refused to work, he or she was sent to the house of correction. Olney, and

Figure 10
Wisbech Workhouse was erected on Albion Terrace in 1720. Since this photograph was taken, in 1954, the building has been demolished.
[Wisbech & Fenland Museum WM/095]

THE WORKHOUSE

*Figure 11
Augustus Pugin
(Senior) depicted this
day-room in the work-
house of St James,
Westminster, for
Ackermann's*
Microcosm of
London, *published in
1808. The building,
erected on Poland Street
in 1725–7, was initially
run by the professional
workhouse contractor,
Matthew Marriott.*
[From Ackermann
1808–10, by permission of
the Syndics of Cambridge
University Library]

many other parishes which employed Marriott, claimed substantial savings as a result of his work.

Although the experiment at Olney was well known and influential, the workhouses of Theydon Garnon (1704), Meldreth (1707) and Thaxted (1711) pre-dated it, and at least five others were founded in the same year (1714), namely St Martin's, Leicester, Witham (Fig 9), Chelmsford, Good Easter and Abingdon.[92] Soon, the idea of the test workhouse spread beyond Essex and surrounding counties.[93]

Like Olney, many of these early 18th-century establishments must have occupied converted houses and cottages, but some were purpose built. Wisbech Workhouse, for example, was built on a 3-acre site between the horse fair and the quay in 1720. The tenant of the land was persuaded to surrender his lease for 2 guineas and the first year's production of hemp from the workhouse.[94] Only those capable of work were admitted into the building (Fig 10), which was a large block-like structure, thirteen bays long and three storeys high, but with little in the way of architectural adornment.

Sir Edward Knatchbull's Act, or the Workhouse Test Act, of 1723 thus codified existing practice.[95] It empowered parish overseers 'to purchase or hire any house or houses . . . and to contract with any person or persons for the lodging, keeping, maintaining and employing any or all such poor persons . . . as shall desire to receive relief'. While large poor-law districts were not contemplated, two or more small parishes were allowed to unite in purchasing or hiring such houses, and parishes without workhouses were permitted to enter into contract with other parishes to accommodate their poor. The Act further stipulated that if a person refused to enter the workhouse, he or she was no longer entitled to request relief. This established a legal destitution test for the first time.

Knatchbull's Act did not make the provision of a workhouse obligatory, and most parishes continued to dispense outdoor relief. It has been estimated that 300 parish workhouses were set up between 1723 and 1732, and another 300 by 1750.[96] Many parishes would have fitted up an existing building and farmed out its management. The details of contracts varied enormously but, whatever their management system, most parishes claimed immediate savings upon setting up a workhouse. This was especially true when a 'workhouse test' was instituted, but in the longer term it was found that the cost of maintaining a workhouse caused poor rates to rise: the rate for Witham was £230 shortly after the workhouse opened, but it had risen to £2,899 by 1785.[97]

An Account of the Workhouses in Great Britain, first published in 1725 but reissued in 1732, contains invaluable descriptions of some new workhouses in London and the provinces, including some which were purpose built. It was published by the Society for the Promotion of Christian Knowledge (SPCK), an organisation which had been deeply involved in the provision of charity schools since its foundation in 1698, and was now interested in workhouses and closely associated with Marriott. The anonymous author, possibly Marriott or one of his associates, regarded workhouses as a boon. He claimed:

> *workhouses, under a prudent and good management, will answer all the Ends of Charity to the Poor, in regard to their Souls and Bodies; and yet at the same time prove effectual Expedients for encreasing our Manufactures, as well as removing a heavy Burden from the Nation.*[98]

Memories of the Great Fire had receded, but in several cases the author of *An Account* made a point of noting that a new building was of brick. The London parish of St Andrew, Saffron Hill, built a brick extension to several old houses in 1730. The extension contained a working-room, where the inmates spun candlewick, with a dining-room on the upper floor. In 1726, the guardians of St Margaret, Westminster hired a house and garden 'to which they added a new brick Fabrick, for receiving the Spinners and other Workers'. New 'Brick-Houses' were built for St Botolph, without Bishopsgate (1730), St Giles, Cripplegate (1724), St James, Clerkenwell (1727), St James, Westminster (1728) and St Mary, Lambeth (1726).

Unfortunately, the appearance of these London workhouses was not recorded. Most held fewer than 100 inmates, but a few held over 150, rivalling contemporary urban incorporation workhouses in size. By 1732 the largest belonged to the united parishes of St Giles-in-the-Fields and St George, Bloomsbury (260 inmates in summer and 300 in winter), St James, Westminster (302 inmates; Fig 11), St Margaret, Westminster (326 inmates) and St Martin-in-the-Fields (344 inmates). Many of these were managed by Matthew Marriott who, for some unrecorded misdemeanour, was dismissed from all of his London posts, with the exception of St Giles-in-the-Fields, in 1728.[99]

One of the workhouses initially entrusted to Matthew Marriott was that of St George's, Hanover Square. The building, designed by Benjamin Timbrell and Thomas Phillips and erected on Mount Street in 1725–6, could accommodate 250 (Fig 12). Although described as 'plain, strong and very commodius', it was surmounted by a graceful cupola and, architecturally, seems to

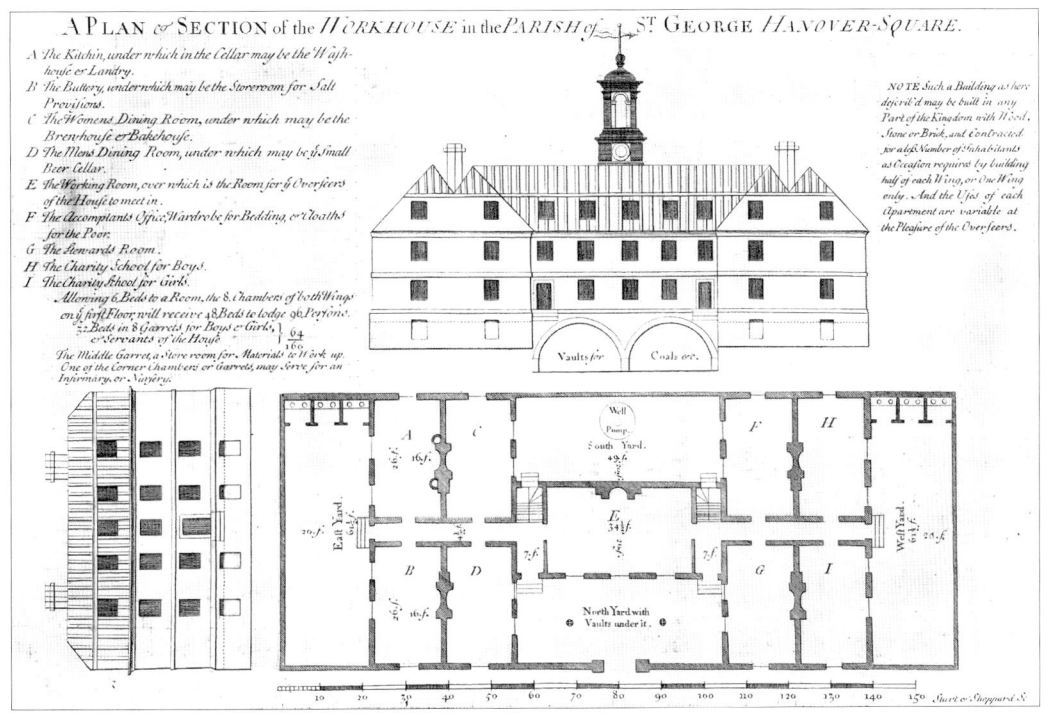

*Figure 12
The design of the workhouse of St George's, Hanover Square, drawn up by Benjamin Timbrell and Thomas Phillips in 1725–6, was circulated by the Society for the Promotion of Christian Knowledge as a model for other workhouses.
[British Museum, Grace Views, Supp Portfolio XXIX, 23]*

The Workhouse

*Figure 13
Chatham Workhouse in Kent was erected in 1725. The building was still in use in Charles Dickens's youth and is thought to have inspired the workhouse in* Oliver Twist.
[*Ground-floor plan and elevation redrawn from an original drawing (U480/P17) held in Medway Archives and Local Studies Centre*]

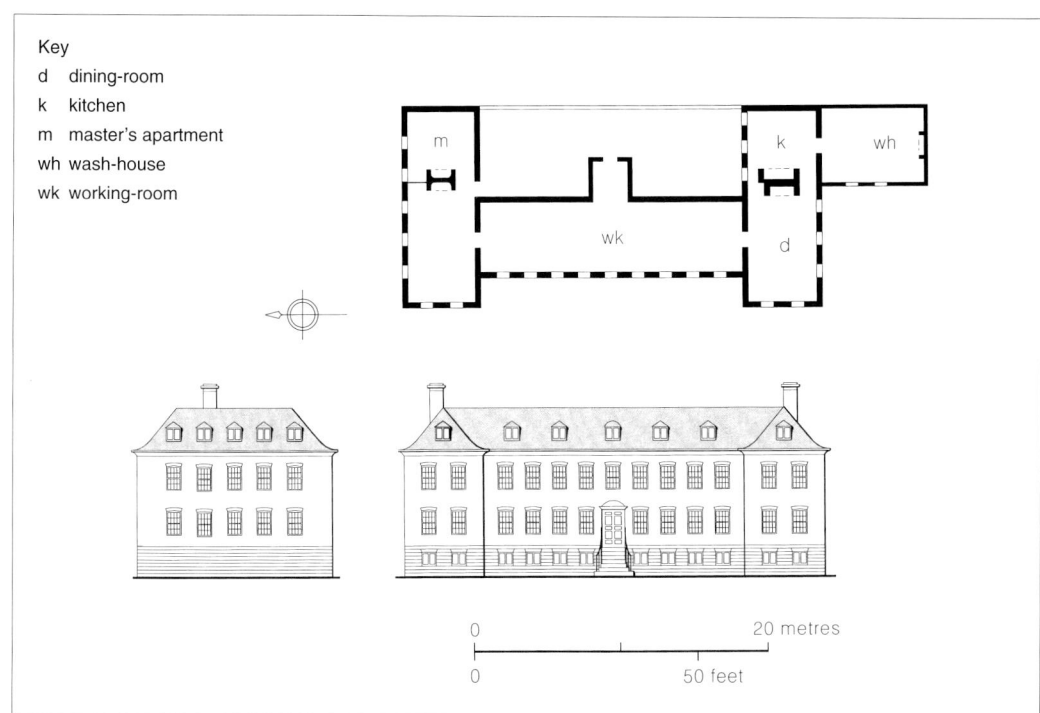

*Figure 14
This token, issued by Birmingham Incorporation for the Poor in 1811, bears an image of the workhouse, which was built 1733–4 and later extended.*
[AA97/01319]

have been grander than most of its contemporaries.[100] In 1726, the SPCK decided to publish its plan, together with that of Strood Workhouse, 'for the Service of the Publick'.[101] It was an H-shaped building with double-pile cross-wings which included, on the ground floor, a working-room, dining-rooms and charity schools. The upper-floor dormitories each contained six double beds – for men as well as women – each of which was surrounded by curtains to afford its occupants some privacy. The extent to which this block design influenced other new workhouses is not clear, but it is said to have inspired Beverley Workhouse, a building which was erected by three parishes in 1726.[102]

Every parish workhouse in London contained large numbers of children who were expected to work for much of the day but also received rudimentary teaching, either in the workhouse or in a nearby charity or parish school. At the workhouse of St Andrew, Holborn, they attended school 'in Rotation as they can be spared from their work'.[103] Children were usually employed in spinning, while a common task for adult inmates, including the elderly, was oakum-picking. It is uncertain whether these workhouses still hoped to profit from pauper labour, and work may have been exacted primarily as a means of urging the idle to support themselves. At St Andrew, Holborn there was little hope of making a profit as over half of the inmates were employed 'in Nursing and other necessary Attendance on the House'.[104]

Information about parish workhouses outside London in this period is less accessible. Provincial reports published in *An Account* are less consistent than those for London as they were elicited from diverse correspondents. Some parishes were clearly reluctant to adopt a harsh stance against their poor. Luton workhouse was called the House of Maintenance for the Poor, 'to soften the Appellation of a Workhouse, against which the Poor might be prejudiced'.[105] Similarly, the workhouses at Harrow-on-the-Hill and Chertsey were known by the same euphemism.

The provincial reports impart much less information about workhouse buildings, or the employment of workhouse inmates, than the London reports. Drawings, however, survive for one, the Chatham Workhouse (Fig 13), which was erected in 1725.[106] Despite the absence of a pediment, cupola or other adornment, it was clearly an impressive structure. Like the workhouse of St George's, Hanover Square, it comprised a basement, two storeys and an attic and had an H-shaped plan.[107] In the centre of the building was a large working-room; the master's apartments occupied one cross-wing, the kitchen and dining-room the other.

Workhouse activity was concentrated in the South, but a number of workhouses are known to have been built in the cities of the North and the Midlands after the passage of Knatchbull's Act. Liverpool Workhouse was erected in 1732. That of Birmingham (Fig 14), built in 1733–4, stylistically resembled the workhouses of Chatham and Kingston-upon-Hull and was extended by an

*Figure 15
Harefield Workhouse in
Middlesex, like many
other parish workhouses
set up in the 18th
century, closely resembled
contemporary houses.
[London Metropolitan
Archives 20.61 HAR
69/35/77/8]*

infirmary wing in 1766 and a workshop wing in 1779.[108] Leeds set up a new workhouse in 1738 and two years later extended the building by adding a brewhouse, wash-house, coal-house, workroom, granary and infirmary; by 1771 it included five or six lunatic cells.[109]

The majority of parish workhouses set up in the mid-18th century were smaller than those of Chatham, Liverpool or Birmingham and, whether converted or purpose built, were domestic in appearance and planning. Albury Workhouse, in Surrey, was typical.[110] It was a red-brick building of two storeys and an attic, erected in 1732. When an inventory was taken in 1739, its rooms comprised a kitchen, hall, pantry, cellar, brewhouse, seven 'chambers' and two attics. Nine beds were in use and three were 'at John Denche's, together with a cradle'. There was little difference between this purpose-built workhouse and adapted houses. Similar house-like workhouses, often with attics lit by small dormer windows, were built at Lingfield (1729), Walthamstow (1730), Cudham (1731), Horncastle (1734) and elsewhere during this period (Fig 15).[111]

Despite the difficulties involved in collating information on 18th-century parish workhouses, it has been argued that fewer new establishments were formed during the 1730s and 1740s than during the 1720s.[112] If so, the reason is unclear. In 1731, a pamphlet by the anonymous 'Christian Love-Poor' accused Marriott, or one of his relations, of outrageous cruelty to paupers in St Giles-in-the-Fields Workhouse (Fig 16). It was claimed that several inmates had been starved to death in the 'Dark Hole', and that the corpse of a woman who had died in childbirth was mutilated – her fingers were cut off, her eyes gouged out and their sockets stuffed with sawdust.[113] In the following year, under the shadow of these allegations, Marriott died. A new edition of *An Account*, published in 1732, may have partially tempered such adverse publicity, but its optimistic view of workhouses no longer mirrored public opinion. The administration of workhouses came under increasing attack and numerous proposals were offered for the reform of the poor law in general, and workhouses in particular.

Mid-18th-Century Schemes for Reform

Numerous pamphlets were published on the subject of poor-law reform in the mid-18th century, and a number of unsuccessful bills were presented to Parliament. Like Sir Matthew Hale a hundred years before, the majority agreed that the parish did not form a large enough unit for effective poor-law provision, but there was no consensus on a viable alternative. While some thought that the county would be ideal, others advocated the Hundred, or simply a convenient grouping of neighbouring parishes. The scale and administration of workhouses were considered by some would-be reformers, but few made suggestions concerning their physical form.

Figure 16
This woodcut illustrated 'The Workhouse Cruelty', a pamphlet which exposed the ill-treatment of inmates in the St Giles-in-the-Fields Workhouse around 1730.
[By permission of the British Library 816M9 Vol 80]

Most assumed that the workhouse would house both impotent and able-bodied paupers, and a few continued to suggest that it should include, or lie adjacent to, a house of correction. The failures of the early 18th-century urban incorporations rarely touched the discourse.

As early as 1735, William Hay, MP, proposed the division of each county into one or several poor-law districts, each managed by twelve guardians. These districts would erect a hospital, workhouse and house of correction, either contiguous or close together. The buildings were to be 'commodious, but destitute of all Ornament, to avoid Expence'.[114]

County institutions were suggested by others, including the Earl of Hillsborough, Sir Richard Lloyd and Henry Fielding, but the only proposal to assume an architectural form was Fielding's scheme for a County House and House of Correction for Middlesex, which was published with a plan by the architect Thomas Gibson in 1753 (Fig 17). With reference to this plan, Fielding was later accused of trying 'to effect the reformation of manners and the employment of the poor, by brick and mortar, and architectural devices'.[115] The proposed building was conceived on a grand scale, in a Classical style, with a steeple rising from the centre. The largest of five residences standing opposite the main entrance was reserved for the governor and included a Justice Hall. The main building encompassed three courtyards: the outer two, forming the 'County-House', could accommodate 3,000 men and 2,000 women; the innermost, the 'County-House of Correction', held 600. The ranges of the County-House included workrooms with wards above, an infirmary ward, stores and lodges for watchmen and attendants. Each of its 160 wards was seven bays long, with windows along one side, a hearth at both ends and a ridge ventilator over the centre. The ranges surrounding the prison court included wards, cells, a keeper's house, and lodges for attendants; in the yard were 'prisons or fasting rooms' and a whipping post. Separate buildings to either side of the men's court were leased to sutlers, or shopkeepers; each included a stall for victualling the inmates of the County-House on the ground floor and accommodation for the tradesmen-tenants above.

The idea that workhouses should be provided by each Hundred, rather than county, was proposed by the writer and clergyman Thomas Alcock in 1752. He suggested that every Hundred erect a workhouse consisting of three parts: one for the impotent, able and industrious poor, one for the sick and one for the vagrant and idle poor.[116] Shortly afterwards his idea was realised by Carlford and Colneis Hundreds in Suffolk, which erected a joint workhouse 'containing an infirmary for the sick, and such poor as are unable to work; a workhouse for those who are able; and a house of correction for those who are not willing'.[117] The scheme produced a saving of over £2,000 between 1758 and 1762, and the publication of this success in 1763 prompted the establishment of other rural incorporations in Suffolk and elsewhere (*see* Chapter 3).

The importance of separating children from adults in workhouses was stressed in a pamphlet by the Quaker poet John Scott, published in 1773. Scott approved the idea of 'orphan houses' for children, but thought it necessary to provide separate 'houses for relief of adults' and 'houses for confinement of habitual beggars and sturdy vagabonds'.[118] He heartily

Old Poor Law Institutions, c 1550–1750

disapproved of the 'parish prisons' set up under the 'dreadful engine of oppression' that was Knatchbull's Act, maintaining:

that those workhouses are scenes of filthiness and confusion; that old and young, sick and healthy, are promiscuously crouded into ill-contrived apartments, not of sufficient capacity.[119]

Furthermore, Scott suggested that 'orphan houses' be designed as 'an oblong quadrangle or double L, the sides composed of a number of low cottages'.[120] The cottages would be separated from one another by party walls of brick or by short gaps, their upper rooms would be ventilated by opposing windows – 'a circumstance more essential to the salubrity of all lodging places than is commonly apprehended' – and would each house five or six children under the care of a matron. This proposal was ahead of its time, pre-dating the introduction of children's cottage homes by 100 years (*see* Chapter 8).

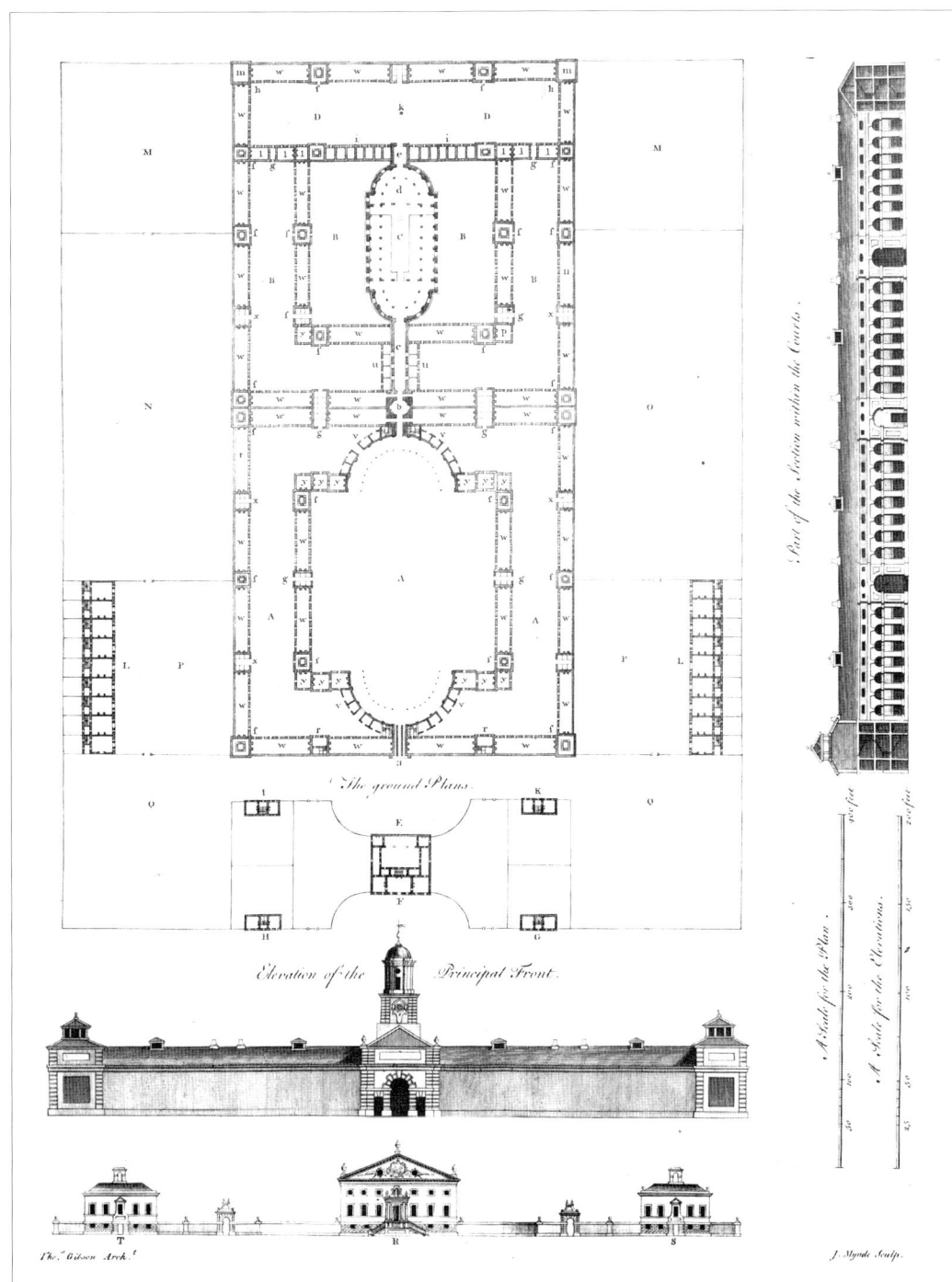

Figure 17
The architect Thomas Gibson produced this design to illustrate Henry Fielding's scheme of 1753, to erect a Middlesex County Workhouse and House of Correction on a site at Acton.
[From Fielding 1753, by permission of the Syndics of Cambridge University Library]

Scott's observations on ventilation were echoed by Edmund Gillingwater, the author of *An Essay on Parish Workhouses* (1786), who recommended that workhouse windows 'should be placed opposite to each other, on the different sides of the house; each window should have a casement which should always be left open, whenever the weather permits, to promote as much as possible, that free circulation of air through every part of the house, so essentially necessary for the health'.[121] This plea was premature. In England, the efficacy of cross-ventilation was not universally understood before the 1860s, when it was adopted as part of the pavilion system of hospital design (*see* Chapter 7).

A few interested parties disapproved of the concept of large Hundred or county workhouses. In 1752, Charles Gray, MP, published a pamphlet arguing that the parish system could work well but was generally badly executed. In 1764, Richard Burn published his history of the poor laws, with observations on poor-law schemes over the preceding century. He disapproved of recent proposals and clearly distrusted architects: if advertisements were placed for a large workhouse 'in order to shew their absurd skill in architecture, they will produce to you models fitter for a royal palace'.[122] Instead, Burn recommended humble house-like establishments capable of expansion. He envisaged 'several small houses contiguous, so as to receive separate families; with rooms or apartments therein, some more some fewer, some larger others smaller, according to the number and circumstances of a man's family that may be brought to lodge there'. Paupers' houses, a governor's house or manufactories could be added to the complex 'as practice and experience shall dictate'. Burn argued that such an establishment would be cheap, congenial to the poor and healthy. He argued: 'the conubial state will not be infringed; nor, consequently, the nation thereby depopulated'.[123] As a final recommendation, if the scheme failed, the building could be turned into houses. It is not known whether anything like this was achieved in Westmorland, where Burn served as a Justice of the Peace, or, indeed, in other parts of England.

Gray and Burn were in the minority: the move towards large poor-law districts was gaining momentum and soon received the sanction of Parliament. In 1765, Thomas Gilbert, MP for Lichfield, presented a bill which aimed to reorganise poor relief on a county basis, each county being divided into large districts corresponding to Hundreds, or to a large number of parishes. These poor-law districts would provide large houses of industry to accommodate the impotent poor. Undeterred by the defeat of this bill, Gilbert made further proposals for poor-law reform in 1776 and 1782. His 1782 bill, which he regarded as a 'temporary expedient', passed into law.[124] Usually known as Gilbert's Act, it allowed numbers of neighbouring parishes to group together for poor-law purposes and set up a poorhouse under a board of guardians. The able-bodied who were willing to work were to be employed by the parish outside the workhouse; those unwilling to work were to be punished, if necessary in a house of correction.

One aspect of Gilbert's proposals which distinguished him from most of his contemporaries, and brought him closer in spirit to the philanthropists of the 17th century, was his emphasis that workhouses should be for the impotent pauper, who was to be treated with leniency:

> *It is not the object of this Plan to have many Persons capable of Labour kept in the Work-houses; it is rather wished to have them placed or hired out to such Employments as they are most capable of; and if they cannot earn their whole Subsistence, the Deficiency to be made up out of the County Fund.*[125]

Marshall called the Act: 'a gesture of revolt against the domination of the parish officer', and indeed it aspired to eliminate the possibility of inefficiency and corruption by setting up boards of elected guardians of the poor.[126] Despite the failure of Gilbert's bolder proposals, the Act of 1782 encouraged the formation of poor-law unions throughout the country and over seventy Gilbert unions, of all shapes and sizes but generally rural in character, had been established by 1834. Many survived until the abolition of remaining Gilbert unions in 1869.

3
Old Poor Law Institutions, *c* 1750–1834

One of the principal themes in the story of the English Poor Law, as it is generally related from the mid-18th century to the introduction of the New Poor Law in 1834, is that of increasing discontent with the existing system. Essentially, there was no unified national policy. Both outdoor and indoor relief methods diversified with the formation of incorporations and unions in rural areas and the proliferation of parish workhouses of all shapes and sizes. More than ever, the treatment of a pauper depended on the simple factor of where he or she had been born. It was generally the case, however, that many more paupers were relieved in their own homes than in the workhouse. Despite their name, workhouses increasingly accommodated children, the disabled, the mentally handicapped, the sick and the aged, and not the unemployed labourers for whom they had been intended.

A more humanitarian approach towards the poor, adopted by some reformers and commentators in the last quarter of the 18th century, informed Gilbert's Act (1782) and Sir William Young's Act (1795). The first attempted to turn workhouses into poorhouses while the second enabled parishes with workhouses to distribute outdoor relief. However, by the end of the century, the tide of public opinion had turned yet again. Fear of escalating poor rates and widespread disapproval of outdoor-relief systems brought cries for a harsher, more universal system of indoor relief. The 'workhouse test' was developed into the 'deterrent workhouse' by several authorities, with results which were to inspire the Poor Law Commission, set up by Parliament to investigate the existing poor law in 1832.

Rural Incorporation and Gilbert Union Workhouses

In the second half of the 18th century, a number of Hundreds in East Anglia obtained special acts enabling them to unite for poor-law purposes and build large workhouses, or houses of industry, each of which could hold several hundred paupers. Typically, the 1775 Act of Incorporation for East and West Flegg in Norfolk stated its purpose as 'The Relief and Assistance of such as by Age or Infirmities are rendered incapable of supporting themselves, the better Employment of the Able and Industrious, the Correction of the Profligate and Idle and the Education of the Poor Children'.[1] This was echoed in the inscription over the doorway of the workhouse at Rollesby (Fig 18) which, perhaps significantly, omitted to mention correction.

Carlford and Colneis, the first rural Hundreds to be incorporated, obtained a local Act in 1756 and erected a workhouse in a rural situation at Nacton, south-east of Ipswich, which opened in 1758.[2] The building comprised three ranges around a quadrangle. A private benefactor, Admiral Vernon, had donated most of the site and loaned £1,000 at low interest to launch the scheme, which swiftly proved successful. Although the workhouse had cost over £4,500 to build and furnish, within four years £2,000 had been saved and the poor rates halved. Moreover, 'many children are rendered useful who otherwise would have figured nowhere

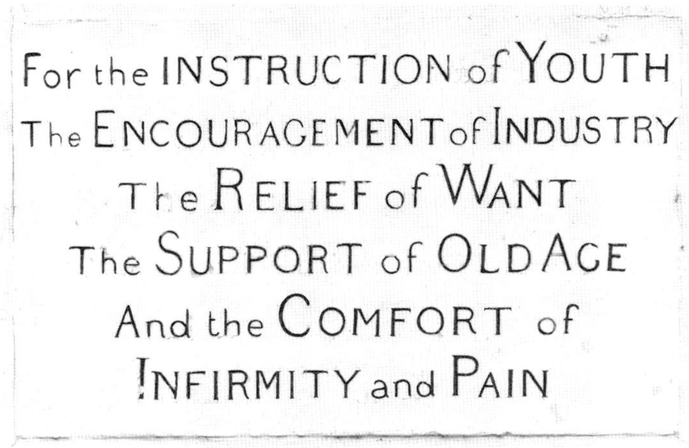

Figure 18
This inscription was displayed over the doorway of Rollesby House of Industry (1775) in Norfolk.
[BB96/3509]

For the INSTRUCTION of YOUTH
The ENCOURAGEMENT of INDUSTRY
The RELIEF of WANT
The SUPPORT of OLD AGE
And the COMFORT of
INFIRMITY and PAIN

but in a landscape of Gainsborough's'.[3] When this achievement was published in 1763, other East Anglian Hundreds were inspired to pursue the same course.[4] By 1800, no less than fourteen Hundred Houses had been set up throughout the region (see Table 1).

The houses of industry erected in East Anglia during the 1760s were large brick buildings in a simple Georgian style, with the bare minimum of ashlar dressings but often incorporating a plain, shallow pediment over the main entrance. Most had open courtyard plans, either U-shaped (as at Tattingstone and Oulton) or H-shaped (as at Shipmeadow and Bulcamp). Wings were generally only one room deep and two storeys high, sometimes, as at Heckingham and Tattingstone (Fig 19), with garrets. The front wings of Heckingham (Fig 20) incorporated open arcades which lent interest to an otherwise plain building, and may have been designed to provide paupers with an exercise area when the weather was bad. Heckingham is the only East Anglian house of industry for which the original plans, of 1765, survive.[5] On the ground floor, the central range contained the dining-hall, committee room and schoolroom. In the centre of one wing was a surgery, in the centre of the other the governor's room. The remainder of the ground floor was occupied by workshops, a 'prison', the kitchen and two infirmary wards. The 'prison' was very small and was probably used as a punishment cell for refractory inmates rather than convicted offenders; it had its own attached workroom.

As well as dormitories for the inmates, two more infirmary wards and a bedroom for the governor, the first floor included sixteen cubicles for married couples. A total of twenty-eight cubicles appear over the dining-hall on a later plan of Smallburgh Workhouse, suggesting that these were a standard feature of 18th-century East Anglian workhouses.[6] In 1836 the typical arrangement for married couples in these establishments was described as follows:

> *A long room was usually divided into small 'huts', each capable of containing one bed. These huts were narrow enclosures from the area of the room, created by thin boarded partitions about six feet high, between the tops of which and the ceiling, the ventilation of the apartment was not obstructed by any other division. In such apartments married people have lived 30 or even 40 years.*[7]

This was an improvement on the quarters set aside for able-bodied married couples in some Kent workhouses. In 1835, the shocked Assistant Commissioner, Sir Francis Head, reported that the beds were often separated merely by blankets, an arrangement which led him to fancy the following promiscuous scenario: 'if husband A should happen unintentionally to make a mistake, the position of his shoes might perchance throw B.C.D. and the rest of the connubial alphabet, all wrong'.[8]

Like many contemporary workhouses, Heckingham had no day-rooms as distinct from workrooms, indicating that all classes of inmate were expected to work throughout the day. The outbuildings included hog houses, a slaughter house and a brewhouse; these were the standard

Figure 19
The attic dormitory for 'young men' in Tattingstone House of Industry (1765–6), Suffolk, photographed in 1991.
[BB91/5471]

Table 1 The Rural Incorporations of East Anglia

Date	Hundred(s)	Location of Workhouse
1756	Carlford and Colneis (Suffolk)	Nacton
1764	Mutford and Lothingland (Suffolk)	Oulton
1764	Bosmere and Claydon (Suffolk)	Barham
1764	Samford (Suffolk)	Tattingstone
1764	Blything (Suffolk)	Bulcamp (or Blythburgh)
1764	Loddon and Clavering (Norfolk)	Heckingham
1764	Wangford (Suffolk)	Shipmeadow
1764	Loes and Wilford (Suffolk)[a]	Melton
1775	East and West Flegg (Norfolk)	Rollesby
1775	Mitford and Launditch (Norfolk)	Gressenhall
1776	Forehoe (Norfolk)	Wicklewood
1778	Stow (Suffolk)	Onehouse
1779	Cosford and Polsted (Suffolk)	Semer
1779	Hartismere, Hoxne and Thredling (Suffolk)	(No house of industry built)
1785	Tunstead and Happing (Norfolk)	Smallburgh

[a]Melton House of Industry, NMR File No. 100047. For other sites in this table, see Appendix 2: Catalogue A.

Key	
bk	bakery
bw	brewhouse
cis	cistern house
com	committee room
d	dining-room
ds	drying shed
gov	governor's room
hog	hog house
inf	infirmary ward
k	kitchen
pr	prison
sch	schoolroom
sg	surgery
slg	slaughter house
stb	stable
wh	wash-house
wk	workroom
y(inf)	infirmary yard

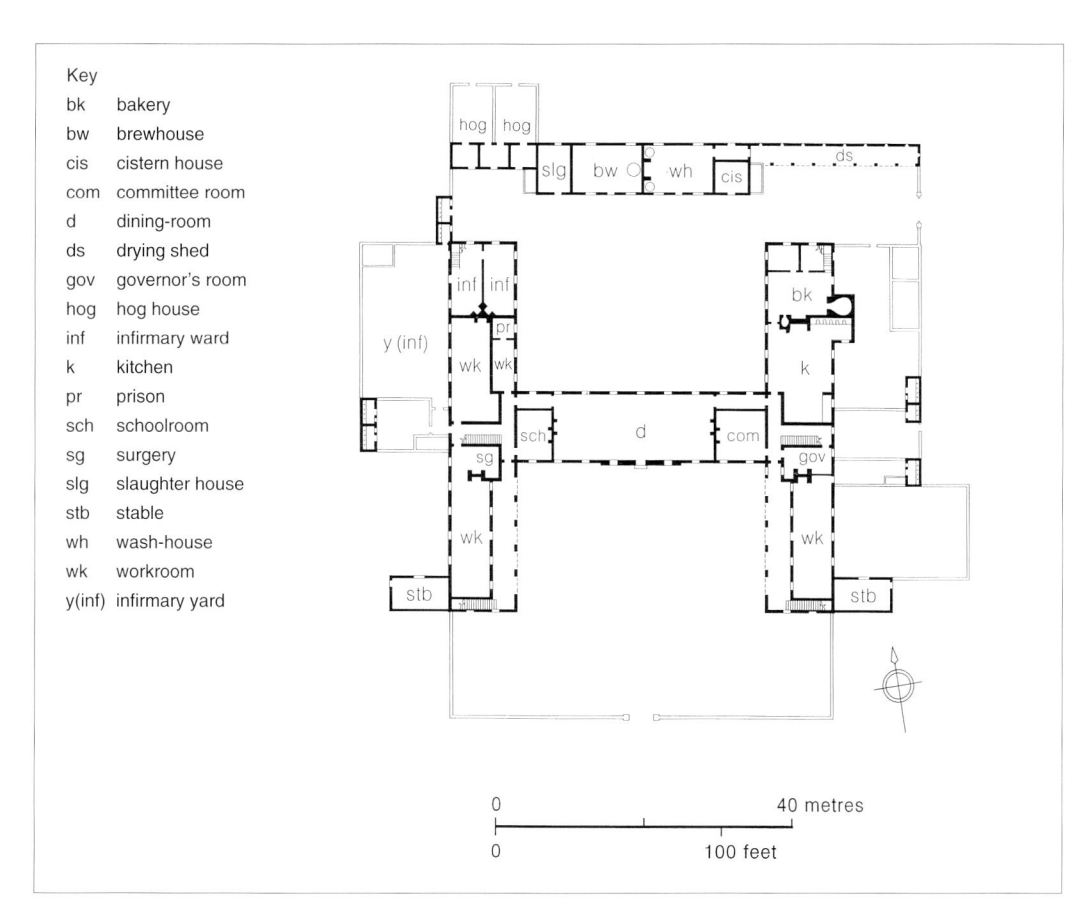

Figure 20
The original plans of Heckingham House of Industry (1765), Norfolk, have survived, providing vital evidence for the original function of the rooms.
[Ground-floor plan redrawn from Norfolk RO C/GP12/274]

domestic appendages of the period, and do not necessarily reflect a special attempt to achieve self-sufficiency. The plan of Smallburgh Workhouse indicates that many rooms in the main building were set aside for labour: on the ground floor was a sack-factory, a twine-spinning room, a mill and a labour wheel; on the first floor a hemp store, a hemp-dressing room, a laundry and another mill; and on the second floor a second twine-spinning room.

The East Anglian houses of industry erected in the mid-1770s and 1780s were very similar in plan and style to their predecessors, but some had greater architectural pretension. Arcades on the façades of Gressenhall, Wicklewood and Onehouse workhouses probably contributed to the appellation 'pauper palace'. Those of Gressenhall (Fig 21) were likened to 'those of the streets of Bologna' by Assistant Commissioner Dr James Kay in 1836.[9]

The unknown architect of Gressenhall adopted a plan similar to that of Ralph Mitchell's early 18th-century Exeter Workhouse. No direct contacts are known which might explain this. However, as Mitford and Launditch Incorporation, which erected Gressenhall House of Industry, was burdened with huge debts, only the U-shaped central block and one wing were ever completed.[10]

While Gressenhall could boast arcades and even a cupola, Onehouse (Fig 22) was undoubtedly the most splendid house of industry to be built in the region. The three-bay centre of the carefully proportioned façade was dominated by a pediment with a full entablature. To either side, a five-bay wing terminated in a two-bay pavilion. When, in 1836, Dr Kay expressed his surprise at the 'palatial' character of this building he was told 'that it was in the immediate vicinity of the country seats of some of the directors, who were naturally inclined to adorn rather than to disfigure the landscape'.[11]

In the early 1790s a Suffolk gentleman, Thomas Ruggles, reported favourably on the East Anglian houses of industry:

> In the incorporated hundreds, the houses of industry . . . are all of them built in as dry, healthy, and pleasant situations, as the vicinity affords; the offices . . . are all large, convenient, and kept exceedingly neat, the workrooms are large, well-aired, and the sexes are kept apart, both in the hours of work and recreation . . . The interior of these houses must occasion a most agreeable surprise, to all those who have not before seen poverty, but in its miserable cottage, or more miserable workhouse.[12]

Ruggles's accounts of East Anglian houses of industry indicate that they housed very few sick

THE WORKHOUSE

Figure 21
Gressenhall House of Industry (1775) now houses the Norfolk Rural Life Museum.
[BB95/2560]

Figure 22
Onehouse House of Industry, erected by Stow Hundred in Suffolk between 1778 and 1781, had an H-shaped plan with a central corridor, similar to that of contemporary voluntary hospitals and some urban workhouses.
[BB91/5091]

Figure 23 Montgomery and Pool House of Industry (1791–2), situated just over the Welsh border, was one of several large workhouses erected in and around Shropshire at the end of the 18th century. It is now Forden Hospital. [BB97/6358]

paupers, and that the majority of inmates were children and the elderly. Usually, children and able adults spun wool for manufacturers in Norwich, but in the mid-1790s this activity was suffering from the dislocation triggered by the French Revolutionary War. By then only two incorporations had cleared the debt incurred by their establishment, in one the debt had increased while in all others at least part of the debt had been paid off. The poor rate had remained stable in most incorporations, rising in two and decreasing in two. On balance, Ruggles proclaimed them an economic and social success.

Other commentators shared Ruggles's opinion of the East Anglian Hundred Houses.[13] The poet George Crabbe, however, described these institutions from the pauper's perspective in his poem *The Borough*, published in 1810:

> Your plan I love not; – with a number you
> Have plac'd your Poor, your pitiable few;
> There, in one House, throughout their Lives to be,
> The Pauper-Palace which they hate to see:
> That Giant-Building, that high bounding Wall,
> Those bare-worn Walks, that lofty thund'ring Hall!
> That large loud Clock, which tolls each dreaded
>   Hour,
> Those Gates and Locks, and all those Signs of
>   Power:
> It is a Prison, with a milder name,
> Which few inhabit without dread or shame.[14]

Few rural incorporations were set up outside East Anglia. The Isle of Wight Corporation, set up in 1770–1, followed their model although it imposed a strict ban on outdoor relief. Its huge, red-brick house of industry, erected near Newport in 1771, was also inspired by its East Anglian predecessors in having a courtyard plan rather than the more compact block plans favoured by urban authorities.[15] It could hold 700 persons, but usually accommodated 500, most of whom were either very old or very young. The long north range was lit by opposing windows and included a large storeroom, a steward's room, a dining-hall (118 ft by 27 ft), and a sitting-room which was shared by the impotent and aged. Under the east end were the governor's and matron's apartments, the laundry, nurseries and sick wards. The east range housed the schoolrooms, apothecary's shop, kitchen, scullery, bakehouse, bread room, governor's and matron's sitting-room and pantry on the ground floor; above were lying-in rooms, sick wards and twenty separate rooms for married men and their wives, with two common sitting-rooms adjoining for the old and infirm who were unable to go downstairs. Such concern for the elderly, and especially aged married couples, was still uncommon outside East Anglia. The south range and the gateway block to its west housed workshops, including weaving-rooms, spinning-rooms, shoemakers' and tailors' shops. To the east, a dairy, wash-house, brewhouse and other domestic offices were arranged around a secondary courtyard. A chapel lay to the north. In the grounds were a vegetable garden, a pest-house with its own burial ground, a four-roomed building for persons who had just been inoculated (probably against smallpox), barns, stables and hogsties.

In 1791–2, the three rural houses of industry of Oswestry, Ellesmere and Atcham were set up in Shropshire, and a fourth, for Montgomery and Pool (Fig 23), just over the Welsh border. These were generally more compact than the East Anglian and Isle of Wight workhouses, resembling contemporary block-plan voluntary hospitals such as Worcester (1766–70) and urban workhouses like Oxford (1772–5; *see* Figure 27). The Atcham workhouse, designed by John H Haycock and built for 300 inmates in 1792–3, was H-shaped with a corridor through the centre and single-depth dormitories in the cross-wings.[16]

THE WORKHOUSE

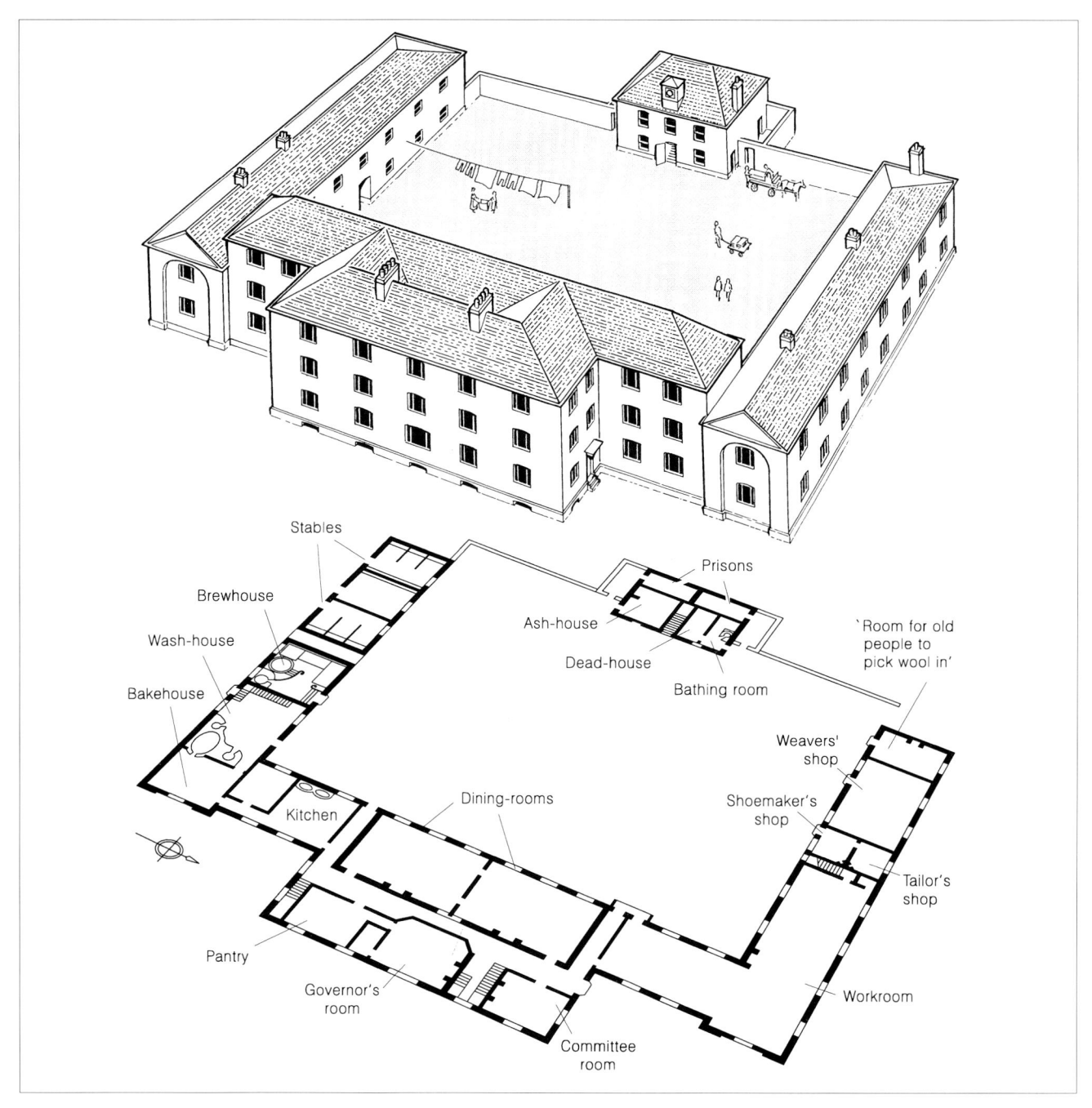

Figure 24
Easebourne Workhouse in Sussex was built in 1793–4. This shows the uses of the rooms in the early 19th century.
[Perspective view and plan based on Young 1813 and Public Record Office MH14/24]

No architectural conformity can be identified amongst the ninety or so workhouses erected throughout the country as a result of Gilbert's Act of 1782 (*see* Chapter 2). This was largely because the unions themselves varied enormously in size and character. They tended to be rural, were scattered all over the country, and varied in size from one to fifty-two parishes (Table 2).

A good example of a middle-sized workhouse established under Gilbert's Act was erected by Easebourne Union in Sussex. The Union was formed by sixteen parishes in July 1792 and the workhouse was built in 1793–4. It was a U-shaped building (Fig 24), arranged around three sides of a courtyard, with stables at the end of one cross-wing and workshops at the end of the other. A detached building in the middle of the fourth side of the courtyard featured two 'prisons', entered through small yards, and the dead house. The buildings were relieved from extreme plainness by their coursed stonework, galleted pointing, red and blue brick dressings, tripartite sash glazing and recessed arches which rose under a dentilled gable on the front of each cross-wing.

True to Gilbert's belief that workhouses should be for the impotent poor, the inmates of Easebourne were aged under 14 and over 60 with the exception of some women with children and those suffering from mental and physical infirmity.[17] A linen and woollen manufactory was set up, but in the first year it was discovered that the outgoings, including raw materials and the salaries and maintenance of the instructors, far exceeded any income generated by selling cloth. The manufactory was intended to provide industrial training for the children, but the elderly were also involved: the ground-floor plan of the building shows, next to a large weaving-room, a smaller heated room in which old people picked wool. Women were occupied with the domestic chores of the house; men in shoemaking, tailoring, gardening and other outdoor work, although some inmates were hired out to local farmers.

The workhouse of Brinton and Melton Constable, two Norfolk parishes united under Gilbert's Act in 1783, was necessarily much smaller than that of Easebourne. The two-storeyed, red-brick building (Fig 25), now a private dwelling, appears to have been erected soon after the parishes were united and, as the union survived the introduction of the New Poor Law, remained in operation until 1869. It had a linear plan, with separate staircases for men and women. One interesting feature, a squint between the central rear wing (kitchen) and the stair bay of the west wing, may have been a crude method of supervision.

Surviving Gilbert workhouses are usually rather plain buildings. It is therefore surprising to read Assistant Commissioner Sir Francis Head's account, in 1835, of the old River Workhouse near Dover. It was:

Table 2 Gilbert Unions and Parishes in England[a]

BERKSHIRE
Wallingford
 	
CUMBERLAND
Whitehaven
 	
DERBYSHIRE
Brassington
Rosliston
Shardlow
 	
DURHAM
Darlington
 	
ESSEX
Ongar
 	
HAMPSHIRE
Aldershot and Bentley
Alverstoke and Gosport
Farnborough
Headley
Winchester
 	
KENT
Archbishop's Palace
Bearstead
Birchington
Eastry
Elham
Farnborough
Harbledown
Martin
Petham
St Mary Cray and
  Orpington
River
Selling
Teyham and Linstead
Tudeley and Capel
Whitstable
 	
LANCASHIRE
Caton
	LEICESTERSHIRE
	Appleby
	Ashby-de-la-Zouch
	Barrow-on-Soar
	Glenn Magna
	Lutterworth
	Melton Mowbray
	Ratby
	Sapcote
	Stathern
	Stretton
	Ullesthorpe
	
	LINCOLNSHIRE
	Caistor
	Claypole
	Winterton
	
	NORFOLK
	Acle
	Aldborough
	Bawdeswell
	Booton
	Brinton and Melton
	  Constable
	Gimingham
	Hackford
	Oulton
	Reepham-cum-Kerdistone
	St Faiths
	Taverham
	
	NOTTINGHAMSHIRE
	Arnold/Basford
	Thurgarton/Upton
	Ruddington
	Bingham
	
	STAFFORDSHIRE
	Alstonefield
	Tutbury
		SURREY
		Ash
		Farnham
		Hambledon
		Reigate
		
		SUSSEX
		Arundel
		Easebourne
		Eastbourne
		East Preston
		Glynde
		Sutton
		Thakeham
		Westhampnett
		Yapton
		
		WARWICKSHIRE
		Bedworth
		Exhall
		Meriden
		Rugby
		
		WESTMORLAND
		Eamont Bridge
		Kirkby-Lonsdale
		Kirkby-Stephen
		Milnthorpe
		
		YORKSHIRE
		Bainbridge
		Barwick
		Bolton-by-Bowland
		Carlton
		Giggleswick
		Great Ouseburn
		Lawkland
		Leyburn
		Lockington
		Paghill/Paul
		(Great) Preston

[a]Principal sources: *PP* 1836 (595), XXIX, Part 1, 9, (2nd Annual Report of PLC); *PP* 1837–8 (447), XXVIII, 151, (4th Annual Report of PLC); *PP* 1844 (578), XL, 331–4. This list may be incomplete.

Figure 25
Brinton and Melton Constable Workhouse (c 1783) in Norfolk – like many other small rural workhouses – was erected under Gilbert's Act of 1782. It has been converted into a single house.
[BB95/1758]

a splendid mansion . . . [the] dignity of its elevation, the elegant chasteness of its architecture, the massive structure of its walls, its broad double staircase, its spacious halls, its lofty bedrooms, and its large windows, form altogether 'a delightful retreat', splendidly contrasted with the mean little ratepaying hovels at its feet which . . . are lost in the splendour of the gilded spectacle.[18]

This was probably a gross exaggeration, serving to validate Head's personal theories about workhouse buildings (*see* pages 54–7).

Urban Workhouses, 1750–1800

In the second half of the 18th century small towns preferred to erect a workhouse under Knatchbull's Act. At the same time, about seventeen new urban poor-law incorporations were formed by local acts.[19] At Birmingham (1783), Chichester (1752) and elsewhere, this involved the introduction of a new administrative system but not the replacement of the existing workhouse. Occasionally, new incorporations set up workhouses in converted buildings: Southampton (1773) took over a range of almshouses while Shrewsbury (1783) purchased a suitably institutional building (Fig 26) which had been erected as a regional branch of the Foundling Hospital in 1760–5. A few incorporations, such as Oxford and Bedford, erected new buildings.

Regardless of the legislation underlying their foundation, late 18th-century urban workhouses had a number of features in common. Due to the cost of land, they generally occupied smaller sites than rural workhouses, and consequently had more compact plans which resembled voluntary hospitals. In architectural terms they tended to be just as conservative as their rural counterparts, usually rising to two or three storeys and having formal façades. Several, such as the large Liverpool Workhouse of 1769–72, were surmounted by pediments and cupolas (*see* Figure 28). Original plans indicate that these urban buildings contained a similar proportion of working to living space as in rural houses of industry.

The ground-floor plan (Fig 27) of Oxford House of Industry (1772–5), a building designed by John Gwynn and erected on the site of Henry I's palace, is a rare survival.[20] The building itself has been demolished, but the plan shows that a central corridor ran from one end to the other, connecting the central block with the end cross-wings. The centre contained the chapel and boardroom; beyond these were dining-rooms, a carding-room for men and a spinning-room for women; finally, the cross-wings contained wards, the kitchen and accommodation for the porter, clerk, and housekeeper. In addition to the workrooms in the main building, single-storeyed ranges to the rear contained long workshops, each with a supervisor's room: a foreman in the men's case, a mistress in the women's. Presumably these were paid employees. A small detached building to the rear of the workhouse contained the rather curious mixture of a 'correction room', washhouse, schoolhouse, salting-room and larder.

Workhouse Provision in the Late 18th and Early 19th Centuries

Parliamentary returns of 1776, 1802–3 and 1813–15 provide a number of statistics which illustrate the extent to which the workhouse system had spread through England by the beginning of the 19th century. These must, however, be treated with caution. On each occasion, the official questionnaire posed a different set of questions, some of which could be interpreted in a variety of ways. Moreover, none of the questionnaires succeeded in eliciting a response from every parish in the country.

The 1776 survey posed three questions of relevance to workhouses: how much rent was paid for workhouses and habitations for the poor, how many workhouses existed, and how many inmates each establishment could accommodate.

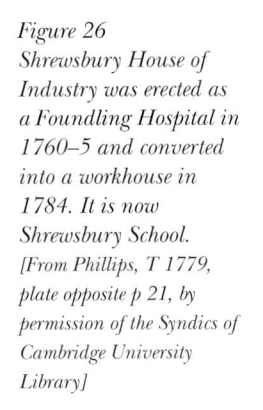

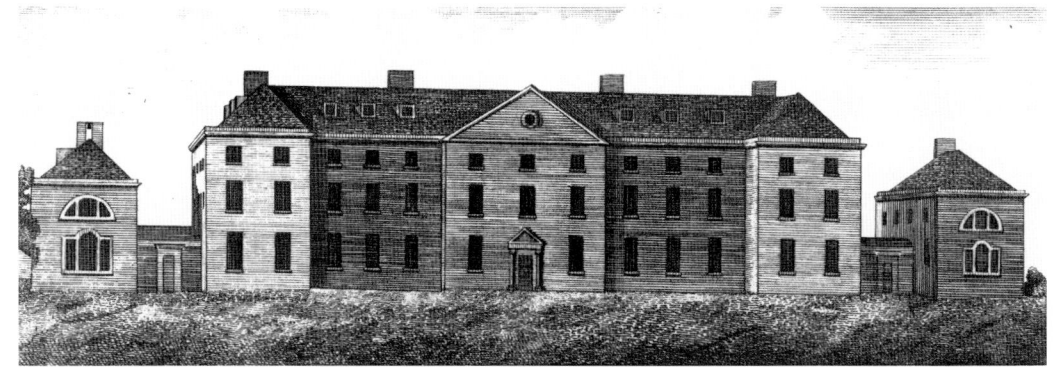

*Figure 26
Shrewsbury House of Industry was erected as a Foundling Hospital in 1760–5 and converted into a workhouse in 1784. It is now Shrewsbury School.
[From Phillips, T 1779, plate opposite p 21, by permission of the Syndics of Cambridge University Library]*

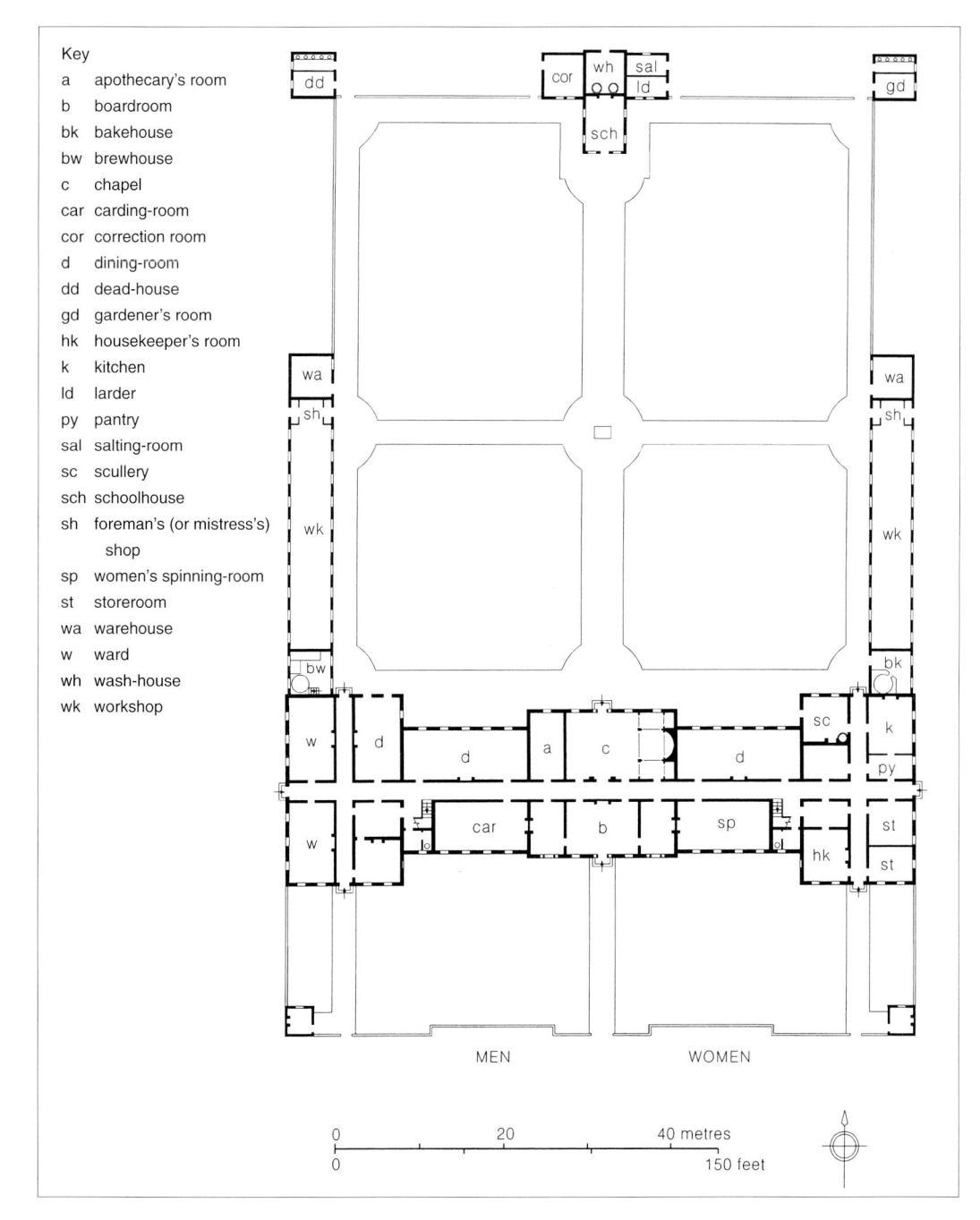

Figure 27
Oxford House of Industry was built in 1772–5 to a design by John Gwynn. It was superseded by a new building on a different site in 1865.
[Ground-floor plan redrawn from British Library Kings Maps XXXIV.33.1]

Key
a   apothecary's room
b   boardroom
bk bakehouse
bw brewhouse
c   chapel
car carding-room
cor correction room
d   dining-room
dd dead-house
gd gardener's room
hk housekeeper's room
k   kitchen
ld larder
py pantry
sal salting-room
sc scullery
sch schoolhouse
sh foreman's (or mistress's) shop
sp women's spinning-room
st storeroom
wa warehouse
w   ward
wh wash-house
wk workshop

Answers revealed the existence of 1,970 workhouses which, together, could hold a total of 90,000 paupers.[21] The actual number of pauper inmates in 1776 was not, however, recorded in the returns.

The more comprehensive survey conducted in 1802–3 revealed that 3,765 of the 14,611 parishes which responded to the questionnaire used a workhouse.[22] In fact, the number of workhouses would have been considerably smaller than 3,765, as many establishments were shared by several parishes.[23] Carlisle Workhouse, for example, was used by at least thirteen adjoining parishes in the 1790s.[24] The 1802–3 return confirmed that outdoor relief was the preferred option for most parishes: out of 725,566 paupers, only 83,468 were returned as 'in workhouses or houses of industry'. It has been calculated that half of all workhouse inmates at this time lived in the South East, an area which held only a third of the population.[25]

The inquiry covering the years 1813, 1814 and 1815 showed that pauperism had risen to 939,977, with an average of 93,141 relieved in workhouses each year.[26] Examined from another point of view, however, the figures clearly show that the number

29

Figure 28
Liverpool Workhouse (1769–72), depicted in this topographical view, was demolished around 1930 to make way for Sir Edwin Lutyens's Roman Catholic Cathedral.
[From a view of 1770, Liverpool RO, Liverpool Libraries and Information Services]

of those receiving indoor relief was beginning to decrease: the number in workhouses stood at 97,223 in 1813, 94,085 in 1814 and 88,115 in 1815. As in 1802–3, the total number of workhouses in existence was not given.

In 1797 Sir Frederick Eden published *The State of the Poor*, an invaluable source of information on late 18th-century workhouses, with accounts which included an assessment of their location, the quality of their beds and bedding, their dietaries and other random information. The majority of the institutions Eden described were simple parish workhouses with under fifty inmates; the biggest workhouses inevitably belonged to urban or rural incorporations, or the largest urban parishes. Liverpool Workhouse (Fig 28) could hold 1,220 paupers by 1790 and must have been one of the largest institutions in the country. Elsewhere in Lancashire, Manchester kept 319 people in a workhouse, Lancaster 57 and Bury 37. Workhouses serving agricultural parishes in the county typically held fewer than twenty inmates.

Many parishes, such as Louth, Spilsby and Leicester, still farmed or contracted out their poor rather than assume direct responsibility for them. Arrangements with 'farmers' or 'contractors' varied, but usually they provided inmates with accommodation, food and clothing, sent them out to work in local manufactories if they were able-bodied, but kept a high proportion or all of their wages. Dissatisfaction with this administrative system probably encouraged pamphleteers to overstate the dirty, overcrowded conditions in workhouses: these were invariably blamed on the contractor system, or corruption on the part of overseers of the poor.[27]

The notion that appalling conditions reigned in most Old Poor Law workhouses was grasped with eagerness by the Commissioners who drafted the *Poor Law Report* of 1834 (*see* Chapter 4). They described the typical Old Poor Law workhouse as:

a large almshouse, in which the young are trained in idleness, ignorance and vice; the able-bodied maintained in sluggish sensual indolence; the aged and more respectable exposed to all the misery that is incident to dwelling in such a society, without government or classification.[28]

Architectural plans indicate that Old Poor Law workhouses were designed to permit a high degree of classification, separating boys and girls from adult paupers, and often separating the aged from the able-bodied. Segregation was required to reduce possibilities of moral contamination as much as to impose an ordered and disciplined regime, but in practice it was frequently neglected. There are several reasons for that. First of all, workhouses do not seem to have admitted different classes of pauper in the proportions which architects and governors had expected, a factor which placed a great strain on available accommodation, especially in small institutions which served only one or two parishes. But more significantly, workhouse masters seem to have disregarded segregation as a result of their own ignorance or laziness.

Surviving plans also reveal that the larger workhouses, which might not be able to employ all inmates on domestic chores or with local employers, invariably included workrooms: it was certainly intended that labour would be an integral element of the institutional regime, although in reality such intentions often fell by the wayside. When inmates worked within an institution, rather than being hired out to local employers, it was usually to produce goods for internal consumption. There is little evidence for the existence of large-scale workhouse factories, even in incorporation workhouses, in the later 18th century. One of the last commercial enterprises had been embarked on by Tiverton Incorporation in 1740, when a large woollen factory was set up in the workhouse by means of a voluntary subscription of £1,020.[29] The project made such heavy losses, caused by wastage and by keeping manufactured goods on hand without an opportunity of sale, that in 1741 it was abandoned. Large workrooms were probably included in later workhouses as much to encourage the work ethic as to make a profit for the contractor or governing authority. It has already been seen that many urban and rural incorporation workhouses included workrooms. At Oxford, however, the working-rooms shown on John Gwynn's plan (*see* above) must have fallen into disuse by the 1790s, when Eden reported that inmates were employed outside the workhouse in a sacking factory and sweeping the streets.

While many workhouses had definite policies aimed at the able-bodied, others were run almost exclusively for the aged and infirm, or had distinct policies for such inmates. Empingham Workhouse in Rutland, built on 'an extensive plan' by Sir Gilbert Heathcote, was 'called the *House of Protection*, both to obviate prejudice against the name of *Poor* or *Workhouse*, and because it is *a protection to the aged sick and infirm*'.[30] In Liverpool Workhouse:

> *The old people in particular are provided with lodging, in a most judicious manner: each apartment consists of three small rooms, in which are 1 fire-place and 4 beds, and is inhabited by 8 or 10 persons. . . . [they] may consider themselves as comfortably lodged as in a secluded cottage; and thus enjoy, in some degree (even in a Workhouse,) the comfort of a private fire-side. The most infirm live on the ground floors: others are distributed through two upper stories. They all dine together in a large room, which serves occasionally for a chapel.*[31]

Although Gilbert's Act envisaged workhouses for the impotent rather than the able-bodied poor, Gilbert unions did not differ markedly from other workhouses in their admission policies: most of them preferred to offer outdoor relief to the able-bodied as it was the cheaper option.

The few statistics provided by Eden show that children often made up over half of workhouse populations. These children were expected to work, but basic schooling was also provided. At New Windsor children were instructed in reading until they were 7 years old, and then attended a free school, where they were clothed and educated until they reached 14. At Sutton Coldfield children were taught to read by a schoolmistress and put out as apprentices when 12 years old. There were schoolrooms on the ground floor of Isle of Wight House of Industry and Heckingham House of Industry, and in a detached building to the rear of the Oxford workhouse.

The Workhouse Discredited

By the end of the 18th century, workhouses were viewed as economic failures. Although most continued to put able inmates to work, either in the house or with an outside employer, it was now clear that attempts to profit from pauper labour entailed expensive supervision and caused an excess of production harmful to independent workers. In most cases pauper labour did not even cover the general running costs of a workhouse. Many authorities which had hoped to effect a reduction in the rates by erecting a large workhouse were now saddled with huge debts and even those which had been initially successful, such as Carlford and Colneis Incorporation, failed to maintain low poor rates after prices began to rise in the 1790s.

While the poor rates have been estimated at £700,000 in 1700, they amounted to £1,500,000 in 1776.[32] Rising rates had been apparent for some time and were frequently blamed on the lax, or even corrupt, management of overseers. Overseers, usually busy tradesmen, were distrusted: as they held office for just one year and received no salary, it was assumed that they were inexperienced, lacked incentive and seized any opportunity to line their own pockets.[33] The preface to the 1786 edition of *An Account of the Workhouses in Great Britain* found the increase in poor rates since 1732 'very alarming', and urged gentlemen and the clergy to take a renewed interest in the management of the poor.[34] Meanwhile, the poor rate continued to rise: in 1795 it stood at around £3,000,000, but by 1803 it had risen to just over £4,000,000 and by 1818 was approaching £8,000,000. It was widely believed that workhouses had failed to provide the economic control which reformers and entrepreneurs of earlier generations had so confidently predicted, particularly in the agrarian south, where economic changes were causing much hardship.

The workhouse came to be seen as a moral and social, as well as an economic failure. While in reality workhouses took in large numbers of helpless children and old people, there was a widespread notion that they were filled with undeserving paupers who lived promiscuously together, without discipline or classification.

The workhouse of St James, Westminster has been cited as a classic example of the 'unreformed workhouse', probably because an ambiguous view of a day-room interior, published in 1808, appears to show interaction between the sexes (*see* Figure 11).[35] But life in St James's Workhouse must have been far from pleasant: by 1814 the buildings were described as 'very dilapidated and dangerous', and severe overcrowding contributed to an outbreak of contagious fever in the following year.[36]

Indeed, images of contagion were often used to describe the workhouses of this period. Poor-Law Commissioner George Nicholls retrospectively described them as 'a sort of pest-houses where diseases, social, moral, and physical, were generated and nurtured, and whence they spread into and contaminated the surrounding districts'.[37] In 1791, the historian and topographer William Hutton of Derby, where there were four parish workhouses with between thirty and sixty-three inmates apiece, was highly critical of contemporary workhouses:

> *according to the present mode of conducting workhouses, they are completely destructive: they are the nurseries of idleness, the corrupters of manners, the receptacles of vulgarity, the sink of rudeness, the destroyers of health, the slaughterhouses of infants, and the plagues of old age: if there is hell upon earth, as taught by our old nurses, it must be in a crowded prison, where corruptions grow with hasty shoots: if there is a purgatory, as taught by a venerable church, many of whose adherents I esteem, it must be in a workhouse, where order is routed by discord.*[38]

Hutton's language contrasts strongly with that of the 1732 *Account of Workhouses*, which had proclaimed workhouses 'Nurseries of Religion, Virtue and Industry'.[39] A general disillusionment had set in over the course of the intervening sixty years, and paupers had lost the sympathy of the rate-paying public.

From the beginning of the French Revolutionary War the proliferation of lenient relief practices increased discontent with the current system. From the 1780s, poor rates were used to subsidise wages in many parts of southern England. Various methods of dispensing outdoor relief included the roundsman system, the labour rate and, most notoriously, the Speenhamland system or Berkshire Bread Scale. This last, introduced by the magistrates of Berkshire in 1795, provided a supplementary allowance that was proportionate to the ruling price of bread and dependent on the number of children in a family. It was widely claimed that such practices had a demoralising effect on the populace, but they seemed to receive official sanction in 1795 when an amendment to Knatchbull's Act made it lawful, in certain cases, for an overseer to give paupers relief in their own homes, even if they refused to enter a workhouse.[40] At the same time, Justices were given the power to enforce outdoor relief. In reality, this made little difference, as few parishes had ever possessed sufficient accommodation to impose a total ban on outdoor relief.

Allowances systems, especially allowances for labourers' children, led the Revd T R Malthus to conclude that all statutory relief to the poor should be abolished. In his *Essay on the Principles of Population* (1803), he argued that a poor law damaged the poor by encouraging an increase in population without a corresponding increase in food for its support.[41] Although few adopted such an extreme stance, Malthus's views attracted a sizeable following.

After the Napoleonic Wars, severe unemployment and a still-rising poor rate triggered official intervention. In 1817, a Select Committee chaired by Sturges Bourne, MP, was appointed to investigate means of controlling expenditure. Its report, dated July 1817, was critical of the very principle of poor relief, but offered few constructive suggestions. The Committee was 'aware how very frequently workhouses have been condemned, as little corresponding with the denomination they have received; and being rather in truth, in many instances, houses of idleness and vice'.[42] Nevertheless, workhouses were deemed necessary, and the Committee expressed its approval for the union system, administered by principal local inhabitants.

The *Report* of the Select Committee led to the Select Vestry Act, or Sturges Bourne's Act, of 1819, which tackled the problems attendant on poor-law administration by allowing parishes to appoint either a permanent salaried assistant overseer or a parish committee ('select vestry') of five to twenty persons, to provide a continuous review of poor-law affairs.[43] The system was introduced in certain parts of the country, notably throughout Lancashire, and by 1831 as many as 3,249 parishes had appointed assistant overseers, reportedly with beneficial results.

The general dissatisfaction with poor-law administration and workhouse management culminated in the Poor Law Amendment Act of 1834, which sought to establish deterrent workhouses throughout the country. The notion of the deterrent workhouse, however, was not new. It had been expounded by several reformers from the end of the 18th century, and had been put into practice by some poor-law authorities in the East Midlands. Closely associated with it was a new approach to workhouse architecture, in which the form of the building facilitated the control of its occupants.

BUILDING AND FURNITURE
FOR AN
INDUSTRY-HOUSE
ESTABLISHMENT,
For 2000 Perfons, of all Ages,
ON THE
PANOPTICON OR CENTRAL-INSPECTION PRINCIPLE.

☞ For the Explanation of the feveral Figures of this PLATE, fee " Outline of a Work, intitled PAUPER MANAGEMENT " IMPROVED;" by *Jeremy Bentham*, Efq. as printed in ANNALS OF AGRICULTURE, Vol. XXX.

The Ranges of Bed-Stages and Cribs are refpectively fuppofed to run from End to End of the *radial* Walls, as exhibited in the GROUND PLAN: they are here reprefented as cut through by a Line parallel to the Side of the Polygon: in the Bed-Stages, what is reprefented as *one* in the Draught, is propofed to be in *two* in the Defcription.

FIG. I.—ELEVATION.

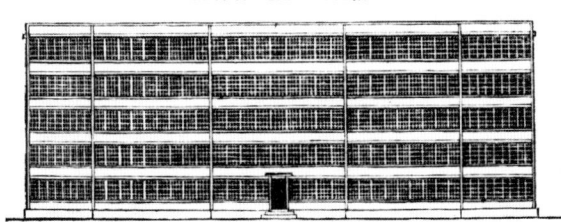

FIG. II.—SECTION.

FIG. III.—GROUND PLAN.

SAMUEL BENTHAM, Knight of the Order of St. George of Ruffia, Brigadier-General in the Ruffian Service, and Infpector-General of his Majefty's Naval Works, *invenit*.
SAMUEL BUNCE, Efq. Architect of his Majefty's Naval Works, *delineavit*.

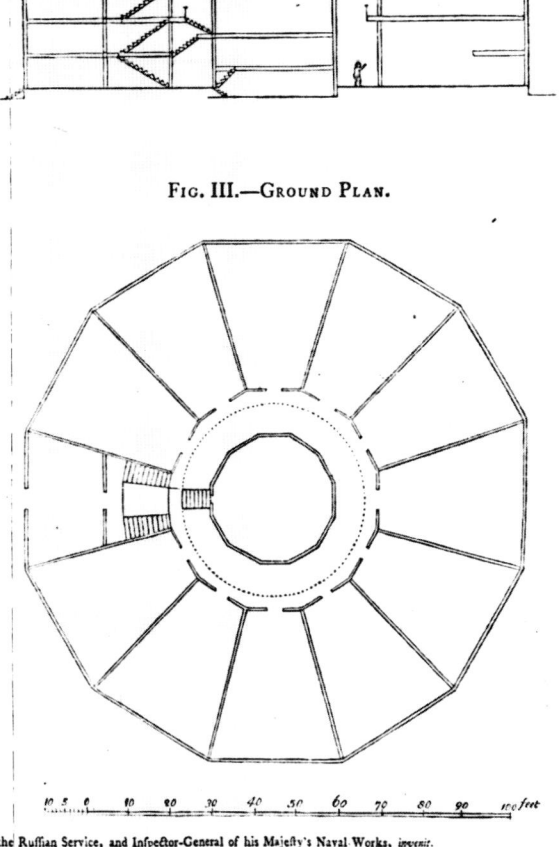

The New Deterrent Workhouse

In the early 19th century stricter workhouses were presented as a solution to the problems of rising poor rates and weak administration. Several new 'deterrent' workhouses incorporated features derived from recent prison architecture which made it easier to supervise and control the inmates. These buildings embodied the belief that architecture could fulfil a moral function – or at least make a substantial contribution to the reformatory intent of an institution.

THE PRINCIPLE OF CENTRAL INSPECTION
A new approach to workhouse architecture seems to have been inspired by the Utilitarian philosopher Jeremy Bentham (1758–1832) who, in 1798, extended his interest from the institutionalisation of convicts to that of paupers.[44] Estimating that there were about half a million paupers in the country, he proposed the construction of 250 panopticons, or buildings on the Central Inspection Principle, evenly distributed throughout England and Wales and administered by a single National Charity Company. Each panopticon would hold 2,000 people. Designed by Bentham's brother Samuel, together with Samuel Bunce, the panopticon was to be a regular 12-sided polygon constructed of iron frames with glazed wall surfaces, both internally and externally (Figs 29 and 30). Internally, the 'universal transparency' of the structure would aid inspection, and mirrors were to be fixed around the centre to direct extra light into the governor's apartments and give him views of the paupers at work. Although the panopticon had been devised by Samuel Bentham in Russia, where he planned to build a circular arsenal for Prince Potemkin in the late 1780s, it was Jeremy who thought it could be applied with success to

Figure 29
The Panopticon House of Industry was designed by Samuel Bentham and Samuel Bunce and published in Jeremy Bentham's Pauper Management *in 1798. No such building was ever built.*
[From Bentham 1798, by permission of the Syndics of Cambridge University Library]

33

*Figure 30
Different types of bed were designed for the inmates of Jeremy Bentham's Panopticon House of Industry.
[From Bentham 1798, by permission of the Syndics of Cambridge University Library]*

FIG. IV.—BED-STAGES for Single Persons.

FIG. V.—BED-STAGES for Married Couples; alternating with sets of Cribs for Children, four in a set.

FIG. VI.—CRIBS for Infants.

schools, hospitals, lazarettos, poor-plan buildings, houses of correction, lunatic asylums, orphanages, nurseries, institutions for the blind and deaf, homes for deserted young women, factories, and even a gigantic chicken-coop.[45]

In the event, no true panopticons were built, but the inspection principle was established as a requisite of effective workhouse buildings. In prison architecture that idea was already well established, one of the earliest examples being the radial *Maison de Force* at Ghent, begun in 1773.[46] After the passage of the 1779 Penitentiary Act, William Blackburn designed a number of English gaols with cellular wings radiating from the governor's quarters, and after 1800 radial and concentric designs became increasingly popular.[47] In these new prisons, the governor could usually watch prisoners in their yards, but not in their cells.

Blackburn's Ipswich County Gaol (1786–90; Fig 31) and New Bailey Prison, Salford (1787–90) were both based on a Greek cross, with four wings attached to an octagonal centre, while the Littledean Bridewell (1787–91) simply had a central block flanked by two wings. The larger Liverpool Borough Gaol (1785–6), like Blackburn's earlier winning design for a National Penitentiary (1782), had detached wings, an idea which was never adopted for workhouse design.

Several architects are known to have designed both prisons and workhouses in the late 18th century. Blackburn was not one of them but, in 1792, his under-surveyor at Stafford Gaol, William Leigh, was instructed to prepare plans for Stone Workhouse 'according to the Plan of the Romford Workhouse omitting only the workshops'.[48] Romford Workhouse had been designed by James Wyatt in 1785, the same year as his rectangular Sussex County Bridewell at Petworth, but the building was demolished in 1840 and nothing is known of its form.[49] George Byfield's Worcester House of Industry was erected in 1793–4, some years before his radial gaols at Bury St Edmunds (1803), Worcester (designed 1802) and elsewhere.[50] Similarly, John Wing designed the Bedford House of Industry (1795–6) before his Bedfordshire County Gaol (1801), a building with a stubby cruciform plan.

None of the aforementioned architects, despite their familiarity with prisons, seems to have imported the concept of central inspection into the field of workhouse design. Throughout the 18th century it had been usual for master's rooms to occupy a peripheral position, but in the early 1790s the benefits of locating him in the centre of an institution were recognised, amongst others, by the guardians of Oxford Incorporation (*see* Figure 27), possibly under the influence of Bentham's and Blackburn's publicised projects. The guardians complained that:

> the master's and matron's apartments [were] situated in one corner of one of the wings of the building, at a distance from, and out of the sight and hearing of every part of the house, where their attention was more particularly demanded.[51]

This was soon sorted out: the master's accommodation was moved to the centre of the building, 'in view of the entrances in front, and at the same time commanding the yard and offices backward'.

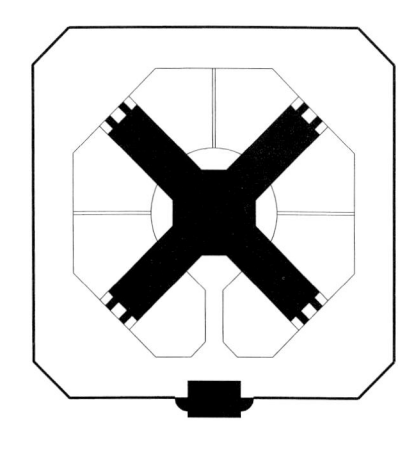

*Figure 31 (right)
Ipswich County Gaol (1786), designed by William Blackburn, the well-known prison architect, had a hub with radial wings.
[Block plan based on plan in Evans 1982, fig 68]*

Old Poor Law Institutions, c 1750–1834

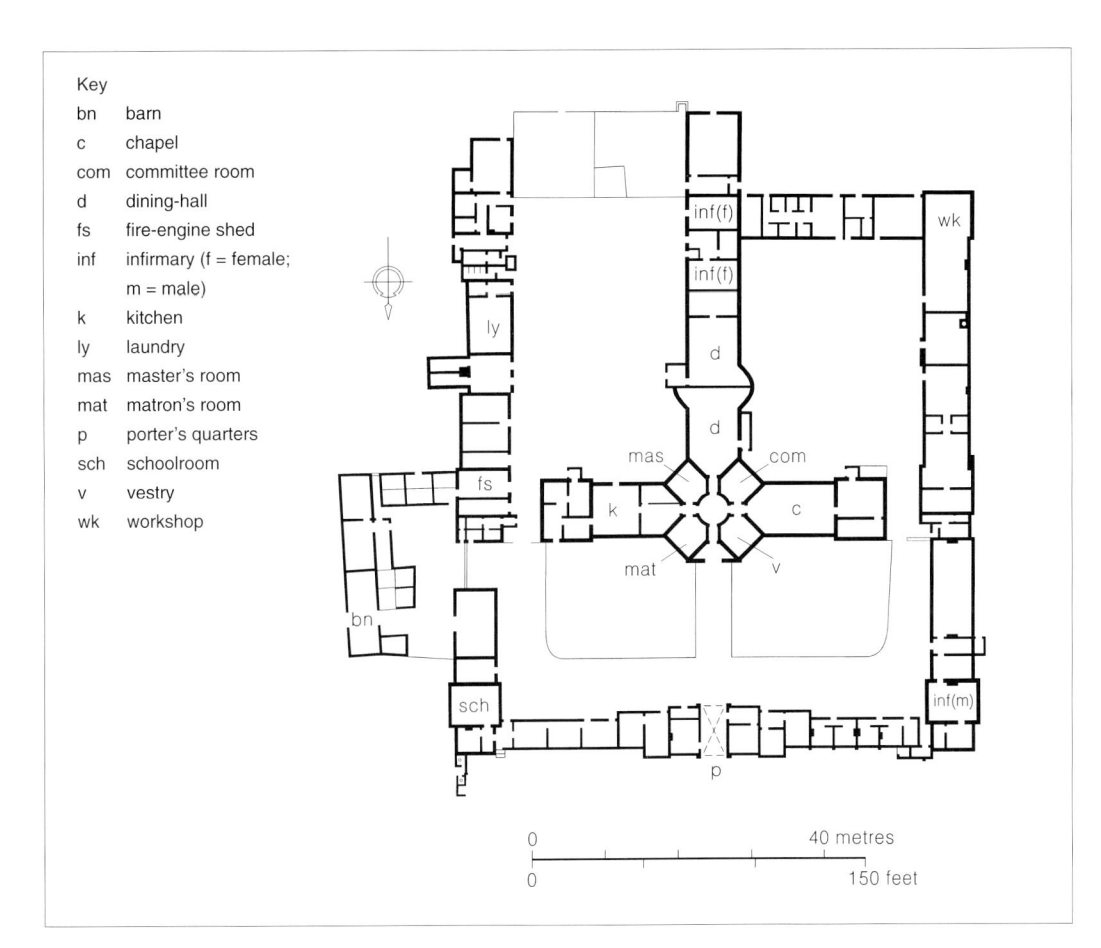

Key
bn   barn
c   chapel
com committee room
d   dining-hall
fs   fire-engine shed
inf infirmary (f = female; m = male)
k   kitchen
ly   laundry
mas master's room
mat matron's room
p   porter's quarters
sch schoolroom
v   vestry
wk   workshop

Figure 32
Alverstoke House of Industry (1799–1801) in Hampshire may have been the first radial workhouse. This plan shows the building as it existed in 1861; unfortunately, it no longer survives.
[Redrawn from 1:500 OS (Hants), LXXXIII.10.15, surveyed 1861]

Figure 33
This perspective drawing of Caistor House of Industry (1800–2) in Lincolnshire, with the entrance block at the top, shows how the corners of the projecting central block were canted to provide the governor with a good view over the yards.

The first workhouses known to have included a central supervisory core, or hub, were Alverstoke House of Industry in Hampshire, erected for 250 paupers in 1799–1801, and Caistor House of Industry, built in 1800–2 by William Dixon's Society of Industry. This is surprising, as each institution belonged to an authority set up under Gilbert's Act, and would have accommodated 'impotent' rather than 'able-bodied' paupers.

Alverstoke House of Industry was designed by Francis Carter of Finsbury Square, London, about whom little else is known.[52] Although it has been demolished, maps show that the 'cross-in-square' plan of the building (Fig 32) was very similar to that of some New Poor Law workhouses built in the 1830s.[53] It was entered from the north, where a path led to a fully octagonal hub containing the vestry, committee room and governor's rooms. Three wings emanated from the hub: in 1861, on the ground floor, the chapel lay to the west, the kitchen to the east and the dining-halls to the south.[54] The outbuildings included infirmaries and lunatic cells.

The hub of the three-storeyed Caistor House of Industry (Fig 33) was rectangular to the front and canted to the rear, and would have been less

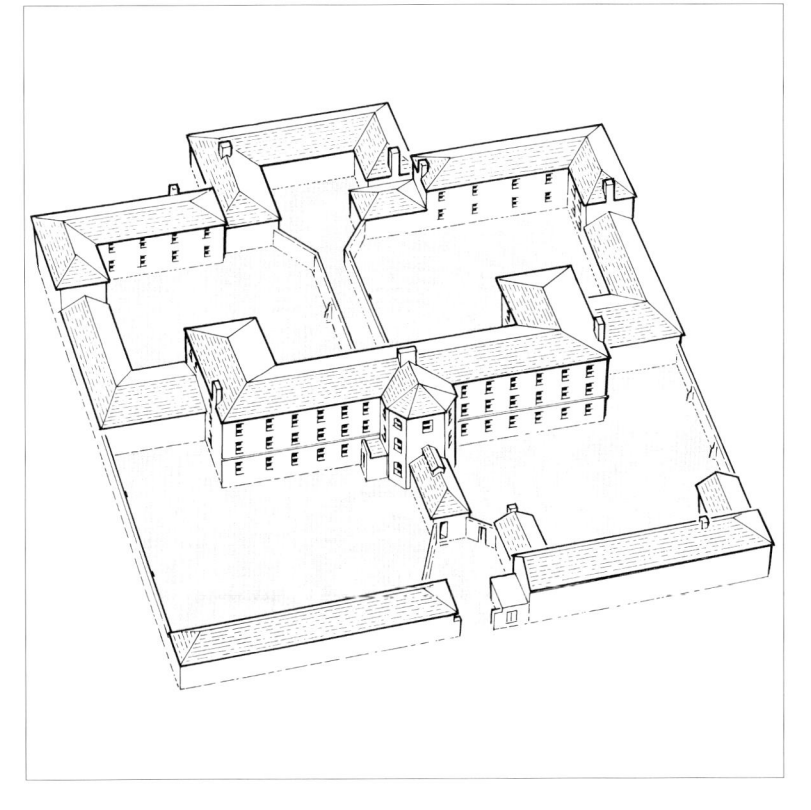

35

effective for surveillance – or architectural impact – than that of Alverstoke. Its ground floor appears to have housed the kitchen, while its upper floors could have provided vantage points overlooking the paupers' yards. As in contemporary prisons, the hubs of neither Alverstoke nor Caistor enabled the governor to watch the inmates in their day-rooms or dormitories.

THE NOTTINGHAMSHIRE EXPERIMENTS
In the early 19th century, more poor-law authorities became insistent about refusing outdoor relief to some classes of pauper. Despite the passage of Sir William Young's Act of 1795, which permitted parishes to grant outdoor relief, Eden's reports of 1797 showed that some authorities, for example Portsmouth, the Isle of Wight and Shrewsbury, still refused it to all classes.[55] Again in 1797, Bentham declared that his panopticon workhouse should be the sole means of receiving aid from the poor rates.

A number of parishes in Nottinghamshire introduced a deterrent poor-law policy in the years following the Napoleonic Wars. In 1818 the Revd Robert Lowe of Bingham refused outdoor relief to the able-bodied paupers of his parish, instead offering them admittance to the workhouse, where a strict regime operated.[56] As a result, the poor were deterred from applying for relief and the cost of relief in Bingham fell markedly. The physical form of the Bingham parish workhouse, which could hold only thirty inmates, did not play a key role in the introduction of the new policy.[57] Assistant Commissioner Wylde, reporting in 1833, complained that:

> Its construction does not admit of that discipline which the law requires. There is neither separation of sexes, classification, employment nor education. It is merely a place of irksome confinement, which the labouring classes will not accept in a parish like Bingham, where sufficient employment may be procured by proper exertion.[58]

The crucial experiment, involving a building which permitted inspection, classification and segregation, took place in the Minster town of Southwell, where Captain George Nicholls was invited to become overseer of the poor in 1821. Nicholls, who had recently retired to Nottinghamshire following a successful career with the East India Company, claimed that the existing workhouse 'had been of little use to the parish, if indeed it was not a positive evil, for it had become the resort of the idle and profligate of both sexes'.[59] It was:

> insufficient for any useful purpose. It was under charge of an elderly female, was at all times open to ingress and egress, and although in its construction provision had been made for the separation of the sexes, the rule had not been observed; in short the workhouse not only occasioned great expense, but was also a source of demoralisation in the parish.

This lax administration, however, had not always prevailed. The building (Figs 34 and 35) had been designed by Lowe's cousin, the Revd John Thomas Becher of Southwell, and was erected in 1808 with room for eighty-four inmates. Becher maintained that it had been 'constructed and governed upon a principle of Inspection, Classification, and Seclusion'[60] and, despite its small size, the building was clearly designed with that intention. The governor's rooms were situated centrally, in the oval hub, and separate accommodation was provided for men, women and children. The founding principles, however, had weakened over the years, and Nicholls lost no time in reinstating them: the building and yards were enclosed by walls sufficiently high to prevent persons entering or leaving the premises without permission, a competent master and matron were appointed and a new set of rules drawn up, involving the classification and segregation of inmates. Once these restraints were put into practice, the number of inmates fell.

Nicholls further reduced the Southwell poor rate by withdrawing assistance to the poor outside the workhouse. Outdoor relief to the aged, infirm and impotent continued, but parish employment outside the workhouse was discontinued, as were allowances to people in employment and the payment of rents out of the poor rate. Nicholls claimed that, under this new system, the labouring class 'improved both socially and morally'.[61] It has been suggested that the system did not result in large-scale distress simply because, at the time, the poor of Southwell were easily able to find work in nearby Nottingham.[62]

Nicholls broadcast his success at Southwell in eight letters published by the *Nottingham Journal* in 1821, later republished as a pamphlet entitled *Eight Letters on the Management of the Poor*. He left Southwell in 1823 to help Thomas Telford supervise the construction of the Gloucester Ship Canal and, until 1834, when he became a Poor Law Commissioner, had little more to do with poor-law affairs.

In 1824, following Nicholls's departure, the Revd Becher instigated the formation of the Thurgarton Hundred Incorporation, comprising forty-nine parishes in the vicinity of Southwell. The Incorporation operated a deterrent system modelled on that of Southwell, based on strict economy and supervision 'tempered with tenderness towards the Infirm and Guiltless Poor, but opposing by every legal effort the overwhelming Advances of idle, profligate, and sturdy Pauperism'.[63] A workhouse, designed by Becher with the help of a

OLD POOR LAW INSTITUTIONS, c1750–1834

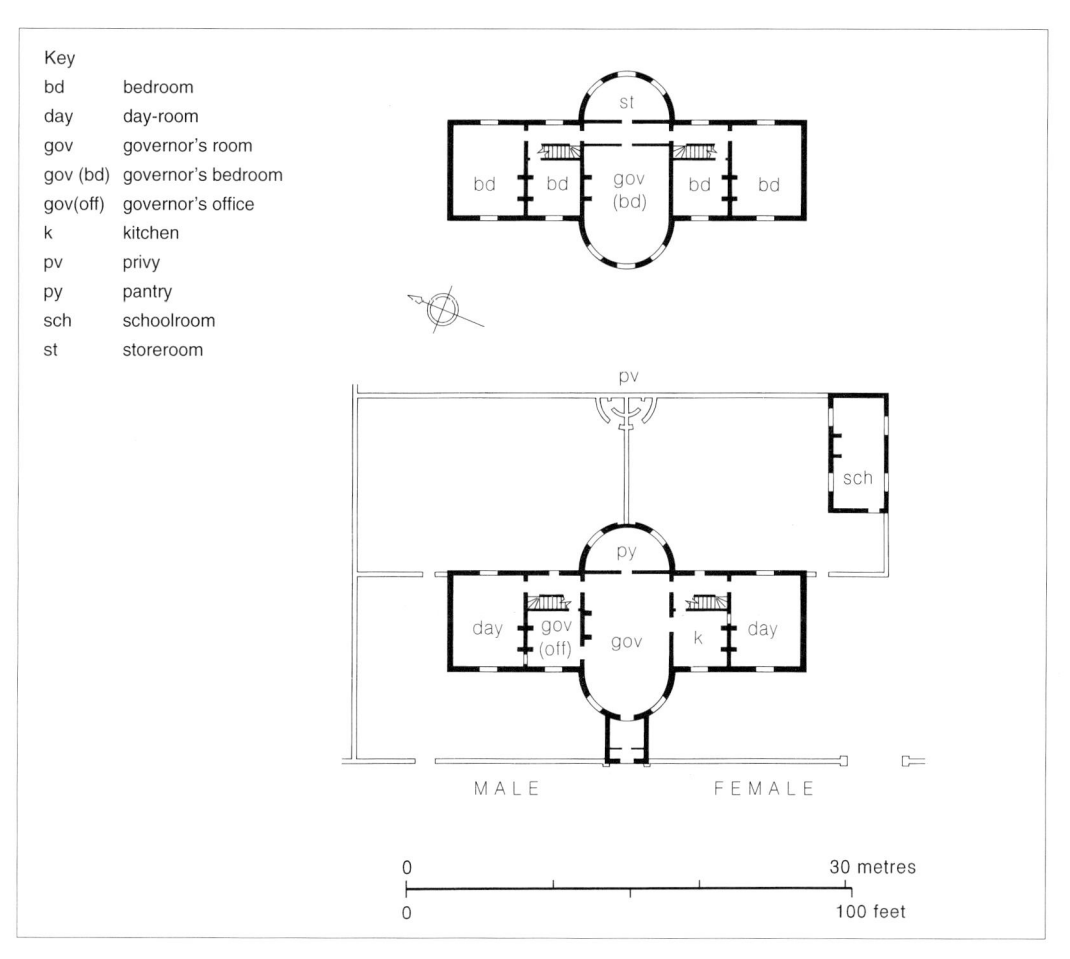

*Figure 34
Plans of the Southwell Parish Workhouse (1808) in Nottinghamshire were published by the Revd Becher in 1828, but the oval 'hub' never became popular.
[Ground and first-floor plans based on Becher 1828]*

*Figure 35
Southwell Parish Workhouse was converted into a Baptist Chapel after the passage of the Poor Law Amendment Act and the creation of Southwell Union in 1836. Thurgarton Hundred Workhouse then became Southwell Union Workhouse.
[BB93/26827]*

The Workhouse

Figure 36
Thurgarton Hundred Workhouse, built just outside Southwell in 1824, had widespread influence after being publicised by the Revd Becher in 1828, despite the fact that poor-law reform was already in the air. Its architect, William Nicholson, later went on to design several New Poor Law workhouses, including Lincoln.
[Ground and first-floor plans largely based on Becher 1828 and RCHME survey]

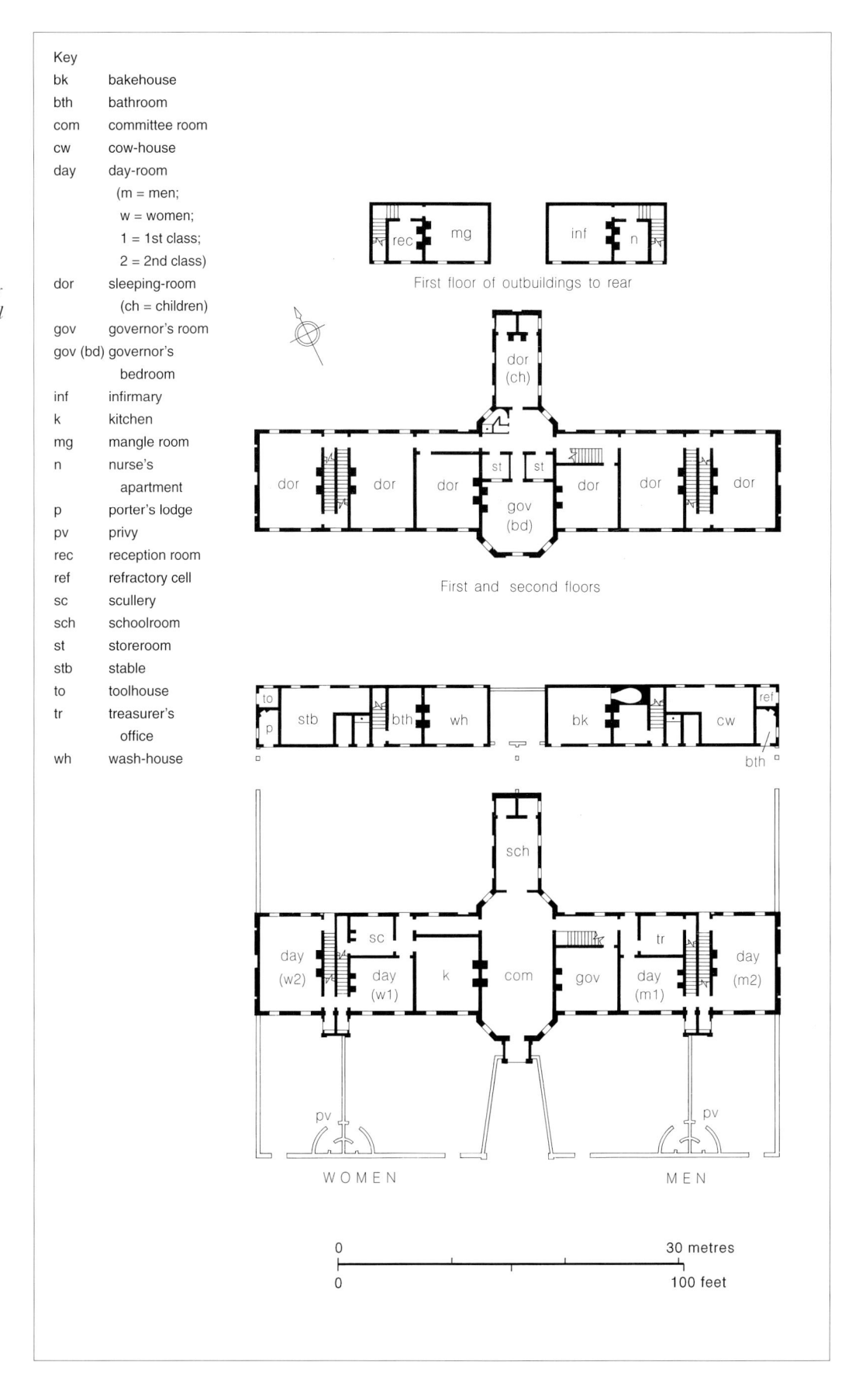

Key
bk	bakehouse
bth	bathroom
com	committee room
cw	cow-house
day	day-room
	(m = men;
	w = women;
	1 = 1st class;
	2 = 2nd class)
dor	sleeping-room
	(ch = children)
gov	governor's room
gov (bd)	governor's bedroom
inf	infirmary
k	kitchen
mg	mangle room
n	nurse's apartment
p	porter's lodge
pv	privy
rec	reception room
ref	refractory cell
sc	scullery
sch	schoolroom
st	storeroom
stb	stable
to	toolhouse
tr	treasurer's office
wh	wash-house

*Figure 37
The walls flanking the path to the main entrance of Thurgarton Hundred Workhouse were part of the original scheme, as was the porch. After 1834 workhouse walls were usually much higher, but these later proved inconvenient and few survive.
[BB93/26856]*

local architect, William Nicholson, was promptly erected in the parish of Upton, on the outskirts of Southwell, at a cost of £6,596. It opened in December 1824 and could hold 158 paupers.

Thurgarton Hundred Workhouse (Figs 36, 37, 38), an important forerunner of the radially planned workhouses of the New Poor Law, adapted the Southwell plan to an altogether larger scale. It was a three-storeyed, red-brick building, comprising three ranges emanating from an octagonal hub. The windows of the committee room and governor's living-rooms in the hub overlooked the four separate exercise yards, aiding inspection. The central position of these rooms also meant that the governor had equal access to the three wings, which were assigned to men, women and children. Men and women were subdivided into first and second-class inmates: those of 'good character and conduct' and those deemed 'idle, immoral and improvident'.[64] Each class had its own day-rooms, dormitories, staircases and yards, to prevent them mixing (Fig 39). While water-closets were installed on each landing for the governor, the inmates were merely supplied with quadrant-shaped privies in their yards. Outbuildings to the rear contained the laundry and bakehouse. Above the bakehouse was an infirmary for the isolation of infectious cases, and next to it were the cow-house and a cell where those who misbehaved could be temporarily incarcerated.

By 1828, when Becher published *The Anti-Pauper System*, a highly influential account of the policies operated by Southwell parish and

Figure 38
This view along the second-floor corridor of Thurgarton Hundred Workhouse gives an impression of the spartan conditions existing in most workhouses.
[BB93/26865]

Figure 39
This drawing shows how the double staircase in the female wing of Thurgarton Hundred Workhouse kept able-bodied (second-class) and elderly (first-class) women apart.

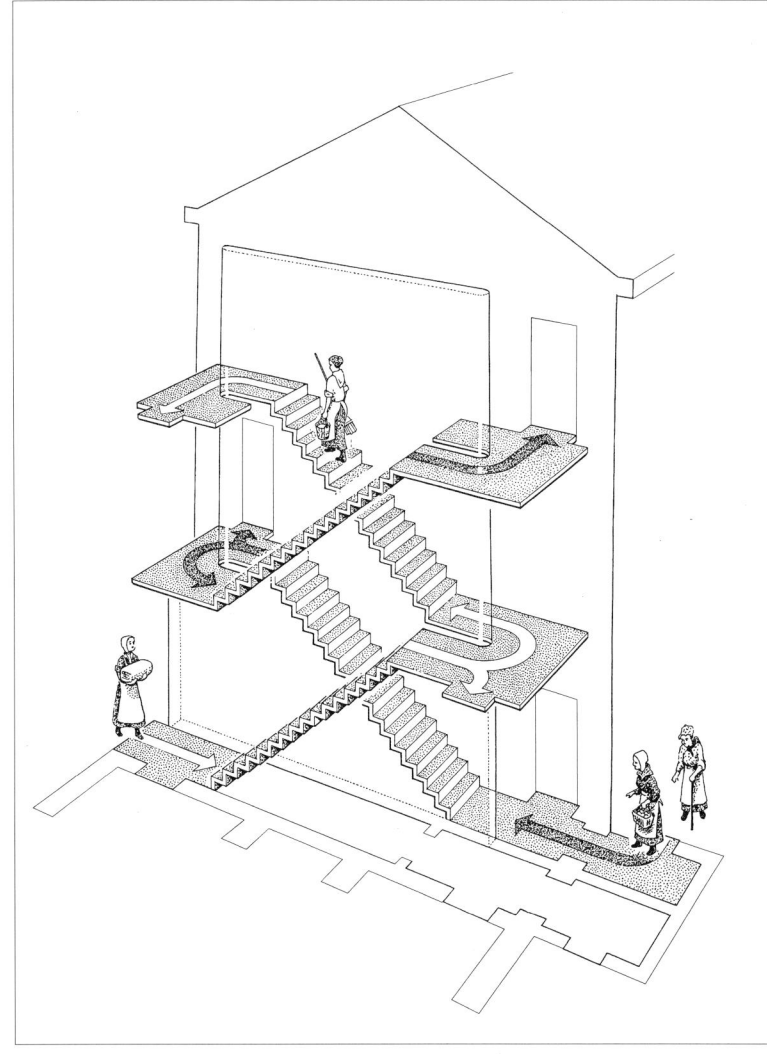

Thurgarton Hundred Incorporation, there were no able-bodied men in the Thurgarton Hundred Workhouse. The deterrent had worked. Male inmates nevertheless cultivated the garden and undertook 'such laborious Work as may be required', while women performed domestic chores. All attempts to set inmates to work for a profit had been abandoned.

Becher further expounded his ideas on poor-law administration in evidence presented to the Poor Law Committee of 1831, revealing stronger humanitarian impulses than Nicholls. While he favoured a large workhouse capable of classifying inmates, he agreed with poor-law expenditure on cottages for the 'guiltless poor', small gardens for the industrious, employment for the able-bodied and medical dispensaries for the poor.[65]

In 1834 the question of whether Becher or Nicholls had pioneered the deterrent workhouse system was hotly debated. In the *Report* of the Poor Law Commission, published in 1834, Assistant Commissioner Cowell attributed it to Lowe and Nicholls, while Wylde gave the credit to Becher.[66] A second edition of *The Anti-Pauper System*, also published in 1834, included an unfortunate attack on Cowell, inspiring retaliation in the form of 'A Letter to the Revd J T Becher'. Cowell also persuaded Nicholls to draft a statement for the Commission, presenting his side of the story, and was probably responsible for recommending Nicholls's appointment as a Poor Law Commissioner.[67]

Despite Nicholls's ultimate victory, owed largely to the intervention of Cowell, the design of Southwell workhouse demonstrates that Becher was aware, as early as 1808, of the role which architecture could play in establishing a well-regulated workhouse. Wylde's evidence to the Poor Law Commission further reveals that Becher had instigated the rebuilding of the Southwell House of Correction, a building which was erected on radial principles to a design by Richard Ingleman in 1807–8.[68] In fairness, Becher and Nicholls can be attributed with joint responsibility for the system: the reforms introduced by Nicholls at Southwell in 1821 seem to have built upon the foundations laid by Becher in 1808, and Becher, in turn, adopted many of Nicholls's ideas for the Anti-Pauper System which was operated by Thurgarton Hundred Incorporation, under his guidance, from 1824. The critical difference between the two men involved their attitude to paupers outside the workhouse: it was Nicholls's punitive approach, rather than Becher's paternalism, which appealed to the law-makers of 1834.

Thurgarton Hundred Incorporation did not manage to effect a material reduction in the rates, but its deterrent workhouse was presented as a means of preventing their increase and a few parishes in other parts of England, including Uley in Gloucestershire, St Werburgh in Derby, and Penzance and Redruth in Cornwall, were motivated by Becher to introduce a similar system.[69] As radical poor-law reform was already anticipated, few of these authorities took the economic risk of erecting a new workhouse. One building, however, which was certainly inspired by the Nottinghamshire experiments belonged to Ongar Hundred (Fig 40), an incorporation of ten Essex parishes formed under Gilbert's Act.[70] The workhouse, erected at Stanford Rivers in 1830, was a large, brown-brick structure with restrained Tudor-style details. The governor's rooms lay in the centre, and his powers of inspection were assisted by a canted semi-hub similar to that at Caistor.[71] Although the interior has been greatly altered, the wings appear to have housed two cross-lit dormitories on each floor.

Another workhouse erected 'from a plan of the Reverend J.T. Becher of Southwell . . . and conducted on the principle of proper and legal restraint' was the new Stoke-upon-Trent parish workhouse of 1832, known locally as the 'Spittals'.[72] The new workhouse, which could accommodate between 500 and 700 inmates, drew criticism for its harshness in separating husbands from wives and children from parents. It was a two-storeyed building with the master's quarters, boardroom, kitchen and chapel in the centre, female accommodation to the west and male to the east. Following the Thurgarton model, the children were accommodated behind the master's rooms, and two sick-rooms were provided on the upper floor of a rear workshop range.

But while the notion of establishing a deterrent workhouse to effect a reduction in the poor rates spread, the architectural form of the workhouse did not often allow for such sophisticated segregation of inmates as Thurgarton, Ongar and Stoke-upon-Trent. In 1834 the Revd D Capper published his *Practical Results of the Workhouse*

*Figure 40
Ongar Hundred
Workhouse in Essex was
built in 1830. After
1834 the building was
extended and adapted to
serve Ongar Union; it
was altered yet again in
the 1920s, when it
became a tent and flag
factory.
[BB94/8107]*

THE WORKHOUSE

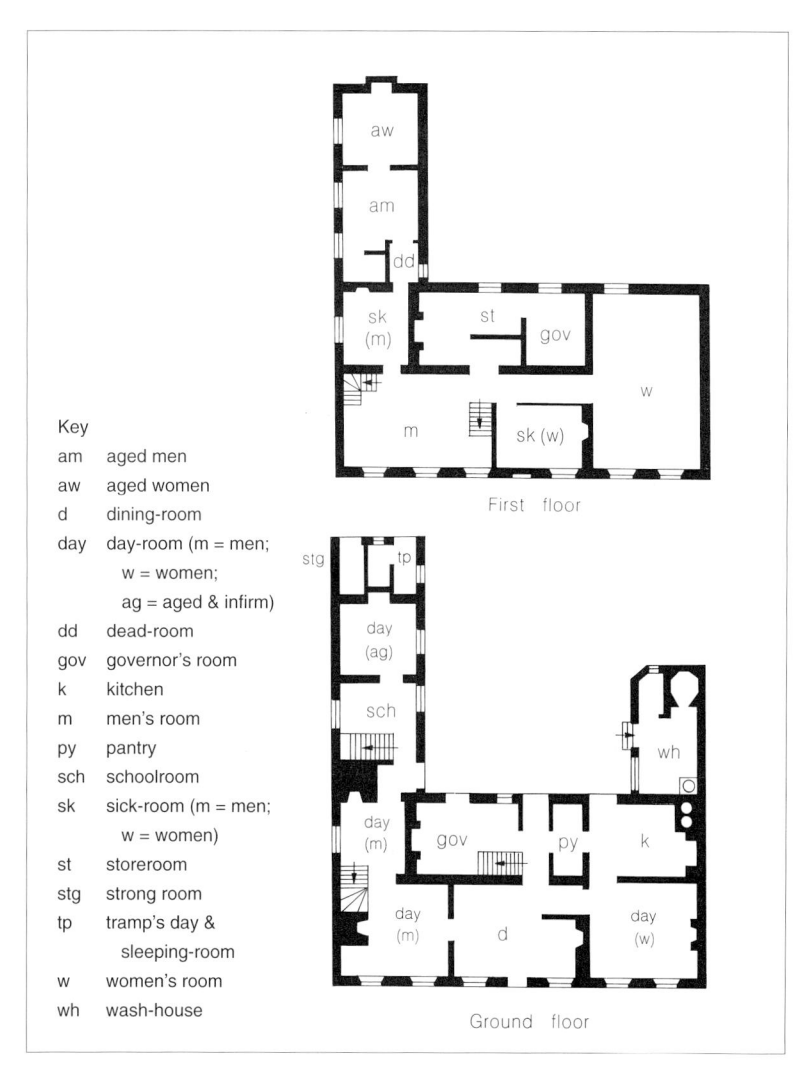

Key
am   aged men
aw   aged women
d   dining-room
day   day-room (m = men;
           w = women;
           ag = aged & infirm)
dd   dead-room
gov   governor's room
k   kitchen
m   men's room
py   pantry
sch   schoolroom
sk   sick-room (m = men;
           w = women)
st   storeroom
stg   strong room
tp   tramp's day &
           sleeping-room
w   women's room
wh   wash-house

Figure 41
In 1832 the parish workhouse of Great Missenden in Buckinghamshire was rearranged under the influence of the Revd Becher's 'anti-pauper system'.
[Ground and first-floor plans based on Capper 1834]

System as adopted in the Parish of Great Missenden, Bucks, during the Year 1833–34.[73] Inspired by Becher and the deterrent workhouses of Berkhampstead and Cookham – where the parish was 'the hardest taskmaster' and 'the worst paymaster' the pauper could find – the parish workhouse of Great Missenden was altered and enlarged at a cost of £756 in 1832.[74] While describing the workhouse as 'a commodious and comfortable house, well-ordered', Capper published plans (Fig 41) showing a two-storey and attic building with a domestic layout, allowing little segregation of its twenty-four inmates. On the first floor, for example, the aged women's room could only be reached by walking through the aged men's room, and the dead room was a small compartment between the aged men's room and the men's sick-room, accessible from both. Capper seems to have been oblivious to these defects.

It may be suspected that Great Missenden publicised the ordering of its workhouse in a vain attempt to retain independence after the passage of the Poor Law Amendment Act. Some other parishes certainly attempted to forestall centralisation by providing, at the eleventh hour, a new workhouse. The parishioners of Glossop must have experienced some qualms when large sums were expended on a new workhouse in 1834, but as the town became the centre of a union the new building was retained.[75] Burslem was less fortunate. In 1835, £1,400 was spent on an addition for male inmates at the workhouse, which could then house 300 paupers. Burslem Select Vestry argued for the retention of its workhouse:

> *the earnings of the Paupers in the Poor House employed in the local manufactures have for many years past averaged more than £100 per annum and considerably exceeded that sum when the House has been most thronged, and this benefit would be lost to the Parish in case the Poor House were fixed at any inconvenient distance.*[76]

In the event, the Wolstanton and Burslem Union was formed and a central workhouse erected. Thenceforth, all pauper labour was conducted within the workhouse and none of it for profit. No doubt to the chagrin of the parish, the building of 1835 was let to the government as an army barracks.

Like Great Missenden, Glossop and Burslem, most English parishes had no option but to join a union and come under the control of the Poor Law Commission after 1834. Many existing incorporations, however, resisted efforts to make them disband, thus impeding the formation of new unions. Some were successful in this, but Thurgarton Hundred Incorporation, upon which the new unions were largely modelled, succumbed in 1836, much to the dismay of the Revd Becher – who was reportedly '*almost raving at the result*' – and to the delight of his old adversary, the former Captain, now Commissioner, George Nicholls.[77]

4
The New Poor Law of 1834

Discontent with the *modus operandi* of the existing poor laws, and particularly the notion that corrupt overseers were profligate in the distribution of outdoor relief, culminated in the *Report* of the Royal Commission on the Poor Laws (1834) and the subsequent Poor Law Amendment Act.[1] This inaugurated the era of the New Poor Law, introducing throughout England and Wales a revised attitude towards the institutionalisation of indoor paupers, largely based on the principle of deterrence as applied in the preceding decade by authorities such as the parish of Southwell and Thurgarton Hundred Incorporation.

The effectiveness of a deterrent policy would depend on the existence of a national system of workhouses, each with the physical capability to segregate different classes of inmate and to implement a disciplined regime which would prove distasteful to would-be paupers. The enormous task of setting in place a new administrative framework and initiating a programme of reconstruction confronted the newly appointed Poor Law Commissioners in 1834. Undaunted by setbacks and regional opposition, however, within five years they were in a position to claim that the new law was operational throughout most of the country.

Steps towards a New Poor Law

In February 1832 Lord Grey's Whig government set up the Royal Commission on the Poor Laws. Nine Commissioners were appointed and directed to:

> make a diligent and full inquiry into the practical operation of the laws for the relief of the poor in England and Wales, and into the manner in which those laws are administered; and to report whether any or what alterations, amendments, or improvements may be beneficially made in the said laws, or in the manner of administering them, and how the same may be best carried into effect.[2]

The Commissioners began their inquiry by sending questionnaires to parishes throughout England and Wales. As these elicited a poor response, twenty-six Assistant Commissioners were swiftly dispatched to report at first hand on one-fifth of the country's parishes. *The Poor Law Report*, based on a selection of evidence collected by these men, was drafted by two Commissioners, the political economist Nassau Senior (1790–1864) and Jeremy Bentham's protégé, Edwin Chadwick (1800–90), and was published in February 1834.[3] It condemned all forms of outdoor relief to able-bodied men, on moral as well as economic grounds, insisting on 'the restoration of the pauper to a position below that of the independent labourer'.[4] The recommended policy of 'less-eligibility' meant that the living conditions of paupers in the workhouse would be rendered less comfortable than those of the self-sufficient poor. As well as the loss of freedom and privacy experienced in the workhouse, its spartan material conditions and monotonous daily regime would make it less attractive to the poor than the hardest existence they could sustain independently.

As the chief instrument of the new policy was to be the 'well-regulated' workhouse, it is surprising that the *Report* did not dwell at any length on the physical form of existing or future workhouses. It did, however, lay down certain functional requirements. Thenceforth, at least four classes of pauper would have to be segregated in workhouses, namely: the aged and impotent; children; able-bodied females and able-bodied males. In many areas, a number of existing buildings, such as old workhouses or empty houses, could each be used to house a separate class of pauper, creating a 'combined workhouse':

> It appears to us that both the requisite classification and the requisite superintendence may be better obtained in separate buildings than under a single roof. If effected in the latter mode, large buildings must be erected, since few of the existing buildings are of the requisite size or arrangement, and as very different qualities, both moral and intellectual, are required for the management of such dissimilar classes, each class must have its separate superintendent. Nothing would be saved, therefore, in superintendence, and much expense must be incurred in buildings.[5]

This arrangement would benefit pauper inmates as well as the poor-law authority:

> Each class might thus receive an appropriate treatment; the old might enjoy their indulgences without torment from the boisterous; the children be educated, and the able-bodied subjected to such courses of labour and discipline as will repel the indolent and vicious.[6]

A single district, or union, might, therefore, run at least four, and perhaps as many as five or six separate workhouses. Former workhouse buildings were thought most appropriate for the able-bodied, while 'proper objects of relief might be accommodated temporarily in ordinary dwelling-houses, and it is a fortunate district in which there are no empty tenements available for their reception'.[7]

The *Report* nevertheless acknowledged that some unions would need to erect new buildings.[8] Several new workhouses for one union might be supplied under a single contract at wholesale prices. Accommodation for 500 paupers, the *Report* estimated, would cost £10 per head, or £5,000, and for 1000 would cost £9 per head, or £9,000.[9] In the event, these figures proved unrealistically low.

Putting the Act into Operation

The Poor Law Amendment Act received Royal Assent on 14 August 1834 and a new administrative system was inaugurated.[10] While the parish remained the unit of settlement and finance, most of the 15,500 parishes of England and Wales were grouped into New Poor Law unions, to be administered by boards of guardians elected annually by ratepayers. Unions, rather than parishes, would now provide workhouses but central control was to be exercised by three Poor Law Commissioners based in London. The Act stated that guardians were to build or enlarge a workhouse 'according to such plan and in such manner as the Commissioners shall deem most proper for carrying the provisions of the Act into execution'.[11]

The three Commissioners appointed immediately after the passage of the Act were the one-time overseer of Southwell, Captain George Nicholls (1781–1865; *see* Chapter 3), the former Tory MP, Thomas Frankland Lewis (1780–1855), and the Whig barrister, John George Shaw-Lefevre (1797–1879). Edwin Chadwick had hoped to become a Commissioner but, instead, became the resentful Secretary to the Commission. Assistant Commissioners were appointed to shape unions from 1835 onwards. By 1841, the year in which the Poor Law Commission issued its first General Order for the Prohibition of Outdoor Relief, 586 unions had been created.[12]

The first unions were formed in the agricultural counties of the South East, but by 1841 most of the manufacturing towns in the Midlands and the sparsely populated counties of the North had also been unionised. A typical union comprised twenty to thirty parishes, ideally including a market town and surrounding rural parishes, but some unions were formed with as few as one or two parishes, and others with as many as a hundred. Before the Union Chargeability Act of 1865,[13] parish contributions to a union depended on the cost of relieving its own poor, thus poorer parishes paid higher rates. To the chagrin of the Poor Law Commission, about a thousand parishes, many of them previously united under Gilbert's Act or local acts, remained independent of the central authority until 1869. This phenomenon significantly impeded the formation of workable unions in some areas.

Guardians usually were businessmen, shopkeepers or local farmers. In the first few years of the New Poor Law, magistrates served as *ex officio* members of boards, but many of them soon tired of tedious union business and left it to the elected representatives. Once a new board had appointed paid officers, such as a receiving officer, medical officers and a clerk, the provision of suitable workhouse accommodation became its most pressing concern. Not all boards followed the correct procedure and in 1838 the Poor Law Commission complained that thirty-eight unions, mostly in Wales, had failed to take any measures to secure suitable workhouse accommodation; ultimately, the central authority did not have the power to force a reluctant union to provide an adequate workhouse and relied heavily on the persuasive tactics of the Assistant Commissioners.[14]

After 1834, several newly created unions found themselves in immediate possession of a large workhouse, generally one that had been erected for an incorporation or a Gilbert union within the past hundred years but which needed to be altered to meet stricter standards of classification and segregation. Typically, as at Semer House of Industry in Suffolk,[15] this entailed the erection of extra yard walls and the blockage of inter-communicating doorways. In some cases a non-purpose-built Old Poor Law workhouse was adapted or enlarged, for example monastic buildings at Coventry and Leominster, barracks at Eastbourne and a Napoleonic prisoner-of-war camp at Bristol. Many unions which did not inherit a suitable building decided to operate a 'combined' or 'divided workhouse', as suggested in the *Poor Law Report*, by redeploying a number of former parish workhouses. Attempts were made to justify this procedure on both economic and political grounds. In May 1836, for example, Assistant Commissioner Richard Hall argued for the retention of four existing parish workhouses in Leicester:

> It will be a great point to avoid all new buildings; many attempts have been made to prejudice the Ratepayers against the Union on those grounds; the enormous central Workhouse, with its Gaol discipline, has been held out to the apprehensions of both Poor and Rich, as the first product of our System at Leicester; and I am peculiarly gratified with the prospect of bringing it into efficient operation, by means of such Workhouses only as will find ready built.[16]

However, the anticipated expense of running a 'combined workhouse' led the Leicester guardians to reconsider. They estimated that existing workhouses could be adapted to the requirements of the new Act at a total cost of £3,000 but, if sold, these buildings would raise £3,650. Moreover, a new workhouse could be built for £6,000, plus the cost of the site, and the union could save £300 a year in administrative costs by housing its paupers under one roof. These factors led the Leicester guardians, and many others throughout the country, to approve the construction of a new 'central' workhouse. Indeed, the idea of separate workhouses, which had been described in the *Report* of 1834, was soon supplanted by the concept of the general mixed workhouse, wherein all classes were housed together. That happened for a variety of reasons.

The psychological advantages of a general mixed workhouse were outlined by Sir Francis Bond Head, Assistant Commissioner for Kent, in reply to a Kentish magistrate who had advocated the retention of existing buildings:

> The very sight of a well-built efficient establishment would give confidence to the Board of Guardians; the sight and weekly assemblage of all servants of their Union would make them proud of their office: the appointment of a chaplain would give dignity to the whole arrangement, while the pauper would feel it was utterly impossible to contend against it. In visiting such a series of Unions, the Assistant Commissioner could with great facility perform his duty, whereas if he had eight establishments to search for in each Union, it would be almost impracticable to attend to them.[17]

Practical considerations also augured in favour of the central workhouse. The board of guardians of Westhampnett in Sussex, for example, found difficulty in adhering to the rule that a family must be admitted and discharged together if its members were split between several establishments.[18]

The classification of workhouse inmates outlined in the first Annual Report of the Poor Law Commission lent further support to the establishment of general mixed workhouses. It directed that paupers be divided into seven rather than four classes: aged or infirm men; able-bodied men and youths aged over 13; boys aged 7 to 13; aged and infirm women; able-bodied women and girls aged over 16; girls aged 7 to 16 and, finally, children under 7 years of age.[19] This extensive classification may have swayed the decision of several boards of guardians to erect a new workhouse: certainly, if all seven classes were to be housed in separate establishments, the cost to a union would have been very great indeed.

From 1836 onwards, the annual reports of the Poor Law Commission included lists showing the expenditure authorised for unions to provide workhouses; these are a major source for the study of New Poor Law workhouses. In 1836, separate lists were published for 'workhouses ordered to be built' and 'workhouses to be altered and enlarged'.[20] Between 1837 and 1839 the first list was expanded to include 'workhouses to be purchased' but in 1840 it reverted to 'workhouses to be built'.[21] The Annual Report of 1839, when 583 English and Welsh unions were in operation, included a return 'shewing the Progress which has been made in providing adequate Workhouse Accommodation'. That distinguished between new and old buildings, and between those completed and those which were still under construction or in course of alteration.[22] In total, 252 new and 175 old workhouses were in operation; 67 new workhouses were under construction and 9 old workhouses were undergoing alteration. A few of the authorisations for expenditure listed between 1836 and 1841 were never put into effect, and some workhouses listed as 'to be built', for example Tewkesbury, were in fact purchases or conversions. Despite that, the authorisation lists are highly accurate.

By 1841, the year of the General Order for the Prohibition of Outdoor Relief, 320 new general mixed workhouses had been built, or were being built, in England and many more had been altered and extended. By that year, however, fewer new workhouses were being started. According to Poor Law Commission figures, expenditure was approved for only fourteen new workhouses in 1840, six in 1841 and three in 1842.[23] The geographic spread of new building during the boom period of 1835 to 1841 is shown in Figure 48 (page 54). Areas with remarkably little new building included London, where many old parish authorities survived, and the North, where the New Poor Law was widely regarded as an irrelevance.

Each union followed a similar procedure in establishing a new workhouse. After examining existing workhouses and agreeing that a new building was necessary, a site had to be identified and purchased. In accordance with the rule that no pauper should have to walk more than 10 miles from his or her parish boundary to the workhouse, sites generally lay in the centre of a union, creating a national network of workhouses positioned approximately 20 miles apart. Workhouses were not symbols of civic pride to adorn urban centres, and so sites generally lay on the outskirts of towns, on greenfield sites.

Having acquired a suitable site, a board of guardians either appointed an architect outright, or held a competition for plans and specifications. Some architects, for example John Plowman and Samuel T Welch, lobbied boards by offering to show their plans free of charge; in the 1830s there were no professional rules of conduct to control such practices.[24]

In addition to accommodating seven classes of pauper, workhouses had to include a number of rooms for staff. The idea of hiring a different superintendent to care for each class, mentioned in the *Report* of 1834, had been forgotten, and in some cases the only resident members of staff were the master and matron. If the porter, schoolmistress and schoolmaster were not simply plucked from the pauper inmates, they too required separate accommodation in the building. Workhouses also had to include offices for non-residential staff, such as the clerk, a boardroom in which the guardians could meet weekly and a waiting-room for applicants for relief. Advertisements for plans usually stated the number of paupers the board wished to accommodate and occasionally specified the type of design they had in mind. Lichfield Union, for example, advertised for 'Plans and Specifications for a Workhouse to hold two hundred paupers, in accordance with Mr Kempthorne's Model'.[25] This referred to a number of designs for general mixed workhouses which were published in the first two annual reports of the Poor Law Commission, but which had been made available through the Assistant Commissioners from the spring of 1835.

Four model designs were published with the first Annual Report in 1835, and another in 1836 (*see* Appendix 3, Figures 1–15).[26] The first design, for a courtyard-plan workhouse, was by Assistant Commissioner Sir Francis Head, but all of the others were by a young, inexperienced architect who had recently returned from his European tour, Sampson Kempthorne. Kempthorne owed his position as official architect to the Poor Law Commission to his father, a friend of Commissioner Nicholls. Possibly under Nicholls's influence, he produced two radial designs, known as the 'square' and 'hexagon' plans, which respectively involved cross-shaped ranges within a square and Y-shaped ranges within a hexagon. Both of these designs had polygonal hubs from which the workhouse master could watch the paupers when they were in their exercise yards. Kempthorne's remaining designs, the '200-pauper' plans, were cruciform but not truly radial as they had no supervisory hub. That published in 1836 was an adaptation of the 1835 design, specifically for areas with low pauper numbers.

In 1835, the model workhouse plans were praised in Loudon's *Architectural Magazine*:

[they] appear to us, from a cursory inspection, excellently arranged; and it is most gratifying to see the attention that has been paid by the architect to the principles of separation and classification, to cleanliness, to ventilation, and to general convenience.[27]

Generally, however, the plans were received with little comment.

Kempthorne's sole exposition of the ideas underlying his workhouse designs, published with the second Annual Report of the Poor Law Commission, was a recommendation of natural ventilation by favouring rooms with opposed windows.[28] That feature, then being advocated for new hospitals on the Continent, occurred in all of his designs. In England it had been urged for workhouse dormitories by John Scott as early as 1773, and by Edmund Gillingwater in 1786 (*see* pages 19–20). Cross-ventilation had also been a feature of wards in several 18th-century military and voluntary hospitals.[29] Kempthorne had nothing to say, however, on the principles of supervision and control inherent in his designs. He would have been aware, through Nicholls, of Thurgarton Hundred Workhouse which had embodied similar inspection principles in the 1820s. He would also have known of recent prisons and asylums designed with radial plans and would have been familiar with Bentham's theories through Chadwick, who had lived in Bentham's house as his secretary in 1831–2. The architect Sir George Gilbert Scott later claimed that Kempthorne had unhappily sought help from his old master, Annesley Voysey, 'who, though a clever and ingenious practical man, had not one spark of taste, and took a very exaggerated view of the necessity for economy'.[30] Whatever his inspiration, Kempthorne's elevations were as plain – and cheap – as possible.

Of all the model plans, Kempthorne's 'square' and 'hexagon' plans proved the most popular. Head persuaded a number of unions in Kent to adopt his courtyard plan, but it was never taken up in that exact form elsewhere. The '200-pauper' plan was only occasionally selected, usually on Kempthorne's recommendation: presumably few unions considered themselves 'less pauperised'. Of all the designs, the 'hexagon' plan was best suited to the segregational requirements of the Poor Law Commission, with its six separate yards. The 'square' plan provided six internal divisions, but only four yards. Head's workhouse had only two yards, providing a simple division by sex which would have been inadequate to meet the rules and regulations without some manipulation. In practice, the yards in all of these designs required further subdivision, and it seems likely that they were produced before the Poor Law Commission decided on seven instead of four classes of inmate. Every design provided strategically placed accommodation for the master and matron, allowing them to observe the paupers in their yards but not within the buildings. The 'square' and 'hexagon' designs, having polygonal hubs, did this the most efficiently.

Guided by the model plans, architects entered competitions for new workhouses. These were not always conducted with scrupulous fairness. In 1836, the *Architectural Magazine* published a letter from Bishop's Stortford which made the following complaint:

> *new workhouses are erecting at Saffron Walden, Lexden, and Manningtree. From the latter place, the plans were returned to the unsuccessful candidates unpacked, and completely exposed to the curious, with the descriptive particulars lost or detained. We would contrast this with the polite and gentlemanly conduct of the Stortford Union. The architects received their plans back after the decision, carefully packed, and each bearing a letter of thanks from the Board of Guardians.*[31]

The same journal published a notice concerning the competition for Chesterton Union Workhouse: 'In this instance, architects were solicited to follow designs, but only *seven days* were allowed for preparing them'.[32] The perusal of guardians' minute-books reveals that this was far from being an uncommon, or unrealistic, expectation.

In his autobiography, George Gilbert Scott described his efforts to chase workhouse commissions, or 'Union-hunting', a strategy shared by many of his contemporaries. In January 1835 Scott had spent several weeks working for Kempthorne, when the death of his father spurred him to set up in independent practice. At first family contacts secured him commissions from clients in his home area of Buckinghamshire and Northamptonshire, but this was followed by:

> *an era of turmoil, of violent activity and exertion. For weeks I almost lived on horseback, canvassing newly formed unions. Then alternated periods of close, hard work . . . with coach journeys, chiefly by night, followed by meetings with guardians, searching out new materials, and hurrying from union to union, often riding across unknown bits of country after dark.*[33]

Few architects covered such a wide area as Scott and his partner, William Bonython Moffatt, or found such success. Occasionally, a guardian was appointed architect to a board, but that was not always deemed honourable. At Leicester, Guardian William Parsons was considered ineligible on account of his position, but the Weymouth Board did not quibble about allowing two of its members, Thomas Dobson and Thomas Hill Harvey, to design the workhouse jointly.[34] Thomas Trubshaw, Guardian for Colwich parish in the Stafford Union, also prepared plans for his local workhouse.[35] At Watford, a guardian named Mr Weedon drew up plans which were rejected by the Poor Law Commission although they had been referred to an architect, Mr Grover; eventually plans by the architect T L Evans were adopted in their stead.[36]

Once a design had been selected by the board of guardians, plans and specifications were laid before the Poor Law Commission for approval. This procedure also had to be followed for the adaptation or extension of existing buildings. If all went well, plans were returned within a couple of weeks, bearing the Commission's stamp and requisite signatures.[37] The board could then apply for loans, appoint a clerk of works, advertise for tenders from building contractors, and initiate the construction work. Builders were usually local, but George Myers and Richard Wilson of Hull seem to have worked for several unions, especially in the Midlands.[38]

The progress of new workhouses can be followed in guardians' minute-books, documents which often reveal an indecisive or parsimonious attitude. In January 1836, for example, Sampson Kempthorne was appointed architect by the guardians of Epping Union in Essex. It is not known which of Kempthorne's plans was accepted, but it was to be a workhouse for 300 paupers, probably on the 'hexagon' plan. Detailed specifications, dated March 1836, survive and include a number of sketches, probably by Kempthorne, showing fixtures and fittings such as windows, drains and lavatories.[39] In July, a tender for £5,139 was accepted from the builder, S Hubert of Lambeth. In November 1836 both Kempthorne and Hubert were invited to a board meeting, ostensibly to sign the contract. However, when Hubert asked for an advance the guardians voted to abandon the entire project and ordered advertisements to be placed in the *Morning Chronicle* and other newspapers for fresh plans and specifications, this time for a workhouse to hold 220 paupers.[40] Kempthorne was discharged, and in January 1837 a plan by Lewis Vulliamy was adopted.[41] Similar stories are related in the minute-books of other unions. As several involve ploys to replace Kempthorne, it seems that many unions had initially felt obliged to employ him but, realising that a degree of free choice would be condoned by the Poor Law Commission, regretted their decision and wriggled out of their contract. In many cases disputes arose between the guardians and their architect regarding remuneration, sometimes because the architect had been required to prepare several sets of working plans, at other times because the initial estimate had been unrealistically low. Architects usually received between 2·5 and 3·5 per cent of the total expenditure, sometimes as much as 5 per cent.

On the whole, workhouses cost rather more than had been anticipated. The *Poor Law Report* had estimated that new workhouses would cost £10 per inmate to build but the cost was usually much higher. Scott complained that for some time architects felt unable to venture beyond Kempthorne's extremely low estimates.[42] In 1835 the Poor Law Commission criticised the architect William T Nash of Royston for coming up with a design costing £20 per head for Buntingford Union Workhouse (*see* Figure 52); Nash retaliated by claiming that it would be impossible to reduce the sum to £15 in the Royston area.[43] In fact, the average cost per head in 1836 was £18 5s, rising to £19 17s in 1839.[44] Builders' tenders for workhouses housing 300 to 400 paupers usually amounted to at least £5,000 and some were much higher.[45] The successful tender of £8,570 for the 600-pauper Leicester Union Workhouse seemed reasonable at the time, but within ten years the workhouse proved too small and had to be rebuilt, bringing the total cost to £25,000.[46]

The Poor Law Amendment Act stated that money for building was to be raised from the poor rate, and that borrowing was to be charged on future rates. Sums borrowed and expended were not to exceed the average annual rates for the three preceding years. Workhouse building was largely financed through the exchequer loan system, although loans were sometimes obtained from other sources, especially from local banks, insurance companies and private individuals, including guardians. Sometimes funds were readily available. Income from the sale of old parish workhouses and land was often set against the cost of a new union workhouse, or more specifically against that individual parish's contribution towards the overall cost. The lists published by the Poor Law Commission show that over £2,000,000 had been authorised for building workhouses by 1840.[47]

Workhouse construction did not attract private charity to the same extent as institutions run by voluntary subscription, such as hospitals, but several donations are documented. For example, the ashlar for the north front of Alcester Union Workhouse (Fig 42), erected in 1837, was given by Charles Throckmorton of Coughton, a benefaction recorded by an inscription on the façade. Lord Talbot gave the

Figure 42
The façade of Alcester Union Workhouse (1837) was faced with ashlar donated by Charles Throckmorton of Coughton, but the rear and side elevations were of brick. The building was converted into flats in 1984 and is now known as Oversley House.
[BB94/5466]

stone for the dressings of Stafford Union Workhouse, but it had to be quarried at the expense of the Union.[48] Mr Ham, a local landowner, offered a clock tower for the Dore Union Workhouse provided the board would agree to a cupola being erected upon it,[49] and the Revd Henry Ducane offered, without success, to build a chapel on the site of the new Witham Union Workhouse.[50]

As soon as a union was operating a suitable workhouse, the Poor Law Commission ordered it to stop issuing outdoor relief to the able-bodied poor. Although the full operation of the New Poor Law was smoother in the South than in the North, some protests were encountered. A common grievance was the removal of paupers from their own parish workhouses. Inmates being transferred from Chesham Parish Workhouse to the union workhouse in Amersham were 'rescued' by a crowd, and at Uckfield paupers broke into the union workhouse, apparently with the purpose of returning paupers to their own parishes.[51] Unrest in Eastbourne resulted from the separation of married paupers in the workhouse, although that had been a common procedure in many areas before 1834. Workhouses, as the physical expression of new relief practices, were the prime target of discontent. In Suffolk, a number of workhouses were damaged and one in particular, St Clement's Workhouse in Ipswich, was partially demolished.[52] At the end of 1835, workhouses at Bishop's Stortford and Saffron Walden were set on fire.[53] Such incidents, however, were isolated, and the New Poor Law was imposed throughout southern England without encountering orchestrated opposition.

The situation in the textile towns of northern England was very different. They had not experienced the soaring poor rates prevalent in the South throughout the late 18th and early 19th centuries, and seldom had recourse to the despised allowance system (*see* page 32). The workhouse test therefore seemed superfluous: it was argued that workhouses in manufacturing areas would stand empty in good times and overflow in bad. Anti-Poor-Law factions were better organised than in the South, and in 1836–7 riots occurred in Huddersfield, Bradford, Todmorden and elsewhere. Ashton, Oldham and Rochdale (Fig 43) Unions failed to administer relief under a board of guardians before the mid-1840s. Other unions resisted pressure to erect new workhouses or to administer existing ones in accordance with the new rules and regulations. Todmorden expressed the feelings of many northern authorities, categorically refusing 'to place these poor, whom we love and respect, and who have been guilty of no crime, in a workhouse and under a discipline and restraint more intolerable than is allotted to felons in a gaol'.[54] In 1844, Todmorden was, exceptionally, permitted to completely abandon the workhouse system, a situation which endured until the 1870s.

The Anti-Poor-Law movement had been closely bound up with the movement for factory reform, and became subsumed by Chartism after 1840. Active opposition died down, but the power of the central authority had been effectively weakened and for many years the workhouse test could be applied only half-heartedly throughout much of the North. Adequate workhouse provision was resisted, particularly in the West Riding and Lancashire, and the Poor Law Commission was forced to make a number of concessions. The General Order for the Prohibition of Outdoor Relief of 1841 was never enforced universally, and was often modified by a Labour Test Order, enabling unions to give outdoor relief to able-bodied men in exchange for labour. One of the first unions permitted to do this was Nottingham, which was affected by depression in the textile industry in 1837. Northern unions exploited the exceptions listed in the outdoor relief prohibition order and often distributed outdoor relief in the guise of medical relief or 'sudden and urgent necessity'. There is evidence that some unions in the South did likewise.[55]

Meanwhile, in a situation reminiscent of the attacks on the workhouse contractor Matthew Marriot in 1730, the Anti-Poor-Law press began

Figure 43
This cartoon, published in the Rochdale Spectator *on* 1 November 1844, depicts an imaginary 'bastile', with a skull and cross-bones displayed as a warning on its lintel.
[Metropolitan Borough of Rochdale Community Services Department]

The Workhouse

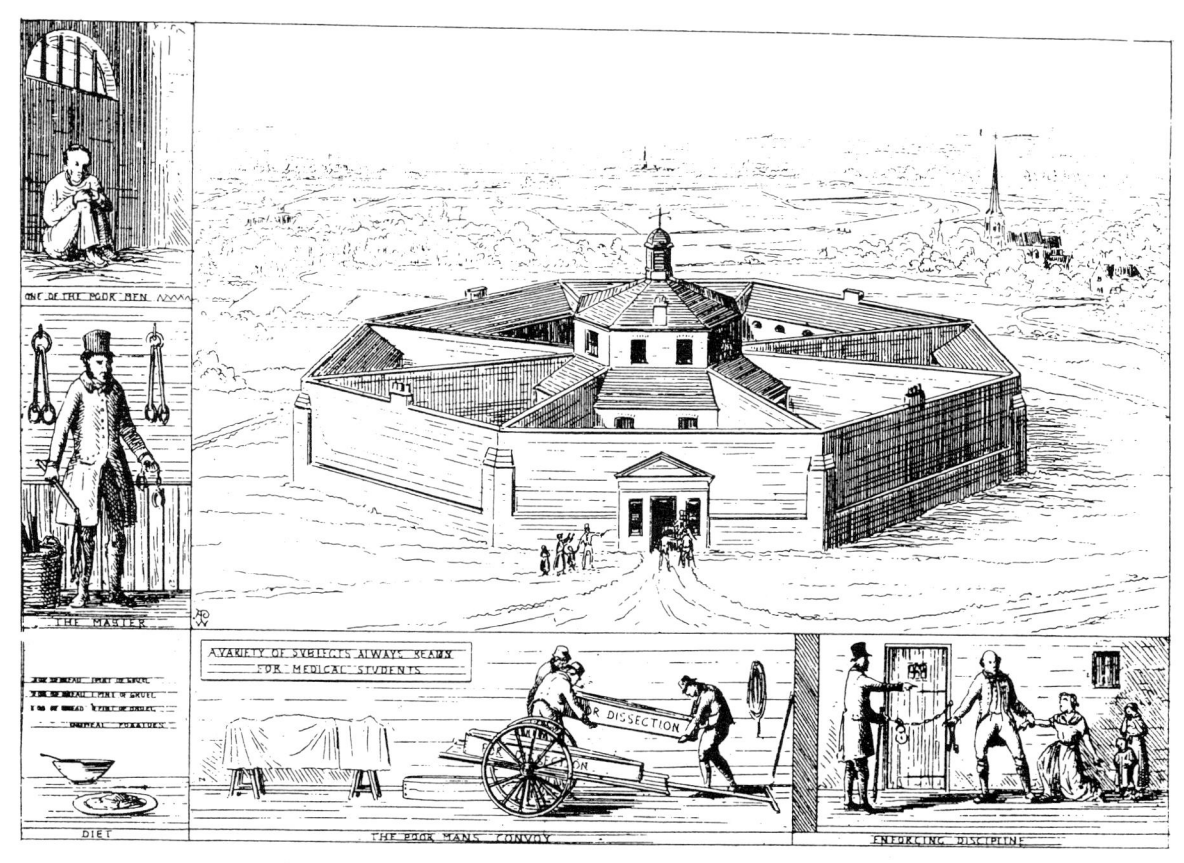

CONTRASTED RESIDENCES FOR THE POOR

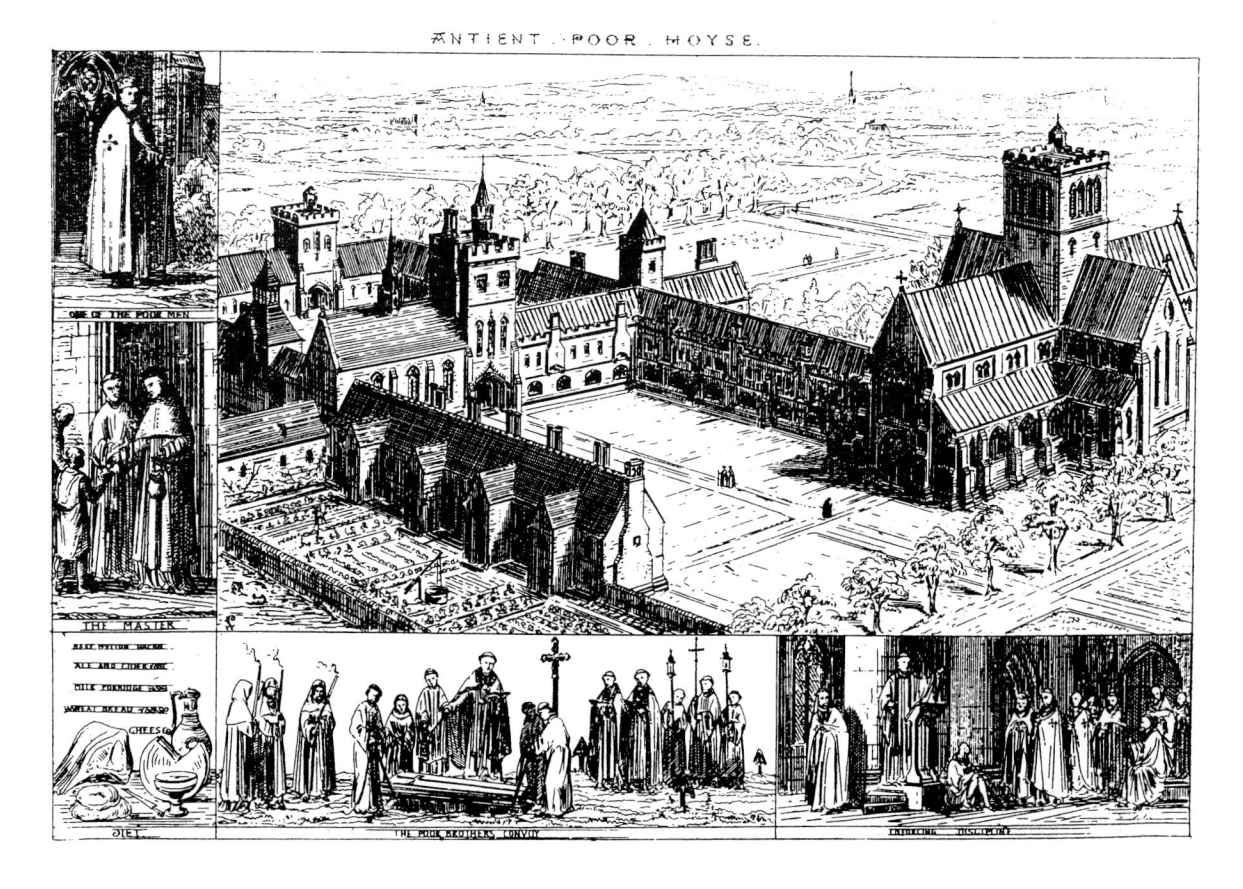

ANTIENT POOR HOYSE.

50

THE NEW POOR LAW OF 1834

to publish tales of alleged cruelty in workhouses throughout the country. These included *The Times*, owned by John Walters MP, and *Blackwood's Magazine*, which made the morbid suggestion that official poor-law registers were bound with the skin of dead paupers. Amongst other publications, one of the best known was the 1841 edition of Pugin's *Contrasts*, which juxtaposed the image of a cloistered 'antient poor hoyse' with that of a 'modern poor house' to highlight the degeneration of English values (Fig 44). In 1842, following an epidemic in Bridgwater Union Workhouse, John Bowen emotively described the new workhouses as 'murderous pest-houses' and 'murder holes' (Fig 45). He particularly objected to the low cubic space which the plans gave to able-bodied paupers in their dormitories, the absence of separate sick-rooms and the poor dietary. Under these conditions, he argued, fevers were rife, resulting in a scandalously high mortality rate. He compared the annual mortality rate of convicts (2·3 per cent in hulks; 2·5 per cent in penitentiaries) with that of paupers in the Bridgwater Workhouse (41·5 per cent).

The Book of the Bastilles or The History of the Working of the New Poor Law, written by G R Wythen Baxter and published in 1841, was a compilation of published criticisms of the new workhouse system and showed that campaigners generally focused on the workhouse establishment rather than its architectural form. Three

Figure 44 (opposite) Augustus W N Pugin's 'Contrasted Residences of the Poor: "Antient Poor Hoyse" and "Modern Poor House"' was an undisguised attack on the New Poor Law.
[From Pugin 1841, by permission of the Syndics of Cambridge University Library]

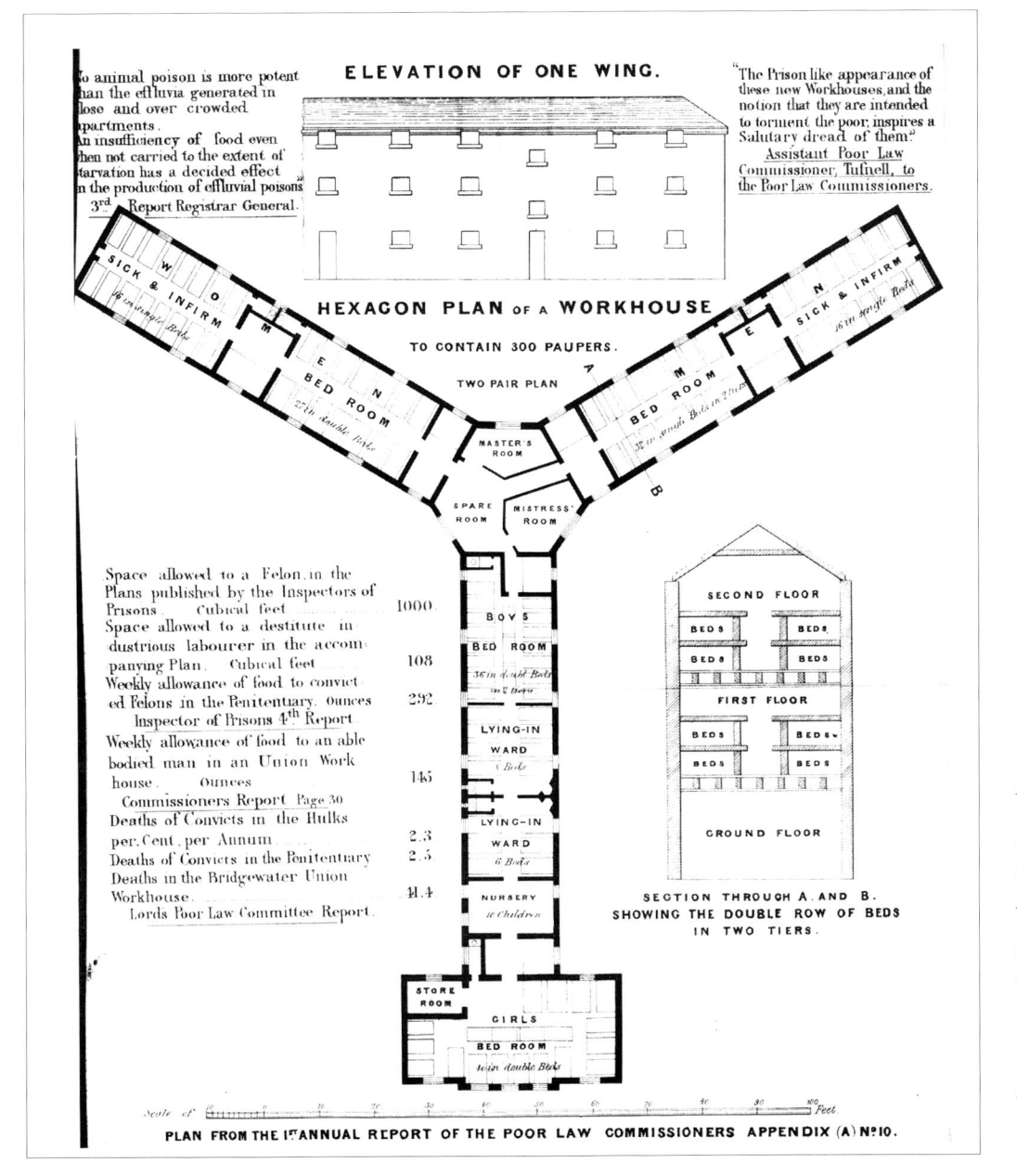

Figure 45 This critical interpretation of the 'hexagon' workhouse, was published by John Bowen of Bridgwater, Somerset, in 1842, after a tragic outbreak of fever at Bridgwater Union Workhouse.
[From Bowen 1842, by permission of the Syndics of Cambridge University Library]

The Workhouse

Figure 46 (right) Andover Union Workhouse was designed by Sampson Kempthorne on the 'square' plan and erected in 1836. The discovery that starving inmates gnawed rotting bones supplied for grinding created a scandal which led, ultimately, to the downfall of the Poor Law Commission.
[BB95/17301]

Figure 47 (below) 'The Poor Picking the Bones to Live', from The Penny Satirist. *Rumour had it that the bones fought over by the Andover paupers included some 'from churchyards'.*
[From The Penny Satirist, *6 September 1845, by permission of the British Library]*

years later, a scandal at Andover Union Workhouse (Fig 46) seized the public imagination and led, ultimately, to the demise of the Poor Law Commission. At Andover, male paupers were habitually employed at bone-crushing (Fig 47), a common workhouse occupation in the early 1840s. Bones were placed in a box and pounded to dust with a heavy iron bar. Because much dust was generated, work was carried out in an open shed in a yard rather than in an enclosed workshop. In August 1845, it was revealed that the inmates of Andover were so starved that, despite the revolting smell, they gnawed marrow and rotting meat from bones supplied for crushing. Details of an inquiry held in Andover under the aegis of Assistant Commissioner Parker were published in *The Times* and succeeded in arousing public indignation.[56] The Poor Law Commission, displeased with Parker's handling of the affair, called for his resignation, but he was cleared following an appeal. This brought the workings of the Poor Law Commission within the scope of a Select Committee of the House of Commons, appointed to look into the Andover scandal, which published its findings in August 1846. Internal conflicts between Chadwick and the Commissioners, and also between Nicholls and his two colleagues, were exposed; *The Times* eloquently declared: 'The Poor Law Commission has burst like a shell . . . Somerset House is in the air, and Commissioners, secretaries, Dukes, Ministers, things great and small, are tumbling down, rather the worst for their forced aerial expedition.'[57] In the following year the Poor Law Commission was replaced by a new authority, the Poor Law Board, but within the period of its office it had brought great changes to the implementation of institutional relief in England and Wales.

5
New Poor Law Workhouses, 1835–1840

By 1841 a network of workhouses answering the requirements of the New Poor Law extended over England (Fig 48), enabling the Poor Law Commission to prohibit outdoor relief in 454 of the 586 unions then in existence.[1] By the same year, of the workhouses then in operation, 320 had been erected as a result of the 1834 Act. Their construction had presented builders and architects alike with fresh opportunities and challenges.

Emulating Sampson Kempthorne's model elevations, most of the new buildings were extremely plain, limiting ornamentation to a pedimental lintel over the main doorway or channelled ashlar on the ground storey of the entrance block. Austere Georgian Classicism, although threatened by a growing interest in Gothic, Tudor, Elizabethan and Jacobean styles, was still as acceptable as it was inexpensive.

The architectural simplicity of the first new workhouses, however, was inspired by economy and decorum rather than aesthetics. Guardians needed little incentive to eliminate superfluous decoration, as they held the financial interests of the rate-payers, their electorate, close to their hearts. Moreover, it was felt that simple buildings would mirror the basic comforts offered within New Poor Law workhouses and, at the same time, fend off critical appellations such as 'pauper palace'. Most guardians were equally anxious not to be accused of erecting 'bastiles'. The Board of Chesterfield Union, for example, placed a cautious advertisement for 'a good, efficient Workhouse which shall not have the appearance of either a prison or a palace'.[2]

A workhouse with the appearance of a prison, however, was exactly the ideal of Assistant Commissioner Sir Francis Head. The blind outer walls of the Kent workhouses erected to his courtyard plan presented a forbidding aspect to the outer world. They made an unmistakable statement about the culpability of pauperism, and warned would-be paupers to expect no comforts within.

In contrast, the workhouses designed by George Gilbert Scott & William Bonython Moffatt, William J Donthorn, Samuel T Welch and a few other architects, with their diamond-paned casements, shaped gables and diapered brickwork, hinted at charitable benevolence. There is little evidence that these architects, or their patrons, consciously alluded to the Tudor, Elizabethan or Jacobean almshouses which existed in most English towns, but it is indisputable that an atmosphere of security and domesticity was achieved through the use of an architectural language associated with such familiar buildings.

New Poor Law workhouses resembling prisons or almshouses represented extreme approaches, as the widespread adoption of Kempthorne's designs gave the workhouse, as a building type, a distinct architectural identity of its own for the first time in its history. Nevertheless, the sanctioning of architectural diversity seriously threatened the institutional uniformity desired by central government, even before the new regime was fully operational. The architectural style of a workhouse must have had a profound psychological impact upon a new inmate: that factor alone would have rendered the experience of a pauper in, for example, Bridge or Blean Union Workhouses (*see* Figures 50 and 51), very different from that of an inmate of Windsor or Amersham (*see* Figures 72 and 73).

Visual allusions to either prisons or almshouses were largely superficial: ultimately, planning had a much greater effect than architectural style on the daily existence of those compelled, for whatever reason, to reside within workhouse walls. The majority of the new workhouses erected between 1835 and 1840 were based on one of the model workhouse plans issued by the Poor Law Commission, especially Sampson Kempthorne's radial plans, which were capable of endless variation. The model plans were not, of course, obligatory, and architects tended to take them as a starting-point,

The Workhouse

Figure 48
This map shows the geographical distribution of new workhouses erected between 1835 and 1840. At the same time many old workhouses were converted to meet the needs of the New Poor Law.

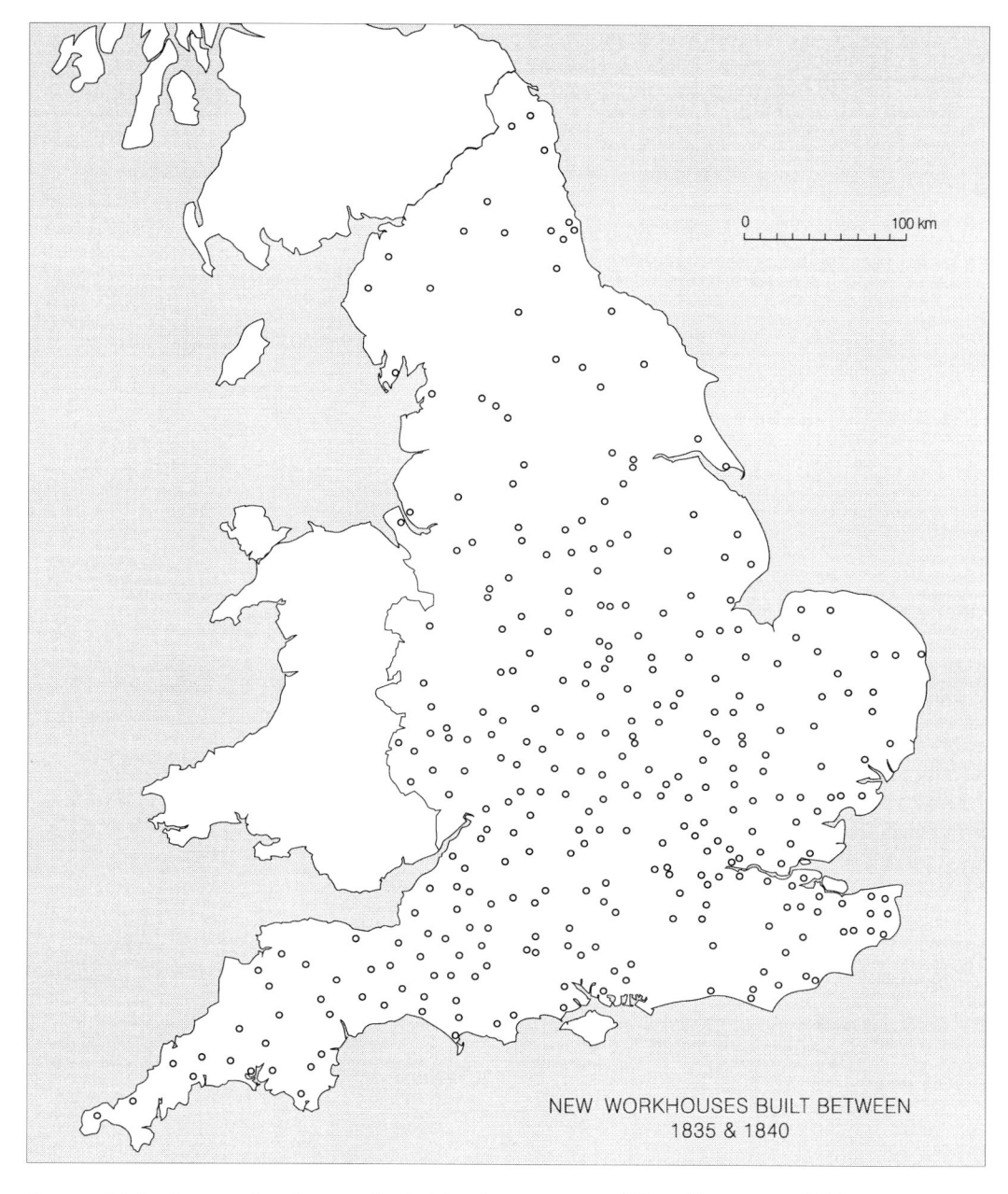

NEW WORKHOUSES BUILT BETWEEN 1835 & 1840

from which they evolved more individual designs.[3]

Despite diversity in architectural style and planning, all New Poor Law workhouses operated oppressive regimes, based on the rigorous separation and classification of inmates, drab workhouse uniforms, strictly observed timetables and monotonous dietaries. In practice, masters and matrons enjoyed some latitude in the manner in which they chose to interpret the rules and regulations laid down by the Poor Law Commission, and some were certainly harsher than others. Country-wide uniformity in the treatment of paupers was never achieved in the New Poor Law workhouses, and was in reality quite unachievable.

The Courtyard Plan: Sir Francis Head's Workhouses

The very first unions to erect new workhouses in 1835 and 1836 included twelve in Kent which all adopted the same 'low, cheap, homely building' (Fig 49), designed by Sir Francis Head.[4] These were East Ashford, West Ashford, Blean, Bridge, Dover, Eastry, Elham, Faversham, Hoo, Maidstone, Milton Regis and the Isle of Thanet.[5] No original floor plans survive for these buildings, but they were all closely based on Head's ground-floor plan, published by the Poor Law Commission in 1835 (*see* Appendix 3, Figure 1).[6]

Head's plan provided numerous small dormitories in two-storeyed ranges around three sides of a large quadrangle. Very little living space was allotted to individual paupers: each dormitory measured 15 ft by 10 ft, was lit by a single window and slept eight. Head originally envisaged four double iron bedsteads in each dormitory but, meeting objections to double beds for men, he urged guardians to adopt tiered 'suspended' beds of his own design.[7] The first-floor dormitories were entered from a narrow, iron gallery, reached by external stairs (Fig 50). As the windows of all dormitories overlooked the courtyard, those on the ground floor were overshadowed by the galleries. They received much-needed additional ventilation through cast-iron gratings in their courtyard walls.

The quadrangle was divided by an axial 12-feet-high wall to create male and female exercise yards, but Head clearly considered that guardians could erect extra walls to suit their individual needs. Sanitation was minimal: each side of the workhouse was provided with a single, unlit privy. Assuming that privies occupied corresponding positions on the upper floor, each would have served 112 inmates. In the absence of lavatories, paupers would have pumped water from a well in the yard for washing purposes. At the junction of the main accommodation ranges, L-shaped halls were used as day-rooms or workrooms and, like the dormitories, had no windows or doors in their outer walls.

While three ranges of Head's model workhouse accommodated pauper inmates, the fourth housed offices and services. The prominent entrance block or governor's house, in the centre of the range, was bisected by an archway. Beyond that lay a yard, surrounded by 9-feet-high walls, containing the coal-house and stabling for the guardians' horses. To one side of the archway lay the kitchen, storeroom, cooking-room and wash-house; to the other, the stairs, governor's room, committee room and waiting-rooms. Even the committee room, where the board of guardians met fortnightly, was deprived of outward-looking windows. The intention may have been to produce a blind façade, or to deprive paupers summoned before the board of a last glimpse of the outside world.

Head's drawing supplied only one clue to the arrangement of the upper floor of the entrance block, a note reading 'the bow window over the Gateway commands a view of the whole establishment'. Surviving Head workhouses retain that

Figure 49
This perspective view of a Kent workhouse built according to Sir Francis Head's model design is partly based on Head's own ground-floor plan ('Plan of a Rural Workhouse for 500 persons' (PP 1835 (500), XXXV, Appendix A, No. 10. 1); see Appendix 3, Figure 1), and partly on surviving buildings.

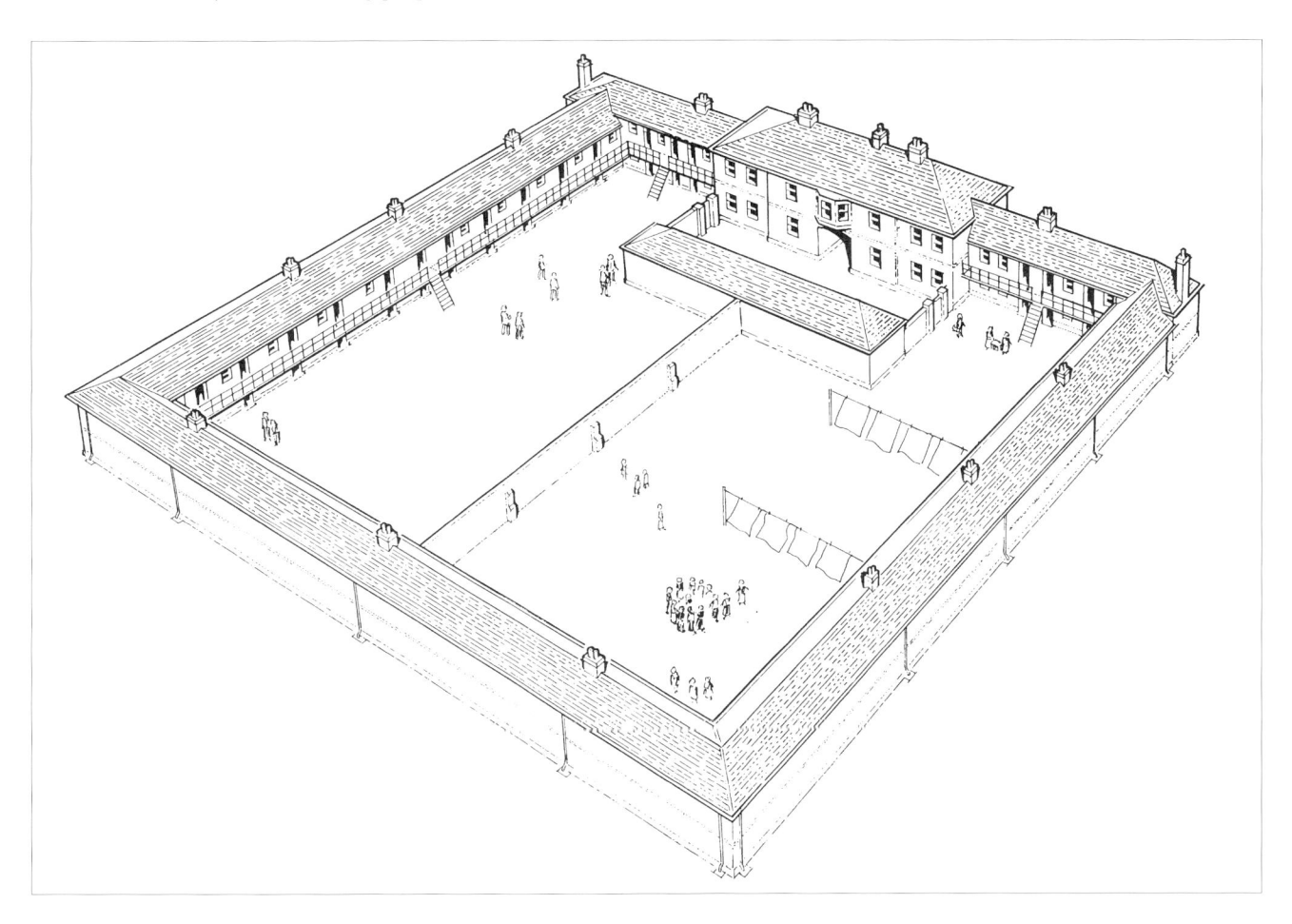

feature, usually in the form of a canted oriel rather than a bow, which theoretically allowed the master to supervise the paupers' yards from his office. In practice, the stable yard concealed the nearest parts of each yard from his vision.

In a letter to the Poor Law Commission, Head explained why he had opted for a courtyard plan:

> *My principle for a poorhouse is this, build poor men's cottages; but, instead of having one long street, bend it into a quadrangle, which forms also a prison, having within itself an area of ground in which the board can introduce any system it may choose.*[8]

This seems to have been an original notion for a workhouse although it has been suggested that it derived from contemporary army-barrack blocks, an influence which could be explained by Head's previous career in the Royal Engineers.[9] A number of demolished Old Poor Law workhouses in Surrey and Sussex, such as those of Farnham, Hambledon, Reigate and Thakeham, had courtyard plans and conceivably served as models, while contemporary prisons would have demonstrated the effectiveness of windowless perimeter walls.

Head laid his model plan before each board of guardians in his district. Once it was accepted, the board appointed a surveyor to prepare working drawings, draft specifications and superintend the erection of the building. Local men involved in this work included John Whichcord of Maidstone, who was later appointed architect of Cranbrook, Dartford, Malling and Tonbridge workhouses. Although these buildings followed his own individual design, they reveal the strong influence of Head's model plan.

Head quit his position to become Lieutenant-General of Canada at the end of 1835, by which time the defects of his design were becoming apparent. At East Ashford, Whichcord had to introduce a number of changes to the building when it was nearing completion, greatly adding to its cost.[10] Not surprisingly, the stables for the guardians' horses were moved to the rear of the building to improve the master's view of the yards. Head had not provided a chapel, and one of the dining-halls was converted for that purpose: the sexes were strictly separated by a high partition and, in an arrangement typical of the period, the pulpit was placed with its back to the end wall, above the partition, so that the preacher could be seen by both men and women, although they remained hidden from one another. A sick-room and a lying-in room were also provided, and the positions of the kitchen, girls' laundry and privies were changed. Finally, it was realised that two yards provided inadequate segregation, and so they were bisected by diagonal walls. Other unions experienced similar practical problems with Head's design and had to introduce dormitory fireplaces and extra privies to make their new buildings habitable.

The Anti-Poor-Law movement attacked Head's workhouses with even more venom than Kempthorne's. In February 1839, for example, *The Times* published the following, slightly exaggerated, description of Blean Union Workhouse (Fig 51):

> About a quarter of a mile from the village of Herne . . . stands a horrible instance of the Poor Law Amendment Act. It is a newly-erected building, forming a square, and covering an acre of ground, and on the sides not a single window or air-hole has been constructed to allow its unfortunate inmates the least glimpse of the surrounding countryside, and nothing is to be seen but dead walls. The place has the appearance of nothing but a prison . . . This workhouse is divided into a great number of cells, in each of which are four iron bedsteads, each destined to receive four unfortunate Paupers, so that sixteen human beings are packed in every cell.[11]

Like all other Head workhouses, Blean has been greatly altered over the years but some window apertures still contain multi-paned iron glazing of mid-19th-century date. A great improvement was achieved in 1843, when a single window was inserted into the outside walls of the old men's and old women's dining-halls. This was a significant advance: at Gravesend and Milton Union Workhouse, another Kent workhouse built with blind outer walls, windows were not inserted in the perimeter walls until 1867.[12]

In the later 19th century, sanitary blocks were built against the outer walls of most Head workhouses, the galleries were replaced by internal staircases and, as at Blean, windows were inserted, often irregularly, into outer walls.[13] In 1896, J S Davy, the poor-law inspector for the South East, recommended that a service block with a dining-hall, boiler house, kitchen and other offices, be built across the quadrangle of each Head workhouse.[14] A chapel had already been erected in that position at Bridge,[15] but Davy's recommendation may have been directly inspired by the central dining-hall then being erected at Elham, to designs by Joseph Gardner & John Ladds.[16]

Inspector Davy presented a rare and unexpected defence of Head workhouses: the small rooms were convenient for sub-classification and were 'more liked by the old people than modern wards of the pavilion type'. He concluded:

> That in one respect they have done their work well is shown by the fact that there are now extremely few able-bodied paupers in the county; in fact the want of able-bodied women is a constant source of embarrassment in the management of the Kent workhouses.[17]

The Courtyard-Plan Workhouse Outside Kent

Although Head's design was not adopted beyond his particular sphere of influence, a distinct group of East Anglian workhouses, designed by William T Nash of Royston, also had courtyard plans. Caxton and Arrington, Buntingford (Fig 52), St Ives (Fig 53) and Royston had single courtyards while Halstead had a double courtyard; all five were erected in

Figure 50 (opposite, top)
Remnants of iron galleries survive in the courtyard of Bridge Union Workhouse (1836), Kent, which has been converted into flats. This photograph shows a corner of the old men's yard.
[BB96/5725]

Figure 51 (opposite, below)
The arcaded main block of Blean Union Workhouse (1835), Kent, contained the master's rooms. The projecting bay window of a later boardroom can be seen in the background.
[BB93/26106]

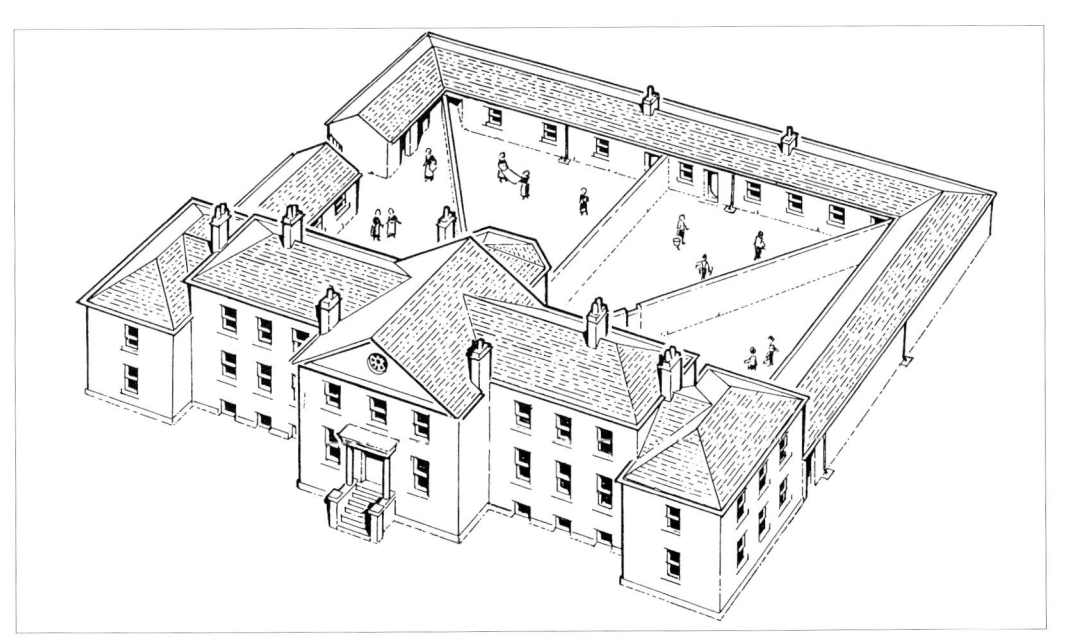

Figure 52
William T Nash of Royston designed a number of courtyard-plan workhouses including that of Buntingford (1836–7) in Hertfordshire, most of which survives as offices.
[Perspective view based on drawings in the Cockett and Nash Collection, Cambridgeshire RO Ref 296]

Figure 53
St Ives Union Workhouse (1836–8) was designed by William T Nash. Like the 'Head' workhouses in Kent, it depended on iron galleries for access to the upper floors of the wings. The master's quarters, shown here, bear scars caused by the removal of yard walls.
[BB96/2711]

the local yellow brick. The presence of first-floor galleries at Royston and St Ives suggests that Nash was inspired to some degree by Head's model plan but, in other respects, his workhouses bore little resemblance to the courtyard-plan workhouses of Kent.

In Nash's single courtyard plan, one side of the yard was closed by the main building, while the other three sides were bounded by lower structures. The buildings did not, therefore, seem as enclosed as the Kent workhouses. The master's rooms occupied a square or polygonal projection on the rear of the central block. Yard walls radiated either directly from the master's quarters or from a 'general yard of communication', defined by railings, which encircled the master's quarters, enabling him to observe every yard while obstructing the view from one yard into the next.

Nash shared a taste for Italianate detail, especially grouped round-headed windows, with a few other workhouse architects, for example James Clephan and, less consistently, T L Evans. These architects were undoubtedly aware of one another's work, as they were often rivals in the same competition. Nash's papers include tracings of winning designs, by his competitors, for Saffron Walden, Bishop's Stortford (where Nash acted as surveyor and modified the original scheme), Luton and Biggleswade workhouses.[18]

Leighton Buzzard Union Workhouse, a single-courtyard building designed by the surveyor of the Woburn estate, William P Roote, was similar in many ways to Head's and Nash's workhouses. It featured round-headed windows, dentilled eaves and wrought-iron first-floor galleries (Fig 54). The institution, however, was not confined to the courtyard. The outside of an octagonal supervisory block in the centre of the rear range, aligned with an archway in the front range, was ringed by single-storeyed workshops (*see* Figure 61e). Roote repeated this unusual arrangement at Newport Pagnell, and possibly at Newmarket, which was extensively remodelled in 1899–1902.[19]

Another Bedfordshire workhouse, designed by John Williams for Luton Union, fused elements of Head's courtyard plan and Kempthorne's 'square' plan in a unique fashion (Fig 55). Two-storeyed accommodation ranges formed a square, but instead of being open, the quadrangle was occupied by a hub and three 'spokes'. A rectangular dining-hall in the centre of the courtyard was flanked by single-storeyed buildings containing a kitchen and wash-house on one side and a schoolroom and laundry on the other. It was connected to the entrance block by a two-storeyed range. Arches within the dining-hall carried a two-storeyed octagon which contained the master's rooms. From this eyrie

New Poor Law Workhouses, 1835–1840

*Figure 54
Designed by the surveyor of the Woburn Estate, William P Roote, Leighton Buzzard Union Workhouse (1836) has a courtyard plan with a gallery which is just visible in this view. The large polygonal block allowed the master to supervise workshops to one side and the main courtyard to the other.
[BB96/2889]*

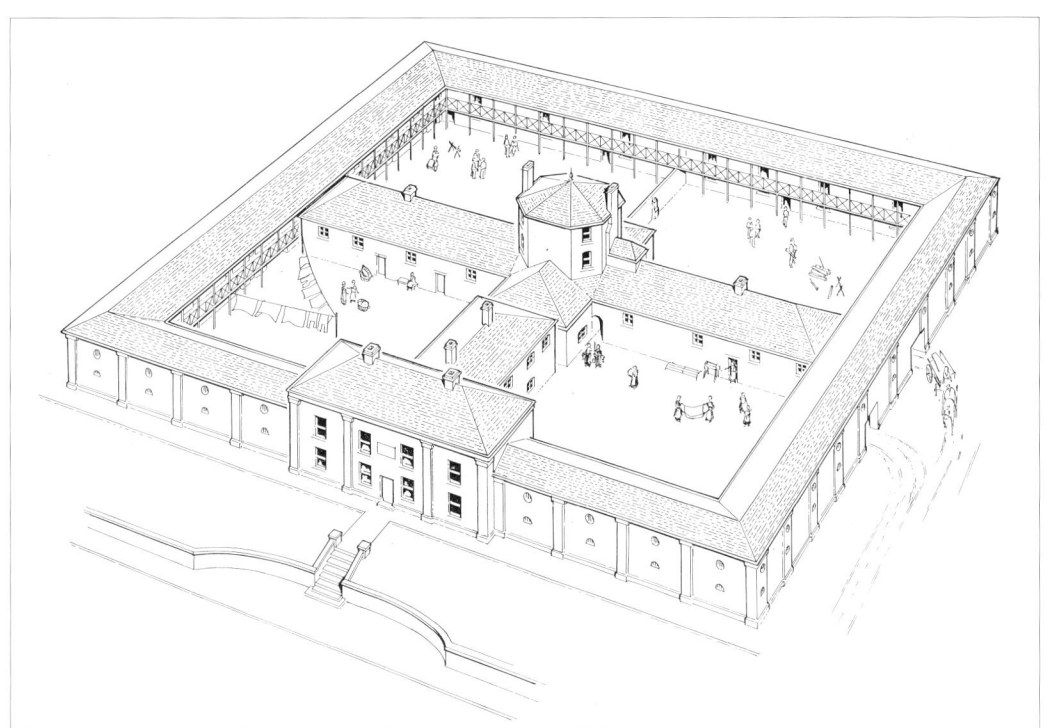

*Figure 55
This perspective view of Luton Union Workhouse (1836) is based on original drawings by the architect John Williams. Later, as St Mary's Hospital, the building was greatly altered.
[Based on a drawing in the Cockett and Nash Collection, Cambridgeshire RO Ref 296]*

he could survey all four workhouse yards. Access to the upper storeys of the four boundary ranges was, once again, by means of a gallery. The ground-floor rooms were lit by barred lunettes placed high in the outer walls, and by rectangular windows overlooking the yards; the first-floor rooms were merely lit by barred oculi in the outer walls and by transom lights, which opened for ventilation, over the doorways. The external elevations of Luton, divided by pilasters, closely resembled Head's design.

Three double-courtyard plan workhouses in Lincolnshire, those of Bourne, Spalding and Stamford unions, were by a local architect, Bryan Browning, who also designed the 'square'-plan Peterborough Union Workhouse. Of these buildings, only Bourne survives. Its courtyards, now infilled, were bounded by single-storeyed ranges across the front and sides and by a linear accommodation block to the rear.[20] Outside the South East, few courtyard-plan workhouses were built.

Radial Workhouses: The 'Square' Plan

Sampson Kempthorne's 'Square Plan of a Workhouse to Contain 300 Paupers' was the plan most commonly adopted after 1835; it proved capable of endless variation, and was adapted for buildings to hold as few as 150 and as many as 500 paupers (*see* Appendix 3, Figures 2–5). Four three-storeyed ranges emanated from an octagonal hub, set within a rectangle defined by a three-storeyed entrance block and single-storey outbuildings. The four yards enclosed by these buildings were assigned to boys, girls, men and women, but greater segregation could be achieved within the house. Unlike Head, Kempthorne did not totally deprive inmates of a view of the outside world. There were no outward-looking windows in the outbuildings, or in the gable ends of the main ranges; indeed, only the girls' dormitory, on the upper floor of the entrance block, benefited from directly outward-looking windows. However, the upper-floor windows of the main ranges, lighting the dormitories, potentially enjoyed views over the roofs of the single-storeyed outbuildings which formed the perimeter of the workhouse.

The façade of the entrance block had some modest architectural embellishment, including rusticated window heads and a shallow pediment over the main doorway. The central three of its five bays were set forwards, with a string-course at first-floor level. The remainder of the building was extremely plain.

On the ground floor of the entrance block was a large waiting-room for paupers, flanked by a searching-room and porter's room on one side and a bread room on the other. The outbuildings adjoining the bread room housed the bakehouse and flour and mill room, while on the other side were stores. Stairs behind the waiting-room led up to the boardroom, off which opened a clerk's room, a strong room and an ante-room. On the upper floor was the girls' bedroom, with a mistress's room opening off it. The girls' bedroom, although with a view of the outside world, was the only dormitory in the house not to have cross-ventilation.

The four ranges emanating from the central hub are most easily referred to in relation to the entrance block as front, side and rear ranges. The front range contained one room on each floor: on the ground floor was the boys' and girls' schoolroom and dining-room, on the first floor the boys' bedroom and on the second floor a women's sick and infirm ward with a nurses' room opening off it. The schoolroom was by-passed by two passages on the outer sides of the range, leading directly from the entrance block to the hub.

The side ranges contained the main accommodation for adult paupers. Their day-rooms were located on the ground floor, their bedrooms and sick and infirm wards above. The sleeping-rooms had access to water-closets but during the day paupers had to use privies, or earth closets, in the yards. The water-closets and privies were 'so contrived as to be continually cleansed by passing water through them'.[21] Day-rooms and bedrooms were allotted to first and second-class men and women, meaning the aged and able-bodied respectively, but there is no indication that the sick and infirm were

Table 3 Workhouses by Sampson Kempthorne
(* = *attribution only. Workhouses erected to the '200-pauper' plan were not necessarily for 200 inmates*)

Union	Plan Type
Abingdon	hexagon
Andover	square
Axminster	square
Banbury	hexagon
Barnstaple	square
Basingstoke	square
Bath	hexagon
Bradfield	hexagon
Bridgwater	hexagon
Chertsey	hexagon
Crediton	hexagon
Droitwich	200-pauper
Droxford	hexagon
Eton	square
Frome	hexagon
Grantham	hexagon
Hastings	square
Huntingdon	200-pauper
Lymington	200-pauper
Mansfield	square
Market Harborough	square
Martley*	200-pauper
New Forest*	hexagon
Newbury	square
Newhaven	block
Okehampton	200-pauper
Orsett	200-pauper
Pershore	200-pauper
St Thomas	hexagon
South Molton*	200-pauper
Taunton	hexagon
Thornbury	200-pauper
Ticehurst	hexagon
Torrington	200-pauper
Upton-on-Severn	200-pauper
Wantage	square
Warminster	hexagon
Winchcomb	200-pauper
Yeovil	hexagon

classified in the same way. Kempthorne seems to have expected first and second-class paupers to mix freely in the yards.

Sleeping arrangements throughout the workhouse varied according to gender and state of health. Men and boys slept in single beds in two tiers, presumably bunks, while women and girls shared double beds. Only the sick and infirm enjoyed single beds in one tier. Their wards were less crowded than the others, housing twelve, while equivalent ordinary wards accommodated twenty-one or more. The sick and infirm wards, moreover, were the only paupers' rooms to be equipped with fireplaces, although chimney-stacks are omitted from Kempthorne's elevation drawings. Other rooms were to be heated by means of hot-water pipes.

The kitchen and scullery were located on the ground floor of the rear range, with the dining-hall and chapel above, and first and second-class lying-in wards and a nursery on the top floor. It can be assumed that the first and second-class lying-in wards were for married and unmarried women, respectively.

The octagonal hub was partitioned rather awkwardly to provide suitable accommodation for the master. His parlour, occupying the entire ground floor, had a window overlooking each of the four exercise yards. On the first floor were the master's bedrooms, and on the second floor another bedroom and a surgery, presumably the room used by the medical officer during his visits to the institution. Stair bays separating the four ranges from the hub were inset, to maximise the light and the view.

The single-storeyed ranges around the perimeter of the workhouse included four separate three-bed receiving wards with adjoining bathrooms and washing-rooms. These were provided for new admissions: here paupers were stripped of their own clothes, bathed, examined by the medical officer and dressed in workhouse garb, before being assigned to the appropriate workhouse ward. The provision of one receiving ward off each of the four yards implies that some degree of classification, probably simply by age and sex, had already occurred before the new inmates were examined. There was a refractory ward for solitary confinement and a dead house or mortuary in the men's and women's yards, but not in the boys' and girls'. Every yard included privies and workrooms. The latter would usually have been for oakum-picking, sack-making, corn-grinding or, until it was banned after the Andover scandal in the 1840s, bone-crushing (*see* page 52). The laundry and wash-house were on the women's side of the house; the piggery had access from the women's and men's yards, but the adjoining slaughter house was on the men's side.

Many boards of guardians approached the Poor Law Commission directly for advice about workhouse design in 1835 and 1836, and throughout those years Sampson Kempthorne's office in Carlton Chambers was kept busy, outlining schemes and producing plans for different unions. Kempthorne was usually employed as architect but often delegated a clerk of works, for example James Humphries at Wantage, to discuss the details of a scheme with the guardians and contractors on site. Some of his letters and personal appearances at board meetings are recorded but only one set of his plans, for the 'hexagon' Crediton workhouse, has survived.[22]

The ten 'square' workhouses known to have been designed by Kempthorne were all erected between 1835 and 1837 (*see* Table 3). Of those which survive, Hastings (Fig 56) and Eton followed the model most closely. The only apparent deviation at Hastings, the blind second-floor windows of the entrance block, may have been introduced by Annesley Voysey who drew up the working plans and specifications in his role as Kempthorne's agent. His motive may have been the elimination of the view from the girls' dormitory. At Eton, Kempthorne was instructed to lower the workhouse, as the board wished to make 'the new Building as little injurious to the view from [Windsor] Castle as the nature of it will permit', and required Kempthorne to communicate with Sir Jeffry Wyattville, who was then transforming the castle for King William IV, on the subject.[23]

Figure 56
The entrance block of Hastings Union Workhouse (1836) is now disused.
[BB92/29716]

Figure 57
The entrance block is all that survives of Winslow Union Workhouse (1835) by George Gilbert Scott.
[BB91/2130]

Nothing came of that loyal gesture, however, and Eton workhouse was erected with the usual three storeys throughout.

At Newbury, the entrance block was reduced to two storeys while the ranges behind it remained three storeys high, but in all other respects it followed the model design closely, having channelled ashlar on the ground floor, a flat, bracketed canopy over the doorway, plain stone bands at first-floor and eaves levels, and shallow slated roofs.

Kempthorne adopted a new design of entrance block from 1836, for example at Andover, where the block was extended laterally, with a gable framing a name plaque ('Andover Union Workhouse') over the central three bays (*see* Figure 46). This seems to have responded to a general demand from guardians for more office accommodation.

Some architects, such as Edward Hunt at Alresford and Wilton, produced workhouses which faithfully reproduced the model 'square' plan. In certain cases the guardians specifically instructed their architect to draw up plans based on Kempthorne's 'square' plan. At Fareham the board asked Mr Owen, probably the speculative builder Thomas Ellis Owen of Southsea, to base his design on Poor Law Commission Plan 'F'.[24] The elevation of the three-storeyed entrance block followed Kempthorne's model exactly, as did the arrangement of the hub. When guardians were less rigid in their instructions, architects preferred to use the 'square' plan as a basis for more individual designs which might attract attention and win competitions.

George Gilbert Scott worked briefly with Kempthorne in 1835 and adhered to the 'square' plan more closely than most throughout 1835, perhaps because he continued to occupy an office in the same building as Kempthorne.[25] Six of his early workhouses, those of Brackley, Buckingham, Kettering, Northampton, Oundle and Winslow unions, had a 'square' plan. The elevations of Scott's entrance blocks, however, departed from the model. At both Winslow (Fig 57) and Oundle the centre of the block was canted for its full height, as though an octagon had been dropped into a rectangle. The entrance blocks of Kettering and Northampton, on the other hand, were both dominated by a full, triangular pediment which gave the air of an imposing civic building. In each case the ground storey of the block received greater enrichment than its upper floors.

By 1836, architects were more prepared to modify both the internal arrangements and the physical appearance of 'square' workhouses. Lewis Vulliamy's approach at both Epping and Brentford was fairly typical, and is well documented. Brentford,[26] designed to be seen from Syon Park, has been demolished but Epping (Figs 58 and 59), where Vulliamy displaced Kempthorne as architect, survives together with the architect's original plans.

Vulliamy had already completed a plain 'hexagon' workhouse for Sturminster Newton Union in Dorset (*see* pages 76–7), but at Epping he designed a red-brick building in an Elizabethan style, with copious stone dressings, diamond-paned casements, numerous gables and grouped chimney shafts. The octagonal hub was covered by a double-pitched roof and dominated by a tall cupola. If this was how the Epping guardians wished their workhouse to look, it is no surprise that they had found Kempthorne's plain designs unsatisfactory (*see* pages 47–8).

More fundamental changes at Epping involved a redistribution of functions throughout the institution. The single-storeyed rear range contained the dining-hall/chapel, which was thus brought down to the same level as other day accommodation. The kitchen was removed to the ground floor of the women's range, depriving them of a day-room, and the lying-in ward was relocated to the upper floor of the entrance block. This displaced the girls' dormitory, which in turn displaced a women's sick and infirm ward. To answer this need, and to enable the sick and infirm to be separated from one another, each of the main ranges was augmented by a short cross-wing which contained a dormitory on each floor: for the infirm on the ground floor and for the sick on the first and second floors. This had the additional advantage of enabling the infirm to move

New Poor Law Workhouses, 1835–1840

Figure 58 Epping Union Workhouse was greatly altered over the years: the entrance block was enlarged, the yards used as car parks and most of the original diamond-pane glazing replaced. [BB92/26589]

Figure 59 (below) Epping Union Workhouse (1837) in Essex was designed by Lewis Vulliamy. [Ground-floor plan redrawn from Essex RO G/E 25/2]

around the establishment without having to climb stairs, and in this respect evinced a considerably more thoughtful attitude towards the elderly and disabled than did the model plan.

Much of the reorganisation of Epping attempted to correct widely recognised deficiencies in the model plan. It was only practical, for example, to locate dining-halls at ground level, next to the kitchen, particularly as the upper-floor dormitories were out-of-bounds during the day. In many cases, for example at John Smith's Chesterton Union Workhouse, this was achieved by shifting the kitchen into the hub and bringing the dining-hall down to the ground floor of the rear range.[27] An alternative solution was to locate the dining-hall in the hub, leaving the kitchen in the rear range. As dining-halls were used as chapels, this created a centralised space for worship which sometimes spread into the side and rear ranges, for example at William Thorold's Walsingham workhouse (Fig 60), where the pulpit abutted a partition separating men from women,[28] and at a number of the 'square' workhouses designed by George Wilkinson of Oxford. End cross-wings became another common feature of new workhouses, housing children, the sick or the infirm, all of whom could be supervised by schoolteachers or nurses, while the able-bodied, who required the direct supervision of the master and matron, remained close to the hub.

One other modification worth noting at Epping is the treatment of the rear yards. Their outer corners were canted, and they were divided by diagonal walls, allowing the establishment to provide six yards rather than four. Vulliamy was not the only architect to play with the geometric relationship between the main buildings and surrounding yards. Occasionally, a cruciform-shaped main building was enclosed by a full octagon rather than a square, allowing the perimeter to repeat the form of the hub, as it did in the 'hexagon' plan. William Thorold chose this design for Depwade and Walsingham workhouses in Norfolk (Fig 61b). He effectively chopped off the corners of the yards, an idea executed much more timidly at his Wayland and Guiltcross workhouses.[29] Lexden and Winstree Union Workhouse in Essex, by Foden &

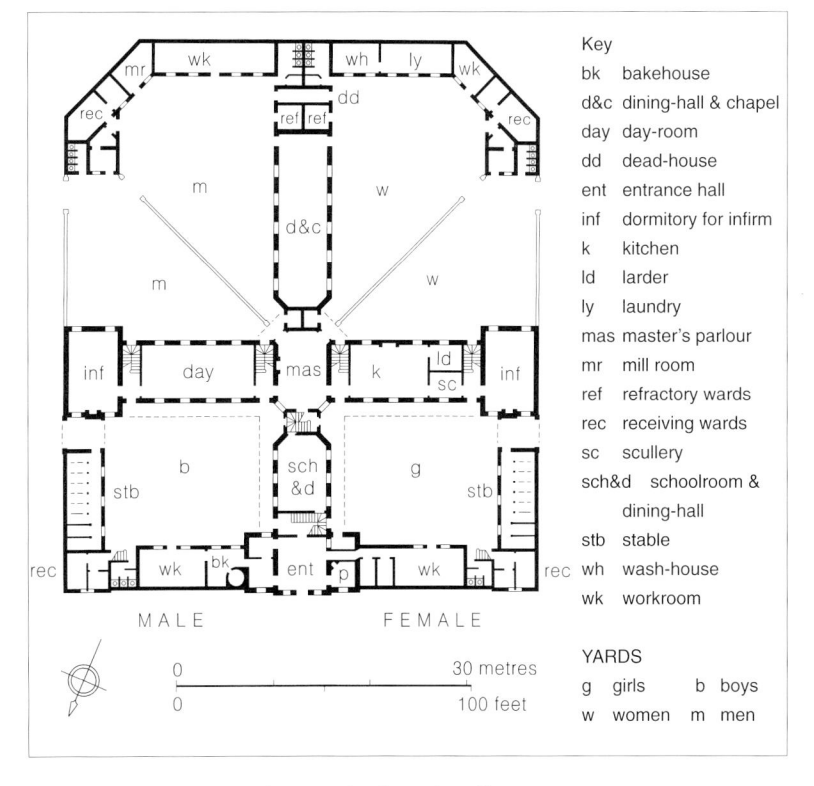

Key
bk   bakehouse
d&c dining-hall & chapel
day day-room
dd   dead-house
ent entrance hall
inf dormitory for infirm
k   kitchen
ld   larder
ly   laundry
mas master's parlour
mr   mill room
ref refractory wards
rec receiving wards
sc   scullery
sch&d schoolroom & dining-hall
stb stable
wh   wash-house
wk   workroom

YARDS
g girls   b boys
w women   m men

THE WORKHOUSE

Figure 60
In New Poor Law workhouses, the dining-hall/chapel was the only communal room. Usually, as in the central chapel of Walsingham Union Workhouse, screens prevented the different classes of inmate from seeing one another. In some institutions, the master read from the raised pulpit during mealtimes.
[Conjectural reconstruction based on Norfolk RO C/GP19/174]

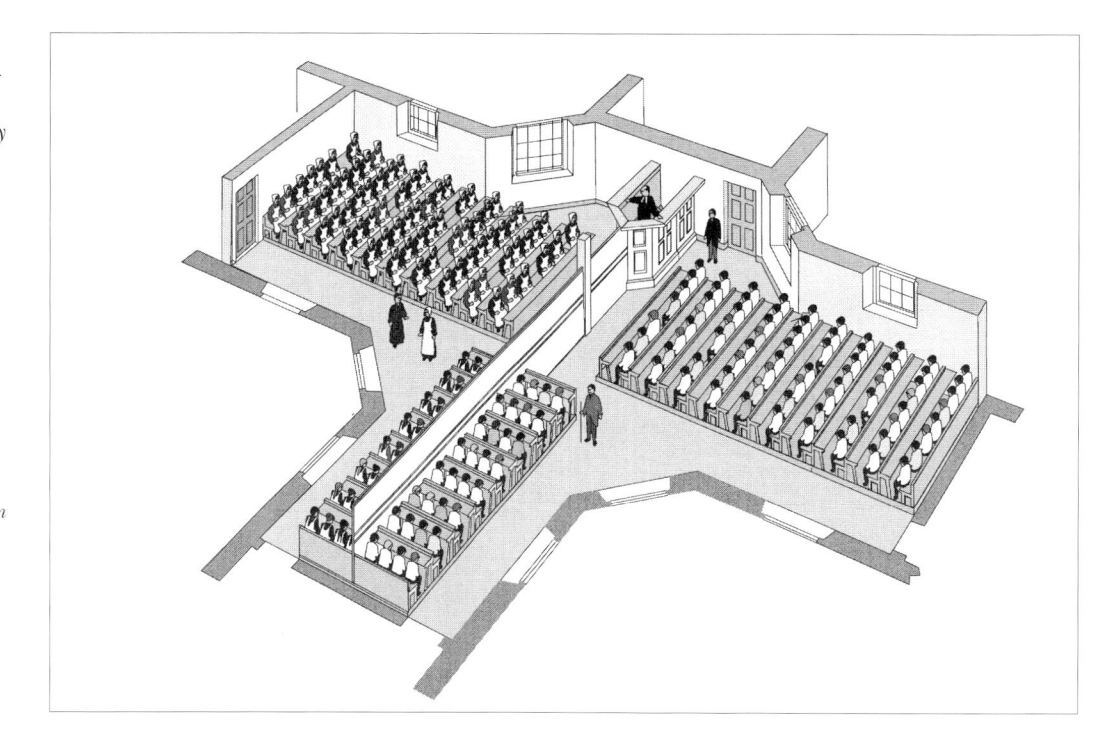

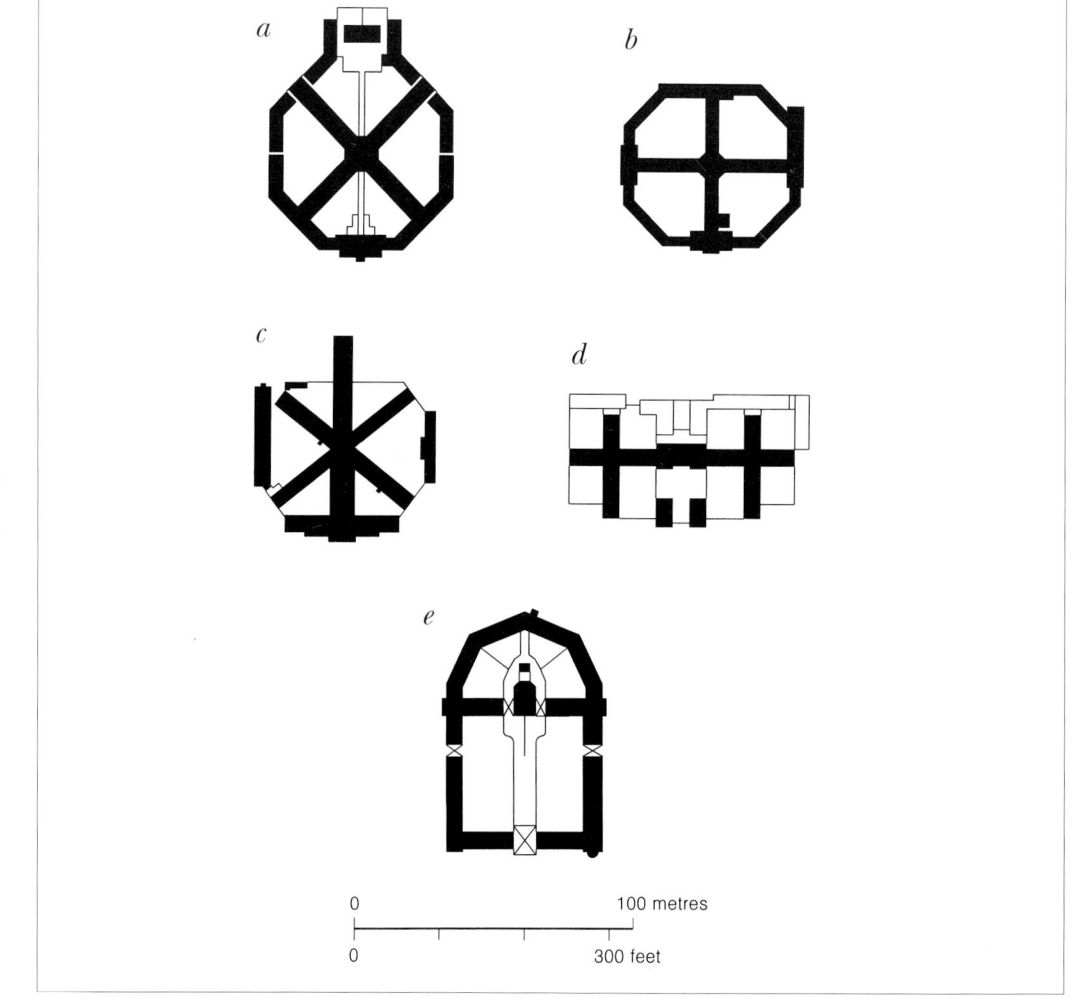

Figure 61
These comparative block plans show variations on the radial workhouse. They are:
a. *Lexden and Winstree Union Workhouse (1836; S O Foden & W Henman);*
b. *Depwade Union Workhouse (1836; William Thorold);*
c. *Chipping Norton Union Workhouse (1836; George Wilkinson);*
d. *Colchester Union Workhouse (1836–7; J Brown);*
e. *Leighton Buzzard Union Workhouse (1836; William P Roote).*

Henman, illustrates a variation on this in which the cruciform-shaped building was spun round 45 degrees within the octagon, detaching the entrance block from the front range (Fig 61a and 62). Severing the connection between these elements meant that the entrance block could not include pauper accommodation and had to include a staircase, but otherwise the arrangement of the rooms fulfilled all the requirements of the model plan, having a waiting-room with a side entrance for paupers on the ground floor, and a large boardroom with separate clerk's office upstairs. The master's accommodation in the hub was linked to the entrance block by a pathway across the front yard, rather than by covered ways or paths running to either side of a front range. He now had the advantage of being able to watch over the main entrance of the institution at all times.

A number of workhouses were built to a double-cruciform plan (Figure 61d), with a central boardroom and kitchen block flanked by miniature 'square'-plan complexes, each with four ranges emanating from an octagonal hub, one for males and the other for females. John Brown, the County Surveyor of Norfolk, employed this plan at Blofield, Colchester, Docking, Henstead, Sudbury and Wickham Market, and appears to have been its originator. It was copied at Stroud, Epsom and Kingston-upon-Thames by William Mason of Ipswich, who emigrated to the Antipodes in 1838,[30] and by W Watson, the architect of Walsall and Warwick workhouses. The double-cruciform plan of these buildings had the benefit of separating yards by buildings rather than walls, making communication between different classes of pauper impossible.

Both Mason and Brown indulged in the new fashion for Tudor architecture at some of their workhouses. The squat centre of Mason's Epsom Union Workhouse, where the boardroom and offices were located, comprised a broad crenellated projection flanked by gabled bays. The board had deliberately favoured this design over sixteen other contenders as it presented 'the appearance of an Almshouse rather than of a Prison'.[31]

The massive hubs of two workhouses in Oxfordshire, Chipping Norton and Witney, both designed by the young Oxford architect George Wilkinson, were irregular octagons sprouting ranges in the form of a St Andrew's cross, creating two small and two large yards (Fig 61c).[32] At both sites, the large yards were bisected by single-storeyed ranges or covered ways, rather than walls, to create a total of six yards. Most of Wilkinson's other workhouses (see Table 4), including Dorchester, Northleach, Stow-on-the-Wold and Honiton, were more closely based on the 'square' plan. These were probably the workhouses the Commissioners had in mind in 1839, when they reported that of all workhouse architects, Wilkinson had 'given the greatest satisfaction as regards arrangement and economy'.[33]

Following the passage of the Irish Poor Law Act in 1838 Wilkinson was employed to design 130 workhouses, all of which had been built by

Table 4 Workhouses by George Wilkinson
(*attribution only)

Union	Plan Type
Bromyard	square
Chard	square
Chipping Norton	St Andrew's cross
Devizes	square
Dorchester	square
Gainsborough	square
Honiton	square
Ledbury	square
Leominster	200-pauper
Malmesbury	not standard
Northleach	square
Stow-on-the-Wold	square
Tenbury	double courtyard
Thame	not standard
Weobley	square
Wincanton	square
Witney	St Andrew's cross
Woodstock	not standard
Wolverhampton*	St Andrew's cross

Figure 62
The graduated massing of Lexden and Winstree Union Workhouse, with low peripheral workshops, a two-storeyed entrance block and a three-storeyed hub, was typical of radial workhouses but has usually been disrupted by later alterations and additions.
[BB93/27197]

THE WORKHOUSE

*Figure 63
The Oxford architect George Wilkinson designed several English workhouses before being given responsibility for building workhouses in Ireland. This is one of his standard designs for an Irish workhouse.
[From* PP *1839 (239), XX, Appendix B, No. 10. C, by permission of the Syndics of Cambridge University Library]*

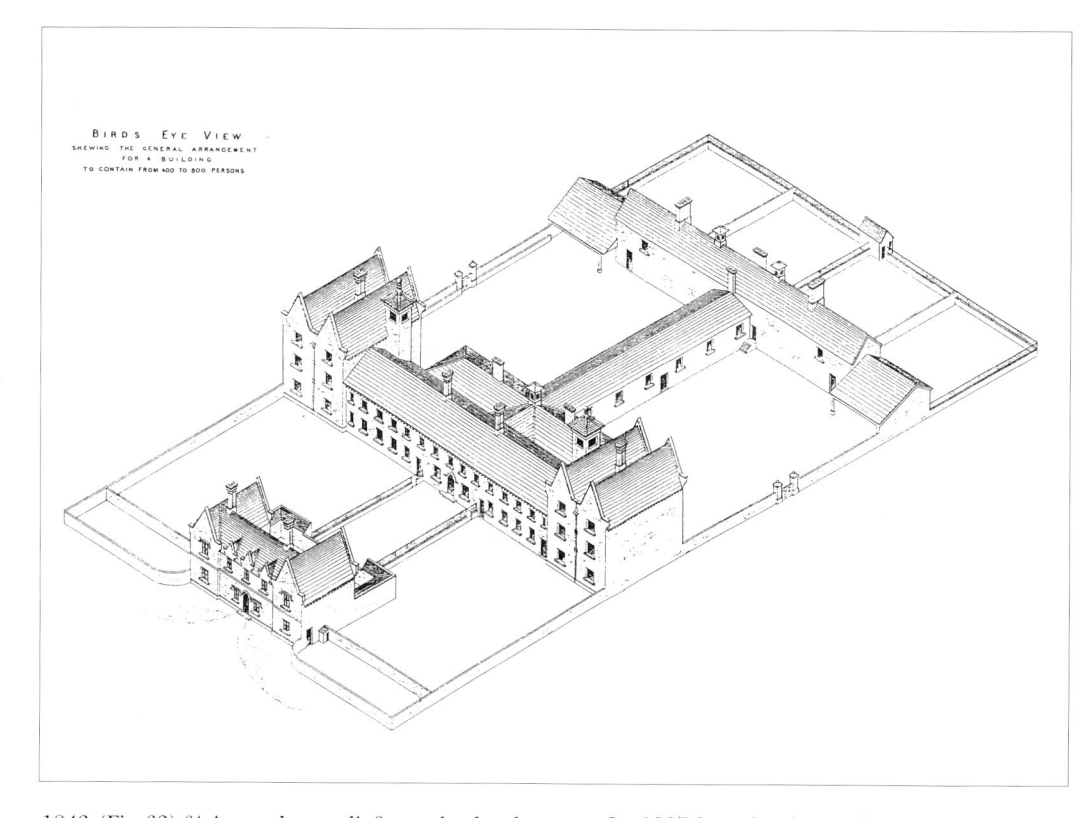

*Figure 64
The register office (1839) on the High Street of Thornbury, designed by S W Daukes, was probably built and administered by the guardians of Thornbury Union.
[BB96/10278]*

1843 (Fig 63).[34] As outdoor relief was absolutely prohibited in Ireland, workhouses there were much larger than their English counterparts. They were erected for one-third of the cost and provided a lower standard of accommodation. The day-rooms, for example, had earthen floors and most dormitories, except those for the aged and infirm, were equipped with sleeping platforms rather than bedsteads.[35]

In 1837 boards of guardians were given the responsibility of administering the registration of births, marriages and deaths in their union and had to provide a register office.[36] This was often located at the workhouse, explaining why many entrance blocks were larger than Kempthorne had initially anticipated. At Shepton Mallet Union Workhouse the register office was combined with a porter's lodge in a small, single-storeyed building by the workhouse gate.[37] It was designed in 1836 by Jesse Gane, whose 'square' plan for the workhouse had been preferred to Kempthorne's.[38] In contrast, Thornbury Union register office of 1839 (Fig 64) was a small Grecian building located some distance away from the workhouse, on the High Street.

By and large, workhouse architects adhered to Kempthorne's utilitarian Classicism throughout the late 1830s, but a few managed to persuade guardians to adopt designs of mixed Gothic or Tudor inspiration. One of the first to achieve this was William J Donthorn, who was already an architect of some standing in his native Norfolk by 1835. After training under Jeffry Wyattville between 1817 and 1820, Donthorn had designed a number of large country houses, some of which were Classical in style, others Gothic. His first workhouse, for his home town of Swaffham, followed the model 'hexagon' plan, but those he designed in 1836 and 1837, including Downham Market, Ely (Fig 65), Freebridge Lynn, Oakham, Sleaford,

Thrapston, Uppingham and Wisbech, were all loosely based on the 'square' plan.[39] In more than one instance, Donthorn had designed a house for the chairman of the board of guardians in the course of the previous ten to fifteen years, and he may have been permitted a freer hand than usual on account of these established relationships.[40]

The contrast between Kempthorne's and Donthorn's elevations could not have been more extreme. The long E-shaped frontages of Donthorn's 'square' workhouses were all treated in an appropriate Gothic, Tudor or Elizabethan style, although never with strict historical accuracy. Typically, the façade of the central range was flanked by polygonal turrets and lit by a huge, mullioned-and-transomed window, filled with diamond-paned casements. Inside, of course, the buildings were as humble as other workhouses of the 1830s, and many of their straw and plaster floors still survive.[41] Their octagonal hubs included ambulatories or circulation passages with corresponding windows which allowed the master to look, from his central room, into the yards. These passages must have considerably impeded his vision but, compared with the model plan, improved communications throughout the building.

A far more fundamental reorganisation of the 'square' workhouse was achieved by Samuel T Welch in Somerset (Fig 66). At his Perpendicular-style Wells and Axbridge workhouses he slid the main accommodation ranges forward, from the sides of the hub to the sides of the entrance block, but he retained the front and rear ranges and the hub itself in a manner not dissimilar to the Alverstoke House of Industry of 1799–1801 (*see* page 35, and Figure 32). This had the advantage of providing the buildings with long, continuous façades. Welch took full advantage of this, and may even have devised the plan principally to permit grand frontages. The façade of Wells (Fig 67), for example, was faced in ashlar and included much Tudor and Gothic detailing, such as mullioned-and-transomed windows with Tudor-arched heads and prominent hoods, tall stone finials, and cusped 'spherical triangles' which ventilated the roof spaces of the wings. In contrast to the ornate frontage presented to the town, the rear elevations were extremely plain and faced in uncoursed rubble (Fig 68). As the paupers' accommodation was at the front of the site, and as it was not considered proper to provide the able-bodied with a view of the world beyond the institution, Welch had to depart from the single-pile arrangement advocated by Kempthorne. Head's solution of blind exterior walls was out of the question for aesthetic reasons, but by providing back-to-back day-rooms and dormitories, Welch enabled the 'deserving' aged and infirm paupers to look outwards while non-deserving paupers looked inwards.

A few other architects designed workhouses with double-width or back-to-back wards despite the fact that Kempthorne had expressed his disapproval of them. While John Smith's Chesterton Union Workhouse respected the model 'square' plan, his Cambridge Workhouse occupied a wedge-shaped site and comprised three parallel ranges connected centrally by a covered way. The wings of the central range were angled north-east and north-west and contained back-to-back rooms which housed able-bodied inmates. Similarly, the Hertfordshire workhouses of Hemel Hempstead, Barnet (Fig 69) and St Albans, probably all designed by John Griffin, had deep wings containing back-to-back wards.[42]

Figure 65
William Donthorn's Ely Union Workhouse (1836–7) seems to echo the design of the west front of Ely Cathedral.
[BB91/15685]

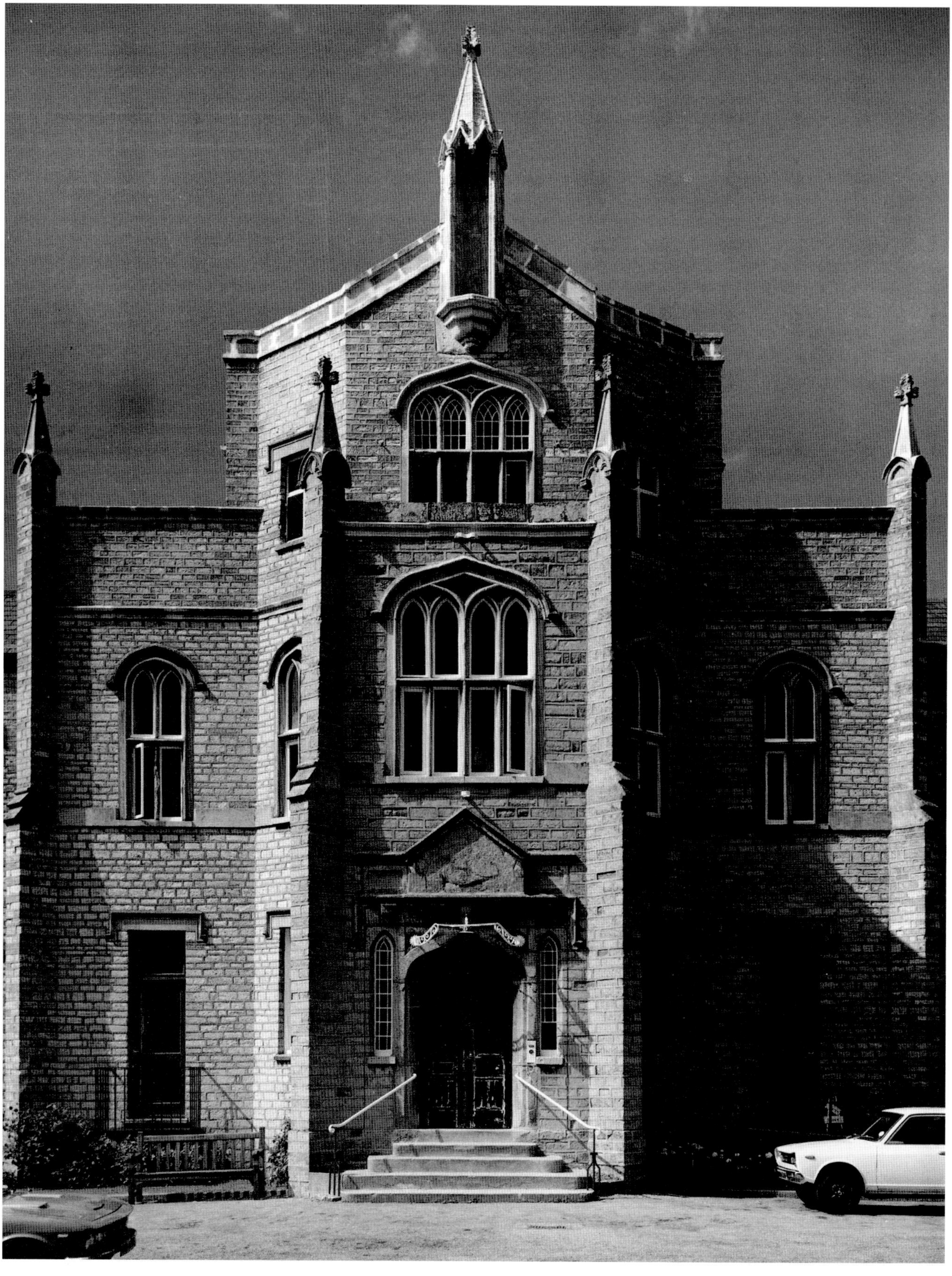

New Poor Law Workhouses, 1835–1840

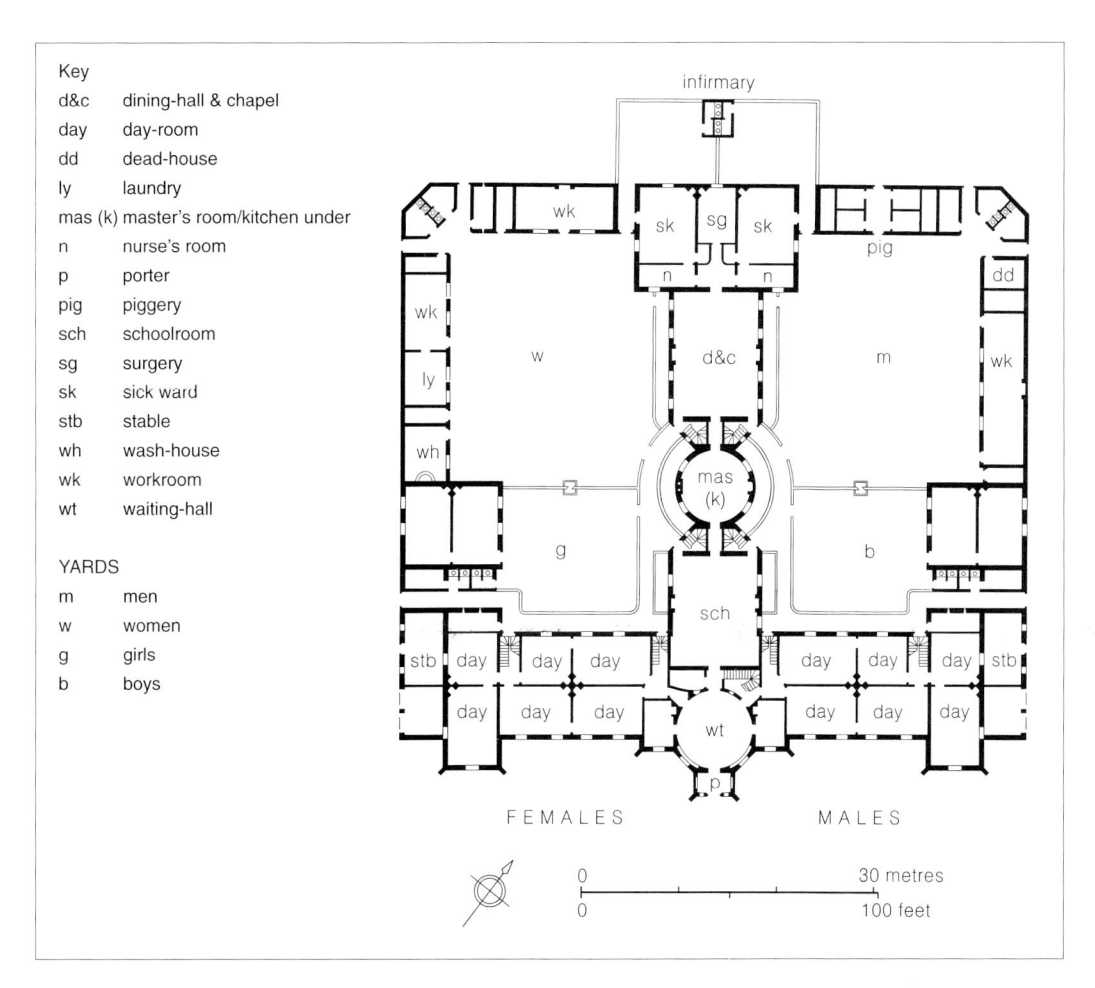

Key

d&c	dining-hall & chapel
day	day-room
dd	dead-house
ly	laundry
mas (k)	master's room/kitchen under
n	nurse's room
p	porter
pig	piggery
sch	schoolroom
sg	surgery
sk	sick ward
stb	stable
wh	wash-house
wk	workroom
wt	waiting-hall

YARDS

m	men
w	women
g	girls
b	boys

Figure 66 (left)
The plan of Wells Union Workhouse (1836–7) was a highly original variation on Kempthorne's model plan by Samuel T Welch.
[Redrawn from Somerset RO D/G/WE 32/1]

Figure 67 (opposite)
Welch adopted an eclectic medieval style, with a strong ecclesiastical flavour, for the façade of Wells Union Workhouse (1836–7). The building, situated on the outskirts of the town, is now Priory Hospital.
[BB98/06543]

Figure 68
The plain rear elevations of Wells Union Workhouse make a stark contrast with its façade.
[BB98/06544]

69

THE WORKHOUSE

*Figure 69
Barnet Union
Workhouse (1836–7),
now part of Barnet
General Hospital,
emulated Hemel
Hempstead Union
Workhouse and included
wards with spine walls.
[Redrawn from a plan in
Barnet Library]*

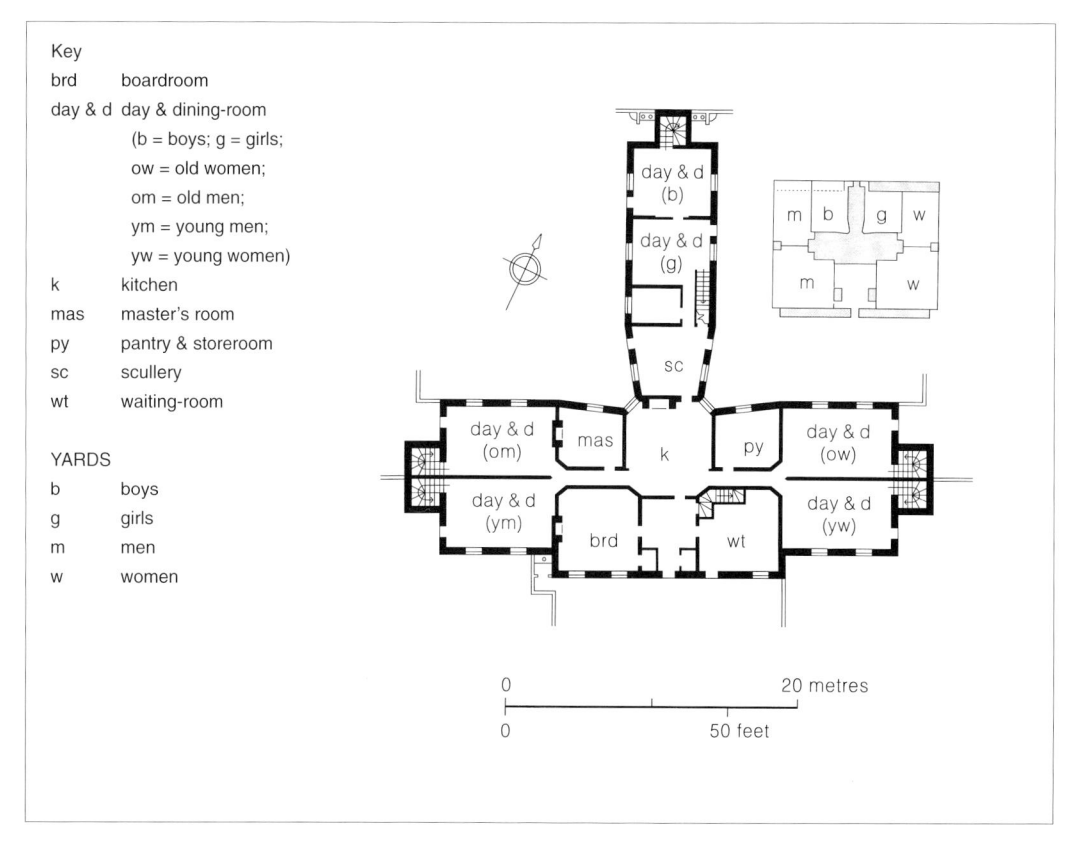

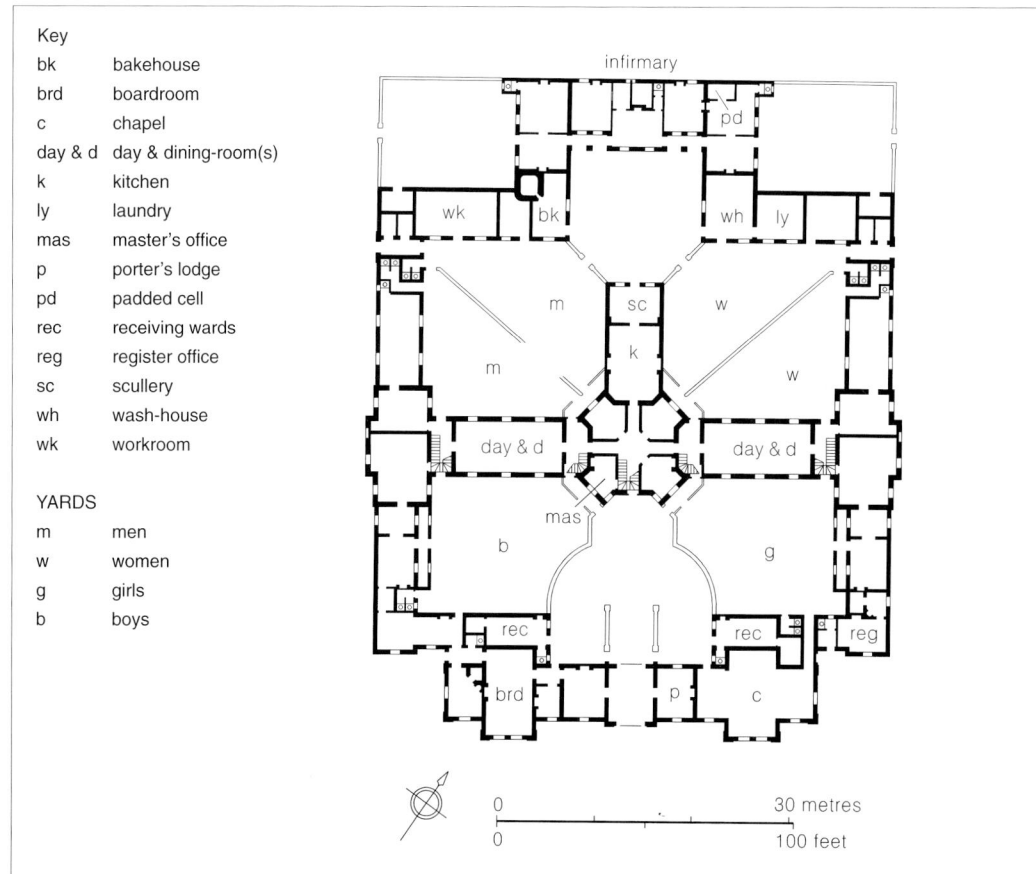

Key
brd   boardroom
day & d   day & dining-room
            (b = boys; g = girls;
            ow = old women;
            om = old men;
            ym = young men;
            yw = young women)
k   kitchen
mas   master's room
py   pantry & storeroom
sc   scullery
wt   waiting-room

YARDS
b   boys
g   girls
m   men
w   women

*Figure 70
The handful of
surviving workhouse
drawings from Scott &
Moffatt's office include a
set for Williton Union
Workhouse (1837–40).
The original ground-
floor plan, on which this
is based, is obscured by
annotations and
modifications, some of
which may date from the
mid-19th century.
[Redrawn from Somerset
RO D/G/WI 32/2]*

Key
bk   bakehouse
brd   boardroom
c   chapel
day & d   day & dining-room(s)
k   kitchen
ly   laundry
mas   master's office
p   porter's lodge
pd   padded cell
rec   receiving wards
reg   register office
sc   scullery
wh   wash-house
wk   workroom

YARDS
m   men
w   women
g   girls
b   boys

70

The Workhouses of Scott & Moffatt

Early in the summer of 1836 George Gilbert Scott teamed up with William Bonython Moffatt,[43] a colleague who had acted as his clerk of works on several occasions and who had independently produced a standard 'square' design for Amesbury Union Workhouse. Together, Scott & Moffatt turned their backs on the 'square' workhouse and produced institutions which were fragmented into three distinct structures: an entrance range, a main building, and an infirmary flanked by workshops (Fig 70). Moreover, instead of being radial, the main building had a linear plan. This 'improved plan' brought the partners much success (*see* Table 5).

Each of Scott & Moffatt's long, low entrance ranges was bisected by a tall archway, usually dominated by a pediment. To one side was the chapel block, to the other the boardroom block; receiving wards and yards lay to their rear (*see* Figures 70 and 71).

The main building was T-shaped. As usual, a large central block housing the master and matron was flanked by accommodation ranges, for male inmates on one side and females on the other. Two different hub designs recurred: in one, the hub was essentially octagonal but four faces were pulled forwards to create square bays diagonally overlooking the paupers' yards (*see* Figures 70 and 71); in the other, two canted bays projected from the front and rear elevations of a rectangular block (Fig 72). As there was no front range, the master and matron enjoyed a clear vista of the receiving wards on the back of the entrance range. Instead of a three-storeyed rear range, there was a single-storeyed kitchen, ventilated through the roof. As if to make up for the loss of accommodation in the front and rear ranges, the lateral ranges of the building were extended by end cross-wings which, as at Vulliamy's Epping Union Workhouse, generally housed boys, girls or the aged. The provision of a small chapel in the entrance range compensated for the absence of a central dining-hall. In an explanatory document for Newton Abbott Union, the architects stated that if efforts were made to segregate inmates in their day-rooms and workrooms, there was no sense in herding them together at mealtimes.[44]

Except when guardians objected to the additional expense, Scott & Moffatt included a semi-detached infirmary to the rear of the workhouse. This building, always very plain architecturally, was positioned centrally, with access from each division of the institution. It was never completely detached: abutting the men's wards were workshops, and abutting the women's were the wash-house and laundry (*see* Figure 70).

Figure 71
Bedminster Union Workhouse (1837) is typical of the workhouses designed by Scott & Moffatt in the late 1830s. The arcade on the left connected the entrance range with a chapel, which was added in 1860.
[BB95/9804]

THE WORKHOUSE

Figure 72
The central block of Scott & Moffatt's Elizabethan-style Windsor Union Workhouse (1839) survives complete with turret and diamond-pane glazing.
[BB97/05763]

Table 5 Workhouses by George Gilbert Scott and William Bonython Moffatt
(M = Moffatt alone; S = Scott alone)

Union	Design Approved by Guardians[a]	Expenditure Authorised by PLC[b]		Union	Design Approved by Guardians[a]	Expenditure Authorised by PLC[b]	
Amersham	–	Apr 1838		Lutterworth	Nov 1838	Apr 1839	
Amesbury	Jan 1836	May 1837	M	Macclesfield	Jan 1843	Feb 1843	
Bedminster	–	May 1837		Mere	May 1836	May 1838	
Belper	Mar 1838	Jul 1838		Newcastle-under-Lyme	May 1838	Jun 1838	
Bideford	–	Nov 1837		Newton Abbot	Sep 1836	Mar 1837	
Billericay	Jul 1839	Jun 1839		Northampton	–	Feb 1836	S
Boston	Nov 1836	Jan 1837	S	Oundle	Apr 1836	Jun 1836	S
Brackley	Jul 1835	Dec 1835	S	Penzance	Oct 1837	Mar 1838	
Buckingham	–	Jun 1836	S	Redruth	–	May 1838	
Burton-upon-Trent	–	Aug 1837		St Austell	–	Apr 1838	
Chesterfield	Feb 1838	Jul 1838		St Columb	Sep 1837	Mar 1838	
Chipping Sodbury	by Jun 1838	Jul 1838		Spilsby	May 1837	Sep 1837	
Dunmow	Jul 1838	Sep 1838		Tavistock	–	Jun 1837	
Edmonton	Nov 1839	Aug 1839		Tendring	Aug 1836	Sep 1837	
Gloucester	Jan 1837	Nov 1836		Tiverton	–	Dec 1836	
Guildford	Jul 1836	Mar 1837		Towcester	Jun 1835	Jan 1836	S
Horncastle	Mar 1837	May 1837		Uttoxeter	–	May 1838	
Kettering	–	Mar 1837	S	Williton	Aug 1836	Sep 1836	
Lichfield	Mar 1837	Jun 1836		Windsor	–	Feb 1839	
Liskeard	–	Oct 1837		Winslow	Jun 1835	Jul 1835	S
Loughborough	Jan 1837	Oct 1837		Witham	May 1837	Nov 1837	
Louth	May 1837	Jun 1837		Wycombe	–	–	

[a] This information is extracted from guardians' minute books.
[b] This information is from the unpublished Registers of Authorizations for Workhouse Expenditure (PRO MH 34/1–3).

In 1836 and throughout most of 1837, Scott & Moffatt designed numerous workhouses to their 'improved plan', all in a restrained Classical design, with architectural embellishment focused on the entrance range and the upper storey of the hub, the parts of the building visible to the public. In 1837, however, they adopted a neo-Elizabethan or neo-Jacobean style, extending an enriched architectural treatment across the front and sides of the main building. Their Amersham (Fig 73), Belper, Billericay, Dunmow, Macclesfield, Mere and Windsor (*see* Figure 72) workhouses were amongst the most expensive and ostentatious of all New Poor Law workhouses.

Scott & Moffatt's later workhouses dispensed with the long entrance range running parallel to the main building. Instead, at Billericay, Mere, Windsor and elsewhere, single-storeyed chapel and board-room blocks extended forward from the front of the end cross-wings, completely opening up the workhouse façade. This new arrangement was usually accompanied by a centrally placed porter's lodge, although that at Billericay had to be sited asymmetrically due to a railway cutting running in front of the building. The partners' last workhouse, Macclesfield, marked a new departure. Not only did the main building, rather surprisingly, include a central dining-hall/chapel, but the offices were concentrated in a detached block to one side.

The linear layout popularised by Scott & Moffatt was adopted by a few other architects, including Boulton & Palmer, who defeated Scott & Moffatt in the competition for Wolstanton and Burslem Union Workhouse at Chell, but had to redesign their elevations as the board requested the 'Elizabethan' rather than the 'Italian' style.[45] The linear layout was also adopted for three workhouses in the South West: Totnes, Bodmin and Kingsbridge. At Totnes, Scott & Moffatt were initially appointed but fell out with the Board, who substituted Thomas Ponsford. As at Bodmin and Kingsbridge, which may have been by the same architect, the hub comprised a small octagon dropped into a rectangle. Another architect to adopt a linear plan was William Adams Nicholson of Lincoln, whose Lincoln and Glanford Brigg workhouses have now been demolished. Melton Mowbray Workhouse had an elongated H-plan and should also be regarded as a member of this group. It was one of the few New Poor Law workhouses to display a plaque recording not just the date of construction (1836) but the name of its architect (Charles Dyer).

Figure 73
The entrance range of Amersham Union Workhouse resembles late-medieval almshouses and must have made the institution more welcoming than many other workhouses of the 1830s. The date '1838' is picked out in red brick above the central gateway, which is now blocked.
[BB92/26783]

Radial Workhouses: The 'Hexagon' Plan

Kempthorne's 'hexagon' workhouse (*see* Appendix 3, Figures 7–10) embodied the same principles as the 'square' workhouse and accommodated the same number of inmates in much the same way. The greatest difference was that three, rather than four, ranges emanated from the hub, which was now hexagonal. The hexagonal hub had the advantage of longer sides, and so the stair bays separating it from each range did not have to be recessed. This plan produced three rather than four yards, but each was bisected by a wall to create a total of six yards. This permitted first and second-class adults to be separated from one another outside as well as inside. Accommodation that was provided in the rear range of the 'square'-plan workhouse, including the kitchen, dining-room/chapel and lying-in wards, was added to the front range, but otherwise the arrangement scarcely differed. There were slight modifications in the arrangement of the outbuildings: the piggery was now in the first-class women's yard, the laundry in the second-class women's yard. Again there were four receiving wards, corresponding to the main divisions of the house.

In all, twenty-six 'hexagon' workhouses were erected between 1835 and 1838 (*see* Table 6), sixteen of which are known to have been designed by Kempthorne, or can be attributed to him with some measure of confidence. Of these, Abingdon, Banbury, Bradfield, and Warminster were designed in 1835. Abingdon (Fig 74), the very first New Poor Law workhouse to be completed, was for 500 paupers and had four-storeyed, rather than three-storeyed, ranges.[46] This experiment was never repeated, possibly because the towering 11-bay ranges overshadowed the yards. The ranges of Bath, the only other 'hexagon' workhouse which Kempthorne designed for 500 paupers, were longer and lower than those of Abingdon. St Thomas's held 450 paupers, Taunton 400 and Frome 350, but the others were built for only 200 to 300. The layout of all these workhouses was similar, but the height and length of the ranges varied according to the needs of the individual union.

While the entrance blocks of Abingdon and Bradfield followed the model plan, those of Warminster, Chertsey, New Forest, Ticehurst, Crediton (Fig 75) and others, like that of the 'square'-plan Andover, were two storeys high and nine bays long, with a gable over the central three bays. As indicated by the surviving plans of Crediton, these long entrance blocks would have concentrated all the union offices, including the boardroom, registry, clerk's office and waiting-hall, on the ground floor, and housed the girls' bedroom, surgery, nursery and lying-in room upstairs.[47] Behind them, the main ranges rose to three storeys, except at New Forest, where the front range was only two storeys high.

At the bigger workhouses of Taunton, St Thomas's and Bath, the entrance blocks were all three storeys high. St Thomas's had the recommended five bays, but Taunton and Bath (Fig 76) were both longer, with twelve and nine bays respectively. All three had a gable or pediment over the central three bays. Constructionally, Bath was of superior quality to Kempthorne's other workhouses, with coursed ashlar facings throughout. It was particularly expensive, costing £12,350,

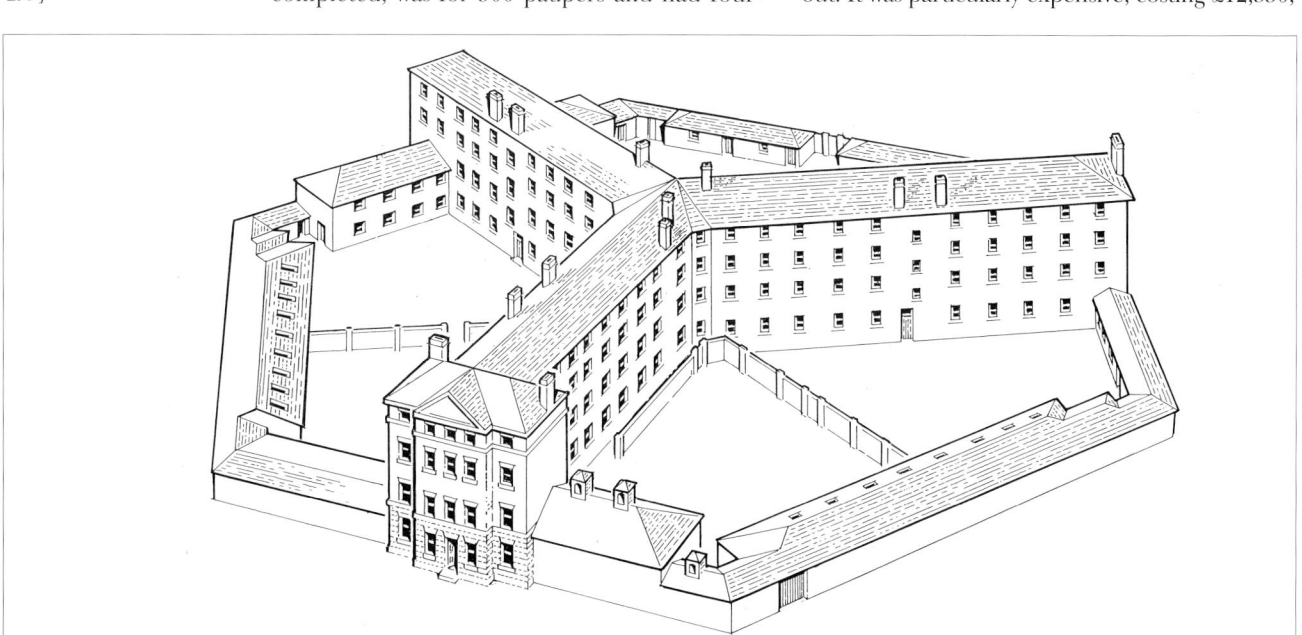

Figure 74
This is an isometric view of Sampson Kempthorne's 'hexagon'-plan Abingdon Union Workhouse, which was built in 1835 and demolished in the 1930s.
[Redrawn from The British Almanac *1836, 235]*

*Figure 75
Crediton Union
Workhouse (Sampson
Kempthorne; 1836–7)
is one of the best-
preserved 'hexagon'-plan
workhouses.
[BB96/10368]*

*Figure 76
Bath Union Workhouse
(1837–8) has ashlar
facings and was
undoubtedly the most
expensive workhouse
designed by Sampson
Kempthorne. It is now
St Martin's Hospital.
[BB96/5422]*

whereas Abingdon, with the same capacity, had cost just £8,500.[48]

Architects other than Kempthorne seem to have been loath to adopt the 'hexagon' plan. Those who did modified it in a number of ways, but it was never fundamentally revised in the way of the 'square' plan. One building which appears to have adhered to the model 'hexagon' plan in most respects, including the design of the entrance block, was Holbeach Union Workhouse. Its architect, Robert Ellis Jnr, like Thomas Owen at Fareham, must simply have produced working drawings and specifications from the published design.[49]

After beating thirty-three other entrants in the competition to design Bishop's Stortford Union Workhouse, T L Evans failed to secure the position of surveyor due to his poor references.[50] Surviving plans bear his signature, but it is clear from the guardians' minutes that the appointed surveyor, William T Nash, introduced several modifications.[51] Evans, however, was responsible for easing the rear ranges apart and running a walled walkway out to a detached infirmary with cross-lit wards (Fig 77).[52] Nash borrowed Evans's idea for his own Braintree Union Workhouse, although all of his earlier workhouses had had courtyard plans and he expressed his disapproval of the 'hexagon' plan in a letter:

> *I have prepared working drawings for 400 paupers upon the Hexagon plan. The faults of it appear to me to consist in allowing all the windows above the ground floor a command of the surrounding country, in allotting to the Master a much larger room than he requires or, if his room is reduced, confining his view to half of the yards.*[53]

THE WORKHOUSE

Table 6 Hexagon-Plan Workhouses
(* = attribution)

Union	Architect
Abingdon	Sampson Kempthorne
Banbury	Sampson Kempthorne
Bath	Sampson Kempthorne
Beaminster	H J Whitling
Bishop's Stortford	T L Evans
Bradfield	Sampson Kempthorne
Braintree	William T Nash
Bridgwater	Sampson Kempthorne
Chertsey	Sampson Kempthorne
Crediton	Sampson Kempthorne
Droxford	Sampson Kempthorne
East Retford	H J Whitling
Frome	Sampson Kempthorne
Grantham	Sampson Kempthorne
Holbeach	Robert Ellis Jnr
Langport	–
Leicester	William Flint
New Forest	Sampson Kempthorne*
New Winchester	William Cole
St Thomas (Exeter)	Sampson Kempthorne
Sturminster Newton	Lewis Vulliamy
Swaffham	William J Donthorn
Taunton	Sampson Kempthorne
Ticehurst	Sampson Kempthorne
Warminster	Sampson Kempthorne
Yeovil	Sampson Kempthorne

Leicester Union Workhouse, designed for 600 paupers by William Flint in September 1836, also included a detached infirmary, reached via a walled walkway.[54] This workhouse was larger than most, and the kitchen in the hub was spacious enough to incorporate a central flue.[55] The workhouse may also have been particularly elaborate: the ever-watchful Poor Law Commission complained about the 'superfluous decoration' of the front elevation, the expensive bay windows in the master's parlour and the ornamental chimneys. In his defence, Flint claimed that he had been merely following his instructions, 'to save the building from a prison or infirmary like character . . . by the introduction of a style which is not more costly than the rusticated and Italian character, to most of the workhouses already built'.[56] As no 'hexagon' workhouse is known to have been built in anything but a Classical style, it is unfortunate that the elevation of Flint's building was not recorded. Despite its unusually large size, the workhouse proved too small for Leicester, and had to be rebuilt with room for 1,000 paupers in 1850.

Lewis Vulliamy adopted an alternative approach to the 'hexagon' plan for Sturminster Newton Union Workhouse, a small building for just 150 inmates (Fig 78).[57] In particular, the shape of the hub and its relationship to the rear

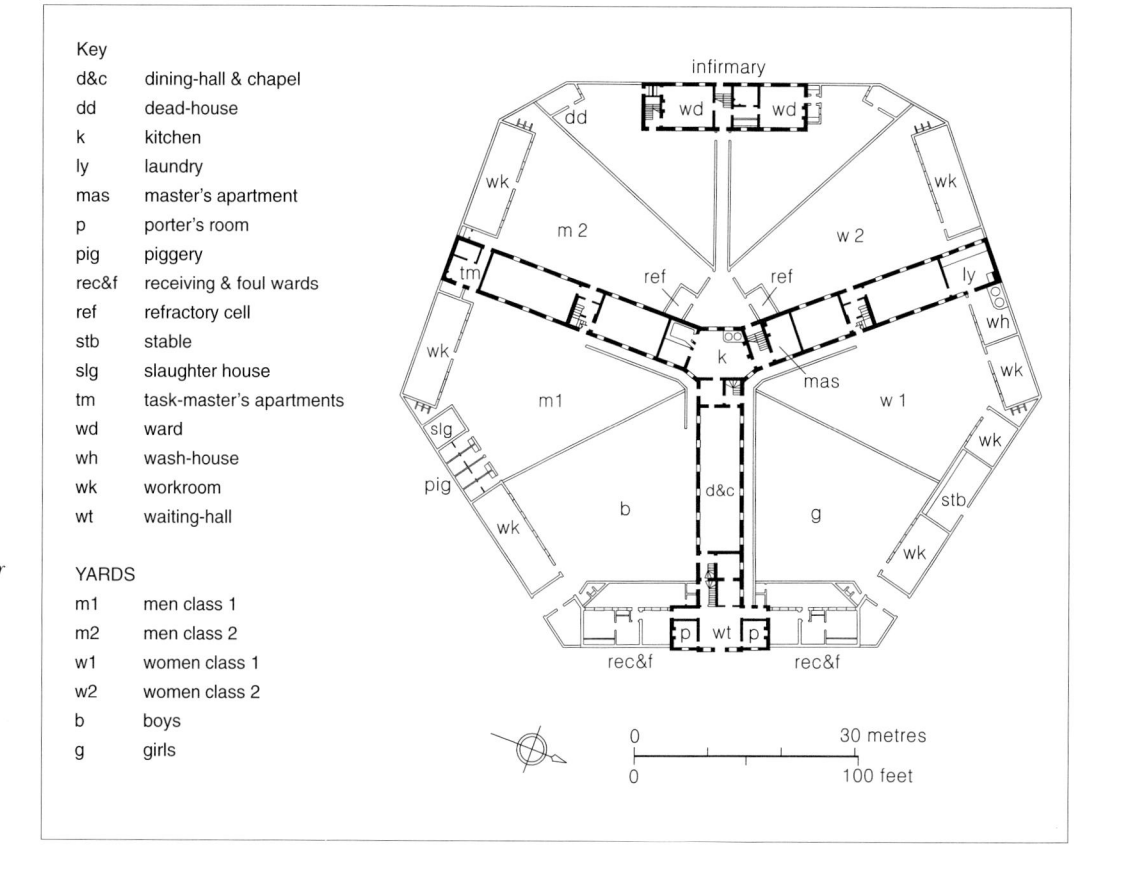

Figure 77
The competition for Bishop's Stortford Union Workhouse was won by T L Evans in 1836, but when Evans failed to secure the post of surveyor due to unsatisfactory references, unsuccessful competitor William T Nash stepped into the breach.
[Based on a drawing in the Cockett and Nash Collection, Cambridgeshire RO Ref 296]

Key
d&c   dining-hall & chapel
dd   dead-house
k   kitchen
ly   laundry
mas   master's apartment
p   porter's room
pig   piggery
rec&f receiving & foul wards
ref   refractory cell
stb   stable
slg   slaughter house
tm   task-master's apartments
wd   ward
wh   wash-house
wk   workroom
wt   waiting-hall

YARDS
m1   men class 1
m2   men class 2
w1   women class 1
w2   women class 2
b   boys
g   girls

wings was altered, and the central 'Y' was enclosed within a rectangle, rather than a hexagon. This did not seriously affect the workings of the institution, although the size of the building left no space for ground-floor dayrooms. Adaptations of the 'hexagon' plan by H J Whitling, for Beaminster and East Retford workhouses, were more faithful to Kempthorne's design but again departed from the geometric regularity of the original concept.[58]

Another building to be mentioned in this context is Clutton Union Workhouse, by Jesse Gane, a building which bore only a passing resemblance to the model 'hexagon' plan. Its perimeter assumed an hexagonal shape, but the main buildings within it formed a single range rather than a 'Y'.

After 1838, although adaptations of the 'square' plan continued to be produced, no more 'hexagon'-plan workhouses were built.

The '200-Pauper' Plan

Kempthorne's '200-pauper' plan workhouse of 1835 was, like the 'square' plan, a cruciform building with separate yards for men, women, boys and girls, but it lacked a supervisory hub (*see* Appendix 3, Figure 6). The master's room, located at the inner end of the men's range, had a single window which looked into the men's yard; the corresponding position on the female side was occupied by the kitchen. Only a ground-floor plan was published, but it shows that the distribution of paupers within the house differed little from the 'square' and 'hexagon' plans.

The '200-pauper' plan 'adapted for the less pauperised districts' was published in 1836 (*see* Appendix 3, Figures 11–13). The outbuildings against the perimeter wall were greatly reduced, and receiving wards were dispensed with altogether. The main ranges only included wards for the sick and infirm and sleeping-rooms for the able-bodied. The adults' dining-hall doubled as the women's day-room, while the men had a single-storeyed day-room in their yard. The girls' bedroom was next to the lying-in ward on the upper floor of the entrance block.

With such a high premium placed on pauper supervision, the hubless '200-pauper' plan failed to become popular. Most of those erected were designed by Kempthorne, but not all housed exactly 200 paupers: Thornbury, for example, was built for 250 and Winchcomb for 180. Lymington (Fig 79) had a five-bay entrance block

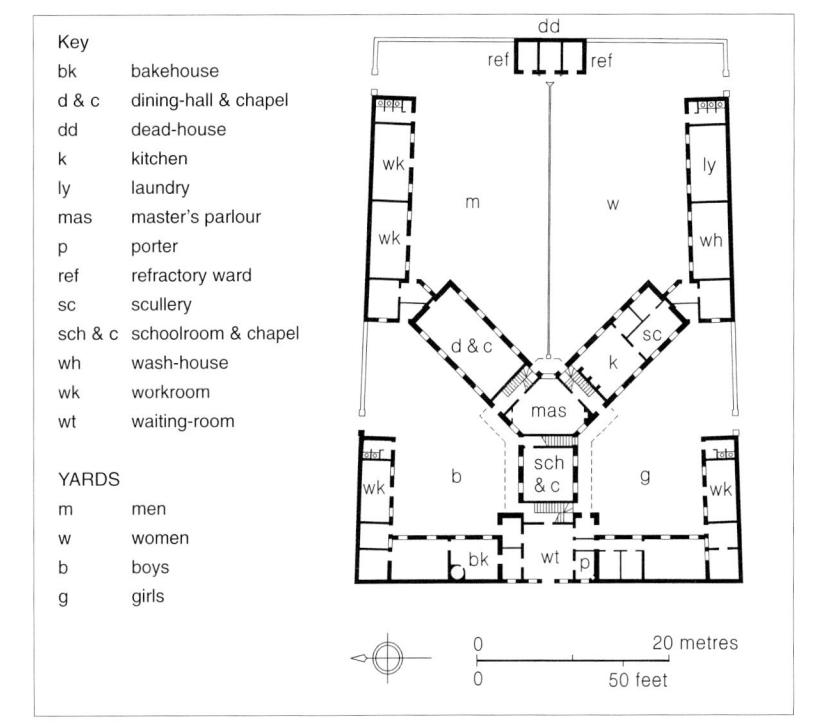

Key	
bk	bakehouse
d & c	dining-hall & chapel
dd	dead-house
k	kitchen
ly	laundry
mas	master's parlour
p	porter
ref	refractory ward
sc	scullery
sch & c	schoolroom & chapel
wh	wash-house
wk	workroom
wt	waiting-room

YARDS	
m	men
w	women
b	boys
g	girls

Figure 78 (above) Sturminster Newton Union Workhouse (Lewis Vulliamy; 1836).
[Ground-floor plan redrawn from Dorset RO BG/SN C.1/1]

Figure 79 (left) Lymington Union Workhouse (1837) is a well-preserved example of Kempthorne's '200-pauper' plan. The end bays of the main ranges were heightened in 1898–9. [BB92/16019]

*Figure 80 (below)
The range on the left in this view of Tonbridge Union Workhouse (1836), now Pembury Hospital, contained the kitchen and terminated in a water tower (now demolished).
[BB91/26198]*

*Figure 81 (bottom)
Newhaven Union Workhouse (1835) was probably Kempthorne's first workhouse commission and did not conform to any of his model plans.
[BB96/5766]*

surmounted by a full pediment, but most of these workhouses had two-storeyed, seven-bay entrance blocks of the Andover type, with a gable enclosing a date or name plaque over the central three bays, a diminutive pediment over the doorway and a plat band underlining the squat upper floor.

A few small, hubless workhouses by other architects show the influence of the '200-pauper' plan. In February 1836, plans for the very plain Cerne Abbas Union Workhouse were drawn up by Charles Wallis 'as nearly as possible conformable to the plan produced by Mr Henry Hodges', one of the guardians.[59] The surviving first and second-floor plans, signed by the contractors, show that the layout was closely based on the model '200-pauper' plans of 1835 and 1836, with certain variations as the building was intended for only 130.[60] Although the building rose to three storeys, the short ranges held only one three-bay room on each floor.

Other hubless cruciform workhouses included Glendale Union Workhouse and Wirral Union Workhouse at Clatterbridge, designed by William Cole for 130 paupers.[61] Map evidence suggests that the demolished workhouses of Cockermouth, Penrith and Hailsham may also have had a '200-pauper' plan.

Some small T-shaped workhouses had a greater affinity with the '200-pauper' plan than the 'square' plan, as they lacked a supervisory hub. One of the simplest examples, Belford Union Workhouse, was only one storey high throughout and had no obvious means of surveillance. At John & William Atkinson's Skirlaugh Union Workhouse, a single-storeyed canted bay on the back of each wing allowed the master and matron to watch over the male and female yards respectively.[62] A similarly limited method of supervision was built into the Kent workhouses of Tonbridge (Fig 80) and Gravesend and Milton, by John Whichcord and John Gould respectively. Each comprised two parallel ranges, with a single-storeyed kitchen range running partially between them to form an incomplete 'H'. The master's rooms lay to one side of a central archway in the front range and his office had a single-storeyed canted bay projecting into a central yard.

The Block Plan

A number of workhouses, of all shapes and sizes, but all adopting a corridor rather than a staircase/lobby access system, and all turning their backs on cross-ventilation, can be dealt with together as block-plan buildings.

The most unexpected workhouse by Sampson Kempthorne is that of Newhaven Union (Fig 81). The building comprised a large block, three storeys high and eight bays long, with no attached single-depth ranges. Not only did it fly in the face of Kempthorne's ideas on ventilation, but stylistically it bore little resemblance to the other workhouses he designed in 1835: the proportions are more graceful than those of his standard entrance block; there are no tell-tale plat bands; the doorways are round-headed with fanlights, and the glazing consists of wooden hornless sashes throughout. No wonder some writers have suggested that this is an Old Poor Law workhouse which was retained after 1834. However, the Newhaven guardians' minutes make it clear that it was built between April and August 1835.[63] Kempthorne's initial plan was received by the board in February 1835; conceivably the model plans had not yet been finalised at that stage.

New Poor Law Workhouses, 1835–1840

Even after the publication of the model plans, a handful of New Poor Law workhouses adopted a block plan. One for which original drawings survive is the Atkinsons' Guisborough Union Workhouse of 1838 (Fig 82). This was a square building with a small open yard, more of a light-well than a courtyard, in the middle. Rooms opened off corridors, and were mostly lit on one side only, a factor which did not deter the Poor Law Commission from approving the plans. Certainly, an absence of cross-ventilation was more acceptable for small workhouses, and Guisborough was to hold only 130 inmates. The even smaller Goole Union Workhouse, also designed in 1839, had the same form and may also have been by the Atkinsons.

Easingwold, erected in 1837 for 130 inmates, had an H-shaped plan. The stairs were positioned in the middle of each cross-wing, and were connected by a corridor, running through the centre. This plan looked backwards to 18th-century workhouses and hospitals, but also forwards to the corridor-plan workhouses which were favoured from the early 1840s (*see* Chapter 6). Bedale workhouse (Fig 83), another designed by the Atkinsons,

Figure 82 (left) Guisborough Union Workhouse (1838–9), now Guisborough General Hospital, was designed by John & William Atkinson, a firm responsible for several Yorkshire workhouses. It had a highly unusual block plan. [Redrawn from a drawing in North Yorkshire RO]

Figure 83 (below) Bedale Union Workhouse was built in 1839 to designs by John & William Atkinson. In plan it was quite different from Guisborough, having an 'H' shape reminiscent of many 18th-century institutions. The site later became Mowbray Grange Hospital. [BB92/9307]

Key	
brd	boardroom
d&c	dining-hall & chapel
dd	dead-house
day	day-room
day&sch	day & schoolroom (b = boys; g = girls)
inf	infirm ward
k	kitchen
ly	laundry
mas	master's room
sc	scullery
wh	wash-house
wk	workroom
vag	vagrant wards
YARDS	
b boys	g girls
m men	w women

The Workhouse

built in 1839 for 100, was very similar but had a canted bay to the rear.

A few workhouses simply comprised a double-pile rectangular block, either under a double or single gabled roof. The domestic-looking Bellingham Union Workhouse of 1839 had proportions very similar to large town houses and farmhouses in the area (Fig 84). It also resembled Old Poor Law workhouses in the North, such as the Bainbridge Workhouse (later Aysgarth Union Workhouse), of 1809–10.

Conversions

While 320 out of a total of 536 English unions had erected a new workhouse by 1841, the remainder occupied existing premises. Only a handful of unions, including Todmorden in Yorkshire, refused to provide a workhouse of any description.

Small Old Poor Law workhouses were often used in the short or medium term, sometimes until the 1870s, before being superseded by a new central workhouse. A number of larger Old Poor Law workhouses, however, particularly those which had served an incorporation or Gilbert union, were retained on a long-term basis. Some of those in rural areas, such as East Anglia, were already large enough to meet the requirements of the new Act, but the majority had to be altered and expanded. This was done in any number of ways. End cross-wings, for example, were added to the recently built Ongar Workhouse (see Figure 40), creating an H-shaped building, and wings were erected behind Cleobury Mortimer Workhouse in Shropshire, forming a 'U' shape.[64] Richmond Workhouse, in Yorkshire, was doubled in depth[65] and George Wilkinson erected a version of the '200-pauper' plan against a medieval range of Leominster Priory (Fig 85).[66]

As at Leominster, many old buildings retained after 1834 had not originally been erected as workhouses. These included the Old Napoleonic Prison at Bristol, a former cavalry barracks at

Figure 84 (above) Bellingham Union Workhouse, built in 1839 and later known as Fountain Cottage, bears more resemblance to the homely parish workhouses of the 18th century than to Kempthorne's model plans.
[BB96/8283]

Figure 85 (right) The north range of Leominster Priory was converted by George Wilkinson in 1836–8, to form part of the Union Workhouse. The tower of the priory church can be seen behind the workhouse.
[BB96/6771]

Eastbourne, recently rebuilt almshouses at Easthampstead and a converted cotton mill in Sheffield. After 1834 the conversion of such buildings for poor-law purposes was seldom, if ever, permitted by the Poor Law Commission.

Life in the Workhouse of the 1830s

Surviving floor plans reveal much about life in New Poor Law workhouses, and show how the buildings enabled the rules and regulations issued by the Poor Law Commission to be put into effect.

Boards of guardians met weekly or fortnightly in a boardroom, usually located in the entrance block. Their clerk, who had an adjoining office with a strong room, attended and minuted the meetings. Paupers requesting relief (Fig 86) waited in a large room on the ground floor whereas those with formal business to transact with the board, including architects and builders, waited in a separate ante-room.

Once admitted, paupers were taken to a small receiving or probationary ward. Usually there were two of these, one for males and the other for females, but some plans provided wards for men, women, boys and girls. At this point families would have been split up. The Anti-Poor-Law faction made much of the enforced separation of families, but in many areas this had been an established policy for generations. In the receiving ward, paupers were searched, stripped and bathed; their own clothes were washed and stored, and they were issued with workhouse uniforms. On many plans, receiving wards adjoined bathrooms and 'washing rooms', the latter possibly for washing clothes rather than people. Separate search rooms could also be provided. Receiving wards seldom had day-rooms, workrooms or yards attached; new arrivals were restricted to their ward and must have led an extremely dull existence. Rather exceptionally, the receiving wards in Scott & Moffatt's workhouses had small yards which were large enough for probationary paupers to take some limited exercise.

Paupers remained in the receiving ward for only one or two days, until the medical officer could examine them. This examination determined whether they were accommodated with the able-bodied, the infirm, the sick, or at some of the larger houses, with the lunatics and/or imbeciles. The position of wards for the sick varied enormously (*see* Chapter 9), but

*Figure 86
Charles West Cope's painting,* Poor Law Guardians, Board Day, Application for Bread, *was based on the artist's attendance at a meeting of the Staines Union guardians. It was exhibited at the Royal Academy in 1841.
[Witt Library, Courtauld Institute of Art]*

The Workhouse

*Figure 87 (above)
A paupers' staircase with plain 'stick' balusters and stone treads in the Bedminster Union Workhouse (1837).
[BB95/9796]*

*Figure 88 (above, right)
The master's staircase in the Bedminster Union Workhouse (1837) is distinguished from the paupers' stairs by its turned newel and moulded string.
[BB95/9795]*

*Figure 89
The interior of a poorly lit dormitory in Williton Union Workhouse.
[BB97/6292]*

the dormitories for other classes were located on the upper floors of the main building. In a few cases, as at Epping, ground-floor wards were furnished for the aged and infirm.

Staircases giving access to the dormitories were built of stone, with metal 'stick' balusters (Fig 87). Those in the master's quarters were similar, but often had discreetly moulded newels (Fig 88). The master's social status was not much higher than that of his charges, and so it was important that the fixtures and fittings of his quarters were suitably modest.

No comforts were introduced into day-rooms and dormitories (Fig 89). Walls were generally unplastered, with a simple dado painted directly on to the brickwork. Uncarpeted floors were usually of wood but some, for example at Ely Union Workhouse, were of plaster. The timber floors of Saffron Walden Union Workhouse lay on top of brick jack-arches, an unusual precaution against fire. Top-floor dormitories were often ceiled at collar level, leaving tie beams exposed; other ceilings usually revealed the undersides of joists and cross beams. Guardians sometimes economised by asking their architect to reduce the number of windows, for example at Stow-on-the-Wold, for which Wilkinson had produced two alternative elevation drawings.[67] Most day-room and dormitory windows contained multi-paned iron-framed panels which either opened as casements or swung on central pivots, while the windows in the hub and entrance block usually held wooden sashes. Perhaps surprisingly, windows were seldom so high that paupers could not see out.

Day-rooms, and sometimes dormitories, were heated by means of open fireplaces, for which fuel was zealously guarded, but many workhouses had a pioneering form of central heating. Water was heated in a coal-fired boiler, usually located in a small cellar under the hub or entrance block, and circulated around the establishment by pipes.[68] The greater part of Barnet Union Workhouse (*see* Figure 69) was heated by means of Mr Weeks's 'Hot Water Apparatus'.[69] Weeks, an engineer from Chelsea, promised the guardians that when the outdoor temperature dropped to 16 degrees (fahrenheit) below freezing, the indoor temperature would not fall below 50 degrees. The apparatus proved unreliable and exploded in January 1838, only nine months after the workhouse had opened. Another system – Dr Arnott's Thermometer Stoves – was widely recommended by the Poor Law Commission, and entries in guardians' minute-books indicate that it was installed in many workhouses.

Dormitories were sometimes provided with toilet and washing facilities, most frequently just with the former, but occasionally with no sanitary facilities whatsoever. Chamber pots would have been provided in the latter instance. Until they were connected with the public system in the last quarter of the century, workhouses generally had their own water supply and means of disposing of sewage. At Dorking, rainwater collected from the roofs was stored in underground tanks, and drains carried waste from the privies and water-closets to a large cesspool in the garden.[70] As well as collecting rainwater, most workhouses also had one or more wells with pumping machinery. Cisterns were usually located in the roof of the main building rather than in water towers.

Paupers followed a strict timetable. In the summer they rose at 5am, ate breakfast between 6am and 7am, worked until 5pm, with a break for dinner between 12am and 1pm, ate supper between 5pm and 6pm, and were in bed at 8pm. In the winter they got up at 7am, ate breakfast between 7.30am and 8am, but thereafter followed the summer timetable. For the majority of able-bodied women, work involved domestic duties in the scullery, kitchen, washhouse, laundry (ironing room) or infirmary. They were also responsible for cleaning and sewing. Able-bodied men were usually put to work on artificially created tasks such as oakum-picking, corn-grinding or sack-making. As these chores had little or no relevance for the day-to-day running of the workhouse, and could not be undertaken on a commercial basis, they eventually tailed off, leaving men with hours of stultifying inactivity. Few plans indicate the precise function of men's workrooms although some, such as those for Nash's courtyard-plan workhouses, included a corn-grinding house next to the bakehouse. The master was usually in charge of setting adult males to work, but the largest workhouses employed a resident taskmaster. At Abingdon, where the workshops included large spinning-rooms, the 'foreman of the work' resided at the end of one of the main wings. At Bishop's Stortford, the task-master's house stood in the centre of the workshop complex (*see* Figure 77) and at Macclesfield the task-master shared the porter's lodge.

For a minimum of three hours each day, workhouse boys and girls attended lessons in the schoolroom, but they also devoted several hours to work. Sometimes a small wash-house and laundry was provided for girls. It is unclear what work boys were expected to undertake, but the model plans often located the bakehouse off their yard.

For the non-able-bodied, days in the workhouse were long and tedious. They were usually

No. 4.—DIETARY for ABLE-BODIED PAUPERS of both SEXES.

		BREAKFAST		DINNER					SUPPER	
		Bread.	Gruel.	Pickled Pork, or Bacon, with Vegetables.	Soup.	Bread.	Meat Pudding, with Vegetables.	Rice or Suet Pudding, with Vegetables.	Bread.	Cheese.
		oz.	pints.	oz.	pints.	oz.	oz.	oz.	oz.	oz.
Sunday	Men	8	1½	-	2	6	-	-	6	2
	Women	6	1½	-	1½	5	-	-	5	1½
Monday	Men	8	1½	-	-	-	-	12	6	2
	Women	6	1½	-	-	-	-	10	5	1½
Tuesday	Men	8	1½	-	2	6	-	-	6	2
	Women	6	1½	-	1½	5	-	-	5	1½
Wednesday	Men	8	1½	6	-	-	-	-	6	2
	Women	6	1½	5	-	-	-	-	5	1½
Thursday	Men	8	1½	-	-	-	-	12	6	2
	Women	6	1½	-	-	-	-	10	5	1½
Friday	Men	8	1½	-	2	6	-	-	6	2
	Women	6	1½	-	1½	5	-	-	5	1½
Saturday	Men	8	1½	-	-	-	12	-	6	2
	Women	6	1½	-	-	-	10	-	5	1½

The vegetables are not included in the weight specified, which is for the meat when cooked.
If it be thought desirable, half an ounce of butter may be given to the women in lieu of cheese, for supper.
Old people of 60 years of age and upwards may be allowed one ounce of tea, five ounces of butter, and seven ounces of sugar per week, in lieu of gruel for breakfast, if deemed expedient to make this change.
Children under nine years of age to be dieted at discretion; above nine, to be allowed the same quantities as women.
Sick to be dieted as directed by the medical officer.

Figure 90
This diet sheet 'for able-bodied paupers of both sexes' was one of six created by the Poor Law Commission for use in New Poor Law workhouses.
[From PP 1836 (595), XXIX, Appendix A, No. 7, 56–9, by permission of the Syndics of Cambridge University Library]

obliged to rise at the same hour as the able-bodied, and sat all day in a day-room, with little to occupy or divert them.

Meals were taken in different places at different workhouses. The model plans provided two dining-rooms, one for men and women and another for boys and girls, but some architects dispensed with dining-rooms altogether, obliging inmates to eat in their day-rooms. The six dietaries (Fig 90) laid down by the Poor Law Commission, boring but sufficient, were heavy in carbohydrates, with meat served once or twice a week. Theoretically the aged and infirm were allowed indulgences, such as tea, and the diet of the sick was determined by the medical officer and administered by the matron and pauper nurses, but these practices were always open to abuse.

A local vicar, appointed chaplain to the workhouse, performed a Church of England service in the workhouse chapel, often the dining-hall, on Sundays. Few workhouses had a chapel exclusively for worship: there is some evidence that Scott & Moffatt's chapels doubled as schoolrooms.[71] The guardians of Cheltenham, unusually, insisted that the chapel of their workhouse should have no secondary function.[72]

If paupers misbehaved or were a nuisance, they were locked in the refractory ward for a period determined by the master. On many plans the refractory ward was a tiny, unlit cell placed next to the mortuary, but sometimes the mortuary itself was used for refractory inmates. When a death occured in the workhouse, the funeral and burial usually took place in the pauper's own parish, at the union's expense, rather than at the workhouse.

6
Corridor-Plan Workhouses, 1840–1870

Between 1847 and 1870 the Poor Law Board sought to consolidate the achievement of its predecessor, the Poor Law Commission, largely by ensuring that unions throughout the country provided adequate workhouse accommodation and operated a workhouse test. The building boom sparked off by the Poor Law Amendment Act had fizzled out by the early 1840s. As many as 320 new workhouses had been erected, or at least begun, by 1841, but the average for each of the next two decades was 60, with only 35 new projects being initiated in the 1860s (Fig 91).

During the period 1840 to 1870, the geographic concentration of new workhouses shifted from the South to the North, partly because manufacturing unions submitted to political and economic pressure to provide a large, central workhouse, but also because numerous new unions were created in the North. At the same time, Metropolitan London began the lengthy and expensive process of replacing its cramped Old Poor Law institutions.

As one would have expected, expenditure on workhouse buildings plummeted at the end of the 1830s then remained relatively steady for the following 30 years.[1] Nevertheless, much piecemeal building work was going on, as more and more unions were compelled to extend existing workhouses, either to meet a growing need for accommodation or to provide a more stringent classification of inmates.

After 1840, the spatial arrangement of new workhouses was radically changed by the introduction of wider ranges with central corridors. Furthermore, following the pattern established by Scott & Moffatt in the late 1830s, architects began to distribute the functions of new workhouses between at least three detached buildings: an entrance block, a linear main building and an infirmary. These elements usually lay parallel to one another, separated by the paupers' exercise yards. Throughout the 1850s and 1860s the process of institutional fragmentation gradually accelerated: detached chapels became more usual, as did separate buildings for children, infectious cases and vagrants.

The Main Building

Between 1840 and 1870, workhouse architects continued to explore the fashionable styles of the day within the constraints of poor-law propriety. Medieval, Tudor and Elizabethan styles were all selected for poor-law buildings, but an Italianate style was generally preferred. Several first-generation workhouses had been crowned by simple pediments, cupolas or ventilation turrets, but it now became standard procedure to erect a grand cupola or clock tower over the central block (Fig 92). Gables, pinnacles, projecting bays and tall chimney-stacks became increasingly popular, and the façades of end cross-wings often competed with those of the central block. This was all for show: away from the public gaze, hidden rear elevations were always of the utmost simplicity.

Principal workhouse buildings now comprised a more commodious central administration block or master's house, with a single-storeyed back wing containing the kitchen or dining-hall/chapel. Accommodation ranges flanked the administration block and, as in some workhouses of the 1830s, often terminated in short cross-wings. But internal planning was very different from the 1830s, when most workhouses had adhered to Kempthorne's ideal of rooms that occupied the full width of the building, and which were lit and ventilated by opposing windows and reached via separate lobbies and staircases.

Ranges were now wide enough to contain central corridors with rooms opening off both sides. These corridors usually ran the full length of a building, with large windows lighting and ventilating them at either end. The termination of corridors at shallow cross-wings was a less-favoured option, as it necessitated indirect or artificial corridor lighting.

THE WORKHOUSE

*Figure 91
This map shows the distribution of new workhouses erected between 1840 and 1870.*

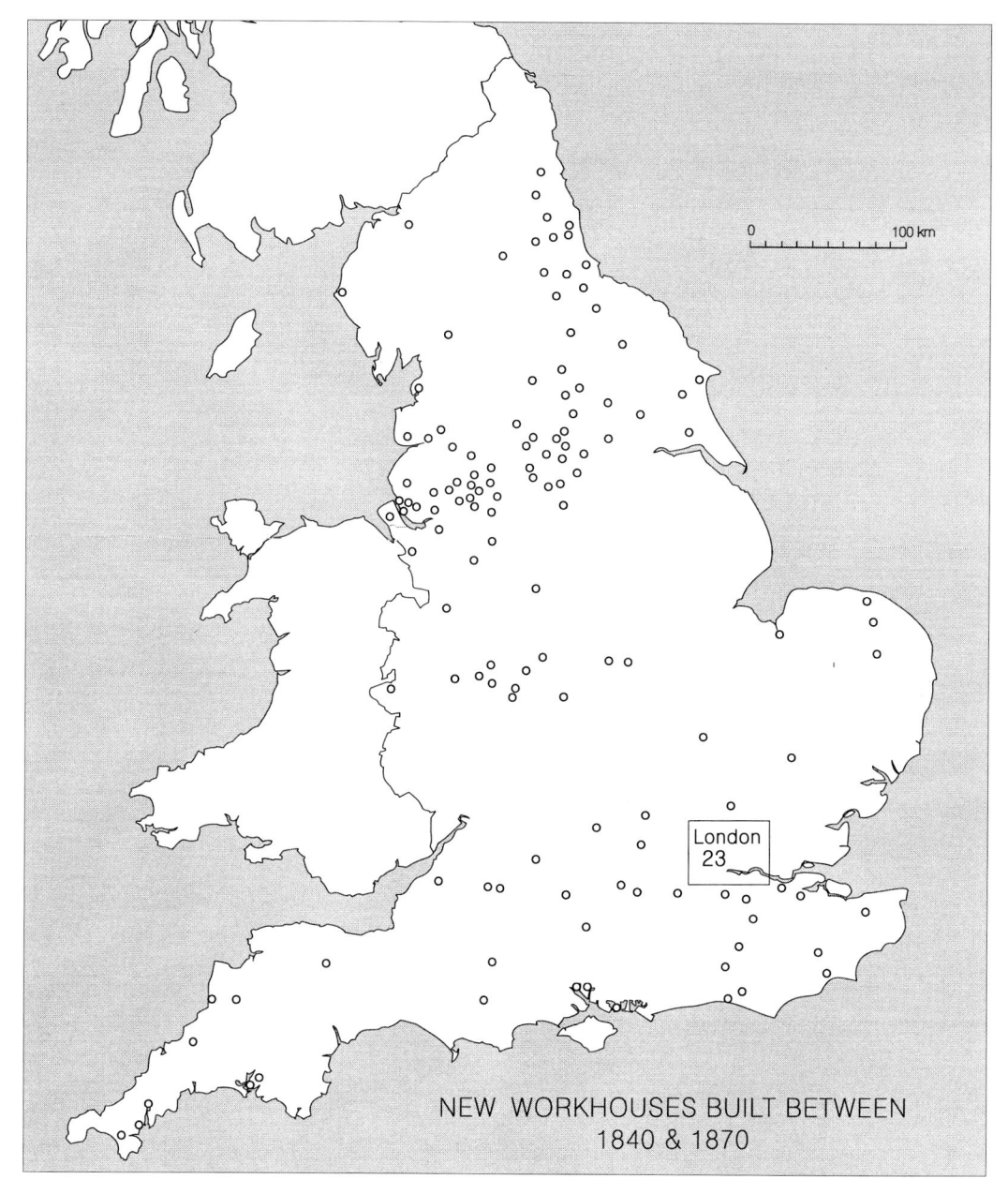

NEW WORKHOUSES BUILT BETWEEN 1840 & 1870

Rooms opening off access corridors were lit on one side only and thus lacked cross-ventilation. Concern for ventilation did not altogether vanish, but there was an increased reliance on systems which supplemented the fresh air admitted through doorways, windows and fireplaces. These ranged from simple iron air-bricks and air-shafts containing perpetually burning gas jets, to perforated zinc tubes, recommended by Assistant Commissioner Walsham in 1849, which ran through the external walls and across the ceilings of rooms.[2] In general, however, ventilation systems were neglected by workhouse staff and were often blocked up by inmates, who used them as hiding-places for their meagre possessions or as receptacles for rubbish. In 1866, after encountering many instances of such behaviour, Poor-Law Inspector Dr Smith recommended that ventilation systems should lie beyond the control of inmates and nurses alike.[3]

One of the earliest corridor-plan buildings was Greenwich Union Workhouse, designed by R P Browne and erected in 1840 (Fig 93). It may have been influential in disseminating the corridor plan, as Browne published his design in 1844, claiming that the 'plain but cheerful and almshouse-like' building had been 'frequently termed the "Model Workhouse"'.[4] Flanking the main entrance were the boardroom, relief offices, porter's lodge, probationary wards, refractory wards and vagrant wards. The master's rooms occupied the centre of the main building,

*Figure 92
The main building of
Rochdale Union
Workhouse (1873–7),
despite being tucked
away on the outskirts of
town, was dominated by
an imposing tower.
[BB96/2267]*

where an octagonal stairwell, considered necessary for the circulation of air, formed the only break in the continuous corridor.[5] Rooms for the able-bodied opened off either side of a corridor in each wing, but rooms for the aged invariably faced the front, in this case south, a feature already noted in 1830s workhouses with back-to-back day-rooms and dormitories. Behind the master's house was a T-shaped chapel: the men sat in one wing, women in another and boys and girls in the third.

Approximately 150 corridor-plan workhouses were erected between 1840 and 1875. The reason why this design so suddenly and comprehensively supplanted the radial designs of the 1830s is not well understood and, rather surprisingly, neither the Poor Law Commission nor the architectural press commented on the phenomenon at the time. Economy does not appear to have been a factor, as workhouses became increasingly ornate and expensive in the 1840s and 1850s. Health was similarly disregarded, as it had been recognised as early as the 1770s that cross-ventilated rooms were preferable to those which opened off corridors. It is also obvious that corridor planning did not make it easier to inspect and control inmates.

One reason for the appeal of the corridor plan may have been the ease of access it allowed throughout an institution, for officials if not for pauper inmates. Corridors, however, presented the danger that inmates of different classes

The Workhouse

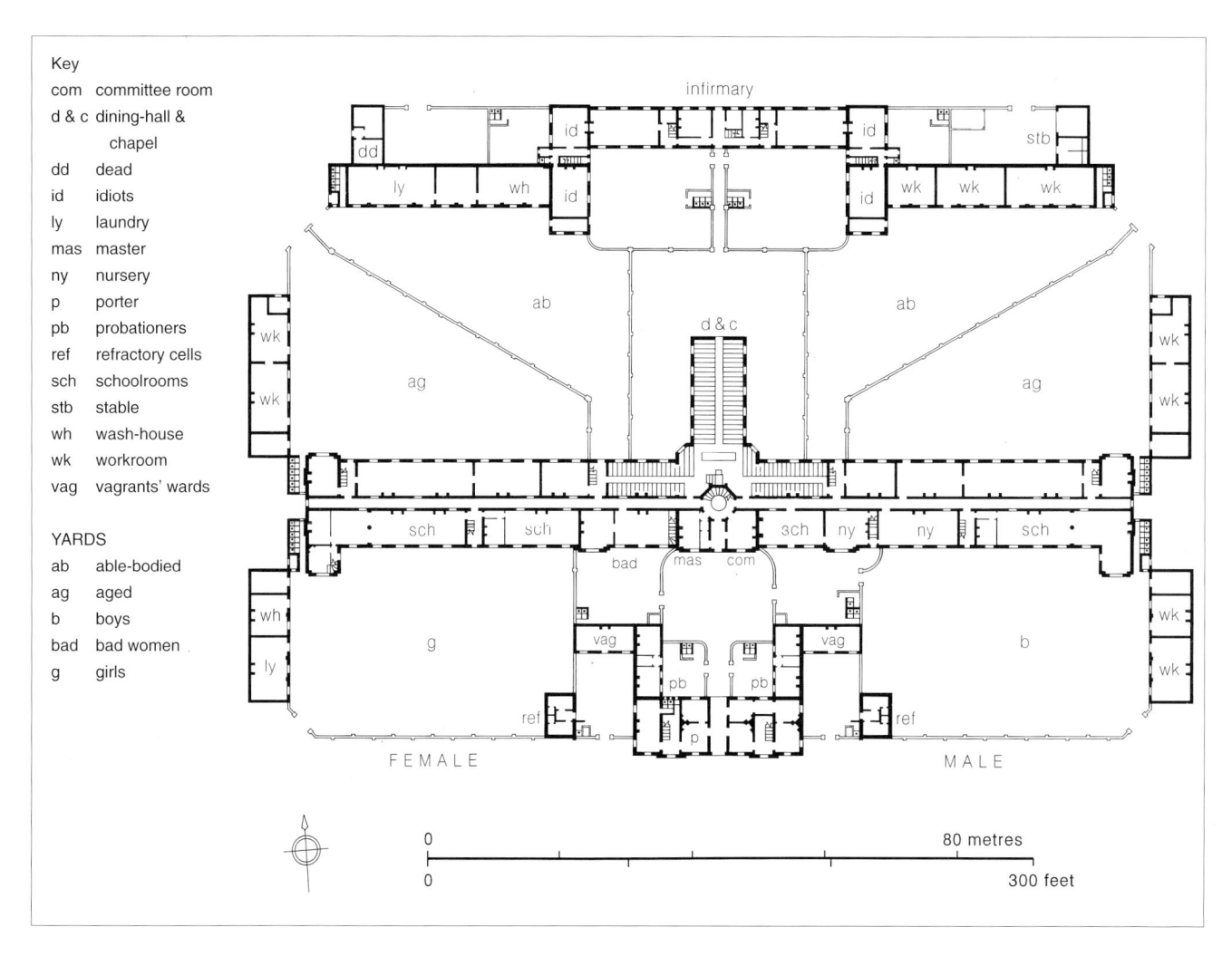

Key
com	committee room
d & c	dining-hall & chapel
dd	dead
id	idiots
ly	laundry
mas	master
ny	nursery
p	porter
pb	probationers
ref	refractory cells
sch	schoolrooms
stb	stable
wh	wash-house
wk	workroom
vag	vagrants' wards

YARDS
ab	able-bodied
ag	aged
b	boys
bad	bad women
g	girls

Figure 93
Greenwich Union Workhouse (1840) was one of the first workhouses to have a corridor running from one end to the other.
[Ground-floor plan based on Browne 1844]

Figure 94
This is a reconstruction of the iron gallery in the centre of Birmingham Union Workhouse (1850–2). The exterior of the workhouse can be seen in Figure 104. The building was demolished in the early 1990s.

could communicate with one another more freely and, in an effort to prevent this, they were barred by gates which divided buildings into sections. Gates separated male wings from female wings and, within each wing, separated the able-bodied from the aged and infirm. They were of doubtful efficiency as they were usually of openwork wrought iron in order to maintain a through draught from one end of the long workhouse corridor to the other.[6]

Corridors usually ran straight through a building but, as at Greenwich, could be interrupted by central light-wells or staircases. William J Donthorn's late workhouses, Erpingham and Aylsham, of 1848–51 and 1848–9 respectively, had central halls with galleries.[7] The square centre of Birmingham Union Workhouse, erected in 1850–2, contained an open rectangular well which rose through the full height of the building. On each floor, a cantilevered cast-iron gallery was supported by openwork brackets and protected by criss-cross railings (Fig 94); the arches to the male and female corridors were barred by two-leaf wrought-iron gates, one of which still survived just before the building was demolished in 1992.

In corridor-plan workhouses the master still occupied the centre of the building, but the polygonal hub, and with it the notion that the paupers could be supervised from a single vantage point, was modified or abandoned. In practice, the polygonal hub may not have proved as useful as had been expected. Paupers could only be observed in their yards, and masters had neither the time nor the capability to observe every yard at once. Nevertheless, vestiges of the hub system can be seen in the canted bay windows of several masters' offices, for example those overlooking the able-bodied yards at Tenterden (1843) and Hungerford (1847; Fig 95).

Variants on the straightforward corridor plan soon emerged. In several London workhouses, the access corridor was positioned along one side of the building, rather than through its centre. The first of these was probably Kensington (Fig 96), a building designed by Thomas Allom and erected in 1846–8. The main wings had open arcades along their west sides on the ground floor but enclosed corridors along their east sides on the upper floors. The Jacobean-style block which Allom designed with Henry F Lockwood for Liverpool Workhouse in 1842–3 had suggested a more uncertain, or experimental, approach to planning. Although it had a corridor along one side of the main range, one of the rear wings had back-to-back wards, the other had a central corridor and both of the forward-projecting wings were one room deep, with cross-ventilation. The City of London Union Workhouse (Fig 97), designed by R Tress and built in 1848–9, had some side and some central corridors and, in addition, an arcade on the front of the main building. At the workhouse of the joint parishes of St Margaret and St John, Westminster, built immediately to the south of Kensington Workhouse in 1851–3, an open arcade ran along the south side of the ground floor, but the upper floors were cross-lit, without corridors. Half of one cross-wing had corridors on the ground floor only. These buildings demonstrate that architects did not adopt central corridors all at once, but were prepared, for some time, to combine lobby and corridor access systems throughout institutions.

A number of T-shaped workhouses in the South had wings with back-to-back wards rather than corridors, continuing the tradition of Welch's workhouses at Wells and Axbridge.

Figure 95 (below)
A small bay window (shown on the left, abutting the dining-hall) enabled the master of Hungerford Union Workhouse (1847) to keep an eye on the rear yards. Its effect was feeble compared with the intimidating supervisory hubs of 1830s workhouses.
[192M(21)]

Figure 96 (bottom)
This watercolour shows the Jacobean-style Kensington Workhouse (1846–8).
[BB96/5605]

The Workhouse

Figure 97
The City of London Union Workhouse, erected on Bow Road in 1848–9, later became St Clement's Hospital.
[Based on The Builder, *25 August 1849, 400]*

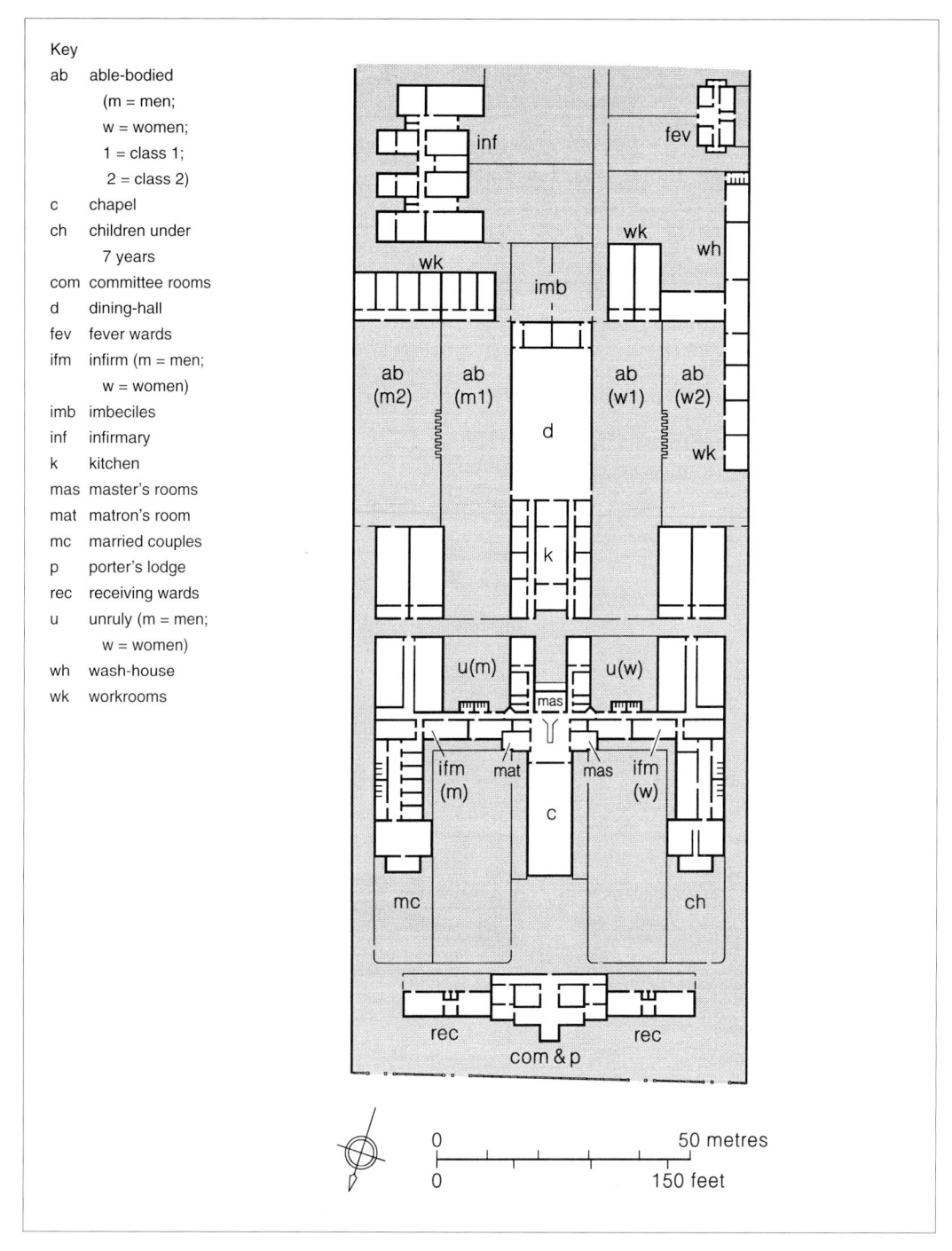

Key
ab	able-bodied (m = men; w = women; 1 = class 1; 2 = class 2)
c	chapel
ch	children under 7 years
com	committee rooms
d	dining-hall
fev	fever wards
ifm	infirm (m = men; w = women)
imb	imbeciles
inf	infirmary
k	kitchen
mas	master's rooms
mat	matron's room
mc	married couples
p	porter's lodge
rec	receiving wards
u	unruly (m = men; w = women)
wh	wash-house
wk	workrooms

The architect S O Foden was responsible for those at Rye (1843), Cuckfield (1843), Bromley (1844), Aylesbury (1844; Fig 98) and Highworth & Swindon (1845–6), as well as an unexecuted project for Canterbury (1846; Fig 99). Usually, Foden's plans were recommended to boards of guardians by Assistant Commissioner Parker, much as Sir Francis Head had urged guardians to adopt his own courtyard plan in 1835, and Foden was subsequently employed for the relatively low fee of 2·5 per cent of the cost of the workhouse. This procedure was successful until 1845, when Parker was dismissed as a result of his involvement in the Andover scandal. In the following year an anonymous attack on the Poor Law Commission, and on the first wave of New Poor Law workhouses, was published in the *Illustrated London News*.[8] The author, possibly Parker himself, blamed Kempthorne's designs for the apparent failure of the new deterrent workhouses. These:

*Figure 98
Aylesbury Union Workhouse (1844) was one of the workhouses which resulted from collaboration between the architect S O Foden and Assistant Poor Law Commissioner H W Parker.
[BB96/3521]*

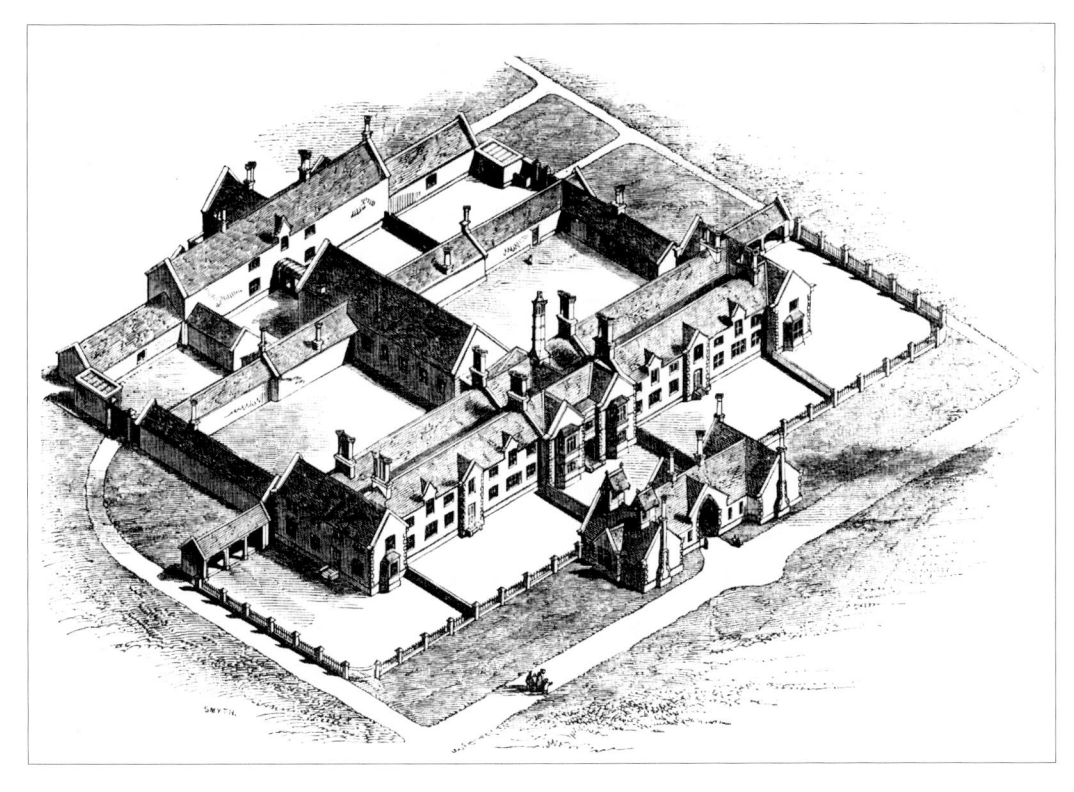

*Figure 99
This design for Canterbury Union Workhouse, by Foden and Parker, was highly commended by an article in the* Illustrated London News *in 1846, but was never built.
[From* Illustrated London News, *7 November 1846, 304, by permission of the Syndics of Cambridge University Library]*

in fact, are tracings from designs for American prisons. The young and inexperienced architect who appropriated these prison plans to a purpose for which they were never intended, was not, it may be supposed, overmuch startled when Cobbett denounced the new buildings as 'Bastiles'.⁹

The author continued to report how Parker had objected to 'the prison-like appearance of the Commissioners' plans and designed four or five Workhouse plans, which possess some claims to architectural taste'. The author made it plain that, unlike Kempthorne's buildings, these workhouses did not incorporate a test for 'the youthful and aged poor'. In particular, the yards for these classes lay at the front of the site; they were bounded by open fences rather than walls and the children's yards included covered play-sheds. The relaxation of the workhouse test for these classes had been apparent in some first-generation New Poor Law workhouses, such as Wells, but never quite so blatantly. The evidence of guardians' minute-books certainly suggests that Parker and Foden collaborated to some extent in the promulgation of this design, but their exact working relationship remains unclear.[10] After Parker had emigrated to Australia in 1847, Foden went on to win competitions for Whitchurch (Hampshire) and Hungerford (see Figure 95) workhouses.

Foden was not the only workhouse architect after Welch to favour back-to-back wards. They were a feature of Wokingham Union Workhouse (1848–50), by Richard Billings of Reading and, in the early 1850s, Edward Ashworth designed two workhouses with back-to-back wards, Dulverton (Fig 100) and Holsworthy, both in the South West.[11] In each case, the rear wing was designed in a particularly ingenious way. It was approached from the main entrance by a corridor which ran past the kitchen, boardroom and dining-hall, and was divided lengthwise into two distinct units, each with its own entrance and staircase. Each unit contained two intercommunicating rooms: the inner rooms were for the able-bodied and the outer ones for the sick and aged.

Figure 100
Dulverton Union Workhouse (1854), in Somerset, was one of two workhouses designed by Edward Ashworth.
[Redrawn from Somerset RO D/G/D 32/1]

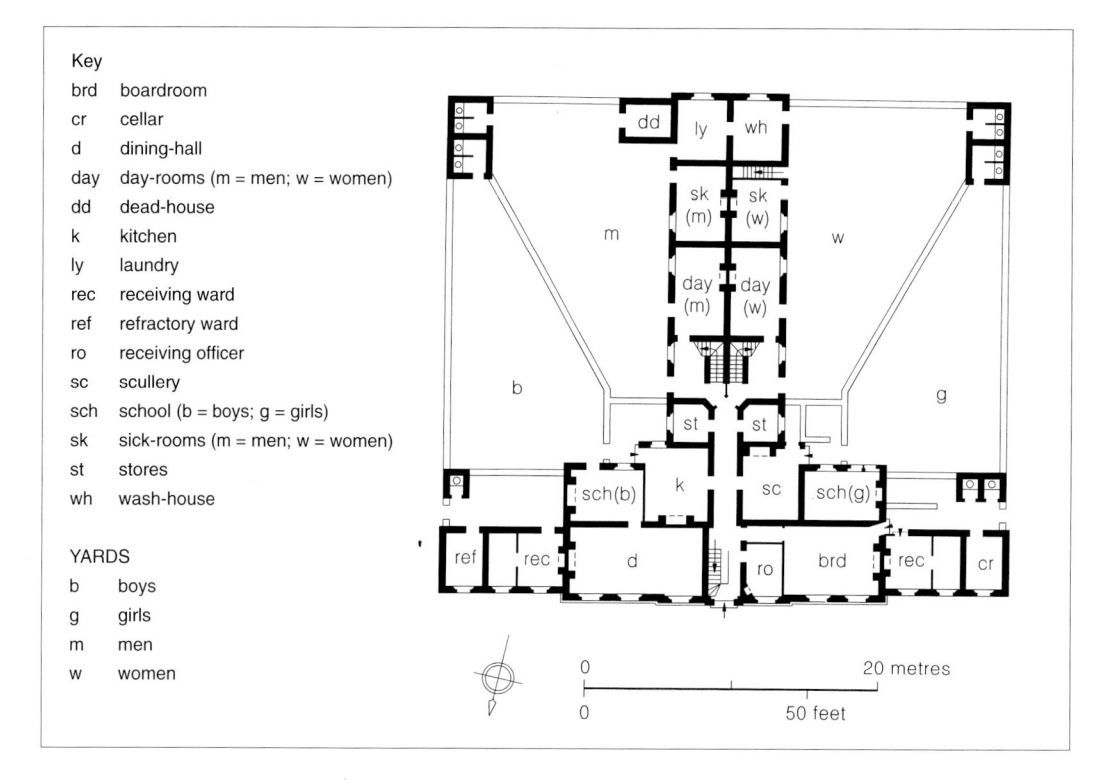

Key
brd   boardroom
cr   cellar
d   dining-hall
day   day-rooms (m = men; w = women)
dd   dead-house
k   kitchen
ly   laundry
rec   receiving ward
ref   refractory ward
ro   receiving officer
sc   scullery
sch   school (b = boys; g = girls)
sk   sick-rooms (m = men; w = women)
st   stores
wh   wash-house

YARDS
b   boys
g   girls
m   men
w   women

Figure 101
The new Huddersfield Union Workhouse at Crosland Moor was designed in a Gothic style by John Kirk in 1870.
[BB96/2359]

The system of appointing architects remained unchanged from 1840 to 1870. In some cases, an architect developed a relationship with a board and achieved the status of a semi-official employee. Thus, when Huddersfield decided to erect a new workhouse at Crosland Moor in 1870 (Fig 101), it was a matter of course to employ John Kirk, who had designed the Deanhouse workhouse in 1860–2 and, in the interim, had provided plans for an abortive scheme on a site at Birkby. It was convenient to have a local architect allied to a union, as he could be called on sporadically to make small alterations and additions or dispense advice. As a general rule, when planning a new workhouse, small unions appointed architects on the basis of recommendation or foreknowledge, while larger unions held competitions. These attracted as many applicants as the workhouse competitions of the 1830s. That held for Scarborough workhouse in 1858, for example, attracted twenty-six applicants with estimates ranging from £3,300 to £10,000.[12] Needless to say, the guardians preferred the plan estimated to cost £3,300, by

Figure 102
The central block of Aylsham Union Workhouse (1848–9) in Norfolk, a late workhouse by William J Donthorn, retains much of its original diamond-paned glazing. Despite its resemblance to Donthorn's earlier workhouse at Ely, this building had a fully developed corridor plan. It is now St Michael's Hospital.
[BB96/3495]

George Styan of York. On the whole, competitions seem to have been conducted along professional lines. It was now usual for building committees to select plans identified only by mottoes. But it was still not unheard of for architects to lobby boards: when the new Knaresborough Union was formed in 1854 both William L Moffatt of Doncaster and Henry F Lockwood of Bradford offered their services, though prematurely and unsuccessfully in each case.[13]

Most of the architects whose names had cropped up repeatedly in the workhouse competitions of the 1830s changed direction after 1840. The few who remained in the field adapted their designs to provide corridor, rather than lobby, access. In Norfolk, William J Donthorn's Aylsham (Fig 102) and Erpingham workhouses closely resembled his earlier workhouses but had corridor-plan main ranges; the residual octagonal hubs were subdivided by corridors into four rooms around an 'octagon hall'.[14] Both had forward-projecting ranges, as did the Perpendicular-style Risbridge Union Workhouse of 1855–6, designed by J F Clark, possibly under the influence of Donthorn's buildings. The central front range housed the porter's lodge, paupers' waiting-room and receiving wards, while the lateral front ranges accommodated children, and included ground-floor schoolrooms.

Another architect who continued to design workhouses was H E Kendall. Kendall had designed the 'square' workhouses of Trowbridge and Melksham and Uckfield in the 1830s, but in 1849–50 he produced the Baroque, corridor-plan Hampstead Workhouse (Fig 103) to

Figure 103 Hampstead Workhouse (1849–50), by H E Kendall, later became New End Hospital. It is one of the most attractive workhouses now surviving in London. [BB91/14940]

CORRIDOR-PLAN WORKHOUSES, 1840–1870

*Figure 104
This perspective view of Birmingham Union Workhouse (1850–2) was drawn by the architects, Bateman & Drury. The children's yards and the chapel can be seen on the left.
[From* The Builder, *31 January 1852, 73, by permission of the Syndics of Cambridge University Library]*

*Figure 105
Kirkby Moorside Union Workhouse (1850) was a small institution by the now established workhouse architect John Atkinson.
[BB79/948]*

replace a parish workhouse of 1800. That building bore little resemblance to his earlier work, in terms of either style or planning. Like Kendall, J Bateman & G Drury of Birmingham, who had designed 'square' workhouses for Bromsgrove, Leek and Stratford-on-Avon in the 1830s, also adapted their approach. They were responsible for one of the largest workhouses of its day, the new Birmingham Union Workhouse of 1850–2 (Fig 104; *see* Figure 94). The institutional character of the site was reinforced by the proximity of three other large and relatively new complexes: Winson Green Prison, the City Lunatic Asylum and the City Fever Hospital.

A large number of new workhouses erected in the 1850s were located in Lancashire and Yorkshire, and one of the most prolific workhouse practices in these counties was John & William Atkinson of York. The Atkinsons had designed some small block-plan workhouses in the late 1830s (*see* Figs 82 and 83) but now adopted a corridor layout. They did not, however, adhere to a single formula, but experimented with different arrangements and styles for different unions. The York workhouse (1848–9) was extremely plain, although the end windows of the main corridor were recessed within tall arches, a motif used at the Atkinsons' earlier workhouses. Kirkby Moorside (1849–50) was a much smaller and more attractive building, with a part corridor (Fig 105). Beverley (1860) seems to have been the Atkinsons' only workhouse in an Elizabethan style. Wetherby (1863) had a medieval-style doorway with a pointed, moulded arch, and a heavily rusticated elevation with mullioned-and-transomed windows.

The Workhouse

*Figure 106
North Bierley Union Workhouse, built between 1855 and 1858 to designs by Henry F Lockwood & William Mawson, closely resembles woollen mills designed by the same architects for Sir Titus Salt at Saltaire.
[BB90/9734]*

*Figure 107 (right)
The new Leeds Union Workhouse (1858–60), an ornate building by William Perkin & Elisha Backhouse, was built next to the earlier Leeds Industrial and Moral Training School. It later became St James's Hospital.
[BB90/9942]*

Alongside continuing workhouse practices, new ones emerged. One particularly prolific duo were Lockwood & Mawson of Bradford. Henry Lockwood had collaborated with Allom on the Liverpool Workhouse, and was also responsible for the Sculcoates Union Workhouse (1843–5) which, despite its intrinsic plainness, had been described with pride, and the merest hint of disapproval, in the local press: 'Not many passengers along the Beverley Road would imagine that the beautiful and immense structure which is in the course of erection, on the ground just beyond the town, is intended for the reception of paupers. Its front aspect would not disgrace the residence of a nobleman.'[15] Later workhouses designed with his partner William Mawson, for example Bradford (1849–52), North Bierley (1855–8; Fig 106) and Carlisle (1863), were in a bold Italianate style. All three had gabled administration blocks flanked by towers, and façades lit by rows of round-headed windows with continuous sill and impost bands. At Carlisle, ornamental details such as the bell turret, central turrets and angle piers were nearly omitted for reasons of economy.

Another important northern partnership was William Perkin & Elisha Backhouse of Leeds, who were responsible for the workhouses of Ripon, Leeds and Chester. The largest of these, the Leeds Workhouse (Fig 107), was erected beside the Industrial and Moral Training School, an earlier building by the same architects, in 1858–60 (*see* pages 138–9; Figures 172 and 173). It was one of the most imposing and elaborate workhouses ever erected in England. Rising above the squat central block was a tall stair-tower, adorned with corner turrets carrying ogee caps and finials. The building was further enriched by Dutch gables, balustraded parapets, and mullioned-and-transomed windows. It could hold 800 inmates, and cost £32,000 to build. That can be compared with the cost of the slightly earlier Birmingham Workhouse, which had twice the capacity yet cost only £41,000.

Prior to 1850, London unions accounted for only 11 per cent of total authorised workhouse expenditure, but between 1851 and 1866 the proportion rose to 26 per cent.[16] In fact, many Old Poor Law workhouses in London had been retained after 1834. Only two new workhouses were built in the Metropolitan area during the

CORRIDOR-PLAN WORKHOUSES, 1840–1870

1830s, but about twenty were erected between 1840 and 1870. The major rebuilding of London's poor-law institutions, however, was postponed until after 1870.

Workhouses erected in London between 1840 and 1870 differed little from contemporary institutions outside the metropolis, although some compensated for their constricted sites by building upwards. The main building of St Leonard's Workhouse, Shoreditch (1861–5; Fig 108), was four storeys high, with an attic and basement, whereas workhouses outside London seldom rose over three storeys. London workhouses accommodated fewer children than those elsewhere, but were still of the 'general mixed' variety, housing large numbers of the aged, the sick, lunatics and imbeciles, as well as the able-bodied. Sometimes, as at the new West London Union Workhouse of 1864 (Fig 109), the sick and imbeciles were provided with detached buildings. The main building at West London housed only the able-bodied, the aged and infirm, 'incorrigibles' and aged married couples; the children of the Union were sent to the Central London District School at Hanwell (see page 140).

Figure 108 (left)
Only in big cities, where new sites could not be afforded, did workhouses impinge directly on the street line. This is St Leonard's Workhouse, Shoreditch (1861–5) in London.
[BB92/15285]

Figure 109 (below)
In 1864, five years before being amalgamated with the City of London Union, West London Union erected this new workhouse in Holloway. The architects were Searle, Son & Yelf.
[Based on The Builder, 3 December 1864, 883]

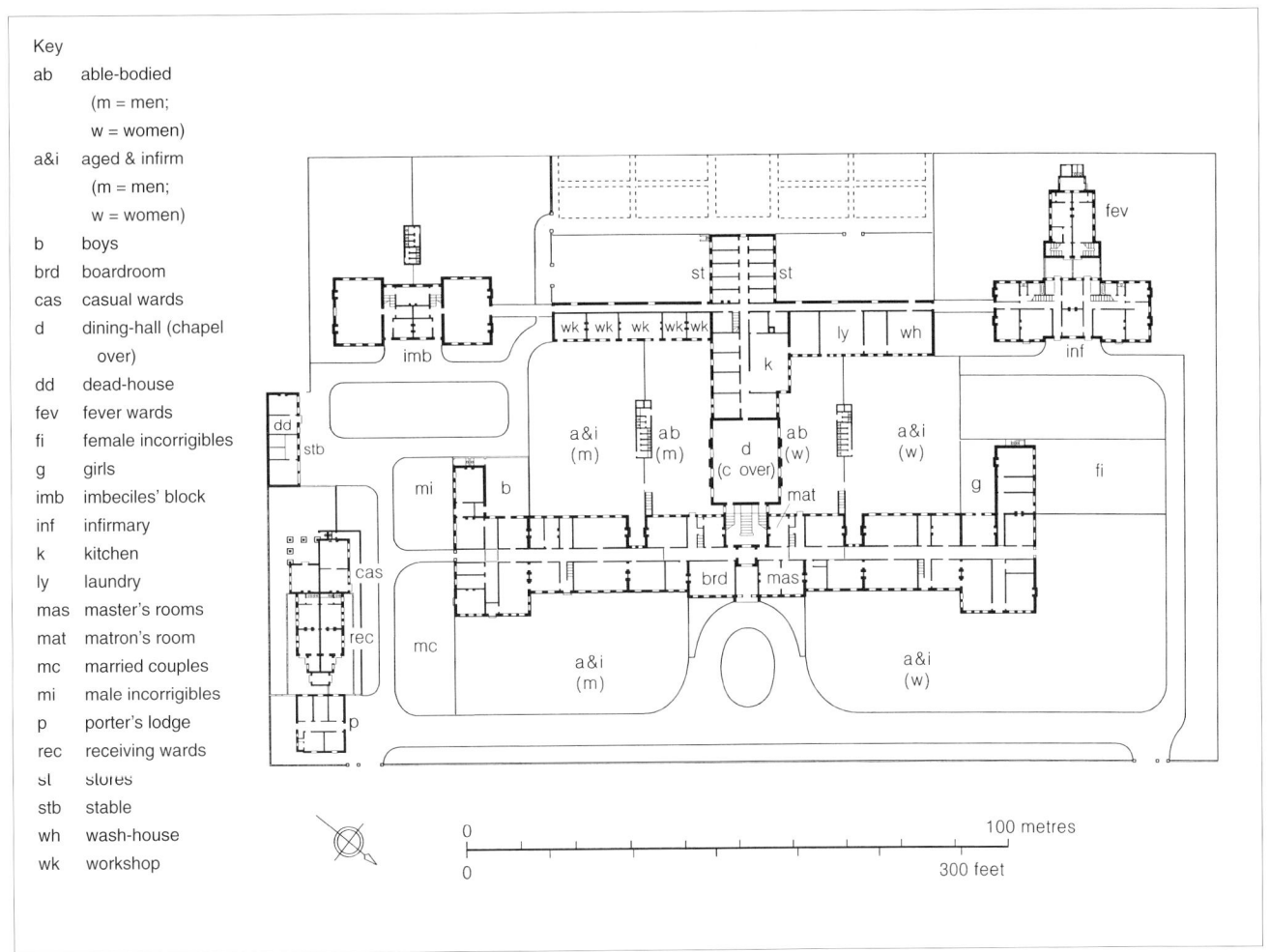

Key
ab	able-bodied (m = men; w = women)
a&i	aged & infirm (m = men; w = women)
b	boys
brd	boardroom
cas	casual wards
d	dining-hall (chapel over)
dd	dead-house
fev	fever wards
fi	female incorrigibles
g	girls
imb	imbeciles' block
inf	infirmary
k	kitchen
ly	laundry
mas	master's rooms
mat	matron's room
mc	married couples
mi	male incorrigibles
p	porter's lodge
rec	receiving wards
st	stores
stb	stable
wh	wash-house
wk	workshop

97

Inspecting London workhouses in 1866, Poor-Law Inspector Dr Smith recognised that corridors did not supply wards with sufficient air and were often, as at Greenwich, too narrow and too long. He made clear his preference for buildings which were only one ward in depth, yet made general recommendations for corridor-plan buildings:

> there should be a wide central corridor, open at both ends, and made light and airy by cross corridors, also leading to the outer air at the end of each set of wards in length. The upper corridor should be ventilated by louvre lights; and all the corridors made light and airy. They should also be fitted up, and used as exercising grounds or day-rooms. They should have as many windows in their walls on both sides as there are windows in the outer walls;

and, for the purpose of ventilation, should be so fixed that they cannot be quite shut.[17]

Smith also suggested that bathrooms occupy cross-corridors, but that water-closets, ideally Jennings tip-up closets (Fig 110), occupy projections from these.

Cross-ventilation and projecting sanitary towers were key elements of the pavilion system, and as the defects of corridors became more widely understood, so the influence of pavilion or separate-block planning began to creep into workhouse design (*see* Chapter 7). Briefly, the main principles of pavilion planning, devised primarily for hospitals, were the division of an institution into separate blocks, and the introduction of a number of features, such as opposing windows, to enhance ventilation.

The first poor-law building with a full pavilion plan, the infirmary of Chorlton Union Workhouse near Manchester, had no immediate impact, and pavilion-plan poor-law buildings did not become usual before the 1870s (*see* Chapter 9). Despite that, some corridor-plan workhouses designed in the 1850s and 1860s incorporated minor features associated with pavilion planning. A few, such as East London, Stepney, Brighton, Medway and Blackburn were designed with recesses to either side of the central block, on the rear of the building. This provided additional lighting at the entrance of the corridors leading into the accommodation wings. It was a feature which had appeared in several hospital designs, for example at the Royal Victoria Hospital, Netley (1856–61), where it was a rare indication that the architect was aware of Continental pavilion planning. Elsewhere, for example at Hungerford (1847; *see* Figure 95), Manchester (1855–6) and West London (1864; *see* Figure 109), the rear wing of the workhouse, containing the dining-hall, chapel or kitchen, was connected to the central block by a narrow lobby. This was a practical step, as it decreased the chance of fire spreading from the kitchen, through the dining-hall, to the rest of the establishment.

As in Scott & Moffatt's workhouses of the 1830s, Manchester Union Workhouse, which rivalled Birmingham in size, had no dining-hall. Under the chapel, in the basement of the rear wing, was a kitchen and a 'cutting-up room', from which food was distributed to the day-rooms via a system of hoists. Although common dining-halls were usual by this time, they still aroused some concern. The Poor Law Board worried that, as the dining-hall of the new Huddersfield workhouse (*see* Figure 101) had only one doorway, men and women would meet on their way in and out.[18] The guardians' response, that one sex would be seated before

Figure 110 (right) Jennings Closets were recommended by Poor-Law Inspector Dr Edward Smith in his 'Report on Metropolitan Workhouse Infirmaries and Sick Wards', in 1866. [From PP 1866 (372), LXI, 39, by permission of the Syndics of Cambridge University Library]

Figure 111 (below) Bramley Union Workhouse (1871–2), by C S & A J Nelson, was one of the last corridor-plan workhouses to be built in England. [BB92/9687]

*Figure 112
This photograph shows
the women's dining-hall
of St Pancras Workhouse
in the 1890s.
[Hulton Getty]*

the other entered the room, appears to have settled the matter.

Despite the introduction of workhouses on a separate-block plan around 1870, corridor-plan workhouses were still built. Late examples include two by C S & A J Nelson, pupils of Lockwood & Mawson: Bramley Union Workhouse (1871–2) and Wharfedale Union Workhouse (1871–3). Bramley (Fig 111) was typical of small, provincial workhouses of this time. Its entrance block housed a porter's lodge, probationers' ward, vagrants' wards, a disinfector, offices and the boardroom. All classes of inmate were accommodated in the main building, with the master and matron in the centre, but separate buildings were provided for the sick and those with infectious diseases.

Workhouse Chapels 1841–1870

Under the Old Poor Law, workhouse inmates had often been permitted to attend services at the local parish church, but that practice ceased with the passage of the Poor Law Amendment Act in 1834. Henceforth, a Church of England chaplain held divine service at the institution each Sunday. Catholics and Nonconformists were permitted to attend their own place of worship, if convenient, or receive visits from their priest or minister. In 1860 a series of *Workhouse Papers* campaigned on behalf of Catholic inmates.[19] One particular demand, met by the central authority at a later date, was that Catholic children should be sent to Catholic boarding-schools which could be certified by the Poor Law Board, and not brought up in the Protestant faith, as was so often the case. The sacrament of marriage did not arise in the workhouse but several chapels had fonts, indicating the performance of baptisms. The dead were usually sent back to their own parish for burial but a few workhouses, such as Bath, had burial grounds. It was unusual for a workhouse chapel to be consecrated, but it was always licensed by the proper authorities.

In the 1830s most boards had thought it unnecessary to set aside a room for exclusive use as a chapel, preferring instead to adapt a dining-room for the purpose. Long, thin benches and tables were arranged so that paupers faced the pulpit for eating as well as worshipping (Fig 112). The dual use of these rooms must have proved inconvenient.

Plainly, detached chapels were not indispensable appendages to workhouses, and so it is uncertain why some unions decided to erect them while others did not. The pattern of chapel provision was determined neither by geography nor by the size of an institution. In some cases, as the workhouse population expanded, the dining-hall might have become inadequate to hold congregations, but the devotion of individual boards of guardians and other local worthies may have been a more significant factor. Some guardians believed that catering to the spiritual needs of the inmates, if only by improving the environment in which they worshipped, would bring about reformation of character. The construction of workhouse chapels was urged in the pages of the *Journal of*

Figure 113 (top)
The chapel of Bath Union Workhouse was built by an elderly inmate, John Plass, in 1843.
[BB96/5432]

Figure 114 (above)
This simple building at Pewsey Union Workhouse (1873) may be regarded as typical of workhouse chapels. On most workhouse sites these buildings have been demolished or are used as stores.
[BB93/21673]

the Workhouse Visiting Society, which issued a pious plea for their erection in 1859 and thereafter published several progress reports.[20] Necessary finance was raised by voluntary contributions.

One of the earliest detached workhouse chapels, a simple structure in the Gothic style, was erected at Bath Union Workhouse in 1843 (Fig 113). It is not known who designed it, but a tablet inside the chapel records how John Plass, a former master builder and an inmate of the workhouse, 'at the age of 78, working with much zeal and industry, laid all the stone of this building'. The participation of paupers in the decoration of chapels is recorded elsewhere. An inmate of Macclesfield workhouse decorated the dining-hall/chapel with 'frescoes containing the Decalogue, the Apostles' Creed, the Lord's Prayer, encircled in floriated borders', and the old men of the workhouse further embellished it with mottoes, such as the appropriate 'No Cross, No Crown'.[21]

Chapels erected in the third quarter of the century ran the whole gamut of contemporary architectural styles, including neo-Norman, Perpendicular and Italianate. The majority, however, opted for an economical and highly restrained version of Early English. The small chapel at Pewsey in Wiltshire (Fig 114), erected in 1873, represents the form and style most commonly adopted for workhouse chapels, being essentially an austere box lit by single lancets. At the other end of the spectrum lies Perkin & Backhouse's chapel, erected at Leeds Union Workhouse in 1858–61 (Fig 115), which is an extraordinarily eclectic confection with borrowings from Romanesque, Italian Gothic and Georgian architecture.

As was the case with other workhouse buildings, chapels were generally built of local materials. That erected at Cuckfield in 1858 was of brick with tile-hanging and had steep roofs with decorative tiling, typical of Sussex. Chapel architects were usually local, but some of national repute were employed: G E Street, for example, designed the rather plain Gothic chapels at Woodstock and Chipping Norton in Oxfordshire and that at Shipmeadow in Suffolk.[22]

The correct orientation of chapels often came second to a rational positioning which related to the divisions of the workhouse. The arrangement of furnishings and fittings, however, usually followed traditional liturgical patterns. Naves contained two rows of pews, one for males and the other for females, with no physical barrier to prevent them seeing or communicating with one another. Dr Edward Smith noted in 1866 that the 'unnecessary and unseemly' screens which had been common in the 1830s (*see* Figure 66) had by now virtually disappeared. Children sat to the rear and the master's pew was located at the east end of an aisle, facing the pulpit.

Workhouse chapels had few unique features but, like dining-halls, they often had separate entrances for males and females. Rather than having a central west doorway, the neo-Norman chapel erected at West Ham (Fig 116) in 1849 had two lateral doorways. The brick chapel at Tonbridge, built at a cost of £650 in 1864 with seating for 300, was entered through two separate porches, one on either side of the square chancel; there were no entrances in the west wall, which actually faced north west.

Although it was tucked away in a corner beside the workhouse laundry, and was clad externally in a plain Gothic style, the interior of the Tonbridge chapel was highly decorative and, unusually, incorporated arcades (Fig 117). The nave and aisles were covered by a single roof, without the interruption of a clerestory. The arcades were composed of three broad

Figure 115 (far left) The chapel of Leeds Union Workhouse (1858–61) was designed by William Perkin & Elisha Backhouse. With typical disregard for true liturgical orientation, it was turned towards the north west.
[BB93/22911]

Figure 116 (left) This shows the west façade of the chapel built at West Ham Union Workhouse in 1849.
[BB91/20840]

Figure 117 (left) In layout, from the 1840s onward, there was very little to distinguish workhouse chapels from ordinary parish churches. This is the view looking down the nave of Tonbridge Union Workhouse chapel (1864), towards the altar.
[BB91/26209]

THE WORKHOUSE

Figure 118
This building, designed by John Norton in 1860, superseded the original chapel at Scott & Moffatt's Bedminster Union Workhouse. The arcaded covered way on the right connected the chapel to the entrance block of the workhouse (see Figure 71).
[BB95/8217]

Figure 119
The original fittings of Bedminster Union Workhouse chapel of 1860 survive intact, including the pulpit, which carries the text 'REPENT YE AND BELIEVE THE GOSPEL'.
[BB95/8221]

arches of banded brickwork, carried by squat marble columns on high plinths, crowned by crocket capitals.

The flint and ashlar chapel added to Bedminster Union Workhouse (Fig 118) in 1860 was, like Tonbridge, unusually large.[23] It did not have arcades, but had transept arms that projected from the east and west sides of the nave, which was orientated north–south. While the liturgical 'south' transept contained the organ, the 'north' transept and nave were entered through separate doorways and contained pews. Those in the 'north' transept may have been for the use of the master and other members of staff. A covered colonnade linked the workhouse to the chapel.

At Bedminster, the pulpit (Fig 119), font and other chapel fittings have survived *in situ*. This is unusual, as many chapels fell into disuse when workhouses became hospitals in the mid-20th century. Then, bedridden patients took the place of mobile inmates, and the only religious provision an institution needed to make was a vicar to visit the sick and a small mortuary chapel for the bereaved. No longer places of worship, workhouse chapels faced an uncertain future: some were demolished and others were stripped of their fittings and converted into stores. Bedminster chapel is, consequently, something of a rarity.

7
Separate-Block Workhouses, 1870–1914

The late 1860s and early 1870s proved a time of transition for workhouse design. The corridor plan was regarded with increasing disfavour and separate-block schemes, designed on pavilion principles, were adopted in its stead (Fig 120). This coincided with a period in which new legislation and improved financial conditions encouraged unions to build extra accommodation for indoor paupers, especially the sick[1].

The erection of a new infirmary often created extra room in the main workhouse building. With this in mind, the central authority launched its so-called 'crusade against out-relief', reinforcing the principles of 1834. Officially, the only class for whom outdoor relief had been strictly prohibited since 1834 was able-bodied men. In practice, however, the respectable unemployed often received outdoor relief while the more disreputable were sent to the workhouse. In 1868, Lord Goschen, the new President of the Poor Law Board, stressed the advantages of a more rigorous application of the workhouse test, and a few years later Inspector Longley urged unions to extend it to other classes, especially to able-bodied women and impotent paupers of bad character.[2] That policy was never enshrined in law, and the urban unions which acted upon Longley's suggestions were severely limited by the capacity of their workhouses. In times of depression, especially in the mid-1880s, many set up labour yards as an alternative to the workhouse test.

After 1870, many unions began to classify workhouse inmates, not just according to their age, sex and state of health, but on the basis of character. The provision of separate accommodation and harsher conditions for the 'undeserving' was not entirely new, as several Old Poor Law workhouses had segregated good and bad inmates. That practice had continued in urban workhouses after 1834, but was applied exclusively to the able-bodied, and sometimes just to able-bodied women: while Greenwich Union Workhouse (1840) had wards for women of 'irredeemably bad character', there were no equivalent wards for men (*see* Figure 93). After 1870, such categorisation was reinforced by giving 'bad' inmates particularly unpleasant work to perform, such as corn-grinding or stone-breaking, often in isolation. By the 1890s, even aged and infirm inmates were classified and segregated on the grounds of morality or behaviour.

At the beginning of the 20th century, many of the tenets of 1834 were being questioned. Even the central poor-law authority was showing uneasiness about the applicability of the workhouse test to many social groups once considered undeserving but now absolved from blame for their poverty, especially the respectable unemployed and most elderly people. Poor-law inspectors constantly reiterated the need to remove the mentally handicapped and children from the workhouse environment, but limited action was taken. In this climate of uncertainty, the Royal Commission on the Poor Laws of 1905–9 failed to agree on a solution. The subsequent Liberal welfare reforms had little immediate effect on workhouse populations and yet, on the eve of the First World War, the transformation of the poor-law system seemed imminent.

The Adoption of the Pavilion, or Separate-Block, Plan

The term 'pavilion' is applied, often rather loosely, to certain aspects of hospital planning adopted in England after the Crimean War.[3] At its most basic, 'pavilion planning' refers to the division of a hospital which, in the past, would have been erected as a single building, into separate blocks connected by covered walkways. Separate-block planning was devised chiefly as a means of inhibiting the spread of disease from one building to another, at a time when contemporary theory maintained that infections were carried in the air.

THE WORKHOUSE

*Figure 120
This map shows the distribution of separate-block, or pavilion-plan, workhouses and infirmaries, newly erected after 1870.*

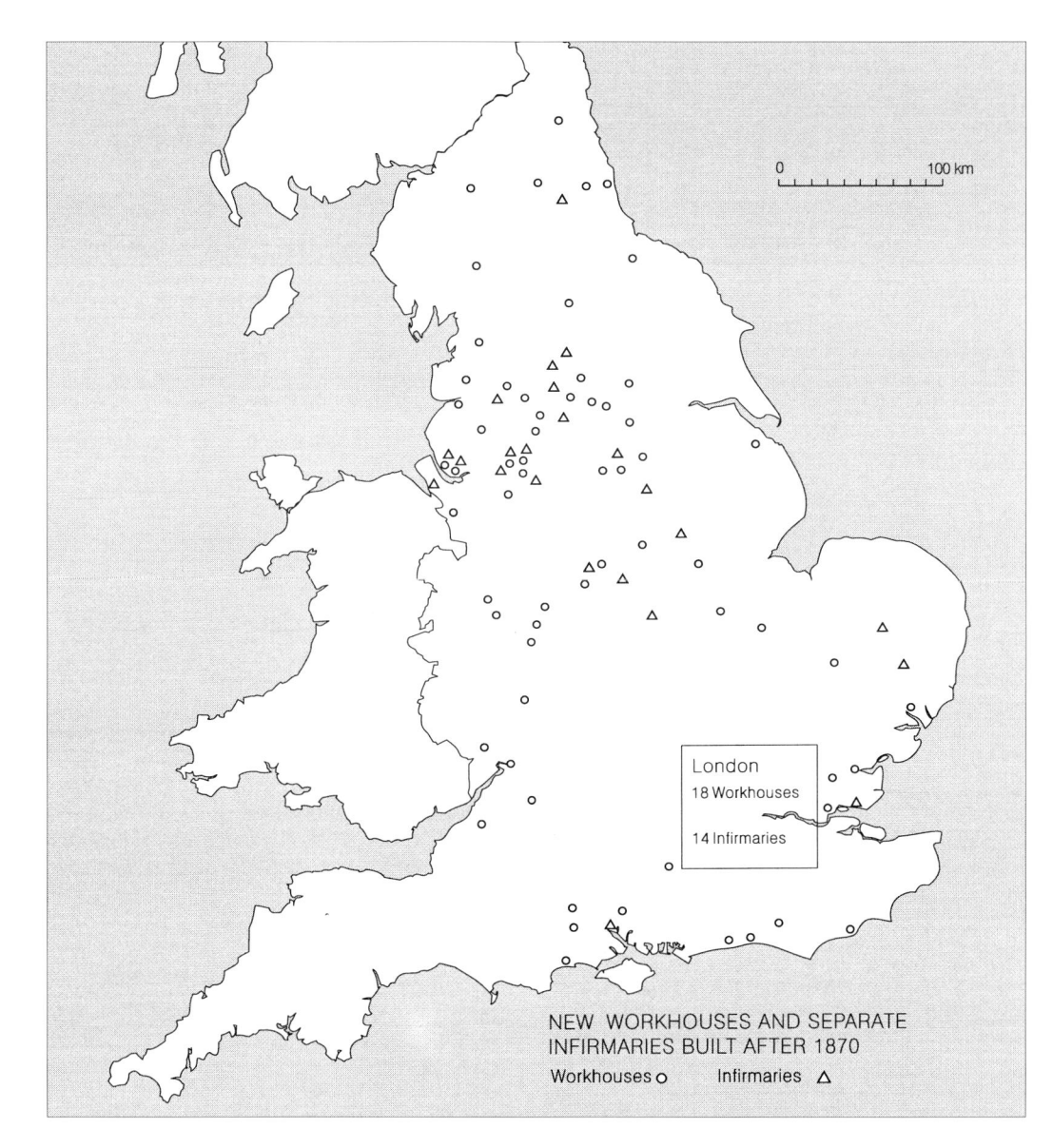

NEW WORKHOUSES AND SEPARATE INFIRMARIES BUILT AFTER 1870
Workhouses ○   Infirmaries △

London
18 Workhouses
14 Infirmaries

Individual hospital ward blocks were referred to as 'pavilions' and incorporated a number of 'pavilion principles' which created a healthier environment for invalids. Most importantly, wards were lit by opposing windows to create a through draught and beds were arranged, either singly or in pairs, between windows. The optimum number of beds in a hospital pavilion ward was decreed to be thirty-two, and each patient was allowed approximately 800 cu ft of air.[4] These criteria dictated long narrow wards, sometimes called 'Nightingale' wards, which were recognisable from the exterior by their rows of tall sash and hopper windows. To prevent sanitary facilities becoming a source of airborne infection, toilets and sinks were removed to towers, or annexes, attached to the outer ends of wards by short, cross-ventilated, stem-like lobbies. Square or polygonal sanitary towers carrying water cisterns, often with decorative roofs, became the most prominent architectural features of pavilion ward blocks.

If guardians were slow to adopt the separate-block plan for workhouse infirmaries, which were still viewed by many boards of guardians as repositories for the sick poor rather than hospitals for their treatment and cure, they were even slower to introduce pavilion principles into buildings for ordinary inmates. Indeed, many features of separate-block planning must have appeared irrelevant for buildings which housed healthy people, but guardians could not ignore the extent to which the acceptance of pavilion principles by the world at large had discredited corridor planning. Corridors were now equated with poor ventilation and the easy transmission of disease: an alternative design had to be discovered for new workhouses.

Points to be Attended to in the Construction of Workhouses, a Poor Law Board circular first issued in June 1868, stated that new infirmaries must incorporate pavilion principles, but assumed that main buildings would continue to be erected with corridors.[5] The document expressed some concern for the ventilation of workhouses and recommended that water-closets occupy projections with cross-ventilated lobbies. Although the Local Government Board failed to take the initiative, outside pressure persuaded some poor-law authorities to adopt the separate-block system for workhouses in the early 1870s, not just because it inhibited the spread of infections, but because it offered a convenient alternative means of segregating different classes of inmate. These local authorities also accepted, in general terms, that cross-ventilated rooms were healthier than those with windows on one side only, but were probably ignorant of the fact that this involved a return to the principles of Sampson Kempthorne, abandoned thirty years before. In other ways, hospital pavilion principles were flouted in workhouses. As most inmates did not occupy their sleeping-rooms during the day, fewer cubic feet could be allotted to each person, both in dormitories and day-rooms.[6] It was also less important for windows to be as large as they were in hospitals, or to incorporate hoppers which would direct the air flow upwards. The position of beds did not have to correspond to window bays, and sanitary facilities did not have to occupy towers.

Provincial separate-block workhouses were designed along different lines from those in London. One reason for this was the availability of spacious, greenfield sites outside London. The general principle that the distance between two blocks should equal twice the height of the tallest one, and that no block should be more than two storeys high, was difficult to respect in the crowded metropolis.[7] Another factor which caused differences to emerge between metropolitan and provincial institutions was the removal of children, the mentally handicapped and the mentally and physically sick from London workhouses while the general mixed workhouse endured elsewhere.

Between 1870 and 1914, at least forty-six new pavilion-plan workhouses had been erected throughout the country and many older workhouses had been remodelled along pavilion, or separate-block, lines. Pavilion principles had also been adopted for many other types of poor-law institution, including asylums, infirmaries and schools.

Pavilion-Plan Workhouses in London, 1870–1914

Conditions within London's workhouses were fiercely attacked throughout the 1860s and, with the attention of sanitary reformers firmly fixed on hospital accommodation, sick wards came in for particular criticism. In 1867, following a number of official enquiries, the Metropolitan Poor Act was passed, creating the Metropolitan Asylums Board.[8] The Board was instructed to relieve London workhouses of harmless lunatics, imbeciles and infectious cases by setting up special asylums and fever hospitals (*see* Chapter 9). Moreover, poor-law authorities were pressed to separate infirmaries from workhouses, administratively if not always physically, and were aided in this by the establishment of a Common Poor Fund. The reorganisation of London poor-law institutions continued apace

Figure 121
In this perspective view of Islington Workhouse (1869–70), the roofs of the pavilion-plan infirmary can be seen behind the larger, corridor-plan, main building.
[*From* The Builder, *12 June 1869, 467, by permission of the Syndics of Cambridge University Library*]

THE WORKHOUSE

ST MARYLEBONE WORKHOUSE
NORTHUMBERLAND STREET W. – INFIRM WARDS.

FIRST FLOOR PLAN.
SECOND FLOOR IS SIMILAR

GROUND PLAN.
Scale of Feet

Figure 122 (above) These wards at St Marylebone Workhouse were designed for aged and infirm inmates in 1867 by Henry Saxon Snell. The bay windows were used as seating areas during the day. [From Snell, H S 1881, 2, by permission of the Syndics of Cambridge University Library]

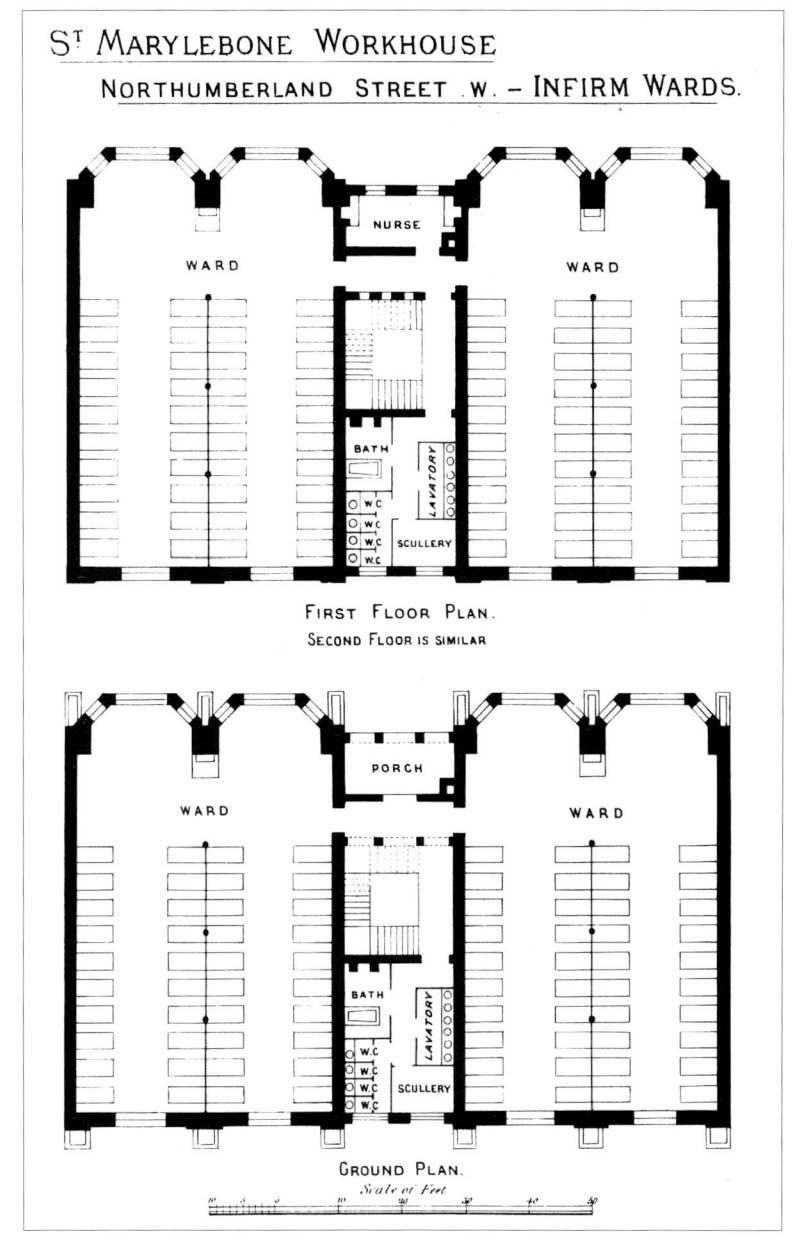

throughout the 1870s and 1880s, and involved the creation of numerous new workhouses, as well as asylums and infirmaries.

While reorganisation and rebuilding were in progress, many authorities resorted to temporary measures. Thus, St Mary, Lambeth, hired Price's Candle Factory for infirm paupers and the joint parishes of St Margaret and St John, Westminster, hired a Working Men's Club for infectious and venereal cases.[9] Others, such as St Mary, Islington, and Kensington, set up cheap iron or wooden buildings on their old workhouse sites.[10]

Several new metropolitan workhouses erected in the late 1860s had pavilion-plan infirmaries and corridor-plan main buildings, a combination which first arose at Chorlton Union Workhouse with the addition of a pavilion-plan infirmary to an older corridor-plan workhouse in 1864–6 (*see* Figure 201). Its architect, Thomas Worthington, designed a complete workhouse along similar lines for the new Prestwich Union in 1866–70. Examples of this type of institution in London included the new Islington Workhouse (Fig 121), built at Holloway in 1869–70, and the Woolwich Union Workhouse of 1869–70. But while corridor-plan workhouses like these continued to be erected in the provinces throughout the 1870s, London architects soon abandoned that design in favour of the separate-block system, albeit without a rigorous adherence to hospital principles.

The majority of London authorities continued to house their able-bodied and aged paupers on restricted urban sites which had been extended piecemeal since the 18th century and were now greatly in need of redevelopment. Architects were faced with the task of squeezing new accommodation blocks, capable of holding large numbers of paupers, on to these sites. The solution they produced, double-width wards, was an old one. Double-width wards had been a feature of several Old Poor Law workhouses in

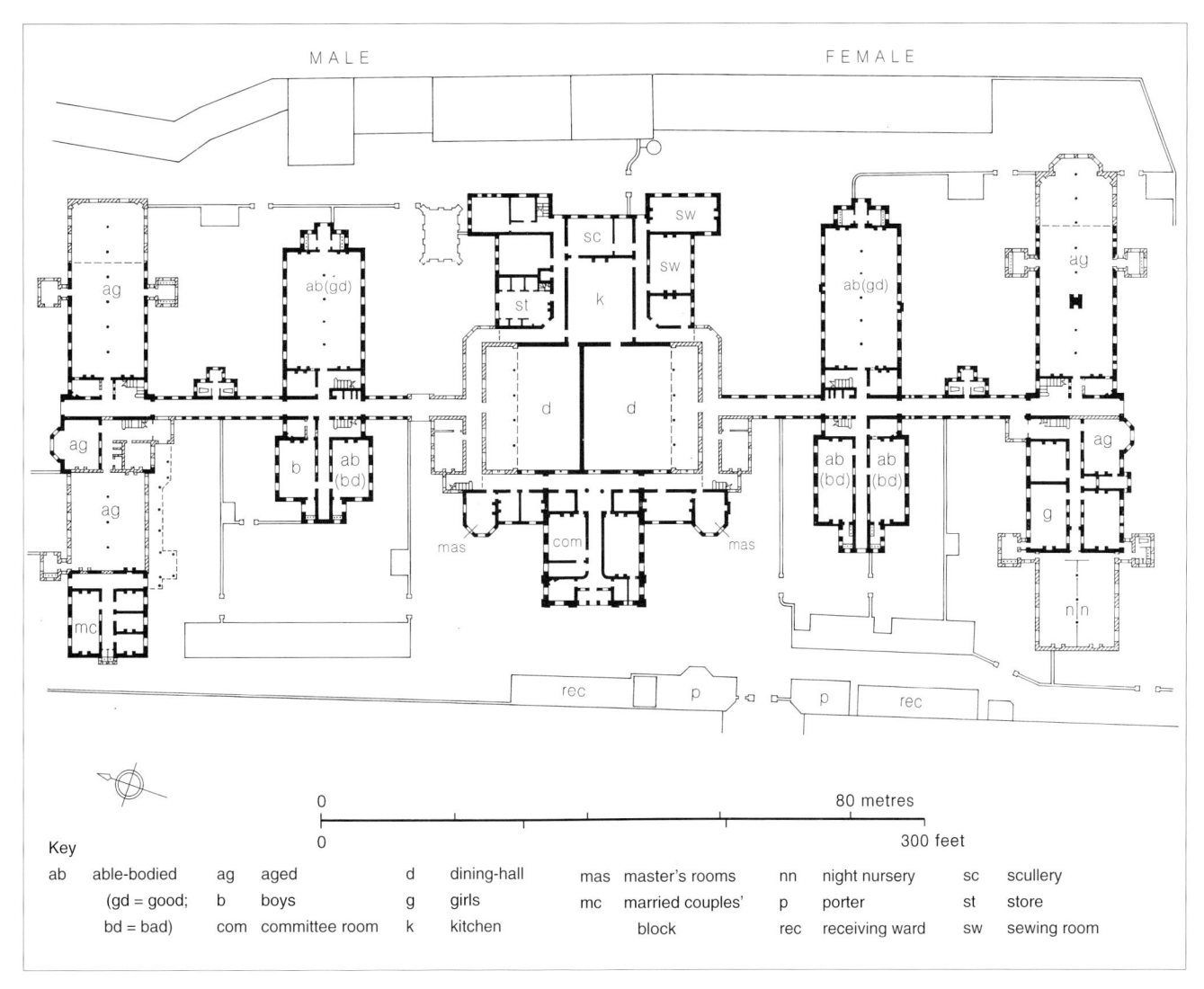

Separate-Block Workhouses, 1870–1914

Key

ab	able-bodied	ag	aged	d	dining-hall	mas	master's rooms	nn	night nursery	sc	scullery
(gd = good; bd = bad)		b	boys	g	girls	mc	married couples' block	p	porter	st	store
		com	committee room	k	kitchen			rec	receiving ward	sw	sewing room

London, such as Camberwell, but after being criticised by Sampson Kempthorne in 1835 they appear to have been largely abandoned.[11] The reintroduction of such wards can be attributed to Henry Saxon Snell, who was appointed architect to St Marylebone in 1866.[12] Snell soon became established as one of the foremost poor-law architects in the capital and was employed by several unions and parishes to design buildings for all classes of pauper.

Snell had noticed that some new infirmaries with opposing windows were so overcrowded that beds had to be placed very close to windows, or even directly under them, where patients suffered from draughts.[13] To avoid this problem he produced a novel design of building for the aged and infirm inmates of St Marylebone Workhouse, whose guardians were reportedly 'anxious that their aged poor should be made as comfortable as the rules of a workhouse will permit'.[14] The resulting three-storeyed block (Fig 122) contained two wards on each floor, separated centrally by stairs, a room for a paid nurse and sanitary facilities.[15] The 40-bed wards, measuring 40 ft by 60 ft, were twice as wide as typical pavilion wards and contained four rather than two rows of beds. Contrary to pavilion principles, the beds were ranged along the dead walls and 5 ft 6 in.-high partitions, rather than between the windows. The partitions were hollow and contained flues for the introduction and expulsion of warm air. Additional heating was supplied by stoves.

Shortly afterwards, Snell designed similar buildings (Fig 123) for the infirm inmates of the City Road workhouse which had formerly belonged to St Luke's, Middlesex, but was now in the hands of Holborn Union.[16] These included triple, and even quadruple-width wards. The largest wards, for infirm women, held no less than 56 beds in eight rows and were fronted by four bay windows; they would have been considered huge and unmanageable by contemporary hospital standards. Snell introduced hydraulic

Figure 124
Lambeth Workhouse was erected in 1871–4. Extensions made in 1880 have a hatched outline.
[Ground-floor plan redrawn from Public Record Office MH14/18]

Figure 123 (opposite)
New wards were erected for the aged and infirm of St Luke's Workhouse on City Road in 1870–1.
[From Snell, H S 1881, 4, by permission of the Syndics of Cambridge University Library]

THE WORKHOUSE

lifts for transporting the bedridden to the upper floor and for the conveyance of coals and meals. Holborn guardians were so impressed with this building that, in the late 1870s, they insisted that Snell include wards of the same type in their new infirmary at Archway (*see* page 167). That building had little impact on hospital design, and few new sick wards were built with double-width wards.[17] The design, however, remained popular for healthier classes of inmate, especially the aged and infirm, and was chosen for additions to many London workhouses, including those of Chelsea, St Pancras, Greenwich, Whitechapel and St Marylebone. It was also adopted for new workhouses, such as those designed by Thomas W Aldwinckle for St Mary, Lambeth (Fig 124), Wandsworth and Clapham, and Camberwell (Fig 125; *see* Figure 127b). Berriman & Son adopted it for a second new Camberwell workhouse, on Gordon Road (Fig 126), and Snell used

Figure 125 (right)
The interior of this double-width women's ward at Camberwell Workhouse on Constance Road (1892) was photographed around 1930. Even at that late date, the brick walls were unplastered and the floor uncarpeted.
[London Metropolitan Archives 84/2997]

Figure 126 (below left)
The administration block of Camberwell Workhouse on Gordon Road (1878) was linked to the flanking pavilions by covered ways and escape bridges. These have survived, despite the conversion of the buildings into flats.
[BB96/550]

Figure 127 (below right)
These block plans show the layout of three separate-block workhouses in London, each designed by a well-known workhouse architect. They are:
a. Holborn Union Workhouse, Mitcham (1885–6; Henry Saxon Snell);
[Based on OS rev edn 1:2500 map 1894]
b. Camberwell Workhouse, Constance Road (1892; T W Aldwinckle);
[Based on OS rev edn 1:2500 map 1912–14]
c. Greenwich Union Workhouse, Grove Park (1899–1902; Thomas Dinwiddy).
[Based on The Building News, 9 June 1899, 777]

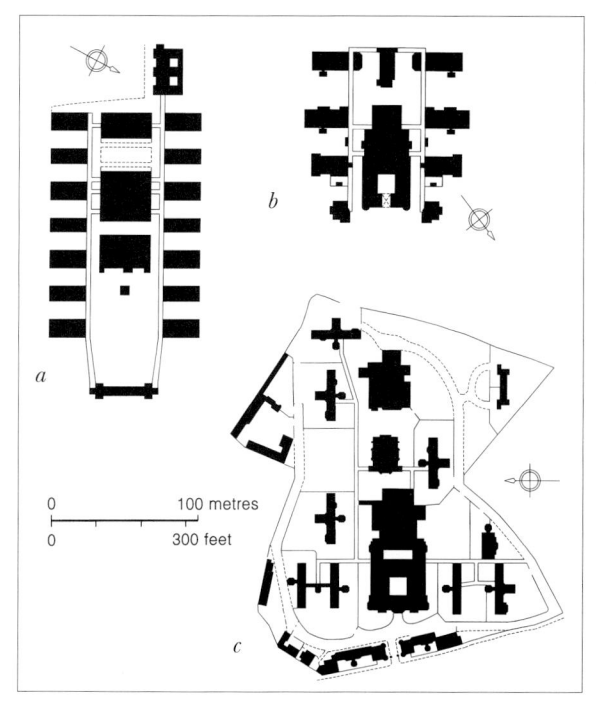

Separate-Block Workhouses, 1870–1914

it for the new Holborn Workhouse at Mitcham (Fig 127a). On all of these new sites, buildings were arranged in the manner of pavilion-plan hospitals, with accommodation blocks for the able-bodied and aged lying parallel to one another, on either side of a central administration block, to which they were connected by covered ways. Covered ways were never enclosed, but sometimes a central screen was provided, allowing nurses and patients to walk in the lee of the wind.

Until the 1890s, most of the New Poor Law buildings erected in London were utterly plain. The façade of the administration block of Aldwinckle's Lambeth workhouse (Fig 128), one of the few exceptions, was executed in polychrome brickwork, in an eclectic, almost palatial, style. The tall, canted bays of Snell's blocks at St Marylebone and City Road workhouses (*see* Figure 123), overlooked the workhouse yards rather than the street, but their long, gabled

Figure 128
The ornate administration block is practically all that survives of Lambeth Workhouse, Renfrew Road, Kennington (1871–4).
[BB96/557]

façades were enlivened by banded brickwork and Gothic details typical of mid-Victorian public architecture. The façade of the five-storeyed Cook's Terrace block of St Pancras Workhouse (Fig 129), erected in 1882–4, was dominated by a central tower and punctuated by rows of canted bays, a feature clearly derived from Snell's recent poor-law buildings.[18]

A pair of elaborate three-storeyed blocks was added to St Marylebone Workhouse in 1898–9 to accommodate 555 old and infirm men, 21 male and female imbeciles and 6 male and female lunatics (Fig 130).[19] The architect was Alfred Saxon Snell, who had taken over his father's practice in 1896.[20] Both buildings were in an ornate Queen Anne style, in red brick and stone, with rusticated facings on the ground floor, and white ashlar window surrounds, balustrades and banded quoining. They adjoined one another at basement and ground-floor level, and were linked at higher levels by open bridges. Flat roofs were 'available for such of these inmates as may be able to take advantage of them'.[21]

Although the St Marylebone wards of 1898–9 had double-width wards, these were seldom erected after 1900. Albert C Freeman, an architect who published a book about the planning of poor-law buildings in 1904, voiced his disapproval of them: 'From observation, I cannot say I should recommend this form; there are not the facilities for cleaning, and the partitions are found to harbour dirt and vermin'.[22] For the three new workhouses in London completed after 1900,

Greenwich, Hammersmith and Willesden, large greenfield sites were found and, liberated from the congested conditions which had necessitated double-width wards, their architects designed widely separated single-width pavilions of the type which had been popular outside London for many years.

The new Greenwich Union Workhouse, erected at Grove Park in 1899–1902 to designs by Thomas Dinwiddy, won a diploma of merit at the Paris Exhibition of 1900 (*see* Fig 127c).[23] Described in *The Builder* as a 'poor-law village', it was destined to receive 816 aged and able-bodied inmates.[24] The need for it, however, had evaporated by the time of its completion and it remained empty for two years.[25] When attempts to sell it failed in 1904, it was partly occupied by the Union. It continued to be under-occupied as a workhouse until the outbreak of the First World War, when it was transferred to the Armed Forces. It never reopened as a workhouse.

The institutions built for the newly formed authorities of Hammersmith and Willesden each included an infirmary as well as a workhouse, something rarely permitted in London since 1870. Indeed, at Willesden, the infirmary (1900–2) was erected some years before the workhouse proper (completed 1908). The architects of the Hammersmith institution (1903–5; Fig 131) were Giles, Gough & Trollope, a firm which had designed several lunatic and imbecile asylums, including two for the Metropolitan Asylums Board.[26] Allegations of extravagance provoked an inquiry in 1907, at

Figure 129
The Cook's Terrace building was added to St Pancras Workhouse in 1882–4. The building on the extreme left, which it dwarfs, is the Town Hall.
[BB90/05760]

Separate-Block Workhouses, 1870–1914

Figure 130 (left)
This huge ward block accommodated the aged and infirm, imbeciles and lunatics of St Marylebone Workhouse on Baker Street, London. It was designed by Alfred Saxon Snell and built in 1898–9. The building was demolished in 1966 to make way for the new London Polytechnic, directly opposite Mme Tussaud's.
[London Metropolitan Archives 20.61 LUX]

Figure 131 (below)
In this view of Hammersmith Union Workhouse (1903–5), designed by Giles, Gough & Trollope, the buildings to the front comprised the infirmary, those to the rear were the workhouse, and service buildings in the middle were shared by both sides of the institution.
[From The Builder, 9 December 1905, 623, by permission of the Syndics of Cambridge University Library]

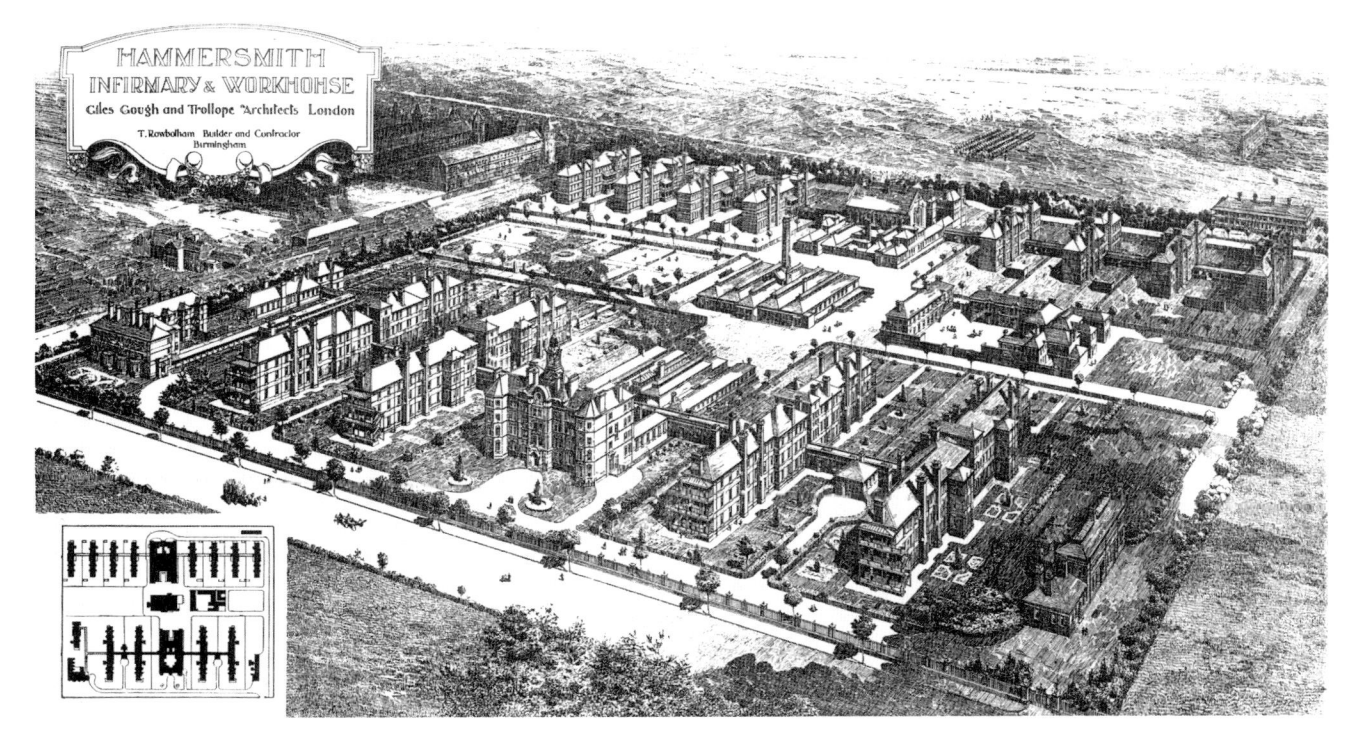

THE WORKHOUSE

Figure 132
Madeley Union Workhouse of 1871–5 may have been the first pavilion-plan workhouse outside London. The large building at the top of the picture is a nurses' home, added in the 1930s.
[4818/19]

Figure 133
These block plans of workhouses built outside London are:
a. *Madeley Union Workhouse (1871–5; Messrs Haddon);*
   [Based on OS rev edn 1:2500 map 1901]
b. *Sheffield Union Workhouse (1877–80; James Hall);*
   [Based on OS 1 edn 1:2500 map 1890]
c. *Middlesbrough Union Workhouse (1877–8; Perkin & Son);*
   [Based on OS rev edn 1:2500 map 1913]
d. *Barrow-in-Furness Union Workhouse (1879; J Y McIntosh);*
   [Based on OS rev edn 1:2500 map 1911]
e. *South Shields Union Workhouse (1877–80; J H Morton).*
   [Based on OS rev edn 1:2500 map 1912–13]

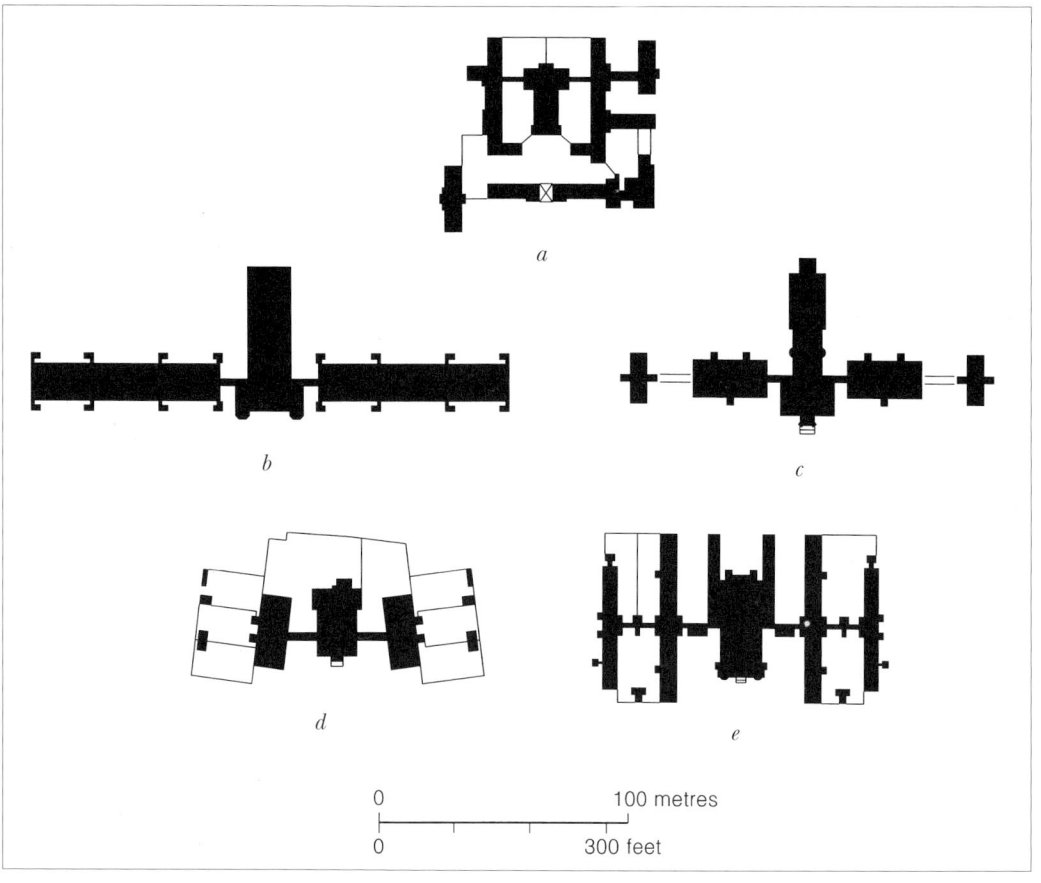

which the architects and guardians blamed one another for the high cost of the institution. Rebutting claims made in the House of Commons that the buildings had cost £335 per bed, the architects argued that the cost was actually £183.[27] The architect Albert Freeman had stated, only three years previously, that the average cost of a workhouse or infirmary in London was between £150 and £200 per bed and £120 to £150 elsewhere.[28] If that was so, the Willesden institution, which cost only £90 per bed, must have been extremely inexpensive.

Pavilion-Plan Workhouses Outside London, 1870–1914

The first separate-block English workhouse, a small institution erected by Madeley Union in Shropshire in 1871–5, received no national publicity. Initially, the Madeley guardians had wished to enlarge their old workhouse, but they were denied permission by the Poor Law Board and were eventually served with an Order to close their institution. In 1870, after a period of procrastination, the guardians approved a new workhouse, determining 'to accept a ground plan offered by a member of the [Building] Committee and to appoint Messrs Haddon as the architects to complete and carry the same into effect'.[29]

A central block of one storey, containing a kitchen and dining-hall, was linked to two-storeyed accommodation pavilions by covered ways (Figs 132 and 133a). Other buildings on the site included an infirmary, an infectious diseases block, an entrance range and workshops. The architecture was decorative, even picturesque in poor-law terms, with banded, polychrome brickwork and leaded ridge ventilators. At the time, Madeley Union Workhouse was not recognised as a new departure, and it had no imitators. Small regional workhouses continued to be built on the corridor plan throughout the 1870s, the adoption of the pavilion plan by large urban authorities coming slowly, and without reference to Madeley.

In 1874, James Hall drew up plans for a huge new workhouse for Sheffield Union. The Local Government Board, however, disapproved of the proposed 900-ft-long main building and invited Hall, together with a number of Sheffield guardians, to London, where poor-law inspectors Dr Mouat and Mr (or more probably, Dr) Smith explained the disadvantages of congregating large numbers of people under one roof and recommended the separate-block system for the main building as well as for the detached lunatic wards and infirmary.[30] The deputation was then invited to Lambeth, to see the system in operation there.

Although Hall subsequently adopted the separate-block system for the new Sheffield workhouse, erected between 1876 and 1880, he did not renounce the corridor plan for the main building (see Figure 133b; Fig 134). Short links connected the administration block to the accommodation blocks, which were arranged 'in-line', with a 645-ft-long central corridor running from one end to the other. This was, in effect, a corridor-plan workhouse with detached wings. The infirmary, to the rear, comprised a row of parallel, pavilion-plan ward blocks. There were additional H-shaped pavilion complexes for imbeciles, fever cases and children.

The separate-block system was taken further by Perkin & Son at Middlesbrough Union Workhouse (see Fig 133c), built in 1877–8. There, the main building comprised five blocks: a central administration block, two ordinary accommodation blocks and two imbecile blocks, all threaded together by a continuous corridor. Only the imbecile wards, however, took the form of cross-lit pavilions.

Double-width ward blocks, generally eschewed outside the metropolis, were erected at Barrow-in-Furness Union Workhouse of 1879 (see Figure 133d; Fig 135) and at Christchurch Union Workhouse of 1881–6. Christchurch was one of only two new workhouses to be built on the separate-block plan in the South, outside London, during the 1870s and 1880s, the other being the new workhouse erected for Chelmsford Union following a fire in 1886. A number of separate-block workhouses were erected in the North, however, and several specialised architectural practices soon emerged

Figure 134
This view shows the administration block and north wing of Sheffield Union Workhouse (1876–80), now the Northern General Hospital, which was designed by James Hall following consultation with the Local Government Board. The south wing has been demolished.
[BB92/9768]

there, taking over from the older generation of workhouse architects.

J H Morton of South Shields was one of the first architects to adopt the separate-block plan, with pavilion principles, for all three elements which typically constituted a large workhouse complex: the main building or 'house', the infirmary and the school. Morton's South Shields Union Workhouse of 1877–80, having a purely administrative central block and pavilions without internal corridors, set the pattern for future workhouses (*see* Fig 133e; Fig 136). It also reflected his sober architectural style, characterised by a sparing use of decorative details but often including shaped parapets. While the components of South Shields and most other late 19th-century workhouses were laid out in regimented rows, the school and workhouse buildings of Morton's Burton-upon-Trent Union Workhouse radiated from a curving covered way. That was echoed in an angular string of entrance buildings, including the offices, receiving wards and casual wards. As usual, the infirmary stood at the back of the site.

Figure 135
Barrow-in-Furness Union Workhouse, built in 1879 to designs by the local architect J Y McIntosh, stood on a hilltop commanding views over the town. Although the Union had only 84 indoor paupers at the time, the new building was capable of accommodating 350. It is now known as Roose Hospital.
[BB92/8870]

Figure 136
The administration block of South Shields Union Workhouse (1877–80), dominated by a water tower bearing the inscription 'MAIN BUILDING', was designed by the local architect, J H Morton, who went on to design workhouses throughout northern England.
[BB93/34478]

Later workhouses by Morton included those of Gateshead (1885–9; with W L Newcombe & W H Knowles), Doncaster (1897–1900) and Hunslet (1900–3). At the opening of the Doncaster Union Workhouse in 1900, the Chairman of the Board of Guardians claimed that the buildings were considered the most up-to-date in England:

> Their fame had spread so wide that the Emperor and Empress of Russia had asked for plans in order to build a similar sort of place in their own country, and he was given to understand that representatives of the Russian government would visit the place.[31]

The workhouse erected by Steyning Union (Fig 137) between 1898 and 1901 can be regarded as typical of new workhouses at the turn of the century.[32] With accommodation for 480 inmates, it cost £65,000 to build, or £135 per bed. The entrance block was two storeys high, rising to three storeys over the entrance arch, where the porter's bedroom was situated. To one side, beyond the porter's lodge and paupers' own clothes store, were tramp wards; to the other side were eight 2-bed receiving wards, each provided with its own toilet annexe. The first-floor wards were reached via an external staircase and a white, wooden veranda (Fig 138). This, together with half-framed gables and a steep, tiled roof, presented the outside world with a very different image of a workhouse than that projected by its predecessor in the 1830s.

The administration block of Steyning Workhouse included the master's house (Fig 139), offices, dining-hall, kitchen and stores. The size and design of the master's house indicated the transformation which had occurred in his status since 1834. He was now a professional, entitled to a two-storeyed family home, albeit one which opened off the main corridor of the administration block. On the ground floor was a kitchen, a dining-room and a sitting-room. Upstairs were three bedrooms. A single-storeyed canted bay on the south elevation did not facilitate surveillance, as it might have done in the 1830s, but contained glazed doors opening from the dining-room into the master's private garden. Reflecting the increase in paid workhouse staff, Steyning also included a residence, in its own walled grounds, for the

Figure 137
Steyning Union Workhouse, in Shoreham, comprises numerous separate buildings in a restrained Arts & Crafts style. Designed by Clayton & Black and built in 1898–1901, it is typical of late 19th-century workhouse complexes. In 1932 it became Southlands Hospital.
[Based on The Building News, 27 May 1898, 742–3]

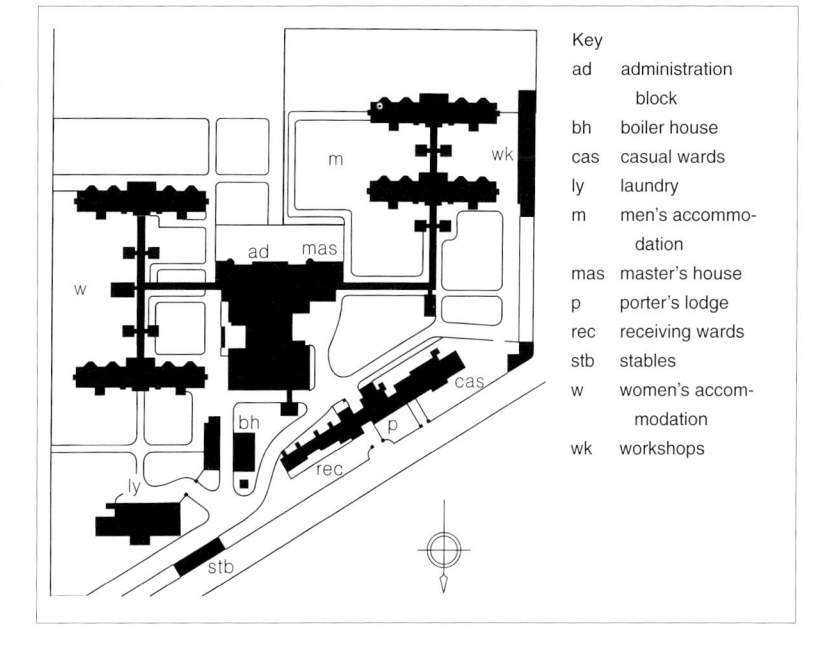

Key
ad administration block
bh boiler house
cas casual wards
ly laundry
m   men's accommodation
mas master's house
p   porter's lodge
rec receiving wards
stb stables
w   women's accommodation
wk workshops

Figure 138
New inmates would have been accommodated in the receiving wards of Steyning Union Workhouse, before being assigned to one of the main wards. This building, in the vernacular tradition, presented the public face of the workhouse.
[BB93/28462]

The Workhouse

Figure 139 (right)
The master's accommodation in Steyning Union Workhouse can be contrasted with that provided in the first New Poor Law workhouses, both in terms of its domestic scale and its position. Here, the canted bay with French windows overlooked the master's garden rather than inmates' yards.
[BB93/28473]

Figure 140 (top right)
Dilapidated toilet blocks survive in the overgrown yards of Steyning Union Workhouse, flanking the covered ways.
[BB96/2813]

Figure 141 (right)
Compared with the large complex built for 480 paupers by Steyning Union at Shoreham, the contemporary Hursley Union Workhouse (1899–1900) in Hampshire was a small building for sixty inmates, which housed the sick and the able-bodied under one roof. It later became a sanatorium.
[BB92/16036]

Figure 142
This is a ground-floor plan of Rothbury Union Workhouse in Northumberland, erected for only fifty inmates in 1900–5. As at Hursley, every function of the institution, except the casual wards and guardians' boardroom, was located in the main building.
[Redrawn from Public Record Office MH14/30]

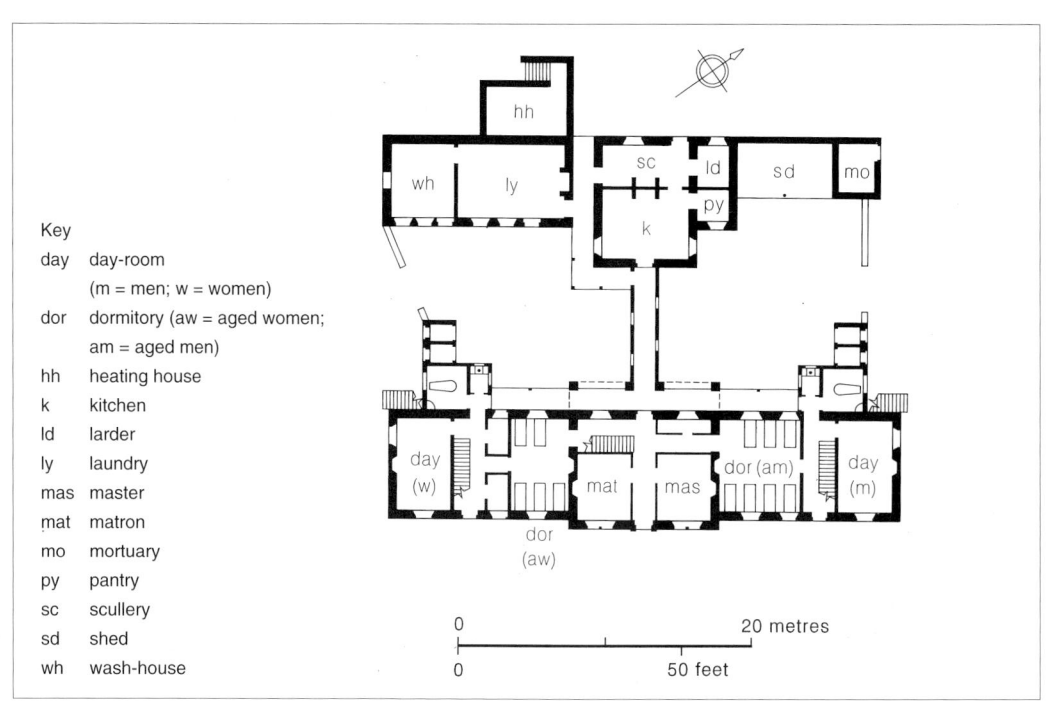

Key
day   day-room (m = men; w = women)
dor   dormitory (aw = aged women; am = aged men)
hh   heating house
k   kitchen
ld   larder
ly   laundry
mas   master
mat   matron
mo   mortuary
py   pantry
sc   scullery
sd   shed
wh   wash-house

engineer and his assistant, and a two-storeyed nurses' home.

Architecturally, the inmates' accommodation blocks at Steyning were plainer than the administration block, to which they were connected by flat-roofed covered ways. They formed double pavilions with separate accommodation to either side of a central staircase. The day-rooms on the ground floor were divided by wooden partitions allowing classification, and each section opened into an expansive canted bay. The dormitories were served by toilet facilities, which projected from the north side of the buildings, and had open fireplaces as well as hot-water radiators. Detached toilet blocks (Fig 140) were provided in each yard, for day use.

Other buildings at Steyning included a chapel, laundry, boiler house, workshops and a cottage for aged married couples (*see* Figure 146). The infirmary, with a capacity for 240, was built after the workhouse, in 1904–6. No water tower was required, as the institution was connected to the mains of Brighton Corporation, and there was no children's section, as the old workhouse had been converted into a children's home.

After 1880, only a few very small workhouses departed from the layout represented by Steyning and followed the in-line plan which had been favoured for small workhouse infirmaries since 1870. These included Hursley (Fig 141) and Rothbury (Fig 142) workhouses, both built at the turn of the century.

The Aged and Infirm in the Workhouse, 1870–1914

The 1834 *Poor Law Report* had expressed the belief that the aged and infirm should be treated with greater lenience than able-bodied paupers in the workhouse. Nevertheless, after 1834 they were generally assigned to ordinary wards in the main workhouse building, under the same roof as able-bodied inmates but with their own dormitories, day-rooms (Fig 143) and exercise yards. Officially, they were eligible for indulgences, such as visiting rights, but their regime and diet were frequently identical to those of able-bodied inmates. After 1870, more accommodation was provided for married couples over 60 years of age, but it was only in the 1890s that more enlightened authorities realised that many people were becoming pauperised in old age through no fault of their own, and began to treat them accordingly.

Aged and infirm paupers were the subject of a Royal Commission inquiry between 1893 and 1895.[33] This coincided with the publication of Charles Booth's *Pauperism and the Endowment of Old Age* (1892), which argued that the aged formed the largest single group drawing relief, and proposed the introduction of a non-contributory old-age pension. His *Aged Poor in England* (1894) attempted to demonstrate that current relief practices, including the deterrent workhouse, did not reduce pauperism. The findings of the Royal Commission, reflecting the

Figure 143
Eventide: A Scene in the Westminster Union *was painted by Hubert von Herkomer in 1878. Although there are still no carpets on the floor of the old women's day-room, and no comfortable armchairs, pictures hang on the walls and tea is in evidence. In many workhouses, such luxuries did not arrive for the elderly before the 1890s.* [National Museums and Galleries on Merseyside, Walker Art Gallery, Liverpool WAG 260]

more sympathetic attitudes dawning at the time, prompted a Local Government Board circular (1896) which encouraged the subdivision of the aged and infirm with reference to their 'moral character or behaviour or previous habits' and suggested that separate day-rooms and individual sleeping cubicles should be provided for those of good character.[34] The idea of subdividing classes of pauper by character and conduct had seldom been applied to elderly inmates in the past. Workhouse rules were now relaxed for the deserving aged: they were to have special rights to receive visitors, to leave the workhouse during the day and to attend their own church on Sundays. Their dress and dietary, however, were to remain the same as those of other aged inmates. In a second circular, issued in 1900, it was suggested that the removal of children from workhouses would create sufficient room to put this new policy into practice without the need to erect new buildings.[35]

In London, the only new workhouse to be built specifically for the elderly was erected in 1897–1900, at Ladywell, for St Olave's Union.[36] It was designed by the hospital architects Newman & Newman, and could house a total of 812 aged and infirm poor. As usual, the ward blocks were arranged formally, to either side of a covered way, flanking an administration block. Each 'pavilion' was attached to the covered way by a short stem, and followed one of three different designs. Four blocks of 'type A' accommodated the bedridden or chronic infirm; six of 'type B' and two of 'type C' housed the healthy infirm. Not surprisingly, accommodation for the bedridden at Ladywell closely resembled that in contemporary hospital wards. The Ladywell wards held 22 beds, arranged in pairs between opposing windows, and were served by corner sanitary towers framing small verandas (Fig 144). Rooms at the inner end of each main ward included a 6 bed ward, a day-room and an attendant's room with an inspection window overlooking the wards. Blocks of 'type B' and 'type C', for healthy inmates, had smaller dormitories, larger day-rooms and integral sanitary

Figure 144
St Olave's Union Workhouse for the Aged at Ladywell (1897–1900), around 1930. The inmates are playing bowls. In the background is an old men's 'type A' ward block, with a 'type B' block on the far right.
[London Metropolitan Archives 20.61 LAD B7579]

SEPARATE-BLOCK WORKHOUSES, 1870–1914

*Figure 145
This asymmetrical building was erected for the aged and infirm inmates of Reading Union Workhouse in 1909–11, to designs by W Roland Howell. The men's wing was longer than the women's wing, reflecting the proportion of male to female inmates, and a flat roof was provided for the open-air treatment of phthisis.
[BB96/8654]*

*Figure 146
Aged married couples lived in this small 'bungalow' block at Steyning Union Workhouse. It later accommodated maids.
[BB96/2810]*

facilities instead of towers. The 'type C' blocks appear to have been reserved for the more deserving class: the dormitories held 5 rather than 10 or 12 beds, and verandas ran along one side of each building.

West Derby was the only union outside London to erect a separate workhouse for the chronic infirm. That was built at Alder Hey between 1911 and 1915, again on the separate-block system. However, the buildings opened in 1914 as a children's hospital, and were never used for their intended purpose.

Accommodation recently vacated by children was not always available for the aged and infirm, and so specially designed buildings were added to several workhouses at the turn of the century. These incorporated only some of the characteristics of poor-law infirmaries. The windows, for example, were usually ordinary double-hung sashes, without hoppers. Sometimes, as at St Marylebone Workhouse (*see* Figure 130), which included rooms for imbeciles and lunatics, these blocks had mixed functions. A building erected at Reading Union Workhouse in 1909–11 (Fig 145), chiefly for the aged and infirm, also accommodated convalescents and had flat roofs with shelters for the treatment of inmates with incipient phthisis (pulmonary tuberculosis).

Throughout the 1880s and 1890s the Local Government Board issued reminders to unions that aged married couples, those over 60, had a right to be housed together in the workhouse. While some unions insisted that old couples preferred to be split up, a few responded positively by providing cubicles in the main building or erecting detached blocks of 'cottages'. These cottages were usually one storey high and catered for only a few deserving couples. A building designed for four couples at Hastings Union Workhouse in 1891 had a steep, hipped roof, a timber-framed gable, a bay window and verandas.[37] Inside, four bedrooms were arranged around a central day-room; there was a shared toilet annexe to the rear. The equivalent block built at Steyning Union Workhouse around 1900 had a similarly picturesque appearance (Fig 146). In some cases, however, buildings for aged couples departed from the 'cottage' ideal. That erected at Sheffield Union Workhouse in 1897 included a two-storeyed caretaker's house flanked by single-storeyed wings, each containing four rooms for couples. At Ladywell, a two-storeyed building housed six couples on each floor. The couples had their own bedsitting rooms but shared a general day-room and sanitary facilities.

Although only two workhouses are known to have been built especially for the aged and infirm, several were created by a simple process of moving other categories of inmate out of a mixed workhouse. That was achieved by the City of London Union in 1870, when the former West London Union Workhouse was taken over for the aged and infirm, and at Lambeth in 1887, when the able-bodied were moved to a new workhouse on Princes Road.

The Able-Bodied in the Workhouse, 1870–1914

Throughout the last quarter of the 19th century, efforts to increase the comfort of the deserving elderly poor in the workhouse were counterbalanced by attempts to impose a stricter and more unpleasant regime on able-bodied 'loafers', generally defined as those who were able, but unwilling, to earn their own living outside the workhouse. Since the 1840s, poor-law authorities in urban and manufacturing districts had found it difficult to operate a deterrent regime for the able-bodied in times of stress. In practice, it had been impossible to reserve sufficient space in the general mixed workhouse for periods of mass unemployment. When workhouses were full, many authorities set task work for temporarily unemployed men, as a condition of receiving outdoor relief, usually by opening labour yards (Fig 147) at the workhouse or elsewhere. The work was generally stone-breaking, wood-chopping, corn-grinding or oakum-picking, all of which were carried out in simple sheds. The quantity of work varied from union to union, as did the required hours, but generally such task work was restricted to men with dependants – single men would have been offered a place in the workhouse, whenever possible.

Labour yards had even less deterrent value than workhouses, and after 1870 the Local Government Board adopted tougher strategies. In particular, the ban on outdoor relief to certain categories of the able-bodied poor was extended to include even widows with one child, and relieving officers were encouraged to treat all paupers, whether in receipt of indoor or outdoor relief, according to their character. However, such policies had limited impact, and the cost of all poor relief continued to spiral upwards. More successful were a number of experimental able-bodied test workhouses, the first of which was set up by Poplar Union as an indirect consequence of the Metropolitan Poor Act of 1867.

In 1868, while the pavilion-plan infirmary of the Poplar and Stepney Sick Asylum was being erected in Bow for the sick and the aged (*see* page 166), Poplar guardians embarked upon a rebuilding of their early 19th-century workhouse premises, exclusively for the able-bodied.[38] Plans were drawn up by John Morris &

Figure 147
In response to the exceptional distress experienced in 1867–8, Bethnal Green Employment and Relief Association opened this Stone-Breaking Yard underneath three vacant railway arches. It offered an alternative to poor relief, providing employment in return for a paltry wage. Workhouse labour yards would have been similar.
[From Illustrated London News, *15 February 1868, 156, by permission of the Syndics of Cambridge University Library]*

Figure 148
This building at Poplar Union Workhouse was part of the extensions of 1869–72 by John Morris & Son. The wards were unusually large, having 40 beds apiece. The institution, which had occupied the same site on Poplar High Street since 1757, was extensively bombed during the Second World War, and later demolished.
[Plans redrawn from London Metropolitan Archives PoBG 283]

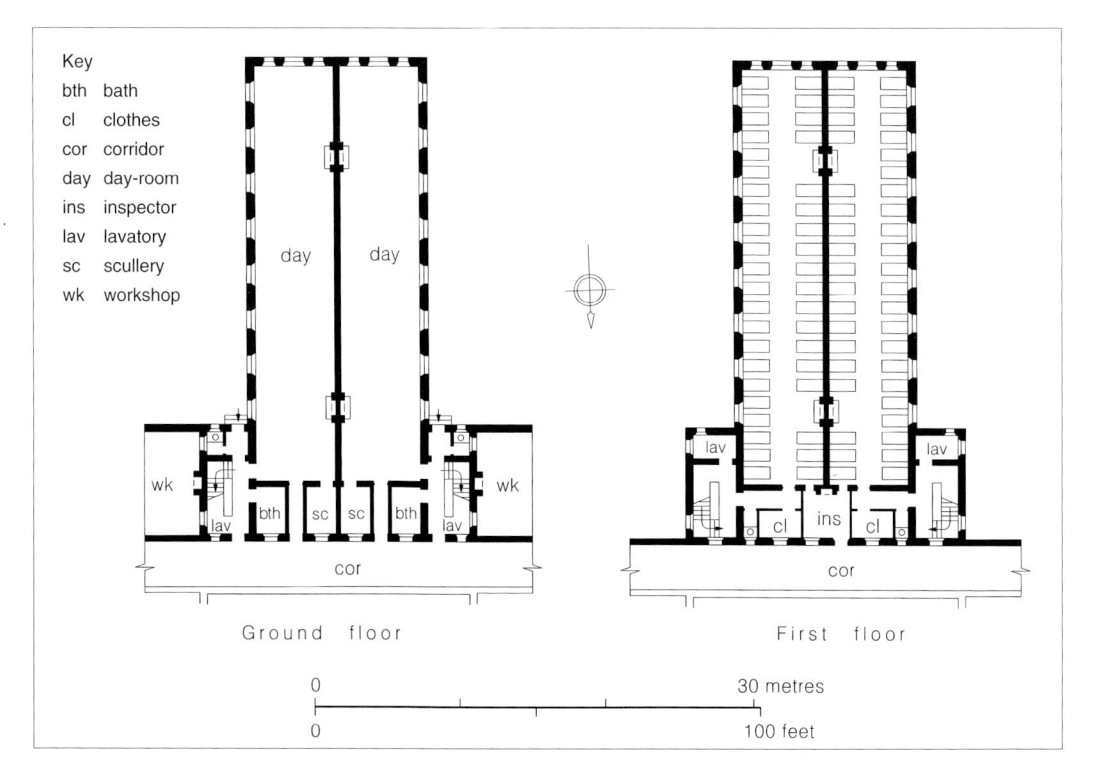

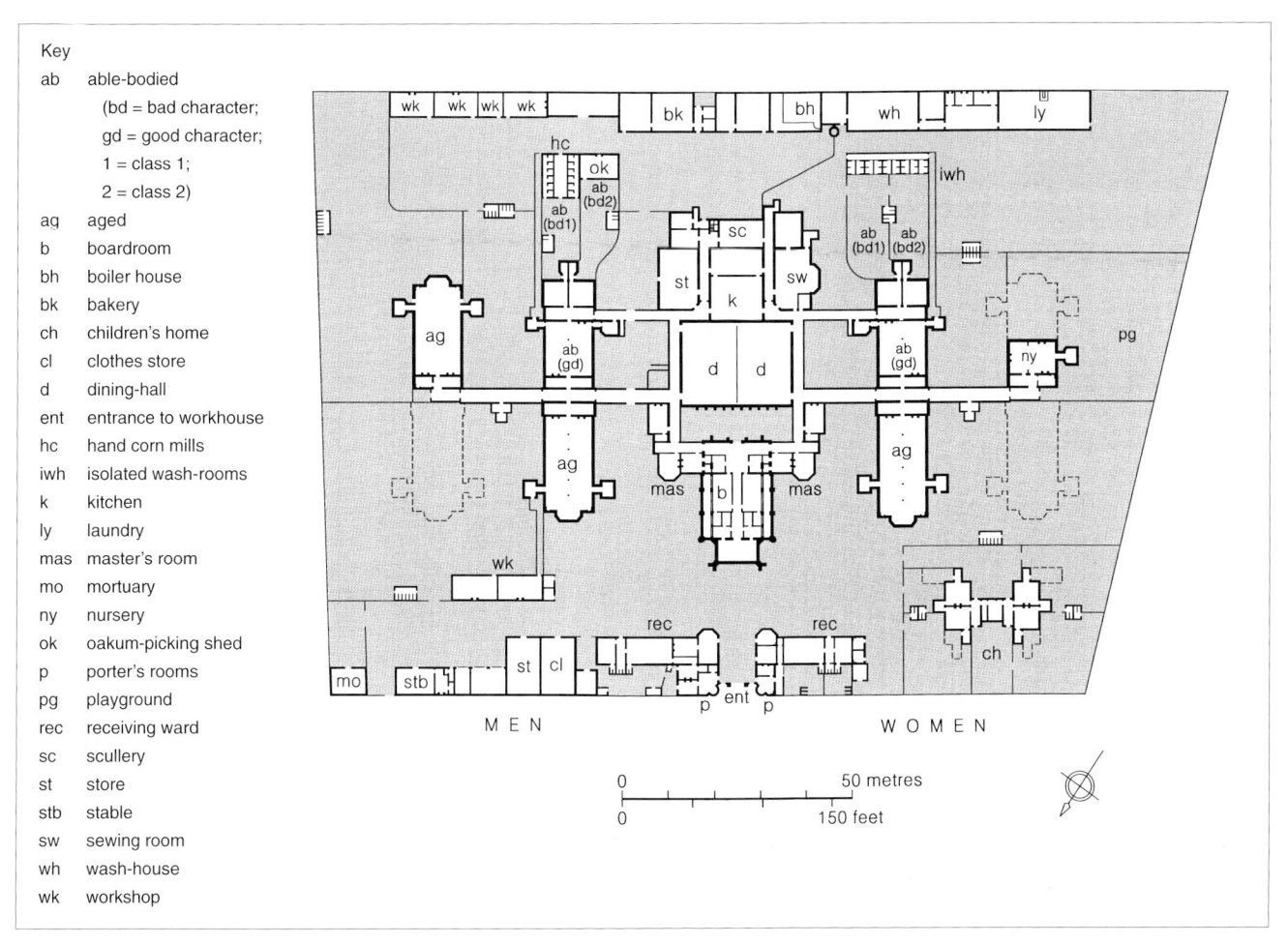

Key	
ab	able-bodied
	(bd = bad character;
	gd = good character;
	1 = class 1;
	2 = class 2)
ag	aged
b	boardroom
bh	boiler house
bk	bakery
ch	children's home
cl	clothes store
d	dining-hall
ent	entrance to workhouse
hc	hand corn mills
iwh	isolated wash-rooms
k	kitchen
ly	laundry
mas	master's room
mo	mortuary
ny	nursery
ok	oakum-picking shed
p	porter's rooms
pg	playground
rec	receiving ward
sc	scullery
st	store
stb	stable
sw	sewing room
wh	wash-house
wk	workshop

Son, and the austere new buildings were erected between 1869 and 1872. Until pressure of space put an end to the system in 1882, the workhouse accepted able-bodied paupers from other London unions and operated a harsh, deterrent regime sometimes referred to as the 'Poplar experiment'.

On the central axis of the Poplar institution were the administrative offices, kitchen, two dining-halls and a chapel. To either side of the dining-halls were double-width 'pavilions', with spine walls rather than colonnades or partitions (Fig 148). Abutting the main corridors were workshops. The stoneyard included no less than 120 individual bunks, or stalls.[39] If an inmate refused to work, he or she was either brought before the magistrates and convicted, or locked in the refractory cell on a diet of bread and water.

The very fact that it was never full demonstrates that the Poplar experiment was a success. However, when the Poplar guardians required additional accommodation for aged and infirm paupers in 1882, the empty rooms in the workhouse caught their eye, and the experiment was stopped. Sidney and Beatrice Webb plausibly blamed the failure of the experiment on the fact that it was administered by an authority with responsibility not just for one but for several different classes of pauper.[40]

Most Metropolitan workhouses erected after 1870 included a stricter test element than their forerunners. Aldwinckle's new pavilion-plan workhouses for St Mary, Lambeth (Renfrew Road, 1871–4) and Wandsworth and Clapham (Garratt Lane, 1883–6) both included buildings in which a labour test could be implemented for the able-bodied (*see* Figure 124; Figs 149 and 150).[41] Both had separate divisions for inmates of 'good' and 'bad' character, and instituted strict discipline for the able-bodied. Whereas those of 'good' character were allowed to work together in open-plan workshops, those of 'bad' character were made to complete a certain quota of work each day in isolation. At Wandsworth and Clapham a hand corn-mill with individual stalls was provided for men classed 'able-bodied, bad, 1' and an oakum-picking shed for those labelled 'able-bodied, bad, 2'. Female inmates still did the laundry, but here 'able-bodied women, bad, 1 and 2' worked in a building divided into a series of isolated washrooms with an inspection corridor along one side.[42]

Figure 149
This ground-floor plan of Wandsworth and Clapham Union Workhouse, Garratt Lane (1883–6), based on the original plan by T W Aldwinckle, shows the complex arrangement of yards and workshops for different classes of inmate. Intended future extensions are shown with dotted lines.
[Based on The Building News, *26 February 1886, 356*]

The Workhouse

*Figure 150
The interior of the wood-chopping shed at Wandsworth and Clapham Union Workhouse, Garratt Lane, photographed earlier this century.
[London Metropolitan Archives 20.61 WAN B1007]*

Greenwich Union intended to implement a similarly rigorous workhouse test at its new Grove Park institution (*see* Figure 127c). Workshops were provided for carpenters, tailors, bricklayers, painters and shoemakers, and labour shops were built for oakum-picking, sawing and wood-chopping. A hand corn-mill comprised ten cubicles provided with cranks, and opening off it was a labour-master's office. A smaller workshop was built for aged men. As at Poplar, a long open shed was divided into stalls, so that stone-breaking could be carried out in isolation.

It was difficult to enforce the workhouse test in an institution which housed aged and infirm paupers as well as the able-bodied, and some large authorities followed Poplar's example and set up a test workhouse exclusively for the able-bodied. Lambeth guardians erected a test workhouse on the old Princes Road site in 1887–8, leaving only the aged and infirm on Renfrew Road.[43] The buildings, designed by Thomas Aldwinckle, were of the 'plainest possible character' and could house 200 men and 150 women. As before, those of good character were permitted to work together while the 'bad' had to work in isolation.

A few test workhouses were set up outside London. In 1881, Birmingham erected a building, designed by W H Ward, to accommodate 100 men, with a courtyard surrounded by stone-breaking and wood-chopping cubicles, corn-grinding sheds, and tailors' and shoemakers' workshops.[44] The complex included a laundry in which men had to wash their own clothes. As at Poplar, this strategy was so successful that the empty rooms were eventually requisitioned for another class of inmate, and in 1889 the scheme was abandoned.

A few other test workhouses are worth noting. In 1889–90, West Derby erected an extensive pavilion-plan workhouse on Belmont Road for able-bodied paupers and boys on remand. Manchester rebuilt its New Bridge Street Workhouse for the able-bodied around 1880, but in 1897 joined forces with Chorlton Union and converted a mill at Ancoates into casual wards and a test workhouse. When that burned down a few years later a new test workhouse was built. One of the last test workhouses was erected by Bradford Union, at Daisy Hill, in 1910–12. The architecture of all of these institutions, like that of Lambeth, was of the 'plainest possible character'.

Ironically, while many unions struggled to find suitable work for the able-bodied to perform in test workhouses and labour yards after 1870, workhouse tasks traditionally assigned to the able-bodied were becoming increasingly mechanised. Steam laundry machinery, pumps and sawing-machines were replacing manual labour in the laundry, boiler-house and maintenance workshops. New technology was introduced because a steady supply of able-bodied pauper labour could not be guaranteed. Indeed, in many workhouses, there were no longer enough able-bodied women to perform basic domestic chores, and servants had to be recruited from outside.

In the 1890s, with the socialists and future Labour party politicians Will Crooks and George Lansbury on the board, Poplar began to adopt a kindlier attitude towards paupers of all classes. At the same time the publication of Charles Booth's *Life and Labour of the People of London* (1902–4) promoted the argument that most poverty was involuntary. The benefits of stone-breaking and oakum-picking were questioned, and Poplar proposed to purchase a farm where men could be employed more profitably than in the labour yard and encouraged to become self-sufficient. At first the Local Government Board opposed the scheme, but in 1904 Poplar was permitted to set up a farm colony for 100 men near Laindon in Essex. In sharp contrast to Poplar's Training School, then being erected at Hutton (*see* Figure 196), little was expended on new buildings. Farm buildings already on the site were augmented by two second-hand iron buildings to be used as a dormitory and dining-hall. New buildings, including a laundry, a lavatory block and a superintendent's house, were of equally cheap construction.

Poplar Union's apparently extravagant policies, particularly its lavish distribution of outdoor relief in 1904–5 ('Poplarism'), led to an official inquiry at which the Laindon colony was denounced as a social and economic failure.[45] Nevertheless, farm colonies were established by some of the distress committees which were set up in the wake of the Unemployed Workmen Act of 1905,[46] for example those of West Ham, Manchester and the Central (Unemployed) Body for London.[47] Colonies seldom involved new building work and were, generally, short-lived; that at Laindon folded in 1912.

The Royal Commission of 1905–9 and the Liberal Welfare Reforms

At the beginning of the new century, confidence in the existing poor-law system, and particularly its treatment of the unemployed, had waned. In 1905, at a time of rising unemployment, the Conservative government appointed a Royal Commission to 'Investigate the Poor Laws and the Relief of Distress'. The twenty Commissioners carried out the most detailed poor-law inquiry since 1834, visiting 200 unions and 400 institutions, hearing 450 witnesses and reading 900 statements.[48] Its investigations took three years to complete, but failed to present unanimous findings. Four Commissioners, namely Beatrice Webb, George Lansbury, Francis Chandler and the Revd Russell Wakefield, broke away and published an alternative 'Minority' report in February 1909. That differed from the 'Majority' report in several respects.

Both the 'Majority' and 'Minority' reports proposed to disband boards of guardians, enlarge areas of administration, and replace the many surviving 'general mixed workhouses' with specialised institutions for different classes of pauper. They disagreed, however, about how that was to be achieved. The 'Majority' Report suggested that boards of guardians be replaced by Public Assistance Committees of county and borough councils, who would liaise with voluntary aid councils to provide relief for all classes of pauper. In addition, labour exchanges would be established under the Board of Trade, and agricultural, labour and detention colonies would be set up under the Home Office. The 'Minority' Report argued that different committees under the local authorities should assume responsibility for the non-able-bodied, but proposed that a new Ministry of Labour deal with the able-bodied. Unemployed men would be examined at reception centres and assigned to a suitable day-training depot or residential farm colony. 'Professional' vagrants would be sent to a detention colony of a reformatory nature. The essence of their disagreement was that the Majority wished to preserve the poor law intact while the Minority wished to fragment it, and in so doing to separate the able-bodied from the non-able-bodied for good.

The split in the Commission contributed to the maintenance of the *status quo*. Despite extensive lobbying for reform by supporters of both the Majority and Minority, the Local Government Board continued to promote the creation of specialised institutions within the existing administrative system. It encouraged the formation of joint, or district, committees to deal with the mentally deficient, epileptics, vagrants and cases of phthisis, but progress was extremely slow and little was achieved before 1914.

Meanwhile, the Liberal Government introduced several welfare reforms which slowly eroded the existing system. In 1908, before receiving the findings of the Royal Commission, it introduced the Old Age Pensions Act.[49] At first the Act applied only to those aged over 70, with an income of less than £31 10s a year, who had never been pauperised.[50] The removal of that last qualification in 1910 caused a marked reduction in the cost of outdoor relief but did little to reduce the number of elderly people living in workhouses, most of whom were incapable of caring for themselves at home.[51] The national network of labour exchanges, set up in 1909, and the National Insurance Bill of 1911,[52] operative by 1913, similarly had little immediate effect on workhouse populations. Despite that, the years immediately preceding the First World War were marked by relative prosperity and a general fall in the cost of poor relief.

Workhouse Alterations and Additions, 1870–1914

Much of the expenditure on poor-law buildings in the last quarter of the 19th century was accounted for by additions to existing establishments. Basic accommodation was enlarged by the erection of separate blocks, or pavilions, and improved in terms of safety and comfort by the addition of fire escapes and sanitary towers. Increased capacity necessitated the enlargement of service buildings, and numerous new chapels, dining-halls, kitchens, laundries, boiler houses and water towers were erected during this period. New residences for the master reflected his increased status and, at the turn of the century, many unions built large boardroom blocks, including committee rooms and other administrative offices.

After 1870, several existing institutions were rebuilt, remodelled or extended on the separate-block system. In 1880–3, J H Morton converted

THE WORKHOUSE

Figure 151
Todmorden in Yorkshire was the last English union to provide a workhouse. The building was erected on a corridor plan in 1877, and extended by detached pavilions in 1889–90. [BB92/9332]

Figure 152
In September 1862 fire devastated the children's dormitory of Liverpool Workhouse. Because no means of escape had been provided for the north end of the room all of its occupants – twenty-one children – died.
[From Illustrated London News, *20 September 1862, 304, by permission of the Syndics of Cambridge University Library]*

the 1839 workhouse of Hexham Union into a pavilion-plan building by replacing the central range with a new administration block. In 1889–90 a single pavilion was erected on each side of the main building of Todmorden Union Workhouse (Fig 151), one of several small corridor-plan workhouses which had been built in Yorkshire in the 1870s. The corridor-plan workhouses of Burnley and Aston were extended in a similar fashion.

Surviving drawings demonstrate that unions throughout the country were adding fire escapes to all types of poor-law accommodation during the early 1890s. Despite a number of fires in the 1850s and 1860s (Fig 152), *Points to be Attended to in the Construction of Workhouses* had merely requested that there be one fire escape in each workhouse. A Local Government Board circular of 1882 had urged guardians to take precautions and make proper arrangements for escape in the event of a fire. The catalyst for practical measures, however, was a series of conflagrations during the 1880s and early 1890s: Guiltcross Union Workhouse was damaged in 1883, Erpingham in 1888, Chelmsford in 1886, Forest Gate School in 1890, Newcastle-under-Lyme in 1890 and South Molton in 1892. Several of these incidents involved fatalities, most tragically twenty-six boys aged under 12 who were suffocated during the New Year's fire at Forest Gate.[53] A circular issued to inspectors on 8 December 1891 urged the importance of leaving dormitory doors unlocked at night, conducting fire drills with voluntary workhouse fire brigades, maintaining telephonic communication with fire stations wherever possible and providing fire escapes.[54]

No particular type of fire escape was advocated by the Local Government Board but one poor-law inspector recommended an apparatus invented by a Mr Bailey, which comprised a tubular canvas chute attached to two iron arms fixed to the floor of an upper room, beneath a window.[55] This was apparently adopted by several schools, including Lambeth School, Norwood, but more conventional fire escape stairs of simple iron construction were generally favoured. Alternatively, modern workhouses and infirmaries on the separate-block principle could be equipped with escape bridges. These appeared in the late 1870s, for example at Camberwell's Gordon Road Workhouse of 1878 (*see* Figure 126). Escape bridges connecting Henry Saxon Snell's new infirmary blocks at the Fulham Road workhouse of St George's Union doubled as verandas in fine weather and included sunrooms (Fig 153).[56] Most new workhouses had covered ways with flat roofs which served as escape routes, in addition to escape stairs.

Improved sanitation also had an effect on the appearance of accommodation blocks. Sanitary towers or annexes became increasingly common additions to blocks for healthy inmates, generally hidden away on end or rear elevations. These were merely one factor in the general improvement of workhouse sanitation which was achieved at this time. Large numbers of surviving workhouse plans between 1870 and 1900 show new drainage systems, generally connecting the institution to main drains and public water supplies.

Although the notion of surveillance from a central vantage point had long since been abandoned, workhouse masters continued to live in the centre of their institutions for reasons of economy and convenience. At new workhouses, such as Steyning and Hexham, substantial master's houses still formed part of the main building, but the master's quarters in older workhouses often seemed inadequate by the turn of the century, and detached residences were provided. The master's house built at Manchester Union Workhouse, Crumpsall (Fig 154), in 1905 stood in its own grounds, to one side of the main workhouse building.[57] It clearly illustrates the enhanced status of the workhouse master, and the relaxation of his role in the surveillance of inmates.

A large number of unions erected new boardrooms in the 1890s and early 1900s. It was not simply that old boardrooms had become too small; they were insufficiently grand. The refurbished boardroom of North Bierley Union Workhouse (Fig 155) resembled a court room or council chamber. The guardians' benches were arranged in the shape of a horseshoe, facing the chairman's dais, which was framed by a decorative arch. The elaborate plaster ceiling was coved, and contained a cupola filled with stained glass. All of the other fixtures and fittings were of high quality. North Bierley was not unique: throughout the country large sums were spent on boardrooms which were meant to be impressive both inside and out. In such rooms, the gulf between the well-heeled middle-class guardians and the paupers who appeared before them must have seemed wider than ever. Some boards sought to place an even greater distance between themselves and indoor

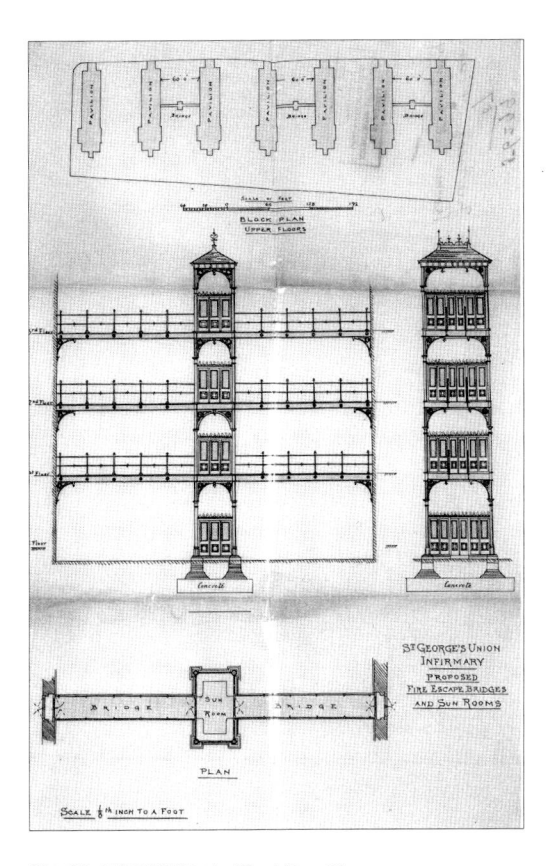

Figure 153 (left)
Unusually, the fire-escape bridges at the infirmary (1887) of St George's Union Workhouse, Fulham Road, Chelsea, incorporated sunrooms.
[Public Record Office MH14/30]

Figure 154 (below)
The master's house at Manchester Union Workhouse, designed in 1905 by A J Murgatroyd, was a large detached dwelling some distance from the main building.
[BB96/2187]

paupers by erecting union offices (Fig 156), including the boardroom, on a separate site from the workhouse.

Points to be Attended to in the Construction of Workhouses required guardians to provide a central dining-hall for all inmates able to leave their wards. The design of dining-halls hardly changed over the years: almost invariably they were single-storeyed rectangular buildings, lit on both sides by large windows and open to the rafters. Like the new dining-hall erected at Ashton-under-Lyne in 1878 (Fig 157), they often resembled chapels. Dining-halls continued to occupy a central position, to the rear of the main building, close to the kitchen. Kitchen extensions were seldom of high architectural quality and were usually erected piecemeal, creating a jumble of interconnected, single-storeyed blocks to the rear of the main building.

The Local Government Board also specified that the general wash-house and laundry should occupy a detached, single-storeyed building with an open roof carrying a louvred ridge ventilator.[58] These basic design precepts scarcely varied over the years, although steam-driven machinery (Figs 158 and 159) eventually

Figure 155
The boardroom of North Bierley Union Workhouse was refurbished c 1900. This view looks towards the chairman's table.
[BB90/9696]

replaced wash-tubs and ironing tables. A boiler house with a tall chimney, and sometimes a water tower, were located close to the laundry. Smaller wash-houses were usually provided for infectious diseases blocks.

Fire prevention measures did not just involve escape stairs and bridges. Water towers were sometimes erected specifically for the purpose of fire prevention rather than simply to provide the site with a regular water supply. Designs of 1891 for a water tower at Alverstoke are captioned 'for prevention of fire'.[59] Awareness of the dangers of fire led to the construction of 'fireman's shops', for example those which stored fire-extinguishing equipment at Atcham and Stoke-upon-Trent.[60]

Several workhouse chapels were built after 1870, but it was still unusual for a new institution to include a detached chapel. Chapels continued to be presented by donors, as at Sturminster Newton, or funded by private subscription, as at Gressenhall (1868) and Thingoe (1898), rather than being paid for out of the poor rates.

The need for a new chapel was felt at Maidstone around 1860, but it was not until 1880 that the guardians appointed a committee to establish a chapel fund. The scheme attracted

*Figure 156
Wandsworth and Clapham Union Offices on East Hill, Wandsworth, were designed by C A Sharp and built in 1899.
[From* The Building News, *16 June 1899, np, by permission of the Syndics of Cambridge University Library]*

*Figure 157
This modest Gothic design was produced for a new dining-hall at Ashton-under-Lyne Union Workhouse in 1878.
[Public Record Office MH14/2]*

THE WORKHOUSE

*Figure 158
Macalpine's steam-powered washing-machine and Manlove's dash-wheel and hydro-extractor were adopted by the workhouses of St Pancras and Nottingham in the late 1850s. The same machinery had been used in the military hospital at Scutari during the Crimean War.
[From* Illustrated London News, *3 October 1857, 341, by permission of the Syndics of Cambridge University Library]*

*Figure 159
The interior of Hackney Union Workhouse laundry was photographed in 1938. This long building was erected between 1914 and 1916 to serve both the workhouse and the infirmary, and was demolished in the early 1990s.
[London Metropolitan Archives B6604]*

donations amounting to £1,700 and the building, designed by Henry Cheers of Bagshot, was erected in 1883–4 (Fig 160). Several of its fittings, including the font, credence table, chancel screen and altar cloth, were gifts from individuals, mostly local ladies. The reasons presented for building this chapel reveal how the general expectations of a place of worship had altered since 1830:

> *The room in which Divine service was held was over the entrance to the workhouse, and was low-pitched and otherwise unsuited for this sacred purpose, besides lacking in the decorum which is an eminent and gratifying feature of all the churches rising and being restored throughout the land.*[61]

Attitudes towards the poor had also changed. At the dedication service, the Archbishop of Canterbury preached about poverty:

> *the chapel in which they now were was a message to the poor present, whether it was God's will that they should be poor in order that they might be rich hereafter, or whether it was their own fault that they were poor – a message of God sent to do them good, sent straight from Him through the loving hearts of those who had put their money together to build so beautiful a House of Prayer for them.*[62]

Figure 160 (above) The Gothic-style chapel of Maidstone Union Workhouse (1883–4) is now all that survives of that institution. [BB96/5413]

Figure 161 (left) The chapel of Whitchurch Union Workhouse in Shropshire was built in 1881. It could seat 150 and cost £639 to build. [BB93/1310]

Figure 162
This shows the interior of Ninian Comper's chapel at Oundle Union Workhouse in Northamptonshire before it was converted into a house. The building was erected in 1896.
[BB98/6502]

Gothic was firmly established as the style for ecclesiastical buildings in Victorian England by the 1870s, and few workhouse chapels strayed from that norm. One of the first to adopt a vernacular Arts & Crafts style was the half-timbered chapel of Whitchurch Union in Shropshire (Fig 161), built in 1881.

One of the finest workhouse chapels was designed by Ninian Comper for Oundle Union Workhouse (Fig 162). This tall, narrow stone building had a simple rectangular plan. Pilaster buttresses rose to about two-thirds of the height of each side wall, while the upper third contained twinned lancets. Panelling masked the lower walls of the interior, and a medieval-style screen divided the four western bays from the chancel. A number of more modest chapels were built in the early 20th century, but few date from after 1918.

Towards the turn of the century some urban authorities, generally those in areas with large numbers of Irish immigrants, even provided permanent chapels for Catholics. There is mention of a Roman Catholic chapel at Swinton School, Manchester in 1880. Ladywell Workhouse had two chapels, one for the Established Church accommodating 200 and the other for Catholics seating 150. Two chapels were added to St Pancras Workhouse in 1899, the larger for Anglicans and the smaller for Catholics. Separate chapels do not seem to have been provided for Nonconformists, although in some rural unions these would have formed the majority of workhouse inmates.

8
Poor-Law Buildings for Children

The first workhouses, set up in the 17th century, provided their young residents with training in a manual skill, often one connected with the textile trade, which would help them to maintain their independence through adult life. Despite a secondary profit-making motive, these formative institutions can be counted amongst the earliest English industrial schools. But the schooling and training of pauper children was a lower priority in later workhouses of the 'general mixed' variety. Very often children were placed in the charge of an unsuitable adult pauper, and in many areas it was difficult to identify relevant industrial training, or find the resources and will-power to put it into effect.

In the middle of the 19th century the idea of the industrial school, or workhouse for children, was revived. Several urban poor-law authorities banded together to erect impressive 'barrack' schools in which hundreds of children could be accommodated, educated and trained. These stood in semi-rural positions, often with agricultural land and farm buildings attached. By the late 1870s, however, it was clear that children in industrial schools were prone to behavioural and health problems, and the European cottage-home system was hailed as a superior alternative. Cottage homes, either grouped in twos and threes on the edge of a workhouse site or forming separate 'villages', permitted children to be housed in an environment which was considered more natural than workhouse or barrack schools, but which was still overwhelmingly institutional.

The last quarter of the 19th century was marked by a profound change in the schooling of children who still lived in workhouses. In 1870 they were likely to receive their education in a school on the workhouse site, but by 1900 the vast majority left the workhouse every day to attend a local elementary school. By the 1920s many had left the workhouse to live in scattered homes, usually houses in residential areas where children could use local amenities such as schools, parks and swimming-baths. The scattered homes system could be set up simply by purchasing a few suitable terraced or semi-detached houses and installing a number of children under the care of a house-father and house-mother in each one.

A wide variety of children's homes and schools was inherited by local authorities in 1930. The few industrial schools which had survived until then soon closed, but cottage-home villages and scattered homes remained operational for decades. Often, they became specialist homes for children taken into care by local authorities, those on remand, or with learning difficulties. Many homes and schools are still owned by local authorities, but fulfil a variety of new functions. Others, including most cottage-home villages, have been successfully converted into housing.

The Old Poor Law: Pauper Children in London

The plight of pauper children, whether orphaned, abandoned, disabled or merely the unfortunate offspring of criminals or adult paupers, was always more acute in London than in the provinces. The first public institution to cater specifically for children was Christ's Hospital, which opened in 1552 and could accommodate 380 orphans over 4 years of age. From the 1560s it was supplemented by Bridewell, which developed into a reformatory and industrial school for children as well as providing a house of correction for vagrants, idlers and prostitutes.

Such specialist institutions for children were rare in London before the 18th century, although some 17th-century workhouses had accommodated children while adults either attended daily or worked at home. In general, throughout the 17th and 18th centuries, London parishes usually fostered out babies and infants to 'nurses' while older children received industrial training and rudimentary education in mixed parish workhouses. The treatment of children in Bishopsgate Workhouse in the early 18th century was probably typical: they were employed in spinning, sewing and knitting, but were also taught reading, writing and arithmetic.[1] Many workhouse children attended charity schools on a daily basis, instead of receiving lessons in the workhouse.

In the middle of the 18th century, increased awareness of the high mortality rate amongst pauper children in London, particularly infants in the care of parish 'nurses', prompted attempts to improve their condition.[2] In 1741, Captain Thomas Coram established the Foundling Hospital by voluntary subscription, and in 1762 an Act 'for keeping poor children alive' required metropolitan parishes to maintain proper records of all children admitted into their workhouses.[3] Five years later, Jonas Hanway, a governor of the Foundling Hospital, steered legislation through Parliament stipulating that all pauper infants and children under 6 years of age from metropolitan parishes were to be sent to school in the countryside, not less than 3 miles from any part of the cities of London and Westminster.[4] After reaching the age of 7, children were to be apprenticed to private employers. In some cases this could be achieved by offering the potential master a premium of £10; in other cases only by threatening him with a £10 fine.[5] Some older children remained in the care of the parish. In 1781, for example, St James, Westminster, set up a boarding-school near St James's Square, in which several hundred children were educated and trained.[6]

After 1767, a few metropolitan parishes chose to operate their own out-of-town schools for young children. Lambeth, for example, rebuilt Norwood House of Industry in 1809 and used it as a residence for the very old as well as the very young. Metropolitan schools, however, were generally run by private contractors for a profit and admitted children from several parishes. By 1834, the largest were undoubtedly Mr Aubin's establishment at Weston Hill, Norwood, which opened in 1821, and Mr Drouet's at Mount House, Tooting.[7] Little is known about either institution but their inmates were described as follows in 1839:

> Their physical conformation and physiognomy betray that they have inherited from their parents physical and moral constitutions requiring the most vigorous and careful training to render them useful members of society . . . Visitors invariably remark the prevalence of a singular formation of their heads; that the boys have almost universally coarse features, and that the girls are almost all plain.[8]

The Old Poor Law: Pauper Children Outside London

Outside London, a few towns established children's 'hospitals' on the model of Christ's Hospital and Bridewell in the late 16th and 17th centuries. Rare examples of institutions set up exclusively for children in the late 17th and 18th centuries included Bristol's 'new workhouse' of 1696 – where girls were taught spinning until they joined other paupers in the 'Mint Workhouse' in 1709 – and the Asylum for the Infant Poor which opened in Summer Lane, Birmingham, in 1797.[9]

It was more usual for children to share a 'hospital' or 'workhouse' with other classes of pauper. Sir Frederick Eden's description of English workhouses in 1796-7 makes it clear that children often accounted for well over half the total number of inmates.[10] They divided their time between work, in the guise of industrial training, and basic schooling. In many cases, for example in the workhouses of Southwell parish and Thurgarton Hundred Incorporation, the workhouse school was available to the children of poor labourers as well as inmates of the house (see pages 36–40).

Children in the Workhouse, 1834–1914

The situation of pauper children was not immediately altered by the Poor Law Amendment Act of 1834. Retrospectively, Nassau Senior, one of the original Poor Law Commissioners, claimed that the *Poor Law Report* had recommended:

> that in every Union there should be a separate school; we said that the children who went to the workhouse were hardened if they were already vicious, and became contaminated if they were innocent. We recommended that in every Union there should be a building for the children . . . We never contemplated having the children under the same roof with the adults.[11]

But a careful reading of the *Report* reveals that no special case was presented for children. It suggested that unions run separate workhouses for all the different classes of pauper, not just children, arguing that separation would allow each class to be treated according to its particular needs. For children, one benefit of being housed separately from adults might be a 'cheaper and more wholesome' diet.[12] The idea of separate children's establishments was not pursued by the newly created Poor Law Commission, and the 'general mixed workhouse' became the rule during the great workhouse building boom of the late 1830s.

Although most of the new workhouses provided ground-floor schoolrooms for boys and girls, and appointed a schoolmaster and/or a schoolmistress to look after them, the first union schools were set up in a most half-hearted manner. As guardians were not permitted to pay for the education of pauper children on outdoor relief before 1855, the fear that workhouse children would receive a better education than other poor children affected the attitude of many boards. In 1836, the Bedford guardians expressed the extraordinary wish that their charges learn reading, but not writing, 'as they were desirous of avoiding greater advantages to the inmates of the workhouse than to the poor children out of it'.[13] The standard of teaching in many workhouse schools was appalling, even by the standards of the time. Some of the worst cases were exposed in 1842, by an investigation into those parishes which had continued to operate independently under local acts.[14] At Salisbury, the pauper schoolmaster drank to excess, while the schoolmistress could not write; at Southampton, the aged schoolmaster was deaf.[15] Only after grants in aid of salaries were introduced in 1846 were professional teachers habitually employed by guardians. Even then it was difficult to attract and retain a high calibre of teacher, and from 1850 a pupil-teacher system was widely adopted.

Vocational training was given a higher priority than schooling in the workhouse: it would prepare children for situations or trades in the outside world, arming them with the means to rise above pauperism and unburden the rates. Kempthorne's plans provided a workroom in the girls' yard and a workroom, a bakehouse and a flour and mill-room in the boys'. It soon became common for girls to be supplied with their own wash-house and laundry, so that they could learn domestic duties. Boys' work usually included shoemaking and tailoring, crafts which were never undertaken on a commercial basis, but contributed towards the needs of the house.

In rural areas, unions were encouraged to put workhouse boys to work on the land and train girls as dairymaids. In 1852, Assistant Commissioner Walsham reported that cows had been acquired and a dairy added to several workhouses in East Anglia, including those at Guiltcross, Plomesgate and Saffron Walden.[16] By the 1850s several unions throughout the country had purchased land specifically for the agricultural training of boys.[17]

Sampson Kempthorne, in his model workhouse plans, had located children's schools and dormitories in the centre of the main workhouse building, and that was the arrangement initially adopted by most unions (*see* Appendix 3, Figures 2 and 7). In Scott & Moffatt's workhouses, and in most of the corridor-plan workhouses erected after 1840, children were placed at either extremity of the main accommodation ranges, in cross-wings. Throughout the 1830s and 1840s very few workhouses included a detached school. One of the first, that at Skirlaugh Union Workhouse (1838–9), was part of the original design by John & William Atkinson. It stood centrally, behind the main building, in the position often occupied by an infirmary.[18] It included girls' schoolrooms and bedrooms on one side and boys' on the other. The plan of the detached school erected at York Union Workhouse in 1848 was also symmetrical. Each wing included a schoolroom and a school-mistress's or schoolmaster's room, with a triangular bay projecting into the yards for supervisory purposes. There was a wash-house on the girls' side and a 'school of industry' – probably no more than simple workshops – on the boys'. In the late 1840s and 1850s, the growing tendency to erect detached schools on the workhouse site reflected a desire to sever all contact between children and adult paupers, but even in detached buildings children were often placed in the care of ill-selected paupers.

For the workhouse child, time set aside for play must have been a highlight in the monotonous round of daily existence. On several early workhouse plans, girls' and boys' yards are identified as 'playgrounds', and, from the 1840s, open, arcaded play-sheds formed an integral and potentially decorative element of several new workhouses, for example Ashbourne Union Workhouse (1846–7) in Derbyshire. At William Donthorn's late workhouses of Aylsham (1848–9) and Erpingham (1848–51), single-storeyed ranges, including open play-sheds and workrooms for children, stretched beyond the main building.[19] J F Clarke adopted similar arrangements for Risbridge Union Workhouse (1855–6) in Suffolk. One of the latest examples of a main workhouse building with open play-sheds was Maldon Union Workhouse (1872–3) in Essex, designed by F Peck. Like every other example cited, the sheds were bricked-up in later years and converted to other uses.

One authority which attempted to provide suitable accommodation for children was the parish of Stoke-upon-Trent. Henry Ward, the Borough Surveyor of Stafford, designed a school (Fig 163) which was erected on the workhouse site in 1842. It was a long, two-storeyed building with Italianate details and, as usual, one wing was devoted to boys, the other to girls. For some years it eased the severe overcrowding which the children had suffered in their previous dormitories

*Figure 163
The enlargement of Stoke-upon-Trent (Parish) Workhouse in 1842 involved the addition of several detached buildings, including this school. The architect was Henry Ward.
[BB93/27795]*

and schoolrooms, but did not prevent them from making contact with able-bodied inmates. In 1850, the Poor Law Inspector declared it:

> a hopeless task to endeavour to raise [children] from a state of pauperism, dependence and crime to one of honest independence and correct moral conduct in the present [workhouse], as the children were continually in contact with the adult inmates, who were generally of depraved habits.[20]

By 1866 the problem of overcrowding had recurred at Stoke-upon-Trent and the guardians erected a new, Elizabethan-style school (Figs 164 and 165), designed by the local architect Charles Lynam, for 250 children. Its tall central tower and multi-gabled wings contrasted with the austerity of the earlier school, which was now adapted for infirm women. The bathrooms were in the basement, the teaching rooms on the ground floor and dormitories, separated by apartments for the teaching staff, above. A back wing contained a dining-room, kitchen, washhouse and laundry.

A number of other detached workhouse schools were built in the 1850s and early to mid-1860s, for example at Guildford (1856), Exeter (1860) and Portsea Island (1860), but few of these have survived. At the time, these buildings must have contrasted markedly with the typical workhouse schoolroom, described by Poor Law Inspector H E Bowyer in 1868. Bowyer declared that workhouse schools:

> cannot in general be compared, for roominess, ventilation, or cheerfulness, with the National Schools erected according to the plans sanctioned by the Committee of Council on Education. An ordinary workhouse school does not, in truth, produce on the mind of a visitor a very exhilarating impression. It generally opens on a yard enclosed by a high wall, with a circular swing in its centre for exercise during play hours. The room is usually about twenty feet long by ten broad, with a flat ceiling ten or eleven feet high, imperfectly ventilated by means of openings high up in the wall, or perforated zinc tubes traversing the room from wall to wall and opening outside. The windows are small and square, and if they should look upon an adult ward, they are darkened by whitewashing the panes . . . The floors are generally of brick or stone, but wooden flooring has supplanted the colder material in many instances.[21]

The architect's perspective view of Birmingham Workhouse (*see* Figure 104), built in 1850–2, shows a circular swing in the girl's yard, much like that described by Bowyer. In one nameless union, the board of guardians refused to erect a swing despite one of its more charitable members offering to bear the cost.[22] Sadly, the majority argued that exercise on a swing would expensively increase children's appetites and that their clothes and shoes would suffer from too much wear and tear.

An Act of 1862 enabled guardians to send certain classes of children, such as the refractory, the blind, the crippled and Roman Catholics, to certified schools.[23] Again from 1862, they could send workhouse children to the National Schools lauded by Inspector Bowyer, where the fee was usually 2*d* to 9*d* a week per child.[24] This solution had the appeal of cheapness, as it saved guardians from employing their own teachers and equipping their own schools. Under such a scheme, children continued to live in the workhouse but left the institution each weekday morning to attend school. Theoretically, this afforded them the opportunity to mix with non-pauper children but, in practice, they were often segregated in the classroom, or effectively set apart from their classmates by their distinctive workhouse dress. Back in the workhouse, their care was often entrusted to adult paupers.

Slowly but surely, an increased use of public elementary schools brought about the demise of the workhouse school. Only 30 unions used elementary schools in 1861, but that rose to 70 in 1868, 98 in 1874 and 419 in 1894. After 1870, education became compulsory in areas with adequate school places, and in 1880 school attendance became obligatory everywhere. The tendency for guardians to use local schools was boosted by the abolition of elementary-school fees in 1891. By 1898–9, 493 unions used public elementary schools, 28 used district schools, 38 used separate schools, 26 used schools belonging to other unions and only 63 unions wholly or partly educated their children in a workhouse school.[25] Despite the rush to use

Poor-Law Buildings for Children

*Figure 164
In 1866, when the earlier school could no longer meet the needs of Stoke-upon-Trent Workhouse, this larger Elizabethan-style building was erected to a design by C Lynam.
[BB93/27792]*

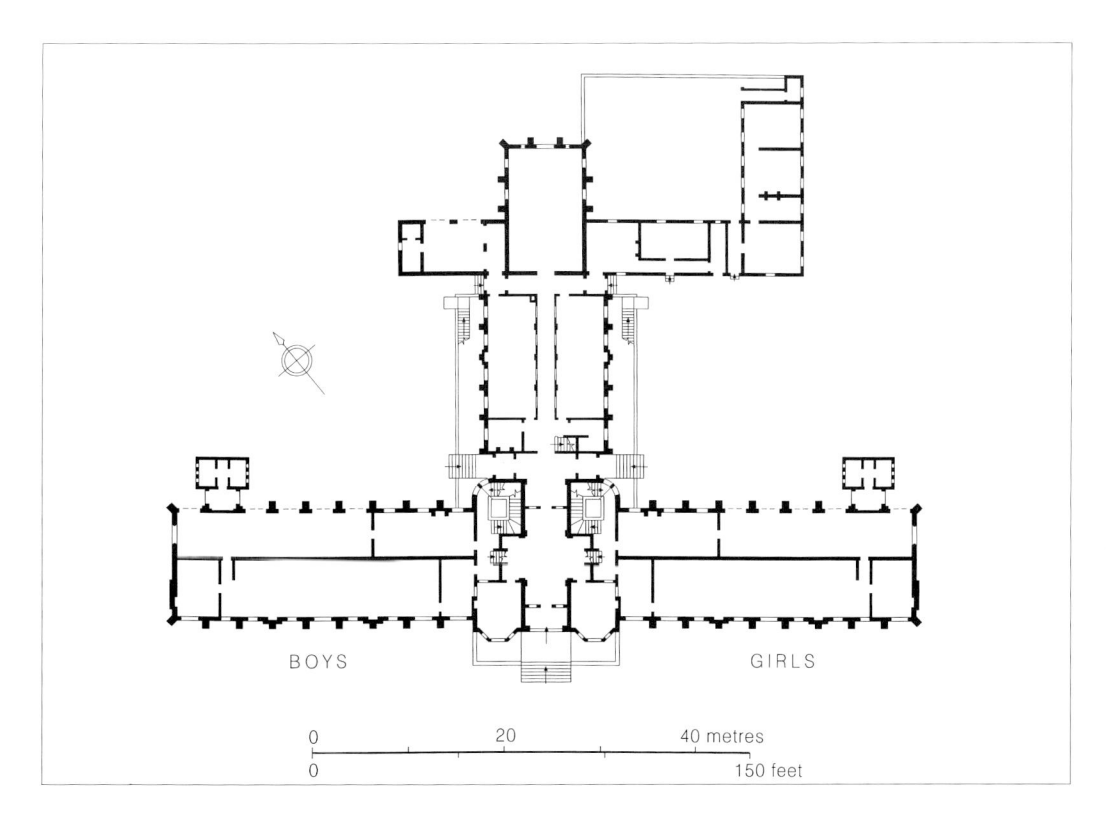

*Figure 165
The 1866 school at Stoke-upon-Trent Workhouse, shown in this ground-floor plan, included an infants' school as well as boys' and girls' schools.
[Based on Baker 1984, 21]*

public elementary schools, of the 52,207 children in receipt of indoor relief in 1898–9, no less than 25,401 still lived in workhouses or poor-law infirmaries.[26]

Perhaps surprisingly, in view of the growing tendency to use local schools, many new workhouse schools were built from the late 1860s to the mid-1880s. Those at Stockton-on-Tees (1868; Fig 166), Rochdale (1873–7; Fig 167) and Maidenhead (1878–9) were all plain buildings on a linear plan, closely resembling contemporary infirmaries but distinguishable by their smaller sash windows and more modest sanitary facilities.

From the late 1860s onwards some of the largest workhouse schools were designed on the separate-block system, comprising a central block flanked by detached pavilions. The school of the new Alderbury Union Workhouse (1877–9; Fig 168), designed by the Birmingham architect George B Nicholls, had small 'cloisters' for boys and girls between the schoolroom and accommodation blocks. J H Morton's school at Burton-on-Trent (1880–4; Fig 169) comprised two separate pavilions to either side of a central administration block.

New buildings erected for children on workhouse sites after 1890, for example at Hastings (1891) and Grimsby (1892–4), were sometimes casually referred to as schools but seldom included schoolrooms. The term 'school' probably lingered as boys and girls continued to receive some industrial training on the workhouse site. At the same time, the trend to remove children altogether from workhouse sites meant that many schools, some of which

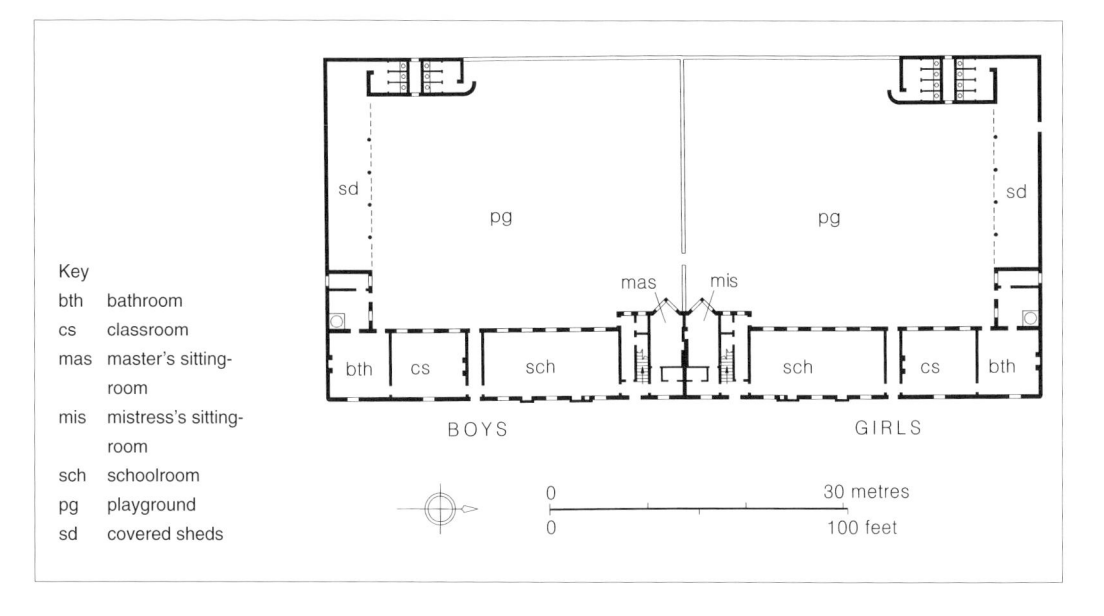

Figure 166
At Stockton Union Workhouse school (1868), the V-shaped windows in the centre enabled the schoolmaster and schoolmistress to supervise the boys' and girls' playgrounds respectively.
[Plan redrawn from Public Record Office MH14/34]

Figure 167
Rochdale Union school formed part of a new workhouse complex designed by G Woodhouse & E Potts and built in 1873–7.
[BB96/2268]

were still relatively new buildings, became redundant. This coincided with moves to separate the elderly from the able-bodied, and so a large number of schools, for example that at Stoke-upon-Trent, were converted for the aged and infirm.

As well as children's blocks, some early 20th-century workhouses had nurseries for babies and infants. The care of young children was criticised by the Royal Commission of 1905–9. It was found that infants were often looked after by 'feeble-minded' inmates, that new arrivals were not quarantined and that some nurseries had no access to the open air.[27] Guardians were slow to respond to a Local Government Board circular of 1910 which directed that attention be paid to 'a sufficiency of light and ventilation, a good supply of hot and cold water, means of airing and exercise, proper floor-covering, means of sterilising milk, etc'.[28] Unusually, in 1912, Nottingham Union reportedly set up a 'nursery for indoor babies' in a house adjoining the workhouse grounds.[29] Infant care generally improved after the First World War, and new maternity blocks with purpose-built nurseries were added to some workhouses, for example that of Cambridge, in the 1920s.

In the 1890s, the Local Government Board announced that it would no longer sanction plans for new workhouses which included children's accommodation, and in 1900 it issued a circular to all boards of guardians urging the removal of all children from the workhouse proper. That stance was supported by the Majority and Minority Reports of the Royal Commission of 1905–9, and by an Order of 1913 prohibiting the maintenance of children over 3 years of age in any 'institution containing adults' for more than six weeks.[30] The Order could not be fully

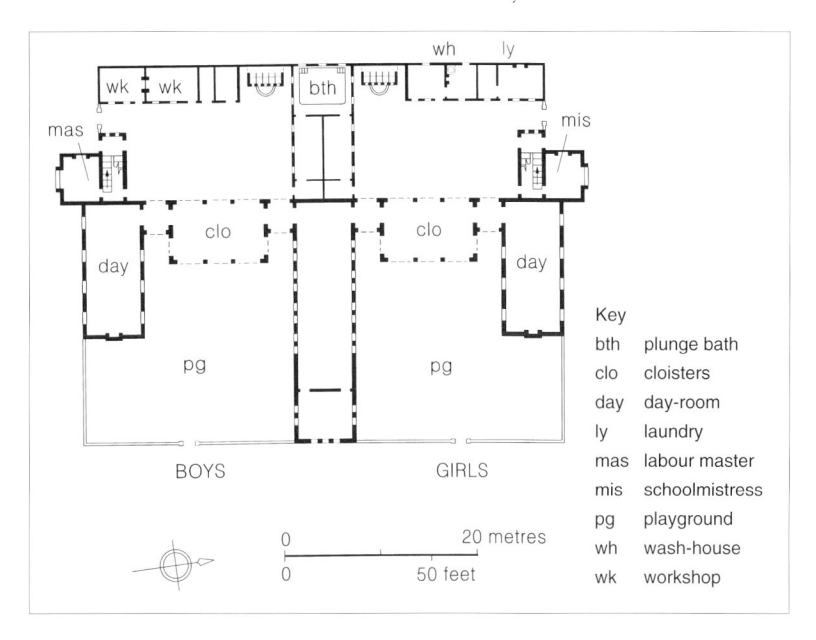

Key
bth plunge bath
clo cloisters
day day-room
ly laundry
mas labour master
mis schoolmistress
pg playground
wh wash-house
wk workshop

Figure 168 (above) Alderbury Union Workhouse, outside Salisbury, was rebuilt in 1877–9 to designs by George B Nicholls, an architect who was responsible for several new workhouses during the 1870s. The school, together with the rest of the institution, was demolished in the 1970s.
[Redrawn from Public Record Office MH14/31]

Figure 169 (left) Scott & Moffatt's Burton-upon-Trent Union Workhouse was superseded by a new institution, designed by J H Morton of South Shields in 1880–4. The school, for 125 children, comprised a central block, shown here, separate blocks for boys and girls, a laundry, workshops and a 'farm homestead'.
[BB96/2343]

Figure 170 (below)
The Dower House of Dudmaston Hall, at Quatt in Shropshire, housed the South-East Shropshire District School, otherwise known as Quatt School, from c 1850. This photograph was taken in 1946.
[AA47/8921]

Figure 171 (bottom)
Like most 19th-century poor-law industrial schools, Kirkdale Industrial School in Liverpool (1843–50) has been demolished.
[From Illustrated London News, 27 April 1850, 296, by permission of the Syndics of Cambridge University Library]

implemented because of the outbreak of war and resistance by rural guardians. Thus, on the eve of the First World War, on 1 January 1914, no less than 15,951 children under 16, out of a total of 68,039 in institutions, still lived in workhouses throughout England and Wales.[31] Just over 300 of them, however, still attended a workhouse school.

Separate Schools, District Schools and Cottage Homes

SEPARATE SCHOOLS IN THE 1830S AND 1840S

Contrary to the general trend in the 1830s, a handful of unions decided to run separate establishments for children. By definition, these occupied a different site from the workhouse and were administered by a superintendent rather than the workhouse master.

In many cases a separate school was an interim measure, to tide the union over while a general mixed workhouse was being built. This was the case, for example, in Cambridge between 1836 and 1838.[32] Edmonton Union, however, retained the former Enfield Parish Workhouse of 1827 as a school, even after a new workhouse had been erected in 1839. The practice of retaining a 'workhouse for children' was most common in London: Stepney Union, for example, used the old Limehouse House of Industry for that purpose. But more influential than any of these establishments was an initiative by a Bridgnorth guardian, Mr Wolrych Whitmore, who offered a house on his estate, the former dower house of Dudmaston Hall at Quatt (Fig 170), to be used as an industrial school for about eighty children.[33] The boys cultivated the land and managed the farm stock while the girls did the housework. By the 1850s the so-called Quatt system was demonstrably successful; it inspired the inception of numerous other industrial schools which purchased land and taught agricultural practices.

Aubin's and Drouet's huge schools (*see above*), with upwards of 1,000 children, inspired Assistant Commissioner James Kay-Shuttleworth (formerly Dr Kay), to advocate the formation of school districts, each to be composed of several unions, under the control of the Poor Law Commission. Kay's 'Report on the Training of Pauper Children' of 1837–8 included a plan and elevation for a district school to accommodate 300 children and 150 infants (*see* Appendix 3, Figures 16 and 17), drawn by Sampson Kempthorne, who had continued to serve as architect to the Poor Law Commission and, in 1839, also produced plans for the Committee of Council on Education.[34] Kempthorne's design of 1837–8 included large rooms with galleries, in which the master could address the entire school, and four smaller classrooms with fixed desks. It was a few years, however, before authorities were permitted to form school districts and, in the meantime, a number decided to erect their own schools away from workhouses.

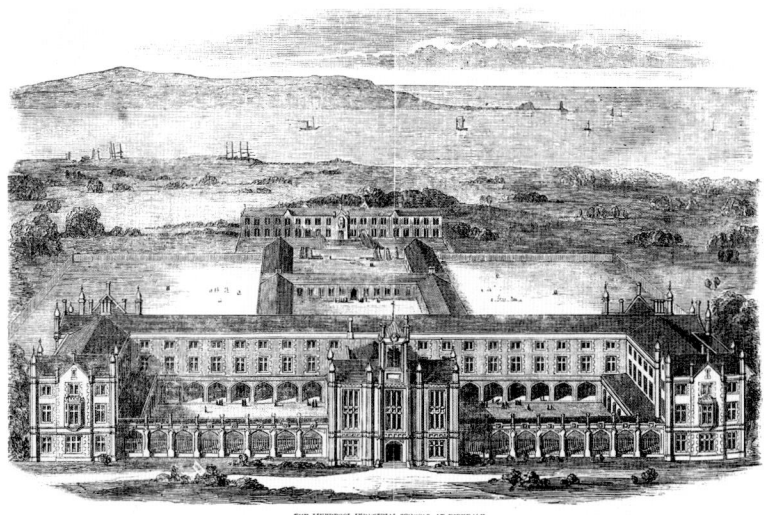

In 1842–3, the guardians of Manchester Township, the Select Vestry of Liverpool, and Sheffield Union all agreed to set up large establishments for their children.[35] Manchester set about erecting its school at Swinton only after a delegation had visited Aubin's and Drouet's establishments in London and plans had been examined by Kay-Shuttleworth.[36] The resulting building had a long symmetrical façade, dominated by two tall towers and adorned by Dutch gables, more elaborate in style than most contemporary workhouses. Kirkdale Industrial School (Fig 171) was erected by Liverpool at the same time. Its E-shaped ranges were open to the front rather than the rear, and each wing was adorned by an elaborate Perpendicular façade. Sheffield, instead of erecting a new and expensive school in the manner of Manchester and Liverpool, established its children in the old Brightside Township Workhouse at Pitsmoor.

Between 1846 and 1848, Leeds Union was also moved to erect an Industrial School. That relieved the overcrowded workhouse, in which almost half of the inmates had been children, and was considered a cheaper remedy than the erection of a larger workhouse. Architects were instructed to produce a design that should be 'calculated to banish from the minds of the inmates all idea that the Institution partakes in any degree of the character of a workhouse'.[37]

The successful architects, William Perkin & Elisha Backhouse, created a building in the Elizabethan style, of brick with ashlar dressings (Figs 172 and 173). On the central block and at the ends of the wings, three-storeyed canted bay windows were crowned by shaped gables flanked by tall octagonal turrets. The centre housed the boardroom, headmaster's apartment, teachers' dining-room and apartments. The wings contained boys' accommodation on one side and girls' on the other; schoolrooms and day-rooms were at the ends of the wings. A chapel, dining-hall, kitchens and infants' schoolroom occupied a rear wing. Children over 6 spent half their time in elementary-school work, the other half in occupations such as gardening, tailoring, shoe-making, domestic duties and sewing. On leaving school at the age of 16, the children were sent out to service or apprenticed.

Despite the objectives of its founders, the Leeds Industrial School did not maintain complete separation from adult paupers for long, as a new workhouse was erected on the same site in 1861.

Meanwhile, in 1844, Hanway's Act was repealed and metropolitan authorities were no longer compelled to send their youngest children into the countryside. New legislation

Figure 172
The central block of Leeds Moral and Industrial Training School (1846), designed by William Perkin & Elisha Backhouse, is now part of St James's Hospital.
[BB90/9937]

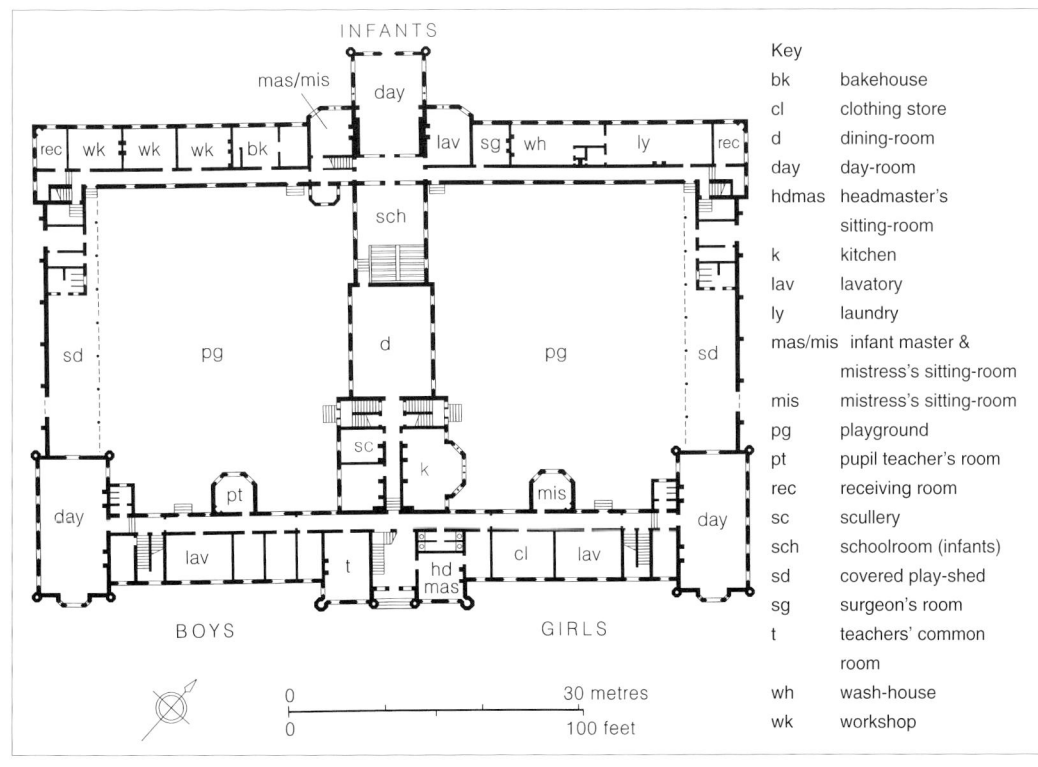

Figure 173
This ground-floor plan of the Leeds Moral and Industrial Training School is based on mid-19th-century drawings.

Key
bk	bakehouse
cl	clothing store
d	dining-room
day	day-room
hdmas	headmaster's sitting-room
k	kitchen
lav	lavatory
ly	laundry
mas/mis	infant master & mistress's sitting-room
mis	mistress's sitting-room
pg	playground
pt	pupil teacher's room
rec	receiving room
sc	scullery
sch	schoolroom (infants)
sd	covered play-shed
sg	surgeon's room
t	teachers' common room
wh	wash-house
wk	workshop

empowered unions and parishes to combine in school districts, as Kay-Shuttleworth had recommended.[38] It was argued that children in district schools would benefit from the salubrity of their situation, separation from adult paupers and proper industrial training.[39] At first, authorities were slow to embrace the new legislation, largely because of restrictions on the size and expenditure of each district, but progress accelerated after January 1849, when a tragic outbreak of cholera at Mr Drouet's school killed 180 of the 1,400 resident children.[40] Further legislation ensured that the few remaining contract-run poor-law establishments now came under the control of the Poor Law Board and lifted the restrictions which had discouraged authorities from combining to form school districts.[41] By the end of 1849, three school districts had been formed in London.[42] Initially, the Central London School District purchased Mr Aubin's establishment at Norwood for £10,000, retaining Aubin as superintendent; the North Surrey School District erected a school in Upper Norwood in 1849–50 and the South Metropolitan School District began building at Sutton in 1852. Both the North Surrey and South Metropolitan schools, now demolished, had a central administration block flanked by separate quadrangles, or playgrounds, for boys and girls; the form of Aubin's school is not known.

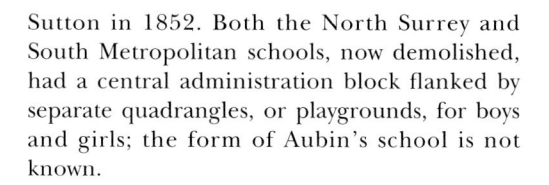

THE SPREAD OF THE SEPARATE-SCHOOL SYSTEM
After 1850, the Poor Law Board tried repeatedly to persuade Metropolitan authorities to form new school districts but for twenty years they met with no success, as guardians preferred the more economical option of establishing or improving their own schools. In the 1850s, new children's institutions were built on the outskirts of London by seven authorities. In addition, St Mary, Newington, erected a school in Newington itself, rather than out in the country, but upon completion that building was considered more suitable for use as a workhouse.

Few mid-Victorian industrial schools survive today, but that erected by St George-in-the-East at Plashet (Fig 174) was typical of its kind. It could accommodate 150 boys, 120 girls and 80 infants. The building, designed by Andrew Wilson, was E-shaped, with the kitchen, dining-hall and administrative offices in the centre, girls and infants in one end cross-wing and boys in the other. It was built of stock brick with some Italianate details executed in cement. As usual, there was a wash-house and laundry behind the girls' wing and workshops behind the boys'. Animal husbandry would have been taught to boys and girls alike in the farm complex on the girls' side of the establishment. This included piggeries, a stable and cow-houses. Other detached buildings on the site included a bailiff's house, a porter's lodge and an infirmary. Although in open countryside at the time of its construction, the school had been engulfed by the spreading suburbs of East London by the 1890s.

Central London School District served five unions and erected a large new school (Figs 175 and 176), with considerable architectural pretension, at Hanwell in 1856–8. The huge, arcaded central block was dominated by a water tower, with a clock installed in 1879. The school rapidly expanded, and accommodated over 1,000 children by the end of the century.

The Royal Commission on Education, reporting in 1861, recommended that district schools become compulsory, but that had little effect.[43] The provision of new metropolitan schools slowed down in the 1860s but, in 1867–8, as part of the general reorganisation of Metropolitan workhouses, two more school districts were formed: Forest Gate took over the Whitechapel school, and West London erected a

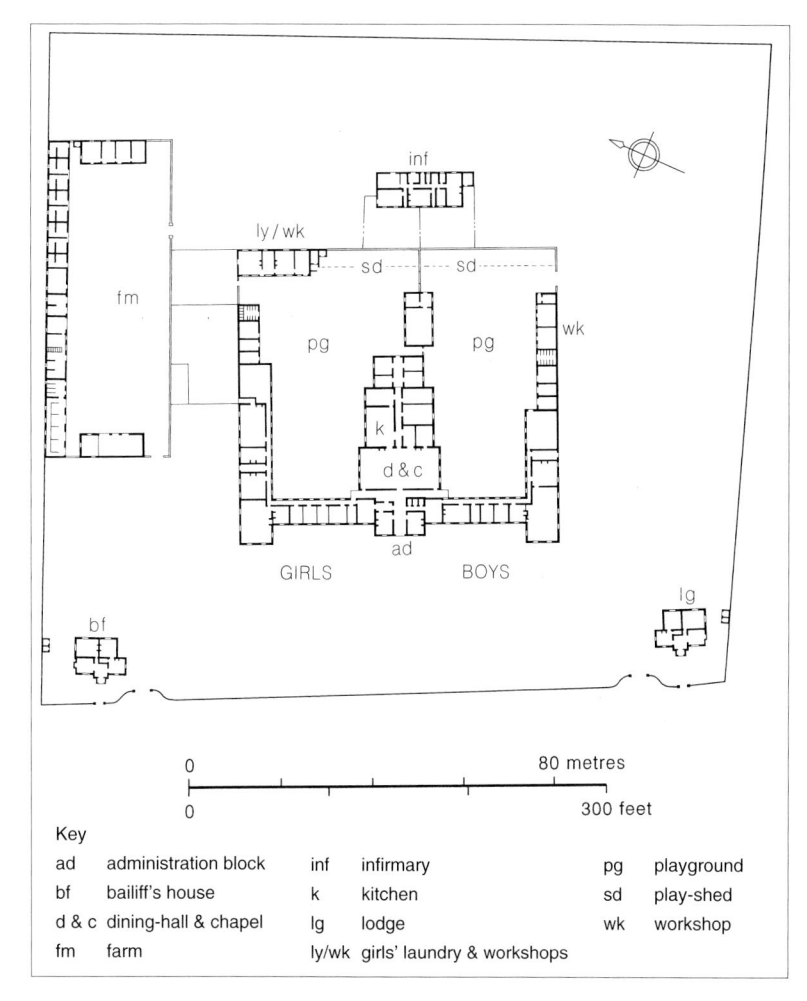

Figure 174
This is the ground-floor plan of St George-in-the-East Industrial School (1851–2), at Plashet, East Ham. The school was engulfed by late-Victorian developments, and became the Carlton Cinema before being demolished.
[Redrawn from Public Record Office MH14/31]

Key
ad	administration block
bf	bailiff's house
d & c	dining-hall & chapel
fm	farm
inf	infirmary
k	kitchen
lg	lodge
ly/wk	girls' laundry & workshops
pg	playground
sd	play-shed
wk	workshop

POOR-LAW BUILDINGS FOR CHILDREN

*Figure 175 (left)
The huge Central London District School at Hanwell was built in 1856–8 to a design by Tress & Chambers. This photograph of the ivy-clad central block was taken in 1935, shortly after the school closed. The building survives today, but the remainder of the site has been levelled and is used as a public park.*
[London Metropolitan Archives 22.54 HAN B1791]

*Figure 176 (below)
This photograph of c 1900 shows the dining-hall of the Central London District School (1856–8). The girls (at the back) are seated separately from the boys.*
[BB96/543]

141

*Figure 177
The West London
District School
(1869–72) at West
Ashford, near Staines,
was photographed in
1931. The children in
the foreground, tending
flower-beds or playing
with hoops, appear to
have been carefully
posed. The school closed
in 1955 and has been
demolished.
[London Metropolitan
Archives 22.54 ASH
A8310]*

large school at Ashford, near Staines (1869–72; Fig 177). Around the same time, Henry Saxon Snell was appointed architect to two abortive school districts, Finsbury and Kensington, and although his designs were never executed, he published them in 1881.[44] In both cases, the buildings were conceived along traditional lines. The last metropolitan school district to be formed with any success, Brentwood, existed between 1877 and 1885 and took over the existing Shoreditch Industrial School.

St Pancras, meanwhile, erected a school for 700 children at Leavesden (1869–72) and Bethnal Green purchased Leytonstone House (1868). By 1870, Hampstead and the joint authority of St Giles-in-the-Fields and St George, Bloomsbury were the only metropolitan authorities which did not run a separate school or belong to a school district.[45]

Outside London, the provision of separate institutions for children was slow. The few school districts formed after 1849 were small and made do with existing buildings. Initially Farnham and Hartley Wintney School District purchased the former Gilbert Union workhouse in Aldershot, a parish which had been subsumed by the new Farnham Union in 1846, but when that building was bought by the Board of Ordnance for Aldershot Camp in 1855, the district erected a new school at Crondall.[46] The South-East Shropshire School District occupied Bridgnorth Union's school at Quatt (*see* Figure 170) and the Reading and Wokingham School District used the defunct Wokingham Union Workhouse at Wargrave.

In the same period, some individual urban authorities established schools on separate sites from their workhouses, but none are known to survive. In 1852–4, Oxford erected a building for the reception and employment of 200 infant paupers at Cowley, on a site which would later be redeveloped for motor-car manufacture.[47]

Brighton erected Warren Farm Industrial Schools near Woodingdean, in 1862–3. Other boards of guardians paid to send pauper children to small, private industrial homes, the first of which was set up by a Mrs Way at Brockenham in Surrey in 1851.[48] These homes were a successful merger of state and private benevolence, but were never available to large numbers of children.

In 1869–70 the Walsall and West Bromwich School District was formed. The new school at Wigmore was an Elizabethan-style building, designed by S E Bindley of Birmingham. It was very much in the architectural tradition of the Kirkdale and Swinton schools, dominated by a massive central tower with an ogee-shaped roof, and adorned by steep, shaped gables and tall chimney-stacks with exaggerated caps. No further provincial school districts were formed, but from the late 1870s to 1897, the East Anglian unions of Hoxne, Hartismere and Guiltcross entered into an arrangement whereby children from all three unions were accommodated together in an old building at Wortham.[49] Inspector Bowyer reported, with approval, that the building was:

nothing but an old, rough farm house, with small windows and whitewashed walls . . . I believe, indeed, that a certain degree of roughness . . . in the arrangement of such schools (especially in an agricultural district) is a better preparation for the duties of a labourer, or artisan, and for those of their wives, than the theoretically more perfect appliances so much in vogue.[50]

Separate-site schools remained rare beyond London, but in 1878 Ipswich erected St John's school on the east side of the town. The school received eighty boys and fifty girls from Ipswich, Sudbury, Wangford and other neighbouring unions, but once again no school district was formally created. As a building, it was completely plain, in the architectural tradition of the first union workhouses.

NEW APPROACHES: BOARDING-OUT AND
COTTAGE HOMES

By 1870, the concept of herding children into large institutions was being openly questioned. District schools proved expensive and difficult to administer, and their long-term benefits were doubted. It was observed that industrial-school children were dull and listless, and those apprenticed were often rejected or absconded. Moreover, fevers and eye and skin diseases spread alarmingly whenever large numbers of children were massed in a single building.

Poor-law authorities began to search for ways to create a healthier and more natural environment in which to raise their charges, and some initiated programmes of 'boarding-out' or fostering children. Fostering became an option in England and Wales, following experiments in Scotland and Ireland, during the 1860s, and by 1898–9, 7,087 children from a total of 163,097 receiving outdoor relief, boarded out.[51] To put this in context, at the same time 52,207 children remained in institutions: these were favoured over fostering by the central authority, as foster parents could exploit or mistreat children, often using them as unpaid servants. From the late 1870s, however, the Local Government Board recommended that new children's institutions be erected on the cottage-home system rather than as old-style industrial schools.[52]

The first English cottage-home villages, erected in the late 1860s and early 1870s, were modelled on German and Swiss examples such as Hamburg and Mettrai.[53] Most notably they included Princess Mary's Village Homes for Little Girls at Addlestone in Surrey (1871), the Home for Little Boys at Farningham in Kent (1865) and Dr Barnardo's Village Home for Orphan, Neglected and Destitute Girls at Barkingside, Essex (1876–9).[54] In each case, a site had been selected in open countryside, but with easy access to a railway station. The buildings were formally arranged around greens and the children lived in self-contained groups, or 'households', varying in size from ten to thirty, under the care of a 'house-mother' and 'house-father'. The ideal family-sized group, comprising no more than twelve or so children, was seldom achievable due to its cost and, despite their name, the 'cottages' in which the children lived more closely resembled large, suburban villas. While most early cottage-home sites were single-sex, or housed girls and boys in separate homes on one site, some, such as the Children's Home on Bonner Road in East London, mixed boys and girls in each home.

The idea that pauper children would benefit from the cottage-home system was mooted in 1874 by Mrs Nassau Senior, the first woman poor-law inspector, who recommended 'schools of a more home-like character . . . each house containing not more than twenty to thirty children of all ages'.[55] In 1878, the Local Government Board commissioned an official report on cottage homes which, although favourably disposed to the system, expressed some reservations about its anticipated cost.[56] It recommended that mixed or all-female 'families' comprise twelve to twenty children, and families of boys aged over 10 comprise twenty-five to thirty.

Between 1874 and 1878 three English unions, West Derby, West Ham and Bolton, experimented with the cottage-home system. West Derby and West Ham erected buildings on their workhouse sites which could each house fifty children; these were not true cottage homes. The four homes erected at Bolton, however, each accommodated thirty, a number which became typical for poor-law homes in years to come. These homes (Fig 178) were built to either side of a school, around a central green on a walled site immediately south of the workhouse. Unions which followed this example and grouped homes on the edge of their workhouse site included Chorlton (1879–80), Burnley (1880s), Dewsbury (1893), Christchurch

Figure 178
The cottage homes to the south of Bolton Union Workhouse, known as Hollins Cottage Homes, were erected in several phases. The two homes on the extreme left in this view were built in 1878, the next was added in 1881 and that on the right in the early 20th century.
[BB96/2253]

The Workhouse

(1895–6) and Blackburn (1891–2). Rural unions seldom looked after enough children to make such a scheme viable, and retained their small workhouse schools.

Many urban authorities established large cottage-home villages at a distance from the workhouse. The first to undertake this was the newly created Kensington and Chelsea School District, which erected homes on a site near Banstead between 1878 and 1880 (Fig 179a). The long site, which trailed along the side of a railway line, gave the impression of 'a well-designed model village'.[57] In all, twenty-three detached homes were built, the girls' homes capable of holding twenty-six, the boys' homes, forty. Each home had a sitting-room, playroom, kitchen, scullery, bathroom and lavatory on the ground floor, two dormitories, a linen closet and a private bedroom upstairs. There was a flower garden to the front, and a playground and kitchen garden to the rear. Industrial training was built into the home system as much as possible. Boys received training from their 'house-father' while girls assisted the 'house-mother' with domestic chores and helped to care for the infants who were evenly distributed between the girls' homes. It was hoped that the wash-houses attached to the girls' homes would cope with the washing for the entire institution, but that proved over-optimistic. By 1898 a central laundry had been added to the site.

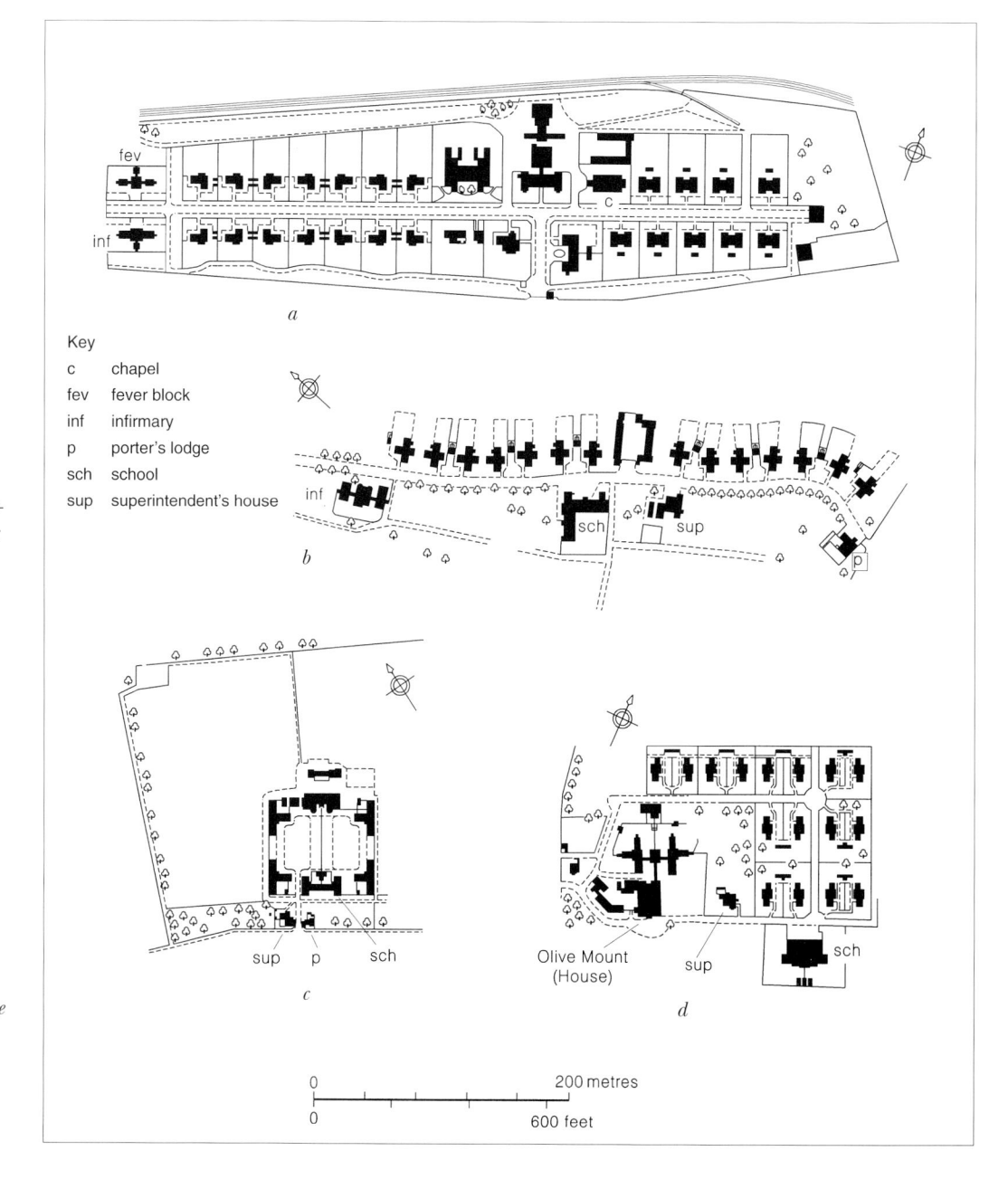

Figure 179
These block plans illustrate several of the standard layouts which were adopted for cottage-home villages. They are:
a. *Banstead Cottage Homes (Kensington and Chelsea School District, 1878–80);*
   [Based on OS rev edn 1:2500 map 1894]
b. *Marston Green Cottage Homes (Birmingham Parish, 1878–9);*
   [Based on OS 1 edn 1:2500 map 1886]
c. *Padgate Cottage Homes (Warrington Union, 1881);*
   [Based on OS 1 edn 1:2500 map 1893]
d. *Olive Mount Cottage Homes, Wavertree (Liverpool Parish, 1898–9).*
   [Based on OS rev edn 1:2500 map 1908]

Key
c   chapel
fev fever block
inf infirmary
p   porter's lodge
sch school
sup superintendent's house

Before the Banstead homes had been completed, Birmingham had undertaken the construction of a smaller cottage-home village at Marston Green (1878–9; Fig 179b). That comprised fourteen cottages, seven for girls and seven for boys, with thirty in each home. The range of buildings on the site, typical of cottage-home villages, included an infirmary, a school, a superintendent's house, workshops, a bakehouse, stores and swimming-baths. While the homes at Banstead had been arranged on either side of a long street, at Marston Green they were arranged in a single, gently curving line facing south west. The opening of Marston Green enabled the pauper children of Birmingham to be removed, not just from the huge parish workhouse, but from their parents, 'as the influence of these forms the greatest drawback on workhouse education'.[58]

Throughout the 1880s and 1890s, grouped cottage homes were erected by many populous unions, including Warrington (Padgate, 1881; Fig 179c), Leicester (Countesthorpe, 1884), St Leonard, Shoreditch (Hornchurch, 1887–8), Wolverhampton (Wednesfield, 1888), West Derby (Fazakerley, 1888–9), Chorlton (Styal, 1895) and Liverpool (Olive Mount, 1898–9; Fig 179d). The arrangement of buildings varied from village to village and was often dictated by the shape of the chosen site. The probationary wards and superintendent's house usually lay close to the main entrance, while the schools, workshops and swimming-baths occupied a central position. At Hornchurch and Fazakerley the homes stood in regimented lines, on either side of a street. At Padgate they bounded a quadrangle, at Wednesfield they formed curved lines and at Olive Mount they were paired on a grid system. At Hornchurch the girls' cottages were named after flowers and governed by a single woman or widow, whereas the boys' cottages were named after eminent men and presided over by a married couple, the husband providing industrial training for the boys. Both sexes were responsible for their own washing, but they were aided by three washerwomen, or charwomen.[59] Boys and girls alike were taught to swim, an opportunity restricted to boys in many other poor-law schools.

THE LAST 'BARRACK' SCHOOLS
Towards the end of the century a few unions adapted existing buildings as schools, for example Nottingham (1882) and Cockermouth (1887–9), but most opted for the cottage-home system. The popularity of cottage homes, however, did not prevent four London authorities from building old-style industrial schools, on what was referred to as the 'aggregate' or 'barracks' system, in the 1880s. While the groupings of children in these institutions, for the

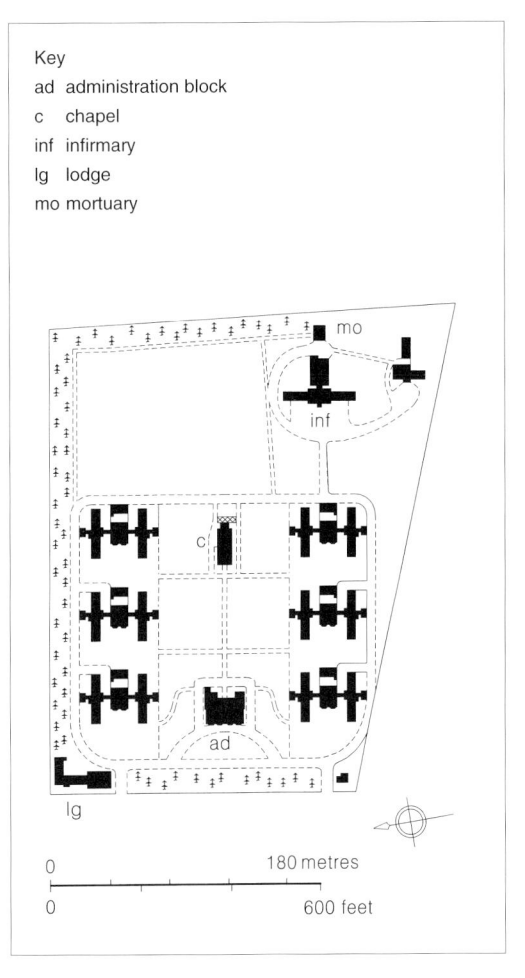

Key
ad administration block
c chapel
inf infirmary
lg lodge
mo mortuary

Figure 180
The South Metropolitan District School (1881–3) on Banstead Road, Sutton, was purchased by the Metropolitan Asylums Board c 1900 and became Downs Hospital; it is now the Royal Marsden and Sutton Hospitals.
[Redrawn from OS 1:2500 (Surrey) XIX.3, revised 1895]

South Metropolitan School District, Bethnal Green, Edmonton and Lambeth, could never pretend to approximate to the size of a normal family, features derived from pavilion and cottage-home planning distinguished the buildings from the massive industrial schools of the preceding thirty years.

By 1881, the South Metropolitan District School at Sutton was full, and a site on Banstead Road was purchased for expansion. The new buildings, initially designated for 600 infants but eventually occupied by girls, comprised two formal rows of three double pavilions flanking a main administration block and hall-cum-chapel (Fig 180). Each two-storeyed double pavilion housed eighty children, forty to either side of a central administration block. This pavilion layout, more closely related to contemporary hospitals than schools, probably offered a more economical use of the site than cottage homes. Lambeth employed a similar system for its new school buildings at Norwood.

A different approach was adopted by Bethnal Green which, between 1881 and 1889, set about replacing the iron buildings of its school at Leytonstone with permanent structures

145

(Fig 181). The architects, A & C Harston, had already designed a number of good, but simple, buildings for metropolitan poor-law authorities, such as the Banstead Cottage Homes (*see* Figures 179a and 189) for Kensington and Chelsea School District. Their solution for the restricted Leytonstone site was a formal arrangement of six closely spaced 'homes' to either side of a central dining-hall and kitchen. Each home was semi-detached and held four 12-bed dormitories and a day-room. Although sometimes referred to as 'cottage homes', the Leytonstone school represented a compromise between the cottage-home and barrack systems which was never repeated elsewhere.

Yet another compromise was reached by Edmonton Union which, in 1884–6, erected Chase Farm Schools (Fig 182) close to its existing children's home, the former Enfield Workhouse. The architect, T E Knightley, produced two schemes for the guardians: one on the separate-block system, the other on the cottage-home system. The former was selected as it was the cheaper option, but the site included two cottage homes, one for girls and one for boys.

Figure 181 (above) The guardians of St Matthew, Bethnal Green, built this school at Leytonstone for 576 children in 1881–9. The site has been derelict for some years. [4895/04]

Figure 182 (right) T E Knightley designed Chase Farm Schools (1884–6) for Edmonton Union, to replace its old school in Enfield Workhouse. The administration block, shown here, housed the master's residence. [BB95/7189]

POOR-LAW BUILDINGS FOR CHILDREN

Figure 183 (left)
New arrivals at Chase Farm Schools had to spend several weeks in the receiving and probationary blocks, shown here, before entering the school. The site is now Chase Farm Hospital.
[BB95/7187]

Figure 184 (below)
The workhouse of St Giles and St George, Bloomsbury occupied a typically cramped city site. This four-storey Receiving Home for Children was built nearby in 1900–2.
[Plans redrawn from Public Record Office MH14/31]

Chase Farm Schools occupied an extensive site. Probationary blocks and a lodge lay close to the gateway. The main building comprised a large administration block flanked by boys' and girls' wings with cross-ventilated rooms. The master's residence, in the front of the administration block, was dominated by a clock tower. Behind it lay a number of single-storeyed parallel blocks, all of which were lit by roof lanterns. These were the general store, the bakery, the scullery and kitchen, the dining-hall, the swimming-pool and, finally, the laundry. Lying between the main building and the cottage homes was an infants' school with a half-butterfly plan.

Some efforts were made to impose the separate-block system on older schools. In 1890, open spaces, 16 ft across, were cut through the main ranges of the Central London District School at Hanwell, to create five detached buildings. Open bridges linked the upper storeys of the individual blocks. This was praised by Monnington and Lampard, authors of *Our London Poor Law Schools* (1898), who suggested that the main building of the old South Metropolitan District School be similarly broken up.[60] Children in both schools had suffered from various epidemics and it was believed that the separate-block system, long since *de rigueur* for hospitals, would ease the problem.

GUARDING CHILDREN'S HEALTH

One of the greatest dangers threatening industrial schools and cottage homes was the admission of children with infections, and new arrivals were usually quarantined in probationary or receiving wards for at least fourteen days to make sure that they were not contagious. Probationary wards could be located at the workhouse, but preferably lay close to the entrance of the school site. At the Chase Farm Schools, children passed through a receiving block, then through a probationary block (Fig 183), undergoing double screening before they were admitted into the main building.

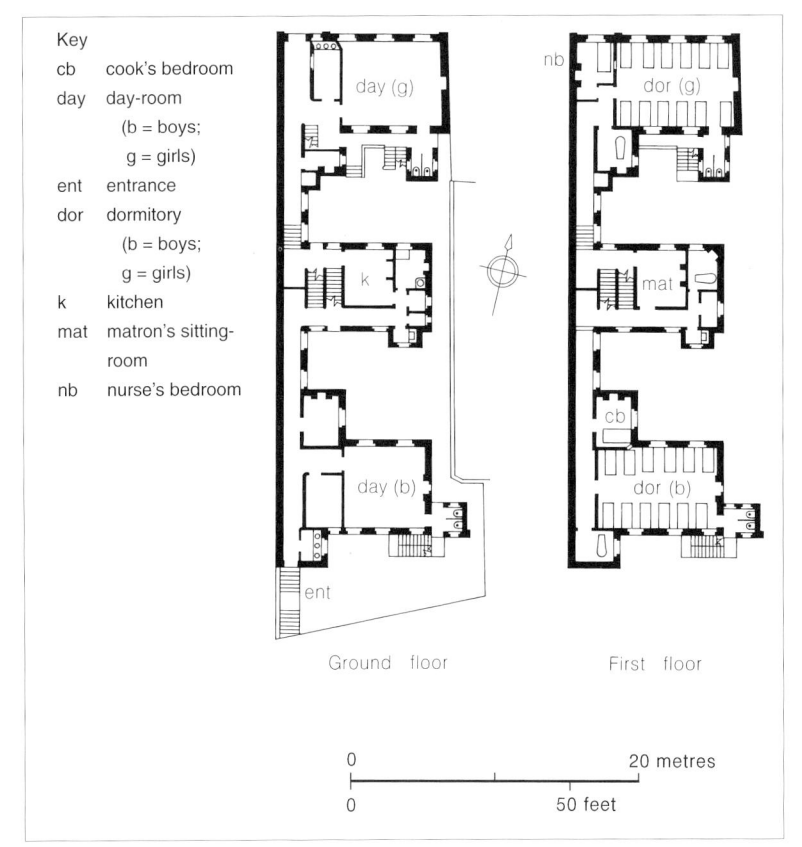

'Branch' or 'intermediate' workhouses augmented probationary wards and helped

Key
cb — cook's bedroom
day — day-room (b = boys; g = girls)
ent — entrance
dor — dormitory (b = boys; g = girls)
k — kitchen
mat — matron's sitting-room
nb — nurse's bedroom

147

THE WORKHOUSE

*Figure 185 (right)
In 1890 a hutted Ophthalmic Institute was erected in the grounds of the Central London District School, for the treatment and education of children with eye infections.
[From PP 1890 (c.6141), XXXIII, opposite p 173, by permission of the Syndics of Cambridge University Library]*

*Figure 186 (below)
Highwood School (1899–1903), Brentwood, was one of two hospital-schools built by the Metropolitan Asylums Board for children with eye infections. This relief on the administration block includes a pair of spectacles.
[BB95/7025]*

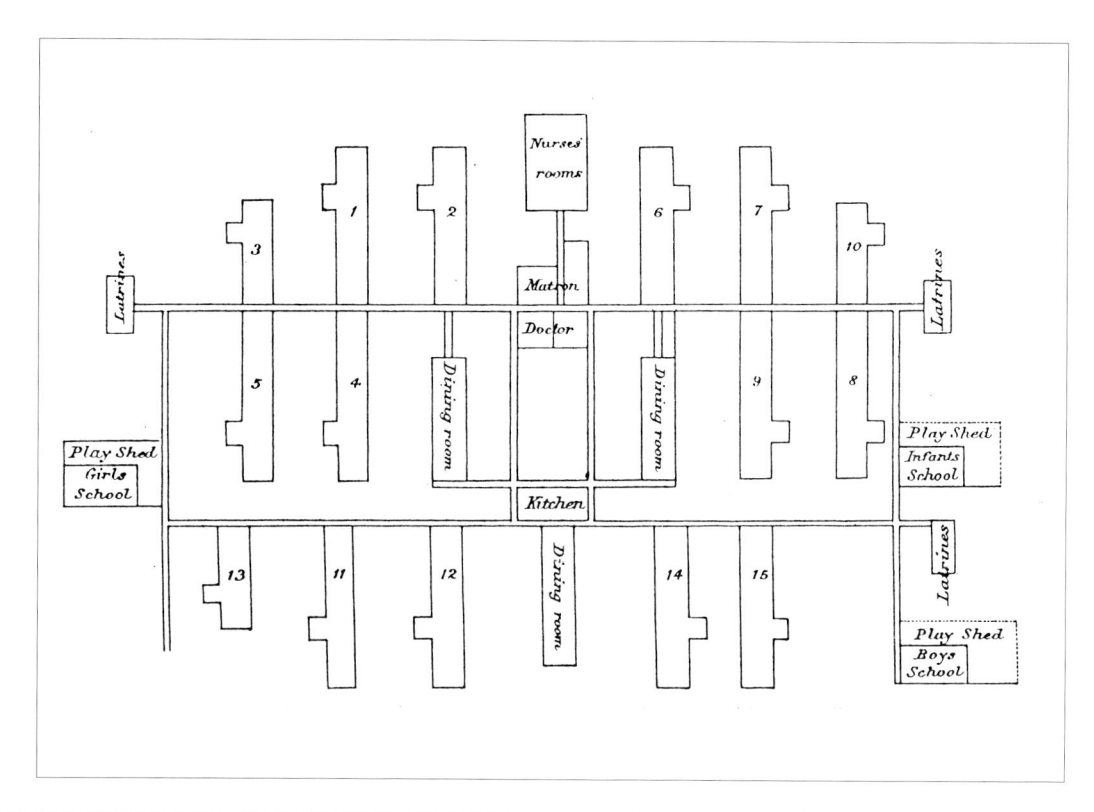

guardians to remove from the workhouse the children of 'ins and outs', who were not candidates for admission into separate schools. The first was opened by Kensington and Chelsea School District in 1883, primarily to act as a stepping-stone between the workhouses and the Banstead Cottage Homes. It was located in Marlesford Lodge, Hammersmith, a private house which at first accommodated 120 girls and infants, but was extended by the erection of a new boys' wing in 1885.[61]

Following pressure from the Local Government Board in 1898, small branch schools, or receiving homes, were set up by several London authorities. Some, for example those of Southwark, Stepney and Woolwich, occupied converted houses but others were purpose built. That of St Giles and St George, Bloomsbury, on Lascelles Place, was designed by J Grafton Izard in 1900 (Fig 184). Typically, it had a pavilion plan, with a central administration block connected to a girls' block on one side and a boys' block on the other.

Despite the network of probationary wards and branch workhouses, ophthalmia posed a huge problem in the largest metropolitan schools throughout the last quarter of the century, threatening the eyesight of many poor children. One of the first positive steps was taken in 1873 by the North Surrey School District, which set up a temporary branch school in Bow for ophthalmic cases. It was supervised by an oculist, Edward Nettleship, and was only discontinued once ophthalmia had all but disappeared. In 1875 the South Metropolitan School District purchased and altered the Pier Hotel, Herne Bay, as a branch school for children suffering from ophthalmia.[62] The Central London District School, the second largest of all the metropolitan schools, had a higher rate of this disease than any other and was strongly criticised for failing to take preventive measures and isolate outbreaks. The erection of temporary iron huts for 100 cases in 1875 did not solve the problem: in 1888 Nettleship identified 375 cases in the school. Eventually, in 1889–90, 11 acres of the site were set aside for the erection of a hutted Ophthalmic Institute (Fig 185), to permit the isolation, treatment and continuing education of up to 400 children.[63] It was available to all London's poor-law authorities, which paid 12s 6d a week per case in 1898. Despite the existence of the Ophthalmic Institute, many authorities continued to care for their own ophthalmic cases. In 1898 the Brentwood school, erected by Shoreditch but now in the hands of Hackney Union, reserved a large house close to the site entrance for ophthalmic cases capable of receiving schooling while more serious cases completely filled the infirmary block.

In 1897, following a report from the ophthalmic surgeon, Sydney Stephenson, the Metropolitan Asylums Board was given responsibility for accommodating children with contagious diseases of the eye, skin and scalp, and those requiring convalescence or sea air for the benefit of their health, children requiring special education, and children remanded in poor-law institutions under the Industrial Schools Act of 1866.[64] Several new institutions were set up as a result, including two hospital-schools for children suffering from ophthalmia, one located at Swanley (opened 1903) and the other at Brentwood (opened 1904). These enabled children with ophthalmia to live in cottage homes, attend school and receive medical attention. The Brentwood establishment, known as Highwood School, was begun in 1899 to designs by C & W Henman (Fig 186). It had a formal layout, with the kitchen, administration block, senior and junior schools in the centre. The fifteen homes were grouped in threes. Each group was clustered around a nurses' cottage and faced south rather than on to a central space. The site was not primarily a hospital, however, and was served by an infirmary with no greater capacity than that of a comparable institution for healthy children.

In 1898, the Metropolitan Asylums Board set up a 120-bed sanatorium at Rustington in Sussex for children who would benefit from sea air, chiefly those suffering from non-pulmonary tuberculosis.[65] After the First World War, Highwood School was turned over to children suffering from non-pulmonary tuberculosis, by then as much of a scourge as ophthalmia had been in the late 19th century. Open verandas capable of taking beds were added to the south side of several cottages (Fig 187). Surviving buildings elsewhere suggest that tuberculosis was a problem at several children's homes in the inter-war period. At Hackney Cottage Homes, Chipping Ongar, an open-air classroom (Fig 188), probably for children suffering from tuberculosis, stands between the school and the porter's lodge. A rare survival, it is a single-storeyed structure with a wooden frame, capable of admitting the maximum amount of light and air.

*Figure 187 (top)
When Highwood School was adapted for tuberculosis cases in 1914, verandas were added to several of the accommodation blocks.[BB95/7034]*

*Figure 188 (above)
Hackney Union abandoned its industrial school in Brentwood and erected a cottage-home village at Chipping Ongar in 1902–5. This open-air classroom may date from the 1930s.[269E/4]*

The Workhouse

Figure 189
This shows the interior of the gymnasium of Kensington and Chelsea Cottage Homes Village, Banstead, in 1931.
[London Metropolitan Archives A8290]

Figure 190
Swimming-baths formed an important part of industrial schools and cottage-home villages, but seldom survive. This one is at the Greenwich Union Cottage Home Village at Sidcup (1902), which is now a housing estate. The architects were Thomas Dinwiddy & Sons.
[BB96/294]

Physical exercise was important to the health of pauper children, and many more facilities were available in industrial schools and the larger cottage-home villages than in workhouses. Playgrounds, open play-sheds and recreation rooms were supplemented by gymnasia (Fig 189) and swimming-baths (Fig 190) in the larger schools from 1870 onwards. Together with bandrooms, these facilities enabled poor boys to train for the navy. In 1874, North Surrey School District erected a heated swimming-bath and an outdoor gym with the special feature of 'a mast and shroud taken from a man-of-war somewhat similar to the one at Greenwich Hospital'.[66]

Between 1870 and 1875 Forest Gate School District offered boys from all metropolitan authorities naval training on board the *Goliath*, moored on the Thames. This proved highly successful, but the ship was destroyed by fire on 22 December 1875 with the loss of twenty-one lives. It was succeeded by the *Exmouth*, a three-decker battleship dating from the Napoleonic Wars which was moored off Grays in Essex. The *Exmouth* was managed by the Metropolitan Asylums Board but accepted boys from unions throughout the country.[67] The original ship was scrapped in 1903, and an exact replica (Fig 191) built by Vickers.

Scattered Homes, and the Spread of the Cottage-Home System

In 1890, Elham Union in Kent broke new ground by establishing fifty children on a small cottage-home site, 3 miles from the workhouse, and sending them to the local elementary school.[68] The homes were designed in 1888 by Joseph Gardner & John Ladds, architects responsible for numerous additions to Elham Union Workhouse in the 1890s.[69] To some extent this development had been foreshadowed as early as 1845 by Norwich's practice of sending older children out of the workhouse, to reside in a house with a schoolmaster and work for various employers in the city.[70] The Elham experiment, however, proved more influential. It inspired other unions to set up homes on residential streets in urban areas, where children had access to the full range of local amenities. The scheme had the additional benefit of being inexpensive.

In 1893, Sheffield rented a number of small houses throughout the city, and filled each of them with boys and girls of mixed ages, but carefully separating Roman Catholics from Protestants.[71] The children attended local elementary schools and, in the case of Protestants, the local Sunday School and parish church. Bath followed suit in 1896, by renting five houses for seventy-five children, and many other unions did likewise in subsequent years.[72] By 1930, Camberwell owned no less than eighteen separate homes, scattered throughout Camberwell and neighbouring Peckham.[73]

The 'Sheffield System', or scattered homes, represented a cheaper urban alternative to the cottage-home village. Most unions purchased and converted existing houses rather than build anew. Purpose-built scattered homes, such as that erected in Clarence Road, Grays (Fig 192), for Whitechapel Union in 1899, were strictly suburban in style, yet conspicuously larger than adjacent semi-detached houses.

As with cottage-home villages, a probationary or receiving house was necessary to ensure that children did not carry infections into scattered

Figure 191 (below)
This photograph shows training in progress on the deck of the MAB training ship Exmouth *c 1930.*
[London Metropolitan Archives B5636]

Figure 192 (bottom)
Park Cottage was one of the scattered homes erected by Whitechapel Union in Grays, Essex, in 1899.
[BB95/7177]

homes. Receiving houses usually adjoined a superintendent's residence and could be located on the workhouse site, as at Sheffield and Middlesbrough, or on a residential street, as at Grays and Royton. The 'headquarters' site at Royton, designed for Oldham Union by Wild, Collins & Wild in 1898, included a detached infirmary as well as a large receiving block (Fig 193) and superintendent's house.

Numerous grouped cottage-home villages were erected in the early 20th century, many of them adopting the then fashionable Arts & Crafts style with panache. The layout of sites still varied enormously. Aston Union homes, located next to the workhouse, adopted the street layout used earlier at Fazakerley and Hornchurch, but with the infirmary as the focal point at the end of the 'street'. Curving rows of homes, either facing south or encircling a green, were favoured by Salford, Hackney and Stepney. The centrepiece of the Stepney Union homes at Stifford was a tapering water tower, behind which lay the swimming-pool, workshops and laundry (Fig 194).

Efforts were made to individualise homes in some of the earliest cottage-home villages – for example each home at Marston Green had a distinctive terracotta pattern embedded in its walls. This tendency developed after 1900. In 1903, the architects Holmes & Watson alternated two different designs around the site of Ecclesall Bierlow Union's homes at Fulwood, outside Sheffield. Much greater variation was displayed on the façades of Salford Union's homes at Culcheth (Fig 195), where the positioning of elements such as projecting bays, chimney-stacks and decorative gables alternated from home to home, as did the use of rendering,

Figure 193 (above) The buildings of Oldham Union's scattered homes headquarters, erected at Royton in 1898, included this receiving block.
[BB96/2170]

Figure 194 (right) This photograph shows the water tower and workshops at Stepney Union Cottage Homes (1901), Stifford, before the flanking buildings were demolished.
[London Metropolitan Archives 22.54 ARD 64179]

red and pink brick and half-timbering. As with late-20th-century housing estates, this approach was effective but superficial; to the rear every cottage was identical, and internally the only differences concerned the respective positions of fireplaces and bay windows.

Architecturally, the most lavish cottage-home site was probably that of Poplar Union, designed by Holman & Goodman and erected in 1906 at Hutton in Essex. Five cottages for boys and five for girls were arranged on opposing sides of a wide green. A detached dining-hall (Fig 196) was erected for the boys, and a laundry for the girls. The girls prepared, served and ate meals in their own cottages as part of their domestic training. The swimming-baths, gymnasium, water tower and boiler house were situated in a large complex to the north of the green, and the school, administration block and superintendent's house lay to the south. The school was a T-shaped building with classrooms in the bar of the T, and a large assembly hall to the rear. All of these buildings were much more ornate than most poor-law buildings, reflecting the ethos of 'Poplarism' (*see* pages 122–123). The boys' dining-hall, for example, had shaped gables with stone capping and a terracotta frieze including depictions of poplar trees and St Leonard; the five-bay hall had a wooden hammerbeam roof.

The Royal Commission's Majority Report of 1909 suggested that the practice of boarding-out should be extended. While admitting that cottage homes were effective, it noted that scattered homes were cheaper. The large industrial schools that had been condemned by the Committee on the Care of Poor Law Children in 1896 were not subjected to much criticism in the report, for they were already viewed as institutions of the past.[74]

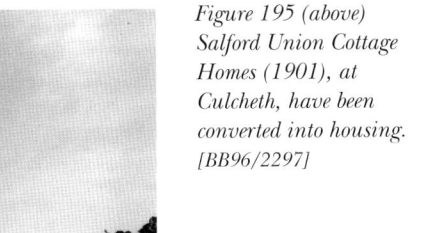

Figure 195 (above)
Salford Union Cottage Homes (1901), at Culcheth, have been converted into housing.
[BB96/2297]

Figure 196 (left)
The boys' dining-hall at Poplar Union Training School (1906), Hutton, was lavishly decorated.
[BB95/6947]

Figure 197 Horncastle Cottage Homes were erected on land next to the workhouse, by the local council, in 1932. [BB95/2467]

After the First World War, many unions adopted the scattered-home system by purchasing and adapting houses, rather than by constructing new premises. The notion of grouped children's homes, however, survived the demise of the poor law in 1929, and several were established on or close to former workhouse sites by county or borough councils in the 1930s. Homes erected on a site to the east of the former Horncastle Union Workhouse in the 1930s (Fig 197) differed little from those built elsewhere fifty years before.

Apprenticeship and Adult Life

Children raised in a workhouse school were, in many cases, supremely ill-fitted for employment and independence in adult life and often ended up back in the workhouse, which, according to some sources, they actively liked and regarded as home. This was recognised as a serious problem as early as 1838, and although the moral and industrial training offered in district schools and grouped cottage homes helped to some degree, they still failed to prepare children for the 'real' world beyond institutional walls. In particular, girls who had been taught to cook for hundreds of children in the vast kitchen of an industrial school had difficulty translating their skills to a small-scale domestic environment. And domestic service was the only option for most workhouse girls: of 530 girls placed out in London in 1908, 521 entered domestic service.[75] The fate of the remaining nine is not recorded, but boys placed out at the same time entered a wide variety of careers and trades: many joined the Royal Navy, Mercantile Marine, or a naval or military band; others became shoemakers, bakers, tailors, builders or farm-hands.

One of the first to show concern for the destiny of former workhouse girls was the philanthropist Louisa Twining, a member of the tea-importing family. In 1861 she set up a home on New Ormond Street in London for ex-workhouse girls who had fallen out of service and found themselves without a home or any (respectable) means of support. This was the start of the Metropolitan Association for Befriending Young Servants. Around the same time, Joseph Rowntree advocated the establishment of such homes within the remit of the poor law, complaining that boards of guardians currently had no option but to readmit such young women to the workhouse.[76] A few years later, a vacant building at Liverpool workhouse was fitted up especially for young women out of service, but within the sphere of the poor law that experiment appears to have been unique.[77]

The fate of workhouse boys never exercised philanthropists to the same degree; unlike girls, they were not perceived to be in moral danger, and their industrial or naval training was more appropriate for their life as independent adults. Nevertheless, the Association for Befriending Boys, set up in 1898, kept in touch with hundreds of former workhouse boys from London. As the 19th century progressed, poor-law authorities made greater efforts to maintain contact with their former pupils, both male and female, and keep statistics of their progress through life. This was not an easy task, especially as thousands of pauper children were shipped to the colonies, particularly Canada, to start a new life.

9
Poor-Law Buildings for the Sick, the Mentally Ill and the Mentally Handicapped

Most workhouses, from the early 18th century onwards, housed many sick, mentally ill and mentally handicapped inmates. Under the Old Poor Law specialist accommodation was rarely provided for these classes, although rooms or buildings were often set aside for infectious cases, to prevent the occurrence of epidemics.

Workhouse sick wards were not regarded as hospitals until the late 1860s, when a public scandal compelled poor-law authorities to improve infirmary buildings, medical facilities and nursing standards. Some of the largest authorities erected infirmaries as separate institutions, apart from the workhouse, in the charge of a medical superintendent, while others simply erected a detached infirmary on the workhouse site. Either way, the pavilion principles which had infiltrated military and voluntary hospital design in the early 1860s were adopted. A high degree of segregation and specialisation was observed in these buildings, with separate wards and yards for the ordinary sick, those suffering from venereal disease or itch (scabies), maternity cases, convalescents, and other classes.

A series of Lunacy Acts in the 19th century brought about the establishment of county and borough 'lunatic' asylums which received pauper patients. But because of the asylums' high cost and tendency to overcrowding, many mild, incurable cases had to remain in the workhouse, as did the mentally handicapped, who were referred to at that time as 'idiots' or 'imbeciles'. The Metropolitan Poor Law Amendment Act of 1867 established imbecile asylums for London paupers, but it was not until the eve of the First World War that provincial unions began to band together to provide colonies for 'mental defectives'. Specialised institutions for the mentally handicapped did not become a reality until the 1930s, when workhouse accommodation was rationalised under local authority control.

The Sick in Old Poor Law Workhouses

Before 1834, whenever the poor lost their independence through illness they became eligible for outdoor parish relief. As well as attendance by the parish medical officer, this could entail direct financial support, payment of rent, a supply of 'medical comforts' (such as wine), bread or fuel. The sick, like the aged, were admitted to the workhouse only when they had no friends or relatives who could care for them at home.

In most Old Poor Law workhouses, invalids took to bed in their dormitories, where they were nursed by fellow paupers. *An Account of the Workhouses in Great Britain* (1732) makes it clear that only the largest establishments of that period, particularly in London, had wards for sick inmates. At the 'model' workhouse of St George's, Hanover Square (*see* Figure 12), built in 1725–6, the sick in the infirmary were attended daily by a physician, apothecary and surgeon, and twice a week by a clergyman. A few of the provincial workhouses mentioned in *An Account* also had sick wards, for example Chatham, where former almshouses across the street were used as an infirmary.[1]

Although large infirmaries were constructed by a handful of urban authorities, such as St Marylebone in London,[2] towards the end of the 18th century, provision for the sick remained inadequate in most workhouses. In *The State of the Poor* (1797), Sir Frederick Eden complained about the absence of rooms for the sick in the new house of industry which had been erected at Louth in 1791:

> There is one large lodging-room for the men, and another for the women, each containing 14 beds, which are partitioned from each other by deal-boards at each end, and on one side: the view of a sick neighbour is thereby, in a great measure, obstructed; but, to a feeling mind, the sense of hearing must frequently convey very disagreeable ideas; the smell must, also, be frequently offensive.[3]

For most institutions, a special ward for the isolation of infectious cases was of much greater importance than general sick wards; once a contagious fever arose in an institution it could – and often did – take hold with tragic results. Already in the 1720s, the workhouse shared by the parishes of St Giles-in-the-Fields and St George, Bloomsbury, had special wards for itch (scabies), 'the foul disease' (possibly venereal diseases), smallpox and malignant fevers.

East Anglian houses of industry were provided with purpose-built, detached pest-houses, usually sited about a quarter of a mile from the main building. Drawings and specifications survive for those of Heckingham and Shipmeadow (Fig 198), dating from 1766 and 1767 respectively.[4] These virtually identical brick buildings were both erected by John Harris of Ipswich, carpenter, for the sum of £320. They followed a standard domestic plan: on each floor two rooms with fireplaces opened off either side of a central staircase. A single-storeyed wing housed a 'coal bin' and a 'bogg-house', or earth closet, with a 3-ft-deep pit.

The existence of pest-houses did not prevent epidemics sweeping through houses of industry. No less than 130 inmates of Bulcamp House of Industry died when a 'putrid fever' broke out in 1781, and a second pest-house had to be added to Barham House of Industry when the existing building proved too small to contain a smallpox epidemic in 1790–1.[5]

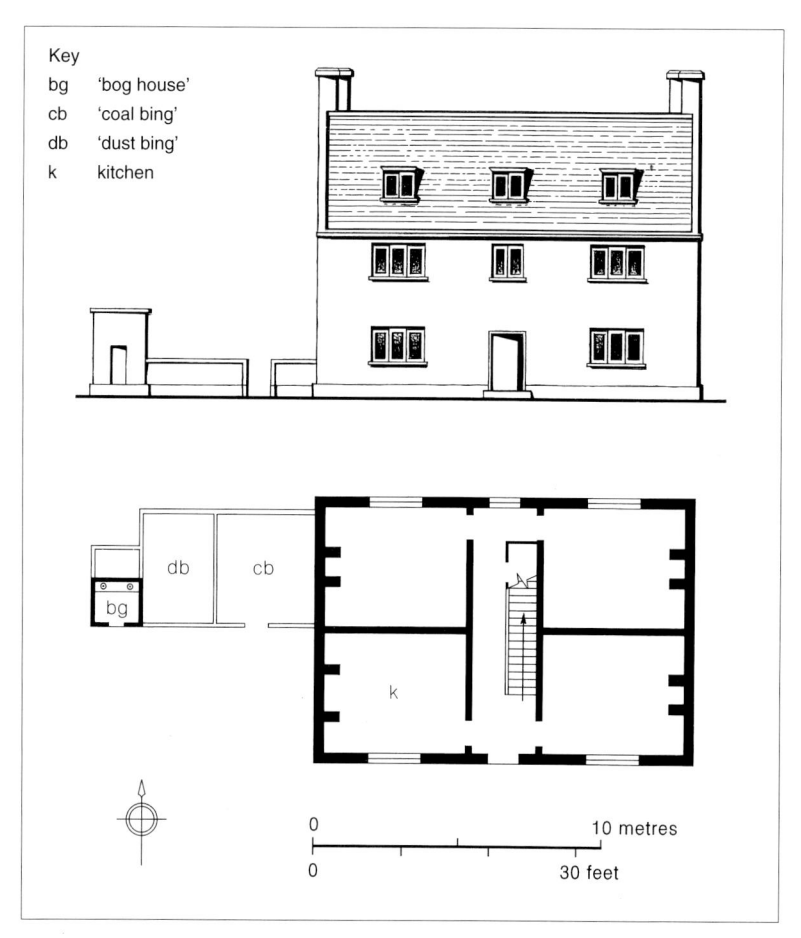

'Lunatics' and 'Imbeciles' under the Old Poor Law

Workhouse populations usually included a number of paupers who would have been classified, throughout the 18th and early 19th centuries, as harmless lunatics, imbeciles or idiots. Generally, they mixed with other inmates, did not require special supervision and were not provided with special accommodation. More problematic were the uncontrollable, even dangerous, lunatics who ended up in workhouses due to a shortage of suitable, affordable asylum accommodation. Although a few private asylums catered exclusively for pauper lunatics, and some counties set up pauper lunatic asylums as a result of legislation passed in 1808 and 1828, there were never enough places to satisfy demand.[6] Boarding-out was another possibility: in a case reported in 1836, a mad woman boarded-out with an old woman of 70 was confined in a wooden cage in which she could neither sit nor lie down.[7]

Before the advent of the New Poor Law, it was not uncommon for a solitary lunatic to be kept in a hut or cell at the workhouse. An early 18th-century account of St Margaret's Workhouse, Westminster, related that 'a lunatic . . . discharged out of Bedlam as an incurable has a brick cell built on purpose for him'.[8] At Atherstone Parish Workhouse, in the first half of the 19th century, a lunatic named 'Poor Joe' was kept in a 'wooden hut with a small enclosure and iron bars' situated close to the site entrance.[9] The treatment of such inmates could be barbarous. Assistant Commissioner Gilbert, making a plea for the creation of pauper lunatic asylums in 1836, related several cases he had come across under the Old Poor Law in Devon:

> At Tiverton I found a female lunatic in the workhouse, who had been there 28 years. She was confined in a small room, having neither furniture, fire-place nor bed; there was not anything in the room but a bundle of straw. She was without a single piece of clothing, perfectly naked, and had been confined in that state, during winter and summer, for the last 28 years.[10]

Some urban poor-law authorities, with specific powers defined by local acts, operated licensed asylums. Sometimes these were separate from the workhouse, but in several cases, for example at Stoke Damerell, Bristol and Exeter,

Figure 198
The pest-house depicted in this drawing was built by John Harris at Shipmeadow House of Industry in 1767.
[Redrawn from Suffolk RO 36/AH5/1/1]

Key
bg 'bog house'
cb 'coal bing'
db 'dust bing'
k kitchen

they were located on the same site. In 1815, Bristol workhouse included a range of underground cells 'in which incurable inmates were allowed to linger out a solitary existence on "plenty of clean straw" '.[11]

In 1823 the provisions of certain Lunatic Acts were extended to Bristol,[12] where St Peter's Workhouse (*see* Figure 6) was deemed to be an asylum. In 1832–3 Bristol Corporation bought a site at Stapleton, formerly used for prisoners of war, and converted and extended the buildings for a large proportion of its inmates. It retained St Peter's Workhouse for others, including lunatics. This accommodation was criticised in 1843 by the house apothecary:

The lunatic wards can only be considered as places of safe keeping, not affording the means of classification even on a limited scale . . . The female wards for lunatics are confined, crowded, and altogether inconvenient; their yard or airing-ground, is exceedingly small, and is moreover the only thoroughfare for carriages to the establishment.[13]

Equally unsatisfactory arrangements existed elsewhere in the country. At Exeter, for example, one female inmate was sometimes restrained by being chained to a fireguard.[14]

Workhouse Infirmaries of the 1830s

Despite the fact that Sampson Kempthorne's model workhouse plans of 1835 and 1836 housed sick and infirm inmates together within the main workhouse building (*see* Appendix 3, Figures 2–15), the first New Poor Law workhouses frequently separated the sick and infirm within the main house, as at Epping (*see* Figures 58 and 59), or provided a detached or semi-detached infirmary for the sick, leaving the infirm under the same roof as the able-bodied, as at Wells (*see* Figures 66–8). The first detached infirmaries were invariably positioned to the rear of the main building, with equal access from the male and female divisions. The usual arrangement housed men in one half of the building and women in the other, but the sexes were occasionally segregated by floor.[15]

For some time workhouse infirmaries remained insignificant structures, in terms of both size and appearance. They contained an assortment of small rooms which typically included general wards, a nurse's room, a surgery, a lying-in ward and a nursery. Unlike ordinary workhouse dormitories of the 1830s, infirmary wards were seldom cross-ventilated: rare examples included the infirmary of Royston, designed in 1835 by William T Nash, and that of Bishop's Stortford, designed in 1836 by T L Evans but built under Nash's supervision (*see* Figure 77). Both buildings had two two-bay wards on each floor, one for men and another for women, each served by water-closets and separated from one another by stairs, a nurse's room and a bathroom. This particularly rational arrangement was followed in the two-storeyed, E-shaped infirmaries which formed part of Scott & Moffatt's workhouse schemes, often with a surgery as well as a nurse's room in the centre (*see* Figure 70). Open verandas between the bars of the 'E' provided nurses with covered access to wards in the cross-wings.

Rightly or wrongly, workhouse medical officers were considered inferior members of their profession at this time. Their powers were limited by the relieving officer and workhouse master, and all too often appointees were inexperienced young men, keen to set up in private practice and consequently negligent in their duties at the workhouse. They generally attended once a week, delegating the daily care of the sick to one or two nurses and the matron, none of whom would have received medical training. Nurses were selected from the pauper inmates and were seldom capable of fulfilling their duties satisfactorily: they were frequently accused of drunkenness, or of pilfering stimulants, and many were unable to read instructions on medicine bottles.

Few early New Poor Law infirmaries survive, as most were superseded by larger buildings in the second half of the 19th century. Those which do, for example those of Bedminster and Braintree Union Workhouses, have been greatly extended and altered.

Workhouse Infirmaries, 1840–1867

No one had anticipated the high numbers of sick cases which would arise within New Poor Law workhouses and, caught unawares, many unions were compelled to build an infirmary shortly after their new workhouse had been completed and occupied. The cheapest solution was to add infirmary wards to the main building, but this raised a problem. If a single infirmary was to be accessible to both men and women it had to be located in the middle of the institution, where the master's quarters, kitchen and dining-hall lay. At Huntingdon, in 1842, an infirmary ward was built over the dining-hall and fever wards were added to its end.[16] This juxtaposition of dining-hall and infirmary would have appeared extraordinary by later 19th-century standards, but Huntingdon was by no means unique in unwittingly creating a health hazard. The first infirmary at Wells Union Workhouse was also attached to the dining-hall, with which it

The Workhouse

Figure 199 (right) Henry Ward's additions to Stoke-upon-Trent Workhouse in 1842 included this 'parish hospital'. Such large detached infirmaries were unusual on workhouse sites before the late 1860s. [BB93/27800]

Figure 200 (below) Pavilion-plan hospitals could adopt one of two alternative layouts, depending on their size. These were: a. the separate-block plan, in which the administrative services occupied a separate building from the wards, and b. the linear, or in-line plan, in which wards were directly attached to the administrative offices.

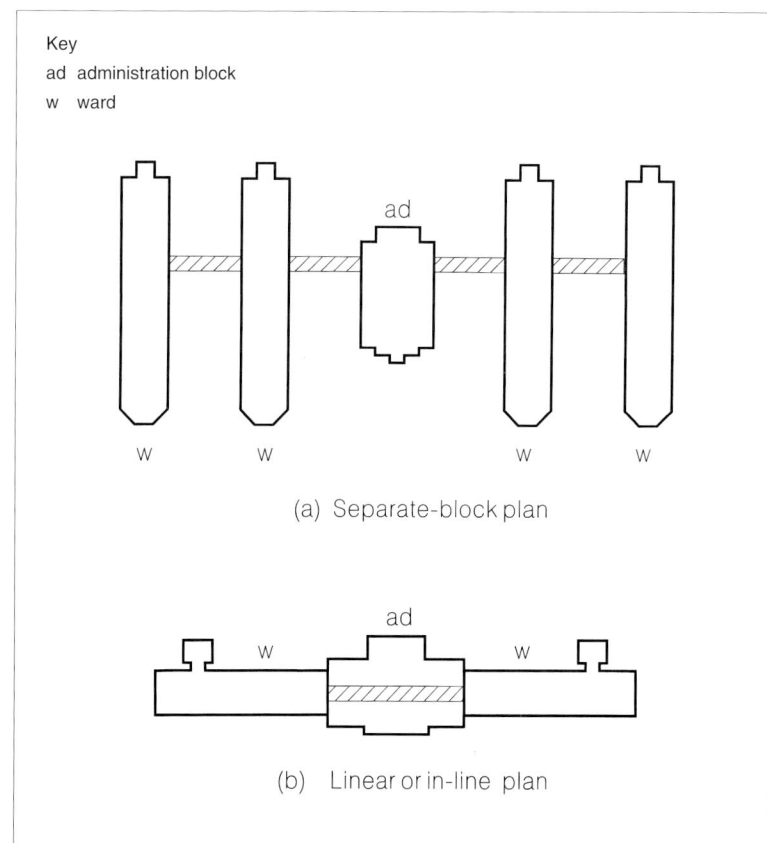

Key
ad administration block
w   ward

(a) Separate-block plan

(b) Linear or in-line plan

communicated directly (*see* Figure 66).[17] As the dangers inherent in such arrangements became apparent, building detached infirmaries was preferred by guardians.

The reason for the unprecedented demand for poor-law infirmary accommodation after 1835 is unclear. Those who were pauperised by sickness continued to be eligible for outdoor relief, but the availability of home care seems to have dropped markedly in the mid-19th century, as industrialisation wrought extreme social changes. Moreover, admission to workhouse infirmaries was encouraged by medical officers, who felt able to provide better care in infirmary wards than in their patients' squalid homes, largely because it involved less travelling for themselves. For whatever reason, it swiftly became standard practice for a new workhouse to include a detached infirmary. Unlike voluntary general hospitals, these infirmaries retained patients on a long-term basis, often until they either recovered or died. That factor partly explains why poor-law infirmaries expanded at a faster rate than voluntary hospitals throughout the late 19th and early 20th centuries.

New infirmaries of the 1840s and 1850s adopted a number of plan types, reflecting the variety found in contemporary general hospitals and main workhouse buildings. Many were

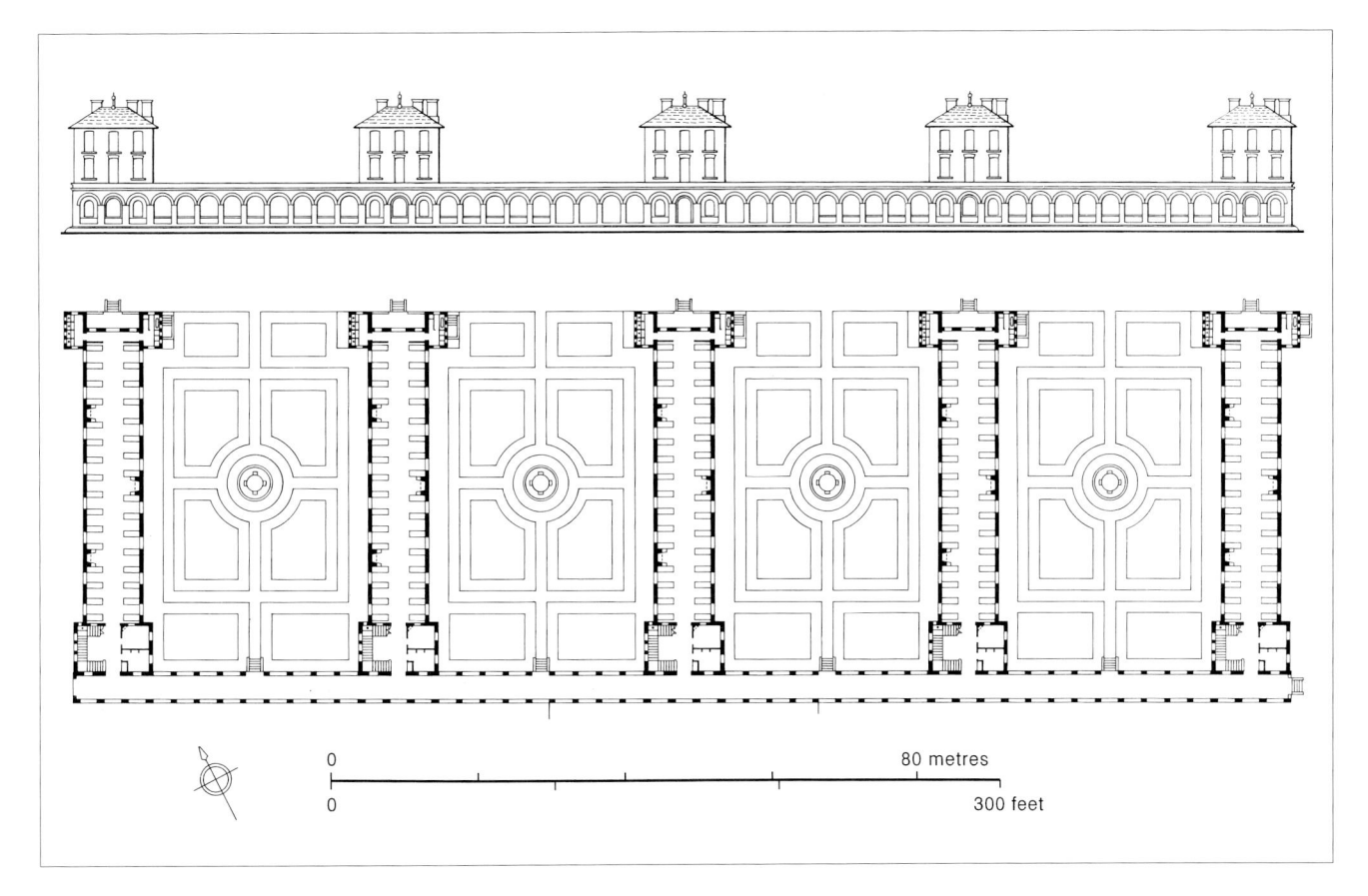

H-shaped, with the main wards in cross-wings and smaller wards and nurses' rooms opening off a corridor through the centre. Wards were sometimes of double-width, separated by a spine wall, or had a corridor along one side. As infirmaries still tended to be erected to the rear of workhouses they had little ornamentation; at most, a modest Italianate effect was achieved by placing round-headed windows beneath gables. The largest infirmaries erected in this period included the austerely Classical 'parish hospital' at Stoke-upon-Trent (1842; Fig 199) and the infirmaries of Portsea Island (1845),[18] York (1848–9), and Stoke Damerell (1850–4). The Stoke Damerell infirmary appears to have been rather advanced in having two large wards with opposing windows on both floors.[19] Even the best workhouse infirmaries, however, had no facilities for surgical and specialist cases and so, from 1852, guardians were permitted to subscribe to voluntary hospitals.[20] Although many pursued that course, the pressure on workhouse infirmaries was not significantly eased.

After the Crimean War, the acceptance of the Continental pavilion plan revolutionised English hospital design (*see* pages 103–4). The first pavilion-plan hospitals to be erected in England included the voluntary general hospital at Blackburn (1857; Smith & Turnbull) and the naval and military hospitals at Woolwich (1858–60, W Scamp and 1861–5, D Galton, respectively). These large establishments adopted the separate-block system, with an administration block connected to parallel ward blocks by single-storeyed covered ways (Fig 200a). For smaller establishments, such as cottage or regimental hospitals, a single building proved more suitable, with a central administration block flanked by ward wings arranged 'in line' (Fig 200b).

A few workhouse infirmaries adopted pavilion principles in the 1860s. The earliest and most whole-hearted of these was the Chorlton Union Workhouse infirmary, designed by Thomas Worthington in 1864–6 (Fig 201).[21] As it relied on the workhouse services, the projected administration block was not needed, and the infirmary simply comprised a row of five ward blocks. Chorlton may have been the unnamed Lancashire infirmary where, in 1869, the guardians made the surprising gesture of erecting a greenhouse specifically to supply the infirmary with flowers.[22]

Few unions acknowledged the need for such a large infirmary, never mind one designed according to the most up-to-date 'scientific' principles. Most guardians still failed to regard workhouse infirmaries as hospitals, and upheld

*Figure 201
One of the first large workhouse infirmaries was erected at Chorlton Union Workhouse in 1864–6, and was praised by Florence Nightingale. The architect was Thomas Worthington.
[Based on* The Builder, *17 June 1865, 430]*

*Figure 202
By the mid-1860s, new workhouses tended to include a detached infirmary. This infirmary formed part of the original scheme for Brighton Parish Workhouse, designed by J C & G Lansdown and erected in 1865–7.
[BB92/26916]*

the notion that sick paupers should not receive better medical attention than the independent sick poor. For some time after the erection of the Chorlton infirmary, new workhouses continued to include a detached infirmary on the outmoded corridor plan. These included the H-shaped infirmaries of Holbeck (1863–4), West London (1864; *see* Figure 109) and Brighton (1865–7; Fig 202). Many new establishments also included a detached fever hospital, generally positioned behind the infirmary. The new Brighton workhouse even included a smallpox hospital, but the fear of that disease was still such that most authorities would not risk looking after its victims in such close proximity to a workhouse.

A limited application of pavilion principles can be detected occasionally in 1860s infirmaries, for example at the Southampton infirmary of 1866, which had an in-line plan with cross-lit wards.[23] The sanitary facilities were located at the outer ends of the wards but were not separated from them by cross-ventilated lobbies, a vital element of the pavilion system. Externally, the toilets and bathrooms were expressed only by their narrow glazing and exposed pipes. A completely different approach was adopted for the contemporary fever hospital which stood behind the infirmary. That was a long building, divided into five distinct sections by stair bays. The central stair bay gave access to rooms used by the nursing staff while the others provided independent access to the wards. This method of separating the wards affected the positioning of the sanitary facilities: instead of lying at extreme ends of the building, they projected into small yards to the rear. This plan was to become standard for workhouse infirmaries, as well as fever hospitals, in the 1870s.

Public attention, and censure, was drawn towards London's workhouse infirmaries from the 1850s onward. The philanthropist Louisa Twining pointed out the shortage of trained nurses in workhouse infirmaries in the *Journal of the Workhouse Visiting Society*, an association which she had founded in 1859. Largely inspired by her work, in 1865, the *Lancet* appointed a Commission to investigate the condition of metropolitan infirmaries. It published highly critical accounts of several institutions. Particularly scandalous was the carpet-beating carried out by able-bodied inmates of Strand Union Workhouse directly beneath the windows of the sick wards, and stone-breaking outside the acute ward of the workhouse belonging to the joint parishes of St Margaret and St John, Westminster, at Kensington.[24] A member of the Lancet Commission, Dr Ernest Hart, went on in 1866 to found the Association for the Improvement of Workhouse Infirmaries and suggested means of providing new, separate infirmaries for the metropolitan area.[25] Florence Nightingale approached her ministerial contacts to urge the cause of these reformers, but maintained a discreet distance from the line of battle.

Under such concerted pressure, Charles Villiers, President of the Poor Law Board, instructed poor-law inspectors H B Farnall and Dr Edward Smith to prepare a report on metropolitan workhouse infirmaries. Farnall and Smith quickly discovered that sick infants and children, sick lunatics and imbeciles, and sick old people were often housed with the able-bodied in ordinary workhouse dormitories, and so they extended their inspection beyond infirmary wards. By now the able-bodied formed a minority of the occupants of London workhouses, and Farnall and Smith predicted that 'the infirmary must ere long become the main building, and the main building become comparatively superfluous . . . the main building is, in fact, the collection of offices, and the hospital or asylum for the aged'.[26] As well as exposing flaws in the design of existing sick wards and nursing arrangements, they drew attention to numerous insanitary practices, such as patients washing in chamber-pots, the lack of waste paper in water-closets and – 'a circumstance connected with the subject just discussed' – the dilapidated state of bibles and prayer-books.[27]

Before Farnall and Smith's reports could be acted upon, the government fell. The new President of the Poor Law Board, Gathorne Hardy, appointed inspectors Uvedale Corbett and Dr William O Markham to present a further report on metropolitan infirmaries, and he sent his assistant, John Lambert, to investigate the dispensary system operating in Ireland.[28] Furthermore, a Cubic Space Committee was appointed under the leadership of Dr Thomas

Watson, President of the Royal College of Physicians.

The subject of cubic space was not new to the Poor Law Board. In 1855 Dr Todd had proposed a minimum requirement of 300 cu ft per person in dormitories and 500 in wards which were occupied both day and night. Dr Smith had studied recent research by Dr Angus Smith and Professor Roscoe of Manchester which seemed to support a minimum of 500, so long as the height of the ward was 10 ft to 12 ft and the space between beds about 3 ft.[29] But Farnall, convinced by the much higher estimates proposed by the Barracks and Hospitals Commission and by Florence Nightingale, recommended a minimum of 1,000 cu ft.[30] A compromise was reached by Watson's Committee, which reported in February 1867 and suggested 850 cu ft in sick wards but 1,200 in fever and lying-in wards.[31] Even lower figures, of 600 to 720 cu ft for sick wards, were enshrined in the 1868 circular, *Points to be Attended to in the Construction of Workhouses*, but those were expressed in terms of floor space and ward height rather than cubic air space.[32]

The Metropolitan Poor Law Amendment Act of 1867 was based on these various official reports. It had significant repercussions for the treatment of the sick in workhouses throughout England, but especially in London, where the Metropolitan Asylums Board was set up to care for the capital's infectious cases, harmless lunatics and imbeciles.

'Lunatics' and 'Imbeciles' in the Workhouse, 1834–1867

The 47th clause of the 1834 Act stated that lunatics and imbeciles were not to be kept in the workhouse for longer than fourteen days.[33] Perhaps as a result of that, the model plans of 1835 failed to allocate space to lunatics or imbeciles, and neither were included amongst the seven official classes of pauper inmate. Lunatic wards, however, were mentioned in the 'Orders and Regulations to be Observed in the Workhouse', issued by the Poor Law Commission in the same year, and by and large the 47th clause was widely ignored.[34]

Most unions mixed lunatics, imbeciles and idiots with other inmates, who often acted as unpaid attendants (Fig 203), but a minority included small lunatic or imbecile wards in infirmaries. The guardians of Gloucester, for example, ensured that their new workhouse, designed by Scott & Moffatt, had a lunatic ward.[35] Architectural plans and maps show that several of Scott & Moffatt's other infirmaries, for example those at Williton (*see* Figure 70) and Macclesfield, included padded cells at a very early date.

Greenwich Union Workhouse infirmary of 1840 included idiots' wards on the ground floor of its cross-wings, and many of the new infirmaries erected in the 1840s and 1850s also included accommodation for imbeciles and/or lunatics. The infirmary to the rear of Bath Union Workhouse had imbecile cells on its ground floor, but elsewhere wards were favoured. The cross-wings of the Portsea Island Workhouse infirmary, built in 1845, contained separate wards and day-rooms for dangerous and harmless lunatics – a distinction which was being made for the first time in this period – with joint keeper's rooms.[36] At the new City of London Union Workhouse, built in 1848–9, imbeciles were provided with two small rooms to the rear of the dining-hall rather than space in the infirmary (*see* Figure 97). The use of the terms 'lunatic', 'imbecile' and 'idiot' in these cases suggests rather more specialisation than actually occurred; in fact, most authorities failed to distinguish between different categories of the 'insane'.

The 1845 Act 'for the Regulation and Care and Treatment of Lunatics' made it compulsory for counties and boroughs to erect pauper lunatic asylums, and further stipulated that dangerous

Figure 203
Despite attempts at rigid classification, the mentally handicapped often mixed with other categories of inmate in workhouse wards. This illustration is 'The Idiot', from Mrs Frances Trollope's novel, Jessie Phillips, *1844.*
[By permission of the Syndics of Cambridge University Library]

Table 7 Numbers of 'Insane' Indoor Paupers, 1859–99.[a]
(The figures are for 1 January in each year)

Year	1859	1869	1879	1889	1899
County or borough asylums	14,481	25,460	36,627	49,158	68,716
Registered hospitals or licensed houses	2,076	1,541	1,303	1,396	1,828
Union or parish workhouses	7,963	11,183	16,005	17,509	17,453
Lodgings or boarded-out or residing with relatives	5,798	6,969	6,230	5,930	5,960
Total	30,318	45,153	60,165	73,993	93,957

[a] *PP* 1860 (2675), XXXVII, xvii (12th Annual Report of PLB); *PP* 1870 (c.123), XXXV, 295 (22nd Annual Report of PLB); *PP* 1880 (c.2681), XXVI, xvii (9th Annual Report of LGB); *PP* 1890 (c.6141), XXXIII, 374 (19th Annual Report of LGB); *PP* 1900 (Cd.292), XXXIII, 60 (29th Annual Report of LGB).

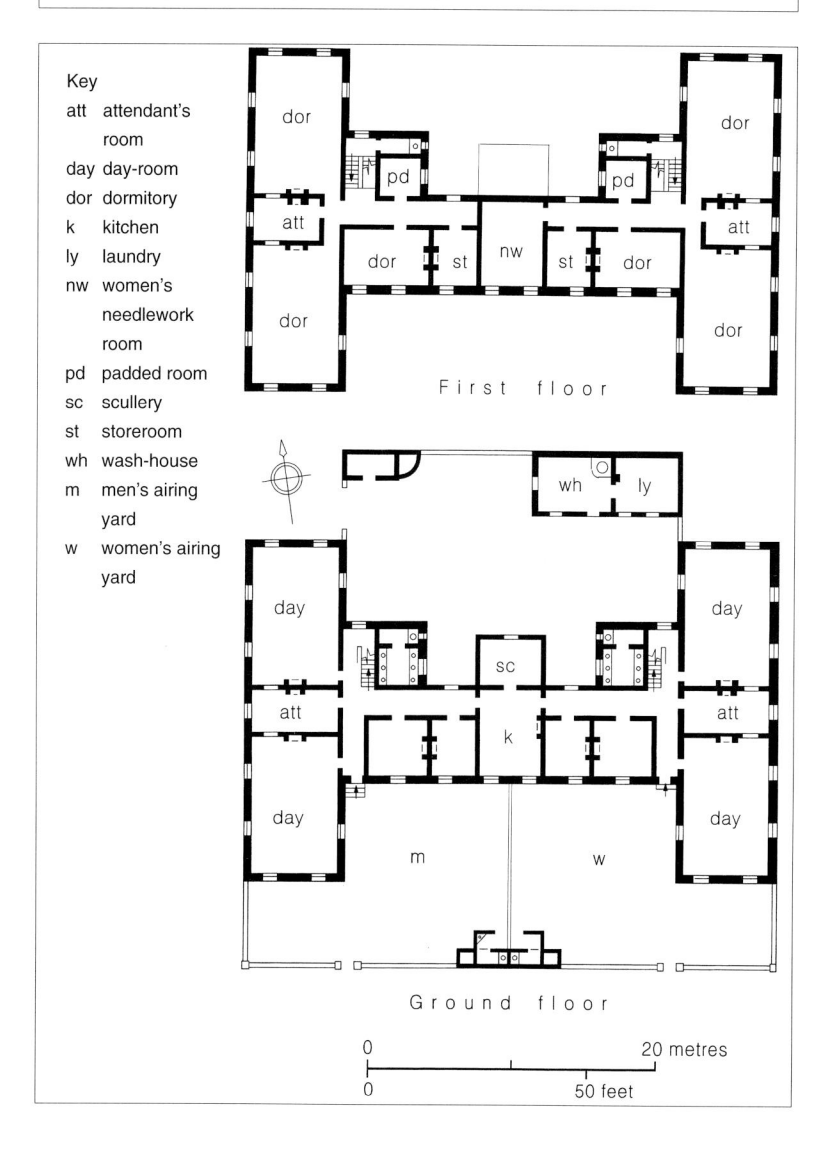

Key
att attendant's room
day day-room
dor dormitory
k kitchen
ly laundry
nw women's needlework room
pd padded room
sc scullery
st storeroom
wh wash-house
m men's airing yard
w women's airing yard

First floor

Ground floor

lunatics be removed from workhouses.[37] However, delays in the erection of the new asylums and resistance from guardians meant that some dangerous lunatics remained in workhouses for many more years. Conditions for the mentally ill in workhouses began to improve, albeit slowly, when the Lunacy Commissioners started to inspect their accommodation in 1842. Nevertheless, without trained staff to attend to these inmates, workhouse masters relied heavily on mechanical restraints such as chains and strait-jackets – often for harmless as well as dangerous lunatics. The banning of such devices in 1853 may have encouraged guardians to send lunatics and imbeciles to asylums, as it became more difficult to control them in the workhouse.[38] On the whole, however, guardians were loath to send patients to asylums, where their care could cost between £100 and £350 a year, instead of £40 in a workhouse. Throughout the second half of the century, the central authorities had to press guardians constantly to send potentially curable cases to asylums.

Despite the erection of county and borough asylums after 1845, and the huge expansion in asylum accommodation throughout the second half of the century, the number of lunatics and imbeciles in workhouses did not fall (*see* Table 7). In 1857, the Lunacy Commissioners, while still urging guardians to send the insane to asylums, emphasised the need for special accommodation to house that class in workhouses.[39] They may have adopted this tactic after realising that the county asylums were filling up with alarming rapidity. Some asylums housed so many 'imbecile and harmless chronic lunatics' that there was not enough room to admit treatable acute cases. The 1862 Lunacy Act recognised that under such circumstances chronic cases could be returned to the workhouse.[40]

A new lunatic block opened at Bath in 1857, and was praised in the *Journal of the Workhouse Visiting Society* as a successful experiment, suggesting that few lunatic wards of this standard yet existed on workhouse sites. The building at Bath could hold 140 and already held 89; with 100 occupants it would allow 620 cu ft per person, slightly over the minimum 576 allowed by the Commissioners in Lunacy in lunatic asylums.[41] With 140 inmates, on the other hand, it would only have allowed 443 cu ft, well below the minimum standard. A few years later, in 1864, the Commissioners in Lunacy laid down slightly less stringent conditions for lunatic accommodation in workhouses, with 600 cu ft in single bedrooms, 500 in dormitories and 400 in day-rooms.[42]

In 1859 only 10 per cent of workhouses provided separate insane wards, but progress was being made in London.[43] By 1866, inspectors

Farnall and Smith were able to remark that facilities for lunatics and imbeciles in London workhouses were much superior to those for other inmates, including the sick.[44] Only ten years previously, Dr Henry Bence Jones had reported on the horrible condition of the insane wards at St Pancras Workhouse: some lay underground, adjacent to a cemetery, while another was ventilated by a single grating opening into a privy.[45] Since then, however, several new lunatic wards had opened in the capital. These included the lunatic block at the new West London Union Workhouse of 1864, which was H-shaped, like many contemporary infirmaries (*see* Figure 109). In the centre were an attendant's room, a padded room and a staircase for each sex, and a shared kitchen. The wings held large day-rooms and dormitories, cross-lit on the short walls, and each had two fireplaces and sanitary facilities.

The so-called lunatic block of Brighton Workhouse, built in 1865–6, (Fig 204) was similar to that of West London Union. According to a contemporary description of the site in the *Brighton and Hove Herald*, the lunatic wards 'may be regarded as the temporary home of those weak, silly and imbecile, devoid of vice and perfectly harmless'.[46] This illustrates how many authorities failed to distinguish properly between lunatics and imbeciles, even by this date, and so it is impossible to be absolutely certain of what is meant by 'lunatic block' or 'imbecile block' without consulting the records of those who actually occupied them.

Metropolitan Asylums Board Fever and Smallpox Hospitals

Before 1867, only Paddington and Poplar Union had retained fever cases in the workhouse; other metropolitan authorities habitually sent cases to special fever and smallpox hospitals, paying 1*s* per day for their treatment.[47] Henceforth, the Metropolitan Asylums Board was assigned the task of establishing and maintaining fever and smallpox hospitals for London's poor.[48] It was only after the passage of the Diseases Prevention Metropolis Act in 1883 that poor patients could enter the Metropolitan Asylums Board's isolation hospitals without becoming disenfranchised and stigmatised as paupers.[49]

Early attempts to set up three district infectious diseases hospitals, each with 200 fever beds and 100 smallpox beds, were hampered by the objections of local residents – particularly by the inventor of the penny post, Sir Rowland Hill, in Hampstead – as well as by the parsimony of both the Poor Law Board and its successor, the Local Government Board.[50] The Metropolitan Asylums Board was scarcely prepared, therefore, for the relapsing-fever epidemic which hit London in 1869. It coped with the emergency by hastily erecting temporary hutted wards at the London Fever Hospital, and on its newly acquired site in Hampstead. By the time of the smallpox epidemic of 1871–3, the Board's two other sites, in Homerton and Stockwell, had become operational. Like Hampstead, these hospitals comprised a row of parallel ward blocks, connected along one side by a covered way. Only the smallpox section of the Homerton Hospital deviated from this layout, with four ward blocks radiating from a core building. On several future occasions the Board was compelled to set up temporary hospitals to deal with epidemics (Fig 205), replacing them with permanent structures once the crisis had abated; few of these temporary ward blocks survive today.

Two new fever hospitals with permanent, brick-built administration and service buildings but semi-permanent ward blocks, the Western Hospital at Fulham and the South-Eastern Hospital at New Cross, were erected in 1877. Shortly afterwards, the Report of the Royal Commission on Smallpox and Fever Hospitals (1881–2), and an official inquiry into the siting of the Fulham hospital, considered the dangers of airborne infection.[51] Their somewhat misconceived concerns, together with local opposition, persuaded the Board to locate its smallpox hospitals away from centres of population. This resulted in the establishment of a river ambulance service and the so-called River Hospitals at Darenth. Two Board hospital ships which had

Figure 205
This photograph of c 1930 shows the interior of one of the huts which originally comprised the Metropolitan Asylums Board North-Eastern Fever Hospital at Tottenham (1892).
[London Metropolitan Archives B1761]

Figure 204 (opposite)
While some unions sent their mentally ill charges to asylums, others preferred the cheaper option of housing them at the workhouse. These 'lunatic wards' formed part of the new Brighton Parish Workhouse, built in 1865–7.
[Plan redrawn from Public Record Office MH14/5]

been moored off Greenwich, the *Atlas* (Fig 206) and the *Endymion*, were moved down the Thames to Long Reach, near Dartford, where they were joined, in 1883, by the *Castalia*. A tented smallpox hospital, the South Smallpox Camp, was set up at nearby Gore Farm in 1883 and replaced by permanent buildings for convalescents in 1887–1902.[52]

The cottage-home, or villa, system influenced the layout of most of the Board's convalescent establishments. The earliest of these was the Northern (Convalescent) Hospital at Winchmore Hill, erected to a design by Pennington & Bridgen in 1885–7.[53] A similar layout was adopted for the more extensive Southern (Convalescent) Hospital at Carshalton, erected for recovering fever patients in the late 1890s but never used as such. Upon completion, it accommodated 1,000 chronically ill and convalescent children and was renamed, first the Children's Infirmary, then in 1910, Queen Mary's Hospital for Children. It included twenty-four double bungalow pavilions in six groups, with one staff block to each group, two infirmary blocks, and administrative buildings. A third Board establishment on the villa system was the small children's sanitorium built at Rustington in Sussex in 1898. These hospitals can be compared with the cottage-home villages erected by the Board, at the turn of the century, for children suffering from ophthalmia (*see* Figure 186), rather than with other fever hospitals.

Five new fever hospitals were built in response to the scarlet fever and smallpox epidemics of 1892–3. The North-Eastern Fever Hospital at Tottenham (*see* Figure 205) and the Fountain Hospital at Tooting comprised timber and corrugated-iron huts, while the Brook Hospital at Shooters Hill, the Park Hospital at Hither Green (Fig 207) and the Grove Hospital at Tooting had permanent brick structures.[54] Without exception, these hospitals were built on the separate-block system, and in each case the architect adopted a utilitarian style.

The site of the shore buildings serving the hospital ships at Long Reach was enlarged by a purchase of land in 1894, and in 1901–3 three new hospitals were erected there: Long Reach and Orchard Hospitals comprised wooden huts, but Joyce Green Hospital was of permanent, brick construction with ward blocks arranged *en échelon* – apparently adopting the fashion of contemporary lunatic asylums, but in fact following the line of the main West Kent Sewer. These institutions, all designed by the experienced poor-law architects Arthur & Christopher Harston, were the last large isolation hospitals to be erected within the remit of the English poor law.

Over the years, the responsibilities of the Metropolitan Asylums Board were extended by several Acts. In particular, in 1897, it was made responsible for children suffering from contagious diseases of the skin and scalp (*see* page 149), and in 1913 it was given responsibility for treating tuberculosis (*see* page 176).

*Figure 206 (above)
The Metropolitan Asylums Board hospital ship*, Atlas, *was one of three floating smallpox hospitals moored off Long Reach between c 1880 and 1904. It could accommodate 300 patients.*
[London Metropolitan Archives 77/1407]

*Figure 207 (right)
These angled sanitary towers stand at the ends of the wards at the Park Hospital, Hither Green (1895–7), designed by Edwin T Hall.*
[BB93/25114]

Metropolitan Asylums Board Asylums for Imbeciles and Harmless Lunatics

As well as fever and smallpox hospitals the Metropolitan Asylums Board established asylums for imbeciles and the chronic insane in the London area.[55] The resulting institutions greatly relieved the problem of housing such cases in workhouses, although some metropolitan workhouses continued, in a small way, to care for the mentally ill.

By 1870 the Board had erected two near-identical asylums, one at Caterham, the other at Leavesden, each with 1,500 beds. Designed by John Giles & Biven (Fig 208), they were on the separate-block system, with huge double-width wards each capable of accommodating eighty inmates. These buildings quickly filled with all classes of mentally ill paupers, from the Middlesex County Asylums as well as workhouses, and both sites soon required extensions.

The training of imbecile children was undertaken by the Board from 1873. In 1878 a school, or training colony, for 600 imbecile children, opened at Darenth. Designed by A & C Harston, the institution included separate blocks for the healthy, infants, the sick, epileptics and the helpless and paralysed. These were arranged on the pavilion plan, together with separate schoolrooms and chapels for boys and girls. In 1880, the school was supplemented by an asylum on a neighbouring site for those over the age of 16. The system of giving children a special education at the school, and then sending them to the adjoining institution, broke down as the Board was forced to admit increasing numbers of untrainable adults.

A later mental hospital erected by the Board was Tooting Bec Asylum (Fig 209), an infirmary for uncertifiable senile patients, infirm epileptics and other 'persons requiring individual attention'. It was designed by the Harstons and deliberately given the same layout as Caterham and Leavesden.[56] The plain, three-storeyed single pavilions were connected by a covered way and escape bridges which doubled as verandas in fine weather. Superficially, they resembled ordinary infirmary wards: the staircase was located on the opposite side of the covered way to the wards, and at the entrance to each 24-bed ward, small rooms such as a duty room and bathroom opened off a central corridor. However, a small 6-bed ward projected from one side of each main ward, a toilet annexe from the other and a wide polygonal day-room from the end. All the wards were lit by tall sash and hopper windows.

As well as these institutions for mental defectives, the Board ran a colony for sane epileptics at Edmonton.

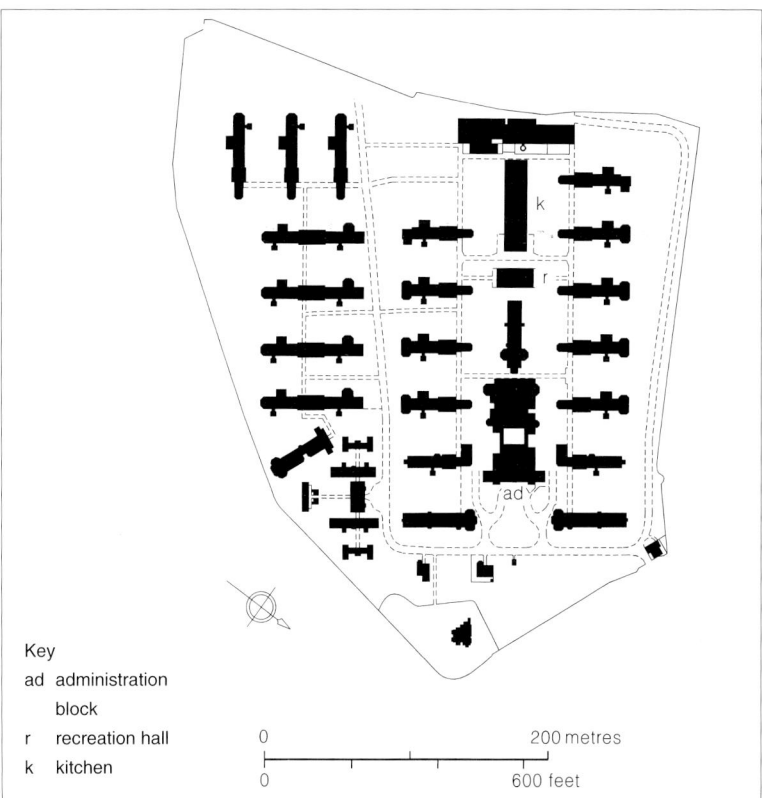

Key
ad administration block
r recreation hall
k kitchen

Poor-Law Infirmaries in London, 1867–1900

The 1867 Metropolitan Poor Act introduced a dispensary system which provided an extensive outdoor medical service and relieved pressure on crowded London infirmaries. By 1887, forty-four dispensaries (Fig 210) had been established.[57] In some cases they were associated with relief offices or workhouses, but they usually comprised a small, converted house with a waiting-room, capable of seating twenty to thirty out-patients, to the rear. Opening off the waiting-room were one or more consulting-rooms and a dispensary with a wicket door, through which medicines were passed. In some cases, the dispenser resided in the building.

The Act of 1867 also initiated the partial reorganisation of London's poor-law authorities with

Figure 208 (top)
The Metropolitan Asylum for Imbeciles at Caterham (1869–70) in Surrey, was designed by John Giles & Biven. The site is now St Lawrence's Hospital.
[BB92/31772]

Figure 209 (above)
Tooting Bec Asylum was built in 1899–1903 as an infirmary for sick mentally handicapped cases.
[Plan redrawn from London Metropolitan Archives AR/CB/3/4/139]

THE WORKHOUSE

*Figure 210
This was one of two dispensaries set up by St Marylebone in the early 1870s.
[From Snell, H S 1881, 46, by permission of the Syndics of Cambridge University Library]*

*Figure 211
This shows the rear of the main building of Holborn Union Infirmary, Archway (1879) by Henry Saxon Snell.
[BB93/11595]*

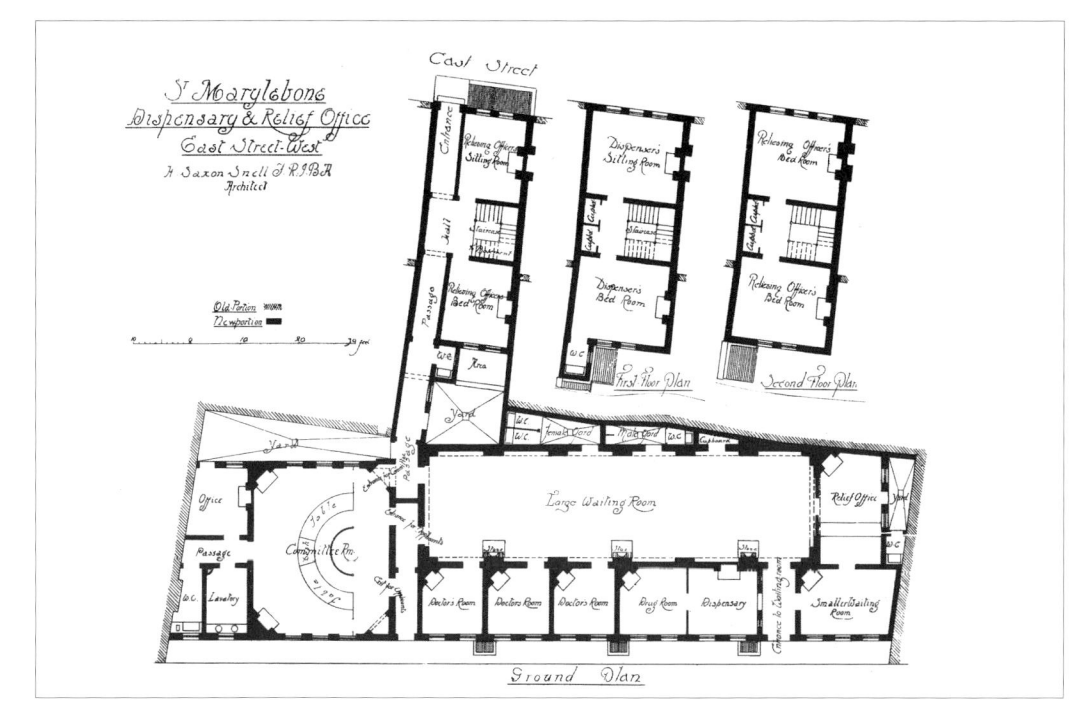

a view to improving infirmary accommodation. Letters were sent to seventeen of the forty metropolitan authorities, requesting them to provide infirmaries on sites separate from the workhouse. Encouragement was provided by a Common Poor Fund for London. The remaining twenty-three authorities were organised into six sick asylum districts but these, with the exception of the Poplar and Stepney Sick Asylum District, failed to become operational.

Two of the first authorities to erect an infirmary on a site separate from the workhouse were St Pancras Union[58] and the Poplar and Stepney Sick Asylum District. Others followed in the 1870s and 1880s, including Holborn Union (Fig 211) and St Marylebone, but the majority of metropolitan authorities, including Fulham, Hackney, Kensington and St George's, merely built new infirmaries on their workhouse sites. Institutionally, these differed from earlier pavilion-plan workhouse infirmaries, such as Chorlton, by having their own separate administrative system, headed by a medical superintendent rather than the workhouse master. They therefore required an administration block, accommodation for the resident medical staff, a separate kitchen and a laundry. The usual arrangement for large infirmaries, such as St Marylebone (Fig 212), comprised a central administration block flanked by separate male and female ward blocks; smaller infirmaries, like those of St John, Hampstead (1869) or St Leonard, Shoreditch (1870–2; Fig 213), occupied a single building with wards attached to the administration block, or in-line.

Poor-Law Buildings for the Sick, the Mentally Ill and the Mentally Handicapped

Figure 212 (left) The St Marylebone Infirmary was built in Kensington in 1879–81.
[From Snell, H S 1881, by permission of the Syndics of Cambridge University Library]

Figure 213 (below, right) The infirmary of St Leonard's Workhouse, Shoreditch (1870–2), abutted an earlier building of 1863. The lane leading into the workhouse site was named 'Land of Promise'.
[BB92/15288]

Most new infirmary wards were long, rectangular rooms which held two rows of beds, but some novel exceptions were created. Henry Saxon Snell included double-width wards, a plan usually reserved for wards occupied by aged or healthy workhouse inmates, in his Holborn Union Infirmary of 1879 (*see* Figure 211).[59] The building was heavily criticised, and attraced few imitators. Snell was also one of the first to advocate circular ward blocks, a form which attracted the notice of hospital architects in England in the early 1880s. He drafted several schemes for hospitals with circular wards, but none were executed and Snell eventually joined the critics of the circular ward block. Other architects, however, used the circular form to expand congested sites, such as those of St John, Hampstead (1884–5)[60] and Camberwell Infirmary (1889–90; Fig 214).

Figure 214 (above, left) A small number of circular ward blocks were erected at poor-law infirmaries in the late 19th century. This building was part of Camberwell Infirmary (1889–90).
[BB92/23900]

167

THE WORKHOUSE

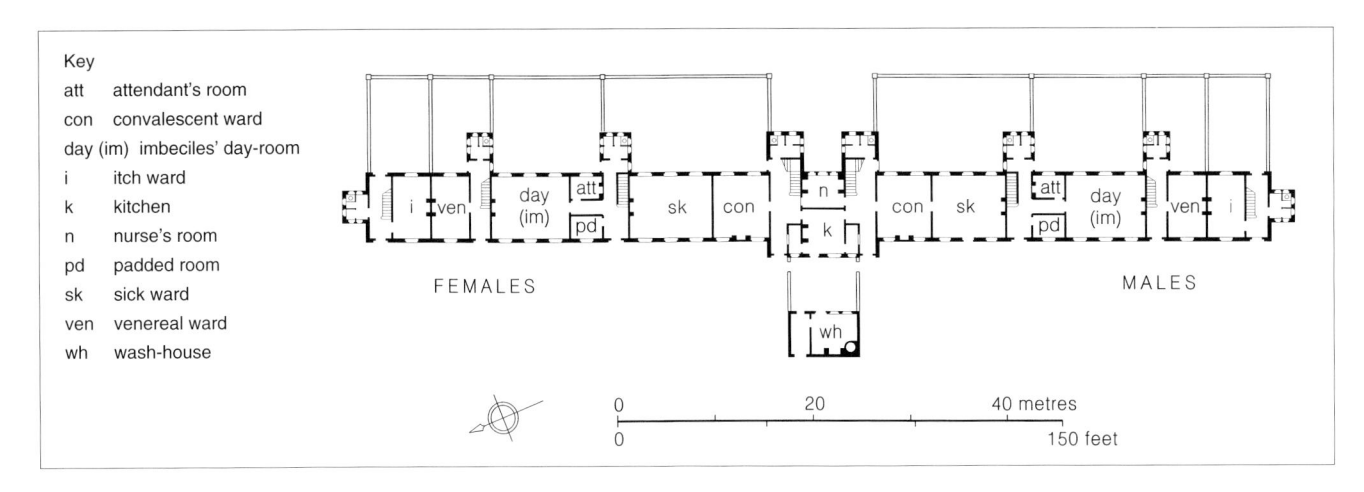

```
Key
att    attendant's room
con    convalescent ward
day (im)  imbeciles' day-room
i      itch ward
k      kitchen
n      nurse's room
pd     padded room
sk     sick ward
ven    venereal ward
wh     wash-house
```

*Figure 215 (above)
The infirmary of
Holbeck Union
Workhouse (1880–1),
designed by W Hill, was
over 300 ft long. The
institution has been
demolished.*
[Plan redrawn from Public
Record Office MH14/15]

*Figure 216 (right)
A new infirmary was
erected at Kingston-
upon-Thames Union
Workhouse in 1868.
The architects were
T H Rushforth &
C L Luck.*
[Plan redrawn from Public
Record Office MH14/17]

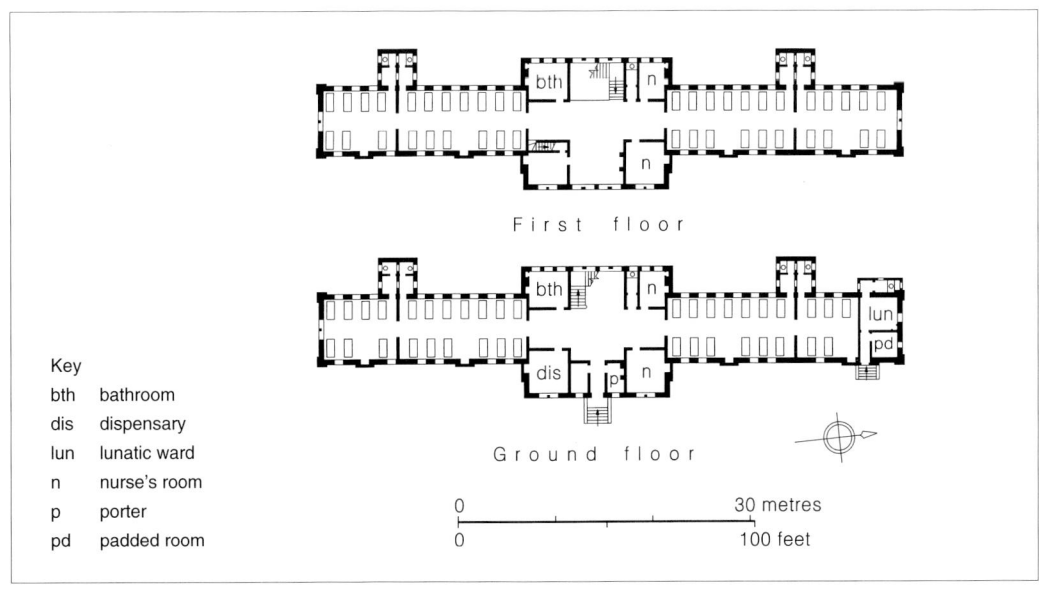

```
Key
bth    bathroom
dis    dispensary
lun    lunatic ward
n      nurse's room
p      porter
pd     padded room
```

Poor-Law Infirmaries Outside London, 1867–1900

In 1867–8, a government inquiry revealed that many provincial workhouse infirmaries were just as inadequate as their metropolitan counterparts.[61] There followed a period of intense infirmary construction throughout the country, despite the fact that no new legislation offered financial aid to improve buildings – or to remove infectious and mentally handicapped patients to specialist institutions – as was the case in London. Many new infectious blocks were erected at the same time, fulfilling a need which was strongly reinforced by a series of epidemics: cholera in 1866, relapsing fever in 1869–70 and smallpox in 1871–3.

A single building on the workhouse site usually fulfilled the infirmary requirements of rural and semi-rural unions. From the late 1860s until well into the 20th century, such buildings usually followed a linear plan, with central nurses' rooms flanked by cross-ventilated ward wings. As in the Southampton fever block, wings were divided into a number of distinct rooms by cross-walls or stair bays, and each ward was served by its own sanitary facilities, characteristically projecting under a monopitch or catslide roof. Although they seldom contained more than 100 beds, linear infirmaries could be extremely long, narrow buildings: that erected behind Holbeck workhouse in 1881–2 (Fig 215), for about 100 patients, had fourteen-bay wings and measured over 300 ft in length.[62]

The division of infirmary ranges into a number of distinct units facilitated classification and separation. Inner rooms could be used as day-rooms, convalescent wards or general sick wards while outer rooms were often assigned to so-called offensive cases, such as those suffering from venereal disease or itch, or to lunatics and imbeciles. Typically, the ground floor of each of the long wings of Hastings infirmary (1868) included a sick ward, a convalescent ward and an infectious ward. The contemporary infirmary of Kingston-upon-Thames (Fig 216) was more unusual in having a large administrative centre containing a nurses' room, a dispensary and a bathroom, together with a wide access corridor which doubled as a day-room, perhaps inspired by the gallery day-room of contemporary lunatic asylums.[63] At one end of the building, on the ground floor, was a small lunatic ward complete with its own water-closet and padded room. The tympanum over the main entrance, carved with works of mercy (Fig 217), gave an unexpectedly decorative touch to the building.

After 1870, most workhouses provided a detached building for the isolation of infectious complaints. That was usually a single-storeyed block, with a central nurses' room flanked by small cross-ventilated wards with end sanitary annexes; larger infectious diseases blocks could closely resemble contemporary infirmaries. The two-storeyed 'Fever Hospital' at Bolton (Fig 218) had two wards on each floor of each wing, enabling the isolation of four different diseases on each side of the building. At a later date, some unions opted for one of the model plans which were issued for local-authority infectious diseases hospitals. In 1893, for example, Ashby-de-la-Zouch adopted Local Government Board plan type B, which had wards with verandas facing in opposite directions (Fig 219).[64]

As well as detached infectious diseases blocks, some workhouses included special buildings for those suffering from venereal disease or itch. These were usually tiny buildings: the lock (venereal disease) and itch wards at Sunderland (1887) and Coventry (1886), for example, held only three or four beds apiece. Larger blocks were erected in some populous urban unions: the so-called 'contagious' block (1881) at West Bromwich workhouse had 44 beds in four wards and resembled an ordinary infirmary. The new Wolverhampton Union Workhouse, designed in 1899 by Arthur Marshall, included two low, detached buildings for 'syphilitic and skin diseases': that for men contained 16 beds, that for women, 10.[65]

Moral considerations, as well as concern for their health and welfare, affected the accommodation and treatment of lying-in cases, most of whom were unmarried mothers. In the last quarter of the century, while it remained common for pregnant women to be separated from 'respectable' female patients, they were more likely to be housed in the infirmary than in the main workhouse building. At Holbeck, the lying-in ward and labour room were situated on the first floor of the female wing of the infirmary, but elsewhere they occupied the upper floor of the administration block, or even a single-storeyed 'bungalow' maternity block, linked to the rear of the infirmary by a covered way.

A number of unions built detached maternity blocks at the turn of the century. That of Ecclesall Bierlow (1896–7), a strong, simple stone building with crenellated sanitary towers (Fig 220), was known as 'The Victoria Diamond Jubilee Maternity Hospital'. Such a name was more typical of voluntary than poor-law hospitals, and its adoption evinces a sympathetic attitude to lying-in cases. The maternity wards of Kensington Workhouse (1888), Halifax Union Infirmary (1897–1901) and Exeter Union Workhouse (1904–5) were all single-storeyed buildings on the separate-block system.

The largest provincial infirmaries, usually those with more than 100 beds, were designed on a separate-block plan throughout.[66] As in London, they had their own administration blocks, with male wards on one side and female

Figure 217 (below)
This carved tympanum is set over the entrance to the Kingston-upon-Thames Union Workhouse infirmary of 1868.
[BB96/528]

Figure 218 (bottom)
The large fever hospital, erected on the site of Bolton Union Workhouse in 1872, resembled contemporary infirmaries. The workhouse is now Bolton District General Hospital.
[BB96/2243]

THE WORKHOUSE

Figure 219
This infectious diseases block was built at Ashby-de-la-Zouch Union Workhouse in 1893.
[Plan and elevation redrawn from Public Record Office MH14/1]

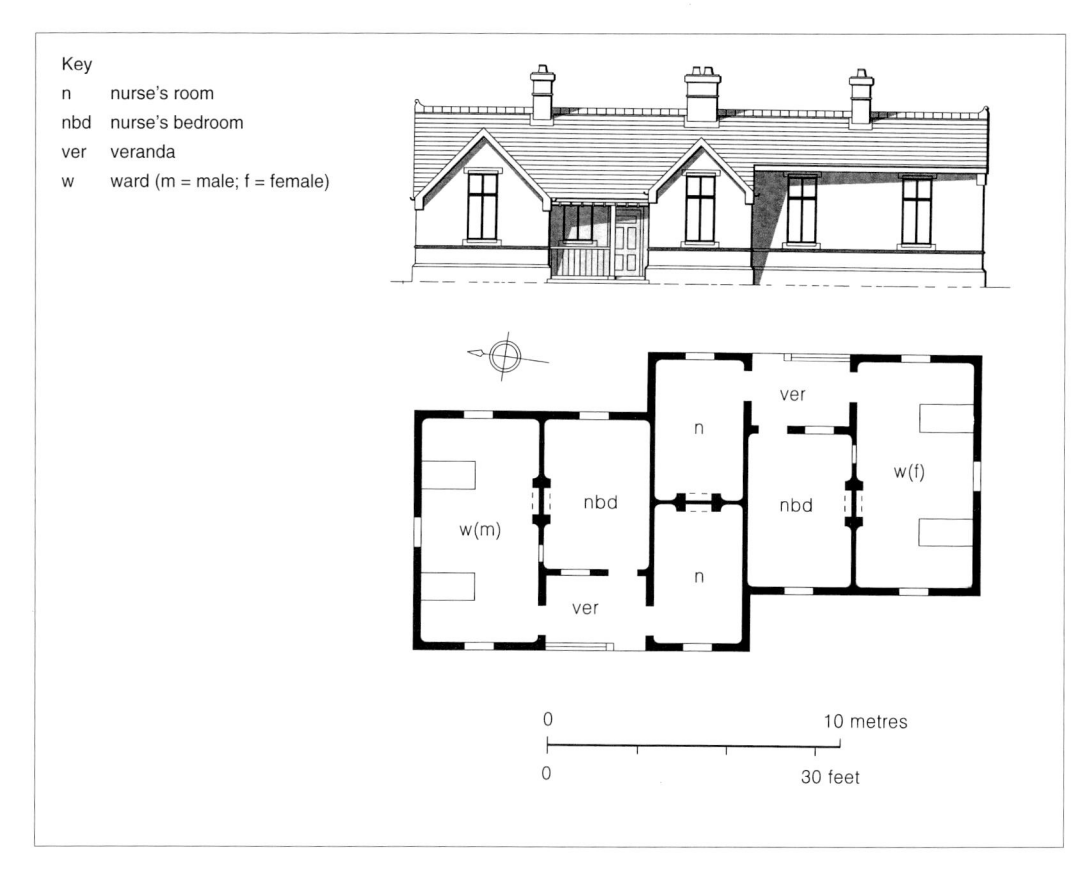

Key
n   nurse's room
nbd   nurse's bedroom
ver   veranda
w   ward (m = male; f = female)

Figure 220
The lying-in block at Ecclesall Bierlow Union Workhouse, with its unusual crenellated sanitary towers, was built in 1896–7. The site is now Nether Edge Hospital.
[BB93/34577]

wards on the other. Ward blocks could be positioned on one or both sides of a covered way. They were usually orientated north–south, and their height was generally limited to two storeys; ideally, each block held no more than sixty or seventy patients. The division of blocks into a succession of wards or rooms, each with its own sanitary facilities, was similar to that found in infirmaries with in-line plans, but individual wards could be much larger. The southern tip of large wards received particularly elaborate architectural treatment, as at Kings Norton (1897; D Arkell), where arcaded verandas ran between polygonal sanitary annexes (Fig 221). The 642-bed infirmary erected for Halifax Union (1897–1901; R Horsfall & W Clement Williams) was one of the few to partake in the brief fashion for circular ward blocks (Fig 222).

Distinctions between wards for 'deserving' and 'non-deserving' classes of pauper, in terms of their location and arrangement, were still marked in infirmaries at the turn of the century. For the new Hunslet workhouse (1900–3), J H Morton designed a separate-block infirmary with wards for bedridden and surgical patients in the south pavilions and venereal and itch cases in those to the north (Fig 223). While the ends of the north pavilions terminated in central sanitary annexes and were extremely plain, the south pavilions, for the bedridden, had polygonal ends with wide eaves sheltering open verandas with wrought-iron supports and railings.

Provincial infirmaries rivalled their metropolitan counterparts in scale, but were seldom erected on separate sites from the workhouse. One of the earliest of these, Keighley Union Infirmary, was a small complex, designed in 1870 and erected in the following year.[67] An infirmary and an infectious block were

170

Poor-Law Buildings for the Sick, the Mentally Ill and the Mentally Handicapped

Figure 221 (above) This contemporary photograph shows the infirmary built at Kings Norton Union Workhouse (now Selly Oak Hospital) in 1897. The architect was D Arkell. [B42/2717]

Figure 222 (left) This postcard dates from the First World War when Halifax Union Infirmary (1897–1901) – now Halifax General Hospital – was used as a military hospital. The circular ward block can be seen on the left. [BB90/9187]

connected to one another by a kitchen and laundry range, both rendered necessary by the remoteness of the workhouse services. Most separate-site infirmaries, however, were much larger than Keighley. The recommended maximum size, 500 to 600 beds, was often exceeded, and by 1900 some establishments had expanded to hold over 1,000 beds – more than any contemporary voluntary hospital.

By the 1890s, most workhouse infirmaries employed trained nurses, rather than pauper nurses. Trained nurses expected accommodation on a par with that offered at voluntary hospitals, and so comfortable nurses' homes were provided, to come under the supervision of a lady superintendent. These were usually decorative buildings in a contemporary Queen Anne or Arts & Crafts style (Fig 224), with generous bay windows lighting the ground-floor sitting and dining-rooms.

171

The Workhouse

*Figure 223 (right)
By the end of the 19th century most large workhouses had infirmaries with separate-block plans and carefully segregated wards. This ground-floor plan shows the layout of the infirmary at Hunslet Union Workhouse (1900–3; J H Morton), which later became St George's Hospital, but is now disused.*
[Redrawn from Public Record Office MH14/16]

*Figure 224 (below)
Detached nurses' homes formed part of infirmary complexes from the 1890s. This one was erected in 1900 at Steyning Union Workhouse, where the infirmary lay adjacent to the workhouse.*
[BB93/28477]

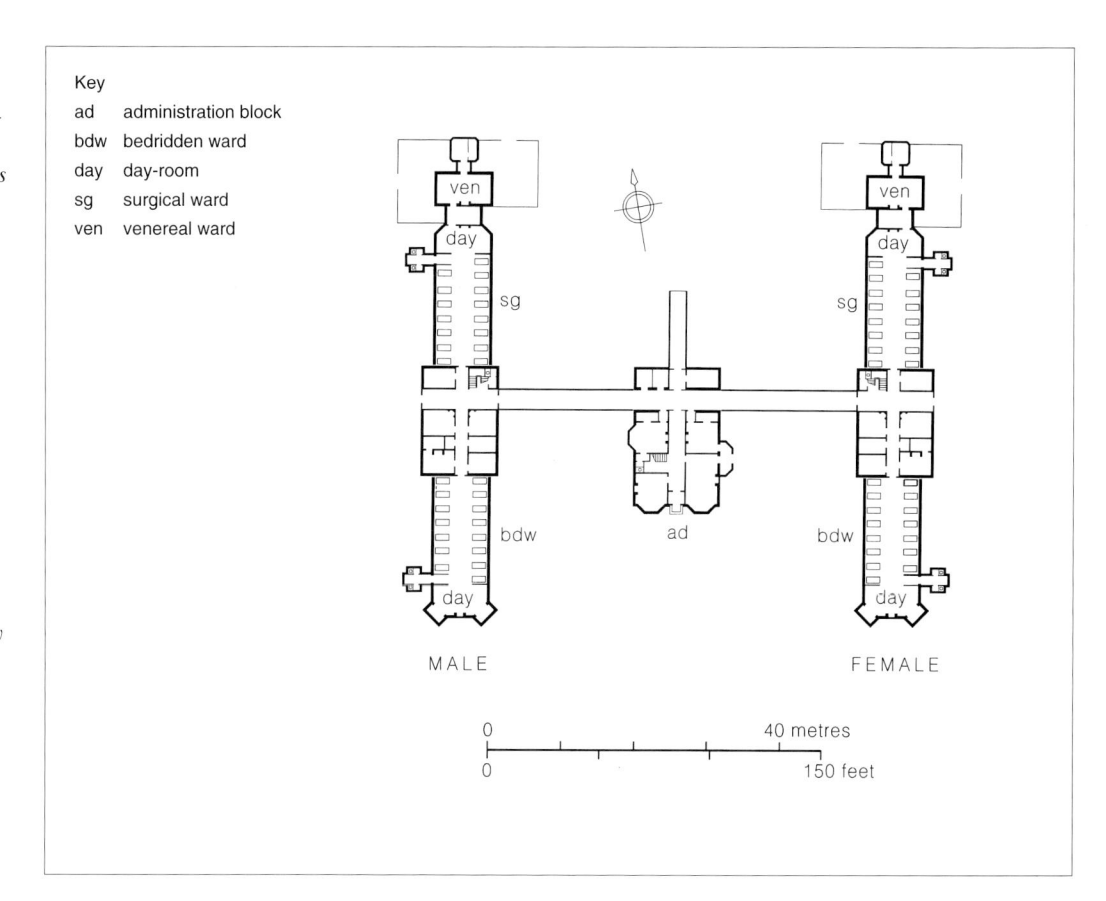

Key
ad administration block
bdw bedridden ward
day day-room
sg surgical ward
ven venereal ward

Lunatics and Imbeciles in the Workhouse, 1867–1914

The numbers of lunatics and imbeciles housed in workhouses rose considerably between 1835 and 1867, but it was only after that date that many buildings were erected for those classes of pauper. Two three-storeyed imbecile blocks were built at Portsea Island Union Workhouse in 1883, facing each other across a yard (Figs 225 and 226). Although slightly different in design, each block was unusually decorative, of red brick with stone and polychrome brick dressings. Bay windows lit the ground-floor day-rooms, but the dormitories had hospital-type sash and hopper windows. For the patients' safety, the stairs were in short flights and had handrails.

Workhouses still housed some curable and incurable lunatics as well as imbeciles and idiots. Under the Lunacy Act of 1890,[68] dangerous lunatics had to be housed in 'short-period' lunatic wards until they could be removed to an asylum by the Lunacy Commissioners. These wards usually occupied a small, detached building with a symmetrical layout. The centre housed an attendant's room and padded rooms; the wards generally held between two to eight patients. While some unions erected buildings especially for this purpose, others converted existing buildings. In 1892, for example, the boardroom of Houghton-le-Spring Union Workhouse was transformed into two wards for 'short-period' lunatics, together with a padded cell and attendant's room.

Despite improved accommodation, the practice of housing lunatics and imbeciles in workhouses remained controversial. The Royal Commission of 1905–9 was shocked to discover that imbeciles still mixed freely with other classes, and their sympathy with the latter, rather than the former, was plainly expressed:

> We have ourselves seen . . . idiots who are physically offensive or mischievous, or so noisy as to create a disturbance by day and by night with their howls, living in the ordinary wards, to the perpetual annoyance and disgust of the other inmates . . .

Figure 225 (left)
This is a view of one of the 'imbecile' blocks erected at Portsea Island Union Workhouse in 1883.
[BB96/4164]

Figure 226 (below)
This ward block was built at Portsea Island Union Workhouse in Hampshire specifically for the mentally handicapped, in 1883. The site is now St Mary's Hospital.
[Redrawn from plans from Hampshire RO]

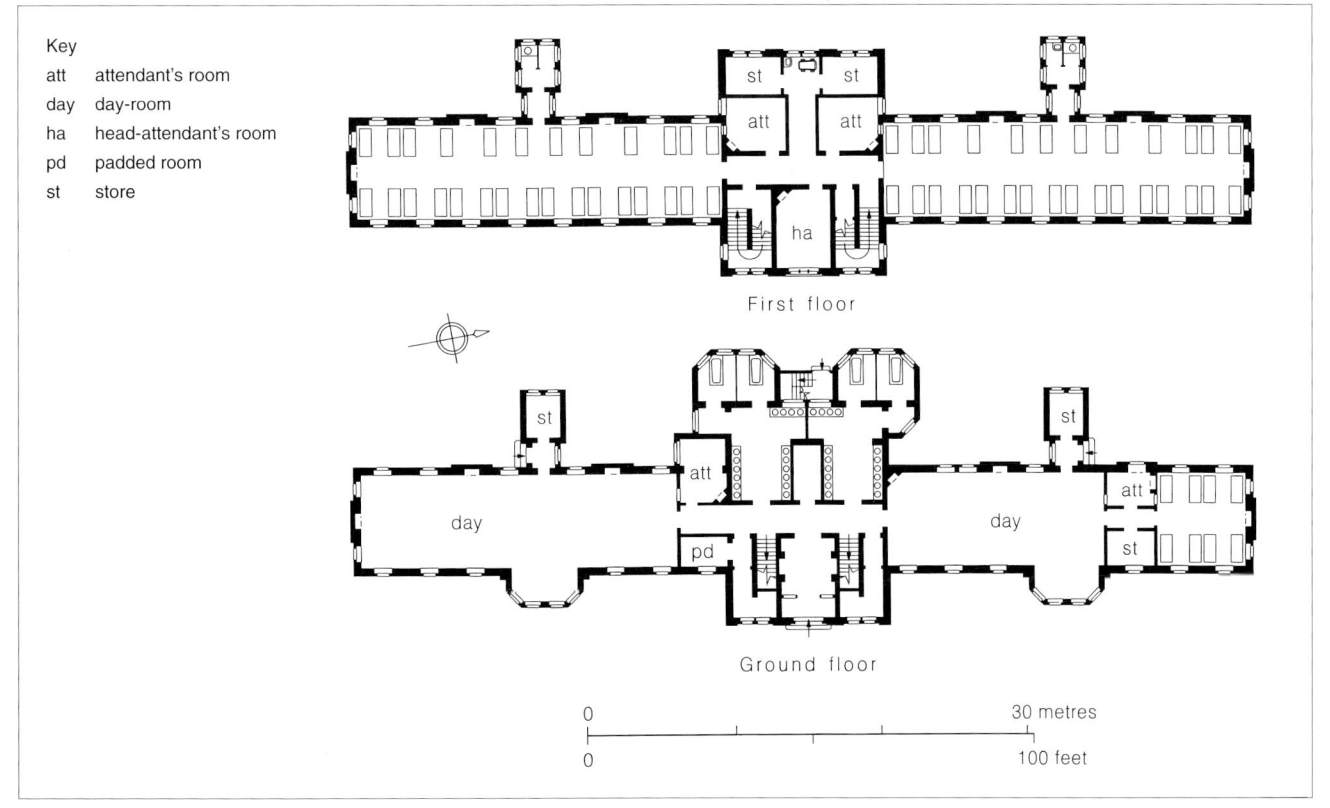

*Figure 227
Pewsey Union
Workhouse in Wiltshire
became a mental-
deficiency colony around
1920, and several villas
were erected in the
grounds.
[BB93/21675]*

We have seen half-witted women nursing the sick, feeble-minded women in charge of the babies, and imbecile old men put to look after the boys out of school hours. We have seen expectant mothers, who have come in for their confinements, by day and by night working, eating and sleeping in close companionship with idiots and imbeciles of revolting habits and hideous appearance.[69]

The search for a practical solution exercised the Local Government Board for many years. The Report of the Select Committee on the Bill for the Providing of Cottage Homes for the Aged Indoor Poor, dated 4 July 1899, had recommended that imbeciles and epileptics be removed from workhouses and cared for in institutions run by county councils, but the expected follow-up legislation was deferred due to the outbreak of the Boer War. In the early years of the 20th century, poor-law inspectors' reports constantly reiterated the problems caused by retaining imbeciles in workhouses, and the desirability of creating separate colonies for them. It was realised that this could only be achieved through the formation of joint committees, or unions of unions. In 1902 the Chorlton and Manchester Joint Asylum Committee took the first step by purchasing a 165-acre site near Langho, outside Blackburn, to set up a colony for sane epileptics. The first six 'homes' on the site could each accommodate forty people, but the administrative and service buildings were erected on a scale which would cope with future expansion. Three years later, Birmingham, Kings Norton and Aston acted together to purchase Monyhull Hall, a 185-acre estate, and develop it into an industrial colony for imbeciles and epileptics.[70] This set the pattern for subsequent so-called 'mental-deficiency colonies' by converting an old house into an administration block and staff residence, while more modest 'cottages' or 'villas' were erected for the patients. In 1913 the Northern Counties Joint Poor-Law Committee, comprising Cumberland, Durham, Northumberland and the North Riding of Yorkshire, purchased Prudhoe Hall in Northumberland, where the Prudhoe Hall Colony opened for mental defectives in August 1914. Plans for villas and other additions by J H Morton and J G Burrell were not put into effect until after the First World War.[71] Other initiatives to create joint committees on the eve of the war were stifled, as was the 1913 Mental Deficiency Act,[72] which would have encouraged local authorities to set up mental-deficiency colonies. Financial constraints during the 1920s meant that the establishment of

*Figure 228
The ends of the wards at Townley's Hospital were fitted with verandas and fire escapes (1896; Bradshaw & Gass).
[BB96/2247]*

mental-deficiency colonies progressed very slowly (Fig 227). A solution was not found until the 1930s, when many of the workhouses which had been handed over to local authorities were transformed into hospitals for the mentally handicapped, a compromise which lasted until the advent of 'care in the community' in the 1980s.

Poor-Law Infirmaries and Sanatoria, 1900–1948

The pavilion plan remained popular for infirmaries at the turn of the century, but advances in plumbing, fire safety and medical theory brought about small architectural refinements. As offensive smells were less likely to cause a problem, it became possible to locate bathrooms at the entrance of wards, leaving only toilets and slop sinks in end or side projections. Verandas or balconies were now provided with fire-escape stairs (Fig 228) and the upper floors of ward blocks on large sites were linked by escape bridges (*see* Figure 153). But more significantly, the curative effects of fresh air and sunshine were generally accepted, and some ward blocks were aligned east–west, rather than north–south, allowing verandas to run the full length of their south sides. Some deflection towards the east was recommended, to avoid the heat and glare of a westering sun.

Exposure to fresh air was thought particularly beneficial for those suffering from tuberculosis of the lungs, or 'phthisis'. As most of the phthisis cases entering workhouses were advanced and incurable, the primary aim of the authorities was isolation, not treatment. Despite that, some

*Figure 229
This phthisis ward was built at Sunderland Union Workhouse in 1911. The site is now Sunderland District General Hospital.
[BB93/35343]*

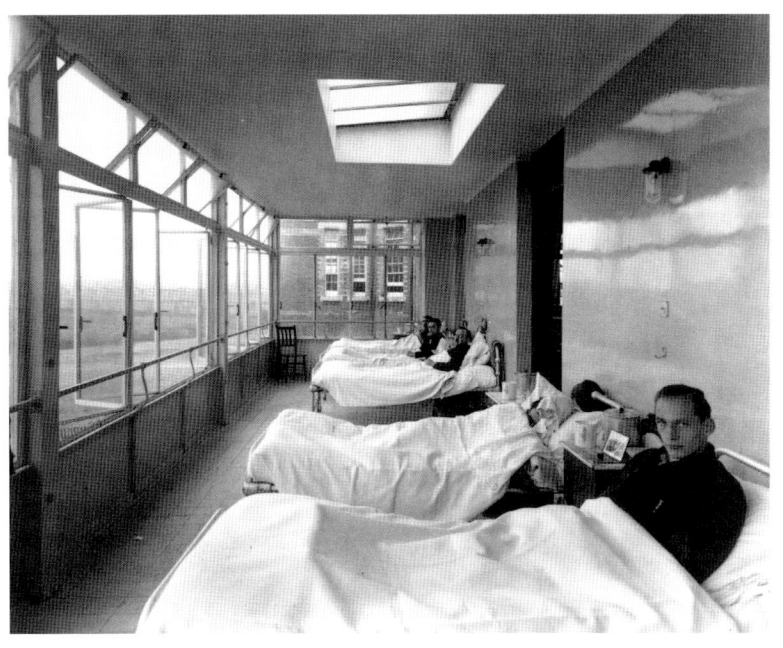

Figure 230
The Central London Sick Asylum was built in 1898–1900, and verandas were added c 1920.
[London Metropolitan Archives B1847]

unions made modest provision for the treatment of phthisis in the early 1900s. Early experiments included adapted wards at Bath and Bristol (1902), an open-air ward for males at Portsmouth (1900–3) and, more substantially, a detached 'veranda ward' for twenty cases at Kettering (1903). Ordinary wards could be converted into phthisis wards simply by the addition of open verandas with glazed roofs. Revolving huts, and sometimes tents, became a common sight outside infirmaries. By 1911, as many as 167 unions provided some accommodation for phthisis cases (Fig 229) and another 19 were planning to do so.[73] Despite these initiatives, most workhouse cases were still hopeless: patients whose condition was curable were generally sent to sanatoria, to which guardians subscribed.

The Public Health (Prevention and Treatment of Disease) Act of 1913 sanctioned the treatment of tuberculosis by the Metropolitan Asylums Board,[74] but the Board did not establish many sanatoria before the end of the First World War. Most of the Board's sanatoria did not involve new building work: several institutions already in its possession were adapted and other properties were purchased, including the Empire Hotel at Lowestoft (which now became St Luke's Hospital), the superfluous Greenwich Union Workhouse at Grove Park (*see* Figure 127c), and the former Central London Sick Asylum at Hendon (Fig 230). Additions to these buildings included verandas for open-air treatment. The Board did, however, build some new sanatoria, notably the King George V Sanatorium near Hambledon, of 1920–2.

Separate-site sanatoria for the treatment of phthisis were erected on occasion by poor-law authorities outside London. The first, built at Heswall between 1901 and 1902, was jointly established by Liverpool Parish, West Derby Union and Toxteth Park Township. The building adopted the sun-trapping half-butterfly plan characteristic of many early 20th-century sanatoria, with verandas on the south side of each wing. Extensive gardens, provided with numerous seats and a shelter for convalescents, overlooked the Dee estuary.

In 1902 Bradford Union commenced the construction of a sanatorium at Eastby. Like the Heswall Sanatorium it was primarily, but not exclusively, intended for inmates of the workhouse and most of the patients were comparatively healthy men in the early stages of tuberculosis – in other words, those most capable of retrieving their status as independent workers and unburdening the poor rates. The Board's architect, Frederick Holland, designed the buildings which, with the exception of the stone administration block, were of wood. The single-storeyed wards, raised on stone pillars, were painted white and had red tiled roofs, reminding the regional poor-law inspector of 'an enlarged seaside bungalow for pleasure purposes'.[75] The wards had unglazed windows opening into a continuous rear corridor.[76] Rather unusually, verandas were excluded from the design because Holland believed 'that such structures cut off light, increase the heat of the wards in summer, and encourage patients to spend their time in the vicinity of the rooms'.[77] Despite these unorthodox notions, verandas were added to many workhouse infirmaries between 1900 and 1940, and remained a prominent feature of sanatoria.

Under the poor law, more beds were provided for men with tuberculosis than for women, because the cure of the breadwinner might remove an entire family from the relief lists. Thus the new phthisis ward built at Scarborough in 1912 had 10 beds for men and 6 for women.[78] The small Badsley Moor Sanatorium, set up by Rotherham Union on the site of an old Corporation fever hospital in 1910–11, was exclusively for male patients.[79]

Sick children were usually cared for in the workhouse infirmary, but towards the end of the 19th century separate children's hospitals appeared on some workhouse and infirmary sites. When the Metropolitan Asylums Board assumed responsibility for children suffering from contagious eye and skin complaints it set up distinct institutions for ophthalmia and ringworm cases (*see* page 149). Many of these occupied buildings which had been erected for quite a different purpose. A similar situation arose in Liverpool, where the new workhouse erected for chronic and infirm inmates at Alder Hey opened as a children's hospital in 1915.[80]

At the outbreak of the First World War many poor-law infirmaries, such as Halifax (*see* Figure 222), were handed over to the military authorities, and by 1918 no less than 74,000 poor-law beds were being put to wartime uses. In military hands, both staffing and facilities were upgraded: Alder Hey Hospital, for example, acquired a new orthopaedic department.

When institutions were returned to poor-law authorities after the war there seemed to be a surplus of infirmary accommodation. Knowing that general voluntary hospitals were suffering from an acute shortage of beds, and ignoring potential legal problems, some boards of guardians entered into agreements with local health authorities which made their excess accommodation available to paying patients. One of the most successful schemes was in Bradford, where the Council leased St Luke's Hospital from the Union, on the understanding that the guardians would have first claim on available beds.[81] The status of poor-law infirmaries continued to improve in the 1920s but little building work was carried out due to lack of funds. The provision of modern nurses' homes was made a priority so that poor-law institutions could attract a trained, professional staff. By 1920, eighty poor-law institutions were recognised as training schools for nurses, and another twenty-four, none of which had a resident medical officer, were designated 'minor training schools'.[82] As probationary nurses were not permitted to live off site, the provision of ample staff accommodation was vital. At the same time, infirmary extensions tended to be modest, but a few completely new hospitals were erected, notably Davyhulme Hospital, built by Barton-upon-Irwell Union in 1925–6.[83] Characteristically, the pavilion-plan wards of Davyhulme Hospital had flat roofs, no sanitary projections, and extensive side verandas.

In the 1920s money was spent on upgrading and extending facilities rather than buildings. In 1928, Beatrice and Sidney Webb reported, with a hint of disbelief, that 'the Ministry of Health has actually sanctioned a Poor Law Authority [the MAB] providing and equipping a most costly "Radium Treatment Ward" for the reception of female paupers suffering from uterine cancer'.[84] As well as radium treatment, X-ray facilities and operating theatres became common features of poor-law hospitals for the first time.

After 1930 many poor-law infirmaries, including Hereford and Uxbridge, were rebuilt and extended by county and county borough councils to create modern municipal hospitals. The extensive new buildings at Rochford Hospital (1938–40), formerly Rochford Union Workhouse, were in the International Modern style, of brick with flat roofs and large expanses of metal-framed glazing. The main wards, still on the separate-block system, had semicircular terminations with sunrooms and balconies to the south. The two-storeyed tuberculosis block (Fig 231) had a staggered, V-shaped plan. A wide semicircular bay in the centre and the flanking

Figure 231
Rochford Hospital was designed by F W Smith in the mid-1930s in a distinctive Modern style. This is the tuberculosis block.
[BB92/5878]

oblique bays were provided with continuous balconies, with opaque glass between the rails, and flat canopies. The complex included a new kitchen, boiler house (Fig 232), laundry, mortuary with post-mortem facilities, and nurses' home.

During the Second World War 'temporary' Emergency Medical Service hospitals, destined to receive both military and civilian casualties, were erected on many former workhouse sites by the Ministry of Health. Like the hutted military hospitals of the First World War they comprised regimented rows of single-storeyed ward blocks, connected by open-sided covered ways (Fig 233). Different materials were used, including asbestos, timber, concrete and brick, and some took the form of corrugated-iron Nissen huts. The commonest type of huts to survive today have a concrete frame, brick infill, metal-framed windows and corrugated asbestos roofs, but many have been completely recased in modern materials. The largest Emergency Medical Service hospitals included cheaply erected staff accommodation, such as the concrete-block nurses' home at Bishop's Stortford.

Since the Second World War, poor-law infirmaries have been modernised and improved considerably, but in a haphazard manner. Older buildings have been retained, rather than replaced, and the alterations and additions which made them feasible as modern hospitals under the National Health Service have often destroyed their original plan and architectural character.

Figure 232 (above) The boiler house at Rochford Hospital (mid-1930s) has a monumental design. [BB92/5873]

Figure 233 (right) These Emergency Medical Service huts were erected at Windsor Public Assistance Institution in 1939. Similar huts were added to public assistance institutions throughout the country in 1939–40 in anticipation of extensive air-raid casualties. [BB93/22000]

10
Poor-Law Buildings for Vagrants and the 'Houseless Poor'

The most despised *habitués* of 19th-century workhouses were vagrants, usually referred to as 'casuals', a category which included an assortment of seasoned tramps, itinerant labourers and homeless persons. After 1834 most workhouses provided accommodation, set apart from that of regular inmates, where vagrants could sleep for one or two nights. Before moving on they were expected to perform a task such as stone-breaking, wood-chopping, corn-grinding or oakum-picking. The system was designed to have a deterrent effect on vagrancy, but could never be so harsh that the majority of vagrants would prefer to sleep rough: it proved difficult to strike the right balance.

The number of vagrants applying for shelter in workhouses fluctuated according to weather conditions and trade cycles, but was unusually high in the 1860s. The use of local police stations as receiving offices had little deterrent effect, and so cellular wards were introduced. As well as denying opportunities for tramps to socialise, these offered a means of controlling their behaviour during their stay. Campaigns to set up labour colonies for hardened tramps, leaving casual wards to those travelling in search of work, came to nothing and cells continued to be the favoured method of accommodating tramps until the middle of the 20th century.

Vagrancy and the Old Poor Law

Workhouses did not play a significant role in the control of vagrancy before the mid-19th century. Vagrancy, an age-old problem, had escalated in the late-medieval period, as feudalism declined and the ties binding servants to masters were loosened. As it posed a threat to public order, it was combated by punitive legislation which prescribed harsh punishments for offenders and prohibited almsgiving to beggars.[1] Attempts to restrict vagrants to their parish of settlement failed, largely because no arrangements were made for their accommodation or maintenance.

The main reason for introducing parish relief in the mid-16th century was to prevent the poor from begging. Parish officers were directed to find work for vagrants, but found it difficult to prevent them from resuming their old habits. In 1572 an Act was passed which decreed that a first-time offender was to be whipped and burnt through the right ear and a repeat offender was to 'suffer death as a felon'.[2] By the end of the century, this severe punishment had been modified to imprisonment in a house of correction.

Houses of correction, modelled on London's Bridewell, were set up throughout England from the late 16th century until the 18th century. They were provided on a county basis, but also seem to have been established by individual towns, often in association with workhouses. Any person convicted of vagrancy was sent to the house of correction and set to work until he or she could be placed in service or, if incapacitated, in an almshouse.[3] The juxtaposition of houses of correction and workhouses continued throughout the 18th century, for example at the Poor Priest's Hospital in Canterbury, where the workhouse master used the bridewell as a lock-up for refractory paupers.[4] Ultimately, the prevalence of vagrancy was little affected by the threat of physical punishment, the prohibition of almsgiving, or the prospect of incarceration in a house of correction.

Throughout the 18th and early 19th centuries great, though often futile, efforts were made to convey vagrants back to their parish of settlement. Contractors or constables were employed by parishes to escort vagrants on such journeys, and overnight accommodation had to be secured at cheap lodging-houses or in parish workhouses *en route*. In the 1820s, in North Yorkshire, the parishes of Easingwold, Scarborough and Bedale fitted up outbuildings in their workhouse yards for this purpose.[5] Other towns set up a separate Vagrant Office or

Vagrant House to accommodate tramps on a short-term basis. Doncaster and York did this around 1816, and Hereford in 1831.[6]

Vagrancy and the New Poor Law

The *Poor Law Report* of 1834 and the subsequent Act both neglected the problem of vagrancy, and the model workhouse plans of 1835 had no tramp wards. Guardians, understandably, interpreted this to mean that they should not admit tramps, and workhouses built immediately after the Act had no facilities to receive them.

Guardians were all too ready to ignore tramps, not least because vagrancy had been considered a police rather than a poor-law matter in the past. Moreover, it was regarded as an urban problem, and rural guardians did not see why their parishes should contribute to the cost of building and maintaining vagrant wards at the union workhouse. Some argued that the very existence of vagrant wards would attract, rather than repel, tramps. Despite the currency of such attitudes, Hereford guardians continued to rent their Vagrant House on Quakers Lane at £8 per annum.[7] A police constable resided in the house, which his wife cleaned.

The law had turned its back on them, yet vagrants persisted in claiming relief at the new union workhouses, which they found conveniently distanced by a day's tramping. Cases of tramps who died of exposure or starvation after being turned away from the workhouse door by the relieving officer or porter were added to the catalogue of complaints lodged against the New Poor Law by its opponents. The Poor Law Commission attempted to remedy the situation in 1837 by recommending that cases of 'sudden or urgent necessity' should be granted shelter and a meal in return for a task of work.[8] As a result, many unions allocated inferior accommodation to tramps, usually in outbuildings adjacent to receiving wards.

By the late 1830s, plans for new workhouses generally included rooms for tramps, but infectious wards were often requisitioned for that purpose. Although Scott & Moffatt had designed tramp wards for Dunmow Union Workhouse, the Building Committee decided to omit them, 'there being an Itch and Infectious Ward beside the probationary ward'.[9] This reflected the fact that tramps often carried contagious diseases into the workhouse: tragically, when they introduced measles into Thirsk Union Workhouse in 1842, fourteen children died.[10]

In 1840, typical tramp accommodation was described as single-storeyed buildings, attached to the back part of the yard:

In general they have brick floors and guard-room beds, with loose straw and rugs for the males and iron bedsteads with straw ties for the females. They are generally badly ventilated and unprovided with any means of producing warmth. All

*Figure 234
The Refuge for the Destitute and Houseless Poor in Playhouse Yard, London, was one of many 'asylums' provided for the homeless in the 1840s. Women and children, shown here in December 1843, slept on straw in trough beds and were fed half a pound of bread at night and in the morning.
[From* Illustrated London News, *30 December 1843, 418, by permission of the Syndics of Cambridge University Library]*

holes for ventilation in reach of the occupants are sure to be stuffed with rags and straws; so that the [e]ffluvia of these places is at best most disgustingly offensive.[11]

Two years later, the Poor Law Commission acknowledged that 'the nature of the present workhouse buildings is in many instances ill-calculated for the reception of persons, such as ordinarily present themselves for a night's lodging . . . There is no effectual power to detain them or to require work in the morning in return for lodging given'.[12] This was remedied the following year, by an Act which enabled guardians to detain male tramps, for no more than four hours, so that they could perform a task of work in exchange for food and lodging.[13] The task was to be completed after breakfast on the morning following admission. At first, taskwork was seldom enforced and, in the absence of a uniform policy, tramps tended to congregate at the more lenient workhouses, where they would not be set to work and would be reasonably well fed. Workhouse authorities were now permitted to search tramps upon their arrival, leading to the notorious practice of tramps concealing their belongings under a hedge before applying to the receiving officer.

Vagrancy was aggravated in the mid-1840s by trade depression, the potato famine and Irish immigration. The problem was greater in London than elsewhere and by 1843 several makeshift refuges (Fig 234) had been set up by philanthropists. The response of the poor law to the crisis proved ineffectual despite an attempt, in 1844, to organise the metropolitan poor-law authorities into six districts which would be responsible for relieving the casual poor.[14] The principles of casual relief were to remain unchanged, but its cost would be more evenly spread. Instead of each workhouse having its own casual ward, an asylum or 'cheap workhouse for a limited purpose', was to be established in each district. Only the homeless and wandering poor would be admitted, and their stay would be for a limited period. Upon admission they would be bathed, and a task of work would be imposed prior to their departure. In 1847, before any of these district asylums were set up, the Poor Law Commission calculated the quantity of accommodation required for casuals on the basis of 216 cu ft per person, or a space measuring 8 ft by 3 ft by 9 ft; very little by any standards.[15] In the event the scheme was not a success and individual authorities soon returned to the practice of maintaining their own vagrant wards. St Marylebone, for example, erected vagrant wards at its workhouse in 1846; St George's, Hanover Square, took the same step in 1846–7, and St Leonard, Shoreditch, in 1848. Much to the annoyance of the central authority, few metropolitan authorities instituted a labour test.

Outside London, a few cities established asylums for the houseless poor, but provision for tramps at workhouses was swiftly becoming the norm.[16] A plan of Trowbridge and Melksham Union Workhouse, dated 1847, shows two small rooms in an outbuilding labelled 'tramps ward'.[17] These lay beyond the square periphery of the workhouse, and opened on to the men's work yard, which was supplied with an open shed marked 'stone house'. More typically, at the York workhouse of 1848–9, vagrant wards were located in either wing of the entrance block. This arrangement had two benefits: it kept tramps on the periphery of the institution and, with a single entrance for all-comers, precluded the need to employ a second porter.

Accommodation for tramps, known for their boisterous, alcohol-fuelled behaviour, was distanced from that of permanent inmates for a good reason. It was common for tramps to tear up their clothes and bedding, either to obtain new clothes or to protest against conditions in the workhouse. The idea of housing tramps in individual cells to prevent riotous behaviour originated in the 1850s and was no doubt inspired by prison planning. The long entrance block of the Norwich Incorporation Workhouse, designed by James Medland & Alfred W Maberley in 1857, included a few tramp cells as well as wards with sleeping platforms.[18] It was some time, however, before cells were recommended by the central authority for casuals, and became widespread.

The *Journal of the Workhouse Visiting Society*, established by Louisa Twining in 1859, was primarily concerned with the condition of the sick and the young in workhouses, but also criticised the harsh treatment meted out to vagrants, who were frequently in ill-health. Despite this, there was never a concerted campaign to improve their condition, as was the case for the sick, children, the aged and, eventually, the mentally handicapped. Tramps inspired little sympathy from guardians, the public or philanthropists, but over the years numerous reformers and journalists posed as vagrants in order to write sensationalist first-hand accounts of the casual lifestyle. In virtually all of these reports, the writer expressed his or her shock at finding all types of wayfarer, ranging from the honest itinerant labourer to the 'professional' tramp, crowded together in insanitary conditions. They also found the taskwork hard going. James Greenwood of the *Pall Mall Gazette*, who spent a night in Lambeth casual ward in the 1860s, found cranking a flour mill almost intolerable.[19] In 1887, C W Craven complained that 'the most aggravating part of the affair [ie: corn-grinding

THE WORKHOUSE

*Figure 235
The male casual ward of
West London Union
Workhouse, c 1860.*
[Hulton Getty]

*Figure 236
The female casual ward
of West London Union
Workhouse, c 1860.*
[Hulton Getty]

in Keighley Union Workhouse] was that none of us could observe how much work had been accomplished'.[20] Later in the century the urge to reform tramps led organisations such as the Salvation Army to set up refuges which relieved, to some extent, the overcrowded poor-law casual wards.

A Poor Law Board circular of 1857 laid down that those applying for a night's shelter in London must be received in one of six 'asylums for the houseless poor'.[21] As in 1844, these did not fully materialise and metropolitan authorities continued to deal with vagrants separately. Illustrations of the West London Union casual wards around 1860 show men huddled in stall-like sleeping cubicles in groups of three or more (Fig 235), whereas women shared a sleeping platform (Fig 236).

In the mid-1860s many London unions were erecting new casual wards or extending old ones in response to the Metropolitan Houseless Poor Act of 1864,[22] which made central funding available for casual wards, managed by the Metropolitan Board of Works. At the same time, guidelines were set down for casual accommodation. At least two wards were to be provided, one for men and another for women and young children: 'there should be a yard containing a bathroom and water-closet attached to each apartment and a shed should be provided for the vagrants to work in'.[23] The guidelines continued:

> *The most convenient form for a vagrant ward is, perhaps, a parallelogram, and each ward, besides being of sufficient capacity with respect to width and height to accommodate the number of persons required to sleep in it, should be fitted up with a*

sleeping platform or barrack bed, of adequate depth along each side of it, with a convenient gangway down the middle. The platform should be divided by means of boards, and the space allotted to each person should be at least two feet three inches wide. Above the head of each platform there may be a shelf the whole length of the room, and divided into corresponding spaces for the deposit of clothes.

These stipulations were followed incompletely by Searle, Son & Yelf, who designed the new West London Union Workhouse of 1864 (*see* Figure 109).[24] There, a small heated sleeping-room and outside water-closet was provided for each sex, but no bathroom. The men's sleeping-room was entered through the stone yard and an open work-shed, the women's through their oakum-picking room. The erection of new casual wards throughout London after 1864, as well as economic depression, may have contributed to the rise in the numbers of tramps receiving relief in the late 1860s.[25]

Religious inscriptions on the walls and roof trusses of the temporary casual ward (Fig 237 and 238) designed for St Marylebone by Henry Saxon Snell in 1867 were certainly an attempt to 'improve' inmates. Displayed on the trusses were the mottoes: 'God is Truth', 'God is Good',

'God is Holy', 'God is Just' and 'God is Love'. Fuller inscriptions on the walls included one beginning 'Thou God Seest Me'. None were so morbid, however, as the thought-provoking inscription which adorned the walls of a late-Victorian Salvation Army shelter for women in

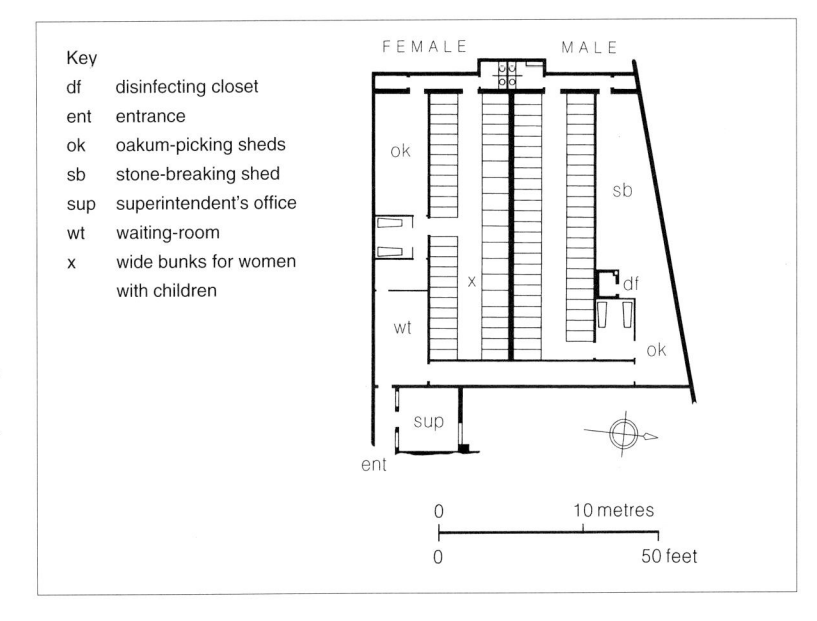

Key
df   disinfecting closet
ent   entrance
ok   oakum-picking sheds
sb   stone-breaking shed
sup   superintendent's office
wt   waiting-room
x   wide bunks for women with children

Figure 237 (above) Temporary casual wards were erected at St Marylebone Workhouse by Henry Saxon Snell in 1867. [Plans based on Snell, H S 1881, 1]

Figure 238 (right) The interior of the St Marylebone temporary casual wards (1867). [From Illustrated London News, *28 September 1867, 353, by permission of the Syndics of Cambridge University Library]*

Figure 239 (left)
One of the first casual ward blocks on the double-cell system was that designed by Henry Saxon Snell for St Olave's Union Workhouse, Rotherhithe, in 1870.
[Based on Snell, H S 1881]

Figure 240 (below)
Gustave Doré's etching shows tramps being bathed at the workhouse, c 1872.
[From Doré 1872, by permission of the Syndics of Cambridge University Library]

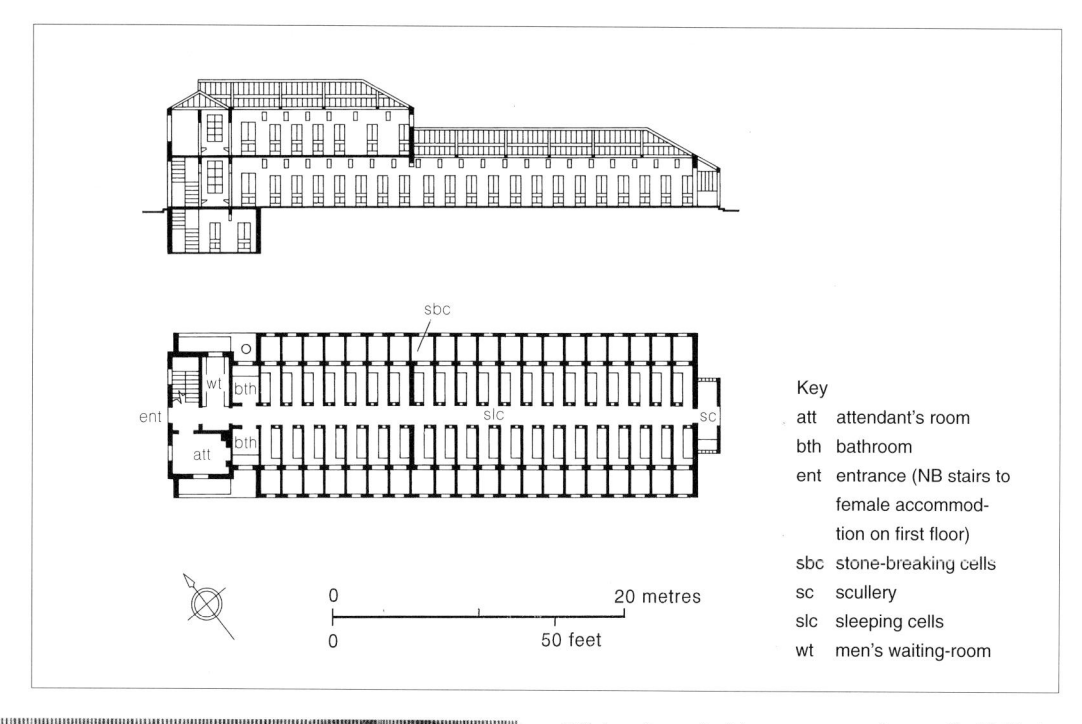

Key
att   attendant's room
bth   bathroom
ent   entrance (NB stairs to female accommodation on first floor)
sbc   stone-breaking cells
sc   scullery
slc   sleeping cells
wt   men's waiting-room

Whitechapel: 'Are you ready to die?'.[26] At St Marylebone, vagrants slept in a continuous row of bunks, placed against the long walls and separated by wooden partitions. There were no windows in the side walls and the room was lit solely by a long ridge lantern.

Soon afterwards, Snell was responsible for introducing a new design of casual ward on the 'cellular' system, in which male vagrants were isolated in separate cells for both sleeping and working. This idea was encapsulated in the new wards which he designed for St Olave's Union Workhouse, Rotherhithe, in 1870, and in others designed shortly afterwards for St George's and St Marylebone.[27] The wards at St Olave's (Fig 239) included forty sleeping and working cells for men on the ground floor and twelve for women above, all of them supplied with hot-water heating and night commodes. Four of the female sleeping cells were large enough to accommodate a woman with a child.

Like many other unions, St Olave's required male casuals to break a certain amount of granite – theoretically anything between 4 cwt and 13 cwt – before leaving the workhouse on the morning following their overnight stay, while women either cleaned the building or picked oakum. The men's labour cells opened directly off their sleeping cells and were equipped with grated openings through which all the crushed stone had to be passed. A cart road was constructed for the delivery and collection of stones. Labour cells were not provided for the women, as they could pick oakum in their sleeping cells if required. Other rooms in

*Figure 241 (far left)
This double casual cell at the Trowbridge and Melksham Union Workhouse, Semington, was erected c 1883 and used until 1947. The upper windows light the sleeping cells while the lower windows light the labour cells. The grilles for stone-breaking survive at the base of the wall.
[BB98/06519]*

*Figure 242 (left)
This shows the interior of a sleeping cell at Trowbridge and Melksham Workhouse, looking through to a labour cell.
[BB98/06521]*

the building included waiting-rooms, sculleries for emptying night commodes, bathrooms, a storeroom for oakum and attendant's accommodation. One bathful of water and a single towel could serve large numbers of vagrants, many of whom suffered from serious skin complaints. Bathing was not a private experience, as there was often more than one bath in each bathroom (Fig 240).

In 1874 the Local Government Board strongly recommended that metropolitan boards adopt Snell's cellular design for casual wards since associated wards, as casual dormitories were known, afforded the opportunity 'for the interchange of intelligence and for the communication of plans for evading the operation of the law'.[28] This was not enforced, however, and the Local Government Board still allowed sleeping platforms to be divided into cubicles. Many unions preferred that option: for example, in 1877 the sleeping platforms at Kirkby Moorside Union Workhouse were divided into cubicles, with four 'beds' per unit, and in the same year Easingwold Union erected casual wards with sleeping platforms divided into twelve compartments for men and five for women.[29] Many unions chose a combination of cellular and associated wards, preferring to use the former for unruly tramps and the latter for overspill. Associated wards could also be used as day-rooms, particularly on Sundays, when no work was performed.

Under the Pauper Inmates Discharge and Regulation Act of 1871,[30] casuals had to stay at the workhouse for one night and were detained to perform a task the following morning. As most casual labour was assigned early each morning, this meant that they could not search for work the following day. Under the Casual Poor Act of 1882,[31] which attempted to remedy this, casuals slept at the workhouse for two nights, completed a task on the middle day and were released early on the morning of the third. Despite these statutes, guardians had discretionary powers which were frequently exercised, meaning that the rules governing the reception and discharge of casuals continued to vary from one union to the next.

Casual ward blocks erected at provincial workhouses after 1870 usually included a mixture of cellular and associated wards, together with a bathroom, disinfector, store and labour master's – or tramp major's – accommodation. Buildings could be one or two storeys high: when accommodation was included for female tramps it was often on the first floor. Central corridors were usually lit by windows placed above the roofs of the sleeping cells, or by a long ridge lantern. Sleeping cells were lit by small, square windows above the roofs of the labour cells (Figs 241 and 242).

Several variations on the standard plan were devised. Cells could be erected on one or both sides of an access corridor. While labour cells usually opened directly off sleeping cells, the casual ward of North Witchford Union Workhouse in Cambridgeshire, designed by William Adams & Son in 1884, had sleeping cells on one side of a corridor and labour cells on the other. When buildings only provided sleeping cells, as

THE WORKHOUSE

*Figure 243 (right)
Spikes on top of the casual yard wall at Ripon Union Workhouse prevented inmates escaping before performing a set task.*
[Dorothy Thelwall 1996]

*Figure 244 (far right)
This restored casual cell at Ripon Union Workhouse shows a folding bed, brought in from the demolished Knaresborough workhouse.*
[Dorothy Thelwall 1995]

at Ripon, vagrants performed their taskwork in sheds or workshops within a yard. The high yard walls were topped by vicious iron spikes to deter escapes or early departures (Fig 243) and it is perhaps from these that many workhouses earned the nickname of 'The Spike'. Few complete examples now survive, as spikes were often removed for use in wartime munition manufacture.

The sleeping arrangements inside casual cells and associated wards varied, but new arrivals were usually handed a hammock or a mattress and left to shift for themselves. Architects' drawings sometimes show hammocks strung across the full length of each cell, and tell-tale hooks often survive. Other drawings, such as those for Berkhampstead casual wards, show beds which folded against the wall when not in use.[32] Beds of that type from the demolished casual cells at Knaresborough have been installed in the restored casual block at Ripon (Fig 244). Sleeping platforms with wooden dividers continued to be favoured in associated wards, for example those of Ashby-de-la-Zouch (1886), Hunslet (1899) and Solihull (1898; Fig 245).

Towards the end of the century, some very large casual wards were erected in cities, especially in London. Those built on Millman Street by St Luke, Chelsea, in 1893, included cellular wards with a stone-breaking shed, a corn-grinding shed (Fig 246) and sixty bunks in a yard.[33] Hackney Union planned to build a large test workhouse on Gainsborough Road, including accommodation for able-bodied men as well as vagrants, but the only part of the scheme to be realised was the casual ward block (1898–1904). That three-storeyed, T-shaped building was capable of holding sixty-two men and forty-four women and children. On the ground floor were separate male and female entrance lobbies, reception wards and bathrooms, attendants' rooms and an office. In a rear wing, twenty-two double sleeping and working cells opened off a central corridor. The upper floors housed accommodation for the attendants, stores, workrooms and more cells, including some double cells for women with children.

In 1904, detailed Local Government Board specifications for casual ward blocks were published by the architect Albert C Freeman, who declared that they 'should be made as cheerless and uninviting as possible'.[34] They were to be of stock brick, with whitewashed interiors. Sleeping cells were to hold 360 cu ft of air space, labour cells to hold 186 cu ft, but in associated wards inmates were allowed 540 cu ft. Ordinary sleeping cells were to be 4 ft 6 in. wide and those for women with children, 6 ft 9 in. wide. The floor of each sleeping cell was to be 6 in. higher than that of the adjoining labour cell, and a raised step across the threshold of the labour cell created a conduit for hot-water pipes as well as providing a seat for vagrants engaged in stone-breaking. Labour cells were to have floors of concrete 'or other hard substance which will withstand the breaking of stone'. In each labour cell, an iron grille was placed in the outer wall, 2 ft above the floor; it measured no less than 18 in. by 3 ft, and was covered by a 2-in. square mesh through which the broken stone had to pass.[35] Cell doors were provided with small perforated iron panels, peep holes 'to prevent cases of suicide'. Recesses with gas jets flanked the doors, lighting both the corridor and cell at night. Freeman also recommended that each cell have an electric bell in case of sudden illness. Other rooms in the building included a mess room, with plain deal seating fixed around the walls and a table in the centre, a store, baths ('No two baths should be fixed in the same room – "decency forbids." '), a labour master's office with an inspection window and a heating apparatus in the basement. Freeman disapproved of 'automatic seat-flushing w-c apparatus' provided in some separate cells, and preferred a basic slopping-out system. A disinfector house, for vagrants' clothes, was to be located in a separate structure.

Freeman also laid down that whenever work had to be carried out in yards, these should include a store for timber or stone and sheds for stone-breaking or wood-chopping. Sheds 'should be erected and divided into bunks about 4 feet wide by 6 feet long with wooden partitions about

Figure 245 (below) The casual ward block and labour master's house at Solihull Union Workhouse (1898), designed by W H Ward, continued to receive tramps until 1941, and was later converted into an outpatients and casualty department. [Plans redrawn from Public Record Office MH14/32]

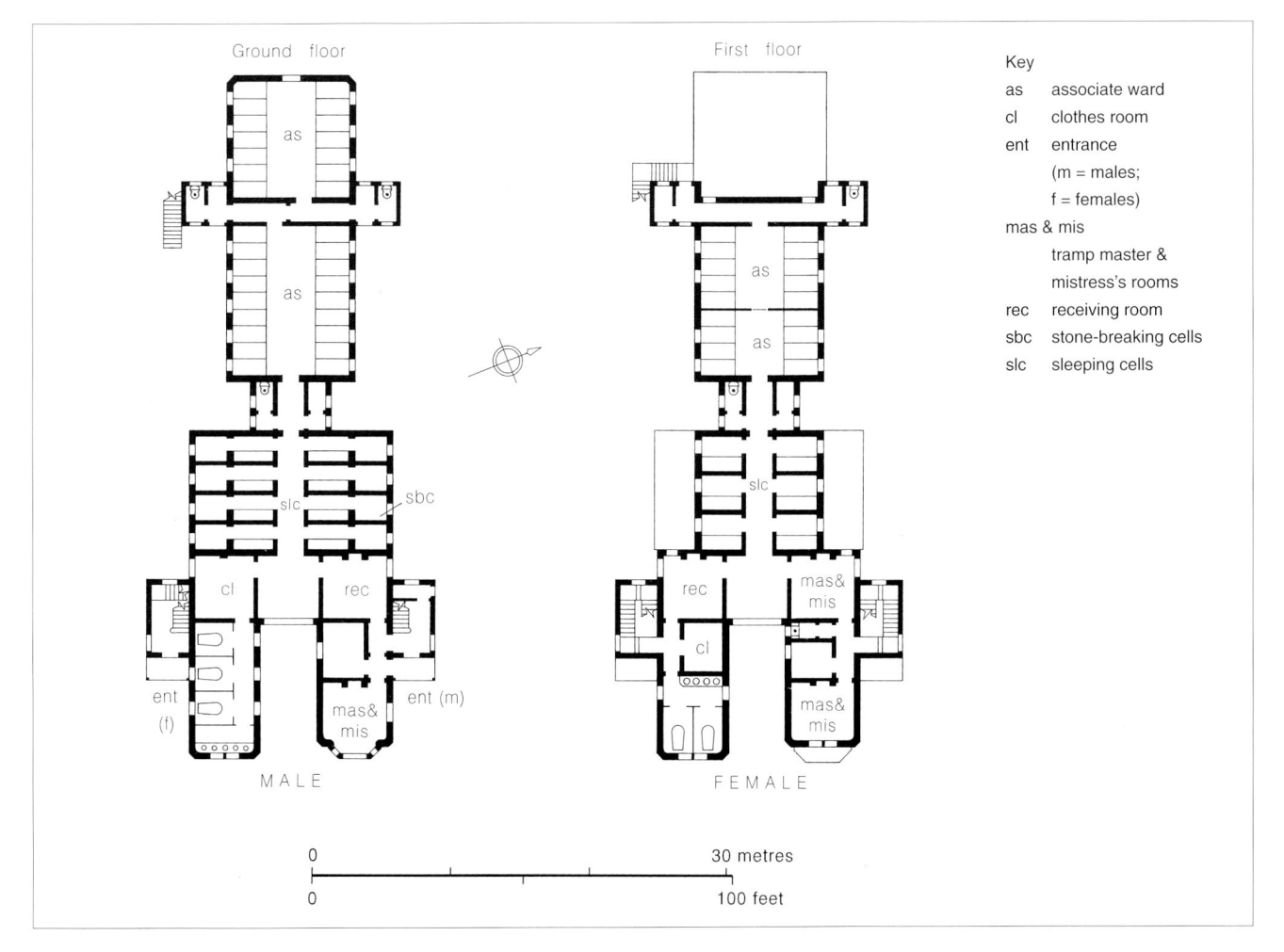

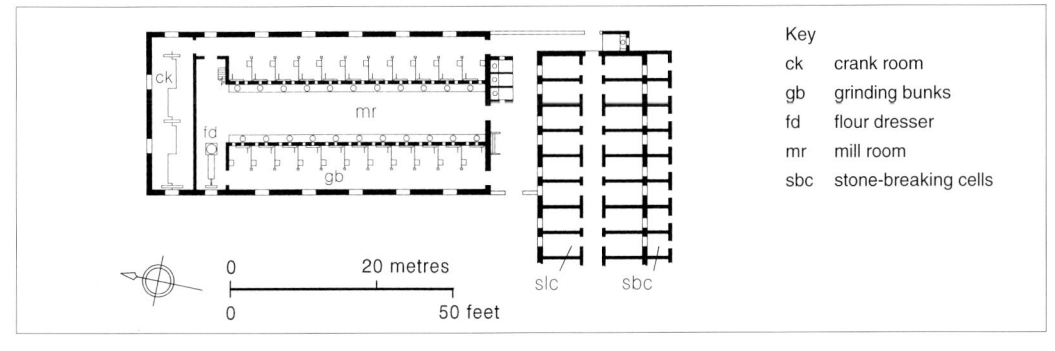

Figure 246 (left) No workhouse corn-grinding sheds are known to survive with their fixtures and fittings. This one was built at St Luke's Workhouse, Chelsea, in c 1888–93. [Plan redrawn from Public Record Office MH14/7]

5 feet 6 inches high, to divide the inmates and check the amount of individual labour'.[36]

The 1906 Report of the Departmental Committee on Vagrancy declared vagrancy an excrescence on the Poor Law and recommended that it be handed over to the police, a view shared by the Majority of the 1905–9 Commission.[37] Vagrancy, nevertheless, remained the responsibility of the poor-law authorities until 1930. The number of vagrants applying to casual wards dropped between 1910 and 1914, probably because of improved economic conditions, but vagrancy was debated in poor-law circles as much as ever.[38] In particular, the idea of setting up compulsory labour colonies for hardened vagrants recurred time and again, but was never put into operation.

In the early 20th century the vagrancy problem was most visible in London, where each authority still ran its own casual wards and some were known to be much harsher than others. Once the lenient wards were full, tramps preferred to sleep rough on the Thames Embankment rather than enter the stricter wards. To remedy this, in 1912, the metropolitan casual wards were transferred to the Metropolitan Asylums Board. Ten wards were closed, and efforts were made to enforce uniform conditions in the seventeen remaining, and also to ensure that regimes were not so hard that vagrants preferred to sleep rough.[39] The immediate impact of this administrative change was a dramatic reduction in applications to London's casual wards.

Outside the capital, it was acknowledged that the soft policies of some unions exacerbated the vagrancy problem of their neighbours. As in London, an authority with a broader perspective was needed to devise a concerted approach, and so county vagrancy committees were born. Although not officially sanctioned by the Local Government Board until 1913, these had been formed in twenty different counties by 1912, and later spread throughout most of England.[40] Despite all of this reorganisation, new buildings were still located on workhouse sites, and followed the traditional mixture of cellular and associated wards.

The number of casuals applying to workhouses continued to drop until the depression of the early 1920s, but never greatly exceeded pre-First World War figures.[41] The wartime closure of many casual wards put a strain on remaining accommodation, especially in industrial areas. As with other types of poor-law building, little money was available for extensions or new structures. Cheap lodging-houses, which had supplemented casual ward accommodation in times of crisis before 1914, had vanished, but philanthropic hostels and training homes helped fill the gap. A few experts on the subject continued to advocate the formation of labour colonies rather than casual wards but, again, no action was taken.[42] Instead, conditions were improved in many wards: mattresses and bedsteads replaced hammocks, clean nightshirts were handed out to new arrivals, and facilities were provided to bathe, to wash underclothes and even to make tea.[43] Showers sometimes replaced baths, both as a time-saving device and as a means of ensuring that casuals washed in clean water. Oakum-picking was banned, stone-breaking discouraged and, all-in-all, life for the casual was much improved.

The piecemeal enlargement of casual wards continued throughout the 1930s, which was a time of severe economic depression and high unemployment. The public assistance committees, which had inherited casual wards from the poor-law authorities in 1930, reorganised facilities by closing some wards and expanding others. On occasion, new casual wards were erected on separate sites from other institutions. These buildings reveal a departure from the cellular system in favour of large dormitories, and permitted greater opportunities for socialising, both in day-rooms and open-plan workshops. The huge ward block of the Irthlingborough Casual Wards, erected by Northamptonshire Public Assistance Committee in 1933, contained eight 20-bed dormitories, lit solely by a high clerestorey and provided with toilet facilities.[44] New institutions like Irthlingborough, which was located on the by-pass road east of the town, kept tramps away from centres of population, and a typical post-1930 alteration to the casual wards of institutions was the creation of separate entrances, so that respectable visitors did not encounter tramps on their way in and out of the site. But for many people today the single abiding memory of the workhouse is the queue of tramps awaiting admission outside its gates, a common sight in English towns and cities into the early 1960s.

11
The Workhouse after 1914

Poor-law construction slowed down in August 1914 – not just for the duration of the war, but for all time. The only ambitious projects initiated after 1918 involved infirmaries and nurses' homes. All other building work, compared with the period prior to the First World War, was of little significance.

Many institutions were emptied during the First World War and handed over to the War Office to be used as hospitals, barracks, or camps for Belgian refugees or German prisoners of war. Displaced civilian inmates were sent to nearby institutions but, as this inevitably caused pressure on space, many of them were encouraged to leave the workhouse and join the war effort. Meanwhile, the military made various additions, usually temporary in nature, to the workhouses it took over. A more lasting effect of the war was the elevated status of workhouse medical facilities and staff. After 1918, poor-law officers expected to work shorter hours for higher salaries, creating a need for extra staff and, consequently, additional staff accommodation.

On 1 April 1919, the Ministry of Health assumed responsibility for poor-law affairs. A brief post-war boom was followed by a period of long-term widespread unemployment: the total number of applicants for relief stood at 576,418 on 1 January 1920, rose above a million in 1921 and soared to nearly 2 million during the General Strike of 1926.[1] At last, the workhouse test was seen as inappropriate for the unemployed, and many unions embraced 'Poplarism' by distributing outdoor relief on an unprecedented scale (*see* pages 122–123). The contributory National Insurance scheme, set up in better times to insure workers against loss of earnings for a limited period of time in cases of sickness, was threatened with insolvency and was supplemented by state aid – the dole. Although most boards of guardians now granted outdoor, or domiciliary, relief when applicants were capable of maintaining themselves out of the workhouse, they granted it on a widely varying scale. The 1926 Board of Guardians (Default) Act enabled the Minister of Health to assume control of authorities whose guardians had distributed outdoor relief too lavishly, and to restrict payments to the families of striking coal-miners.[2] Despite this, by the end of the 1920s, a number of unions were effectively bankrupt.

Money for new buildings was, understandably, in short supply throughout the 1920s. This, together with the high cost of building work, meant that official restrictions on expenditure, enforced during the war, remained in place; only urgent work was carried out. Building work was further inhibited by the expectation that, before too long, the poor-law system would be thoroughly reorganised. As Inspector Lowry phrased it in 1920, boards of guardians were 'under sentence of death'.[3]

Urgent building work involved piecemeal extensions to casual wards and infirmaries as well as nurses' homes. The erection of new children's homes was effectively forbidden, although some unions were allowed to purchase houses on the 'scattered-home' system (*see* pages 151–4). The Order of 1913 (*see* pages 137–8), prohibiting the maintenance of children in the workhouse, could not be enforced, and guardians were encouraged either to board-out children or send them to homes run by other unions.[4] Similarly, few of the joint committees created shortly before 1914 with a view to establishing mental deficiency or epileptic colonies were able to put their plans into operation.

No new workhouses were erected in the 1920s. Indeed, many of those which had been taken over for war purposes, especially in rural East Anglia (for example, Docking, Swaffham and Halstead), never reopened as institutions. Their inmates were despatched to the workhouses of neighbouring authorities, despite complaints that the aged were being distanced from friends and relatives. One of the most noticeable changes to workhouses throughout the 1920s was the lowering or removal of yard walls, a repercussion of the relaxation of those longstanding rules which segregated different classes of inmate.

*Figure 247
This is Rochford House, a new U-shaped 'workhouse' building erected at Rochford Public Assistance Institution by Southend-on-Sea Borough Council after 1930.
[BB95/6761]*

Neville Chamberlain's Local Government Act of 1929,[5] as anticipated for many years, changed the existing system of poor-law administration. Unions and boards of guardians were disbanded, and their responsibilities transferred to various committees of the county and county borough councils. This was not achieved without objections from both boards of guardians and councils, and the change-over was slow. Ultimately, the Act did not abolish the poor law; it merely reformed its administrative basis and changed a few titles.

Public health committees took over the best-appointed infirmaries, which were developed into municipal hospitals during the 1930s. Wirrall Union Workhouse, for example, became Clatterbridge (County) General Hospital under the auspices of Cheshire County Council, which proceeded with a large scheme of alteration and rebuilding. By the early 1940s the workhouse, which had been erected for 130 inmates in 1836, had expanded to become a 300-bed hospital.[6] Cheshire County Council had intended to convert the former Macclesfield Union Workhouse into a hospital serving the east of the county, but that scheme was not realised until war broke out in 1939.[7]

After 1930, many workhouses operated much as before in the hands of public assistance committees. Officially known as Poor-Law Institutions since 1913, workhouses were now re-christened Public Assistance Institutions. At a local level, they were controlled by sub-committees of 'guardians', and were often referred to as 'guardians' institutions'. Plympton-St-Mary Union Workhouse, for example, came under the control of Devon County Council and was managed by the Plympton Guardians' Committee under the direction of the Devon Public Assistance Committee. The day-to-day running of the institution, under its new name of Underwood House Public Assistance Institution, remained in the hands of a master and matron who, in time-honoured tradition, were a married couple residing on the site.[8] The new municipal hospitals, on the other hand, were run by medical superintendents.

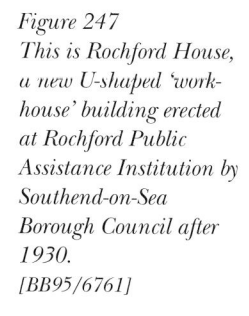

The elderly, the mentally deficient, unmarried mothers and vagrants were still the principal classes of inmate. Ample accommodation was usually available for all of these, with the exception of vagrants, and many casual ward blocks were therefore extended or rebuilt. Only one large new building for able-bodied and aged inmates, in effect a new workhouse, is known to have been erected in this period, at Rochford in Essex (Fig 247), but many others were 'upgraded', a process which entailed redecoration, the enlargement and reglazing of windows, improving sanitary facilities, refurbishing kitchens and laundries, the introduction of central heating and, eventually, lift shafts.

The pattern of change after the First World War can be illustrated by looking closely at one county. Hertfordshire had thirteen poor-law unions. Before 1930, two had been dissolved: Welwyn Union Workhouse became the children's home for Hatfield Union in 1921 and Hertford Union Workhouse became Kingsmead Special School in 1924, at which time its inmates were distributed between the St Albans and Ware workhouses. In the 1930s, only two Hertfordshire institutions shut down: Berkhampstead closed in 1935 and was demolished in 1937; Buntingford closed in 1933 and later became the offices of the Rural District Council. The remainder survived to become hospitals or old people's homes. These were Barnet (Barnet General Hospital), Bishop's Stortford (Haymeads Hospital), Hatfield (Wellfield Hospital), Hemel Hempstead (Hemel Hempstead General Hospital, St Paul's Wing), Hitchin (Hitchin Hospital), Royston (Heath Lodge), St Albans (St Albans City Hospital and Waverley Lodge Old People's Home), Ware (Western Hospital) and Watford (Watford General Hospital). Of these, Hatfield, Hemel Hempstead, Hertford, Hitchin and Royston have since been demolished.

The outbreak of the Second World War had a greater physical effect on workhouses than the First. Most were supplied with air-raid shelters and many became emergency hospitals under the Emergency Medical Service. Large hutted hospitals (*see* Figure 233) were erected on available land – usually on sites which had sufficient administrative and service buildings to cope with a great influx of staff and patients. Several workhouses were damaged or destroyed by bombing, one of the most regrettable losses being the grand, late 17th-century workhouse in Exeter (*see* Figure 8).

The National Health Service Act of 1946,[9] which became operative on 5 July 1948 ('The Appointed Day'), brought further changes. Most of the hospitals in the United Kingdom were taken over by the state and reorganised into groups run by Hospital Management Committees under Regional Hospital Boards. Former workhouse infirmaries, upgraded by county councils in the 1930s and extended during the war, were amongst the largest establishments inherited by the National Health Service. State hospitals, however, included many poor-law sites which had been classified as Public Assistance Institutions rather than hospitals in the 1930s. Bakewell Public Assistance Institution, for instance, was transferred to the Sheffield No. 3 Hospital Management Committee and was renamed Newholme Hospital. The stigma attached to these former workhouses lingered for more than a generation, perhaps understandably as they continued to operate much as they had under boards of guardians. For the majority, their primary function was to house the chronic sick and aged or mentally handicapped, but as a secondary function many maintained a 'Reception Centre for wayfarers' – in other words casual wards – into the 1960s.

Contemporary standards in the 1950s and 1960s decreed that old workhouse buildings, despite the piecemeal alterations and additions of the post-war period, provided unsuitable homes for the elderly and the mentally handicapped. Their steep stone staircases and low upper floors were especially inconvenient for such residents, and so the upper levels of many institutions were sealed off. As a result, many early 20th-century workhouse interiors remained untouched until recent times, for example those at Onehouse Workhouse in Suffolk, Thurgarton Hundred Workhouse in Nottinghamshire and Kensington Workhouse in London.

As buildings fell into disuse throughout the 1960s and 1970s, hospital authorities sold them off, a process which accelerated during the property boom of the 1980s. Many workhouses have since been demolished, and their sites redeveloped. Others have been successfully converted to housing, offices or light industrial units, in which case the main buildings have generally been retained and ancillary buildings demolished. The recession of the early 1990s left a large proportion of former workhouses standing empty, in a forlorn state, awaiting the economic recovery which would inevitably bring about their demolition or redevelopment.

12
Conclusion: The Changing Role of the Poor-Law Institution in English Society

The previous chapters have mapped the series of changes undergone by English poor-law buildings over the course of 350 years, especially in terms of their location, planning and appearance. These processes mirrored shifts in the attitude of those in authority towards the poorest elements of society, those living on the margins. At one time the prevailing view of pauperism might be benevolent, at another time censorious or reformatory. To complicate matters, different classes of pauper were regarded as more deserving of pity or reprobation than others. The revision of ideas on the causes of pauperism, in all its manifestations, was especially significant in introducing new approaches to indoor poor relief, bringing in their wake new designs and types of building.

The story which emerges is not a simple one of linear progression from one form of building to another. At any one time a variety of types co-existed, reflecting a diversity in attitudes which transcended the opposing socio-economic conditions prevailing in urban and rural or agricultural and industrial areas. In the second half of the 18th century, for example, many parishes set up small workhouses in the heart of towns or villages, close to the church or overlooking the green (Fig 248). These buildings were indistinguishable from the houses of other inhabitants, and their location showed a desire to maintain, even nurture, paupers within the community. But at the same time other parishes were grouping together to erect huge, self-sufficient houses of industry which removed the poor from their own town or village to an alien environment. In those cases, the prospect of lowering the poor rate had overwhelmed natural feelings of sympathy for the local poor. The tension between humanitarian concern and the desire to keep costs as low as possible was apparent in the treatment of the poor at all times, and is arguably still a factor in determining the welfare policies of the present day.

No matter what form it assumed, the workhouse was the cornerstone of the poor-law system. The name itself is somewhat misleading as, from the early 18th century onwards, most of its occupants were incapable of much work. The term 'workhouse' originated as a variant on 'workshop', but not necessarily one in which work was carried out. In the 17th century it was a store for materials, a collection point for finished articles and a control centre for administering what was, in effect, a cottage industry. The workshop-workhouse failed, undermined by the poor themselves, who simply could not or would not co-operate. These people were often unemployed for the simple reason that they were unemployable, either through some physical or mental disability. They were also tempted by pilfering, an opportunity readily offered by the cottage-industry system. A suggestion by some optimistic entrepreneurs, that the labour of the poor could be turned into profit in a well-managed workhouse, failed for the same reasons, thereby reinforcing the common assumption that able-bodied paupers were of inherently idle disposition.

By the early 18th century the workshop-workhouse had evolved into a residential institution which accommodated many different classes of pauper. This occurred largely because the parishes which operated workhouses had a number of other responsibilities, funded from the same purse, including the need to shelter and care for those impotent poor who had no friends or relatives to support them, and the obligation to train poor children. It must have seemed logical, and economical, to use the workshop-workhouse, which was already equipped with the necessary materials and administrative system, as a children's home and training school. The new urban incorporation workhouses set up at the turn of the 18th century were still designed primarily with children in mind, but for financial and administrative reasons they were soon being used to accommodate the aged, the mentally ill and the mentally handicapped. The older type of institutions for the impotent poor, which had been referred to as 'hospitals', thus merged with the workshop-workhouse to form a single institution.

The next step was to offer a place in the workhouse to able-bodied paupers. That became desirable as a deterrent: an able-bodied person applying for relief would have to choose between quitting his or her home to enter a workhouse or receiving no relief whatsoever. If this strategy succeeded, the workhouse would contain few able-bodied inmates and numbers on out-relief would be greatly reduced. The idea of the workhouse test was enshrined in Knatchbull's Act of 1723, and from that time the term workhouse was clearly outmoded – the workhouse had become a multi-faceted parish institution, at once an almshouse, an asylum, a hospital, an orphanage and a training school, but above all an instrument to reform the idle and indulgent habits of able-bodied unemployed adults, thereby reducing the poor rate.

Thomas Gilbert and a few other reformers towards the end of the 18th century argued that the able-bodied should be allowed to remain in their own homes and set to work on the roads or in the fields in return for their relief. The character of workhouse populations would not change by this move, but institutions could be officially acknowledged as poor houses for the impotent, rather than workhouses. Unions formed under Gilbert's Act of 1782 followed these principles, but the abandonment of the workhouse test was seen as one of the factors which brought about a rise in the poor rates. The new deterrent workhouses of the 1820s were a reaction to such policies and received official approval by the 1834 Poor Law Amendment Act.

As an attempt to impose national uniformity upon the treatment of pauperism, the New Poor

Figure 248
The indoor paupers of Cardington in Bedfordshire lived in this purpose-built workhouse on the village green until the advent of the New Poor Law, when Cardington became part of Bedford Union.
[BB97/5374]

Law must be judged a failure. Its opponents equated the new workhouses of the 1830s with prisons, although in reality they assumed a variety of guises. While many of the new 'bastiles' certainly bore a superficial resemblance to contemporary prison architecture, others adopted the architectural vocabulary of almshouses. The retention of old buildings, many of which had not been erected as workhouses and were inadequate to the task, added further complications. Regimes operating within these buildings could be as diverse as their physical appearances, as the rules and regulations laid down by the central authority were interpreted in various ways by guardians and by the resident master and matron.

In determining who should enter a workhouse as a condition of receiving relief, the New Poor Law again failed to enforce a national policy. The ban on outdoor relief to all but the impotent poor presented the unemployed and indolent with the option of either entering the workhouse, in which conditions were rendered 'less-eligible' (that is, less comfortable) than those of the humblest worker's cottage, or somehow discovering independent means. It was hoped that the new workhouses would deter able-bodied men from applying for relief, thereby reducing the poor rates. This strategy appeared to be successful until mass industrial unemployment drove huge numbers to the workhouse gates in the mid-1840s. By that time, however, workhouse wards had been filled by impotent paupers, forced to seek refuge with 'the Union', not merely on account of their poverty, but because they required an element of care or supervision which friends and relatives were unable to provide. There simply was not enough room in workhouses to accommodate the able-bodied casualties of economic depression and, rather than approve massive spending on new buildings, the central authority was obliged to adopt a flexible attitude to outdoor relief, enabling many unions to issue doles. From that time, more and more unions were exempted from the General Order for the Prohibition of Outdoor Relief. The attempt to clamp down on outdoor relief in the 1870s met with partial success, as some workhouse capacity had recently been freed up by the provision of separate buildings for children and the sick, but ultimately suffered from the lack of sufficient accommodation.

The dichotomy of sheltering the impotent and deserving poor while deterring and reforming the able-bodied and undeserving is central to our understanding of the workhouse as an institution and as a building type. The irony and ambiguity inherent in that situation ensured that the form of a workhouse was frequently at odds with its function. Indeed, a recurrent theme in the history of the poor law is the use of buildings for functions and classes of pauper for which they were not originally intended, but the case of the first-generation New Poor Law workhouses shows how even purposely designed buildings could be at odds with the reality of indoor pauperism.

The typical workhouse of the 1830s incorporated architectural imagery borrowed from penal institutions, notably in the single entrance, blind outer walls, and disposition of wings radiating from a central, supervisory 'hub'. This was not done simply for effect. Inside, the building was designed to restrict personal freedom and relationships to a degree which would prove intolerable to its occupants. Its planning facilitated the segregation of different classes of inmate, and the judicious positioning of doors, windows and staircases ensured that no two classes could communicate with one another, whether in their dormitories, day-rooms or yards. All of this was calculated to deter the able-bodied, who could avoid the workhouse except in times of exceptional hardship. Almost incidentally, it determined the living environment of those without other options: the aged and infirm, orphaned or abandoned children, the disabled who could not work, the mentally ill or mentally handicapped.

Potentially, the planning of a radial workhouse exerted greater control over the movement of its inmates than did the activities of the official staff. Few Old Poor Law workhouses had incorporated special planning to facilitate the supervision or control of inmates, and in small establishments paupers of all classes and sexes had mixed freely. In the new workhouses of the 1830s, the master's and matron's rooms gave them an overview of the yards, but unlike a nurse in a hospital or a keeper in an asylum, their only means of observing the behaviour of inmates indoors was to patrol the day-rooms, dormitories and workrooms. Workhouses had proportionately smaller staffs than contemporary institutions such as asylums or prisons; no warders were positioned in rooms with observation windows or stationed in the wards themselves. Instead, those in power relied on locked doors, high walls and a restricted lobby access system to the accommodation of different classes. Only when everyone was gathered in a communal space such as the chapel or dining-hall was the presence of the master or matron necessary to ensure the maintenance of discipline.

The rhetoric of supervision and control, of the workhouse as a self-regulating machine which operated to prevent contamination across

Conclusion: The Changing Role of the Poor-Law Institution in English Society

the classes, was contradicted by the practical conditions of workhouse life, and by the frugality with which it was associated. In the absence of paid servants and carers, inmates were expected to perform tasks which involved crossing the barriers that separated the different classes, in effect becoming pauper officials. Women of all ages occupied crucial roles in this process, as they were expected to clean, cook, wash clothes and bedding, nurse the sick and care for the infirm, infants and young children.[1] They did not have to leave their own designated area to enter the kitchen, wash-house or laundry, but required considerable freedom of movement in order to clean the rooms of other classes and to care for the sick and impotent; only the rooms and yards of able-bodied men and boys were out of bounds. With only the master and matron to supervise these activities, a high element of trust was involved. The daily business of the institution, therefore, broke down the physical segregation of its occupants; indeed, the sophisticated planning of the radial workhouse must have impeded daily chores, and it may have been supplanted by the corridor plan for that very reason. Once workhouses began to employ domestic servants and paid nurses, in the last decades of the 19th century, segregation became easier to maintain for all workhouse inmates.

It had been predicted that the New Poor Law workhouse would solve the problem of pauperism and become redundant within a decade but the problem had been wrongly diagnosed and that did not happen. In many areas, outdoor relief, thinly disguised as medical relief, continued to be distributed to the respectable unemployed while workhouses filled with the impotent and disreputable poor. The condition of certain groups of inmate – especially children and the sick – aroused public sympathy, awakening the desire to provide the 'deserving' with specialised accommodation which would offer protection against the 'undeserving'.

In this context, the introduction of the pavilion plan after 1870 can be seen as the culmination of a development spanning almost fifty years. Until the mid-19th century all classes of inmate, although segregated from one another, had been housed under a single roof in a 'general mixed institution'. This continued to be the case throughout the late 19th and early 20th centuries in workhouses with static or dwindling populations, some of which were never extended. But from the mid-19th century, workhouses with increasing populations, particularly those serving manufacturing towns, tended to expand by erecting detached buildings for specific classes of pauper rather than by enlarging the main building. This policy gradually relieved space in the main house which, ultimately, could become a specialised building in its own right, usually devoted to the able-bodied or aged and infirm. The ideal separate-block principle, embodied in new workhouses after 1880, allocated a separate building, or pavilion, to each class of inmate.

Attempts to reinforce the workhouse test in the 1870s and 1880s led to harsher conditions for able-bodied inmates in some urban workhouses. This was reflected in the architecture of new pavilion-plan workhouses, and may have played a role in the proliferation of cellular casual blocks throughout these decades. The workhouse was ill-fitted, however, to cope with periods of boom and slump, or even the seasonal employment patterns of agricultural areas, as it could not set aside sufficient space for hard times. An alternative test, that of task work in the labour yard, offered a cheap solution. It appealed because it prevented the contamination of respectable but temporarily unemployed labourers by the rougher element of workhouse populations.

The surveys of Booth, Rowntree and others contributed to the understanding that environmental and economic factors, such as low wages and large families, were more significant than personal deficiencies as causes of poverty. In the 1890s, aged paupers were no longer regarded as undeserving, and although they were seldom provided with detached buildings or separate institutions, in line with the treatment of children and the sick, the conditions of their life inside the workhouse were considerably improved. This was pivotal in changing the workhouse into a welfare institution. After 1900 fewer poor-law buildings were erected, and there were no further attempts to strengthen the workhouse test. The buildings, like the institutions, came to be seen in a new light, but were still produced with cheap materials, in an economical style.

Most of the institutions erected to serve the New Poor Law formed part of a large, inward-looking complex, but some exceptional building types emerged towards the end of the 19th century which were integrated with the wider community. Scattered homes allowed children to live in houses on ordinary residential streets, attend the local school and parish church, and use public facilities such as swimming-baths and parks. They were the last solution offered by poor-law authorities in their quest for a healthy, 'normal' environment in which to raise pauper children, and show that 'care in the community' is not such a recent concept. Other categories of poor-law building erected in visible positions in town centres were non-residential. They included dispensaries, out-relief offices and, at a slightly later date, union offices. The latter had the added advantage of allowing guardians to attend their regular meetings without setting foot inside the workhouse.

The dole, as a means of relieving the able-bodied, only became an acceptable alternative to the workhouse test in the period of mass unemployment which followed the First World War. Once that break had been made, the *raison d'être* of the workhouse vanished and the collapse of the poor law soon followed.

Fifty years have passed since 'public assistance institutions' went the way of 'workhouses', to be succeeded by 'hospitals', 'children's homes' and an extensive social security system. Surviving poor-law buildings no longer pose a sinister threat to the poor: indeed, many lie empty and derelict, awaiting redevelopment or demolition, while others have been sanitised and converted into desirable modern dwellings. Stripped of their power and tamed to more anodyne uses, these buildings still stand as a physical reminder of a system which has passed into myth.

Appendix 1
The Study of Poor-Law Buildings

Our understanding of the English poor law can be greatly enhanced by studying the buildings which housed its institutions. The plan, style and location of a workhouse, infirmary or children's home reveal much about contemporary attitudes towards the least fortunate members of society, and provide unique insights into the day-to-day lives of those compelled to reside within its walls. For those reasons, standing poor-law buildings must be recognised as a key historical resource.

Extant poor-law buildings have greatly diminished in number in recent years, largely through the processes of demolition and redevelopment. The need to record and interpret a representative selection of poor-law buildings before such a task became an impossibility prompted the Royal Commission on the Historical Monuments of England to launch the project which formed the basis of this book. In the course of the project, a substantial amount of material on workhouses, which had been already collected by the National Monuments Record, was augmented by an intensive programme of fieldwork and documentary research, covering the whole of England and including all poor-law building types. The principal aim of the project was to use the evidence of both standing and demolished buildings to track the history of indoor poor relief from the 16th century until the establishment of the National Health Service in 1948.

Although several hundred poor-law buildings were visited by Royal Commission fieldworkers between 1991 and 1996, it proved impossible to investigate them all or to undertake exhaustive historical research on every site.[1] Detailed studies must be undertaken at a local or regional, rather than national, level. At present, a degree of urgency attends the recording of all types of poor-law building, but those facing the greatest threat are peripheral structures, such as laundries and tramp wards, which are generally swept away when the central building is retained and converted to other uses. Even these modest structures have much to tell us about the poor-law policies of their day.

This book offers a broad historical framework for the study of individual poor-law institutions, but further exploration of primary and secondary sources adds to the interpretation of any site. A good introduction to poor-law sources is provided by Andy Reid's book, *The Union Workhouse, A Study Guide for Teachers and Local Historians* (1994). In addition, lists of poor-law documents held in record offices have recently been published by the Federation of Family History Societies.[2]

Primary Sources for Old Poor Law Buildings
No comprehensive official surveys of workhouse buildings were compiled in the period of the Old Poor Law (pre-1834), but Parliamentary returns of 1776, 1802–3 and 1813–15 provide useful, if incomplete, statistics.[3] Of greater value for the architectural historian are two contemporary accounts of selected 18th-century institutions, namely the anonymous *An Account of the Workhouses in Great Britain* (1725, 1732 and 1786), published by the Society for the Promotion of Christian Knowledge, and Sir Frederick Morton Eden's three-volume *State of the Poor* (1797), which included reports on the relief practices of numerous parishes, incorporations and unions throughout the country. *The Report from the Commissioners for Inquiry into the Poor Laws*, published in 1834, did not include a detailed analysis of the existing building stock, but critical accounts of selected buildings contributed to its general castigation of the Old Poor Law system.[4]

Information on Old Poor Law workhouses is sometimes contained in parish overseers' account books. Other relevant documents include building specifications, contracts, inventories, sales particulars and, less frequently, plans or elevations. Such material is usually held in local record offices. Even if documentary information is found, the site of the workhouse is not always easy to locate. Workhouses were usually identified on large-scale town maps but, with the exception of the early 19th-century tithe and enclosure maps, few surveys were made for rural areas. Despite these problems, approximately 300 buildings which were used as workhouses under the Old Poor Law figure in the Department for Culture, Media and Sport statutory lists.[5] Many more may be unlisted, or have not yet been identified as workhouses.

Primary Sources for New Poor Law Buildings
Between 1835 and 1914, the annual reports of the Poor Law Commission and its successors, the Poor Law Board and the Local Government Board, included tables which listed authorisations for expenditure on poor-law buildings.[6] After 1870, the purpose of each authorisation was noted, whether it was for a workhouse, an infirmary or merely a 'cooking apparatus'. These tables can be used to study patterns of building activity at particular dates.

The unpublished Registers of Authorizations for Workhouse Expenditure, housed in the Public Record Office, contain much the same information as the annual tables, now catalogued alphabetically by union rather than year by year.[7] Although the data is occasionally inaccurate and often vague, the Registers provide an excellent starting-point for research on a specific site by supplying the date and cost of its component parts.

In recent years some historians have used the expenditure records to analyse the extent of the workhouse system after 1834. Karel Williams relied on the authorisation tables in the annual reports, while Felix Driver used the Registers of Authorizations for Workhouse Expenditure.[8] Williams concluded that between 492 and 548 unions in England and Wales erected new workhouses between 1834 and 1870,[9] while Driver counted 511 unions building 521 workhouses in the same period.[10] The Registers also allowed Driver to chart the total authorised workhouse expenditure between 1835 and 1883.[11]

The published annual reports of the central authority were accompanied by numerous other documents of use to the architectural and social historian, in particular the reports of the regional poor-law inspectors, which often included detailed accounts of particular buildings or sites. Special enquiries, such as those which investigated the condition of metropolitan infirmaries in the 1860s or the benefits of cottage homes in the 1870s, are also very informative.

A massive amount of poor-law correspondence survives in the Public Record Office, notably between the central authority, on the one hand, and unions, school districts and poor-law inspectors on the other.[12] Because of its sheer quantity, that material could not be fully exploited for this study but, used selectively, it sheds much light on the activities of individual authorities and fills gaps where guardians' minute-books have not survived.

Unfortunately, 20th-century correspondence was destroyed during the Blitz.

Guardians' minute-books, held in local record offices and libraries, recorded the business of their weekly meetings. Where new building projects were concerned, this involved the purchase of a site, the appointment of an architect, the approval of plans, obtaining sanction for the scheme from the central authority, securing finance, advertising for tenders, the award of contracts and the progress of the work. Not all guardians' minute-books, however, have survived, and some are quite illegible.

Architectural drawings retained by the central authority are housed in the Public Record Office under the classmark MH14. They date mainly from the period 1870 to 1900, with a few earlier or later, and are folded into thirty-eight boxes.[13] Other plans and specifications are retained by local record offices: some of these oddments were deposited via the architect's office, others were from the institution itself. Whenever an institution is still functioning, its estate office or works department may hold substantial collections of drawings.

In the early 1930s, many county and county borough councils undertook surveys of the poor-law institutions which they had just inherited. These included plans and assessments of suitable reuse for buildings. Particularly useful are those carried out by the London County Council in 1929, now held in the London Metropolitan Archives, formerly the Greater London Record Office.[14] Some years later, as a preliminary to the National Health Act of 1946, the Ministry of Health undertook a survey of hospitals, including information about the then usage of former workhouses.[15]

Architects' drawings can be supplemented by the 1:500 (approximately 10 ft to the mile) and 1:2500 (25 in. to the mile) Ordnance Survey maps. The first editions of these were generally published from 1858 onwards, and a comparison of successive editions reveals the physical development of institutions. First edition 1:500 maps show the internal planning of public buildings.

Periodicals and newspapers are another important source of information. From the mid-19th century, architectural journals such as *The Builder* and *The Building News* advertised contracts and published winning tenders for new poor-law buildings, often mentioning the names of the architects and contractors, together with tender prices.[16] The same journals also published articles on significant sites, sometimes accompanied by plans and bird's-eye views. Again from the mid-19th century, entries in trade directories, especially *Kelly's Directory*, often gave the location of an institution, the date of its erection, its cost, the name of the architect and the nature of significant later additions. Local newspapers recorded opening ceremonies and other events, but are rarely indexed. Some record offices hold collections of cuttings which are arranged thematically under the heading 'workhouses' or 'hospitals'.

Finally, several semi-official publications offered guidance for new construction, rather than information about existing buildings. Particularly informative are *Knight's Guide to the Arrangement and Construction of Workhouse Buildings* (1889) by Knight and Co,[17] *Hints and Suggestions as to the Planning of Poor Law Buildings* (1901) by Percival Gordon Smith and *Hints on the Planning of Poor Law Buildings and Mortuaries* (1904) by A C Freeman.

Secondary Sources

For a general introduction to the history of the English poor law, one is spoiled for choice. Histories produced from the 18th century onward provide a useful introduction to the political, social and economic context of poor-law institutions. These works, including *The History of the Poor Laws* (1764) by the Revd Richard Burn, *A History of the English Poor Law* (1854 rcv 1898) by George Nicholls and *English Poor Law History* (1927–9) by Sidney and Beatrice Webb, tend to reflect contemporary attitudes towards poverty and frequently engage in the perennial debate concerning the 'proper' treatment of the poor. Nicholls, a former Poor Law Commissioner and major player in the establishment of the New Poor Law, was anxious to highlight the inadequacies of the Old Poor Law. In a similar way, the Webbs' monumental study of the poor laws is coloured by their own political stance and, in particular, their role in the Royal Commission of 1905–9 and subsequent agitation for reform. Their books, nevertheless, remain the standard general works on poor-law history.

Most modern poor-law historians have ignored poor-law buildings, but there are a few exceptions, notably Ann Digby, Karel Williams and Felix Driver, all of whom recognised their importance for the operation of poor-law policies and as evidence for the social attitudes of their time. Like other types of post-medieval public institution, poor-law buildings have also been shunned by mainstream architectural history. Until relatively recently, architectural historians have concentrated on works of obvious quality and have proved reluctant to examine the marriage of form and function in structures erected for the 'lower orders'. The few modern studies devoted to workhouse architecture are brief, and focus almost exclusively on the New Poor Law workhouses erected during the building boom of the 1830s. These include an essay by Richard Wildman, published as an appendix to Norman Longmate's book, *The Workhouse*, in 1974, and an article by Anna Dickens, 'The architect and the workhouse', which appeared in *Architectural Review* in 1976. Unpublished doctoral theses by Anna Dickens (1982) and Neil Bentham (1993) have used New Poor Law workhouses as a springboard for studies of the architectural profession and building trade, respectively. The architect Thomas A Markus (1993) has contributed to the discourse by subjecting workhouses and industrial schools, amongst other new building types of the Enlightenment and the Industrial Revolution, to spatial analysis adapted from tools first suggested by Hillier and Hanson.[18]

Several studies have been devoted to the workhouses of a particular area and include architectural comment, such as Diane Baker's *Workhouses in the Potteries* (1984) and Ann Digby's *Pauper Palaces* (1984). As well as regional works, local historians have produced many useful studies of individual workhouses, especially of those which were transformed into valued local hospitals in the mid-20th century. These works generally display a greater interest in the personalities who ran the establishments and the regimes which they operated than in the buildings, but nevertheless are a source of useful background information for the architectural historian.

Poor-law buildings were generally designed by obscure local architects or builders, few of whom have been the subject of monographs. One exception is George Gilbert Scott (1811–78) who, in partnership with William Bonython Moffatt (1812–87), began his practice by designing workhouses in 1835. Scott was dismissive of this period in his career in his autobiography, but Cole and Dickens have both published analyses of his workhouse buildings.[19] Another noted architect whose poor-law buildings have been discussed in a monograph is Thomas Worthington (1826–1909).[20]

In addition to the above, poor-law buildings are sometimes discussed in encyclopaedic works such as the Victoria County History, the Survey of London, the Inventory volumes of the Royal Commission on the Historical Monuments of England and the *Buildings of England* series. Descriptions of those protected by statutory listing can be found in the statutory lists of buildings of architectural or historic interest formerly issued by the Department of the Environment, then by the Department of National Heritage and now by the Department for Culture, Media and Sport.

Finally, files on several hundred English poor-law buildings can be consulted in the National Monuments Record, the archive of the Royal Commission. Files for sites in Greater London are held at the National Monument Record's Public Search Room in London and files for sites in the rest of the country are held at the National Monuments Record Centre in Swindon. The range of material held in a typical file might include ground and air photography, copies of historical maps, extracts from documents and a report by the Royal Commission investigators who visited the site.

APPENDIX 2
Catalogue A: Poor-Law Institutions Outside Metropolitan London (post-1834)

This catalogue lists the most significant poor-law institutions set up outside London after 1834, including many Old Poor Law institutions which remained in use. Poor-law infirmaries and industrial schools are included as are most cottage-home villages, but post-1900 children's establishments were too numerous and scattered to be listed comprehensively.

The first column lists poor-law authorities alphabetically, by pre-1974 county. Information about name changes follows the original name of the authority in brackets. The second column gives the locality of the institution. The third is a key to the function of each institution (*see* abbreviations below), and the fourth gives the National Grid Reference of the institution. Dates of original builds and major rebuilds are given in the fifth column and the sixth gives architects' names, with sources in endnotes. The final column gives the National Monuments Record file number. As the contents of the files vary, any person interested in a particular site is advised to make a written or telephone enquiry in the first instance. The files contain information trawled from diverse sources, including poor-law authority documents, local directories, architectural journals and architectural drawings held in libraries and record offices throughout the country. By no means all potential sources have been consulted. Local newspapers, in particular, could reveal a great deal of extra information about the sites listed below.

Abbreviations

ab	able-bodied (test) workhouse or labour colony
alt	altered
ch	children's cottage, scattered or receiving homes
conv	converted
enl	enlarged
est	established
GP	Gilbert Parish
GU	Gilbert Union (indicates those which continued to exist after 1834; all were dissolved 1869)
i	(separate-site) infirmary
men	asylum or colony for epileptics and/or the mentally handicapped
purch	purchased
reb	rebuilt
san	(separate-site) sanatorium
sch	industrial school
SD	School District
w	workhouse

Poor-Law Authority	Location	Type	NGR	Dates	Architect(s)	NMR No
Bedfordshire						
Ampthill	Ampthill	w	TL 033 375	1835–6	James Clephan[1]	100224
Bedford	Bedford	w	TL 055 503	1795–6	John Wing[2]	100234
Biggleswade	Biggleswade	w	TL 200 439	1836	Thomas Gwyn Elger[3]	100221
Leighton Buzzard	Leighton Buzzard	w	SP 923 248	1836	William P Roote[4]	100229
Luton	Luton	w	TL 085 214	1836	John Williams[5]	100249
Woburn	Woburn	w	SP 948 329	1836	–	101673
Berkshire						
Abingdon	Abingdon	w	SU 499 975	1835	Sampson Kempthorne[6]	101636
Bradfield	Bradfield	w	SU 606 717	1835	Sampson Kempthorne[7]	100536
Cookham (Maidenhead)	Maidenhead	w	SU 872 815	1836	Cooper & Son[8]	100387
Easthampstead	Easthampstead, Bracknell	w	SU 864 675	1826	–	100389
Faringdon	Faringdon	w	SU 290 955	1801	–	101655
Hungerford (Hungerford and Ramsbury)	Hungerford	w	SU 340 682	1847	S O Foden[9]	100569
Newbury	Newbury	w	SU 473 655	1836	Sampson Kempthorne[10]	100513
Reading	Reading	w	SU 697 738	1866–7	Mr Woodman[11]	100398
Reading and Wokingham SD	Wargrave	sch	SU 790 786	pre-1834	–	101657

Poor-Law Authority	Location	Type	NGR	Dates	Architect(s)	NMR No
Wallingford	Wallingford	w	SU 600 898	1807	–	100391
Wantage	Wantage	w	SU 397 855	1836	Sampson Kempthorne[12]	101656
Windsor	Crimp Hill, Old Windsor	w	SU 977 737	1839	G Gilbert Scott & W Bonython Moffatt[13]	100237
Wokingham	Wokingham	w	SU 803 685	1848–50	Richard Billings[14]	100327

Buckinghamshire

Amersham	Amersham	w	SU 955 970	1838	G Gilbert Scott & W Bonython Moffatt[15]	100254
Aylesbury	Aylesbury	w	SP 825 146	1844	S O Foden with H W Parker[16]	100290
Buckingham	Buckingham	w	SP 697 343	1836	G Gilbert Scott[17]	101670
Eton	Slough	w	SU 976 794	1835	Sampson Kempthorne[18]	100346
Newport Pagnell	Newport Pagnell	w	SP 886 432	1836	William P Roote[19]	100252
Winslow	Winslow	w	SP 768 281	1835	G Gilbert Scott[20]	100271
Wycombe	Bledlow	sch	SP 781 022	pre-1834	–	101671
Wycombe	Saunderton	w	SU 815 980	1843	G Gilbert Scott & W Bonython Moffatt[21]	101672

Cambridgeshire

Cambridge	Cambridge	w	TL 461 579	1838	John Smith[22]	100186
Caxton and Arrington	Caxton	w	TL 301 590	1836–7	William T Nash[23]	100217
Chesterton	Chesterton, Cambridge	w	TL 460 599	1836–8	John Smith[24]	100187
Ely	Ely	w	TL 533 799	1836–7	William J Donthorn[25]	100157
Linton	Linton	w	TL 558 473	1836–7	Hallett & Newman[26]	83336
Newmarket	Newmarket	w	TL 639 642	1836	William P Roote[27]	100054
North Witchford	Doddington	w	TL 395 912	1838	–	101679
Whittlesey	Whittlesey	w	TL 277 972	1874	–	100219
Wisbech	Wisbech	w	TF 463 101	1837–8	William J Donthorn[28]	100142

Cheshire

Altrincham (Bucklow)	Knutsford	w	SJ 748 784	1836–40 reb 1892–1904	– Robert J McBeath[29]	102116
Birkenhead	Birkenhead	w	SJ 318 875	1860–4	Thomas Layland[30]	102406
Chester	Chester	w	SJ 420 670	1873	W Perkin & Son[31]	100155
Congleton	Arclid	w	SJ 788 624	1844–5	Henry Bowman[32]	102127
Great Boughton (Tarvin)	Great Boughton	w	SJ 424 659	1857	J Harrison[33]	101680
Macclesfield	Macclesfield	w	SJ 909 739	1843–4	G Gilbert Scott & W Bonython Moffatt[34]	102007
Nantwich	Nantwich	w	SJ 654 533	1780	–	102128
Northwich	Northwich	w	SJ 658 731	1837–9	George Latham[35]	102136
Runcorn	Dutton	w	SJ 575 793	1854–7	–	100154
Stockport	Shaw Heath	w	SJ 895 895	1841–2	Henry Bowman[36]	100156
Stockport	Stepping Hill	i	SJ 912 875	1901–5	W H Ward[37]	100164
Wirral	Clatterbridge	w	SJ 320 821	1836–7	William Cole[38]	102401

Cornwall

Bodmin	Bodmin	w	SX 074 673	1839–42	William Dwelly?[39]	100260
Camelford	Camelford	w	SX 101 834	1858	–	100301
Falmouth	Falmouth	w	SW 788 333	1850–2	Fred William Porter[40]	100313
Helston	Helston	w	SW 662 272	1854–7	Fred William Porter[41]	100356
Launceston	Launceston	w	SX 335 838	1838–9	Charles Lang[42]	100352
Liskeard	Liskeard	w	SX 247 640	1837–9	G Gilbert Scott & W Bonython Moffatt[43]	100295
Penzance	Madron	w	SW 450 321	1838	G Gilbert Scott & W Bonython Moffatt[44]	100306
Redruth	Redruth	w	SW 685 416	1838	G Gilbert Scott & W Bonython Moffatt[45]	100357
St Austell	St Austell	w	SX 011 526	1838–9	G Gilbert Scott & W Bonython Moffatt[46]	100338
St Columb	St Columb Major	w	SW 916 637	1838–40	G Gilbert Scott & W Bonython Moffatt[47]	100358
St Germans	Torpoint	w	SX 437 547	1837–8	Charles Lang[48]	101697
Stratton	Stratton	w	SS 226 064	1856	–	101696
Truro	Truro	w	SW 838 456	1849–50	William Harris[49]	100312

Cumberland

Alston (with Gargill)	Alston	w	NY 717 460	pre-1834	–	101628
Bootle	Bootle	w	SD 100 884	1856	–	101631
Brampton	Brampton	w	NY 530 613	1875	Charles S & Alline J Nelson[50]	102275
Carlisle	Harraby Hill	sch	NY 411 547	1809	–	102280
Carlisle	Carlisle	w	NY 409 556	1863	Henry F Lockwood & William Mawson[51]	102279
Cockermouth	Cockermouth	w	NY 118 304	1839–40	–	100170
Cockermouth	Flimby Lodge	sch	–	1887–9	–	No file
Longtown	Netherby	w	NY 410 689	1828	–	101630
Northern Counties Joint Poor-Law Committee: see Northumberland						
Penrith	Penrith	w	NY 504 300	1838	–	100169
Whitehaven	Workington	w	NY 006 270	1792	–	102289
Whitehaven	Whitehaven	w	NX 975 163	1854–6	Mr Porter[52]	100168
Wigton	Wigton	w	NY 248 490	1838–42	–	102285

Appendix 2: Catalogue A

Poor-Law Authority	Location	Type	NGR	Dates	Architect(s)	NMR No
Derbyshire						
Ashbourne	Ashbourne	w	SK 174 464	1846–7	Henry J Stevens[53]	102411
Bakewell	Bakewell	w	SK 220 691	1840	Mr Johnson[54]	102069
Belper	Belper	w	SK 346 470	1838	G Gilbert Scott & W Bonython Moffatt[55]	102413
Chapel-en-le-Frith	Chapel-en-le-Frith	w	SK 051 805	1840	–	100588
Chesterfield	Chesterfield	w	SK 382 715	1838–40	G Gilbert Scott & W Bonython Moffatt[56]	100617
Chesterfield	Brampton	sch	–	1879	–	No file
Derby	Derby	w	SK 357 351	1837–8	John Mason[57]	101637
Derby	Derby	w	SK 327 353	1876	William Giles & Robert & Thomas Brookhouse[58]	102408
Derby	Derby	i	SK 327 350	1926–9	T H Thorpe[59]	102415
Glossop	Glossop	w	SK 043 952	1834	–	100308
Hayfield	Low Leighton	w	SK 008 857	1838–9	Mr Worth[60]	100550
Shardlow	Shardlow	w	SK 429 305	1816		
				enl 1838–9	Henry J Stevens[61]	100185
Devon						
Axminster	Axminster	w	SY 292 979	1836–8	Sampson Kempthorne[62]	101681
Barnstaple	Barnstaple	w	SS 562 332	1837	Sampson Kempthorne[63]	100502
Bideford	Bideford	w	SS 449 263	1837	G Gilbert Scott & W Bonython Moffatt[64]	100499
Crediton	Crediton	w	SS 820 005	1836–7	Sampson Kempthorne[65]	100368
East Stonehouse	East Stonehouse, Plymouth	w	SX 466 546	1801	–	100381
Exeter	Exeter	w	SX 932 927	1699–1707	Ralph Mitchell[66]	100366
Holsworthy	Holsworthy	w	SS 340 042	1853	Edward Ashworth?[67]	100370
Honiton	Honiton	w	ST 164 002	1836	George Wilkinson?[68]	100316
Kingsbridge	Kingsbridge	w	SX 732 444	1837	Thomas Ponsford?[69]	101682
Newton Abbot	Newton Abbot	w	SX 861 710	1837	G Gilbert Scott & W Bonython Moffatt[70]	100372
Okehampton	Okehampton	w	SX 586 946	1836–7	Sampson Kempthorne[71]	100369
Plymouth	Plymouth	w	SX 487 553	1852–8	Oswald C Arthur & William Dwelly[72]	100329
Plympton St Mary	Plympton, Plymouth	w	SX 535 560	1836	–	100378
St Thomas	Exeter	w	SX 907 924	1836	Sampson Kempthorne[73]	100367
South Molton	South Molton	w	SS 711 261	1837–9	Sampson Kempthorne?[74]	100501
Stoke Damerell (Devonport)	Devonport, Plymouth	w	SX 460 565	1850–4	Alfred Norman[75]	100374
Tavistock	Tavistock	w	SX 478 749	1837	G Gilbert Scott & W Bonython Moffatt[76]	101676
Tiverton	Tiverton	w	SS 958 130	1836–7	G Gilbert Scott & W Bonython Moffatt[77]	38934
Torrington	Torrington	w	SS 485 192	1837	Sampson Kempthorne[78]	101683
Totnes	Totnes	w	SX 795 603	1837–9	Thomas Ponsford[79]	100325
Dorset						
Beaminster	Beaminster	w	ST 467 009	1836–7	H J Whitling with Munday[80]	100482
Blandford	Blandford	w	ST 887 069	1856–7	Christopher C Creeke[81]	101684
Bridport	Bridport	w	SY 469 931	1837	H J Whitling[82]	100477
Cerne	Cerne Abbas	w	ST 661 017	1836–7	Charles Wallis[83]	100484
Dorchester	Dorchester	w	SY 687 903	1836	George Wilkinson[84]	100475
Poole	Poole	w	SZ 018 914	1838–9	Mr Clarke[85]	100404
Shaftesbury	Shaftesbury	w	ST 856 227	1836–40	William Walker[86]	100486
Sherborne	Sherborne	w	ST 636 163	1837	Edward Percy[87]	100485
Sturminster	Sturminster	w	ST 787 148	1836	Lewis Vulliamy[88]	100426
Wareham and Purbeck	Wareham	w	SY 918 874	1837	O B Carter & H Hyde[89]	100407
Weymouth	Weymouth	w	SY 675 785	1836	T Dobson & T Hill Harvey[90]	100479
Wimborne and Cranborne	Wimborne Minster	w	SU 010 003	1780	–	101685
Durham						
Auckland	Auckland	w	NZ 208 290	1853–5	–	102207
Chester-le-Street	Chester-le-Street	w	NZ 274 508	1854–6	Matthew Thompson[91]	102216
Darlington	Darlington	w	NZ 301 142	1868	Charles J Adams[92]	102201
Durham	Durham	w	NZ 268 424	1837	George Jackson[93]	102221
Easington	Easington	w	NZ 419 435	1850	–	100672
Gateshead	Gateshead	w	NZ 249 622	1840–1	–	101638
Gateshead	Gateshead	w	NZ 247 612	1885–9	J H Morton with W L Newcombe & W H Knowles[94]	102343
Gateshead	Shotley Bridge	ch	–	1895–1901	W L Newcombe[95]	No file
Gateshead	Shotley Bridge, Consett	san	NZ 103 527	1909–12	W L Newcombe & Newcombe[96]	102213
Hartlepool	Hartlepool	w	NZ 500 345	1861	Matthew Thompson[97]	102181
Houghton-le-Spring	Houghton-le-Spring	w	NZ 343 500	1864	Matthew Thompson[98]	100673
Lanchester	Lanchester	w	NZ 164 475	1863	–	102218
Northern Counties Joint Poor-Law Committee: *see* Northumberland						
Sedgefield	Sedgefield	w	NZ 353 286	1860–1	–	102205
South Shields	Ocean Rd, South Shields	w	NZ 369 675	1837	John & Benjamin Green[99]	101639
South Shields	West Harton, South Shields	w	NZ 366 643	1877–80	J H Morton[100]	102327
Stockton-on-Tees	Stockton-on-Tees	w	NZ 451 196	1849–51	John & William Atkinson?[101]	102184
Sunderland	Sunderland	w	NZ 380 566	1856	J E Oates[102]	102337

The Workhouse

Poor-Law Authority	Location	Type	NGR	Dates	Architect(s)	NMR No
Teesdale	Barnard Castle	w	NZ 054 169	1838	John Green[103]	102200
Weardale	Stanhope	w	NY 999 390	1866–7	Matthew Thompson[104]	100671

Essex

Billericay	Billericay	w	TQ 678 952	1839	G Gilbert Scott & W Bonython Moffatt[105]	100679
Braintree	Braintree	w	TL 751 231	1836–8	William T Nash[106]	100680
Chelmsford	Chelmsford	w	TL 699 049	1837	William Thorold[107]	
				reb 1886–9	Fred Chancellor[108]	101244
Colchester	Colchester	w	TL 991 253	1836–7	John Brown[109]	100719
Dunmow	Dunmow	w	TL 631 212	1838–40	G Gilbert Scott & W Bonython Moffatt[110]	100678
Epping	Epping	w	TL 469 028	1837	Lewis Vulliamy[111]	101344
Halstead	Halstead	w	TL 814 311	1837–9	William T Nash[112]	100677
Lexden and Winstree	Stanway, Colchester	w	TL 959 249	1836	S O Foden & Henman[113]	100723
Maldon	Maldon	w	TL 845 068	1872–3	F Peck[114]	101243
Ongar	Stanford Rivers		TL 541 002	1830	–	100725
Orsett	Orsett	w	TQ 643 817	1837	Sampson Kempthorne[115]	100674
Rochford	Rochford	w	TQ 874 908	1837	William Thorold[116]	
				reb 1933–4	F W Smith[117]	101250
Romford	Romford	w	TQ 510 881	1838	Francis Edwards[118]	100675
Saffron Walden	Saffron Walden	w	TL 550 386	1835–6	James Clephan[119]	101342
Tendring	Tendring Heath	w	TM 135 265	1837–8	G Gilbert Scott & W Bonython Moffatt[120]	100676
West Ham	Leyton	w	TQ 390 860	1839–40	Alfred Richardson Mason[121]	101162
West Ham	Whipps Cross	i	TQ 389 886	1900–3	Francis J Sturdy[122]	101163
West Ham	Aldersbrook	ch	TQ 409 869	1906	–	No file
Witham	Witham	w	TL 815 140	1837–9	G Gilbert Scott & W Bonython Moffatt[123]	101242

Gloucestershire

Barton Regis	Southmead	w	ST 591 777	1902	A P I Cotterell & W H Thorpe[124]	100888
Bristol	St Peter's Hospital, Bristol	w	–	1612	–	No file
Bristol	Stapleton	w	ST 629 762	c 1800	–	
				enl 1858	Medland & Maberley[125]	101326
Bristol	Downend	ch	ST 644 768	1902–5	–	No file
Cheltenham	Cheltenham	w	SP 945 231	1838	Mr Cope[126]	100618
Chipping Sodbury	Chipping Sodbury	w	ST 718 824	1838	G Gilbert Scott & W Bonython Moffatt[127]	100924
Cirencester	Cirencester	w	SP 024 013	1836–7	John Plowman[128]	100641
Clifton (Barton Regis)	Eastville	w	ST 613 748	1847	Samuel T Welch[129]	100886
Dursley	Dursley	w	ST 755 979	1838–9	Mr Fulljames[130]	101686
Gloucester	Gloucester	w	SO 838 186	1836–40	G Gilbert Scott & W Bonython Moffatt[131]	100594
Newent	Newent	w	SO 719 263	1803–4? alt 1836 –		101687
Northleach	Northleach	w	SP 118 144	1836	George Wilkinson[132]	86403
Stow-on-the-Wold	Stow-on-the-Wold	w	SP 195 257	1836	George Wilkinson[133]	100915
Stroud	Stroud	w	SO 863 049	1835–40	William Mason[134]	100622
Tetbury	Tetbury	w	ST 892 931	1790	–	No file
Tetbury	Tetbury	w	ST 892 931	1905–6	V A Lawson[135]	100642
Tewkesbury	Tewkesbury	w	SO 889 321	1792–6	–	100625
Thornbury	Thornbury	w	ST 641 904	1837	Sampson Kempthorne[136]	100887
Westbury (-on-Severn)	Westbury-on-Severn	w	SO 715 141	1789–90		
				reb 1869	A W Maberley[137]	101688
Wheatenhurst	Eastington	w	SO 782 063	1785	–	
				enl 1836	Mr Fulljames[138]	101689
Winchcomb	Winchcomb	w	SP 019 281	1836	Sampson Kempthorne[139]	101690

Hampshire

Aldershot (GP)	Aldershot	w	SU 861 511	17th C;	–	
				enl 1838–40	–	100174
Alresford	Alresford	w	SU 587 315	1835–6	Edward Hunt[140]	76971
Alton	Alton	w	SU 725 400	1793	–	39258
Alverstoke (GP)	Alverstoke	w	SZ 609 992	1799–1801	Francis Carter[141]	100021
Andover	Andover	w	SU 360 457	1836	Sampson Kempthorne[142]	100092
Basingstoke	Basingstoke	w	SU 654 528	1835–6	Sampson Kempthorne[143]	100096
Catherington	Horndean	w	SU 703 129	1835	–	100127
Christchurch	Christchurch	w	SZ 150 939	1881–6	Christopher C Creeke & E H Burton[144]	100461
Droxford	Droxford	w	SU 604 185	1836	Sampson Kempthorne[145]	101691
Fareham	Fareham	w	SU 582 070	1835	Thomas Owen[146]	100109
Farnborough (GU)	–	w	–	1794	–	No file
Farnham: *see* Surrey						
Farnham & Hartley Wintney SD	Aldershot	sch	SU 861 511	purch 1849	–	
				alt 1851	William Young[147]	100174
Farnham & Hartley Wintney SD	Crondall	sch	SU 802 468	1855–6	–	101621
Fordingbridge	Fordingbridge	w	SU 146 143	1884–5	Fred Bath[148]	100112

Appendix 2: Catalogue A

Poor-Law Authority	Location	Type	NGR	Dates	Architect(s)	NMR No
Hartley Wintney	Winchfield	w	SU 781 541	1870–1	Edmund Woodthorpe[149]	100210
Havant	Havant	w	SU 714 063	1819; enl 1835	–	100125
Headley (GU)	Headley	w	SU 825 355	1795	–	100086
Hursley	Hursley	w	–	1828	–	No file
Hursley	Chandler's Ford	w	SU 430 220	1899–1900	Cancellor & Hill[150]	100106
Isle of Wight	Newport	w	SZ 495 905	1770–1	–	100898
Kingsclere	Kingsclere	w	SU 524 592	1836–7	George Adey[151]	100132
Lymington	Lymington	w	SZ 322 959	1837	Sampson Kempthorne[152]	100136
New Forest	Ashurst	w	SU 336 102	1836	Sampson Kempthorne?[153]	100093
New Winchester	Winchester	w	SU 476 298	1836–7	William Cole[154]	100512
Petersfield	Petersfield	w	SU 751 233	1835	–	100147
Portsea Island	Portsea Island, Portsmouth	w	SU 660 005	1843–5	Augustus Livesay & Thomas Ellis Owen[155]	76977
Ringwood	Ringwood	w	SU 138 048	1725	–	101692
Romsey	Romsey	w	SU 362 214	1774; enl 1836	–	100172
Southampton	Southampton	w	–	1776		No file
Southampton	Southampton	w	SU 426 123	1866–7	Thomas A Skelton[156]	100192
Southampton	Shirley Warren, Southampton	i	SU 399 150	1899–1902	A F Gutteridge[157]	100191
South Stoneham	West End	w	SU 474 145	1848	W Henman[158]	100031
Stockbridge	Stockbridge	w	SU 360 349	1836–7	Mr Hopgood[159]	100199
Whitchurch	Whitchurch	w	SU 473 481	1847–8	S O Foden[160]	100201

Herefordshire

Bromyard	Bromyard	w	SO 670 541	1836	George Wilkinson[161]	100519
Dore	Riverdale	w	SO 384 326	1837–9	John Plowman[162]	101693
Hereford	Hereford	w	SO 515 402	1836	John Plowman[163]	100205
Kington	Kington	w	SO 298 558	1837	H J Whitling[164]	100515
Ledbury	Ledbury	w	SO 707 381	1836	George Wilkinson[165]	100524
Leominster	Leominster	w	SO 499 593	enl 1836–8	George Wilkinson[166]	100517
Ross	Ross-on-Wye	w	SO 600 239	1836–7 reb 1872	John Plowman Haddon Bros[167]	100521
Weobley	Weobley	w	SO 393 521	1837	George Wilkinson[168]	100472

Hertfordshire

Barnet	Barnet	w	TQ 235 963	1836–7	John Griffin[169]	100939
Berkhampstead	Berkhampstead	w	SP 986 080	1831	–	101694
Bishop's Stortford	Bishop's Stortford	w	TL 500 209	1836	T L Evans[170]	101343
Buntingford	Buntingford	w	TQ 364 294	1836–7	William T Nash[171]	100991
Hatfield	Hatfield	w	TQ 225 088	1788	J Donowell[172]	100994
Hemel Hempstead	Hemel Hempstead	w	TL 061 079	1835–6	John Griffin[173]	101075
Hertford	Hertford	w	TL 344 131	1867–9	Frederick Peck[174]	100920
Hitchin	Hitchin	w	TL 178 298	1836	Thomas Smith[175]	100682
Royston	Royston	w	TL 351 407	1835–6	William T Nash[176]	100681
St Albans	St Albans	w	TL 144 081	1836–7	John Griffin?[177]	100683
Ware	Ware	w	TL 359 147	1839–40	Brown & Henman[178]	90892
Watford	Watford	w	TQ 105 957	1836–7	T L Evans[179]	101232
Welwyn	Welwyn	w	TQ 231 155	1830	–	100993

Huntingdonshire

Huntingdon	Huntingdon	w	TL 234 723	1836–7	Sampson Kempthorne[180]	100079
St Ives	St Ives	w	TL 307 703	1836–8	William T Nash[181]	100067
St Neots	St Neots	w	TL 173 597	1841–2	W Abbott[182]	100218

Kent

Blean	Hearne Common	w	TR 176 652	1835	Sir Francis Head/William Edmunds[183]	101179
Bridge	Bridge	w	TR 179 544	1836	Sir Francis Head/George Lancefield[184]	100943
Bromley	Locks Bottom	w	TQ 433 650	1844	James Savage & S O Foden[185]	100690
Canterbury	Canterbury	w	TR 150 567	1848–50	H Marshall[186]	101136
Cranbrook	Hartley	w	TQ 760 350	1838	John Whichcord[187]	100947
Dartford	Dartford	w	TQ 538 743	1836	John Whichcord[188]	101216
East Ashford	Ashford	w	TR 034 423	1835–7	Sir Francis Head/John Whichcord[189]	101321
Eastry	Eastry	w	TR 308 545	1836	Sir Francis Head/William Spanton[190]	100685
Elham	Etchinghill	w	TR 167 393	1835	Sir Francis Head[191]	101320
Elham	Cheriton	ch	–	1887–8	–	No file
Faversham	Faversham	w	TR 001 614	1836	Sir Francis Head/John Day[192]	100956
Gravesend and Milton	Gravesend	w	TQ 644 736	1847	John Gould[193]	100686
Hollingbourne	Hollingbourne	w	TQ 820 548	1836	–	100948
Hoo	Hoo	w	TQ 775 721	1836	Sir Francis Head[194]	100950
Isle of Thanet	Minster in Thanet	w	TR 311 655	1836	Sir Francis Head[195]	100945
Isle of Thanet	Manston	ch	TR 348 663	1900–1	–	No file

205

# THE WORKHOUSE

Poor-Law Authority	Location	Type	NGR	Dates	Architect(s)	NMR No
Maidstone	Coxheath	w	TQ 744 509	1836	Sir Francis Head/John Whichcord[196]	101221
Malling	West Malling	w	TQ 671 562	1836	John Whichcord[197]	100944
Medway	Chatham	w	TQ 763 670	1858–9	Frederick Peck & Edward W Stephens[198]	100687
Medway	Rochester	ch	TQ 752 663	1902–3	–	No file
Milton Regis	Sittingbourne	w	TQ 903 650	1835	Sir Francis Head/Mr Bland[199]	100954
North Aylesford (Strood)	Strood	w	TQ 735 695	1837	–	100953
River (Dover)	Dover	w	TR 302 420	1836	Sir Francis Head/George Lancefield[200]	100684
Romney Marsh	New Romney	w	TR 065 246	pre-1834	–	100946
Sevenoaks	Sundridge	w	TQ 482 537	1843	Mr Mason[201]	100952
Sheppey	Minster in Sheppey	w	TQ 955 733	pre-1834	–	100949
Tenterden	Tenterden	w	TQ 874 328	1843	James Savage[202]	100688
Tonbridge	Pembury	w	TQ 615 413	1836	John Whichcord[203]	100689
West Ashford	Hothfield Common	w	TQ 968 464	1835	Sir Francis Head[204]	101324

Lancashire

Poor-Law Authority	Location	Type	NGR	Dates	Architect(s)	NMR No
Ashton-under-Lyne	Ashton-under-Lyne	w	SJ 954 995	1849–50	–	100699
Barrow-in-Furness	Barrow-in-Furness	w	SD 221 689	1879	J Y McIntosh[205]	102084
Barrow-in-Furness	Barrow-in-Furness	ch	SD 213 690	c 1905	–	No file
Barton-upon-Irwell	Patricroft	w	SJ 763 985	1851–3 reb 1892–4	William Mangnall & John Littlewood[206]	102074
Barton-upon-Irwell	Davyhulme	i	SJ 755 953	1925–6	Elcock & Sutcliffe[207]	100698
Blackburn	Blackburn	w	SD 694 268	1861–4	J E & J D Oates[208]	100695
Bolton	Bolton	w	SD 718 064	1858–61	Hall & Woodhouse[209]	100697
Burnley	Burnley	w	SD 851 347	1873–6	William Waddington[210]	100694
Bury	Jericho	w	SD 833 116	1855–6	–	100738
Caton (GU)	Moorgarth	w	SD 546 639	pre-1834	–	101634
Chorley	Chorley	w	SD 592 178	1870–2	T T Bradshaw[211]	102245
Chorlton	Withington	w	SJ 836 924	1855	William Hayley, Son & Leigh Hall[212]	102142
Chorlton	Styal	ch	SJ 844 828	1895	J B Broadbent[213]	102123
Chorlton and Manchester Joint (Asylum) Committee (1897–1915)	Langho	men	SJ 690 339	1902–6	Giles, Gough & Trollope[214]	102621
Chorlton and Manchester Joint (Casual Ward and Test House) Committee (1897–1915)	–	ab	–	1901	–	No file
Clitheroe	Clitheroe	w	SD 755 430	1870–3	–	100732
Fylde	Kirkham	w	–	1843–4	–	No file
Fylde	Wesham	w	SD 420 329	1898	Charles S Haywood & Fred Harrison[215]	100730
Garstang	–	w	–	1795	–	No file
Garstang	Bowgreave	w	SD 497 444	1876	–	100733
Haslingden	Haslingden	w	SD 797 225	1866–9	Henry F Lockwood & William Mawson[216]	100731
Lancaster	Lancaster	w	SD 486 614	1841	–	100696
Leigh	Leigh	w	SD 658 013	1850–1	–	100745
Liverpool	Liverpool	w	SJ 357 902	1769–72 enl 1842–3	Joseph Brooks[217] Henry F Lockwood & Thomas Allom[218]	100746
Liverpool	Kirkdale	sch	SJ 350 941	1843	Henry F Lockwood & Thomas Allom[219]	101675
Liverpool	Olive Mount, Wavertree	ch	SJ 395 898	1898–9	–	102522
Liverpool	Highfield	i	SJ 404 909	1902–6	Edmund Kirby & W E Willink[220]	102382
Liverpool, West Derby and Toxteth Park Joint Committee	Heswall	san	SJ 257 824	1901–2	Charles H Lancaster[221]	102709
Lunesdale	Hornby	w	SD 584 677	1872	–	100735
Manchester	Bridge St	w	SJ 835 983	1793; reb c 1880	–	100743
Manchester	Swinton	sch	SD 775 016	1843	Richard Tattersall[222]	100966
Manchester	Crumpsall	w	SD 849 023	1855–6	Alexander W Mills & James Murgatroyd[223]	100744
Manchester	Tame St, Ancoates	ab	SJ 856 981	Mill conv c 1896 burnt down c 1900	–	No file
Oldham	Oldham	w	SD 920 062	1849–51	Travis & Mangnall?[224]	102509
Oldham	Royton	ch	SD 917 086	1898	Wild, Collins & Wild[225]	100967
Ormskirk	Ormskirk	w	SD 421 080	1851–3	William Culshaw[226]	100736
Prescot	Prescot	w	SJ 479 919	1842–3	–	100741
Preston	Fulwood	w	SD 539 318	1865–8	Leigh Hall[227]	100737
Preston	Ribchester	w	SD 627 366	1856	–	100734
Prestwich	–	w	–	1819	–	No file
Prestwich	Delauney Rd	w	SD 849 025	1866–70	Thomas Worthington & Son[228]	100692
Prestwich	Booth Hall	i	SD 865 031	1909	Thomas Worthington & Son[229]	100747
Rochdale	Marland	w	–	1863–5	–	No file
Rochdale	Dearnley	w	SD 921 161	1873–7	George Woodhouse & Edward Potts[230]	100693
Rochdale	Wardle	ch	–	1898	P Butterworth & Duncan[231]	No file
Salford	Eccles	w	SJ 783 985	1850–2	Pennington & Jervis[232]	100739
Salford	Hope, Salford	i	SJ 786 991	1880–2	Lawrence Booth[233]	100740
Salford	Culcheth	ch	SJ 650 960	1901–3	–	100964
Toxteth Park	Toxteth	w	SJ 378 888	1859	William Culshaw[234]	102393

206

Appendix 2: Catalogue A

Poor-Law Authority	Location	Type	NGR	Dates	Architect(s)	NMR No
Toxteth Park: san *see* Liverpool						
Ulverston	Ulverston	w	SD 284 786	1839	Edward William Trendall[235]	102090
Warrington	Warrington	w	SJ 596 888	1849–51	–	100748
Warrington	Padgate	ch	SJ 636 897	1881	–	100968
West Derby	Mill Rd, Liverpool	w/i	SJ 363 915	1838–45	–	
				reb as i 1890–3	Charles H Lancaster[236]	102391
West Derby	Walton-on-the-Hill	w	SJ 358 954	1864–9	William Culshaw[237]	102381
West Derby	Belmont Rd, Liverpool	ab	SJ 372 924	1889–90	–	100742
West Derby	Fazakerley	ch	SJ 387 977	1888–9	Charles H Lancaster[238]	100963
West Derby	Alder Hey	w	SJ 404 919	1911–15	Charles H Lancaster[239]	102387
West Derby: san *see* Liverpool						
Wigan	Wigan	w	SD 574 060	1855–7	William Mangnall[240]	100691

Leicestershire

Ashby-de-la-Zouch	Ashby-de-la-Zouch	w	SK 367 171	1826; enl 1836	–	101709
Barrow-upon-Soar	Mountsorrel	w	SK 585 142	1838–40	William Flint[241]	101710
Billesdon	Billesdon	w	SK 718 029	1846	–	101711
Blaby	Enderby	w	SP 548 985	1837	William Parsons[242]	101712
Hinckley	Hinckley	w	SP 435 939	1838	J A Hansom[243]	100882
Leicester	Leicester	w	SK 595 042	1836–8	William Flint[244]	
				reb 1850–1	W Parsons & M J Dain[245]	101742
Leicester	Countesthorpe	ch	SP 569 955	1884	I Baradale[246]	100970
Leicester	North Evington	i	SK 622 039	1903–5	Giles, Gough & Trollope[247]	100885
Loughborough	Loughborough	w	SK 525 204	1838	G Gilbert Scott & W Bonython Moffatt[248]	100714
Lutterworth	Lutterworth	w	SP 539 841	1839–40	G Gilbert Scott & W Bonython Moffatt[249]	101678
Market Bosworth	Market Bosworth	w	SK 401 030	1836	Mr Knightley?[250]	100883
Market Harborough	Great Bowden	w	SP 726 883	1836–7	Sampson Kempthorne[251]	100884
Melton Mowbray	Melton Mowbray	w	SK 759 193	1836	Charles Dyer[252]	100713

Lincolnshire

Boston	Boston	w	TF 333 433	1837	G Gilbert Scott[253]	100835
Bourne	Bourne	w	TF 092 199	1836–7	Bryan Browning[254]	100836
Caistor	Caistor	w	TA 102 013	1800–2	–	100837
Gainsborough	Gainsborough	w	SK 819 885	1837	George Wilkinson[255]	100838
Glanford Brigg	Brigg	w	TA 003 074	1835	William Adams Nicholson[256]	100839
Grantham	Grantham	w	SK 912 352	1837	Sampson Kempthorne[257]	No file
Grantham	Grantham	w	SK 904 355	1891–2	Valentine Green[258]	100840
Grimsby	Grimsby	w	TA 263 073	1892–4	Ernest Farebrother & H C Scaping[259]	100841
Holbeach	Holbeach	w	TF 369 249	1836–7	Robert Ellis Jnr[260]	100842
Horncastle	Horncastle	w	TF 265 693	1837–8	G Gilbert Scott & W Bonython Moffatt[261]	100843
Lincoln	Lincoln	w	SK 972 721	1837–8	William Adams Nicholson[262]	100844
Louth	Louth	w	TF 326 878	1837	G Gilbert Scott & W Bonython Moffatt[263]	100845
Sleaford	Sleaford	w	TF 076 463	1836–8	William J Donthorn[264]	100846
Spalding	Spalding	w	TF 248 234	1836–7	Bryan Browning[265]	100847
Spilsby	Hundleby	w	TF 392 662	1837–8	G Gilbert Scott & W Bonython Moffatt[266]	100848
Stamford	Stamford	w	TF 036 069	1836–7	Bryan Browning[267]	100849
Stamford	Stamford	w	TF 037 078	1899–1902	J H Morton[268]	100934

Non-Metropolitan Middlesex

Brentford	Isleworth	w	TQ 164 763	1837–8	Lewis Vulliamy[269]	
				reb 1895–1902	W H Ward[270]	101184
Edmonton	Edmonton	w	TQ 335 923	1839	G Gilbert Scott & W Bonython Moffatt[271]	100891
Edmonton	Enfield	sch	TQ 326 976	1827	–	101253
Edmonton	Chase Farm, Enfield	sch	TQ 312 980	1884–6	T E Knightley[272]	100942
Hendon	Burnt Oak, Edgware	w	TQ 200 908	1838	–	101715
Hendon	Burnt Oak, Edgware	i	TQ 198 912	1925–7	Paine & Hobday[273]	101398
Staines	Ashford	w	TQ 062 724	1840–1	–	101360
Uxbridge	Hillingdon	w	TQ 069 821	pre-1834	–	
				alt 1836–7	W Thorold[274]	101363
Willesden	Harlesden	w	TQ 202 828	1898–1908	A Saxon Snell[275]	100834

Norfolk

Aylsham	Aylsham	w	TG 184 266	1848–9	William J Donthorn[276]	100554
Blofield	Lingwood	w	TG 361 082	1837	John Brown[277]	101665
Brinton and Melton Constable (GU)	Melton Constable	w	TG 038 307	c 1783	–	100729
Depwade	Pulham Market	w	TM 186 876	1836	William Thorold[278]	101658
Docking	Docking	w	TF 749 370	1835–6	John Brown[279]	101659
Downham	Downham Market	w	TF 614 030	1836	William J Donthorn[280]	101660
Erpingham	West Beckham	w	TG 147 386	1848–51	William J Donthorn[281]	100534
East and West Flegg	Rollesby	w	TG 456 151	1775	Charles Elder[282]	101664

Poor-Law Authority	Location	Type	NGR	Dates	Architect(s)	NMR No
Forehoe	Wicklewood	w	TG 079 019	1776	–	100546
Freebridge Lynn	Gayton	w	TF 736 210	1836	William J Donthorn[283]	101661
Guiltcross	Kenninghall	w	TM 019 846	1836–7	William Thorold[284]	101662
Henstead	Swainsthorpe	w	TG 212 012	1836	John Brown[285]	100545
King's Lynn	King's Lynn	w	TF 627 196	1854–6	James Medland & Alfred W Maberley[286]	100530
Loddon and Clavering	Hales, Heckingham	w	TM 386 973	1765	–	100532
Mitford and Launditch	Gressenhall	w	TF 974 169	1775	–	100923
Norwich	Norwich	w	TM 209 090	1859–60	James Medland & Alfred W Maberley[287]	100526
St Faiths	Horsham St Faith	w	TG 218 161	1805	–	101667
Swaffham	Swaffham	w	TF 826 078	1836	William J Donthorn[288]	100531
Thetford	Thetford	w	TL 869 823	1836–7	William Thorold[289]	101669
Tunstead and Happing (Smallburgh)	Smallburgh	w	TG 325 241	1785	–	101668
Walsingham	Great Snoring	w	TF 967 352	1836	William Thorold[290]	100533
Wayland	Rockland All Saints	w	TL 993 969	1836–7	William Thorold or William J Donthorn?[291]	101666
Wayland	Attleborough	i	TM 030 961	1911–12	Herbert J Green[292]	100528
Yarmouth	Great Yarmouth	w	TG 524 084	1838	John Brown[293]	100125
Yarmouth	Gorleston	ch	–	1900–2	Arthur S Hewitt[294]	No file

Northamptonshire

Poor-Law Authority	Location	Type	NGR	Dates	Architect(s)	NMR No
Brackley	Brackley	w	SP 580 372	1836–7	G Gilbert Scott[295]	100504
Brixworth	Brixworth	w	SP 746 705	1835–6	Mr Milne[296]	100474
Daventry	Daventry	w	SP 574 619	1836–7	John Plowman[297]	100507
Hardingstone	Hardingstone	w	SP 764 572	1838–9	Mr Milne[298]	100505
Kettering	Kettering	w	SP 870 780	1837–8	G Gilbert Scott[299]	100456
Northampton	Northampton	w	SP 764 610	1836	G Gilbert Scott[300]	100471
Oundle	Oundle	w	TL 036 887	1836–7	G Gilbert Scott[301]	83285
Peterborough	Peterborough	w	TL 183 987	1836	Bryan Browning[302]	100262
Pottersbury	Pottersbury	w	SP 766 446	pre-1834	–	100436
Thrapston	Thrapston	w	SP 995 782	1836	William J Donthorn[303]	100473
Towcester	Towcester	w	SP 690 486	1836	G Gilbert Scott[304]	8215
Wellingborough	Wellingborough	w	SP 898 675	1836–7	James Clephan[305]	100452

Northumberland

Poor-Law Authority	Location	Type	NGR	Dates	Architect(s)	NMR No
Alnwick	Alnwick	w	NU 190 128	1840	–	102319
Belford	Belford	w	NU 106 338	1834	–	101647
Bellingham	Bellingham	w	NY 839 835	1839	–	101649
Berwick-upon-Tweed	Berwick-upon-Tweed	w	NU 997 534	early 19th C	–	102317
Castle Ward	Ponteland	w	NZ 165 733	1848	John & Benjamin Green[306]	102357
Glendale	Wooler	w	NT 988 281	1839	–	101648
Haltwhistle	Haltwhistle	w	NY 703 642	1837–9	–	101650
Hexham	Hexham	w	NY 941 640	1839	–	
				reb 1880–3	J H Morton[307]	102271
Morpeth	Morpeth	w	NZ 196 862	1865–7	Frederick R Wilson[308]	102306
Newcastle-upon-Tyne	Newcastle-upon-Tyne	w	NZ 228 645	1838–40	–	102355
Newcastle-upon-Tyne	Ponteland	ch	NZ 154 741	1901–3	Thomas Oliver, Richard J Leeson & William H Wood[309]	101646
Northern Counties Joint Poor-Law Committee						
	Prudhoe	men	NZ 106 619	1913–20	J H Morton & J G Burrell[310]	102267
Rothbury	Rothbury	w	NU 063 012	1900–5	J Stevenson & Son[311]	102314
Tynemouth	Tynemouth	w	NZ 354 689	1836	–	
				reb 1884–8	Henry Gibson[312]	102362

Nottinghamshire

Poor-Law Authority	Location	Type	NGR	Dates	Architect(s)	NMR No
Basford	Basford, Nottingham	w	SK 544 443	1817	–	100892
Basford	–	ch	–	1913–15	H Tatham Sudbury[313]	No file
Bingham	Bingham	w	SK 699 396	1837	Henry J Stevens[314]	100895
East Retford	East Retford	w	SK 712 825	1836–8	H J Whitling[315]	100893
Mansfield	Mansfield	w	SK 533 608	1837	Sampson Kempthorne[316]	100896
Newark	Claypole	w	–	1817	–	No file
Newark	Bowbridge Lane, Newark	i	SK 801 529	1878	–	100894
Nottingham	Nottingham	w	–	1840–1	–	No file
Nottingham	Nottingham	w	SK 567 440	1898–1903	Arthur Marshall & Turner[317]	102072
Radford	Hartley Rd, Nottingham	w	SK 556 406	1837	–	101745
Southwell	Upton	w	SK 711 542	1824	William Adams Nicholson & Revd Thomas Becher[318]	100716
Worksop	Worksop	w	SK 587 795	1837	–	100937
Worksop	Kilton Hill, Worksop	i	SK 594 803	1901–4	H C Scaping[319]	100897

Appendix 2: Catalogue A

Poor-Law Authority	Location	Type	NGR	Dates	Architect(s)	NMR No

Oxfordshire

Banbury	Banbury	w	SP 447 411	1835	Sampson Kempthorne[320]	100386
Bicester	Bicester	w	SP 575 233	1836	John Plowman[321]	101716
Chipping Norton	Chipping Norton	w	SP 317 275	1836	George Wilkinson[322]	83991
Headington	Headington	w	SP 552 074	1836–8	–	101717
Henley	Henley	w	SU 756 828	1790	William Bradshaw[323]	100615
Oxford	Oxford	w	SP 510 068	1772–5	John Gwynn[324]	No file
Oxford	Oxford	w	SP 532 058	1865	William Fisher[325]	100455
Oxford	Cowley Fields	sch	–	1852–4	Edward G Bruton[326]	No file
Thame	Thame	w	SP 701 064	1836	George Wilkinson[327]	100509
Witney	Witney	w	SP 345 099	1835–6	George Wilkinson[328]	101718
Woodstock	Woodstock	w	SP 447 168	1836–7	George Wilkinson[329]	101719

Rutland

Oakham	Oakham	w	SK 862 093	1837	William J Donthorn[330]	100712
Uppingham	Uppingham	w	SK 861 998	1836–7	William J Donthorn?[331]	101720

Shropshire

Atcham	Cross Houses	w	SJ 539 076	1792–3	John Hiram Haycock[332]	101298
Bridgnorth	Bridgnorth	w	SO 714 934	1848	–	100978
Church Stretton	Church Stretton	w	SO 455 944	1838	T D Duppa with E Blakeway Smith[333]	101721
Cleobury Mortimer	Cleobury Mortimer	w	SO 669 763	pre-1834	–	101722
Clun	Bishop's Castle	w	SO 322 888	1842–4	H J Whitling & Mr Haycock[334]	101723
Drayton	Market Drayton	w	SJ 661 334	1851	Thomas D Barry[335]	100981
Ellesmere	Ellesmere	w	SJ 404 355	1791–2	–	101724
Ludlow	Ludlow	w	SO 514 753	1836	Matthew Stead[336]	101725
Madeley	Madeley	w	SJ 674 039	1871–5	G C Haddon[337]	100985
Newport	Newport	w	SJ 753 188	1855–6	Mr Haycock[338]	100980
Oswestry	Morda	w	SJ 289 279	1790	–	101304
Shifnal	Shifnal	w	SJ 748 072	1817	–	37504
Shrewsbury	Shrewsbury	w	SJ 486 120	1760–5	Thomas Farnolls Pritchard[339]	No file
South-East Shropshire SD	Quatt	sch	SO 756 883	c 1700	–	101713
Wellington	Wellington	w	SJ 648 109	1874–5	Bidlake & Fleming[340]	100979
Wem	Wem	w	SJ 514 304	1837	Mr Graham[341]	101726
Whitchurch	Whitchurch	w	SJ 545 420	1791–4	–	101309

Somerset

Axbridge	Axbridge	w	ST 428 545	1837	Samuel T Welch?[342]	100605
Bath	Bath	w	ST 742 622	1837–8	Sampson Kempthorne[343]	101257
Bedminster (Long Ashton)	Flax Bourton	w	ST 518 696	1837	G Gilbert Scott & W Bonython Moffatt[344]	100899
Bridgwater	Bridgwater	w	ST 297 373	1836	Sampson Kempthorne[345]	100432
Chard	Chard	w	ST 331 087	1836–8	George Wilkinson[346]	100429
Clutton	Temple Cloud	w	ST 629 577	1836–7	Jesse Gane[347]	101727
Dulverton	Dulverton	w	SS 912 279	1854	Edward Ashworth[348]	101739
Frome	Frome	w	ST 770 475	1837–8	Sampson Kempthorne[349]	100573
Keynsham	Keynsham	w	ST 656 678	1837	William Armstrong[350]	100900
Langport	Picts Hill	w	ST 434 275	1837–9	–	101740
Shepton Mallet	Shepton Mallet	w	ST 612 434	1836	Jesse Gane[351]	100606
Taunton	Taunton	w	ST 236 244	1836–8	Sampson Kempthorne[352]	100492
Wellington	Wellington	w	ST 132 209	1836–8	Richard Carver[353]	100494
Wells	Wells	w	ST 540 455	1836–7	Samuel T Welch[354]	100575
Williton	Williton	w	ST 083 415	1837–40	G Gilbert Scott & W Bonython Moffatt[355]	45613
Wincanton	Wincanton	w	ST 707 287	1836–8	George Wilkinson[356]	101728
Yeovil	Yeovil	w	ST 545 165	1837	Sampson Kempthorne[357]	100488

Staffordshire

Alstonefield (GU)	–	w	–	conv 1817–18	–	No file
Burton-upon-Trent	Burton-upon-Trent	w	SK 248 238	1838	G Gilbert Scott & W Bonython Moffatt[358]	100984
Burton-upon-Trent	Burton-upon-Trent	w	SK 234 244	1880–4	J H Morton[359]	101407
Cheadle	Cheadle	w	SK 007 430	1773–5	–	100878
Leek	Leek	w	SJ 995 562	1838–9	J Bateman & G Drury[360]	100879
Lichfield	Lichfield	w	SK 126 098	1838–40	G Gilbert Scott & W Bonython Moffatt[361]	100877
Newcastle-under-Lyme	Newcastle-under Lyme	w	SJ 838 457	1838–9	G Gilbert Scott & W Bonython Moffatt[362]	100976
Penkridge	Brewood	w	–	c 1800; enl 1838	–	No file
Penkridge (Cannock)	Cannock	w	SJ 975 096	1870–2	–	100875
Seisdon	Trysull	w	SO 856 947	1858–60	George Bidlake & Lovatt[363]	100977
Stafford	Stafford	w	SJ 920 244	1837–8	Thomas Trubshaw[364]	100876
Stoke-upon-Trent	Stoke-upon-Trent	w	SJ 858 452	1832–3	–	
				enl 1842–5	Henry Ward[365]	101402

Poor-Law Authority	Location	Type	NGR	Dates	Architect(s)	NMR No
Stoke-upon-Trent	Penkhull	ch	SJ 866 449	1900	–	No file
Stone	Stone	w	SJ 899 338	1792–3	William Leigh[366]	102044
Tamworth	Tamworth	w	SK 208 058	1856–7	George B Nicholls[367]	100873
Uttoxeter	Uttoxeter	w	SK 084 340	1838–40	G Gilbert Scott & W Bonython Moffatt[368]	100975
Walsall	Walsall	w	SP 003 984	1838	W Watson[369]	101385
Walsall and West Bromwich SD	Wigmore	sch	SK 017 934	1869–70	S E Bindley[370]	101663
West Bromwich	West Bromwich	w	SP 009 921	1855–8	Briggs & Everall[371]	100874
Wolstanton and Burslem	Chell	w	SJ 867 531	1838–40	Boulton & Palmer[372]	100861
Wolverhampton	Wolverhampton	w	SO 925 980	1836–8	George Wilkinson?[373]	101200
Wolverhampton	Wolverhampton	w	SJ 935 004	1901–3	Arthur Marshall[374]	101381
Wolverhampton	Wednesfield	ch	SJ 942 009	1888	G H Stranger[375]	100982

Suffolk

Poor-Law Authority	Location	Type	NGR	Dates	Architect(s)	NMR No
Blything	Bulcamp, Blythburgh	w	TM 440 762	1765–6	Thomas Fulcher[376]	100008
Bosmere and Claydon	Barham	w	TM 122 512	1766	–	100002
Bury St Edmunds	College St, Bury St Edmunds	w	–	1748	–	
				alt 1841	William Mason[377]	No file
Cosford	Semer	w	TM 008 452	1781	–	100064
Hartismere	Eye	w	TM 147 737	pre-1834	–	
				enl 1835–40	William Mason[378]	100040
Hartismere	Eye	i	TM 143 739	1915–16	Herbert J Green[379]	100017
Hartismere & Hoxne	Wortham	sch	–	c 1878	–	No file
Hoxne	Stradbroke	w	TM 250 732	1835	–	100062
Ipswich	Ipswich	w	TM 165 437	1836–7	William Mason[380]	100973
Ipswich	Ipswich	w	TM 192 450	1898–9	Stephen Salter, William L Newcome & Henry P Adams[381]	100029
Ipswich	Ipswich	sch	TM 187 446	1878	–	100971
Mildenhall	Mildenhall	w	TL 708 746	pre-1834; enl 1836	–	101744
Mildenhall	Mildenhall	w	TL 717 749	1895–6	–	100050
Mutford and Lothingland	Oulton	w	TM 523 953	1765		
				enl 1836	John Brown[382]	100060
Newmarket: see Cambridgeshire						
Plomesgate	Wickham Market	w	TM 304 556	1836–7	John Brown[383]	100077
Risbridge	Kedington	w	TL 702 470	1855–6	John F Clark[384]	100038
Samford	Tattingstone	w	TM 135 373	1765–6	–	100074
Stow	Onehouse	w	TM 034 591	1778–81	Thomas Fulcher[385]	100058
Sudbury	Sudbury	w	TL 870 414	1836–7	John Brown[386]	100073
Thingoe (Bury St Edmunds)	Bury St Edmunds	w	TL 847 638	1835–6	–	100009
Wangford	Shipmeadow	w	TM 378 898	1765–7	M Barn[387]	100065
Woodbridge	Nacton	w	TM 223 406	1756–8	John Joshua Kirby[388]	100047

Surrey

Poor-Law Authority	Location	Type	NGR	Dates	Architect(s)	NMR No
Ash (GU)	–	w	–	pre-1834	–	No file
Chertsey	Ottershaw	w	TQ 028 639	1836	Sampson Kempthorne[389]	101618
Croydon	Croydon	w	TQ 316 674	1865	John Berney[390]	101351
Croydon	Croydon	i	TQ 321 675	1882	Berney & Monday[391]	101352
Dorking	Dorking	w	TQ 165 487	1838–41	W Shearburn[392]	101288
Epsom	Epsom	w	TQ 204 598	1836	William Mason[393]	100904
Farnham	Farnham	w	SU 850 475	1770	–	101622
Farnham & Hartley Wintney SD: see Hampshire						
Godstone	Bletchingley	w	TQ 328 509	enl 1839	John Whichcord[394]	101623
Guildford	Guildford	w	TQ 008 495	1836	G Gilbert Scott & W Bonython Moffatt[395]	100901
Hambledon	Hambledon	w	SU 957 381	1786	–	101620
Kingston-upon-Thames	Norbiton	w	TQ 195 697	1837–9	William Mason[396]	100902
Reigate	Reigate	w	TQ 272 491	pre-1834	–	100903
Richmond	Richmond	w	TQ 188 742	1786	–	8218

Sussex

Poor-Law Authority	Location	Type	NGR	Dates	Architect(s)	NMR No
Arundel (GP)	–	w	–	pre-1834	–	8235
Battle	Battle	w	TQ 732 159	1840	Frederick Thatcher[397]	100905
Brighton	Brighton	w	TQ 328 052	1865–7	J C & G Lansdown & George Maynard[398]	101198
Brighton	Warren Farm, Woodingdean	sch	TQ 354 057	1862–3	–	101614
Chailey	South Chailey	w	TQ 383 173	1871–3	Henry Card[399]	101205
Chichester	Chichester	w	SU 861 056	1625	–	101610
Cuckfield	Cuckfield	w	TQ 308 257	1843	S O Foden with H W Parker[400]	101375
Eastbourne	Eastbourne	w	TV 596 994	1793–4	–	100906
East Grinstead	East Grinstead	w	TQ 390 382	1859	Frederick Peck[401]	100996
East Preston	East Preston	w	TQ 070 023	1791–2	–	
				reb 1872	George B Nicholls[402]	101606
Hailsham	Hailsham	w	TQ 588 112	1835	–	100998

Appendix 2: Catalogue A

Poor-Law Authority	Location	Type	NGR	Dates	Architect(s)	NMR No
Hastings	Hastings	w	TQ 832 113	1836	Sampson Kempthorne & Annesley Voysey[403]	100907
Hastings	Hastings	i	TQ 831 114	1898–1903	Alfred W Jeffery & William Skiller[404]	100907
Horsham	Horsham	w	TQ 189 317	1838–9	Hallett & Newman[405]	101373
Lewes	Lewes	w	TQ 407 103	1867–8	Henry Currey[406]	101604
Midhurst	Easebourne	w	SU 890 232	1793–4	–	101611
Newhaven	Newhaven	w	TQ 440 011	1835	Sampson Kempthorne[407]	101195
Petworth	Petworth	w	SU 976 226	1820	–	101612
Petworth	Wisborough Green	w	TQ 052 258	1815	–	101613
Rye	Rye	w	TQ 919 214	1843	S O Foden with H W Parker[408]	100995
Steyning	Shoreham-by-Sea	w	TQ 218 056	1836	Mr Elliott[409]	101608
Steyning	Kingston-by-Sea	w	TQ 227 060	1898–1901	Clayton & Black[410]	101378
Sutton (GU)	Sutton End	w	–	1791	–	No file
Thakeham	Heath Common	w	TQ 110 149	1789–91	'surveyor' Stephen Rowland[411]	100997
Ticehurst	Union St	w	TQ 705 313	1836	Sampson Kempthorne[412]	101603
Uckfield	Uckfield	w	TQ 478 198	1838–9	H E Kendall[413]	101605
Westbourne	Westbourne	w	SU 759 083	pre-1834	–	101609
West Firle	West Firle	w	TQ 484 081	c 1835–6	–	100999
Westhampnett	Westhampnett Place	w	SU 879 059	16th C	–	101607

Warwickshire

Alcester	Alcester	w	SP 094 577	1837	–	100245
Aston	Erdington	w	SP 108 912	1866–9	Mr Thomason[414]	100914
Aston	Erdington	ch	SP 108 912	1898–1901	F Cross & Nicholls[415]	100986
Atherstone	Atherstone	w	SP 310 976	1836	–	101729
Birmingham	Birmingham	w	–	1733, enl 1766 and 1779		No file
Birmingham	Birmingham	sch	–	1797	–	No file
Birmingham	Winson Green	w	SP 047 878	1850–2	J Bateman & G Drury[416]	100400
Birmingham	Marston Green	ch	SP 179 858	1878–9	–	100972
Birmingham, King's Norton and Aston (Joint Committee)	Monyhull	men	–	1905	–	No file
Coventry	Whitefriars, Coventry	w	SP 342 787	purch & enl 1804	–	100715
Foleshill	Foleshill, Coventry	w	SP 344 823	1858–9	Edward Holmes[417]	101730
Meriden	Meriden	w	SP 237 825	1793	–	101731
Nuneaton	Chilvers Coton, Nuneaton	w	SP 356 906	1800	–	100908
Rugby	Rugby	w	SP 510 749	1818	–	100909
Solihull	Solihull	w	SP 154 798	1838	–	100910
Southam	Southam	w	SP 416 621	1836	John Plowman[418]	101732
Stratford-upon-Avon	Stratford-upon-Avon	w	SP 196 553	1837	J Bateman & G Drury[419]	100273
Warwick	Warwick	w	SP 285 659	1838	W Watson[420]	100634

Westmorland

East Ward	Kirkby Stephen	w	NY 776 089	conv 1810	–	100880
Kendal	Kendal	w	SD 512 932	1789	–	102082
Kendal	Milnthorpe	w	SD 504 818	1813	Francis Webster[421]	101632
West Ward	Shap	w	NY 564 142	1877	–	101629

Wiltshire

Alderbury (Salisbury)	Salisbury	w	SU 143 283	1836–7	Edward Hunt[422]	
				reb 1877–9	George B Nicholls[423]	100542
Amesbury	Amesbury	w	SU 157 409	1836–7	W Bonython Moffatt[424]	100540
Bradford (Bradford-on-Avon)	Avoncliffe	w	ST 802 599	1792	–	101733
Calne	Calne	w	ST 994 714	1847–8	Thomas Allom[425]	101734
Chippenham	Chippenham	w	ST 913 727	1858–9	Christopher C Creeke[426]	100607
Cricklade and Wootton Bassett	Purton	w	SU 085 874	1837	George Wilkinson[427]	83102
Devizes	Devizes	w	SU 007 616	1836–7	George Wilkinson[428]	100600
Highworth and Swindon	Stratton St Margaret	w	SU 175 876	1845–6	S O Foden with H W Parker[429]	100231
Malmesbury	Malmesbury	w	ST 926 874	1837–8	George Wilkinson[430]	100645
Marlborough	Marlborough	w	SU 184 695	1837	William Cooper[431]	100565
Mere	Mere	w	ST 809 323	1838–9	G Gilbert Scott & W Bonython Moffatt[432]	101677
Pewsey	Pewsey	w	SU 157 603	1836	William Cooper[433]	100539
Ramsbury: *see* Hungerford, Berkshire						
Salisbury	Crane St, Salisbury	w	–	enl 1728	–	No file
Tisbury	Tisbury	w	ST 941 288	1865–8	Christopher C Creeke[434]	100541
Trowbridge and Melksham	Semington	w	ST 893 603	1838	H E Kendall[435]	82303
Warminster	Warminster	w	ST 864 441	1836–7	Sampson Kempthorne[436]	77985
Westbury and Whorwellsdown	Westbury	w	ST 867 508	pre-1834 enl 1836–7	T L Evans[437]	101735
Wilton	Wilton	w	SU 099 318	1836–7	Edward Hunt[438]	100572

Poor-Law Authority	Location	Type	NGR	Dates	Architect(s)	NMR No
Worcestershire						
Bromsgrove	Bromsgrove	w	SO 965 716	1837–8	J Bateman & G Drury[439]	100597
Droitwich	Droitwich	w	SO 895 635	1836–8	Sampson Kempthorne[440]	100638
Dudley	Dudley	w	SO 930 912	1854–9	George B Nicholls[441]	100912
Evesham	Evesham	w	SP 037 430	1837	John Plowman[442]	100661
Kidderminster	Kidderminster	w	SO 822 764	1836–8	William Knight & J Nettleship[443]	100627
King's Norton	Selly Oak	w	SP 045 821	1870	Edward Holmes[444]	100913
King's Norton	Shenley Fields	ch	SP 015 817	1880s	–	100983
Martley	Martley	w	SO 753 598	1838	Sampson Kempthorne[445]	100639
Pershore	Pershore	w	SO 946 463	1836	Sampson Kempthorne[446]	101736
Shipston-on-Stour	Shipston-on-Stour	w	SP 254 410	1836–8	–	101714
Stourbridge	–	w	–	pre-1834 enl 1836	– Mr Griffiths[447]	No file
Stourbridge	Stourbridge	w	SO 893 874	1903–7	Arthur Marshall[448]	100911
Tenbury	Tenbury Wells	w	SO 596 685	1837	George Wilkinson[449]	101737
Upton-on-Severn	Upton upon Severn	w	SO 855 400	1836	Sampson Kempthorne[450]	100522
Worcester	Worcester	w	SO 857 550	1793–4	George Byfield[451]	100646
Worcester	Worcester	ch	SO 857 545	1894	–	No file
Yorkshire: East Riding						
Beverley	Beverley	w	TA 027 395	1860–1	John & William Atkinson[452]	102108
Bridlington	Bridlington	w	TA 174 682	1846	–	101643
Driffield	Driffield	w	TA 033 585	1866–8	J Oates[453]	102110
Howden	Howden	w	SE 743 280	1839	John & William Atkinson?[454]	101640
Kingston-on-Hull	Kingston upon Hull	w	TA 084 289	1851–2	Henry F Lockwood & William Mawson[455]	102092
Patrington	Patrington	w	TA 310 227	1837	–	102101
Pocklington	Pocklington	w	SE 799 483	1852	John & William Atkinson[456]	101642
Pontefract	Pontefract	w	SE 456 223	1862–4	–	102264
Sculcoates	Sculcoates	w	TA 091 301	1843–5	Henry F Lockwood[457]	102097
Sculcoates	Hessle	ch	TA 043 266	c 1897	–	No file
Skirlaugh	Skirlaugh	w	TA 138 399	1838–9	John & William Atkinson[458]	101641
York	York	w	SE 608 530	1848–9	John & William Atkinson[459]	160266
Yorkshire: North Riding						
Bainbridge (Aysgarth) (GU)	Bainbridge	w	SD 933 901	1809–10	–	101652
Bedale	Bedale	w	SE 269 879	1839	John & William Atkinson[460]	102053
Easingwold	Easingwold	w	SE 534 704	1837	John & William Atkinson?	100863
Guisborough	Guisborough	w	NZ 614 163	1838–9	John & William Atkinson[461]	102177
Helmsley	Helmsley	w	SE 610 839	1859	John & William Atkinson[462]	101645
Kirkby Moorside	Kirkbymoorside	w	SE 693 870	1850	John & William Atkinson[463]	57979
Leyburn	Leyburn	w	SE 115 905	1877	J T Jackman[464]	101644
Malton	Malton	w	SE 791 715	1735 & 1798; enl 1893	–	100866
Middlesbrough	Middlesbrough	w	NZ 485 190	1877–8	Perkin & Son[465]	102171
Northallerton	Northallerton	w	SE 371 942	1858–9	Mr Moffatt[466]	102052
Northern Counties Joint Poor-Law Committee: *see* Northumberland						
Pickering	Pickering	w	SE 801 844	1837	–	100862
Reeth	Reeth	w	SE 039 992	c 1800	–	101651
Richmond	Richmond	w	NZ 166 010	1794 enl 1841	– Ignatius Bonomi[467]	100868
Scarborough	Scarborough	w	TA 039 888	1858–9	George Styan[468]	102055
Stokesley	Stokesley	w	NZ 526 089	1848	–	101653
Thirsk	Thirsk	w	SE 434 822	1838	–	100872
Whitby	Whitby	w	NZ 902 105	1794; enl 1858	–	102061
Yorkshire: West Riding						
Barnsley	Barnsley	w	SE 332 070	1852	Henry F Lockwood & William Mawson[469]	102161
Barwick-in-Elmet (GU)	–	w	–	pre-1834	–	No file
Bradford	Bradford	w	SE 158 320	1849–52	Henry F Lockwood & William Mawson[470]	102316
Bradford	Daisy Hill	ab	SE 129 349	1910–12	Fred Holland[471]	101617
Bradford	Eastby	san	SE 025 550	1902–3	Fred Holland[472]	102376
Bramley	Bramley	w	SE 256 338	1871–2	C S & A J Nelson[473]	102028
Carlton (GU)	–	w	–	pre-1834	–	No file
Dewsbury	Dewsbury	w	SE 233 228	1852–4	Henry F Lockwood & William Mawson[474]	100852
Doncaster	Doncaster	w	SE 570 027	1839	–	101615
Doncaster	Doncaster	w	SE 556 005	1897–1900	J H Morton[475]	102164
Ecclesall Bierlow	Brincliffe, Sheffield	w	SK 337 849	1840	William Flockton[476]	102229
Ecclesall Bierlow	Fulwood	ch	SK 294 857	1903–12	Holmes & Watson[477]	100938
Goole	Goole	w	SE 742 239	1839	John & William Atkinson?[478]	102224
Great Ouseburn	Great Ouseburn	w	SE 435 618	1856–7	–	101616

APPENDIX 2: CATALOGUE A

Poor-Law Authority	Location	Type	NGR	Dates	Architect(s)	NMR No
Great Preston (GU)	–	w	–	pre-1834	–	No file
Halifax	Halifax	w	SE 083 253	1839	–	100855
Halifax	Halifax	i	SE 096 232	1897–1901	Richard Horsfall & W Clement Williams[479]	100859
Hemsworth	Hemsworth	w	SE 429 126	1859	–	100860
Holbeck	Holbeck	w	SE 295 319	1863–4	W Hill[480]	102029
Huddersfield	Crosland Moor	w	SE 126 154	1870	John Kirk[481]	100853
Huddersfield	Deanhouse	w	SE 137 099	1860–2	John Kirk[482]	100854
Hunslet	Hunslet	w	SE 306 317	1760–1	–	102298
Hunslet	Rothwell Haigh	w	SE 330 290	1900–3	J H Morton[483]	102015
Hunslet	Rothwell Haigh	ch	SE 335 290	1895	–	No file
Keighley	Oakworth Rd, Keighley	w	SE 055 408	1858	–	100857
Keighley	Fell Lane, Keighley	i	SE 049 406	1870–1	–	100858
Knaresborough	Knaresborough	w	SE 351 573	1857	Mr Shutt[484]	100865
Leeds	Sheepscar, Leeds	sch	SE 317 347	1846–8	William Perkin & Elisha Backhouse[485]	102018
Leeds	Leeds	w	SE 317 347	1858–60	William Perkin & Elisha Backhouse[486]	102018
North Bierley	Clayton, Bradford	w	SE 124 311	1855–8	Henry F Lockwood & William Mawson[487]	102262
Pateley Bridge	Pateley Bridge	w	SE 158 658	1863–8	John & William Atkinson[488]	100867
Penistone	Penistone	w	SE 244 039	1859	Henry F Lockwood & William Mawson[489]	100850
Ripon	Ripon	w	SE 313 715	1854	William Perkin & Elisha Backhouse[490]	100869
Rotherham	Rotherham	w	SK 430 922	1838–9 reb 1894	– H L Tacon[491]	102150
Rotherham	Rotherham	san	SK 447 928	est 1910–11 (built 1887)	–	102156
Saddleworth	Dobcross	w	SE 006 069	1810–12; enl 1855	–	101654
Sedbergh	Sedbergh	w	SD 659 917	1857	–	101738
Selby	Selby	w	SE 611 320	1837	–	100870
Settle	Giggleswick	w	SD 810 638	1837	–	100864
Sheffield	Sheffield	w	SK 362 907	1876–80	James Hall[492]	102225
Sheffield	Pitsmoor	sch	–	pre-1834	–	No file
Skipton	Skipton	w	SD 985 520	1838–40	–	102070
Tadcaster	Tadcaster	w	SE 479 431	1872	–	100871
Thorne	Thorne	w	SE 682 132	1838	–	102155
Todmorden	Mankinholes	w	SD 962 238	1877	–	102265
Wakefield	Wakefield	w	SE 343 207	1852	J E Oates[493]	100856
Wetherby	Wetherby	w	SE 398 484	1863	John & William Atkinson[494]	102023
Wharfedale	Otley	w	SE 198 465	1871–3	C S & A J Nelson[495]	102024
Wortley	Grenoside	w	SK 335 935	1827 reb 1850–2	– Aicken & Capes[496]	100851

Catalogue B: Poor-Law Institutions for Metropolitan London (post-1834)

This is a list of institutions run by London poor-law authorities under the New Poor Law, including older sites which continued in use for some time after 1834. Authorities are arranged under four separate headings:

a. Single Authority Institutions (ie: unions and parishes)
b. Metropolitan Sick Asylum Districts (SADs)
c. Metropolitan School Districts (SDs)
d. The Metropolitan Asylums Board (MAB)
    i) infectious diseases hospitals
    ii) sanatoria (tuberculosis)
    iii) asylums
    iv) schools/hospital schools

For categories a, b and c, the first column gives the location of the building. The second gives the type of institution it housed (*see* abbreviations, below) and the third gives the National Grid Reference. The fourth gives the date of erection with additional information on dates of purchase, sale, or change of use if relevant. The fifth gives the name(s) of the architect(s), if known, with sources in endnotes. The final column gives the NMR file number.

Abbreviations

ab	able-bodied (test) workhouse or labour colony
enl	enlarged
cas	separate-site casual wards (all transferred to MAB in 1912)
ch	cottage, scattered or receiving homes for children
conv	convalescent home
i	(separate-site) infirmary
men	asylum or colony for epileptics and/or the mentally handicapped
purch	purchased
reb	rebuilt
san	(separate-site) sanatorium
sch	industrial school
w	workhouse

a. Single Authority Institutions

Authorities are listed alphabetically by primary union or parish name (in the case of parish names, this applies to the locality rather than the saint, if these differ), followed by a list of its institutions. Institutions are listed under the authority which first set them up. The entry ends with information in square brackets about changes to the authority. (The main source for this information is the London Metropolitan Archives poor-law catalogue.)

Location	Type	NGR	Dates	Architect(s)	NMR No
Bermondsey (Parish of St Mary Magdalen)					
Tanner/Russell St, Bermondsey	w	TQ 333 797	1791	–	101635
[Added to St Olave's Union 1869 which became Parish of Bermondsey 1904]					
Bethnal Green (Parish of St Matthew)					
Waterloo Rd, Bethnal Green	w	TQ 350 835	1840–2	Mr Bunning[1]	101698
Leytonstone	sch	TQ 397 878	purch 1868; reb 1881–9	A & C Harston[2]	93691
Cambridge Heath Rd, Bethnal Green	i	TQ 350 832	1896–1900	Giles, Gough & Trollope[3]	101229
Camberwell (Parish of St Giles)					
Havil St, Camberwell	w	TQ 332 769	1818	–	101170
Gordon Rd, Camberwell	w	TQ 346 764	1878	Berriman & Son[4]	100749
Constance Rd, Camberwell	w	TQ 333 752	1892	Thomas W Aldwinckle[5]	101153
Chelsea (Parish of St Luke)					
Britten St, Chelsea	w	TQ 271 782	1843	Mr Coleman[6]	101061
Cale St, Chelsea	i	TQ 271 783	1872	John Giles & Gough[7]	101130
Millman St, Chelsea	cas	TQ 268 775	1893–4	A & C Harston[8]	No file
City of London (Union)					
Bow Rd	w	TQ 367 826	1848–9	R Tress[9]	101169
Thavies Inn	cas	TQ 313 815	1892–3	F Hammond[10]	No file
[East London, West London and City of London Unions amalgamated to form the new City of London Union 1869]					

Appendix 2: Catalogue B

Location	Type	NGR	Dates	Architect(s)	NMR No
City of Westminster (Union)					
[Westminster Union, St George's Union (including Westminster, St Margaret and St John), and Strand Union (including St Martin-in-the-Fields) united to become City of Westminster Union 1913]					
Clerkenwell (Parishes of St James and St John)					
Farringdon Rd, Clerkenwell	w	TQ 313 822	1727	–	101702
[Added to Holborn Union 1869]					
East London (Union)					
Homerton	w	TQ 355 853	1852	–	100830
[East London, West London and City of London Unions amalgamated to form the new City of London Union 1869]					
Finsbury (Parish)					
[Part of Holborn Union split off to become Parish of Finsbury 1915]					
Fulham (Union)					
Fulham Palace Rd, Fulham	w	TQ 236 779	1848–9	A Gilbert[11]	100827
Brighton Rd, Sutton	w	TQ 255 626	Belmont Institution leased from MAB 1908	–	100962
[Fulham Union split to form Parish of Fulham and Parish of Hammersmith 1899]					
Greenwich (Union)					
Vanburgh Hill, Greenwich	w	TQ 396 782	1840	R P Browne[12]	100826
Grove Park, Greenwich	w	TQ 410 727	1899–1902; sold to MAB for TB sanatorium 1920	Thomas Dinwiddy[13]	101088
Sidcup	ch	TQ 460 734	1902	Thomas Dinwiddy & Sons[14]	100958
Hackney (Union)					
High St, Homerton	w/i	TQ 361 851	pre-1834; reb 1898–1914	William A Finch[15]	101997
Gainsborough Rd, Hackney Wick	cas	TQ 376 849	1898–1904	William A Finch[16]	101699
Brentwood, Essex	sch	TQ 587 936	purch from Brentwood SD 1885	–	101279
Chipping Ongar, Essex	ch	TQ 553 038	1902–5	William A Finch[17]	100936
Hammersmith (Parish of Hammersmith, formed 1899)					
Du Cane Rd, Hammersmith	w	TQ 225 813	1903–5	Giles, Gough & Trollope[18]	101275
Hampstead (Parish of St John)					
New End, Hampstead	w	TQ 264 860	1800–1; reb 1849–50	H E Kendall[19]	101089
Holborn (Union)					
Greys Inn	w/cas	TQ 310 821	pre-1834; reb as Little Greys Inn Lane Casual Wards 1901	Smith & Coggan[20]	101700
Eagle House, Mitcham	sch	TQ 278 694	purch 1870 from Southwark, St George the Martyr	–	100988
Archway, Upper Holloway	i	TQ 293 870	1879	Henry Saxon Snell[21]	101067
Mitcham	w	TQ 276 693	1885–6	Henry Saxon Snell[22]	100987
[Parish of St Sepulchre added to Holborn Union 1845; Parishes of St Luke's, Middlesex and Clerkenwell, St James and St John added to Holborn Union 1869; Joint parishes of St-Giles-in-the-Fields and St George, Bloomsbury added to Holborn Union 1914; Part split off to form Parish of Finsbury 1915]					
Islington (Parish of St Mary)					
John St (now Barnsby St), Islington	w	TQ 314 842	pre-1834	–	100926
Hornsey	sch	–	1853	Birch or Jones & Parker[23]	No file
Upper Holloway	w	TQ 297 874	1869–70	R H Burden[24]	100828
Highgate Hill	i	TQ 290 869	1898–1900	W Smith[25]	101068
Kensington (Union 1837–45)					
Butt's Field, Kensington	w	TQ 262 794	1778	Thomas Callcott[26]	101129
Marloes Rd, Kensington	w	TQ 256 793	1846–8	Thomas Allom[27]	101126
[Renamed Parish of St Mary Abbots 1845–1930]					
Lambeth (Parish of St Mary)					
Norwood	sch	TQ 322 711	purch 1809; enl 1850s and 1888	–	100957
Princes Rd, Lambeth	w/ab	TQ 308 785	pre-1834; reb as test workhouse 1887–8	Thomas W Aldwinckle[28]	101624
Renfrew Rd, Lambeth	w	TQ 316 788	1871–4	Thomas W Aldwinckle & R Parris[29]	101038
Renfrew Rd, Lambeth	i	TQ 314 788	1875–7	Fowler & Hill[30]	101038
Lewisham (Union)					
Lewisham Rd, Lewisham	w	TQ 378 747	1817	–	100829
Mile End Old Town (Hamlet, formed 1857)					
Bancroft Rd, Mile End	w	TQ 359 825	1858–9	W Dobson[31]	101167
[Added to Stepney Union 1925]					

The Workhouse

Location	Type	NGR	Dates	Architect(s)	NMR No
Newington (Parish of St Mary)					
–	w	–	pre-1834	–	No file
Westmorland Rd, Walworth	sch, used as a w	TQ 328 778	1850	–	101625
[Added to St Saviour's Union 1869]					
Paddington (Union, formed 1845)					
Harrow Rd, Paddington	w	TQ 253 819	1846	–	101035
Poplar (Union)					
High St, Poplar	w	TQ 377 807	1757	–	101212
			enl 1815–17	James Walker[32]	
			enl 1869–72	John Morris & Son[33]	
Forest Gate	sch	TQ 399 852	purch from Forest Gate SD 1897	–	101271
Hutton, Brentwood, Essex	ch	TQ 620 953	1906	Holman & Goodman[34]	100933
Laindon, Basildon, Essex	ab	TQ 661 884	1904	–	101708
[Renamed Parish of Poplar Borough 1907]					
Rotherhithe (Parish of St Mary)					
Lower Rd, Rotherhithe	w	TQ 351 793	1827–9	–	100832
[Added to St Olave's Union 1869]					
St George's, Hanover Square (Parish)					
Mount St, Westminster	w	TQ 285 806	1725–6	Benjamin Timbrell & Thomas Phillips[35]	101001
			reb 1786–8	William Porden[36]	
Fulham Rd/Little Chelsea, Chelsea	w	TQ 263 777	1786–7; reb 1858;	–	101096
			infirmary added 1876–8	Henry Saxon Snell[37]	
[Added to St George's Union 1870 which amalgamated with other unions to form City of Westminster Union 1913]					
St George's (Union)					
Formed 1870 by an amalgamation of the Parish of St George's, Hanover Square and Westminster, Joint Parishes of St Margaret and St John					
St Ermin's Hill, Westminster	i	TQ 297 794	1871	–	101033
Palace St/Wallis Yard	w	TQ 291 794	1883–6	–	101017
Millman St, Chelsea	ch	TQ 268 776	1902; transferred to MAB 1914	–	No file
[Amalgamated with other unions to form City of Westminster Union 1913]					
St George-in-the-East (Parish)					
Prusom St, Wapping	w	TQ 349 804	1824	–	101701
Plashet	sch	TQ 412 842	1851–2	Andrew Wilson[38]	93713
[Added to Stepney Union 1925]					
St Giles-in-the-Fields and St George, Bloomsbury (Parishes)					
Endell St, St Giles	w	TQ 302 813	1727; reb 1878–82	Lee & Smith[39]	101072
Lascelles Place	ch	–	1900	J Grafton Izard[40]	No file
[Added to Holborn Union 1914]					
St Luke's, Middlesex (Parish)					
City Rd, Islington	w	TQ 323 829	pre-1834; largely reb c 1870	Henry Saxon Snell[41]	100921
[Added to Holborn Union 1869]					
St Martin-in-the-Fields (Parish)					
Hemmings Row/St Martin's	w	TQ 300 806	1770–7	Robert Palmer[42]	101010
[Added to Strand Union 1868]					
St Marylebone (Parish)					
Baker St, Marylebone	w	TQ 281 819	1775; reb 1890s	Alfred Saxon Snell[43]	101046
Southall	sch	TQ 127 802	1856–8	–	101707
Kensington	i	TQ 237 818	1879–81	Henry Saxon Snell[44]	101110
St Olave's (Union)					
Parish St/Fair St, Bermondsey	w	TQ 334 799	18th C	–	101621
Lower Rd, Rotherhithe	i	TQ 351 793	1873–5	Henry Saxon Snell[45]	100832
Ladywell, Lewisham	w	TQ 373 745	1897–1900	Newman & Newman[46]	101627
Shirley, Croydon	ch	TQ 357 633	1903	Newman & Newman[47]	100990
[Parishes of Bermondsey, St Mary Magdalen and Rotherhithe, St Mary were added to St Olave's Union 1869; Renamed Parish of Bermondsey 1904]					
St Pancras (Parish)					
Kings Rd, Camden	w	TQ 297 836	1809	T Hardwick[48]	101106
Highgate	i	TQ 288 869	1869	John Giles & Biven[49]	101069
Leavesden, Abbots Langley, Herts	sch	TL 101 014	1869–72	John Giles & Biven[50]	100992

APPENDIX 2: CATALOGUE B

Location	Type	NGR	Dates	Architect(s)	NMR No
St Saviour's (Union)					
Marlborough St	w	–	1834	George Allen[51]	No file
Champion Hill, Dulwich	i	TQ 334 751	1885–7	Henry Jarvis[52]	101154
[Parishes of Southwark, St George the Martyr and Newington, St Mary were added to St Saviour's Union 1869; Renamed Southwark Union 1901]					
St Sepulchre (Parish)					
[Added to Holborn Union 1845]					
Shoreditch (Parish of St Leonard)					
Kingsland Rd, Shoreditch	w	TQ 335 834	1861–5	–	101225
Brentwood, Essex	sch	TQ 587 936	1852–4; sold to Brentwood SD 1877	–	101279
Hornchurch	ch	TQ 529 872	1887–8	Francis J Smith[53]	100940
Southwark (Parish of St George the Martyr)					
Mint St	w	–	–	–	No file
Eagle House, Mitcham	sch	TQ 278 694	1856; sold to Holborn Union 1870	–	100988
[Added to St Saviour's Union 1869 which was renamed Southwark Union 1901]					
Stepney (Union)					
Bromley-by-Bow	w	TQ 379 826	1861–2	H Jarvis[54]	100833
North Stifford, Essex	ch	TQ 597 800	1901	Frank Baggallay[55]	100845
[Briefly known as Parish of Limehouse 1921–5; Parish of St George-in-the-East, Whitechapel Union and the Hamlet of Mile End Old Town added to Stepney Union 1925; Stepney Union renamed Parish of Stepney Union 1927]					
Strand (Union)					
Covent Garden	w	–	–	–	No file
Cleveland St	w	–	–	–	No file
Bear Yard/Sheffield St, nr Aldwych	w	TQ 307 812	c 1870; casual wards built on adjacent site c 1890; reb 1903; sold to MAB 1914 for VD cases	–	101013
Silver St, Edmonton	sch	TQ 329 926	Millfield House purch and enl 1849; sold to MAB 1914	–	101706
Edmonton	w	TQ 334 924	1868–70	–	101705
[Parish of St Martin-in-the-Fields added to Strand Union 1868; Strand Union amalgamated with other unions to form City of Westminster Union 1913]					
Wandsworth & Clapham (Union)					
St John's Hill, Wandsworth	w	TQ 265 751	1838–40	George Ledwell Taylor[56]	101085
Garratt Lane, Wandsworth	w	TQ 260 737	1883–6	Thomas W Aldwinckle[57]	101189
Wandsworth	i	TQ 277 732	1910	James S Gibson[58]	101074
Church Lane, Wandsworth	w	TQ 281 711	1903	–	101703
[Renamed Wandsworth Union 1904]					
West London (Union)					
Holloway	w	TQ 302 867	1864	Searle, Son & Yelf[59]	100831
[East London, West London and City of London Unions amalgamated to form the new City of London Union 1869]					
Westminster (Parish of St James)					
Poland St, Soho	w	TQ 293 812	1725–7	J Ludby	101003
			reb 1858–9	Charles Lee[60]	
Wandsworth	sch	TQ 277 732	1852	Charles Lee[61]	101074
[Renamed Westminster Union 1868 which amalgamated with other unions to form City of Westminster Union 1913]					
Westminster (Joint Parishes of St Margaret and St John)					
Dean St/Gt Smith St	w	–	–	–	No file
Marloes Rd, Kensington	w	TQ 256 793	1851–3	H A Hunt[62]	101126
St Ermin's Hill/Petty France	w	–	1866	–	No file
[Amalgamated with Parish of St George's, Hanover Square to form St George's Union 1870]					
Whitechapel (Union)					
Vallance Rd/Spitalfields	w	TQ 345 820	1842	–	101165
South Grove, Bow	w	TQ 367 825	1871	–	101168
Forest Gate	sch	TQ 399 852	1852–4; sold to Forest Gate SD 1869	–	101271
Grays, Essex	ch	TQ 61 78	1899	Christopher M Shiner[63]	100951
[Renamed Parish of Whitechapel 1921; Added to Stepney Union 1925]					
Woolwich (Union, formed 1868)					
Plumstead	w	TQ 454 784	1869–70	Church & Rickwood[64]	101704
Bostall Heath	ch	TQ 471 777	1899; sold to MAB 1914 (Goldie Leigh Homes)	–	No file

THE WORKHOUSE

b. Metropolitan Sick Asylum Districts

Location	Type	NGR	Dates	Architect(s)	NMR No
Poplar and Stepney Sick Asylum District (1868–1925)					
Bow	i	TQ 379 824	1869	A & C Harston[65]	101387
Central London Sick Asylum District (1868–1913)					
Hendon	i	TQ 211 901	1898–1900; sold to City of Westminster Union 1913; later sold to MAB 1920 for TB sanatorium	Giles, Gough & Trollope[66]	100890

c. Metropolitan School Districts

Brentwood SD (1877–85)
Brentwood, Essex	sch	TQ 587 936	purch from Shoreditch, St Leonard 1877; sold to Hackney Union 1885	–	101279

Central London SD (1849–1930)
Weston Hill, Norwood	sch	–	Mr Aubin's School purch 1849	–	No file
Hanwell	sch	TQ 156 815	1856–8; Ophthalmic Institute (later Park School) added to site 1890	Tress & Chambers[67]	100961

Finsbury SD (1868–9)
No institution (although a site had been purchased at Upton and plans approved)[68]

Forest Gate SD (1868–97)
Forest Gate	sch	TQ 399 852	purch from Whitechapel Union 1869; sold to Poplar Union 1897	–	101271
Goliath	training ship	–	bought 1870, destroyed by fire 1875	–	No file

Kensington & Chelsea SD (1876–1930)
Banstead, Surrey	ch	TQ 240 603	1878–80	A & C Harston[69]	101619
Marlesford Lodge, Hammersmith	branch sch	–	1882–3	A & C Harston[70]	No file

North Surrey SD (1849–1930)
Anerley, Upper Norwood	sch	TQ 342 699	1849–50	Charles Lee[71]	100989
Wainwright Home, Broadstairs, Kent	conv	–	1887–91	–	No file

South Metropolitan SD (1849–1902)
Brighton Rd, Sutton	sch	TQ 255 626	1852–5; sold to MAB c 1904 (Belmont Asylum)	Edwin Nash[72]	100962
Banstead Rd, Sutton	sch	TQ 259 622	1881–3; sold to MAB 1902 (Downs Hospital) used for children with ringworm	William Wallen[73]	100962
Herne Bay, Kent	conv	–	Pier Hotel purch and altered 1875; sold to MAB 1897 (St Anne's Home)	–	No file
Witham, Essex	sch	TL 815 140	purch 1882 from Witham Union, used for children with ringworm; sold to MAB 1901 for ringworm cases (Bridge School)	–	101242

West London SD (1868–1930)
Ashford, Surrey	sch	TQ 058 715	1869–72	H H Collins[74]	100960

d. Metropolitan Asylums Board

Name of Institution	Location	NGR	Dates	Architect(s)	NMR No
i. Infectious Diseases Hospitals					
Brook (Fever) Hospital	Shooters Hill, Woolwich	TQ 423 766	1894–6	Thomas W Aldwinckle[75]	101091
Eastern (Fever and Smallpox) Hospital	Homerton	TQ 356 853	1869–71	John Giles & Biven[76]	102772
Fountain (Fever) Hospital	Tooting	TQ 271 714	1893; from 1911 used for mentally deficient children	Thomas W Aldwinckle[77]	101133
Grove (Fever) Hospital	Tooting	TQ 268 713	1899	A Hessell Tiltman[78]	101134
Joyce Green (Smallpox) Hospital	Dartford, Kent	TQ 546 760	1901–3	A & C Harston[79]	101208
Long Reach (Smallpox) Hospital	Dartford, Kent	TQ 550 773	1901–3	A & C Harston[80]	101210
North-Western (Fever) Hospital	Hampstead	TQ 273 854	1870	Pennington & Bridgen[81]	101099
North-Eastern (Fever) Hospital	Tottenham	TQ 325 885	1892	A & C Harston[82]	102782
Northern (Convalescent) Hospital	Winchmore Hill	TQ 306 957	1885–7	Pennington & Bridgen[83]	101254
Orchard (Smallpox) Hospital	Dartford, Kent	TQ 543 768	1901–3	A & C Harston[84]	101209
Park (Fever) Hospital	Hither Green, Lewisham	TQ 387 741	1895–7	E T Hall[85]	101399
River Ambulance Service	North Wharf, Blackwall	TQ 384 801	1884	–	No file
	South Wharf, Rotherhithe	TQ 366 797	1884	–	No file
Sheffield St Hospital	Bear Yd/Sheffield St, Aldwych	TQ 307 812	purch from City of Westminster Union for VD cases 1914	–	101013
Smallpox hospital ships, *c* 1880–1904: *Atlas, Endymion* and *Castalia*	moored at Long Reach, Dartford	–	–	–	101208
South-Eastern (Fever) Hospital	New Cross	TQ 354 774	1877	J Walker & W Crickmay[86]	102776
Southern (Smallpox) Hospital (South Smallpox Camp, later Southern (Convalescent) Hospital)	Gore Farm, Dartford, Kent	TQ 568 723	1883 reb 1887–1902	– A & C Harston[87]	101218
South-Western (Fever and Smallpox) Hospital	Stockwell	TQ 305 756	1869–70	fever hospital by F Marrable smallpox hospital by T H Wyatt[88]	102755
Western (Fever) Hospital	Fulham	TQ 257 775	1877	J Walker & W Crickmay[89]	101128
ii Sanatoria (tuberculosis)					
Colindale Hospital	Hendon	TQ 211 901	purch from City of Westminster Union 1920 for advanced pulmonary TB in males	–	100890
Downs Hospital	Banstead Rd, Sutton	TQ 259 622	change of use 1913 (previously used for children with ringworm); sanatorium for adults 1913–22 and children 1922–30	–	100962
Grove Park Hospital	Grove Park, Greenwich	TQ 410 727	purch from Greenwich Union 1920	–	101088
Highwood Hospital	Brentwood, Essex	TQ 591 945	change of use 1919 (previously MAB hospital school)	–	101277
King George V Sanatorium	nr Hambledon, Surrey	SU 972 402	1920–3	E S Hall[90]	102761
Millfield Hospital	Rustington, Sussex	–	1898–1904 convalescent home	–	No file
Pinewood Sanatorium	Wokingham, Berks	–	purch 1919	–	No file
Princess Mary Hospital	Margate, Kent	TR 361 709	East Cliff House purch from St Pancras 1898, enl 1919	–	101143
St George's Home	Millman St, Chelsea	–	rented from City of Westminster Union 1914 for advanced cases of TB in women	–	No file
St Luke's Hospital	Lowestoft, Suffolk	TH 542 914	Empire Hotel purch and converted 1920	–	100044
iii Asylums					
Belmont Asylum	Brighton Rd, Sutton	TQ 255 626	purch from South Metropolitan SD *c* 1904 and used for imbeciles; leased to Fulham Union 1908 (Belmont Institution)	–	100962
Bridge School	Witham, Essex	TL 815 140	purch 1901 from South Metropolitan SD; used for ringworm 1901–6; renamed Bridge Industrial Home used as a working colony for feeble-minded boys 1906–22	–	101242
Darenth School for Imbeciles	Darenth, Kent	TQ 571 730	1876–8 school for imbecile children; renamed Darenth Asylum for Imbeciles 1880 used as asylum for imbeciles	A & C Harston[91]	101217

The Workhouse

Name of Institution	Location	NGR	Dates	Architect(s)	NMR No
Edmonton Colony for Sane Epileptics	Silver St, Edmonton	TQ 329 926	Millfield House School purch from City of Westminster Union, (previously owned by Strand Union)	–	No file
Metropolitan Asylum for Imbeciles	Caterham, Surrey	TQ 326 558	1869–70	John Giles & Biven[92]	101292
Metropolitan Asylum for Imbeciles	Leavesden, Abbots Langley, Herts	TL 103 017	1869–70	John Giles & Biven[93]	101186
Tooting Bec Asylum	Tooting Bec	TQ 269 712	1899–1903 & 1906	A & C Harston[94]	101131
iv Schools/Hospital Schools					
Downs Hospital	Banstead Rd, Sutton	TQ 259 622	purch from South Metropolitan SD 1902; used for children with ringworm 1903–13; sanatorium thereafter	–	100962
Exmouth and Land Establishment	Grays, Essex	–	built by Vickers 1904–5, replacing two-decker battleship lent by Admiralty	–	No file
Goldie Leigh Homes	Bostall Heath	TQ 471 777	purch from Woolwich Union 1914	–	No file
Highwood School	Brentwood, Essex	TQ 591 945	1899–1903; converted to TB sanatorium 1919	C & W Henman[95]	101277
St Anne's Home	Herne Bay, Kent	TR 172 681	purch from South Metropolitan SD 1897 (formerly Pier Hotel)	–	No file
The Children's Infirmary/Queen Mary's Hospital for Children	Carshalton	TQ 278 625	1907–9 designed as convalescent fever hospital	–	101395
White Oak School	Swanley, Kent	TQ 511 689	1900–3	Newman & Newman[96]	101597

APPENDIX 3
Model Plans issued by the Central Poor-Law Authority

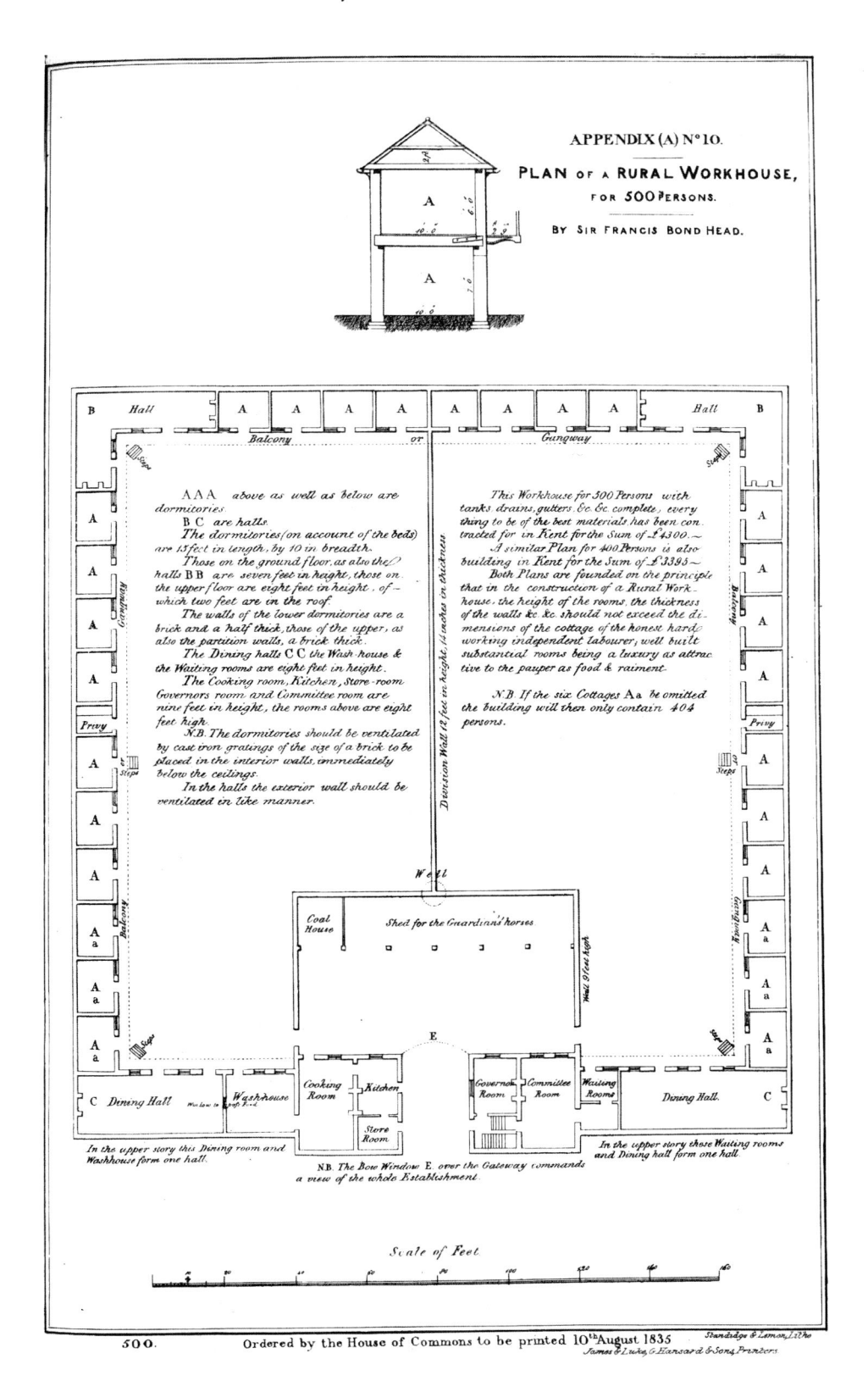

*1
'Plan of a Rural Workhouse for 500 Persons', ground plan, by Sir Francis Head. [By permission of the Syndics of Cambridge University Library, PP 1835 (500), XXXV, Appendix A, No.10. 1]*

THE WORKHOUSE

2
'Square Plan of a Workhouse to Contain 300 Paupers', ground plan, by Sampson Kempthorne.
[By permission of the Syndics of Cambridge University Library, PP 1835 (500), XXXV, Appendix A, No.10. 2]

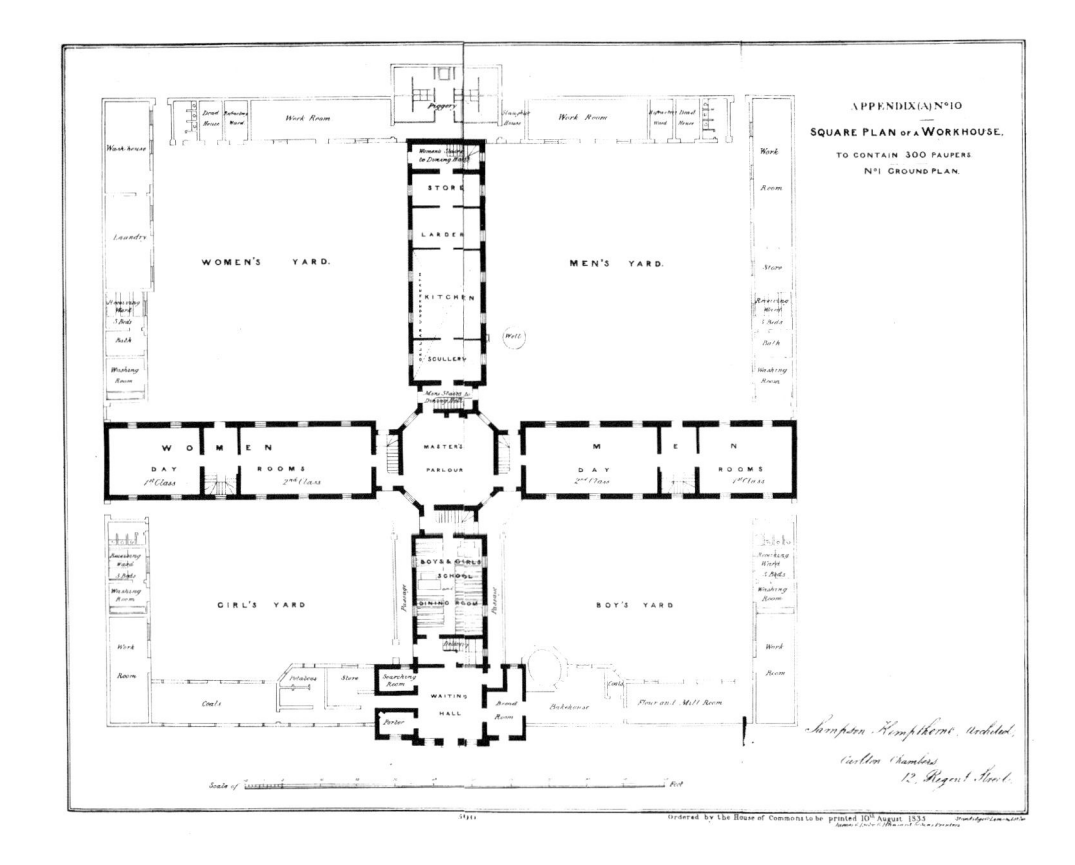

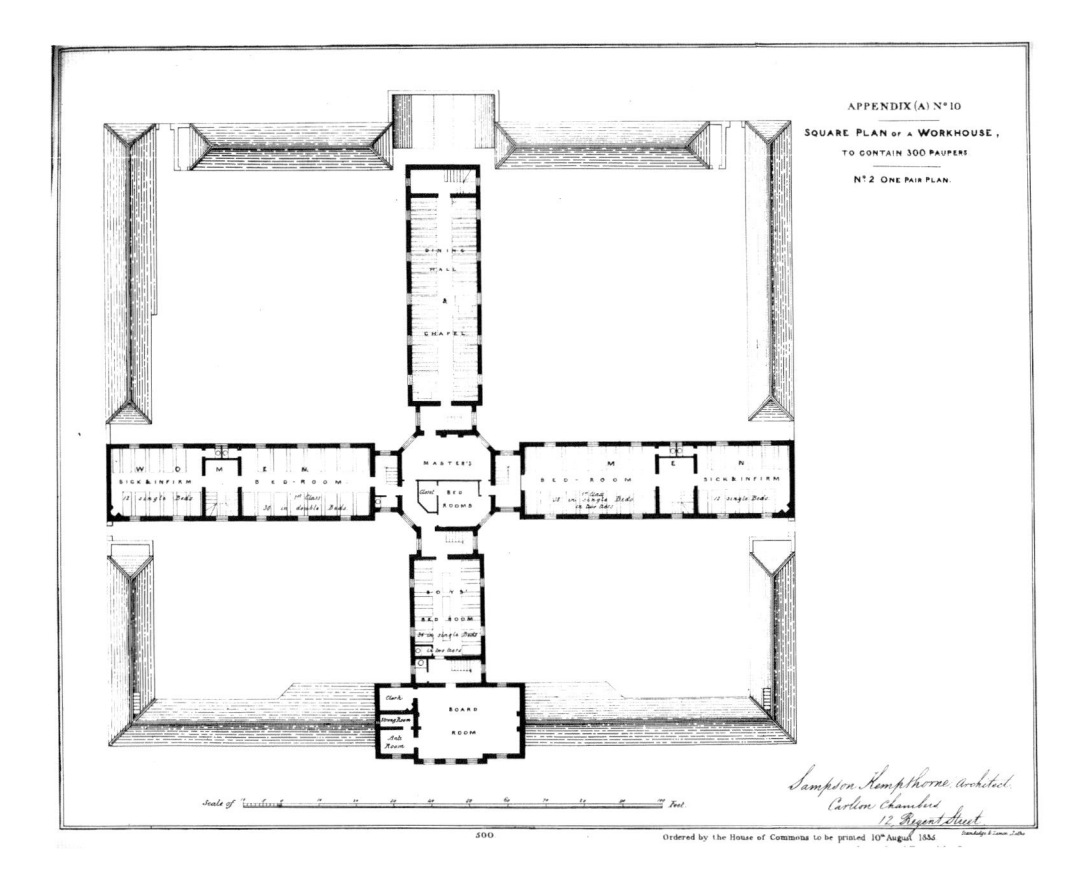

3
'Square Plan of a Workhouse to Contain 300 Paupers', first-floor plan, by Sampson Kempthorne.
[By permission of the Syndics of Cambridge University Library, PP 1835 (500), XXXV, Appendix A, No.10. 3]

APPENDIX 3

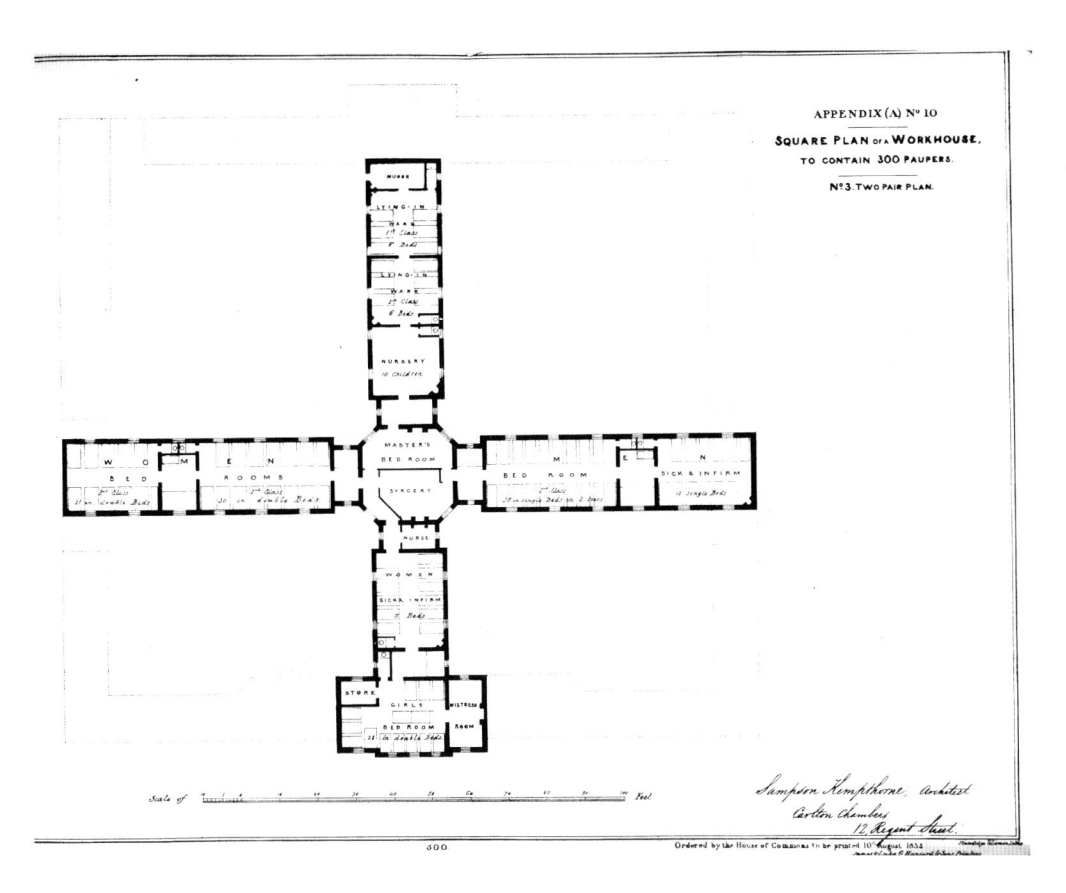

4
'Square Plan of a Workhouse to Contain 300 Paupers', second-floor plan, by Sampson Kempthorne.
[By permission of the Syndics of Cambridge University Library, PP 1835 (500), XXXV, Appendix A, No.10. 4]

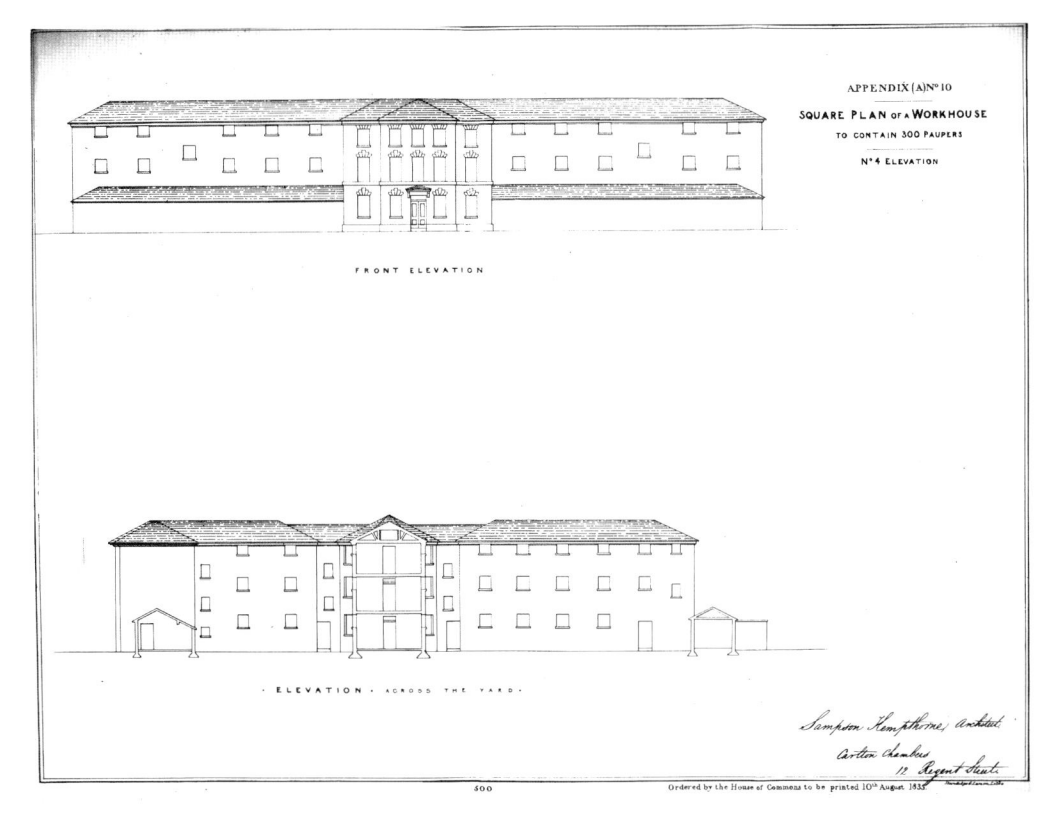

5
'Square Plan of a Workhouse to Contain 300 Paupers', elevations, by Sampson Kempthorne.
[By permission of the Syndics of Cambridge University Library, PP 1835 (500), XXXV, Appendix A, No.10. 5]

223

THE WORKHOUSE

6
'Ground Plan of a Workhouse to Contain 200 Paupers', by Sampson Kempthorne.
[By permission of the Syndics of Cambridge University Library, PP 1835 (500), XXXV, Appendix A, No.10. 6]

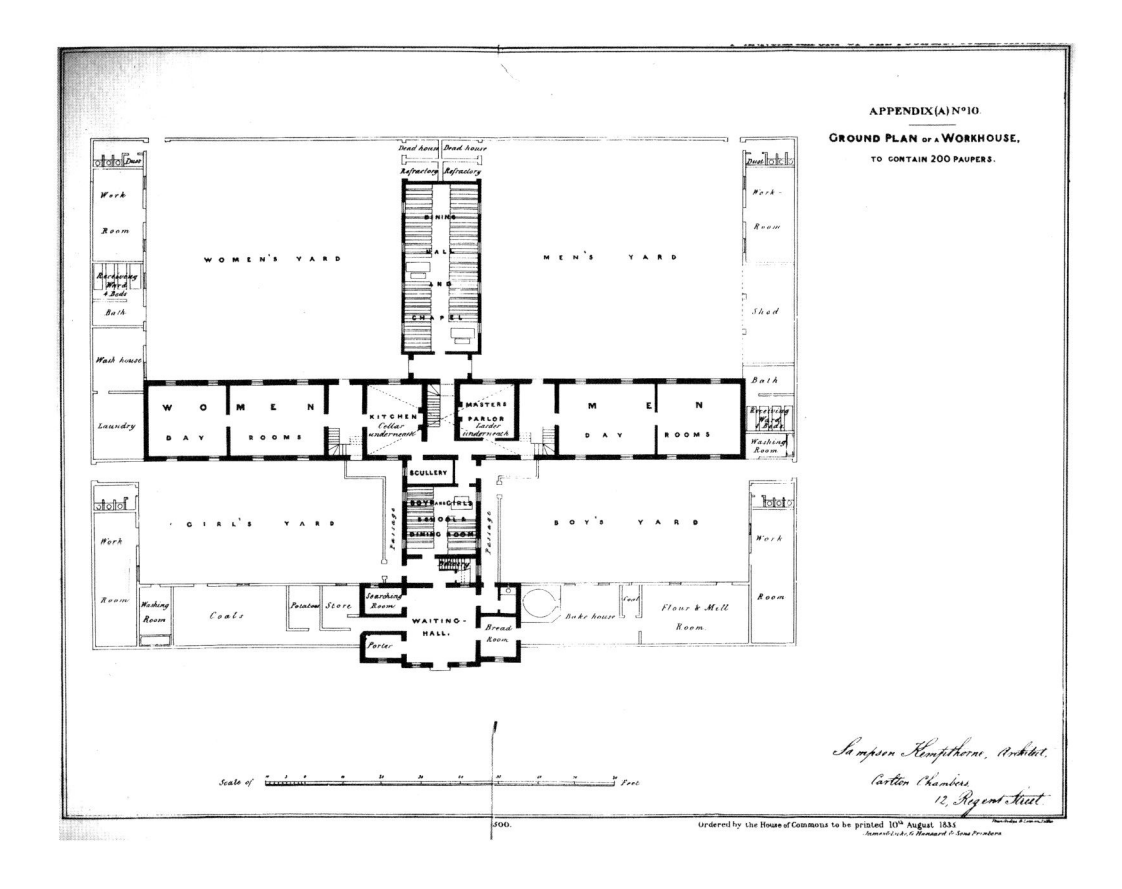

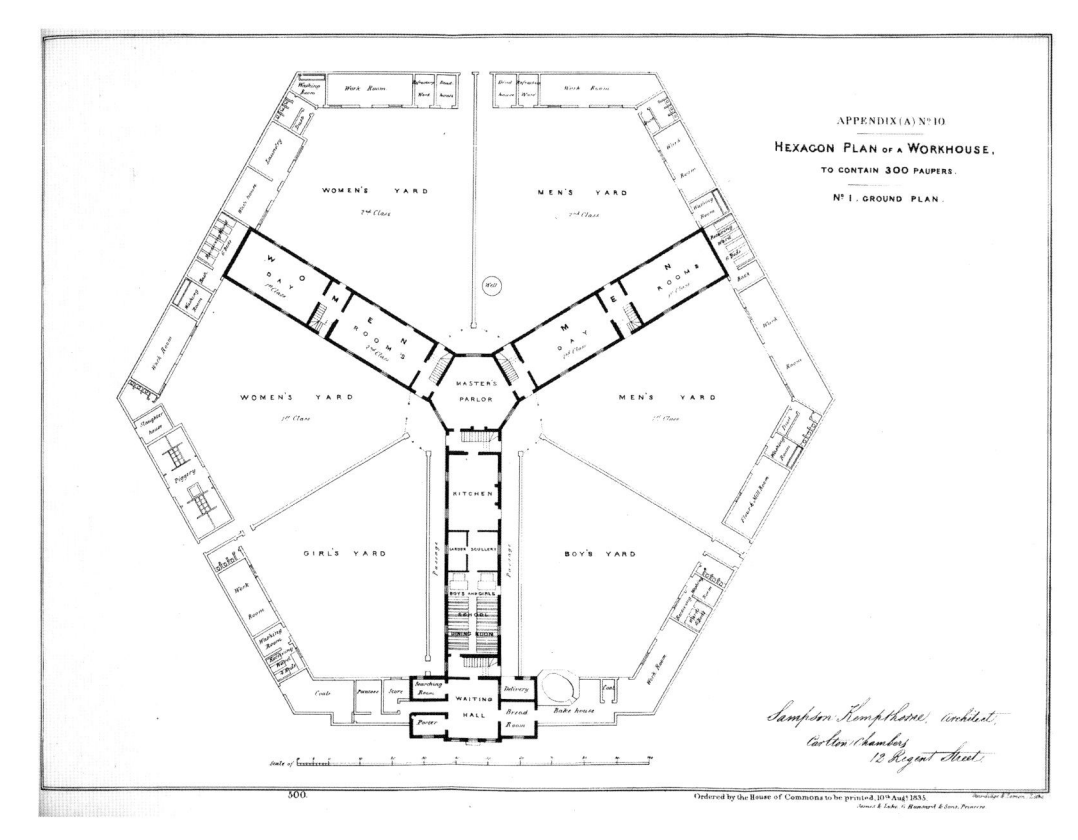

7
'Hexagon Plan of a Workhouse to Contain 300 Paupers', ground plan, by Sampson Kempthorne.
[By permission of the Syndics of Cambridge University Library, PP 1835 (500), XXXV, Appendix A, No.10. 7]

APPENDIX 3

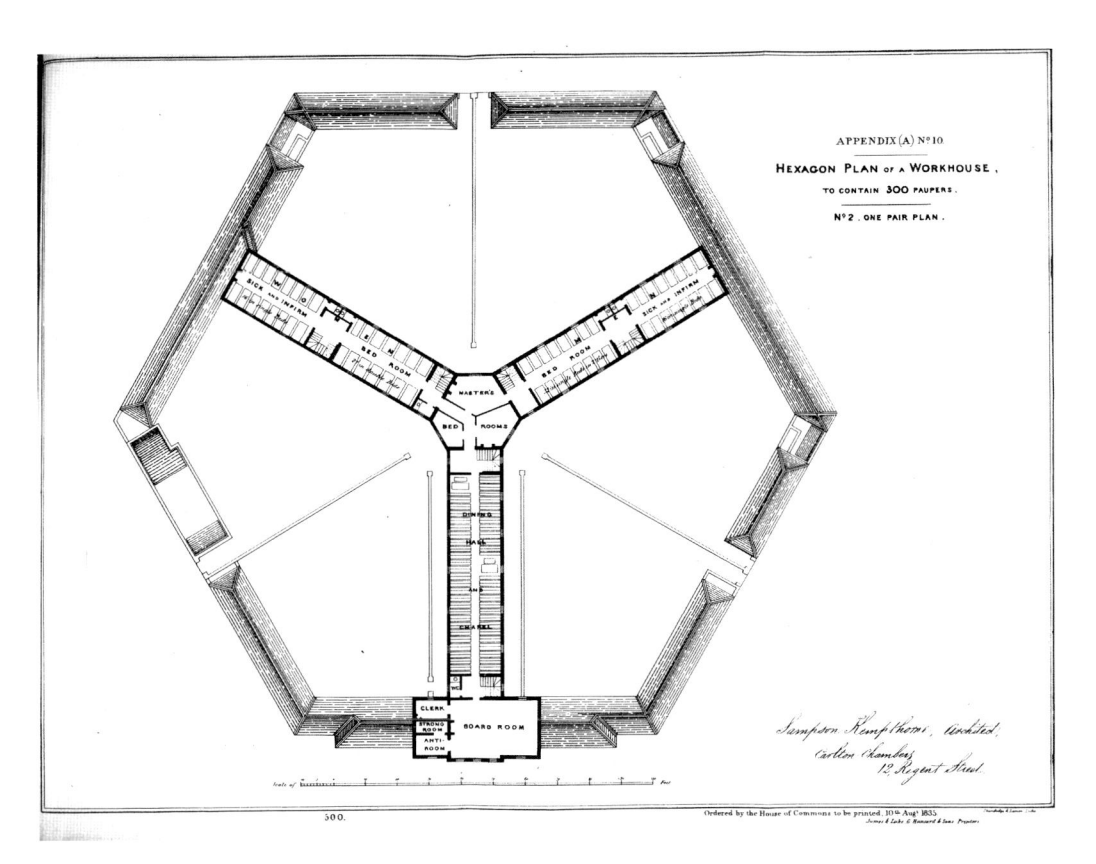

8
'Hexagon Plan of a Workhouse to Contain 300 Paupers', first-floor plan, by Sampson Kempthorne.
[By permission of the Syndics of Cambridge University Library, PP 1835 (500), XXXV, Appendix A, No.10. 8]

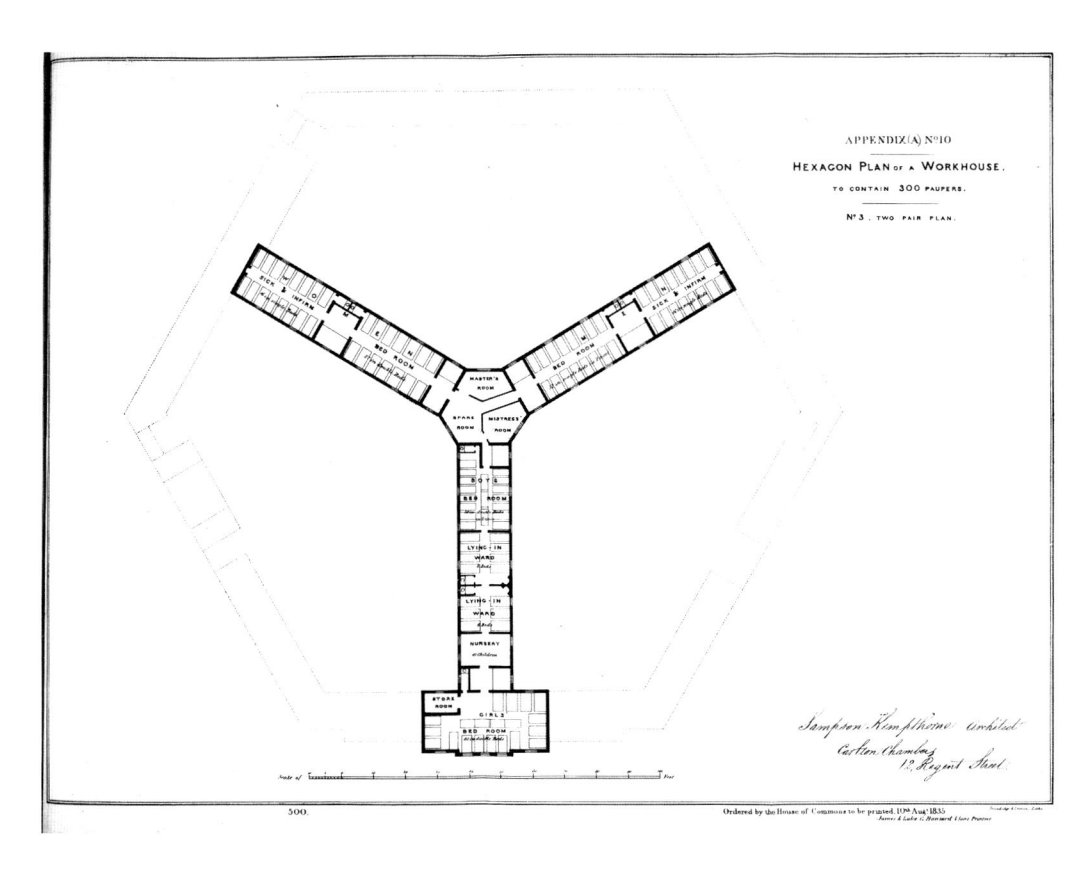

9
'Hexagon Plan of a Workhouse to Contain 300 Paupers', second floor plan, by Sampson Kempthorne.
[By permission of the Syndics of Cambridge University Library, PP 1835 (500), XXXV, Appendix A, No.10. 9]

225

THE WORKHOUSE

10
'Hexagon Plan of a Workhouse to Contain 300 Paupers', elevations, by Sampson Kempthorne.
[By permission of the Syndics of Cambridge University Library, PP 1835 (500), XXXV, Appendix A, No.10. 10]

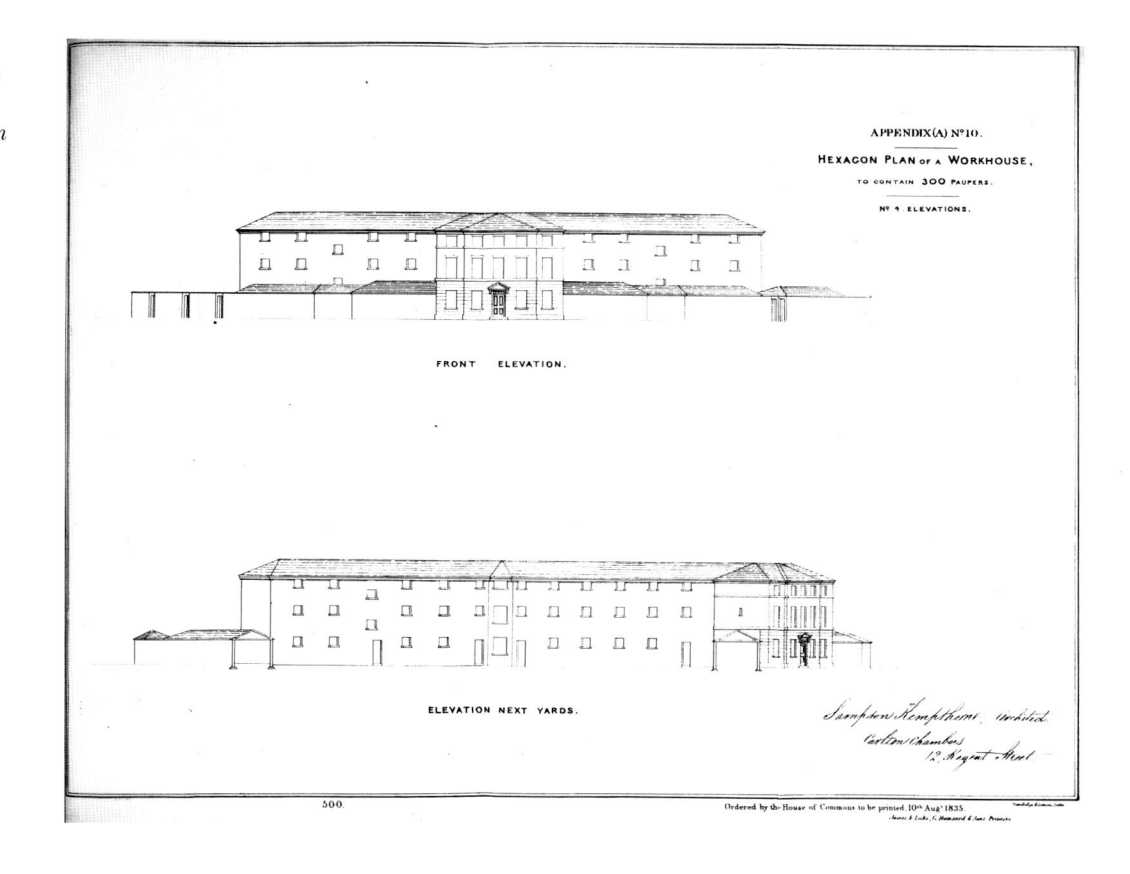

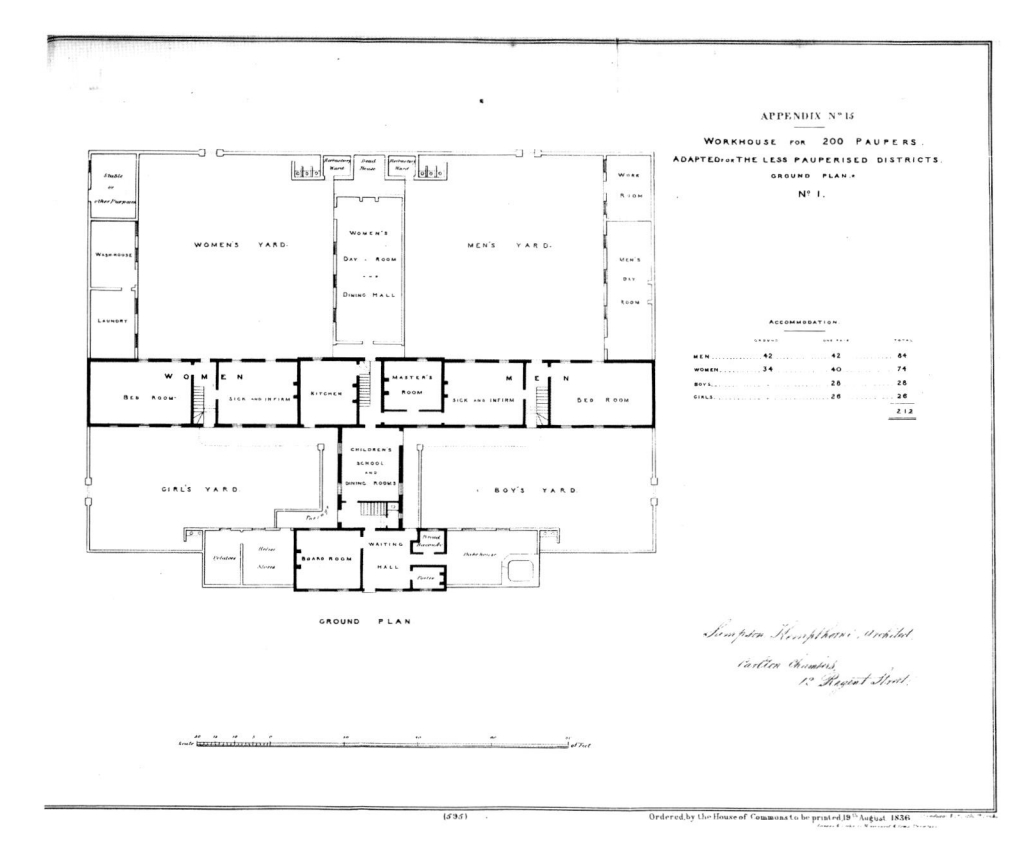

11
'Workhouse for 200 Paupers Adapted for the less pauperised districts', ground plan, by Sampson Kempthorne.
[By permission of the Syndics of Cambridge University Library, PP 1836 (595), XXIX, Appendix No.15, 1]

APPENDIX 3

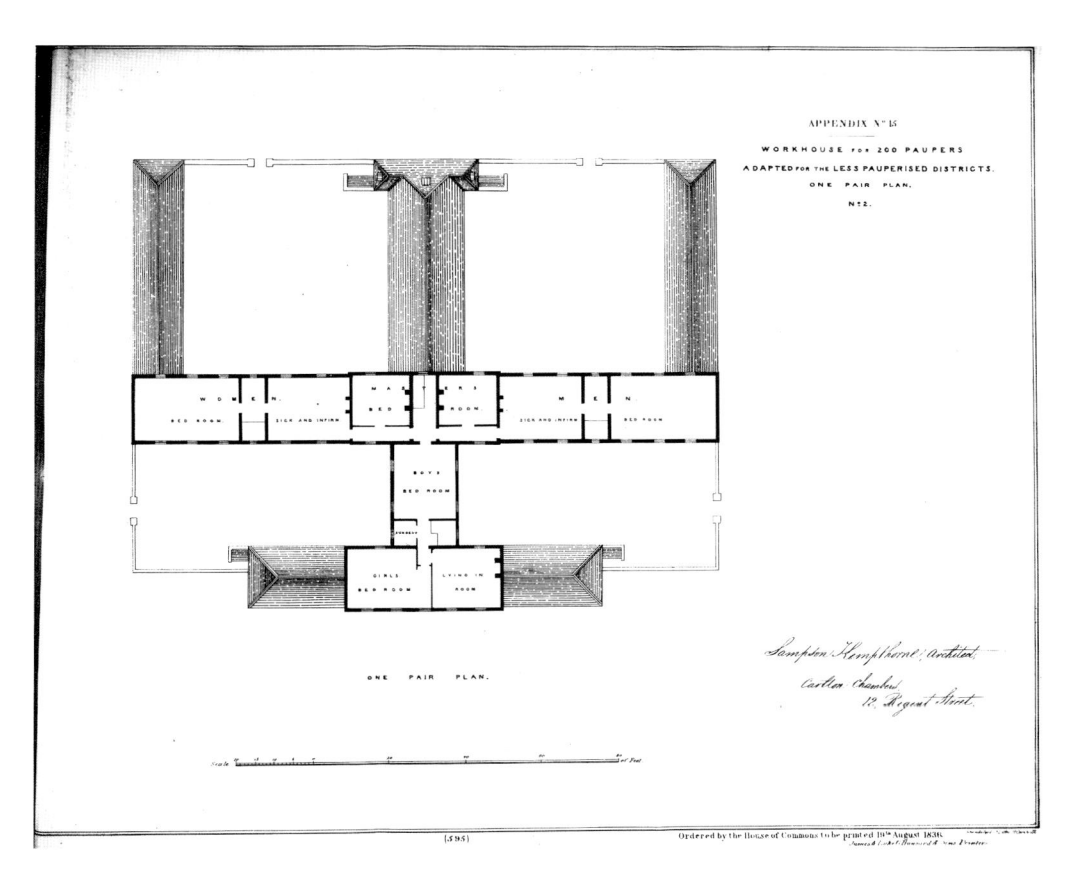

12
'Workhouse for 200
Paupers Adapted for the
less pauperised districts',
first-floor plan, by
Sampson Kempthorne.
[By permission of the
Syndics of Cambridge
University Library, PP
1836 (595), XXIX,
Appendix No.15, 2]

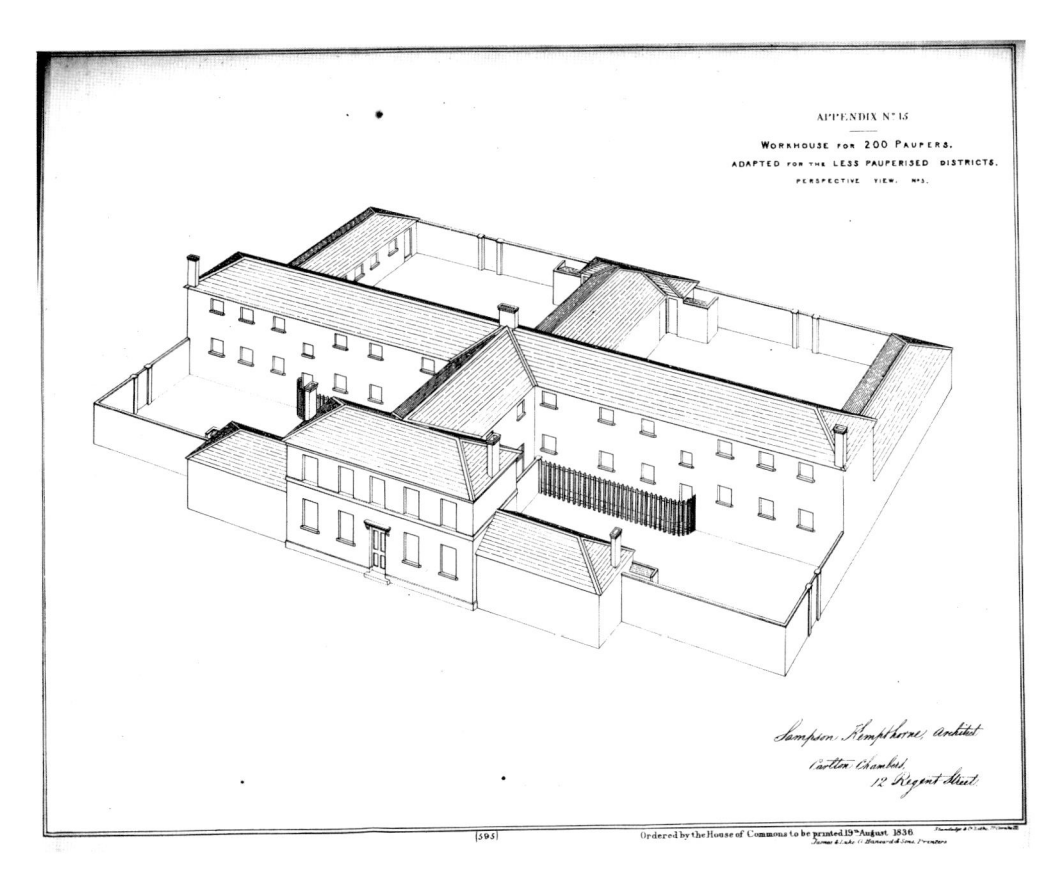

13
'Workhouse for 200
Paupers Adapted for the
less pauperised districts',
perspective view, by
Sampson Kempthorne.
[By permission of the
Syndics of Cambridge
University Library, PP
1836 (595), XXIX,
Appendix No.15, 3]

THE WORKHOUSE

14
Perspective view of a 'hexagon'-plan workhouse. Taken from the small-format editions of the 1st and 2nd Annual Reports of the Poor Law Commission. The drawings in the small-format editions differed from those in the large-format volumes. Perspective views of the 'hexagon' and 'square' workhouses had not appeared in the large-format volumes.
[Copied from small-format editions held at Buckinghamshire RO]

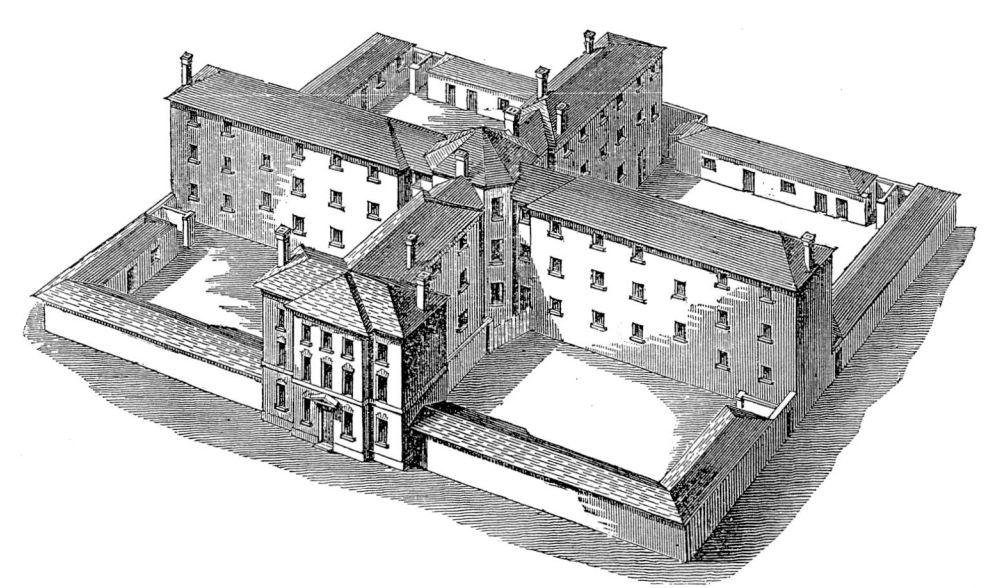

PERSPECTIVE VIEW OF A WORKHOUSE FOR 300 PAUPERS. (E.)

SAMPSON KEMPTHORNE, Architect,
CARLTON CHAMBERS, 12, REGENT STREET.

15
Perspective view of a 'square'-plan workhouse. Taken from the small-format editions of the 1st and 2nd Annual Reports of the Poor Law Commission.
[Copied from small-format editions held at Buckinghamshire RO]

PERSPECTIVE VIEW OF A WORKHOUSE FOR 300 PAUPERS. (F.)

SAMPSON KEMPTHORNE, Architect,
CARLTON CHAMBERS, 12, REGENT STREET.

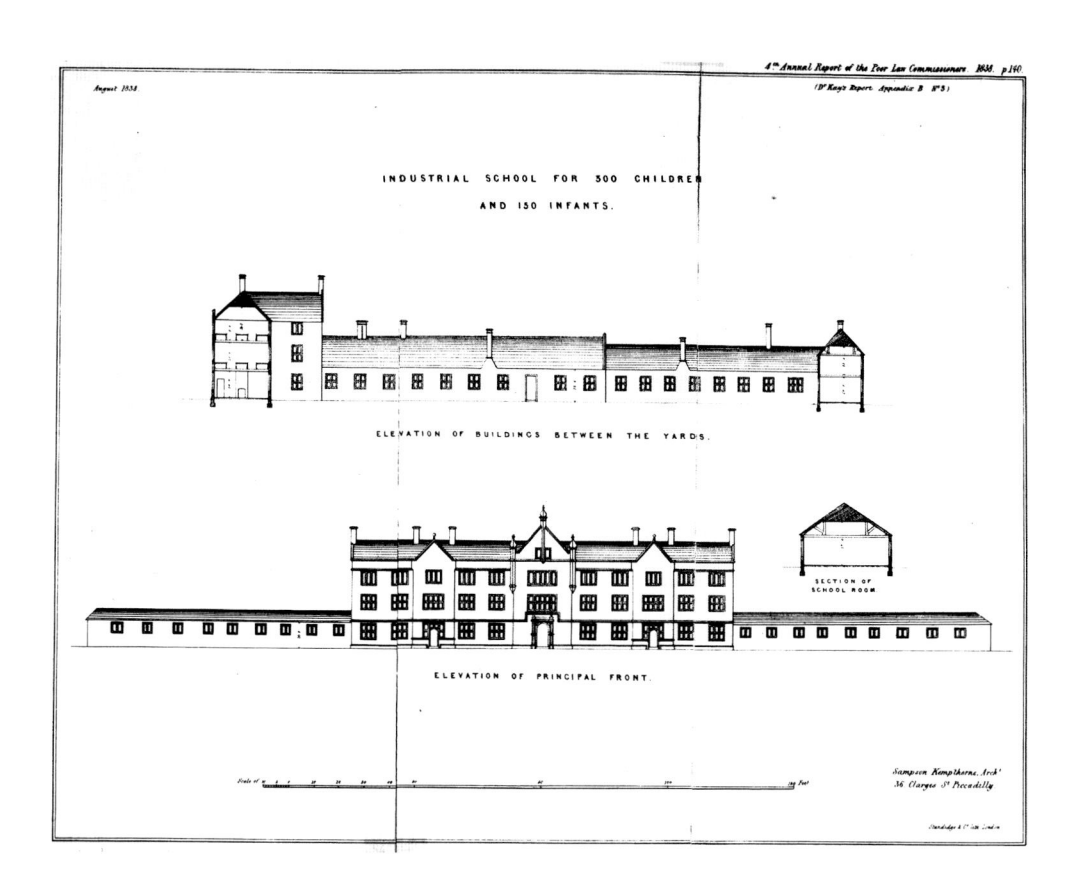

APPENDIX 3

16
'Industrial School for 300 Children and 150 Infants', elevations, by Sampson Kempthorne, August 1838.
[By permission of the Syndics of Cambridge University Library, PP 1837–8 (147), XXVIII, Appendix B, No. 3, 285–7]

17 (below)
'Industrial School for 300 Children and 150 Infants', floor plans, by Sampson Kempthorne, August 1838.
[By permission of the Syndics of Cambridge University Library, PP 1837–8 (147), XXVIII, Appendix B, No. 3, 285–7]

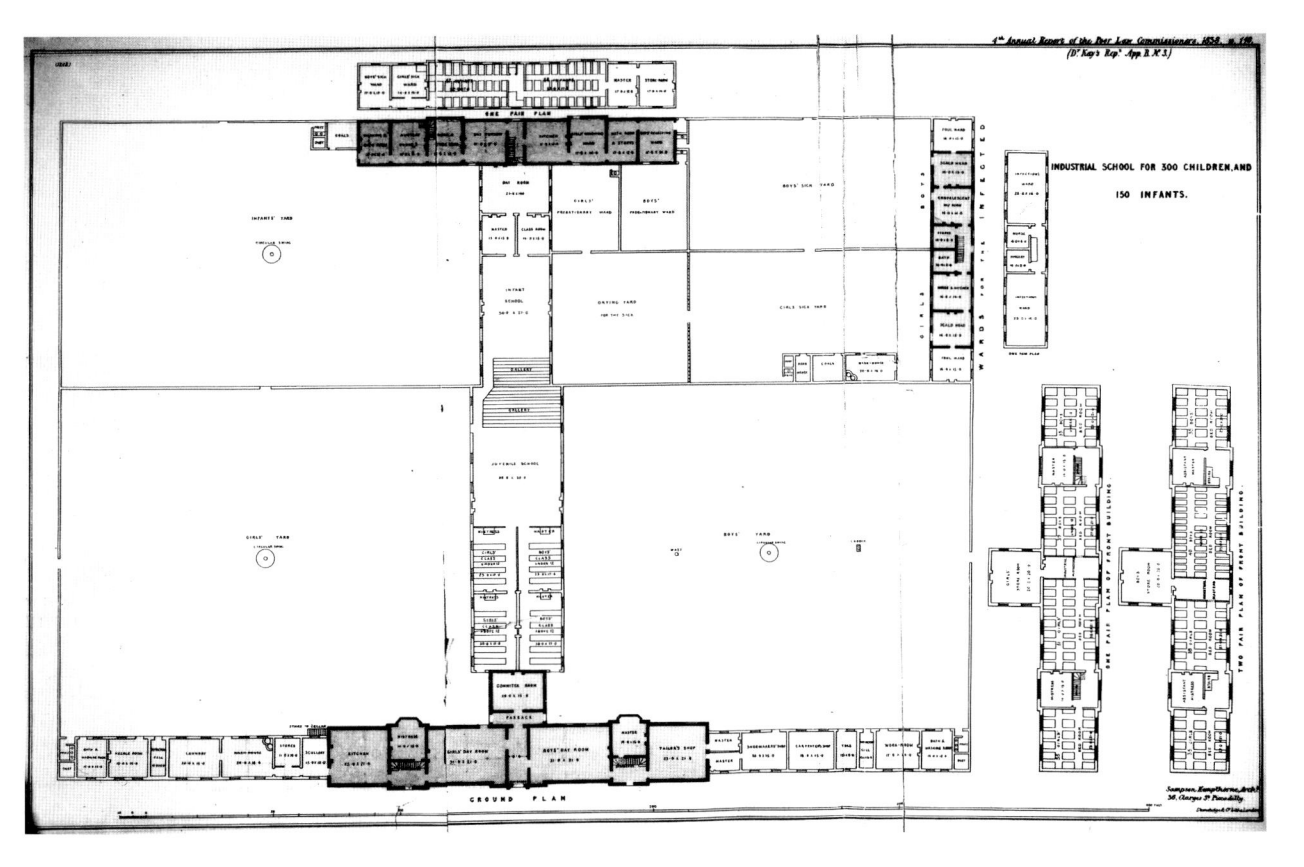

Notes and References

The following abbreviations have been used in the references and bibliography:

LGB	Local Government Board	PRO	Public Record Office	
LMA	London Metropolitan Archives, formerly the Greater London Record Office	RAWE	Registers of Authorizations for Workhouse Expenditure	
MAB	Metropolitan Asylums Board	RCHME	Royal Commission on the Historical Monuments of England	
NHS	National Health Service			
NMRC	National Monuments Record Centre, Swindon	RIBA	Royal Institute of British Architects	
		RO	Record Office	
PLB	Poor Law Board	SPCK	Society for the Promotion of Christian Knowledge	
PLC	Poor Law Commission			
PP	Parliamentary Papers	VCH	The Victoria History of the Counties of England	

Acts of Parliament have been referred to in line with standard historical convention as follows: 14 Elizabeth I c. 5.

Annual Reports of the central authority are listed in the bibliography on pages 240–3. Full references to other documents and *Parliamentary Papers* are given in the notes.

Chapter 2

1. 43 Elizabeth I c. 2.
2. 9 George I c. 7.
3. Checkland & Checkland (eds) 1974; 'Report from the Commissioners for Inquiry into the Poor Laws' (*PP* 1834, XXVII).
4. Webb & Webb 1927, 248. See also Webb & Webb 1906, 593.
5. 27 Henry VIII c. 25 (quoted in Nicholls 1898, I, 123).
6. Pelling 1985, 117; Leonard 1900, 29, 42–3; Webb & Webb 1927, 51.
7. 5 Elizabeth I c. 3; Webb & Webb 1927, 51.
8. 14 Elizabeth I c. 5 (quoted in Nicholls 1898, I, 159–60); Webb & Webb 1927, 52. It is doubtful that a compulsory poor rate was widely introduced before 1601.
9. O'Donoghue 1923, I, 197.
10. Leonard 1900, 42.
11. Phillips, D 1980, 42.
12. Webb & Webb 1927, 53.
13. Ibid.
14. VCH 1948, *Cambs II*, 93.
15. Stokes 1911, 81; Webb & Webb 1927, 57.
16. Guilding (ed) 1892, 403.
17. Westminster City Archives, *Catalogue of Westminster Records*.
18. Marshall, D 1926, 108. Paupers' cottages were not identified and recorded as part of the RCHME Poor-Law Buildings project.
19. In 1844 the PLC declared that such cottages should not be retained by authorities with workhouses (*PP* 1844 (560), XIX, 29).
20. The defining Acts were 39 Elizabeth I c. 3 of 1597–8 and 43 Elizabeth I c. 2 of 1601.
21. Webb & Webb 1927, 80. The pamphlet is sometimes attributed to the dramatist Thomas Dekker (*Dictionary of National Biography*, XIV (1888), 300).
22. 7 James I c. 4 (1608); 21 James I c. 1 (1623). See Nicholls 1898, I, 228, 233 and 252–7.
23. Webb & Webb 1927, 92.
24. VCH 1908, *Dorset II*, 249.
25. *OED* 1989, XX, 548–9.
26. Pearl 1978, 214–15.
27. Phillips, D 1980, 49–53. Only one wing of the Newbury Workhouse, later known as the Cloth Hall and now the Museum, was built in 1626–7.
28. Man 1816, 153.
29. It has been suggested that the name of 'The Oracle' was derived from the word 'Orchal', a substance imported from the Canary Islands for the dyeing process (Man 1816, 151–2).
30. Leonard 1900, 225.
31. VCH 1959 *Cambs III*, 121–2; Leonard 1900, 226; Stokes 1911; Hampson 1934, 20–2.
32. Stokes 1911, 92.
33. Oxley 1974, 80.
34. Southampton purchased a workhouse in 1631 (Southampton City Council Archives SC10/1/17). For Taunton and Abingdon see Leonard 1900, 226. For Totnes see Taverner 1968, 67.
35. Inf from Calderdale District Archives.
36. For Salisbury see Slack 1972; 'A plan of Crane Street Workhouse, Salisbury, made in 1712, showing alterations and new Buildings made AD 1728' (Wilts RO G23/150/24).
37. Taverner 1968, 67.
38. Leonard 1900, 226.
39. Grey (1972, 71) reports that St Giles-in-the-Fields is reputed to have converted a pest-house into a workhouse during the Commonwealth.
40. Longmate 1974, 15.
41. Bush 1649, 18; Pearl 1978, 219.
42. Pearl 1978, 229.
43. Anon 1786, 90. In 1661 the building returned to use as a House of Correction.
44. Marshall, D 1926, 125–6.
45. Dangerfield *et al* 1938, 134.
46. 13 & 14 Charles II c. 12.
47. The registration of births and deaths was required in London before it was extended to the whole country in 1837. Hence the term 'within the Bills of Mortality'.
48. Macfarlane 1986, 258.
49. Anon 1686, 1.
50. McClure 1981, 7.
51. Westminster City Archives, E2414 (catalogue to records destroyed during the Second World War).
52. Survey of London XX, 1940, 113.
53. Hale 1683, 9. This tract was probably written around 1660, although published in 1683.
54. Ibid, 10.
55. Child 1693, 4–5.
56. Ibid, 7.
57. Firmin 1681, 3.
58. Firmin 1678, 4–5.
59. Firmin 1681, 5.
60. Webb & Webb 1927, 105–6.
61. Macfarlane 1986, 259.
62. Clarke (ed) 1987, 43.
63. Hitchcock 1987, x.
64. Braddon 1721, 19–21.
65. Dunning 1686.
66. Survey of London XXXI, 1963, 210.
67. Survey of London XXXIII, 1966, 190.
68. Taylor, J S 1972, 61.
69. Nicholls 1898, I, 352.
70. 7 & 8 William III c. 32.
71. Hitchcock 1985, 53.
72. Cary 1700, 15.
73. Cary 1700.
74. Although it had no Corporation of the Poor, Salisbury set up a new workhouse in 1709 (Slack 1988, 198). The Oracle in Reading was fitted up again for the poor of the three parishes in the town in 1716 (Coates 1802, 147).
75. Slack 1988, 198.
76. Charity Hall was erected in 1615 according to Hadley (1788) but built in 1698 according to Anon (1786), a view shared by Sir Frederick Eden (1797, III, 832).
77. Russell 1976, 76–83; Hitchcock 1985, 59–69.
78. Anon 1702; Roque's Map of London 1746.
79. Anon 1786, 3.
80. Ibid, 56.
81. Hitchcock 1985, 76–82; Roque's Map of London 1746.
82. Ransome 1948.
83. Defoe 1704, 70.
84. VCH 1924, *Worcs IV*, 457–8.
85. VCH 1988, *Glos IV*, 112.
86. Macfarlane 1986, 266–7.
87. Ibid, 269.
88. Gray 1751, 18.
89. Oxley 1974, 81.
90. Hitchcock 1987, x.
91. Bucks RO PR159/1/3; Marshall, D 1926, 134; Anon 1725.
92. Hitchcock 1985, 97–100.
93. These included: Hartist (1718), Kettering (1719), Wellingborough (1719), Oundle (1719), Great Burstead (Billericay) (1719), St Ives (1719), St Neots (1719), Kimbolton (1719), Eaton Socon (1719), Bedford (1720), Maidstone (1720) and Wisbech (1720) (Hitchcock 1985, 101–2; Grey 1972, 71; Grounds 1968, 218; Webb & Webb 1927, 216–17, 244–5).
94. VCH 1953, *Cambs IV*, 260.
95. Knatchbull's Act (9 George I c. 7) became law on 25 Mar 1723.
96. Hitchcock 1985, 218.
97. Longmate 1974, 33.
98. Anon 1786, vii.
99. Hitchcock 1985, 236.
100. Ibid, 228.
101. Anon 1786, 27; Hitchcock 1985, 227–9. The Strood plan was sent to Nicholas Hawksmoor in 1724/25, but he was too ill to respond.
102. VCH 1989, *Yorks E Riding VI*, 133 and 192. The Beverley Workhouse was demolished in the 1960s.
103. Anon 1786, 5.
104. Ibid, 7.
105. Ibid, 87.
106. This may have been the Strood Workhouse, which the SPCK adopted as a model in 1726.
107. Anon 1786, 129.
108. VCH 1964, *Warws VII*, 321–2.
109. Anderson 1981, 79.
110. Report by Surrey Domestic Buildings Recording Group, 12 Oct 1989, NMR file no. 79235.
111. Statutory lists of buildings of architectural or historic interest.
112. Hitchcock 1985, 218.
113. Anon 1731.

114 Hay 1735, 17.
115 Brereton 1823, 37.
116 Alcock 1752.
117 Cooper 1763.
118 Scott 1773, 100.
119 Ibid, 37.
120 Ibid, 87.
121 Gillingwater 1786, 37.
122 Burn 1764, 233–4.
123 Ibid, 234.
124 22 George III c. 83.
125 Gilbert 1786, 15.
126 Marshall, D 1926, 13.

Chapter 3

1 Norfolk RO PD77/25.
2 29 George II c. 79; Cooper 1763. The workhouse became the Woodbridge Union Workhouse after 1834.
3 Webb & Webb 1927, 127.
4 Cooper 1763.
5 Norfolk RO C/GP12/274.
6 Norfolk RO WD117. These plans, signed by Joseph Stannard Junior of Norwich, were approved by the LGB in 1873 but the internal arrangements suggest that they were drawn before 1834.
7 *PP* 1836 (595), XXIX, 161.
8 Head 1835, 8.
9 *PP* 1836 (595), XXIX, 161.
10 Digby 1978, 38.
11 *PP* 1836 (595), XXIX, 154.
12 Young 1794, 85.
13 Marshall, D 1926, 157–9.
14 Crabbe 1810, Letter XVIII, 241.
15 Eden 1797, II, 238–9.
16 PRO MH14/2; Colvin 1978, 407.
17 Young 1813, 449–50.
18 Head 1835, 2.
19 *PP* 1843 (468), XXI, 65–6, 70–1. These were: Chichester (1752); Chester (1761); Maidstone (?); Oxford (1771); Southampton (1773); Plymouth Dock and Stoke Damerel (1780); Birmingham (1783); Shrewsbury (1783); Romford (1785); Highworth (1787); Streatham (1789); Manchester (1789); Sunderland (1790); Stone (1791); Tewkesbury (1791); Whitchurch (1791), and Bedford (1793). Later ones included: Buxton (1805) and Brighthelmstone (1825). In addition, a number of London parishes obtained local acts between 1722 and 1795.
20 British Library Kings Maps XXXIV 33 (1).
21 These figures were not totalled in the Abstract of Returns, 1776 (*Reports from Committees of the House of Commons*, first series, IX, 1774–1802, 297–538). See Williams 1981, 79–80; Taylor, J S 1972, 61–2.
22 Abstract of Returns, 1802–3 (*PP* 1803–4 (175), XIII); Williams 1981, 79.
23 According to Digby (1982, 7) the number of poor-law institutions increased by a fifth between 1776 and 1803.
24 Eden 1797, II, 52–3.
25 Taylor, J S 1972, 63.
26 Abstract of Returns, 1813–15 (*PP* 1817 (50), XVII, 107; *PP* 1818 (82), XIX, 1).
27 Marshall, D 1926, 131ff.
28 Checkland & Checkland (eds) 1974, 127.
29 Eden 1797, II, 143.
30 Ibid, 602.
31 Ibid, 329.
32 Marshall, D 1926, 76–7.
33 The administration of the poor laws was criticised in several pamphlets, eg 'An Inquiry into the Management of the Poor, and our usual policy respecting the common people, with reasons why they have not hitherto been attended with success', 1767, and 'Observations on the number and misery of the Poor, on the heavy rates levied for their maintenance', 1785.
34 Anon 1786, vii.
35 Eg, in Barwell 1994, 11.
36 Survey of London XXXI, 1963, 212.
37 Nicholls 1898, II, 101.
38 Hutton 1791, 60.
39 Anon 1786, vii.
40 'An Act to Amend so much of an Act made in the ninth year of the Reign of King George the First . . . as prevents the distributing occasional relief to Poor Persons in their own Houses, under certain circumstances, and in certain cases', otherwise known as Sir William Young's Act (36 George III c. 23).
41 Huzel 1969, 430–1.
42 Report of the Select Committee on the Poor Laws (*PP* 1817 (462), VI, 20).
43 59 George III c. 12.
44 Bentham, J 1798.
45 Evans 1971, 21.
46 Howard 1777, plate opp page 140.
47 Evans 1982, 118ff.
48 Stone Guardians' Mins 22 Jun 1792 (Staffs RO D 25/2/1–2).
49 VCH 1978, *Essex VII*, 77–8; building contract of 1786 (Essex RO D/DQ 75).
50 Colvin 1978, 177.
51 Eden 1797, II, 594–5.
52 Colvin 1978, 198.
53 Alverstoke Parish Book 1799–1831 (Hants RO PL2/1/1).
54 1:500 OS map Hants LXXXIII.10.15, surveyed 1861.
55 Eden 1797, II, 227, 234 and 623.
56 According to the Webbs, 'what was new in Lowe's experiment was his reliance, not on bad treatment by underfeeding, overcrowding and squalor, but on hygienic treatment under conditions that were unpleasant' (Webb & Webb 1927, 256).
57 Priestland (ed) 1989, 267.
58 Assistant Commissioner Wylde's Report to the Poor Law Commission (*PP* 1834 (44), XXVIII, Appendix A, II, 124).
59 Nicholls 1898, II, 228.
60 Becher 1828, 1.
61 Nicholls 1898, II, 232.
62 Caplan 1984, 2.
63 Becher 1828, 7.
64 Ibid, 9.
65 Ibid, 5.
66 *PP* 1834 (44), XXVIII, Appendix A, I, 610–19, and XXIX, Appendix A, II, 128–30.
67 The document drafted by Nicholls for this purpose was not published. See Nicholls 1898, I, xii, fn 1.
68 Evans 1982, 443–4.
69 Becher 1834, v–vi; Webb & Webb 1927, 258–9.
70 Becher 1834, v.
71 Assistant Commissioner Majendie's Report to the PLC (*PP* 1834 (44), XXVIII, Appendix A, I, 226).
72 Becher 1834, vi–ix; Baker 1984, 15–18. The Stoke-upon-Trent workhouse was demolished in the 1960s.
73 Capper 1834.
74 Checkland & Checkland (eds) 1974, 337.
75 Glossop Overseer's Account Book (Derb RO D2125 A/G2).
76 Baker 1984, 11–14.
77 PRO MH32/28.

Chapter 4

1 Checkland & Checkland (eds) 1974; 'Report from the Commissioners for Inquiry into the Poor Laws' (*PP* 1834, XXVII).
2 Ibid, 29.
3 Webb & Webb 1929, I, 56.
4 Checkland & Checkland (eds) 1974, 337.
5 Ibid, 429.
6 Ibid, 430.
7 Ibid, 437.
8 Ibid, 438.
9 Ibid.
10 4 & 5 William IV c. 76.
11 Nicholls 1898, II, 274.
12 *PP* 1842 (389), XIX, Appendix A.
13 Union Chargeability Act, 1865 (28 & 29 Victoria c. 79); Webb & Webb 1929, I, 431.
14 *PP* 1837–8 (447), XXVIII, 182.
15 Plan of Cosford Union Workhouse, formerly Semer House of Industry, dated 28 Aug 1835 (Suffolk RO 1445/5/38).
16 Thompson 1980, 59–60.
17 Webb & Webb 1929, I, 126–7.
18 Ibid, 130–2.
19 *PP* 1835 (500), XXXV, 170.
20 *PP* 1836 (595), XXIX, 1, Appendix D, 11a and 11b.
21 *PP* 1837 (546), XXXI, Appendix C No.4 and No.5; *PP* 1837–8 (447), XXVIII, Appendix C No.3 and No.4; *PP* 1839 (239), XX, Appendix D No.4, I and II; *PP* 1840 (245), XVII, Appendix E No.3, I and II.
22 *PP* 1839 (239), XX, Appendix D No.4, III.
23 *PP* 1840 (245), XVII; *PP* 1841 (327), XI; *PP* 1842 (389), XIX.
24 Witney Guardians' Mins 15 Jun 1835 (Oxon Archive PLU6/G/1A1/1); Brixworth Guardians' Mins 10 Sept 1835 (Northants RO PL2/1); Wellingborough Guardians' Mins 16 Sept 1835 (Northants RO PL12/1).
25 Leighfield 1978, 1.
26 *PP* 1835 (500), XXXV, Appendix A, No.10, 1–10; *PP* 1836 (595), XXIX, Appendix No.15, 1–3.
27 *Architectural Magazine*, 1835, 511.
28 *PP* 1836 (595), XXIX, 450.
29 Eg, Exeter Infirmary.
30 Stamp (ed) 1995, 77.
31 *Architectural Magazine*, 1836, 481.
32 Ibid, 329.
33 Stamp (ed) 1995, 79.
34 Thompson 1980, 61; RCHME 1970, 340.
35 Stafford Guardians' Mins 23 Feb 1837 (Staffs RO D 659/1/1/1).
36 Watford Guardians' Mins 1835–6 (Herts RO BG/WAT 1).
37 Drawings submitted to this procedure, whether accepted or not, are recognisable as they bear stamps recording the date on which they were received by the PLC.
38 Neil Bentham (1993, 115–55) considers the role of builders in the erection of New Poor Law workhouses in the South West.
39 Specification for Epping Union Workhouse (Essex RO G/E Z1).
40 Epping Guardians' Mins (Essex RO G/E M1, 193).
41 Epping Guardians' Mins and workhouse plans (Essex RO G/E M1, 227; G/E Z2/1–3).
42 Stamp (ed) 1995, 81.
43 Corfield 1990, 13.
44 *The Builder*, VII (1849), 452.
45 Neil Bentham (1993, table 3, 112) tabulated the costs of a number of the 300-pauper workhouses erected in the South West in 1836. The cheapest of these cost £4,600 (Weymouth)

while the most expensive cost £7,000 (Warminster).
46 Thompson 1988, 104.
47 Williams 1981, 81.
48 Stafford Guardians' Mins 23 Feb 1837 (Staffs RO D 659/1/1/1).
49 Elliott 1985, 3.
50 Witham Guardians' Mins, 9 Jul 1838 (Essex RO G/W M1).
51 Edsall 1971, 29–31.
52 Ibid, 35–6.
53 Ibid, 26.
54 Ibid, 146.
55 Digby 1982, 22–3.
56 Anstruther 1973, 22.
57 Ibid, 142.

Chapter 5

1 *PP* 1842 (389), XIX, 12.
2 *N Derbyshire Chronicle and Chesterfield Advertiser*, 28 Apr 1838, quoted in Watson 1981, 12; Bestall & Fowkes, 1979.
3 *PP* 1836 (595), XXIX, 23.
4 *PP* 1835 (500), XXXV, 214.
5 Malling abandoned plans to erect such a workhouse. See Malling Guardians' Mins 1835 (Centre for Kentish Studies G/ML AM1).
6 Drawings of Blean Union Workhouse (RIBA, SE Thames Regional Health Authority Collection).
7 Letter from Head to East Ashford Union, 21 Aug 1835 (Centre for Kentish Studies G/AE AM1).
8 Head's letter is quoted in Davy, J S, 'Report on pauperism and relief' (*PP* 1896 (c.8213), XXXVI, 172).
9 Dickens 1982, 75.
10 Hughes 1836, 98–100.
11 Baxter 1841, 185.
12 Signed drawings in RIBA, SE Thames Regional Health Authority Collection.
13 See PRO plans of 1875 for alterations to Bridge Union Workhouse (MH14/5), and the state of Elham Union Workhouse by 1886 (MH14/10).
14 Davy, J S, 'Report on pauperism and relief' (*PP* 1896 (c.8213), XXXVI, 172).
15 Plans of Bridge Union Workhouse, 1871 (PRO MH14/5).
16 Plans for administration building, dated Feb 1895 and signed by Joseph Gardner and John Ladds (RIBA, SE Thames Regional Health Authority Collection).
17 Davy, J S, 'Report on pauperism and relief' (*PP* 1896 (c.8213), XXXVI, 172).
18 Cockett and Nash Collection (Cambs RO Ref 296).
19 Documents and plans of Newmarket Union Workhouse (Suffolk RO ADA 500/1–127).
20 T L Evans's Watford Union Workhouse and John Plowman's Dore Union Workhouse each had a double-courtyard plan.
21 *Architectural Magazine*, 1835, 511–12.
22 Devon RO PLU Crediton 41.
23 Eton Guardians' Mins 14 Jul 1835 and 21 Jul 1835 (Bucks RO G/8/1).
24 Fareham Guardians' Mins 12 Jun 1835 (Hants RO PL3/8/1).
25 Stamp (ed) 1995, 77; Morrison 1997, 187.
26 Dickens 1982, fig 259: contemporary view of Brentford Union Workhouse.
27 Kempthorne's plans for Crediton Union Workhouse (Devon RO PLU Crediton 41) show that the kitchen was located in the hub.
28 Drawings of Walsingham Union Workhouse (Norfolk RO C/GP19/173–85).
29 Thorold's Chelmsford, Rochford and Thetford workhouses had square plans.
30 Stacpoole 1971.
31 Epsom Guardians' Mins 27 Jul 1836 (Surr RO BG3/11/1).
32 Wolverhampton Union Workhouse had a similar plan and may have been designed by Wilkinson.
33 'Proceedings in Ireland' (*PP* 1839 (239), XX, Appendix, 33).
34 *PP* 1839 (239), XX, Appendix 9, 1. Gould (1983) includes a good selection of illustrations of Irish workhouses by Wilkinson.
35 *PP* 1840 (245), XVII, 668–9.
36 Registration Act, 1837 (6 and 7 William IV c. 86).
37 Shepton Mallet Guardians' Mins 20 Feb 1837 (Som RO D/G/SM 8a/1). Plans of the register office are not signed, dated or approved but the building survives.
38 Colvin 1978, 330.
39 The only known surviving workhouse drawing by Donthorn is a ground-floor plan captioned 'Edmonton Union Ground Plan' (RIBA Drawings Collection, K5). It appears to have been an unsuccessful competition entry, and differed from Donthorn's other plans by having two hubs.
40 O'Donnell 1978, 89.
41 Eg, Ely.
42 Barnet Guardians' Mins 1835 (Herts RO BG/BAR 1).
43 For a fuller discussion of the workhouses of Scott & Moffatt see Morrison 1997.
44 Devon RO PLU Newton Abbott 20, f.3r.
45 Wolstanton and Burslem Guardians' Mins 26 Jun 1838 (Staffs RO 3506/1/1).
46 *The British Almanac* 1836, 234–6, describes Abingdon Workhouse, which was begun in mid-March 1835 and completed in October at a cost of £8,500.
47 Plans of Crediton Union Workhouse, dated '8 Nov 1836 (Devon RO PLU Crediton 41).
48 Dickens 1982, 92; *The British Almanac* 1836, 235.
49 Holbeach Guardians' Mins 1835 (Lincs Archives PL8/102/1).
50 The same happened at Wilton (Wilts RO H17 110/1).
51 Colvin attributed Bishop's Stortford to Kempthorne (Colvin 1978, 487) while Dickens attributed it to Nash (Dickens 1982, 166–7). See Bishop's Stortford Guardians' Mins 1836 (Herts RO BG/BIS 1).
52 Plans of Bishop's Stortford Union Workhouse (Cambs RO Cockett and Nash Collection Ref 296).
53 Letter dated 31 May 1836 (Cambs RO Cockett and Nash Collection Ref 296).
54 The Leicester Workhouse was designed some months after those of Bishop's Stortford and Braintree.
55 PRO MH12/6470 (cited by Thompson 1988, 75 fn 21).
56 Thompson 1988, 75.
57 Plans of Sturminster Newton Union Workhouse (Dors RO BG/SN C1/1).
58 Beaminster Guardians' Mins 1836 (Dors RO BG/BE A1/1).
59 Cerne Abbas Guardians' Mins 1836 (Dors RO BG/CEA A1/1).
60 First-floor plan Cerne Abbas Union Workhouse (Dors RO BG/CEA C1/1). See also Cockburn 1972, 89.
61 Plans of Wirral Union Workhouse (Wirral Archives A/HH/100/1).
62 The original plans of the Skirlaugh Union Workhouse are still kept in the building.
63 Newhaven Guardians' Mins (E Suss RO G7/1a/2).
64 Plans for the enlargement of Cleobury Mortimer Workhouse (Salop RO PL5/66 and PL6/321).
65 Plans for the conversion of Richmond Union Workhouse (N Yorks RO MIC 963).
66 Plans for the enlargement of Leominster Union Workhouse, Jul 1836 (Herefs RO A58/1).
67 Elevations for Stow-on-the-Wold Union Workhouse (Glos RO G/STO 32).
68 Bentham, N 1993, 66–9.
69 Gutchen 1984, 22.
70 'Explanatory Particulars of the Plans of a "Union Poorhouse" proposed to be built at Dorking . . .' (Surr RO BG2/31/248).
71 Plans of Launceston Union Workhouse (Devon RO 1081/81); 1:500 OS map of Chesterfield.
72 Cheltenham Guardians' Mins (Glos RO G/CH 8a/2).

Chapter 6

1 Driver 1993, 76, fig 5.1.
2 *PP* 1850 (1142), XXVII, 82–3.
3 Smith, Dr Edward, 'Report on the Metropolitan Workhouse Infirmaries and Sick Wards' (*PP* 1866 (372), LXI, 53).
4 Browne 1844, 1.
5 Ibid, 4.
6 No gates are known to survive *in situ*.
7 Dickens 1982, 149.
8 *Illustrated London News*, 7 Nov 1846, 304.
9 Ibid, 303–4.
10 Dickens 1982, 174–90.
11 Signed plans for Dulverton Union Workhouse, dated 1854, resemble the surviving Holsworthy Union Workhouse of 1853 so closely that it can be ascribed to the same architect, Edward Ashworth (Som RO D/G/D 32/1–2).
12 Scarborough Guardians' Mins 1858 (N Yorks RO MIC 583).
13 Knaresborough Guardians' Mins (N Yorks RO MIC 1647).
14 PRO MH14/10.
15 *Hull Advertiser*, 17 May 1844, 5.
16 Driver 1993, 77.
17 Smith, Dr Edward, 'Report on the Metropolitan Workhouse Infirmaries and Sick Wards' (*PP* 1866 (372), LXI, 39).
18 Huddersfield Guardians' Mins 4 May 1860 (W Yorks Archive Service).
19 *Workhouse Papers*, Nos 1–7 (1 May–1 Nov 1860).
20 *Journal of the Workhouse Visiting Committee*, III (Aug 1859); VIII (Jul 1860); XXIII (Jan 1864), 150–1; XXX (Jul 1864), 220.
21 Typescript 'History of Macclesfield Union Workhouse', *c* 1888 (Ches RO LGM 3169/4).
22 Pen sketch entitled 'Design for a Workhouse Chapel Chipping Norton', signed 'George Edmund Street, Architect' (Oxon Archives PLU3/G/2A1).
23 The Bedminster chapel was a gift from William Gibbs of Wraxall and designed by John Norton (inf from John McVerry, National Trust).

Chapter 7

1 Wood 1991, 127.
2 Williams 1981, 96–100.
3 Taylor, J 1991, 7–9; Richardson, H 1998, 5ff.
4 Report of the Commission Appointed for Improving the Sanitary Condition of Barracks and Hospitals (*PP* 1861 (2839), XVI).
5 *PP* 1868–9 (4197), XXVIII, 47.
6 Workhouse dormitories occupied only by night

allowed 360 cu ft of air space per person; dormitories occupied by day and night allowed 500. These figures were based on the assumption that rooms were perfectly ventilated.
7 Knight & Co 1889, 19.
8 Metropolitan Poor Act, 1867 (30 & 31 Victoria c. 6).
9 *PP* 1867–8 (4039), XXXIII, 22.
10 Ibid, 21.
11 *PP* 1836 (595), XXIX, 450.
12 Taylor, J 1991, 223.
13 Snell, H S 1872.
14 *The Builder*, 2 May 1868, 323.
15 Snell, H S 1881, 1.
16 Ibid, 3; Richardson, H 1998, 66 & fig 63.
17 Knight & Co 1889, 32, stated that double-width wards were only permissible for 'adult inmates in health'.
18 *The Builder*, 11 Nov 1882, 620.
19 *The Builder*, 5 Nov 1898, 413; *The Building News*, 9 Dec 1898, 823.
20 Taylor, J 1991, 223.
21 *The Building News*, 9 Dec 1898, 823.
22 Freeman 1904, 29.
23 A series of plans survives from 1898 (PRO MH14/11) and others were published by Freeman in 1904 (Freeman 1904, 23, 25, 35).
24 *The Builder*, 19 Apr 1902, 401.
25 Ibid, 23 Aug 1902, 174.
26 Ibid, 9 Dec 1905, 623.
27 *The Building News*, 31 May 1907, 774.
28 Freeman 1904, 12.
29 Madeley Guardians' Mins 11 Feb 1870 (Salop RO PL10/7).
30 *The Builder*, 2 Oct 1875, 893.
31 *The Building News*, 7 Dec 1900, 804.
32 Plans of elements of Steyning Union Workhouse, Shoreham, were published by A C Freeman in 1904 (Freeman 1904, 18, 26).
33 Report of Royal Commission on the Aged Poor, appointed 7 Jan 1893, reported 26 Feb 1895 (*PP* 1896 (c.8212), XXXVI, 156–61).
34 *PP* 1897 (c.8539), XXXVI, lxxxviii.
35 *PP* 1901 (Cd.746), XXV, 17–20.
36 A C Freeman published several plans of Ladywell Workhouse (Freeman 1904, 20, 21, 32, 33, 36, 58).
37 PRO MH14/14.
38 Survey of London XLIII, 1994, 80.
39 *The Architect*, 26 Mar 1870, 149.
40 Webb & Webb 1929, I, 388–9.
41 PRO MH14/18; *The Building News*, 26 Feb 1886.
42 *The Building News*, 26 Feb 1886, 356.
43 *The Builder*, 16 Apr 1887, 585.
44 Webb & Webb 1929 I, 384.
45 Survey of London XLIII, 1994, 6.
46 Unemployed Workmen Act, 1905 (5 Edward VII c. 18); Webb & Webb 1929, II, 650.
47 *PP* 1908 (Cd.4347), XXX, clxxvii. The Unemployed Workmen Act authorised the establishment of distress committees in urban areas with populations in excess of 50,000. The committees included representatives from councils and charities as well as boards of guardians.
48 Rose 1986, 42; Report of the Royal Commission on the Poor Laws and the Relief of Destitution (*PP* 1909 (Cd.4499), XXXVII, 1–718; 719–1238).
49 Old Age Pensions Act, 1908 (8 Edward VII c. 40).
50 *PP* 1909 (Cd.4786), XXVIII, lxxv.
51 Rose 1986, 47.
52 National Insurance Act, 1911 (1 & 2 George V c. 28); Webb & Webb 1929, II, 663–7.
53 *PP* 1890 (c.6141), XXXIII, lxxxv.
54 *PP* 1892 (c.6745), XXXVIII, 72–3.
55 *PP* 1886 (c.4844), XXXI, 199.
56 PRO MH14/10 and 30; drawings dated 1887.
57 *The Builder*, 15 Jul 1905, 80.
58 'Points to be Attended to in the Construction of Workhouses' (*PP* 1868–9 (4197), XXVIII, Appendix, 49).
59 PRO MH14/1.
60 PRO MH14/2.
61 Unidentified press-cutting of 16 Jun 1884 seen on site.
62 Ibid.

Chapter 8

1 Anon 1786, 8.
2 Marshall, D 1926, 98–100.
3 2 George III c. 22.
4 7 George III c. 39.
5 Masters could be compelled to receive a pauper apprentice under 8 & 9 William III c. 30. This was abolished by 7 & 8 Victoria c. 101.s.13 (1844).
6 *Sketch of the State of the Children of the Poor in the year 1756, and of the present state and management of all the poor in the Parish of St James, Westminster, in January 1797*, 1797 (cited in Webb & Webb 1927, 261 fn 2).
7 Arnott, N, 'Report on the Metropolitan Houses for the Reception of Pauper Children' (*PP* 1836 (595), XXIX, 445; Hill 1868, 65).
8 Dr Kay's 'Report on the Training of Pauper Children' (*PP* 1839 (239), XX, Appendix C, 97).
9 Butcher (ed) 1932, 6; Assistant Commissioner Villiers' Report to the PLC (*PP* 1834 (44), XXIX, Appendix A, II, 7).
10 Eden 1797.
11 Webb & Webb 1929, I, 129.
12 Checkland & Checkland (eds) 1974, 438.
13 Chance 1897, 5.
14 *PP* 1843 (468), XXI, Appendix A.
15 Ibid, 81; Chance 1897, 8.
16 *PP* 1852 (1461), XXIII, 11–12.
17 Chance 1897, 18.
18 Original plan held on site.
19 This was a feature of Donthorn's unsuccessful plan for Edmonton Union Workhouse.
20 Baker 1984, 24.
21 *PP* 1867–8 (4039), XXXIII, 139.
22 Longmate 1974, 183.
23 Certified Schools Act, 1862 (25 & 26 Victoria c. 43); Webb & Webb 1929, I, 267–9.
24 Education of Pauper Children Act, 1862–3 (25 & 26 Victoria c. 43). National Schools were run with the help of government grants.
25 *PP* 1899 (c.9444), XXXVII, lxxxvi. In 1911, 588 unions used public elementary schools, 20 used district schools, 62 used separate schools and only 11 used workhouse schools (*PP* 1911 (Cd.5865), XXXI, xxiii).
26 In 1910, 70,316 children lived in institutions, including 24,175 in workhouses (*PP* 1910 (Cd.5260), XXXVIII, xxi). Of these, only 388 were partly or wholly educated in a workhouse school.
27 Webb & Webb 1929, I, 306–9.
28 Ibid, II, 731.
29 Ibid, 755.
30 Ibid, 734; *PP* 1914 (Cd.7444), XXXVIII, xli.
31 *PP* 1914 (Cd.7444), XXXVIII, xlix.
32 Stokes 1911.
33 Hill 1868, 75.
34 *PP* 1837–8 (447), XXVIII, 285–7; Mins of the Committee of Council on Education with Appendices and Plans of School Houses (*PP* 1840, XII, 407).
35 *PP* 1843 (468), XXI, 16.
36 'Report of the Retiring Board of Guardians of the Manchester Union to their Successors, Elected 25 March 1841' (*PP* 1841 (327), XI, Appendix, 135–7). By 1839 Kay-Shuttleworth had introduced improvements to Mr Aubin's school at Norwood, where one room held classes for 400 children, separated only by canvas or green baize screens (Mins of the Committee of Council on Education (*PP* 1840, XII, 16–17)).
37 Pennock 1986, 134.
38 7 & 8 Victoria c. 101.
39 *PP* 1850 (1142), XXVII, 14.
40 Longmate 1974, 175.
41 11 and 12 Victoria c. 83; *PP* 1850 (1142), XXVII, 14–17.
42 *PP* 1850 (1142), XXVII, 14–15.
43 Chance 1897, 12.
44 Snell, H S 1881, 37–9.
45 *PP* 1870–1 (c.396), XXVII, 30.
46 *PP* 1856 (2088), XXVIII, 15.
47 *PP* 1852–3 (1625), L, 15; Kelly 1903, 84.
48 Hill 1867, 86–91.
49 Bowyer, H G, 'Report on the education of Pauper Children in the Midlands and Eastern District' (*PP* 1878 (285), LX, 340); *PP* 1880 (c.2681), XXVI, 204).
50 *PP* 1880, (c.2681), XXVI, 204.
51 *PP* 1899 (c.9444), XXXVII, xlvii.
52 Morrison 1998, 86.
53 Fletcher 1851.
54 *The Builder*, 29 Jul 1871, 594; Mouat, F J and Bowly, Captain J D, 'Report on the Home and Cottage System of Training and Educating the Children of the Poor' (*PP* 1878 (285), LX).
55 Mrs Nassau Senior, 'Report on the Education of Girls in Pauper Schools', 1 Jan 1874 (*PP* 1874 (c.1071), XXV, 311–94; Wood 1991, 139).
56 Mouat, F J and Bowly, Captain J D, 'Report on the Home and Cottage System of Training and Educating the Children of the Poor' (*PP* 1878 (285), LX, 297).
57 Monnington & Lampard 1898, 14–19.
58 *PP* 1880 (c.2681), XXVI, 205.
59 Chance 1897, 144–6.
60 The LGB declared the accommodation of the South Metropolitan School District inadequate in 1897, and its various properties were eventually sold to the MAB (see Appendix 2, Catalogue B).
61 Plans signed by Arthur & Christopher Harston and dated Nov 1880 (LMA KCSD 392C).
62 *PP* 1876 (c.1585), XXXI, 25.
63 Dr Bridges, 'Report on the Health of Metropolitan Pauper Schools for Seven Years, 1883–9' (*PP* 1890 (c.6151), XXIII, 161–74).
64 Industrial Schools Act, 1866 (29 & 30 Victoria c. 118).
65 Ayers 1971, 206.
66 Monnington & Lampard 1898, 4.
67 Ayers 1971, 203; Chance 1897, 30.
68 *PP* 1889 (c.5638), XXXV, 531.
69 Elham Cottage Homes, site plan (RIBA, SE Thames Regional Health Authority Collection).
70 Hill 1868, 79–80.
71 *PP* 1894 (c.7500), XXXVIII, 138.
72 *PP* 1896 (c.8213), XXXVI, 199.
73 LMA AR/CB/3/2.
74 Chance 1897, 38.
75 *PP* 1908 (Cd.4347), XXX, cxxix.
76 *Carlisle Patriot*, 8 Mar 1862.
77 Hill 1868, 97.

Chapter 9

1. Anon 1786, 129.
2. Richardson, H 1998, 54–5 & fig 51.
3. Eden 1797, II, 395–6.
4. Norfolk RO C/GP12/275; Suffolk RO 36/AH5/1/1.
5. Young 1794, 238 and 245.
6. Lunacy Act, 1808 (48 George III c. 96); Lunacy Act, 1828 (9 George IV c. 40); Richardson, H 1998, 159.
7. Hodgkinson 1966, 139.
8. Anon 1786, 65.
9. Watts & Winyard 1988, 159.
10. *PP* 1836 (595), XXIX, 326.
11. Webb & Webb 1927, 263, citing Report of the House of Commons Committee on the State of Madhouses, 1815, 54.
12. 3 George IV c. 24.
13. *PP* 1843 (468) XXI, Appendix A, 113.
14. Ibid, 76.
15. Eg, at Chesterton Union Workhouse, Cambs.
16. Contract for infirmary, 1842 (Cambs RO, Huntingdon 1955/16).
17. Plan of Wells Union Workhouse (Som RO D/G/WE 32/1).
18. Richardson, H 1998, 60–1 & fig 57.
19. Plan of Stoke Damerell Workhouse infirmary (PRO MH14/9).
20. 14 & 15 Victoria c. 105, section 4.
21. Richardson, H 1998, 61–2.
22. *PP* 1870 (c.123), XXXV, 15.
23. Richardson, H 1998, 62 & figs 59 and 60.
24. *Lancet*, 12 Aug 1865, 184–7; 7 Apr 1866, 376–8.
25. Hart 1866.
26. Smith, Dr Edward, 'Report on the Metropolitan Workhouse Infirmaries and Sick Wards' (*PP* 1866 (372), LXI, 35).
27. Ibid, 17.
28. Report of U Corbett and W O Markham to the President of the PLB, dated 18 Jan 1867, relative to the Metropolitan Workhouses (*PP* 1867, (18), LX, 119–83).
29. Smith, Dr Edward, 'Report on the Metropolitan Workhouse Infirmaries and Sick Wards' (*PP* 1866 (372), LXI, 43–7).
30. Farnall, H B, 'Report on Infirmary Wards in Several Metropolitan Workhouses' (*PP* 1866 (387), LXI, 2–3, 7).
31. Report of the Committee Appointed to Consider the Cubic Space of Metropolitan Workhouses (*PP* 1867 (3786), LX, 185–271).
32. Patients in itch and venereal-disease wards were allowed 600 cu ft, the same as those in ordinary wards. Lying-in and 'offensive' wards allowed 960 cu ft per person, and isolation wards allowed 2,000.
33. Hodgkinson 1966, 140.
34. *PP* 1835 (500), XXXV, Appendix A, No.9, 59–65.
35. *PP* 1836 (595), XXIX, 326.
36. Richardson, H 1998, 60 & fig 57.
37. Act for the Regulation and Care and Treatment of Lunatics, 1845 (8 & 9 Victoria c. 126); Richardson, H 1998, 164–5.
38. Hodgkinson 1966, 147.
39. *PP* 1863 (3197), XXII, 22 and 35–7.
40. Lunacy Acts Amendment Act, 1862 (25 & 26 Victoria c. 111); Webb & Webb 1929, I, 339–40.
41. *Journal of the Workhouse Visiting Society*, Aug 1859, 77.
42. *PP* 1864 (3379), XXV, 39.
43. Hodgkinson 1966, 146.
44. Smith, Dr Edward, 'Report on the Metropolitan Workhouse Infirmaries and Sick Wards' (*PP* 1866 (372), LXI, 36).
45. Hodgkinson 1966, 146–7.
46. Gooch 1980, 5.
47. Smith, Dr Edward, 'Report on the Metropolitan Workhouse Infirmaries and Sick Wards' (*PP* 1866 (372), LXI, 4 and 35). In 1857 the PLB had advised metropolitan unions and parishes to use the London Fever Hospital (*PP* 1857–8 (2402), XXVIII, 37).
48. For a fuller discussion of this subject see Richardson, H 1998, 136–8.
49. Diseases Prevention Act, 1883 (46 & 47 Victoria c. 35); Webb & Webb 1929, I, 326.
50. Taylor, J 1991, 109.
51. Report of the Royal Commission on Fever and Smallpox Hospitals, dated 21 Jul 1882 (*PP* 1882 (c.3314), XXIX, 1).
52. *The Builder*, 3 May 1884, 630.
53. Taylor, J 1991, 109–10.
54. Ibid, 115–17.
55. Richardson, H 1998, 173–4.
56. MAB Mins, 1894–5, XXVIII, 150.
57. Dr Bridges, 'Report on Metropolitan Poor Law Dispensaries' (*PP* 1887 (c.5131), XXXVI, 260–6).
58. Richardson, H 1998, 64 & figs 61 and 62
59. Snell, H S 1881, 9–10.
60. Richardson, H 1998, 69 & fig 65.
61. Smith, Dr Edward, 'Report on the Sufficiency of the Existing Arrangements for the Care and Treatment of the Sick Poor in 48 Provincial Workhouses in England and Wales' (*PP* 1867–8 (4), LX, 325–483).
62. *The Building News*, 3 Jun 1881, 655.
63. PRO MH14/17.
64. PRO MH14/1; Richardson, H 1998, 141 & fig 141.
65. Plans of Wolverhampton Union Workhouse (PRO MH14/38).
66. Knight & Co 1889, 65
67. PRO MH14/16.
68. Lunacy Act, 1890 (53 Victoria c. 5); Webb & Webb 1929, I, 344.
69. Webb & Webb 1929, I, 349.
70. *PP* 1912–13 (Cd.6327), XXXV, 97–100.
71. Richardson, H 1998, 179 & fig 179
72. Mental Deficiency Act, 1913 (3 & 4 George V c. 28).
73. *PP* 1911 (Cd.5865), XXXI, lvi.
74. Public Health Act, 1913 (3 & 4 George V).
75. *PP* 1904 (Cd.2214), XXIV, 225.
76. *The Hospital*, 23 Jul 1904, 300–1.
77. Bulstrode, H Timbrell, 'Report on Sanatoria for Consumption' (*PP* 1907, XXVII, 531).
78. Plan signed by the architect, James Iveson (N Yorks RO MIC 3070).
79. *PP* 1912–13 (Cd.6327), XXXV, 126.
80. In 1913 it was reported that Walsall and West Bromwich were providing accommodation for sick children on an estate recently purchased at Great Barr, and Manchester and South Manchester were combining to do something similar (*PP* 1913 (Cd.6980), XXXI, lv).
81. *PP* 1920 (Cmd.932), XVII, 34, 116; *PP* 1921 (Cmd.1446), XIII, 129.
82. *PP* 1920 (Cmd.932), XVII, 35.
83. Richardson, H 1998, 74–5 & fig 73.
84. Webb & Webb 1929, II, 757.

Chapter 10

1. Eg, the Act Against Vagabonds and Beggars, 1495 (11 Henry VII c. 2) and another act with the same name, 1503–4 (19 Henry VII c. 12).
2. An Act for the Punishment of Vagabonds and for the Relief of the Poor and Impotent, 1572 (14 Elizabeth I c. 5); Nicholls 1898, I, 158.
3. Nicholls 1898, I, 183.
4. *PP* 1843 (468), XXI, 121.
5. Hastings 1981, 156.
6. Ibid, 152–6; *PP* 1836 (595), XXIX, 375.
7. Hereford Guardians' Mins 25 Jun 1836 (Herefs RO K42/215).
8. Correspondence between PLC and Commissioners of Metropolitan Police (*PP* 1837–8 (447), XXVIII, Appendix, 96–8).
9. Dunmow Guardians' Mins 1838 (Essex RO G/D M3).
10. Hastings 1981, 162.
11. Longmate 1974, 233.
12. *PP* 1842 (389), XIX, 21.
13. 5 & 6 Victoria c. 57; *PP* 1843 (468), XXI, 8.
14. 7 & 8 Victoria c. 101.
15. *PP* 1847 (816), XXVIII, 15.
16. Asylums were set up in Liverpool, Manchester, Leeds, Birmingham and Bristol.
17. Plan of Trowbridge and Melksham Union Workhouse, 1847 (Wilts RO H11/190/1H).
18. Plan of Norwich Workhouse, 1857 (Norfolk RO N/GP3/3).
19. Longmate 1974, 251.
20. Craven 1887, 6.
21. Report of the Departmental Committee on Vagrancy (*PP* 1906 (Cd.2852), CIII, 11).
22. Metropolitan Houseless Poor Act, 1864 (27 & 28 Victoria c. 116).
23. *PP* 1865 (3549), XXII, 77.
24. While the new West London workhouse was being built, the union sent vagrants to lodging houses (*PP* 1865 (3549), XXII, 81).
25. 2,153 casuals received relief on 1 Jan 1859 (*PP* 1860 (2675), XXXVII, 13) and 7,020 on 1 Jan 1869 (*PP* 1870 (c.123), XXXV, 32). Poor-law records show that numbers of casuals fluctuated considerably throughout the last quarter of the century rather than showing a steady rise.
26. Wood 1991, plates between pp 120 and 121.
27. Snell, H S 1881, 27.
28. *PP* 1874 (c.1071), XXV, 18; *The Building News*, 27 Feb 1874, 242; *PP* 1876 (c.1585), XXXI, 33.
29. PRO MH14/17 and MH14/9.
30. Pauper Inmates Discharge and Regulation Act, 1871 (34 & 35 Victoria c. 108).
31. Casual Poor Act, 1882 (45 & 46 Victoria c. 36); Webb & Webb 1929, I, 413.
32. PRO MH14/3.
33. PRO MH14/7.
34. Freeman 1904, 13.
35. Ibid, 14, with illustrations.
36. Ibid, 13–16.
37. Report of the Departmental Committee on Vagrancy (*PP* 1906 (Cd.2852), CIII); Report of the Royal Commission on the Poor Laws and the Relief of Destitution (*PP* 1909 (Cd.4499), XXXVII, 1–718; 719–1238).
38. Numbers of casuals accommodated in workhouses in England and Wales on 1 Jan 1910: 17,043 (*PP* 1910 (Cd.5260), XXXVIII, xiii); on 1 Jan 1911: 10,474 (*PP* 1911 (Cd.5865), XXXI, ix); on 1 Jan 1914: 7,468 (*PP* 1914 (Cd.7444), XXXVIII, xvii).
39. *PP* 1913 (Cd.6980), XXXI, lxix. By 1929 the remaining casual wards were: Bethnal Green, Chelsea, Hackney, Lambeth, Poplar, St Pancras, Southwark, Whitechapel, Woolwich.
40. Webb & Webb 1929, II, 738.
41. Casual applicants for relief on 1 Jan 1914: 7,568 (*PP* 1914 (Cd.7444), XXXVIII, xvii); 1 Jan 1916: 3,576 (*PP* 1916 (Cd.8331), XIII, 8); 1 Jan 1919: 1,091 (*PP* 1920 (Cmd.932), XVII, 52); 16 Sept 1921: 8,989 (*PP* 1922 (Cmd.1713), VIII, 95).
42. Webb & Webb 1929, II, 953–60.
43. Survey of the Structure, Equipment and Accommodation of Casual Wards in England

NOTES AND REFERENCES

and Wales (outside London) (*PP* 1924 (Cmd.2267), XIX, 595).
44 Plans signed by County Building Surveyor, G H Lewin, dated Dec 1932 (Northants RO NAP 485–91); see NMR file no. 101748.

Chapter 11

1 *PP* 1920 (Cmd.932), XVII, 7; *PP* 1922 (Cmd.1713), VIII, 78–9; *PP* 1927 (Cmd.2938), IX, 112.
2 Board of Guardians (Default) Act, 1926 (16 & 17 George V).
3 *PP* 1920 (Cmd.932), XVII, 73.
4 Ibid, 42.
5 Local Government Act, 1929 (19 George V c. 17).
6 Anon 1966, 4.
7 Siggins 1989, 6.
8 John nd, 8.
9 National Health Service Act, 1946 (9 and 10 George VI c. 81).

Chapter 12

1 'Orders and Regulations to be Observed in the Workhouse' (*PP* 1835 (500), XXXV, 169–70).

Appendix 1

1 Many workhouses and poor-law infirmaries were investigated in the course of the RCHME Hospitals Project, between 1991 and 1994. That work was augmented and expanded by further fieldwork in 1995–6.
2 Gibson *et al* 1993.
3 Abstract of Returns, 1776 (*Reports from Committees of the House of Commons*, first series, IX, 1774–1802, 297–538); Abstract of Returns, 1802–3 (*PP* 1803–4 (175), XIII); Abstract of Returns, 1813–15 (*PP* 1817 (50), XVII, 107; *PP* 1818 (82), XIX, 1).
4 Checkland & Checkland (eds), 1974; 'Report from the Commissioners for Inquiry into the Poor Laws' (*PP* 1834, XXVII).
5 This number was computed by searching the Listed Buildings Database in the National Monuments Record.
6 The annual reports of the central authorities were all published as Parliamentary Papers. The expenditure tables were omitted in 1848, 1873 and 1874, and abandoned after 1914. In general, the LGB reports of 1914–19, and the Ministry of Health reports of 1919–30, were less detailed than earlier reports.
7 PRO MH34/1–10.
8 Williams 1981; Driver 1993, 73ff. The RAWE were also used by Neil Bentham (1993).
9 Williams 1981, 77.
10 Driver 1993, 79.
11 Driver 1993, 78, table 5.1. Approximate authorised expenditure was as follows: 1835–44, £2,908,000; 1845–54, £1,315,000; 1855–64, £1,490,000; 1865–74, £3,718,000; 1875–83, £4,031,000.
12 The most useful classes are: MH12 (correspondence with unions and other local authorities); MH17 (correspondence with asylum districts); MH27 (correspondence with industrial schools) and MH32–3 (reports and correspondence of the assistant commissioners and poor-law inspectors).
13 As with the correspondence files, most of the post-1900 holdings appear to have been destroyed.
14 LMA AR/CB/3.
15 Ministry of Health 1945–6.
16 Harper 1983 offers a useful short cut to information in *The Builder*.
17 Knight's *Guide* is very difficult to find, but a copy is held in the RIBA Library, London.
18 Hillier & Hanson 1984.
19 Cole, D 1980; Dickens 1976; Morrison 1997.
20 Pass 1988.

Appendix 2/Catalogue A

1 Colvin 1995, 254.
2 Ibid, 1070.
3 Biggleswade Guardians' Mins 1837 (Beds RO PU.BW.M.2).
4 Leighton Buzzard Guardians' Mins 1835 (Beds RO PU.LB.M.1); correspondence of C Haedy (Beds RO R3/4105).
5 Signed plans, elevations and sections (Beds RO PU.LV 21/1–5).
6 Colvin 1995, 577.
7 Bradfield Guardians' Mins 1835 (Berks RO G/B 1/1).
8 Cookham Guardians' Mins 1835 (Berks RO G/M 1/1).
9 Hungerford Guardians' Mins 1845 (Berks RO G/H 1/3).
10 Newbury Guardians' Mins 1835 (Berks RO G/N 1/1).
11 Preece 1983, 33.
12 Wantage Guardians' Mins 1835 (Berks RO G/Wt 1/1).
13 Stamp (ed) 1995, 100.
14 Wokingham Guardians' Mins 1848 (Berks RO G/Wo 1/4); signed ground-floor plan, 1848 (Berks RO G/Wo 4).
15 Stamp (ed) 1995, 100.
16 Dickens 1982, 176, citing *Aylesbury News*, 22 Apr 1843.
17 Dickens 1982, 138.
18 Eton Guardians' Mins 1835 (Bucks RO G/8/1).
19 Correspondence of C Haedy (Beds RO R3/4105); Newport Pagnell Guardians' Mins, 1835 (Bucks RO G/4/1).
20 Winslow Guardians' Mins 1835 (Bucks RO G/6/1/1).
21 *Bucks Herald*, 19 Nov 1842 and 10 Dec 1842 (inf from Dr Ian Toplis).
22 Cambridge Guardians' Mins 1837 (Cambs RO G/C/AM2).
23 Cockett and Nash Collection (Cambs RO Ref 296).
24 Chesterton Guardians' Mins 1836 (Cambs RO G/Ch/AM/1).
25 Colvin 1995, 319.
26 Linton Guardians' Mins 1836 (Cambs RO G/L/AM1).
27 Correspondence of C Haedy (Beds RO R3/4105); Newmarket Guardians' Mins 1836 (Suffolk RO 611/11).
28 Colvin 1995, 318.
29 PRO MH14/6.
30 *The Builder*, 16 Jan 1864, 52.
31 *The Builder*, 29 Nov 1873, 956.
32 Congleton Guardians' Mins (Ches RO LGC 1/3).
33 Great Boughton Guardians' Mins 1856 (Ches RO LGT 1/5).
34 Stamp (ed) 1995, 100. Macclesfield Guardians' Mins do not survive before 1880, but documents relating to the building work survive (Ches RO LGM 11), and a typescript history of the workhouse, *c* 1888, appears to be based on the lost minute-books (Ches RO LGM 3169/4).
35 Statutory lists of buildings of architectural or historic interest.
36 Pass 1988, 86.
37 *The Builder*, 16 Dec 1905, 653.
38 Wirral Guardians' Mins (Ches RO, LGW 1/1).
39 Bodmin Guardians' Mins 1842 (Cornw RO, PU Bodmin/1). Dwelly is named as the surveyor, but may not have been the architect. The building has been attributed to Scott & Moffatt in the past (Cole, D 1980, 186), but bears a closer resemblance to Thomas Ponsford's workhouses.
40 Falmouth Guardians' Mins 1851 (Cornw RO PU Falmouth/4).
41 Helston Guardians' Mins 1852 (Cornw RO PU Helston/1).
42 Launceston Guardians' Mins 1839 (Cornw RO PU Launceston/2).
43 St Columb Guardians' Mins 12 Mar 1838 (Cornw RO PU St Columb/1); Dickens 1982, 138.
44 Penzance Guardians' Mins 1837 (Cornw RO PU Penzance/1).
45 Dickens 1982, 138.
46 St Austell Guardians' Mins 1839 (Cornw RO PU St Austell/1).
47 St Columb Guardians' Mins 1837 (Cornw RO PU St Columb/1).
48 St Germans Guardians' Mins 1837 (Cornw RO PU St Germans/1).
49 *The Builder*, 21 Jul 1849, front leaf. Truro was attributed to William Bonython Moffatt by David Cole (1980, 186).
50 Ibid, 18 Nov 1871, 909.
51 Ibid, 13 Sept 1862, 656.
52 Ibid, 11 Jun 1853, 376.
53 Ashbourne Guardians' Mins 1846 (Derb RO D520 C/W 1/1).
54 Bakewell Guardians' Mins 1839 (Derb RO D521 C/W 1/1).
55 Stamp (ed) 1995, 100; Belper Guardians' Mins 1838 (Derb RO D19 C/W 1/1).
56 Chesterfield Guardians' Mins 1838 (Derb RO D522 C/W 1/1).
57 Colvin 1995, 643.
58 *The Builder*, 10 Oct 1874, 858.
59 Ibid, 24 Jan 1930, 214–25.
60 Hayfield Guardians' Mins 1838 (Derb RO D441 C/W 1/1).
61 Shardlow Guardians' Mins 1838 (Derb RO D523 C/W 1/2).
62 Axminster Guardians' Mins 1836 (Devon RO PLU Axminster 1).
63 Ibid, 16 Jun 1836 (Devon RO PLU Axminster 1).
64 Cole, D 1980, 11.
65 Crediton Guardians' Mins 1836 (Devon RO PLU Crediton 1); signed plans dated 1836 (Devon RO PLU Crediton 41).
66 Snell, A S 1905, 9.
67 Stylistic attribution.
68 Stylistic attribution.
69 Stylistic attribution.
70 Documents relating to the erection of Newton Abbot Union Workhouse (Devon RO PLU Newton Abbot 19–23).
71 Okehampton Guardians' Mins 1836 (Devon RO PLU Okehampton 1). Plans survive for a workhouse, designed in 1899 by Herbert W Willis and John Anderson, which was never built (Devon RO PLU Okehampton 198–207).
72 Kelly 1856, 220.
73 St Thomas Guardians' Mins 1836 (Devon RO PLU St Thomas 1).
74 Stylistic attribution.

235

75 *The Builder*, 28 Sept 1850, front leaf.
76 St Columb Guardians' Mins 12 Mar 1838 (Cornw RO PU St Columb/1).
77 Ibid.
78 Axminster Guardians' Mins 16 Jun 1836 (Devon RO PLU Axminster 1).
79 Totnes Guardians' Mins 1836–7 (Devon RO PLU Totnes 1); Dickens 1982, 47. Scott & Moffatt's competition plan was adopted on 7 Sept 1836, but following Moffatt's failure to deliver estimates on time the board appointed Ponsford.
80 Beaminster Guardians' Mins 1836 (Dors RO BG/BE A1/1).
81 Blandford Guardians' Mins 1856 (Dors RO BG/BF A1/8).
82 Bridport Guardians' Mins 1836 (Dors RO BG/BT A1/1).
83 Cerne Abbas Guardians' Mins 1836 (Dors RO BG/CEA A1/1). Plans dated 1836 (Dors RO BG/CEA C1/1).
84 RCHME 1970, 116.
85 The workhouse has been attributed to John Tulloch (ibid, 206; Colvin 1995, 996). Poole Guardians' Mins, 1837–8 (Dors RO BG/PL A1/1), reveal that John Tulloch was initially employed to alter the old workhouse (29 Feb 1836), and later to superintend the erection of the new workhouse (26 Apr 1838), but the approved plans appear to have been those of Clarke, who won the competition in Jan 1837.
86 Shaftesbury Guardians' Mins 1836 (Dors RO BG/SY A1/1).
87 Sherborne Guardians' Mins 1836–7 (Dors RO BG/SH A1/1).
88 Signed plans dated 1836 (Dors RO BG/SN C1/1–2).
89 Wareham Guardians' Mins 1836 (Dors RO BG/WA A1/1).
90 RCHME 1970, 340.
91 *The Builder*, 24 Mar 1855, 141; Chester-le-Street Guardians' Mins 1855 (Dur Co RO U/CS.3).
92 *The Builder*, 29 Feb 1868, 157.
93 Durham Guardians' Mins 1837 (Dur Co RO U/Du.1).
94 *The Building News*, 12 Mar 1886, 439.
95 Ibid, 7 Oct 1898, 518.
96 *The Builder*, 14 Apr 1910, 444.
97 Ibid, 26 May 1860, 335.
98 Houghton-le-Spring Guardians' Mins 1863 (Dur Co RO U/Ho.4).
99 Colvin 1995, 428.
100 *The Builder*, 28 Sept 1878, 1022.
101 Stylistic attribution. Series of plans, ns, nd, for new workhouse (Dur Co RO U/St.100).
102 *The Builder*, 10 Jun 1854, 310.
103 Colvin 1995, 428.
104 Weardale Guardians' Mins 1865 (Dur Co RO U/We/466).
105 Stamp (ed) 1995, 100; Billericay Guardians' Mins 1839 (Essex RO G/Bi M4).
106 Braintree Guardians' Mins 1836 (Essex RO G/Br M1); Cockett and Nash Collection (Cambs RO Ref 296).
107 Chelmsford Guardians' Mins 1837 (Essex RO G/Ch M2).
108 *The Builder*, 26 May 1888, 385.
109 Colchester Guardians' Mins 1836 (Essex RO G/Co M1).
110 Stamp (ed) 1995, 100; Dunmow Guardians' Mins 1838 (Essex RO G/D M2).
111 Epping Guardians' Mins 1837 (Essex RO G/E M2); signed plans (Essex RO G/E Z5). Attributed to Sampson Kempthorne by Colvin 1995, 577.
112 Halstead Guardians' Mins 1837 (Essex RO G/H M2).
113 Lexden and Winstree Guardians' Mins 1836 (Essex RO G/Lw M1).
114 Maldon Guardians' Mins 1872 (Essex RO G/M M10 and M11).
115 Orsett Guardians' Mins 1837 (Essex RO G/Or M1).
116 Jefferies and Lee 1986, 131.
117 Statutory lists of buildings of architectural or historic interest.
118 Romford Guardians' Mins 1838 (Essex RO G/Rm M1).
119 Saffron Walden Guardians' Mins 1835 (Essex RO G/Sw M1).
120 Tendring Guardians' Mins 1836 (Essex RO G/T M1).
121 Inf from English Heritage.
122 *The Builder*, 11 Apr 1903, 396.
123 Witham Guardians' Mins 1837 (Essex RO G/W M1).
124 Ibid, 5 Apr 1902, 349.
125 Ibid, 16 Apr 1859, 274–5.
126 Cheltenham Guardians' Mins 1838 (Glos RO G/CH 8a/2).
127 Chipping Sodbury Guardians' Mins 1838 (Glos RO G/SO 8a/2).
128 Cirencester Guardians' Mins 1836 (Glos RO G/CI 8a/1).
129 *The Builder*, 20 Jun 1846, front leaf.
130 Dursley Guardians' Mins 1838 (Glos RO G/DU 8a/2; G/DU 32).
131 Gloucester Guardians' Mins 1837 (Glos RO G/GL 8a/1).
132 Verey 1979, 343.
133 Stow-on-the-Wold Guardians' Mins 1836 (Glos RO G/STO 8a/1); signed plans and specifications (Glos RO G/STO 32).
134 Stroud Guardians' Mins 1836 (Glos RO G/STR 8a/1). Colvin attributed the building to Charles Baker (Colvin 1995, 93).
135 Plans (Glos RO G/TET 57/1–3).
136 Thornbury Guardians' Mins 1836 (Glos RO G/TH 8a/1).
137 Plans (Glos RO G/WE 32).
138 VCH 1972, *Glos X*, 135. Wheatenhurst Guardians' Mins 1836 (Glos RO G/WH 8a/1).
139 Winchcomb Guardians' Mins 1836 (Glos RO G/WI 8a/1).
140 Alresford Guardians' Mins 1835 (Hants RO PL3/1/1).
141 Alverstoke Parish Records 1799–1831 (Hants RO PL2/1/1).
142 Dickens 1982, 102.
143 Basingstoke Guardians' Mins 1835 (Hants RO PL3/5/1).
144 Newman 1994, 24.
145 Droxford Guardians' Mins 1836 (Hants RO PL3/7/1).
146 Fareham Guardians' Mins 1835 (Hants RO PL3/8/1). The architect is simply referred to as 'Mr Owen'.
147 *The Builder*, 12 Apr 1851, front leaf.
148 Ibid, 24 Mar 1883, 396; signed plan of infirmary (Hants RO 1/1M86/1).
149 *The Building News*, 5 Nov 1870, 891.
150 *The Builder*, 17 Nov 1900, 449.
151 Kingsclere Guardians' Mins 1836–7 (Hants RO PL3/2/1).
152 Dickens 1982, 102.
153 Stylistic attribution.
154 New Winchester Guardians' Mins 1836 (Hants RO PL3/19/1).
155 Colvin 1995, 718; signed plans (Portsmouth City RO BG/WP 1A/2/1).
156 Anstey 1978.
157 *The Builder*, 7 Jan 1899, 23.
158 Ibid, 29 Apr 1848, 210
159 Stockbridge Guardians' Mins 1836 (Hants RO PL3/17/1).
160 Whitchurch Guardians' Mins 1846 (Hants RO PL3/18 43M66 DU23).
161 Bromyard Guardians' Mins 1836 (Herefs RO K42/).
162 Dore Guardians' Mins 1837 (Herefs RO K42/85).
163 Hereford Guardians' Mins 1836 (Herefs RO K42/215).
164 Kington Guardians' Mins 1836 (Herefs RO K42/280). Benjamin Wishlade, identified as the architect by Colvin (1995, 1071), was an unsuccessful competition entrant who was later appointed building contractor for the works.
165 Ledbury Guardians' Mins 1836 (Herefs RO K42/342).
166 Specifications and plans (Herefs RO A58/1–5).
167 Ross Guardians' Mins (Herefs RO K42/406) (Plowman); *The Builder*, 18 May 1872, 381 (Haddon Bros).
168 Weobley Guardians' Mins 1836 (Herefs RO K42/475).
169 Barnet Guardians' Mins 1835 (Herts RO BG/BAR 1).
170 Cockett and Nash Collection (Cambs RO Ref 296); Bishop's Stortford Guardians' Mins 1836 (Herts RO BG/BIS 1). This workhouse was attributed to Sampson Kempthorne by Colvin (1995, 577).
171 Cockett and Nash Collection (Cambs RO Ref 296).
172 Colvin 1995, 317.
173 Barnet Guardians' Mins (Herts RO BG/BAR 1).
174 Signed block plan dated July 1867 (Herts RO BG/HER 70).
175 Hitchin Guardians' Mins 1835 (Herts RO BG/HIT 2).
176 Signed drawings Cockett and Nash Collection (Cambs RO Ref 296); Royston Guardians' Mins 1835 (Herts RO BG/ROY 1).
177 Stylistic attribution.
178 *The Reformer*, 13 Apr 1839.
179 Watford Guardians' Mins 1836 (Herts RO BG/WAT 1).
180 Huntingdon Guardians' Mins 1836 (Cambs RO, Huntingdon 1844/1).
181 Cockett and Nash Collection (Cambs RO Ref 296).
182 WEA 1978, 22–3.
183 Blean Guardians' Mins 1835 (Centre for Kentish Studies G/BL AM1). Drawings signed by the surveyor William Edmunds (RIBA, SE Thames Regional Health Authority Collection).
184 Bridge Guardians' Mins 1835 (Centre for Kentish Studies G/BR AM1). The surveyor was George Lancefield.
185 *The Builder*, 4 May 1844, 234; Colvin 1995, 852. Whichcord and Walker were named as the architects in an earlier advertisement for tenders (*The Builder*, 7 Oct 1843, 428).
186 *The Builder*, 13 May 1848, front leaf. A design by S O Foden, published in *Illustrated London News*, 17 Nov 1846, was abandoned and replaced by Marshall's design.
187 Cranbrook Guardians' Mins 1837 (Centre for Kentish Studies G/C AM1).
188 Dartford Guardians' Mins 1836 (Centre for Kentish Studies G/DA AM1). Attributed to James Savage by Colvin (1995, 852).
189 East Ashford Guardians' Mins 1835 (Centre for Kentish Studies G/AE AM1). The surveyor was John Whichcord.
190 Eastry Guardians' Mins 1835 (Centre for Kentish Studies G/EA AM1). The surveyor was William Spanton.
191 Stylistic attribution.
192 Faversham Guardians' Mins 1835 (Centre for

Notes and References

Kentish Studies G/F AM1). The surveyor was John Day.
193 *The Builder*, 12 Sept 1846, front leaf; signed drawings dated 1846 (RIBA, SE Thames Regional Health Authority Collection).
194 Stylistic attribution.
195 Stylistic attribution.
196 Maidstone Guardians' Mins 1835 (Centre for Kentish Studies G/MA AM1). The surveyor was John Whichcord.
197 Malling Guardians' Mins 1836 (Centre for Kentish Studies G/ML AM1). In 1835 the guardians had planned to erect a workhouse to Sir Francis Head's plan, with Whichcord acting as surveyor, but when Head left his position as Assistant Commissioner in November 1835, that resolution was rescinded.
198 *The Builder*, 6 Mar 1858, 162.
199 Milton Guardians' Mins 1835 (Centre for Kentish Studies G/MI AM1). Mr Bland was one of the guardians.
200 River Guardians' Mins 1835 (Centre for Kentish Studies G/DO AM1). The surveyor was George Lancefield.
201 *The Builder*, 24 Feb 1844, 96.
202 Colvin 1995, 852.
203 Cranbrook Guardians' Mins indicate that the architect was Whichcord (Centre for Kentish Studies G/C AM1). Whichcord is also named as the architect in Nicholson (1986, 2).
204 Stylistic attribution.
205 *Barrow Herald*, 7 Feb 1880.
206 *The Building News*, 7 Aug 1891, 178.
207 *The Builder*, 24 Oct 1924, 634.
208 Ibid, 10 Mar 1860, 157.
209 Ibid, 5 Oct 1861, 689.
210 Ibid, 28 Jun 1873, 504.
211 Ibid, 13 Nov 1869, 916.
212 Pass 1988, 89.
213 *The Builder*, 15 Oct 1898, 349.
214 Ibid, 12 Nov 1904, 499.
215 Ibid, 9 Apr 1898, 351. Crickmay & Sons won a competition in 1897 (Harper 1983, 73).
216 *Yorkshire Daily Observer*, 12 Dec 1904, 6.
217 Colvin 1995, 365.
218 *The Builder*, 22 Jul 1843, 296.
219 Ibid, 26 Oct 1872, 840.
220 Ibid, 22 Feb 1902, 198.
221 Ibid, 2 Nov 1901, 391.
222 Colvin 1995, 958.
223 *The Builder*, 15 Sept 1855, 441.
224 Harper 1983, 131.
225 PRO MH14/26.
226 *The Builder*, 16 Aug 1851, front leaf.
227 Statutory lists of buildings of architectural or historic interest.
228 *The Builder*, 16 Apr 1870, 311.
229 Ibid, 13 Jan 1906, 55.
230 *The Rochdale Observer*, 22 Dec 1877.
231 *The Building News*, 3 Jun 1898, 779.
232 *The Builder*, 5 Apr 1851, 217.
233 Ibid, 15 Jul 1882, 91.
234 *The Building News*, 6 Aug 1858, 805.
235 Colvin 1995, 988.
236 *The Building News*, 21 Oct 1892, 582.
237 *The Builder*, 25 Nov 1865, 842.
238 *The Liverpool Review*, 9 Feb 1889.
239 *The Builder*, 14 May 1910, 569.
240 Ibid, 15 Mar 1856, 146.
241 Barrow-upon-Soar Guardians' Mins 1838 (Leics RO G/2/8a/1).
242 Blaby Guardians' Mins 1836 (Leics RO G/5/8a/1).
243 Francis 1930, 136.
244 Leicester Guardians' Mins 1836–7 (Leics RO G/12/8a/1); Thompson 1988, 71–8.
245 Thompson 1988, 97.
246 Statutory lists of buildings of architectural or historic interest.
247 *The Builder*, 14 Jul 1900, 30–1.
248 Stamp (ed) 1995, 88; Loughborough Guardians' Mins 1837 (Leics RO G/7/8a/1).
249 Lutterworth Guardians' Mins 1938 (Leics RO G/8/8a/2).
250 Market Bosworth Guardians' Mins, which begin in 1838, refer to a Mr Knightley, who might have been the architect or the contractor (Leics RO DE 3640/175).
251 Market Harborough Guardians' Mins 1835 (Leics RO G/10/8a/1).
252 Belper Guardians' Mins, 10 Mar 1838 (Derb RO D19 C/W 1/1); inscription on façade.
253 Boston Guardians' Mins 1836 (Lincs Archives PL1/102/1).
254 Bourn Guardians' Mins 1837 (Lincs Archives PL2/102/1).
255 Signed, undated drawings for workhouse (Lincs Archives PL4/109/2).
256 Dickens 1982, 170.
257 Cited in Belper Guardians' Mins 10 Mar 1838 (Derb RO D19 C/W 1/1).
258 Grantham Guardians' Mins 1890 (Lincs Archives PL6/102/10).
259 Kelly 1937, 243.
260 Holbeach Guardians' Mins 1835 (Lincs Archives PL8/102/1).
261 Horncastle Guardians' Mins 1837 (Lincs Archives PL9/102/1).
262 Lincoln Guardians' Mins 1837 (Lincs Archives PL10/102/1).
263 Louth Guardians' Mins 1837 (Lincs Archives PL11/102/1).
264 Sleaford Guardians' Mins 1836 (Lincs Archives PL12/102/1).
265 Spalding Guardians' Mins 1836 (Lincs Archives PL13/102/1).
266 Spilsby Guardians' Mins 1837 (Lincs Archives PL14/102/1).
267 Stamford Guardians' Mins 1835 (Lincs Archives PL15/102/1).
268 *The Builder*, 2 Sept 1899, 230.
269 Colvin 1995, 1013; unsigned plans of Brentford Union Workhouse, 1837 (LMA B.BG.230).
270 *The Building News*, 7 Nov 1902, 617.
271 Edmonton Guardians' Mins 1839 (LMA E.BG.3). A ground-floor plan in the RIBA Drawings Collection is captioned 'Edmonton Union Workhouse' and signed by William Donthorn (K5). It was probably an unsuccessful competition entry.
272 Graham 1974, 4.
273 Plaque in hall.
274 Uxbridge Guardians' Mins 21 Oct 1836: plan by Thorold selected (LMA U.BG.1).
275 *The Builder*, 1 Jan 1898, 24; signed block plan 1898 (LMA W.BG.130).
276 Colvin 1995, 319.
277 Colvin 1978, 145 (not in Colvin 1995).
278 Colvin 1995, 979.
279 Colvin, 1978, 145 (not in Colvin 1995).
280 Colvin 1995, 319.
281 Ibid.
282 East and West Flegg Incorporation Minute Book, 19 Feb 1776 (Norfolk RO C/GP/7/1).
283 Colvin 1995, 319.
284 Ibid, 979.
285 Colvin 1978, 145 (not in Colvin 1995).
286 *The Builder*, 12 Jul 1856, 388.
287 Digby 1978, 66.
288 Colvin 1995, 319.
289 Ibid, 979.
290 Ibid, 979.
291 Colvin (1995, 979) attributes Wayland to William Thorold; Dickens 1982, 145, to William J Donthorn.
292 *The Builder*, 10 Nov 1911, 548.
293 Pevsner and Wilson 1997, 506.
294 PRO MH14/38.
295 Brackley Guardians' Mins 1835 (Northants RO PL1/1).
296 Brixworth Guardians' Mins 1835 (Northants RO PL2/1).
297 Daventry Guardians' Mins 1837 (Northants RO PL3/1).
298 Hardingstone Guardians' Mins 1838 (Northants RO PL4/2).
299 Kettering Guardians' Mins 1836 (Northants RO PL5/1).
300 Dickens 1982, 138.
301 Oundle Guardians' Mins 1836 (Northants RO PL7/1).
302 Peterborough Guardians' Mins 1836 (Northants RO PL8/1).
303 Thrapston Guardians' Mins 1836 (Northants RO PL10/1).
304 Towcester Guardians' Mins 1835 (Northants RO PL11/1).
305 Wellingborough Guardians' Mins 1836 (Northants RO PL12/1).
306 Colvin 1995, 429.
307 *The Building News*, 16 Nov 1883, 785.
308 *The Builder*, 31 Mar 1866, 153.
309 Ibid, 22 Jun 1901, 612.
310 Ibid, 2 Oct 1914, 315.
311 Signed plan, PRO MH14/30.
312 *The Building News*, 9 Jan 1885, 52.
313 Notts Archives PUB 1/29/18.
314 Bingham Guardians' Mins 1836 (Notts Archives PUD 1/1/1).
315 East Retford Guardians' Mins 1836 (Notts Archives PUE 1/1/1).
316 Belper Guardians' Mins, 10 Mar 1838 (Derb RO D19 C/W 1/1).
317 *The Builder*, 16 Jul 1898, 68.
318 Becher 1828, 8.
319 *The Builder*, 1 Jun 1901, 546.
320 Banbury Guardians' Mins 1835 (Oxon Archives PLU1/G/1A1/1).
321 Bicester Guardians' Mins 1835 (Oxon Archives PLU2/G/1A1/1).
322 Chipping Norton Guardians' Mins 1837 (Oxon Archives PLU3/G/1A1/1).
323 Oxon Archives MSS DD. Henley C. IV.12.
324 British Museum Kings Maps XXXIV 33 (1).
325 Kelly 1883, 647.
326 *The Builder*, 7 Aug 1852, 503.
327 Thame Guardians' Mins 1835 (Oxon Archives PLU5/G/1A1/1).
328 Witney Guardians' Mins 1835 (Oxon Archives PLU6/G/1A1/1). Kempthorne's hexagon plan had initially been adopted.
329 Woodstock Guardians' Mins 1836 (Oxon Archives PLU7/G/1A1/1).
330 Oakham Guardians' Mins 1836 (Leics RO G/R1/8a/1).
331 Stylistic attribution.
332 Colvin 1995, 482.
333 Church Stretton Guardians' Mins 1837–8 (Salop RO PL4/1).
334 Clun Guardians' Mins 1844–5 (Salop RO PL6/23); plans (Salop RO PL6/112).
335 *The Builder*, 22 Nov 1851, front leaf; 4 Oct 1851, 625.
336 Signed plans (Salop RO PL9/2/1–4).
337 Madeley Guardians' Mins 1870 (Salop RO PL10/7).
338 Newport Guardians' Mins 1855 (Salop RO PL11/106).
339 Colvin 1995, 783.
340 Wellington Guardians' Mins 1874–5 (Salop RO PL14/19).
341 Wem Guardians' Mins 1837 (Salop RO PL15/1).

342 Stylistic attribution.
343 Colvin 1995, 577.
344 Bedminster Guardians' Mins 1837 (Som RO D/G/BD 8a/2).
345 Bridgwater Guardians' Mins 1836 (Som RO D/G/BW 8a/1).
346 Chard Guardians' Mins 1836 (Som RO D/G/CH 8a/1a).
347 Clutton Guardians' Mins 1836 (Som RO D/G/CL 8a/1). This workhouse has been attributed to Scott and Moffatt (Cole, D 1980, 186).
348 Dulverton Guardians' Mins 1854 (Som RO D/G/D 8a/3); specifications and plans of May 1854 (Som RO D/G/D 32/1–2 and 57/12/1).
349 Frome Guardians' Mins 1836 (Som RO D/G/F 8a/1).
350 Keynsham Guardians' Mins 1836–7 (Som RO D/G/K 8a/1).
351 Shepton Mallet Guardians' Mins 1836 (Som RO D/G/SM 8a/1); signed plans dated Jan 1836 (Som RO D/G/SM 35/5). Colvin (1995, 1015) attributed the workhouse to Wainwright, who in fact made a small addition in 1871.
352 Taunton Guardians' Mins 1836 (Som RO D/G/TA 8A/1).
353 Wellington Guardians' Mins 1836 (Som RO D/G/W 8A/1); plans dated 1836 (Som RO D/G/W 32/2).
354 Wells Guardians' Mins 1836 (Som RO D/G/WE 8a/1); signed plans dated 1836 (Som RO D/G/WE 32/1–3). Colvin (1995, 1015) attributes the workhouse to Wainwright.
355 Williton Guardians' Mins 1836 (Som RO D/G/WI 8a/1); signed plans dated 1837 (Som RO D/G/WI 32/2).
356 Wincanton Guardians' Mins 1836 (Som RO D/G/WN 8a/1).
357 Yeovil Guardians' Mins 1836 (Som RO D/G/Y 8a/1).
358 *The Building News*, 31 Oct 1884, 722.
359 Ibid, 10 Dec 1880, 687.
360 Leek Guardians' Mins 1838 (Staffs RO D699/1/1/1).
361 Dickens 1982, 138.
362 Newcastle-under-Lyne Guardians' Mins 1838 (Staffs RO D 02/1/1–9; D 339/1/1).
363 Seisdon Guardians' Mins 1858 (Staffs RO D 3268/Add).
364 Stafford Guardians' Mins 1837 (Staffs RO D 659/1/1/1).
365 Baker 1984, 19.
366 Stone Guardians' Mins 1792 (Staffs RO D 255/2/1–2).
367 Tamworth Guardians' Mins (Staffs RO 459/A/G/54).
368 Colvin (1995, 995) attributed this workhouse to Thomas Trubshaw. A pencil sketch by Trubshaw is dated 1838 and may have been part of a competition entry (RIBA Drawings Collection K5/82). The builders' contract names Scott and Moffatt as the architects (Staffs RO D/686/1).
369 Walsall Guardians' Mins 1837 (Walsall Archives, 393/67).
370 VCH 1976, *Staffs XVII*, 45.
371 *The Builder*, 5 Jan 1856, front leaf.
372 Wolstanton & Burslem Guardians' Mins 1838 (Staffs RO 3506/11).
373 Stylistic attribution.
374 *The Builder*, 2 Sept 1899, 229.
375 Ibid, 14 Jul 1888, 30.
376 Colvin 1995, 383.
377 Bury St Edmunds Guardians' Mins 1841 (Suffolk RO DC 1/1/1).
378 Colvin 1978, 540 (not in Colvin 1995).
379 *The Builder*, 13 Oct 1916, 232.
380 Colvin 1978, 540 (not in Colvin 1995).
381 *The Building News*, 3 Aug 1895, 87; 21 Jul 1899.
382 Colvin 1978, 145 (not in Colvin 1995).
383 Ibid.
384 Pevsner 1974, 312.
385 Colvin 1995, 383.
386 Colvin 1978, 145 (not in Colvin 1995).
387 Goodwyn 1987, 13. A plan by John Redgrave had initially been accepted.
388 Colvin 1995, 588.
389 Chertsey Guardians' Mins 1835–6 (Surr RO BG1/11/1).
390 *The Builder*, 10 Jun 1865, 416.
391 Ibid, 23 Apr 1881, 525.
392 Dorking Guardians' Mins 1838 (Surr RO BG2/11/1).
393 Epsom Guardians' Mins 1836 (Surr RO BG3/11/1).
394 Godstone Guardians' Mins 1838–9 (Surr RO BG5/11/2).
395 Guildford Guardians' Mins 1836 (Surr RO BG6/11/1).
396 Broome 1930; *Kingston Hospital 150th Annual Report*, 1993, 5.
397 Battle Guardians' Mins 1840 (E Suss RO G1/1a/2).
398 Signed drawings, 1864 (E Suss RO HB103/1(1–8)).
399 Chailey Guardians' Mins 1871 (E Suss RO G2/1a/4).
400 Cuckfield Guardians' Mins 1843 (W Suss RO G3/1a/4).
401 East Grinstead Guardians' Mins 1859 (W Suss RO G4/1a/5).
402 East Preston Guardians' Mins 1872 (W Suss RO EWG9/1/1); set of plans, signed and dated 1872 (WG9/56/2 (1–4)).
403 Hastings Guardians' Mins 1836 (E Suss RO RC/18/1). Kempthorne is named as the architect, but Voysey acted as his 'agent' and prepared the plans and specifications.
404 Plans dated 1899 and signed by Jeffrey and Skiller (E Suss RO HH77/8 and 9).
405 Horsham Guardians' Mins 1838 (W Suss RO WG6/1/2).
406 Lewes Guardians' Mins 1867 and 1868 (E Suss RO G6/1a/9).
407 Newhaven Guardians' Mins 1835 (E Suss RO G7/1a/1).
408 Rye Guardians' Mins 1843 (E Suss RO G8/1a/5).
409 Steyning Guardians' Mins 1836 (E Suss RO G9/1a/1).
410 *Steyning Union, Sussex. New Workhouse at Kingston, Shoreham (near Brighton)* (E Suss RO HW 70/1).
411 Thakeham Union Mins and Account Book, 1788–91, 51–6 (W Suss RO).
412 Colvin 1995, 577 and Dickens 1982, 102, attributed the workhouse to Kempthorne. E Suss RO Catalogue to Guardians' Records ascribes it to H E Kendall.
413 Uckfield Guardians' Mins 1837 (E Suss RO G11/1a/1); signed elevation and section, dated Nov 1837 in catalogue (R/S6/1). Kendall succeeded Whichcord as architect to the Uckfield board.
414 Aston Guardians' Mins 1865 (Birmingham Central Library Press F1).
415 Foundation stone.
416 *The Builder*, 6 Oct 1849, 474. An earlier competition was won by Mr Hemming (*The Builder*, 10 Feb 1849, 68).
417 Foleshill Guardians' Mins 1858 (Coventry Archives FU/PL/1/4). An initial design by Joseph Neville was abandoned when tenders proved too high.
418 Southam Guardians' Mins 1836 (Warws RO CR51/1388).
419 Stratford-upon-Avon Guardians' Mins 1836 (Shakespeare Birthplace Trust RO DR 252/1).
420 Warwick Guardians' Mins 1837 (Warws RO CR51/1581).
421 Colvin 1995, 1033.
422 Alderbury Guardians' Mins 1836 (Wilts RO H1/110/1); drawings (Wilts RO H1/190/3).
423 Alderbury Guardians' Mins 1876 (Wilts RO H1 110/18). Henry Hall took over from Nicholls in May 1878 (Wilts RO H1 110/19).
424 Stamp (ed) 1995, 80; Amesbury Guardians' Mins 1836 (Wilts RO H2/110/1).
425 Calne Guardians' Mins 1846 (Wilts RO H4/110/4).
426 Chippenham Guardians' Mins 1857 (Wilts RO H5/110/11).
427 Slocombe 1996, 104.
428 Devizes Guardians' Mins 1836 (Wilts RO H7/110/1).
429 Highworth and Swindon Guardians' Mins 1845 (Wilts RO H8/110/4).
430 Malmesbury Guardians' Mins 1836 (Wilts RO H9/110/1).
431 The architect is named on a plaque on the façade; Slocombe 1996, 31.
432 Mere Guardians' Mins 1836–8 (Wilts RO H12/110/1).
433 Slocombe 1996, 31.
434 Tisbury Guardians' Mins 1869 (Wilts RO H14 110/12).
435 Trowbridge and Melksham Guardians' Mins 1837 (Wilts RO H11/110/1).
436 Warminster Guardians' Mins 1836 (Wilts RO H15/110/1).
437 Westbury and Whorwellsdown Guardians' Mins 1836 (Wilts RO H16/110/1).
438 Wilton Guardians' Mins 1836 (Wilts RO H17/110/1). A plan by T L Evans was selected at first.
439 Bromsgrove Guardians' Mins 1837 (Worcs RO 251/400/1).
440 Droitwich Guardians' Mins 1836 (Worcs RO 251/401/1).
441 *The Builder*, 26 May 1855, 251.
442 Colvin 1995, 768.
443 Kidderminster Guardians' Mins 1837 (Worcs RO b251/403/1).
444 King's Norton Guardians' Mins 1868 (Birmingham Central Library Press F15).
445 Colvin 1995, 577.
446 Pershore Guardians' Mins 1836 (Worcs RO 251/409/1).
447 Plans (Staffs RO D 585 A/G 32); Stourbridge Guardians' Mins (Staffs RO D 585/8a).
448 *The Builder*, 30 May 1903, 578.
449 Tenbury Guardians' Mins 1836 (Worcs RO b251/413/1).
450 Upton-on-Severn Guardians' Mins 1836 (Worcs RO 251/414/1).
451 Green 1796, 13.
452 *The Builder*, 7 Sept 1860, 700.
453 Ibid, 10 Nov 1866, 840.
454 Bedale Guardians' Mins 18 May 1839, state that Bedale workhouse followed the internal arrangements of Howden (N Yorks RO MIC 3165).
455 *The Builder*, 7 Jun 1851, 360.
456 Ibid, 8 Nov 1851, front leaf.
457 VCH 1969, *Yorks E Riding* I, 440.
458 Signed drawings seen at site.
459 *The Builder*, 1 Apr 1848, front leaf.
460 Bedale Guardians' Mins 1839 (N Yorks RO MIC 3165).
461 Signed plan (Cleveland Co Archives ZAR 1).
462 Helmsley Guardians' Mins 1859 (N Yorks RO MIC 1821).
463 *The Builder*, 15 Sept 1849, front leaf; signed

plans (present location not known).
464 Signed plans for the new Leyburn Union Workhouse (N Yorks RO MIC 3070).
465 *The Building News*, 12 May 1876, 466.
466 Northallerton Guardians' Mins (N Yorks RO MIC 1014).
467 Richmond Guardians' Mins 1841 (N Yorks RO MIC 1366). Plans for the work are identified 'Durham 1841' (MIC 963).
468 *The Builder*, 6 Aug 1858, 805; Scarborough Guardians' Mins 1858 (N Yorks RO MIC 583).
469 *The Builder*, 8 Mar 1851, 161.
470 Ibid, 14 Jun 1851, 379.
471 Ibid, 9 Aug 1912, 192.
472 *The Hospital*, 23 Jul 1904, 301.
473 *The Builder*, 8 Jul 1871, 524.
474 Ibid, 3 Mar 1855, 102.
475 Ibid, 27 Jun 1896, 557.
476 Flett 1984, 6–7.
477 *The Builder*, 17 Oct 1903, 390–1.
478 Stylistic attribution.
479 *The Builder*, 13 Apr 1901, 374.
480 Ibid, 4 Jul 1863, 484.
481 Huddersfield Guardians' Mins 1868 (W Yorks Archive Service).
482 Huddersfield Guardians' Mins 1860 (W Yorks Archive Service).
483 *The Builder*, 7 Jan 1899, 23.
484 Knaresborough Guardians' Mins 1856 (N Yorks RO MIC 1647).
485 Joseph Thompson won the competition (Harper 1983, 76) but Perkin and Backhouse are named on an engraving of the building published *c* 1847.
486 *The Builder*, 13 Mar 1858, 183.
487 *The Builder*, 24 Mar 1855, 143.
488 Pateley Bridge Guardians' Mins 1862 (N Yorks RO MIC 1906).
489 *The Builder*, 9 Apr 1859, 252.
490 Ripon Guardians' Mins 1853 (N Yorks RO MIC 2483).
491 *The Building News*, 29 Nov 1889, 752.
492 P Speck *et al* 1978, 6.
493 *The Builder*, 9 Aug 1851, front leaf.
494 Ibid, 9 May 1863, 340.
495 Ibid, 16 Dec 1871, 994.
496 Ibid, 30 Mar 1850, 153.

Appendix 2/Catalogue B

1 Bethnal Green Guardians' Mins 1840 (LMA Be.BG.5).
2 *The Building News*, 10 May 1889, 671.
3 *The Builder*, 10 Mar 1900, 243.
4 Ibid, 17 Nov 1877, 1162.
5 *The Building News*, 30 Jan 1891, 185.
6 Chelsea Guardians' Mins 1843 (LMA Ch.BG.2).
7 *The Builder*, 7 Sept 1872, 714.
8 Chelsea Guardians' Mins 22 Aug 1888, 248 and 8 Feb 1893, 341 (LMA Ch.BG.34 and Ch.BG.37).
9 *The Builder*, 11 Aug 1849, 378.
10 Ibid, 1 Jul 1893, 21.
11 Ibid, 17 Mar 1849, 131.
12 Browne 1844.
13 *The Builder*, 3 Jun 1899, 554.
14 Ibid, 1 Nov 1902, 399.
15 Ibid, 4 Dec 1914, 540.
16 PRO MH14/12.
17 *Builder's Journal and Architectural Record*, 29 Mar 1905, 163.
18 *The Builder*, 9 Dec 1905, 622.
19 Statutory lists of buildings of architectural or historic interest.
20 *The Builder*, 7 Sept 1901, 217–18.
21 Ibid, 1 Mar 1879, 227.
22 Ibid, 23 Oct 1886, 588.
23 Harper 1983, 90.
24 *The Builder*, 12 Jun 1869, 464–7.
25 Ibid, 4 Aug 1900, 112–13.
26 Survey of London XXXVIII, 1975, 27.
27 Kensington Guardians' Mins 1 Sept 1846, f 21 (LMA K.BG.10).
28 *The Builder*, 16 Apr 1887, 585.
29 Ibid, 24 Jan 1874, 70.
30 Ibid, 6 Oct 1877, 1004.
31 Cleminson 1983, 10.
32 Survey of London XLIII, 1994, 79.
33 *The Building News*, 26 Mar 1869, 282; signed plans (LMA Po.BG.283).
34 Unpublished history of the school, viewed on site.
35 Westminster City Archives, C766a, D766; Survey of London XL, 1980, 316.
36 Survey of London XL, 1980, 316.
37 *The Builder*, 2 Mar 1878, 227.
38 Inf from English Heritage.
39 *The Builder*, 31 Aug 1878, 924.
40 PRO MH14/31.
41 *The Builder*, 29 Jan 1870, 89.
42 St Martin-in-the-Fields Parish Mins 1770 (Westminster City Archives F4102).
43 *The Building News*, 9 Dec 1898, 823.
44 *The Builder*, 19 Mar 1881, 354.
45 Ibid, 10 Jun 1876, 386.
46 Ibid, 21 Jul 1900, 56–7.
47 Freeman 1904, 55
48 Colvin 1995, 460.
49 *The Builder*, 9 Jan 1869, 28.
50 Ibid, 28 Mar 1868, 234.
51 Colvin 1995, 74.
52 *The Builder*, 7 Mar 1885, 363.
53 Inf from English Heritage.
54 *The Builder*, 13 Jul 1861, 488.
55 Kelly 1906, 500.
56 Wandsworth & Clapham Guardians' Mins 1838 (LMA Wa.BG.3).
57 *The Builder*, 16 Oct 1886, 580.
58 Ibid, 9 Jan 1909, 45.
59 Ibid, 3 Dec 1864, 881–3.
60 Survey of London XXXI, 1963, 211 (Ludby), 213 (Lee).
61 Inf from Battersea Local History Library.
62 Survey of London XLII, 1986, 347.
63 PRO MH14/37.
64 Woolwich Guardians' Mins 1869 (LMA Wo.BG.2).
65 *Illustrated London News*, 2 Dec 1871, 537.
66 *The Builder*, 1 Jun 1895, 404.
67 CLSD Mins 1855 (LMA CLSD 2).
68 A competition for a school was won by Peck in 1868 (*The Builder*, 29 Aug 1868, 640).
69 KCSD Mins 1876–80 (LMA KCSD 1); signed and dated plans (LMA KCSD 354–91).
70 Signed and dated plans 1882 (LMA KCSD 392–401).
71 NSSD Mins 1849 (LMA NSSD 1).
72 SMSD Mins 1850 (LMA SMSD 1).
73 SMSD Mins 1882 (LMA SMSD 16).
74 WLSD Mins 1868 (LMA WLSD1).
75 *The Builder*, 4 Aug 1894, 86.
76 Ibid, 2 Jan 1869, 5.
77 Ibid, 4 Nov 1893, 342–3.
78 Ibid, 2 Oct 1897, 258.
79 Ibid, 7 Apr 1900, 359.
80 See NMR file no. 101210.
81 *The Builder*, 2 Jan 1869, 5.
82 See NMR file no. 102782.
83 *The Builder*, 4 Oct 1884, 477.
84 See NMR file no. 101209.
85 *The Builder*, 17 Jul 1897, 47–9.
86 See NMR file no. 102776.
87 *The Builder*, 23 Nov 1901, 470.
88 Ibid, 2 Jan 1869, 5
89 Mins of the Metropolitan Asylums District 1876 (LMA History Library).
90 See NMR file no. 102761.
91 *The Building News*, 5 Nov 1875, 504.
92 *The Builder*, 21 Mar 1868, 214.
93 Ibid, 21 Mar 1868, 214.
94 Ibid, 28 Oct 1899, 395.
95 Ibid, 10 Jun 1899, 573.
96 Ibid, 22 Jul 1899, 84.

Bibliography
The list below contains works cited in the text and notes and further reading.

Published Works

Ackermann, Rudolph 1808–10. *The Microcosm of London, or London in Miniature*

Alcock, Thomas 1752. *Observations on the defects of the poor laws and on the causes and consequences of the great increase and burden of the poor, with a proposal for redressing these grievances*

Anderson, Philip 1981. 'The Leeds Workhouse under the Old Poor Law: 1726–1834'. *Thoresby Society* **LVI**, Part 2, 75–113

Anon 1686. *An Account of the General Nursery or Colledg of Infants set up by the Justices of the Peace for the County of Middlesex*

Anon 1702. *A Short Account of the Workhouse belonging to the President and Governours for the Poor, in Bishopsgate Street, London*

Anon 1725. *A Case of the Parish of St Giles-in-the-Fields, As to their Poor, And a Workhouse designed to be built for Employing them*

Anon (Christian Love-Poor) 1731. *The Workhouse Cruelty: Workhouses turned Gaols and Gaolers turned Executioners*

Anon (Charles Gray, MP for Colchester) 1751. *Considerations on Several Proposals, lately made, for the Better Maintenance of the Poor*

Anon 1773. *Considerations on the Present State of the Poor*

Anon 1786. *An Account of the Workhouses in Great Britain in the Year MDCCXXXII* (first published 1725; 2nd edn 1732; reprinted with a new preface 1786)

Anon *c* 1852. *The Strand Union Pauper Children at Edmonton: A Statement of Facts*

Anon 1888. *A Walk Through the Public Institutions of Macclesfield* (articles reprinted from *The Macclesfield Courier and Herald*)

Anon 1908. Willesden Workhouse, *Order of Ceremony*

Anon 1966. *A Short History of Clatterbridge Hospitals*

Anstey, Christine 1978. A History of the Southampton Technical College (typescript)

Anstruther, I 1973. *The Scandal of Andover Workhouse*

Ayers, G M 1971. *England's First State Hospitals, 1867–1930*

Baker, Diane 1984. *Workhouses in the Potteries*

Barwell, John 1994. *A Victorian Workhouse*

Baxter, G R Wythen 1841. *The Book of the Bastilles or the History of the Working of the New Poor Law*

Becher, Revd John Thomas 1828. *The Anti-Pauper System, Exemplifying the Positive and Practical Good realised by the Relievers and the Relieved under the Frugal, Beneficial and Lawful Administration of the Poor Laws Prevailing at Southwell*

1834. *The Anti-Pauper System* (2nd edn)

Bentham, Jeremy 1791. *Panopticon; Or the Inspection House*

1798. *Outline of a Work entitled Pauper Management Improved*

Bentham, Neil 1993. The Workhouse Buildings of the New Poor Law in the South-West of England (PhD thesis, University of Brighton)

Bestall, J M and Fowkes, D V 1979. *History of Chesterfield*

Blaug, M 1963. 'The myth of the Old Poor Law and the making of the New'. *Journal of Economic History* **XXIII**, 151–84

1964. 'The Poor Law Report re-examined'. *Journal of Economic History* **XXIV**, 229–45

Blease, W L 1910. 'The Poor Law in Liverpool, 1681–1834'. *Transactions of the Historical Society of Lancashire and Cheshire* **61**, ns, 25, 97–182

Booth, Charles 1892. *Pauperism and the Endowment of Old Age*

1894. *The Aged Poor in England*

Bosworth, Revd J 1824. *The Practical means of reducing the Poor's Rate, Encouraging Virtue and Increasing the Comforts of the Aged, Afflicted and Deserving Poor as well as Repressing Able-Bodied Pauperism by a Proper Application of the Existing Laws Respecting Select Vestries, and Incorporated Houses of Industry*

Bowen, John 1842. *The Union Workhouse and Board of Guardians System as worked under the control of Poor-Law Commissioners; exemplified by official documents and plans, with an address to Sir Robert Peel*

Bradbury, J Bernard 1981. *A History of Cockermouth*

Braddon, Lawrence 1721. *A Proposal for Relieving, Reforming and Employing all the Poor of Great Britain*

Brereton, Revd C D 1823. *An Inquiry into the Workhouse System and the Law of Maintenance in Agricultural Districts*

The British Almanac (Companion to the Almanac), 1836, 234–6

Broome, Herbert 1930. *Kingston Union: The Beginning and the End, 1836–1930*

Browne, R P 1844. 'Greenwich Union Poorhouse'. *Weale's Quarterly Papers on Architecture* **I**, 1–7

Burn, Richard 1764. *The History of the Poor Laws with Observations*

Bush, Rice 1649. *The Poor Mans Friend, or A Narrative of what progresse many worthy Citizens of London have made in that Godly Work of providing for the Poor* (Guildhall Library Pamphlet 4706)

Butcher, E (ed) 1932. *Bristol Corporation of the Poor, 1696–1834* (Bristol Record Society, 3)

Caplan, M 1970. 'The Poor Laws in Nottinghamshire, 1836–1871'. *Transactions of the Thoroton Society* **74**, 82–98

1984. *In the Shadow of the Workhouse*

Capper, Revd Daniel 1834. *Practical Results of the Workhouse System as adopted in the Parish of Great Missenden*

Cary, John 1700. *An Account of the Proceedings of the Corporation of Bristol in Execution of the Act of Parliament for the better Employing and Maintaining the Poor of that City*

Chance, W 1897. *Children under the Poor Law*

Checkland, S G and Checkland, E O A, (eds), 1974. *The Poor Law Report of 1834*

Child, Sir Josiah *c* 1670. *Proposals for the Relief of the Poor*

1693. *New Discourse on Trade* (first published 1669)

Clarke, G (ed) 1987. *John Bellers, His Life, Times and Writings*

Claydon, Rosemary 1991. *The Story of the Royal Liverpool Children's Hospital*

Cleminson, F 1983. *Beyond Recall*

Coates, C 1802. *The History and Antiquities of Reading*

Cockburn, Elizabeth 1972. 'The Cerne Abbas Union Workhouse, 1835–1838'. *Proceedings of Dorset Natural History and Archaeological Society* **94**, 89–94

Cole, David 1980. *The Work of Sir Gilbert Scott*

Cole, John 1984. *Down Poorhouse Lane. The Diary of a Rochdale Workhouse*

Collins, D 1965. 'The introduction of old-age pensions in Great Britain'. *Historical Journal* **VIII**, 246–59

Colvin, Howard 1978. *A Biographical Dictionary of British Architects, 1600–1840* (first published 1954)

1995. *A Biographical Dictionary of British Architects, 1600–1840* (3rd edn)

Cooper, Samuel 1763. *Definitions and Axioms relative to charity, charitable institutions and the poor laws*

Corfield, John 1990. 'Buntingford and the Poor Law (Amendment) Act 1834. I. The building of the Union workhouse'. *Hertfordshire's Past* **28**, Spring, 11–19

Cowell, John W 1834. *A Letter to the Rev. John T. Becher of Southwell in reply to certain Charges and Assertions made in the Introduction to the second edition of his Anti-Pauper System, recently published*

Crabbe, George 1810. *The Borough: A Poem in Twenty-Four Letters*

Craven, C 1887. *A Night in the Workhouse*

Crowther, M A 1978. 'The later years of the workhouse, 1890–1929'. In Pat Thane (ed), *The Origins of British Social Policy*, 36–55

1981. *The Workhouse System, 1834–1929: The History of an English Social Institution*

Dangerfield, M E, Marshall, O, Stringer, E R and Welch, V E 1938. 'Chichester Workhouse'. *Sussex Archaeological Collections* **79**, 131–67.

Defoe, Daniel 1704. *Giving Alms No Charity and Employing the Poor a Grievance to the Nation*

Dickens, A M 1976. 'The architect and the workhouse'. *Architectural Review* **CLX**, No. 958, 345–52

1982. Architects and the Union workhouses of the New Poor Law (PhD thesis, Brighton Polytechnic)

Digby, A 1978. *Pauper Palaces*

1982. *The Poor Law in Nineteenth-Century England and Wales*

Doré, G 1872. *London*

Driver, F 1993. *Power and Pauperism: The Workhouse System, 1834–1884*

Dunning, Richard 1686. *A Plain and Easie Method*

Eden, Sir Frederick Morton 1797. *The State of the Poor or a History of the Labouring Classes in England from the Conquest to the Present Period* (3 vols)
Edsall, Nicholas C 1971. *The Anti-Poor Law Movement 1834–1844*
Elliott, Nancy 1985. *Dore Workhouse in Victorian Times*
Evans, R, 1971. 'Bentham's Panopticon. An incident in the social history of architecture'. *Architectural Association Quarterly* **3**, No. 2, April/July 21–37
—— 1982. *The Fabrication of Virtue: English Prison Architecture, 1750–1840*

Fearn, H 1958. 'The financing of the Poor-Law Incorporation for the Hundreds of Colneis and Carlford in the County of Suffolk, 1758–1820'. *Proceedings of the Suffolk Institute of Archaeology* **27**, 96–111
Fielding, Henry 1753. *Proposal for Making an Effectual Provision for the Poor, for amending their Morals and for Rendering them useful Members of the Society, to which is added a Plan of the Buildings proposed, with proper elevations, drawn by an Eminent Hand*
Firmin, Thomas 1678. *Some Proposals for the Imploying of the Poor, Especially in and about the City of London and For the Prevention of Begging, a practice so dishonourable to the Nation and to the Christian Religion*
—— 1681. *Some Proposals for the imployment of the Poor and For the prevention of Idleness and the Consequences thereof, Begging, A Practice so dishonourable to the Nation, and to the Christian religion*
Fletcher, J 1851. 'Statistics of the Farm School System of the Continent and of its applicability to the Preventive and Reformatory Education of Pauper and Criminal Children'. Statistical Society of London
Flett, Joan 1984. *The Story of the Workhouse and the Hospital at Nether Edge*
Francis, Henry James 1930. *A History of Hinckley*
Fraser, D (ed) 1976. *The New Poor Law in the Nineteenth Century*
Freeman, A C 1904. *Hints on the Planning of Poor Law Buildings and Mortuaries*

Gibson, J et al 1993. *Poor Law Union Records. Part 1, South-East England and East Anglia; Part 2, The Midlands and Northern England; Part 3, South-West England, the Marches and Wales* (Federation of Family History Societies)
Gilbert, Christopher 1991. *English Vernacular Furniture 1750–1900*
Gilbert, Thomas 1786. *A Plan of Police exhibiting the Causes of the present Increase of the Poor and proposing a mode for their future more oeconomical and effectual relief and Support with Objections to the Plan stated and answered and General Observations respecting the Expediency and Practicability of the Whole*
—— 1787 (1). *Heads of a Bill for the Better Relief and Employment of the Poor and for the Improvement of the Police of this Country, With a Supplement submitted to the Consideration of the Members of both Houses of Parliament*
—— 1787 (2). *Considerations on the Bills for the Better Relief and Employment of the Poor, etc., Intended to be offered to Parliament this session*
Gillingwater, Edmund 1786. *An Essay on Parish Workhouses containing observations on the present state of English workhouses with some regulations proposed for their improvement*
Gooch, Janet 1980. *A History of Brighton General Hospital*
Goodwyn, E A 1987. *'A Prison with a Milder Name'. The Shipmeadow House of Industry, 1766–1800*
Gould, Michael H 1983. *The Workhouses of Ulster*
Graham, M 1974. 'The Chase Farm Schools'. *Edmonton Hundred Historical Society*, Occasional Paper New Series No. 28
Gray, Charles (MP for Colchester) 1751. *Considerations on Several Proposals lately made for the better maintenance of the poor*
Green, Valentine 1796. *History and Antiquities of the City and Suburbs of Worcester*. Vol II
Grey, P 1972, 'Parish workhouses and poorhouses'. *The Local Historian* **10**, No. 2, 70–5
Grounds, W M 1968. 'Old Billericay workhouse'. *Essex Journal* **3**, No. 4, 218–22
Guilding, J M (ed) 1892. *Reading Records. Diary of the Corporation. Vol I, Henry VI to Elizabeth (1431–1602)*
Gutchen, Robert M 1984. 'The diary of Benjamin Woodcock, master of the Barnet Union workhouse, 1836–1838'. In P Kingsford and A Jones (eds), *Down and Out in Hertfordshire*, 7–97

Hadley, George 1788. *A New and Complete History of the town and county of the Town of Kingston-upon-Hull*
Hains, Richard 1679. *Proposals for promoting the Woollen Manufacture*
Hale, Matthew 1683 (written c 1660). *Discourse touching Provision for the Poor*
Hampson, E 1934. *The Treatment of Poverty in Cambridgeshire 1597–1834*
Harper, Roger H 1983. *Victorian Architectural Competitions. An Index to British and Irish Architectural Competitions in* The Builder *1843–1900*
Hart, Dr Ernest 1866. 'Metropolitan infirmaries for the pauper sick'. *Fortnightly Review* **IV**, 15 Feb 1866 to 1 May 1866, 459–63
Hartlib, S 1649. *Londons Charitie Stilling the Poor Orphans Cry, Providing places and provision, by the care and indeavour of the Corporation appointed by the Parliament*
Hastings, R P 1981. *Essays in North Riding History*
—— 1983. *More Essays in North Riding History*
Hay, William (MP) 1735. *Remarks on the Laws Relating to the Poor; with Proposals for their Better Relief and Employment* (repr 1751)
Head, Sir F 1835. *English Charity*
Hill, Florence Davenport 1868. *Children of the State*
Hillier, B and Hanson, J 1984. *The Social Logic of Space*
Hitchcock, T V 1985. *The English Workhouse: A Study in Institutional Poor Relief in Selected Counties, 1696–1750* (DPhil thesis, Oxford University)
—— 1987. *Richard Hutton's Complaints Book* (London Record Society 24)
Hodgkinson, Ruth 1966. 'Provision for pauper lunatics 1834–1871'. *Medical History* 10, 138–54
—— 1967. *The Origins of the National Health Service*
Howard, J 1777. *The State of the Prisons in England and Wales*
Hughes, E 1836. *A Compendium of the Operation of the Poor Law Amendment Act, with some Practical Observations on its Present Results and Future Apparent Usefulness*
Hutton, W 1791. *The History of Derby from the Remote Ages of Antiquity to the Year MDCCXCI*
Huzel, James P 1969. 'Malthus, the Poor Law, and population in early nineteenth-century England'. *Economic History Review*, 2nd ser, **XXIII**, 3, 430–52

Innes, J 1987. 'Prisons for the poor: English Bridewells 1555–1800'. In F Snyder and D Hay (eds), *Labour, Law and Crime. An Historical Perspective*, 42–122

Jeffries, M and Lee, J A 1986. *The Hospitals of Southend*
John, Owen nd (c 1946). *A Little Hospital in Wartime*

Kelly 1856. *Kelly's Directory of Devon*
—— 1883. *Kelly's Directory of Oxfordshire*
—— 1903. *Kelly's Directory of Oxfordshire*
—— 1906. *Kelly's Directory of Essex*
—— 1937. *Kelly's Directory of Lincolnshire*
Knight & Co 1889. *Knight's Guide to the Arrangement and Construction of Workhouse Buildings, with notes and diagrams of the Requirements and Recommendations of the Local Government Board in regard to the Erection of Poor Law Institutions*

Lansberry, H C F 1984. 'The Blean Bastile: Blean Poor Law Union, 1835–46'. In K H McKintosh and H E Gough (eds), *Hoath and Herne – The Last of the Forset*, 108–12
Leonard, E M 1900. *The Early History of English Poor Relief*
Leighfield, E J 1978. *The History of St Michael's Hospital, Lichfield*
Longmate, N 1974. *The Workhouse*
Loudon 1834–9. *John Claudius Loudon's Architectural Magazine and Journal of Improvement in Architecture, Building, and Furnishing, and in the Various Arts and Trades connected therewith* (5 vols)

McClure, R K 1981. *Coram's Children: The London Foundling Hospital in the Eighteenth Century*
Macfarlane, S 1986. 'Social policy and the poor in the later seventeenth century'. In A L Beier and R Finlay (eds), *London 1500–1700: The Making of the Metropolis*, 252–77
Mackay, T 1898 *A History of the English Poor Law from 1834 to the Present Time* (Vol III of *History of the English Poor Law* – see Nicholls 1898)
Man, John 1816. *The History and Antiquities, Ancient and Modern, of the Borough of Reading, in the County of Berks*
Markus, Thomas A 1954. 'Pattern of the law'. *Architectural Review* **116**, No. 694, 251–6

1993. *Buildings and Power. Freedom and Control in the Origin of Modern Building Types*
Marshall, Dorothy 1926. *The English Poor in the Eighteenth Century*
Marshall, J D 1985. *The Old Poor Law, 1795–1834* (rev 2nd edn; 1st edn 1968)
Melling, Elizabeth 1964. *Kentish Sources. Vol IV: The Poor*
Ministry of Health 1945–6. *Hospital Survey*
Monnington, W, and Lampard, F J 1898. *Our London Poor Law Schools*
Morrison, Kathryn 1997. 'The New-Poor-Law Workhouses of George Gilbert Scott and William Bonython Moffatt', *Architectural History* **40**, 184–203
1998. 'Cottage Home Villages'. *Transactions of the Ancient Monuments Society*, **42**, 81–102
Mouat, F J and Snell, H S 1883. *Hospital Construction and Management*

Neate, A R 1967. *St Marylebone Workhouse and Institution 1730–1965*
Newman, Sue 1994. *The Christchurch and Bournemouth Union Workhouse*
Nicholls, G. 1822. *Eight Letters on the Management of our Poor and the general Administration of the poor Laws in the two Parishes of Southwell and Bingham*
1898. *A History of the English Poor Law* (vols I & II by Nicholls first published 1854, rev edn 1898; vol III by T Mackay, 1898. Reprinted 1967)
Nicholson, D C 1986. 'Tonbridge Union 1836–1986: Pembury Hospital'. *Pembury Contact*, 8 October

O'Donnell, Roderick 1978. 'W J Donthorn (1799–1859): architecture with "great hardness and decision in the edges"', *Architectural History* **21**, 83–92
O'Donoghue, E G 1923. *Bridewell Hospital. Palace, Prison, Schools*. Vol I
1929. *Bridewell Hospital. Palace, Prison, Schools*. Vol II
OED 1989. *Oxford English Dictionary* (2nd edn)
Oxley, G W 1974. *Poor Relief in England and Wales, 1601–1834*

Pass, Anthony J 1988. *Thomas Worthington: Victorian Architecture and Social Purpose*
Pearl, V 1978. 'Puritans and poor relief: the London workhouse 1649–1660'. In D Pennington and K Thomas (eds), *Puritans and Revolutionaries. Essays presented to Christopher Hill*, 206–32
Pelling, M 1985. 'Healing the poor: Social policy and disability in Norwich, 1550–1640'. *Medical History* **XXIX**, 115–37
Pennock, Pamela M 1986. 'The Evolution of St James's, 1848–94'. *Thoresby Society* **LIX** Part 2 No. 130, 129–76
Pevsner, N 1974. *The Buildings of England. Suffolk* (2nd edn)
Pevsner, N and Wilson, B 1997. *The Buildings of England. Norfolk I: Norwich and North-East*
Phillips, D 1980. *The Story of Reading* (rev edn 1990)
Phillips, T 1779. *The History and Antiquities of Shrewsbury: From its First Foundation to the Present Time*
Poynter, J R 1969. *Society and Pauperism. English Ideas on Poor Relief, 1795–1834*
Preece, P 1983. *Berkshire Old and New* (Berkshire Local History Association **3**)
Priestland, Pamela (ed) 1989. *Radcliffe-on-Trent 1837–1920. A Study of a Village during an Era of Change*
Pugin, A W N 1841. *Contrasts: Or a Parallel between the Noble Edifices of the Middle Ages and Corresponding Buildings of the Present Day; Shewing the Present Decay of Taste* (2nd edn)

Ransome, M 1948. 'The parliamentary career of Sir Humphrey Mackworth 1701–13'. *University of Birmingham Historical Journal* **1**, 232–54
Redford, A and Russell, I S 1939. *The History of Local Government in Manchester*
Reid, Andy 1994. *The Union Workhouse, A Study Guide for Teachers and Local Historians*
Richardson, Harriet (ed) 1998. *English Hospitals 1660–1948. A Survey of their Architecture and Design*
Richardson, Ruth and Hurwitz, Brian 1989. 'Joseph Rogers and the reform of workhouse medicine'. *British Medical Journal* **299**, 1507–10
Rose, Michael E. 1985. *The Poor and the City: The English Poor Law in its Urban Context, 1834–1914*
1986. *The Relief of Poverty 1834–1914* (rev 2nd edn)
RCHME 1970. *An Inventory of Historical Monuments in the County of Dorset. Vol II. South-East. Part II*
Ruggles, Thomas 1797. *The History of the Poor*
Russell, P M G 1976. *A History of the Exeter Hospitals 1170–1948*

Scott, John 1773. *Observations on the State of the Parochial and Vagrant Poor*
Seyer, Samuel 1821. *Memoirs Historical and Topographical of Bristol and its Neighbourhood*
Siggins, G P 1989. *History of West Park Hospital, Macclesfield, 1939–1948*
Slack, Paul 1972. 'Poverty and problems in Salisbury, 1597–1666'. In P Clark and P Slack (eds), *Crisis and Order in English Towns*, 164–203
1988. *Poverty and Policy in Tudor and Stuart England*
Slocombe, 1996. *Architects and Building Craftsmen with Work in Wiltshire*
Smith, Percival Gordon 1901. *Hints and Suggestions as to the Planning of Poor Law Buildings*
Snell, Alfred Saxon 1905. *Opening of the New Infirmary at the Workhouse, Exeter*
Snell, Henry Saxon 1872. *Holborn Union Workhouse Buildings*
1881. *Charitable and Parochial Establishments*
Speck, P 1978. *The Institution and Hospital at Fir Vale: A Centenary of the Northern Hospital*
Stacpoole, John 1971. *William Mason, the First New Zealand Architect*
Stallard, Joshua Harrison 1866. *The Female Casual and her Lodging*
1870. *Pauper Lunatics and their Treatment*
Stamp Gavin (ed) 1995. *Personal and Professional Recollections: The Autobiography of the Victorian Architect Sir George Gilbert Scott*
Stokes, H P 1911. 'Cambridgeshire parish workhouses'. *Proceedings of the Cambridgeshire Antiquarian Society* **15**, 70–123
Survey of London XX, 1940. *Trafalgar Square and Neighbourhood (The Parish of St Martin-in-the-Fields, Part III)*
XXXI, 1963. *The Parish of St James Westminster, Part Two. North of Piccadilly*
XXXIII, 1966. *The Parish of St Anne Soho*
XXXVIII, 1975. *The Museum Area of South Kensington and Westminster*
XL, 1980. *The Grosvenor Estate in Mayfair, Part II. The Buildings*
XLII, 1986. *Southern Kensington: Kensington Square to Earl's Court*
XLIII, 1994. *Poplar, Blackwall and the Isle of Dogs. The Parish of All Saints*

Taverner, R L 1968. 'The administrative work of the Devon Justices in the seventeenth century'. *Reports and Transactions of the Devonshire Association* 100, 55–84
Taylor, Jeremy 1991. *Hospital and Asylum Architecture in England 1840–1914*
Taylor, James S 1972. 'The unreformed workhouse, 1776–1834'. In E W Martin (ed), *Comparative Development in Social Welfare*, 57–84
Thompson, Kathryn M 1980. 'The building of the Leicester Union Workhouse, 1836–39'. In D Williams (ed), *The Adaptation of Change: Essays upon the History of Nineteenth-Century Leicester and Leicestershire*, 59–76
1988. *The Leicester Poor Law Union, 1836–1871* (PhD thesis, University of Leicester)
Turner, J J, 1984. *Guisborough, Middlesbrough and Stockton: Poor Law Union Workhouses, 1837–c 1930. An Introduction* (University of Leeds, Dept of Adult and Continuing Education)
Twining, Louisa 1893. *Recollections of Life and Work*

VCH 1908. *The Victoria History of the County of Dorset. Vol Two*
1924. *The Victoria History of the County of Worcester. Vol Four*
1948. *The Victoria History of the County of Cambridge and The Isle of Ely. Vol Two*
1953. *The Victoria History of the County of Cambridge and The Isle of Ely. Vol Four*
1959. *A History of the County of Cambridge and The Isle of Ely. Vol III. The City and University of Cambridge*
1964. *A History of the County of Warwick. Vol VII. The City of Birmingham*
1969. *A History of the County of York East Riding. Vol I. The City of Kingston upon Hull*
1972. *A History of the County of Gloucester. Vol X*
1976. *A History of the County of Stafford. Vol XVII*
1978. *A History of the County of Essex. Vol VII*
1988. *A History of the County of Gloucester. Vol IV. The City of Gloucester*
1989. *A History of the County of York East Riding. Vol VI. The Borough and Liberties of Beverley*
Verey, David 1979. *The Buildings of England. Gloucestershire I: The Cotswolds*

Vorspan, R 1977. 'Vagrancy and the New Poor Law in Late Victorian and Edwardian England'. *English Historical Review* **XCII**, 59–81

Watson, A F 1981. 'The Chesterfield Poor Law Union, the first 10 years 1837–47'. *Journal of the Bakewell and District Historical Society* **VIII**, January, 10–20

Watts, Brenda and Winyard, Eleanor 1988. *The History of Atherstone*

WEA 1978. *In and Out of the Workhouse*

Weatherly, Lionel A 1904–6. 'Boards of Guardians and the crusade against Consumption'. *Tuberculosis* **3**, January 1904 to January 1906, 66–85

Webb, Sidney and Webb, Beatrice 1906. *English Local Government from the Revolution to the Municipal Corporations Act: The Parish and the County*

   1910. *English Poor Law Policy* (reprinted 1963)

   1927. *English Poor Law History. Part I: The Old Poor Law*

   1929. *English Poor Law History. Part II: The Last 100 Years* (2 vols; references are to the reprint of 1963)

White, R 1978. *Social Change and the Development of the Nursing Profession: A Study of the Poor Law Nursing Service, 1848–1948*

Williams, Karel 1981. *From Pauperism to Poverty*

Wood, Peter 1991. *Poverty and the Workhouse in Victorian Britain*

Young, Arthur 1794. *A General View of the Agriculture of the County of Suffolk*

   1813. *A General View of the Agriculture of the County of Sussex* (2nd edn; facsimile of 1970)

Government Publications

Citations of Select Committees, Royal Commissions, Parliamentary Reports, Returns, etc, are given in full in the references. Below is a complete list of the published full annual reports of the central poor law authorities from 1834 to 1930, giving the page number on which the report starts (the page numbers cited in the notes are those on which the particular information in question appears).

Poor Law Commission (1834–1847)
PP 1835 (500), XXXV, 107 (1st Annual Report of the PLC)
PP 1836 (595), XXIX, 1 (2nd Annual Report of the PLC)
PP 1837 (546), XXXI, 127 (3rd Annual Report of PLC)
PP 1837–8 (447), XXVIII, 145 (4th Annual Report of PLC)
PP 1839 (239), XX, 1 (5th Annual Report of PLC)
PP 1840 (245), XVII, 397 (6th Annual Report of PLC)
PP 1841 (327), XI, 201 (7th Annual Report of PLC)
PP 1842 (389), XIX, 1 (8th Annual Report of PLC)
PP 1843 (468), XXI, 1 (9th Annual Report of PLC)
PP 1844 (560), XIX, 9 (10th Annual Report of PLC)
PP 1845 (624), XXVII, 247 (11th Annual Report of PLC)
PP 1846 (704), XIX, 1 (12th Annual Report of PLC)
PP 1847 (816), XXVIII, 1 (13th Annual Report of PLC)
PP 1847–8 (960), XXXIII, 1 (14th Annual Report of PLC)

Poor Law Board (1847–1868)
PP 1849 (1042), XXV, 1 (1st Annual Report of PLB)
PP 1850 (1142), XXVII, 1 (2nd Annual Report of PLB)
PP 1851 (1340), XXVI, 1 (3rd Annual Report of PLB)
PP 1852 (1461), XXIII, 1 (4th Annual Report of PLB)
PP 1852–3 (1625), L, 1 (5th Annual Report of PLB)
PP 1854 (1797), XXIX, 333 (6th Annual Report of PLB)
PP 1854–5 (1921), XXIV, 1 (7th Annual Report of PLB)
PP 1856 (2088), XXVIII, 1 (8th Annual Report of PLB)
PP 1857 (2241), XXII, 1 (9th Annual Report of PLB)
PP 1857–8 (2402), XXVIII, 1 (10th Annual Report of PLB)
PP 1859 (sess. 1) (2500), IX, 741 (11th Annual Report of PLB)
PP 1860 (2675), XXXVII, 1 (12th Annual Report of PLB)
PP 1861 (2820), XXVIII, 1 (13th Annual Report of PLB)
PP 1862 (3037), XXIV, 1 (14th Annual Report of PLB)
PP 1863 (3197), XXII, 1 (15th Annual Report of PLB)
PP 1864 (3379), XXV, 1 (16th Annual Report of PLB)
PP 1865 (3549), XXII, 1 (17th Annual Report of PLB)
PP 1866 (3700), XXXV, 1 (18th Annual Report of PLB)
PP 1867 (3870), XXXIV, 1 (19th Annual Report of PLB)
PP 1867–8 (4039), XXXIII, 1 (20th Annual Report of PLB)
PP 1868–9 (4197), XXVIII, 1 (21st Annual Report of PLB)
PP 1870 (c.123), XXXV, 1 (22nd Annual Report of PLB)
PP 1870–1 (c.396), XXVII, 1 (23rd Annual Report of PLB)

Local Government Board (1870–1919)
PP 1872 (c.516), XXVIII, 1 (1st Annual Report of LGB)
PP 1873 (c.748), XXIX, 1 (2nd Annual Report of LGB)
PP 1874 (c.1071), XXV, 1 (3rd Annual Report of LGB)
PP 1875 (c.1328), XXXI, 1 (4th Annual Report of LGB)
PP 1876 (c.1585), XXXI, 1 (5th Annual Report of LGB)
PP 1877 (c.1865), XXXVII, 1 (6th Annual Report of LGB)
PP 1878 (c.2130), XXXVII, 1 (7th Annual Report of LGB)
PP 1878–9 (c.2372), XXVIII, 1 (8th Annual Report of LGB)
PP 1880 (c.2681), XXVI, 1 (9th Annual Report of LGB)
PP 1881 (c.2982), XLVI, 1 (10th Annual Report of LGB)
PP 1882 (c.3337), XXX, 1 (11th Annual Report of LGB)
PP 1883 (c.3778), XXVIII, 1 (12th Annual Report of LGB)
PP 1884 (c.4166), XXXVII, 1 (13th Annual Report of LGB)
PP 1884–5 (c.4515), XXXII, 1 (14th Annual Report of LGB)
PP 1886 (c.4844), XXXI, 1 (15th Annual Report of LGB)
PP 1887 (c.5131), XXXVI, 1 (16th Annual Report of LGB)
PP 1888 (c.5526), XLIX, 1 (17th Annual Report of LGB)
PP 1889 (c.5638), XXXV, 1 (18th Annual Report of LGB)
PP 1890 (c.6141), XXXIII, 1 (19th Annual Report of LGB)
PP 1890–1 (c.6460), XXXIII, 1 (20th Annual Report of LGB)
PP 1892 (c.6745), XXXVIII, 1 (21st Annual Report of LGB)
PP 1893–4 (c.7180), XLIII, 1 (22nd Annual Report of LGB)
PP 1894 (c.7500), XXXVIII, 1 (23rd Annual Report of LGB)
PP 1895 (c.7867), L, 1 (24th Annual Report of LGB)
PP 1896 (c.8213), XXXVI, 1 (25th Annual Report of LGB)
PP 1897 (c.8539), XXXVI, 1 (26th Annual Report of LGB)
PP 1898 (c.8978), XXXIX, 1 (27th Annual Report of LGB)
PP 1899 (c.9444), XXXVII, 1 (28th Annual Report of LGB)
PP 1900 (Cd.292), XXXIII, 1 (29th Annual Report of LGB)
PP 1901 (Cd.746), XXV, 1 (30th Annual Report of LBG)
PP 1902 (Cd.1231), XXXV, 1 (31st Annual Report of LGB)
PP 1903 (Cd.1700), XXIX, 1 (32nd Annual Report of LGB)
PP 1904 (Cd.2214), XXIV, 1 (33rd Annual Report of LGB)
PP 1905 (Cd.2661), XXXI, 1 (34th Annual Report of LGB)
PP 1906 (Cd.3105), XXXV, 1 (35th Annual Report of LGB)
PP 1907 (Cd.3665), XXVI, 1 (36th Annual Report of LGB)
PP 1908 (Cd.4347), XXX (37th Annual Report of LGB)
PP 1909 (Cd.4786), XXVIII, 1 (38th Annual Report of LGB)
PP 1910 (Cd.5260), XXXVIII, 1 (39th Annual Report of LGB)
PP 1911 (Cd.5865), XXXI, 1 (40th Annual Report of LGB)
PP 1912–13 (Cd.6327), XXXV, 1 (41st Annual Report of LGB)
PP 1913 (Cd.6980), XXXI, 1 (42nd Annual Report of LGB)
PP 1914 (Cd.7444), XXXVIII, 1 (43rd Annual Report of LGB)
PP 1916 (Cd.8195), XII, 1 (44th Annual Report of LGB)
PP 1916 (Cd.8331), XIII, 1 (45th Annual Report of LGB)
PP 1917–18 (Cd.8697), XVI, 1 (46th Annual Report of LGB)

Ministry of Health (1919–1930)
PP 1920 (Cmd.932), XVII, 283 (1st Annual Report of Ministry of Health)
PP 1921 (Cmd.1446), XIII, 1 (2nd Annual Report of Ministry of Health)
PP 1922 (Cmd.1713), VIII, 1 (3rd Annual Report of Ministry of Health)
PP 1923 (Cmd.1944), XI, 593 (4th Annual Report of Ministry of Health)
PP 1924 (Cmd.2218), IX, 751 (5th Annual Report of Ministry of Health)
PP 1924–5 (Cmd.2450), XIII, 311 (6th Annual Report of Ministry of Health)
PP 1926 (Cmd.2724), XI, 1 (7th Annual Report of Ministry of Health)
PP 1927 (Cmd.2938), IX, 591 (8th Annual Report of Ministry of Health)
PP 1928–9 (Cmd.3185), VI, 597 (9th Annual Report of Ministry of Health)
PP 1929–30 (Cmd.3362), XIV, 1 (10th Annual Report of Ministry of Health)

INDEX

Page references in **bold** refer to illustrations, and those in *italics* refer to Appendix 2. Pre-1974 counties are used in this index.

A

Abbots Langley (Herts) *see* Leavesden
Abbott, W *205*
Abingdon (Berks)
   workhouse (1631) 6
   workhouse (1714) 14
   workhouse (1835) 60, 74, **74**, 75, 76, 83, *201*
able-bodied x, 120–3, 193, 194
   able-bodied test workhouses x, 120–2
   attitudes towards, 18th century 3
   see also deterrent workhouses; labour yards; taskwork; workhouse test; working-houses
Acle (Norf), Gilbert Union 27
Act of Settlement (Act for the Better Relief of the Poor of this Kingdom) (1662) 8
Acton (Mdx), scheme for Middlesex County Workhouse and House of Correction **19**
Acts of Parliament *see* legislation
Adams, Charles J *203*
Adams, Henry P *210*
Adams, William, & Son 185
Addlestone (Surr), Princess Mary's Village Homes for Little Girls 143
Adey, George *205*
aged and infirm, in workhouse, 1870–1914 117–19
'aggregate' system *see* 'barrack' schools
Aicken & Capes *213*
Albury (Surr), workhouse 17
Alcester (Warws), workhouse 48, **48**, *211*
Alcock, Thomas 18
Aldborough (Norf), Gilbert Union 27
Alderbury (Wilts), Alderbury (later Salisbury) Union Workhouse 136, **137**, *211*
Aldersbrook (Essex), receiving homes *204*
Aldershot (Hants), Gilbert Parish (Aldershot and Bentley) 27, *204*
   workhouse (later industrial school) 142, *204*
Aldwincle, Thomas W 108, **108**, *214, 215, 219*
   Lambeth Workhouse **107**, 108, 109, 121, 122, *215*
   Wandsworth and Clapham Union Workhouse 108, 121, **121**, *217*
Aldworth, Robert 10
Allen, George *217*
Allom, Thomas 89, 96, *206, 211, 215*
allowance systems 32, 49
almshouses 179
   workhouses resembling 53, 194
Alnwick (Northumb), workhouse *208*
Alresford (Hants), workhouse 62, *204*
Alston (Cumb), Parish (later Alston with Gargill), workhouse *202*
Alstonefield (Staffs), Gilbert Union 27
   workhouse *209*
Alton (Hants), workhouse *204*
Altrincham (Ches), Altrincham (later Bucklow) Union Workhouse, Knutsford *202*
Alverstoke (Hants), Gilbert Parish (Alverstoke and Gosport) 27
   workhouse 35–6, **35**, 67, 127, *204*
Amersham (Bucks), workhouse 49, 53, 72, 73, **73**, *202*
Amesbury (Wilts), workhouse 71, 72, *211*
Ampthill (Beds), workhouse *201*
Andover (Hants), workhouse 52, 60, 62, 74, 78, *204*
   scandal (1845) 52, **52**, 90

Anti-Poor-Law movement 49–52, 57, 81
Appleby (Leics), Gilbert Union 27
apprenticeship 132, 154
Archbishop's Palace Gilbert Union (Kent) 27
architects, system of appointing 46, 47–8, 93–4
Architectural Magazine 47
Arclid (Ches), workhouse *202*
Arkell, D 170, **171**
Armstrong, William *209*
Arnold/Basford Gilbert Union (Notts) 27
Arnott, Dr Arnott's Thermometer Stoves 83
Arthur, Oswald C *203*
Arts & Crafts style 130, 152, 171
Arundel (Suss), Gilbert Parish 27
   workhouse *210*
Ash (Surr), Gilbert Union 27
   workhouse *210*
Ashbourne (Derb), workhouse 133, *203*
Ashby-de-la-Zouch (Leics)
   Gilbert Union 27
   Union Workhouse 169, **170**, 186, *207*
Ashford (Kent), East Ashford Union Workhouse 54, 56, *205*
Ashford (Surr, formerly Mdx)
   Staines Union Workhouse *207*
   West London District School 142, **142**, *218*
Ashton-under-Lyne (Lancs), Union 49
   workhouse 126, **127**, *206*
Ashurst (Hants), New Forest Union Workhouse 60, 74, 76, *205*
Ashworth, Edward 92, **92**, *203, 209*
Association for Befriending Boys 154
Association for the Improvement of Workhouse Infirmaries 160
Aston (Warws), Union
   cottage homes, Erdington 152, *211*
   workhouse, Erdington 124, *211*
   see also Birmingham, King's Norton and Aston (Joint Committee)
asylums 156–7, 165, *219–20*
Atcham (Salop), workhouse, Cross Houses 25, 127, *209*
Atherstone (Warws), workhouse 156, *211*
Atkinson, John and William, workhouses by
   before 1840 78–80, **79**, 133, *212*
   after 1840 95, **95**, 133, *203, 212, 213*
Atlas, hospital ship 164, **164**, *219*
Attleborough (Norf), infirmary *208*
Aubin, ___, school at Weston Hill, Norwood 132, 138, 140
Auckland (Dur), workhouse *203*
Avoncliffe (Wilts), workhouse *211*
Axbridge (Som), workhouse 67, 89, *209*
Axminster (Devon), workhouse 60, 203
Aylesbury (Bucks), workhouse 90, **91**, *202*
Aylsham (Norf), workhouse 88, **93**, 94, 133, *207*
Aysgarth (Yorks N R) *see* Bainbridge

B

back-to-back (double width) wards
   1835–40 67
   1840–70 89, 92, 151, 165
   1870–1914 106–8, 110, 113, 167
Backhouse, Elisha 96, **96**, 100, **101**, 139, **139**, *213*
Baggallay, Frank *217*
Bagshot (Surr) 129
Bailey, ___, fire escape apparatus 124
Bainbridge (Yorks N R), Gilbert Union (later Aysgarth) 27
   workhouse 80, *212*
Bakewell (Derb), workhouse (later Newholme Hospital) 191, *203*
Banbury (Oxon), workhouse 60, 74, 76, *209*
Banstead (Surr), cottage homes 144–5, **144**, 146, 148, **150**, *218*
baptisms 99
Baradale, I *207*
Barham (Suff), workhouse 22, 156, *210*

Barkingside (Essex), Dr Barnardo's Village Home for Orphan, Neglected and Destitute Girls 143
Barn, M *210*
Barnard Castle (Dur), workhouse *204*
Barnet (Herts), workhouse 67, **70**, 83, 191, *205*
Barnsley (Yorks W R), workhouse *212*
Barnstaple (Devon), workhouse 60, *203*
Baroque style 94
'barrack' schools 145–7
Barracks and Hospitals Commission 161
Barrow-in-Furness (Lancs)
   cottage homes *206*
   workhouse **112**, 113, **114**, *206*
Barrow-on-Soar (Leics)
   Gilbert Union 27
   Union Workhouse, Mountsorrel *207*
Barry, Thomas D *209*
Barton Regis (Glos), Union
   workhouse, Eastville *204*
   workhouse, Southmead *204*
Barton-upon-Irwell (Lancs)
   Davyhulme Hospital 177, *206*
   workhouse, Patricroft *206*
Barwick-in-Elmet (Yorks W R), Gilbert Union 27
   workhouse *212*
Basford (Notts)
   Arnold/Basford Gilbert Union 27
   cottage homes *208*
   workhouse *208*
Basildon (Essex) *see* Laindon
Basingstoke (Hants), workhouse 60, *204*
Bateman, J 95, **95**, *209, 211, 212*
Bath, Fred *204*
Bath (Som)
   scattered homes 151
   workhouse 60, 74, **75**, 76, 99, *209*
      accommodation for lunatics and imbeciles 161, 162
      chapel 100, **100**
      phthisis ward 176
Battle (Suss), workhouse *210*
Bawdeswell (Norf), Gilbert Union 27
Baxter, G R Wythen 51
Beaminster (Dors), workhouse 76, 77, *203*
Bearsted (Kent), Gilbert Union/Parish 27
Becher, Revd John Thomas 36–40, **37–8**, 41, 42, *208*
Bedale (Yorks N R), workhouse 79–80, **79**, 179, *212*
Bedford
   Bedfordshire County Gaol 34
   Incorporation (later Union) 28, 133, **193**
   workhouse 28, 34, *201*
Bedfordshire, poor-law institutions, post-1834 *201*
Bedminster (Som), Bedminster (later Long Ashton) Union Workhouse, Flax Bourton 71, 72, **82**, 157, *209*
   chapel 102, **102**
Bedworth (Warws), Gilbert Union 27
Belford (Northumb), workhouse 78, *208*
Bellers, John 9
Bellingham (Northumb), workhouse 80, **80**, *208*
Belper (Derb), workhouse 72, 73, *203*
Bentham, Jeremy 33–4, **33–4**, 36, 43, 46
Bentham, Samuel 33, **33**, 34
Berkhampstead (Herts)
   workhouse (18th century) 13
   workhouse (1831) 42, 186, 191, *205*
Berkshire
   Gilbert Unions/Parishes 27
   poor-law institutions, post-1834 *201–2*
Berkshire Bread Scale (Speenhamland system) 32
Bermondsey (Lond)
   Parish of St Mary Magdalen *214*
   workhouse, Tanner/Russell St *214*
   St Olave's Union Workhouse, Parish St/Fair St *216*
Berney, John *210*

Berney & Monday *210*
Berriman & Son 108, *214*
Berwick-upon-Tweed (Northumb), workhouse *208*
Bethnal Green (Lond)
   Bethnal Green Employment and Relief Association, stone-breaking yard **120**
   children's home, Bonner Rd 143
   Parish of St Matthew
      industrial school, Leytonstone 142, 145–6, **146**, *214*
      infirmary, Cambridge Heath Rd *214*
      workhouse, Waterloo Rd *214*
Beverley (Yorks E R)
   workhouse (1726) 16
   workhouse (1860–1) 95, *212*
Bideford (Devon), workhouse 72, *203*
Bidlake, George, & Lovatt *209*
Bidlake & Fleming *209*
Biggleswade (Beds), workhouse 58, *201*
Billericay (Essex), workhouse 72, 73, *204*
Billesdon (Leics), workhouse *207*
Billings, Richard 92, *202*
Bindley, S E 142, *210*
Bingham (Notts)
   Gilbert Parish 27, 36
   Union Workhouse *208*
Birch, ___ *215*
Birchington (Kent), Gilbert Union 27
Birkenhead (Ches), workhouse *202*
Birmingham (Warws)
   architects of 95, 136, 142
   Asylum for the Infant Poor, Summer Lane (1797) 132
   cottage homes, Marston Green **144**, 145, 152, *211*
   Incorporation for the Poor **16**, 28
   industrial school *211*
   test workhouse (1881) 122
   workhouse (1733–4) 16–17, **16**, *211*
   workhouse, Winson Green (1850–2) 88, **88**, 95, **95**, 96, 134, *211*
   see also Aston; King's Norton
Birmingham, King's Norton and Aston (Joint Committee), mental colony, Monyhull 174, *211*
Bishop's Castle (Salop), workhouse *209*
Bishop's Stortford (Herts), Union 47
   workhouse 49, 58, 75, 76, **76**, 83, 191, *205*
   Emergency Medical Service hospital 178
   infirmary 157
Biven *see* Giles, John, & Biven
Blaby (Leics), Union Workhouse, Enderby *207*
Black *see* Clayton & Black
Blackburn, William 34, **34**
Blackburn (Lancs)
   voluntary general hospital 159
   workhouse 98, 144, *206*
Blackwall (Lond), North Wharf, River Ambulance Service *219*
Blackwood's Magazine, and Anti-Poor-Law movement 51
Bland, ___ *206*
Blandford (Dors), workhouse *203*
Blean (Kent), Union Workhouse, Hearne Common 53, 54, **56**, 57, *205*
Bledlow (Bucks), industrial school *202*
Bletchingley (Surr), workhouse *210*
block plan (1835–40) 78–80
Blofield (Norf), Union Workhouse, Lingwood 65, *207*
Blything Incorporation (later Union) (Suff), workhouse, Bulcamp (Blythburgh) 22, 156, *210*
Board of Guardians (Default) Act (1926) 189
Board of Trade, report (1697) 10
boarding-out
   children 143, 153
   lunatics 156, 162

Index

boards of guardians
 boardrooms 81, 125–6
 disbanded (1929) 190
 given responsibility for registering births, marriages and deaths (1837) 66
 under Gilbert's Act 20
 under Poor Law Amendment Act 44, 81
Bodmin (Cornw), workhouse 73, *202*
Bolton (Lancs)
 Hollins Cottage Homes 143, **143**
 workhouse 169, **169, 175**, *206*
Bolton-by-Bowland (Yorks W R), Gilbert Union/Parish 27
bone-crushing 52, **52**, 61
Bonomi, Ignatius *212*
Booth, Charles 195
 Aged Poor in England (1894) 117
 Life and Labour of the People of London (1902–4) 122
 Pauperism and the Endowment of Old Age (1892) 117
Booth, Lawrence *206*
Bootle (Cumb), workhouse *202*
Booton (Norf), Gilbert Union 27
Bosmere and Claydon Incorporation (later Union) (Suff), workhouse, Barham 22, 156, *210*
Bostall Heath (Lond), cottage homes (later Goldie Leigh Homes) *217*, 220
Boston (Lincs), workhouse 72, *207*
Boulton & Palmer 73, *210*
Bourne, Sturges 32
Bourne (Lincs), workhouse 59, *207*
Bow (Lond)
 North Surrey School District branch school 148–9
 Poplar and Stepney Sick Asylum 120–1, 166, *218*
 South Grove, Whitechapel Union Workhouse *217*
Bowen, John 51, **51**
Bowgreave (Lancs), workhouse *206*
Bowman, Henry *202*
Bowyer, H E 134, 142
Brackley (Northants), workhouse 62, 72, *208*
Bracknell (Berks) *see* Easthampstead
Braddon, Lawrence 9
Bradfield (Berks), workhouse 60, 74, 76, *201*
Bradford (Yorks W R)
 Anti-Poor-Law riots 49
 architects of 94, 96
 Union
  sanatorium, Eastby 176, *212*
  test workhouse, Daisy Hill 122, *212*
  workhouse (later St Luke's Hospital) 96, 177, *212*
 see also North Bierley
Bradford-on-Avon (Wilts), Bradford (later Bradford-on-Avon) Union Workhouse, Avoncliffe *211*
Bradshaw, T T *206*
Bradshaw, William *209*
Bradshaw & Gass **175**
Braintree (Essex), workhouse 75, 76, 157, *204*
Bramley (Yorks W R), workhouse **98**, 99, *212*
Brampton (Cumb), workhouse *202*
Brampton (Derb), industrial school *203*
'branch' ('intermediate') workhouses 147–8
Brassington (Derb), Gilbert Union 27
Brentford (Mdx), Union Workhouse, Isleworth 62, *207*
Brentwood (Essex)
 Brentwood School District 142, *218*
 Highwood School (later Highwood Hospital) **148–9**, 149, *219*, 220
 industrial school 142, 149, *215, 217, 218*
 see also Hutton
Brewood (Staffs), workhouse *209*
bridewells 3, 179
 see also London, Bridewell
Bridge (Kent), workhouse 53, 54, **56**, 57, *205*
Bridgen *see* Pennington & Bridgen
Bridgnorth (Salop) 138
 workhouse *209*

Bridgwater (Som), workhouse 51, 60, 76, *209*
Bridlington (Yorks E R), workhouse *212*
Bridport (Dors), workhouse *203*
Brigg (Lincs), workhouse *207*
Briggs & Everall *210*
Brighton (Suss)
 Warren Farm Industrial Schools, Woodingdean 142, *210*
 workhouse 98, 160, **160, 162**, 163, *210*
Brinton and Melton Constable Gilbert Union (Norf) 27, *207*
 workhouse 27, **27**, *207*
Bristol (Glos)
 Incorporation 10, 13
 cottage homes, Downend *204*
 'Mint Workhouse' (St Peter's Hospital) 10, **10**, 132, 156–7, *204*
 'new workhouse' (1696) 10, 132
 workhouse, Stapleton (*c* 1800) 44, 80, 157, 176, *204*
 see also Barton Regis
Brixworth (Northants), workhouse *208*
Broadbent, J B *206*
Broadstairs (Kent), Wainwright Home *218*
Brockenham (Surr), industrial home 142
Bromley (Kent), Union Workhouse, Locks Bottom 90, *205*
Bromley-by-Bow (Lond), Stepney Union Workhouse 98, *217*
Bromsgrove (Worcs), workhouse 95, *212*
Bromyard (Herefs), workhouse 65, *205*
Brookhouse, Robert & Thomas *203*
Brooks, Joseph *206*
Brown, John 64, 65, *204, 207, 208, 210*
Brown & Henman *205*
Browne, R P 86, *215*
Browning, Bryan 59, *207, 208*
Bruton, Edward G *209*
Buckingham, workhouse 62, 72, *202*
Buckinghamshire, poor-law institutions, post-1834 *202*
Bucklow (Ches) *see* Altrincham
Bulcamp (Suff), workhouse 22, 156, *210*
Bunce, Samuel 33, **33**
Bunning, ____ *214*
Buntingford (Herts), workhouse 48, 57, **57**, 191, *205*
Burden, R H *215*
burial grounds 99
Burn, Revd Richard 20
Burnley (Lancs), workhouse 124, 143, *206*
Burrell, J G 174, *208*
Burslem (Staffs), workhouse 42
Burton, E H *204*
Burton-upon-Trent (Staffs)
 workhouse (1838) 72, *209*
 workhouse (1880–4) 114, 136, **137**, *209*
Bury (Lancs)
 workhouse (18th century) 30
 workhouse (1855–6), Jericho *206*
Bury St Edmunds (Suff)
 gaol 34
 Incorporation 13
  workhouse (College St) *210*
 parish workshop (1589) 5
 Thingoe (later Bury St Edmunds) Union Workhouse 76, 127, *210*
Bush, Rice 7
Butterworth, P, and Duncan *206*
Byfield, George 34, *212*

C

Caistor (Lincs), Gilbert Union 27
 workhouse 35–6, **35**, *207*
Callcott, Thomas *215*
Calne (Wilts), workhouse *211*
Camberwell (Lond), Parish of St Giles
 scattered homes 151
 workhouse, Constance Rd 108, **108**, *214*
 workhouse, Gordon Rd 108, **108**, 125, 167, **167**, *214*
 workhouse, Havil St 107, *214*

Cambridge
 parish workshop (1582) 5
 'Spinning House' (1628–34) 6, **7**
 workhouse (1838) 67–70, 137, 138, *202*
 see also Chesterton
Cambridgeshire, poor-law institutions, post-1834 *202*
Camden Town (Lond), St Pancras workhouse, Kings Rd **99**, 108, **128**, 130, 163, *216*
Cook's Terrace block 110, **110**
Camelford (Cornw), workhouse *202*
Canada, workhouse children shipped to 154
Cancellor & Hill *205*
Cannock (Staffs), workhouse *209*
Canterbury (Kent)
 Incorporation 13
 workhouse 90, **91**, *205*
 Poor Priests' Hospital 179
Canterbury, Archbishop of 129
Capes *see* Aicken & Capes
Capper, Revd D 41–2
Card, Henry *210*
Cardington (Beds), workhouse **193**
'care in the community' 175, 195
Carlford and Colneis Incorporation (Suff) 21, 22, 31
 workhouse, Nacton 18, 21–2, 31, *210*
Carlisle (Cumb)
 industrial school, Harraby Hill *202*
 workhouse (1790s) 29
 workhouse (1863) 96, *202*
Carlton (Yorks W R), Gilbert Union 27
 workhouse *212*
Carshalton (Surr), Southern (Convalescent) Hospital (later the Children's Infirmary/Queen Mary's Hospital for Children) 164, *220*
Carter, Francis 35, *204*
Carter, O B *203*
Carver, Richard *209*
Cary, John 10, 13
Castalia, hospital ship 164, *219*
Castle Ward Union (Northumb), workhouse, Ponteland *208*
Casual Poor Act (1882) 185
casual wards 185–7, 188, 190, 191
 cellular system 184–7, 188, 195
Caterham (Surr), Metropolitan Asylum for Imbeciles 165, **165**, *220*
Catherington (Hants), Union Workhouse, Horndean *204*
Catholics 99, 130, 134, 151
Caton (Lancs), Gilbert Union 27
 workhouse, Moorgarth *206*
Caxton and Arrington Union (Cambs), workhouse 57, *202*
cellular system *see* casual wards
central heating 83
Central Inspection Principle 33–6
Central London School District
 Central London District School, Hanwell 97, 140, **141**, 147, 149, *218*
 Ophthalmic Institute **148**, 149, *218*
 industrial school, Weston Hill, Norwood 140, *218*
Central London Sick Asylum District, Central London Sick Asylum, Hendon 176, **176**, *218*
Cerne Abbas (Dors), Cerne Union Workhouse 78, *203*
Chadwick, Edwin 43, 44, 46, 52
Chailey (Suss), Union Workhouse, South Chailey *210*
Chamberlain, Neville 190
Chambers *see* Tress & Chambers
Chancellor, Fred *204*
Chandler, Francis 123
Chandler's Ford (Hants), workhouse *205*
Chapel-en-le-Frith (Derb), workhouse *203*
chapels
 1835–40 56, 61, 62, 63, **64**, 71, 73, 84
 1841–70 85, 87, 98, 99–102, **100–2**
 after 1870 127–30, **129–30**
Chard (Som), workhouse 65, *209*

charitable donations, for workhouse building 48–9
Charles I, King 5–6
Chartism 49
Chatham (Kent)
 Medway Union Workhouse 98, *206*
 workhouse (1725) 16, **16**, 155
Cheadle (Staffs), workhouse *209*
Cheers, Henry 129
Chell (Staffs), Wolstanton and Burslem Union Workhouse 42, 73, *210*
Chelmsford (Essex)
 workhouse (1714) 14
 workhouse (1837, rebuilt 1886–9) 113, 124, *204*
Chelsea (Lond)
 Parish of St Luke
  casual wards, Millman St 186, **187**, *214*
  infirmary, Cale St *214*
  workhouse, Britten St 108, *214*
 St George's, Hanover Square Parish Workhouse (later St George's Union Workhouse), Fulham Rd/Little Chelsea 181, 184, *216*
 infirmary 125, **125**, 166
 St George's Union receiving homes (later St George's Home), Millman St *216*, *219*
 see also Kensington & Chelsea School District
Cheltenham (Glos), workhouse 84, *204*
Cheriton (Kent), scattered homes 151, *205*
Chertsey (Surr)
 workhouse (18th century) 16
 workhouse (1836), Ottershaw 60, 74, 76, *210*
Chesham (Bucks), workhouse 49
Cheshire
 County Council 190
 poor-law institutions, post-1834 *202*
Chester (Ches), workhouse 96, *202*
Chester-le-Street (Dur), workhouse *203*
Chesterfield (Derb), Union industrial school, Brampton *203*
 workhouse 53, 72, *203*
Chesterton (Cambs), workhouse 47, 63, 67, *202*
Chichester (Suss), Incorporation (later Union) 28
 workhouse 8, **8**, 28, *210*
Child, Sir Josiah 9
children 131–54
 hospitals 149, 176–7
 imbecile 165
 under Old Poor Law
  John Scott's ideas for reform (1773) 18–19
  London 7, 8, 12, 16, 131–2
  in workhouses (1796–7) 31, 132
 see also industrial schools
Chilvers Coton (Warws), workhouse *211*
Chippenham (Wilts), workhouse *211*
Chipping Norton (Oxon), workhouse **64**, 65, 100, *209*
Chipping Ongar (Essex), cottage homes 149, **149**, 152, *215*
Chipping Sodbury (Glos), workhouse 72, *204*
cholera 168
Chorley (Lancs), workhouse *206*
Chorlton (Lancs), Union
 casual wards and test workhouse, Tame St, Ancoates 122, *206*
 cottage homes, Styal 145, *206*
 workhouse, Withington 98, 106, 143, 159, **159**, *206*
Chorlton and Manchester Joint (Asylum) Committee, mental colony, Langho 174, *206*
Chorlton and Manchester Joint (Casual Ward and Test House) Committee, test workhouse 122, *206*
Christchurch (Hants), workhouse 113, 143–4, *204*
Church & Rickwood *217*

245

Church Stretton (Salop), workhouse 209
circular ward blocks 167, 170
Cirencester (Glos), workhouse 204
City of London Union 119, 214
    casual ward, Thavies Inn 214
    workhouse, Bow Rd 89, **90**, 161, 214
Clapham (Lond) *see* Wandsworth
Clark, John F 94, 133, 210
Clarke, ___ 203
Clatterbridge (Ches), Wirral Union Workhouse (later Clatterbridge (County) General Hospital) 78, 190, *202*
Claypole (Lincs)
    Gilbert Union 27
    Newark Union Workhouse 208
Clayton (Yorks W R), North Bierley Union Workhouse 96, **96**, 125, **126**, *213*
Clayton & Black **115**, *211*
Cleobury Mortimer (Salop), workhouse 80, *209*
Clephan, James 58, *201, 204, 208*
Clerkenwell (Lond)
    Middlesex County Workhouse (1664) 8, 12
    Parishes of St James and St John *215*
        workhouse, Farringdon Rd (1729) 151, *215*
    Quaker workhouse (1702) 12
Clifton (Glos), Clifton (later Barton Regis) Union Workhouse, Eastville *204*
Clitheroe (Lancs), workhouse *206*
Clun (Salop), Union Workhouse, Bishop's Castle *209*
Clutton (Som), Union Workhouse, Temple Cloud 77, *209*
Cobbett, William 91
Cockermouth (Cumb)
    Flimby Lodge, school 145, *202*
    workhouse 78, *202*
Coggan *see* Smith & Coggan
Coke, John 6
Colchester (Essex)
    Colchester Union Workhouse **64**, 65, *204*
    compulsory poor rate (1557) 4
    Incorporation 11, 13
    Lexden and Winstree Union Workhouse, Stanway 47, 63–5, **64–5**, *204*
Cole, William H 78, *202, 205*
Coleman, ___ *214*
Collins, *see also* Wild, Collins & Wild
Collins, H H *218*
Colwich (Staffs) 47
Commissioners for the Poor (17th century) 6
Committee on the Care of Poor Law Children (1896) 153
Common Poor Fund for London 105, 166
Comper, Ninian 130, **130**
competitions, for workhouse architects 46, 47, 93–4
Congleton (Ches), Union Workhouse, Arclid *202*
Consett (Dur) *see* Shotley Bridge
convalescent homes 164, *218*, *219*
conversions of older buildings, 1835–40 80–1
Cookham (Berks)
    Cookham (later Maidenhead) Union Workhouse, Maidenhead 136, *201*
    workhouse (pre-1836) 42
Cooper, William *211*
Cooper & Son *201*
Cope, ___ *204*
Cope, Charles West **81**
Coram, Captain Thomas 132
Corbett, Uvedale 160
corn-grinding 61, 83, 103, 120, 121, 122
    vagrants 179, 181–2, 186
Cornwall, poor-law institutions, post-1834 *202*
corridor-plan workhouses
    1840–70 85–102
    1870s 106, 113
Cosford and Polsted Incorporation (later Cosford Union) (Suff), workhouse, Semer 22, 44, *210*

cottage-home system
    for children 19, 131, 143–5, 149, 151–4, 164
    for convalescent establishments 164
Cotterell, A P I *204*
Coughton (Warws) 48
Countesthorpe (Leics), cottage homes 145, *207*
county, as unit for poor-law provision 17, 18, 20
courtyard plan 46–7, 54–9, **221**
Coventry (Warws)
    Coventry Incorporation Workhouse, Whitefriars 44, 169, *211*
    Foleshill Union Workhouse *211*
Cowell, ___ 40
Cowley Fields (Oxon), industrial school 142, *209*
Coxheath (Kent), Maidstone Union Workhouse 54, 127–9, **129**, *206*
Crabbe, George 25
Cranbrook (Kent), workhouse 56, *205*
Craven, C W 181–2
Crediton (Devon)
    Incorporation 11
    Union Workhouse 60, 61, 74, **75**, 76, *203*
Creeke, Christopher C *203, 204, 211*
Cricklade and Wootton Bassett Union (Wilts), workhouse, Purton *211*
Crickmay, W *219*
Crondall (Hants), industrial school 142, *204*
Crooks, Will 122
Crosland Moor (Yorks W R), Huddersfield Union Workhouse **92**, 93, 98–9, *213*
Cross, F *211*
cross-ventilation 20, 87, 89, 98, 104, 105
    Kempthorne recommends 46, 60
    workhouse infirmaries 157, 168, 169
Croydon (Surr)
    St Olave's Union cottage homes, Shirley *216*
    Union
        infirmary *210*
        workhouse *210*
Crumpsall (Lancs), Manchester Union Workhouse 98, 125, **125**, *206*
Cubic Space Committee 160–1
Cuckfield (Suss), workhouse 90, 100, *210*
Cudham (Kent), workhouse 17
Culcheth (Lancs), Salford Union Cottage Homes 152–3, **153**, *206*
Culshaw, William *206, 207*
Cumberland
    Gilbert Unions/Parishes 27
    poor-law institutions, post-1834 *202*
Currey, Henry *211*

D
Dain, M J *207*
Daisy Hill (Yorks W R), Bradford Union test workhouse 122, *212*
Darenth (Kent)
    Darenth School for Imbeciles 165, *219*
    River Hospitals 163
Darlington (Dur)
    Gilbert Union/Parish 27
    Union Workhouse *203*
Dartford (Kent)
    Dartford Union Workhouse 56, *205*
    Gore Farm, Southern (Smallpox) Hospital (South Smallpox Camp, later Southern (Convalescent) Hospital) 164, *219*
    Joyce Green (Smallpox) Hospital 164, *218*
    Long Reach
        Long Reach (Smallpox) Hospital 164, *218*
        smallpox hospital ships moored at 164, *164, 219*
    Orchard (Smallpox) Hospital 164, *218*
Daukes, S W 66

Daventry (Northants), workhouse *208*
Davy, J S 57
Davyhulme (Lancs), Davyhulme Hospital 177, *206*
Day, John *205*
Deanhouse (Yorks W R), Huddersfield Union Workhouse 93, *213*
Dearnley (Lancs), Rochdale Union Workhouse 87, 136, **136**, *206*
Defoe, Daniel 12
Depwade Union (Norf), workhouse, Pulham Market 63, **64**, *207*
Derby
    parish workhouses (1791) 32
    St Werburgh, workhouse 41
    Union
        infirmary *203*
        workhouse (1837–8) *203*
        workhouse (1876) *203*
Derbyshire
    Gilbert Unions/Parishes 27
    poor-law institutions, post-1834 *203*
detention colonies 123
deterrent workhouses (early 19th century) x, 33–42, 193
Devizes (Wilts), workhouse 65, *211*
Devon
    County Council 190
    poor-law institutions, post-1834 *203*
Devonport (Devon), Stoke Damerell (later Devonport) Parish Workhouse 156–7, 159, *203*
Dewsbury (Yorks W R), workhouse 143, *212*
diet 84, **84**
Dinwiddy, Thomas **108**, 110, *215*
Dinwiddy, Thomas, & Sons **150**, *215*
disease *see* infectious diseases
Diseases Prevention Metropolis Act (1883) 163
dispensaries 165, 196
distribution maps, new workhouses
    1835–40 54
    1840–70 **86**
    after 1870, separate-block (pavilion plan) **104**
Dixon, William 35
Dobcross (Yorks W R), workhouse *213*
Dobson, Thomas 47, *203*
Dobson, W *215*
Docking (Norf), workhouse 65, 189, *207*
Doddington (Cambs), North Witchford Union Workhouse 185, *202*
dole 189, 196
domestic service, workhouse girls entering 154
Doncaster (Yorks W R) 94
    vagrant house 180
    workhouse (1839) *212*
    workhouse (1897–1900) 115, *212*
Donowell, J *205*
Donthorn, William J, workhouses
    before 1840 53, 66–7, **67**, 76, *202, 207, 208, 209*
    after 1840 88, **93**, 94, 133, *207*
Dorchester (Dors)
    workhouse (1617) 6, 7, 10
    workhouse (1836) 65, *203*
Doré, Gustave 184
Dore Union (Herefs), workhouse, Riverdale 49, *205*
Dorking (Surr), workhouse 83, *210*
Dorset, poor-law institutions, post-1834 *203*
double-width wards *see* back-to-back wards
Dover (Kent), River (later Dover) Union Workhouse 54, *206*
Downend (Glos), cottage homes *204*
Downham Market (Norf), Downham Union Workhouse 66, *207*
Drayton Union (Salop), workhouse, Market Drayton *209*
Driffield (Yorks E R), workhouse *212*
Droitwich (Worcs), workhouse 60, *212*
Drouet, ___ 132, 138, 140
Droxford (Hants), workhouse 60, 76, *204*

Drury, G 95, **95**, *209, 211, 212*
Ducane, Revd Henry 49
Dudley (Worcs), workhouse *212*
Dulverton (Som), workhouse 92, **92**, *209*
Dulwich (Lond), Champion Hill, infirmary *217*
Duncan, ___ *206*
Dunmow (Essex), workhouse 72, 73, 180, *204*
Duppa, T D *209*
Durham (city), workhouse *203*
Durham (county)
    Gilbert Unions/Parishes 27
    poor-law institutions, post-1834 *203–4*
Dursley (Glos), workhouse *204*
Dutton (Ches), workhouse *202*
Dwelly, William *202, 203*
Dyer, Charles 73, *207*

E
Eamont Bridge (Westmld), Gilbert Union 27
Easebourne (Suss), Gilbert Union 27
    workhouse (later Midhurst Union Workhouse) 26–7, **27**, *211*
Easington (Dur), workhouse *203*
Easingwold (Yorks N R), workhouse 79, 179, 185, *212*
East Anglia, houses of industry 21–5, 156
East Ashford Union (Kent), workhouse, Ashford 54, 56, *205*
East Grinstead (Suss), workhouse *210*
East Ham (Essex) *see* Plashet
East London Union *215*
    workhouse, Homerton 98, *215*
East Preston (Suss), Gilbert Union 27
    workhouse *210*
East Retford (Notts), workhouse 76, 77, *208*
East Stonehouse (Devon), Parish Workhouse *203*
East and West Flegg Incorporation (Norf) 21, 22
    workhouse, Rollesby 21, **21**, 22, *207*
Eastbourne (Suss), Gilbert Union 27
    workhouse 44, 49, 81, *210*
Eastby (Yorks W R), Bradford Union sanatorium 176, *212*
Easthampstead (Berks), workhouse 81, *201*
Eastington (Glos), workhouse *204*
Eastry (Kent)
    Gilbert Union 27
    Union Workhouse 54, *205*
Eastville (Glos), workhouse *204*
Eccles (Lancs), workhouse *206*
Ecclesall Bierlow Union (Yorks W R)
    cottage homes, Fulwood 152, *212*
    workhouse, Brincliffe (Sheffield) 169, **170**, *212*
Eden, Sir Frederick Morton, *The State of the Poor* (1797) 30, 31, 36, 132, 155
Edgware (Mdx)
    Hendon Union Infirmary, Burnt Oak *207*
    Hendon Union Workhouse, Burnt Oak *207*
Edmonton (Mdx)
    Edmonton Union
        Chase Farm Schools, Enfield 145, 146–7, **146–7**, *207*
        industrial school (former Enfield parish workhouse) 138, 146, *207*
        workhouse 72, 138, *207*
    Strand Union
        industrial school, Silver St (later Edmonton Colony for Sane Epileptics) 165, *217*, 220
        workhouse *217*
Edmunds, William *205*
Edwards, Francis *204*
Elcock & Sutcliffe *206*
Elder, Charles *207*
elderly *see* aged and infirm
Elger, Thomas Gwyn *201*

INDEX

Elham (Kent)
    Gilbert Union/Parish 27
    Union
        scattered homes, Cheriton 151, *205*
        workhouse, Etchinghill 54, 57, 151, *205*
Elizabethan style 53, 62, 67, 73, 85, 95, 134, 139, 142
Ellesmere (Salop), workhouse 25, *209*
Elliott, ___ *211*
Ellis, Robert, Jnr 75, 76, *207*
Ely (Cambs), workhouse 66, **67**, 83, *202*
Emergency Medical Service 178, 191
Empingham (Rut), workhouse 31
Enderby (Leics), workhouse *207*
Endymion, hospital ship 164, *219*
Enfield (Mdx)
    Chase Farm Schools 146–7, **146–7**, *207*
    industrial school (former workhouse) 138, 146, *207*
epidemics *see* infectious diseases
epileptics 165, 174, *220*
Epping (Essex), workhouse 47–8, 62–3, **62**, 71, *204*
    provision for sick, aged and infirm 62, 83, 157
Epsom (Surr), workhouse 65, *210*
Erdington (Warws), Aston Union
    cottage homes 152, *211*
    workhouse 124, *211*
Erpingham (Norf), Union Workhouse, West Beckham 88, 94, 124, 133, *207*
Essex
    Gilbert Unions/Parishes 27
    poor-law institutions, post-1834 *204*
    see also London
Etchinghill (Kent), Elham Union Workhouse 54, 57, 151, *205*
Eton (Bucks), Union Workhouse, Slough 60, 61–2, *202*
Evans, T L 47, 58, 75, 76, **76**, 157, *205*, *211*
Everall *see* Briggs & Everall
Evesham (Worcs), workhouse *212*
Exeter (Devon)
    workhouse 11–12, **11**, 23, 191, *203*
    asylum 156–7
    maternity ward 169
    school 134
    see also St Thomas
Exhall (Warws), Gilbert Union/Parish 27
Exmouth, training ship 151, **151**, *220*
Eye (Suff), workhouse and infirmary *210*

F

factory reform, movement for 49
Falmouth (Cornw), workhouse *202*
Farebrother, Ernest *207*
Fareham (Hants), workhouse 62, 75, *204*
Faringdon (Berks), workhouse *201*
farm colonies 122–3
Farnall, H B 160, 161, 163
Farnborough (Hants), Gilbert Union 27, *204*
Farnborough (Kent), Gilbert Union 27
Farnham (Surr)
    Gilbert Parish 27
    workhouse 56, *210*
    Union 142, *210*
Farnham and Hartley Wintney School District (Surr/Hants), industrial schools
    Aldershot 142, *204*
    Crondall 142, *204*
Farningham (Kent), Home for Little Boys 143
Faversham (Kent), workhouse 54, *205*
Fazakerley (Lancs), cottage homes 145, *207*
fever *see* infectious diseases
Fielding, Henry 18, **19**
Finch, William A *215*
Finsbury (Lond)
    Finsbury School District 142, *218*
    Parish *215*

fire escapes 123, 124–5, 175
fire prevention 127
Firmin, Thomas 9
First World War
    closure of casual wards 188
    poor-law buildings taken over by War Office 177, 189
Fisher, William *209*
Flax Bourton (Som) *see* Bedminster
Fleming *see* Bidlake & Fleming
Flint, William 76, *207*
Flockton, William *212*
Foden, S O 90, **91**, 92, *201*
    and W Henman 63–5, **64**, *204*
    and H W Parker 90, **91**, 92, *202*, *210*, *211*
    and James Savage *205*
Foleshill (Warws), workhouse *211*
Fordingbridge (Hants), workhouse *204*
Forehoe Incorporation (Norf), workhouse, Wicklewood 22, 23, *208*
Forest Gate School District (Essex)
    industrial school (formerly Whitechapel Union) 124, 140, *216*, *217*, *218*
    training ship *Goliath* 151, *218*
fostering 143
Fowler & Hill *215*
Fox, George 9
Freebridge Lynn Union (Norf), workhouse, Gayton 66, *208*
Freeman, Albert 113, 186–8
Freeman, Albert C 110
Frome (Som), workhouse 60, 74, 76, *209*
Fulcher, Thomas *210*
Fulham (Lond)
    Union
        workhouse, Brighton Rd, Sutton (later Belmont Asylum/Belmont Institution) 140, 145, *215*, *218*, *219*
        workhouse, Fulham Palace Rd 166, *215*
    Western (Fever) Hospital 163, *219*
Fulljames, ___ *204*
Fulwood (Lancs), workhouse *206*
Fulwood (Yorks W R), Ecclesall Bierlow Union cottage homes 152, *212*
Fylde (Lancs), Union, workhouses *206*

G

Gainsborough (Lincs), workhouse 65, *207*
Galton, D 159
Gane, Jesse 66, 77, *209*
Gardner, Joseph 57, 151
Garstang (Lancs), Union, workhouses *206*
Gass *see* Bradshaw & Gass
Gateshead (Dur), Union
    cottage homes, Shotley Bridge *203*
    sanatorium, Shotley Bridge *203*
    workhouse (1840–1) *203*
    workhouse (1885–9) 115, *203*
Gayton (Norf), Freebridge Lynn Union Workhouse 66, *208*
General Strike (1926) 189
Germany, cottage-home system 143
Ghent (Belgium), *Maison de Force* 34
Gibson, Henry *208*
Gibson, James S *217*
Gibson, Thomas 18, **19**
Giggleswick (Yorks W R)
    Gilbert Union 27
    Settle Union Workhouse *213*
Gilbert, ___ (Assistant Commissioner) 156
Gilbert, A *215*
Gilbert, Thomas 20, 27, 193
Gilbert Unions 20, 27–8, 41, 44, 193
    workhouses 21–6, 31, 35, 41, 44
Gilbert's Act (1782) 20, 21, 26–7, 31, 193
Giles, John, & Biven 165, **165**, *216*, *219*, *220*
Giles, John, & Gough *214*
Giles, William *203*

Giles, Gough & Trollope 110–12, **111**, *206*, *207*, *214*, *215*, *218*
Gillingwater, Edmund 20, 46
Gimingham (Norf), Gilbert Union 27
Glanford Brigg (Lincs), workhouse 73, *207*
Glendale Union (Northumb), workhouse, Wooler 78, *208*
Glenn Magna (Leics), Gilbert Union 27
Glossop (Derb), workhouse 42, *203*
Gloucester
    Corporation 11, 13
    Union Workhouse 72, 161, *204*
Gloucester Ship Canal 36
Gloucestershire, poor-law institutions, post-1834 *204*
Glynde (Suss), Gilbert Union 27
Godstone (Surr), Union Workhouse, Bletchingley *210*
Goliath, training ship 151, *218*
Good Easter (Essex), workhouse 14
Goodman *see* Holman & Goodman
Goole (Yorks W R), workhouse 79, *212*
Gorleston (Norf), cottage homes *208*
Goschen, George, 1st Viscount 103
Gothic style 53, 66, 67, 110
    workhouse chapels 100, 130
    see also Perpendicular style
Gough *see* Giles, John and Gough; Giles, Gough & Trollope
Gould, John 78, *205*
Graham, ___ *209*
Grantham (Lincs)
    workhouse (1837) 60, 76, *207*
    workhouse (1891–2) *207*
Gravesend and Milton Union (Kent), workhouse, Gravesend 57, 78, *205*
Gray, Charles 13, 20
Grays (Essex)
    scattered homes 151, **151**, 152, *217*
    training ship *Exmouth* 151, *220*
Great Boughton (Ches), Great Boughton (later Tarvin) Union Workhouse *202*
Great Bowden (Leics), Market Harborough Union Workhouse 60, *207*
Great Missenden (Bucks), workhouse 42, **42**
Great Ouseburn (Yorks W R)
    Gilbert Union 27
    Union Workhouse *212*
Great Preston (Yorks W R), Gilbert Union 27
    workhouse *213*
Great Snoring (Norf), Walsingham Union Workhouse 63, **64**, *208*
Great Yarmouth (Norf), workhouse *208*
Grecian style 66
Green, Herbert J *208*, *210*
Green, John *204*
Green, John & Benjamin *203*, *208*
Green, Valentine *207*
Greenwich (Lond), Union
    Cottage Homes Village, Sidcup 150, *215*
    workhouse, Grove Park (later Grove Park Hospital) 108, 110, 122, 176, *215*, *219*
    workhouse, Vanbrugh Hill 86–7, **88**, 98, 103, 108, *215*
    infirmary 161
Greenwood, James 181
Grenoside (Yorks W R), workhouse *213*
Gressenhall (Norf), workhouse 22, 23, **24**, 127, *208*
Griffin, John 67, *205*
Griffiths, ___ *212*
Grimsby (Lincs), workhouse 136, *207*
Grover, ___ 47
guardians *see* boards of guardians
Guildford (Surr), workhouse 72, 134, *210*
Guiltcross Union (Norf) 142
    workhouse, Kenninghall 63, 124, 133, *208*
Guisborough (Yorks N R), workhouse 79, **79**, *212*
Gutteridge, A F *205*
Gwynn, John 28, **29**, 31, *209*
gymnasia 151

H

Hackford (Norf), Gilbert Union/Parish 27
Hackney (Lond)
    casual ward block, Gainsborough Rd, Hackney Wick 186, *215*
    cottage homes, Chipping Ongar 149, **149**, 152, *215*
    industrial school, Brentwood 149, *215*
    workhouse/infirmary, High St, Homerton **128**, 166, *215*
Haddon, G C (Messrs Haddon) **112**, 113, *205*, *209*
Hailsham (Suss), workhouse 78, *210*
Haines, Richard 9
Hale, Sir Matthew 9, 17
Hales (Norf), workhouse *see* Heckingham
half-butterfly plan 176
Halifax (Yorks W R)
    infirmary 169, 170, **171**, 177, *213*
    workhouse (1635) 6
    workhouse (1839) *213*
Hall, E S *219*
Hall, E T *219*
Hall, James **112–13**, 113, *213*
Hall, Leigh *206*
Hall, Richard 45
Hall & Woodhouse *206*
Hallett & Newman *202*, *211*
Halstead (Essex), workhouse 57, 189, *204*
Haltwhistle (Northumb), workhouse *208*
Ham, ___ 49
Hambledon (Surr)
    Gilbert Union/Parish 27
    workhouse 56, *210*
    King George V Sanatorium 176, *219*
Hamburg (Germany), cottage-home system 143
Hammersmith (Lond)
    branch school, Marlesford Lodge 148, *218*
    workhouse, Du Cane Rd 110–12, **111**, *215*
Hammond, F *214*
Hampshire
    Gilbert Unions/Parishes 27
    poor-law institutions, post-1834 *204–5*
Hampstead (Lond)
    North-Western (Fever) Hospital 163, *218*
    Parish of St John 142
    workhouse, New End 94–5, **94**, 166, 167, *215*
Hansom, J A *207*
Hanway, Jonas 132, 139
Hanwell (Mdx), Central London District School 97, 140, **141**, 147, 149, *218*
    Ophthalmic Institute **148**, 149, *218*
Harbledown (Kent), Gilbert Union 27
Hardingstone (Northants), workhouse *208*
Hardwick, T *216*
Hardy, Gathorne 160
Harefield (Mdx), workhouse **17**
Harlesden (Mdx), Willesden Union Workhouse 110, 113, *207*
Harraby Hill (Cumb), industrial school *202*
Harris, John 156, **156**
Harris, William *202*
Harrison, Fred *206*
Harrison, J *202*
Harrow-on-the-Hill (Mdx), workhouse 16
Harston, A & C 145, 164, 165, *214*, *218*, *219*, *220*
Hart, Dr Ernest 160
Hartismere Union (Suff) 142, *210*
    infirmary, Eye *210*
    workhouse, Eye *210*
Hartismere and Hoxne Union (Suff), industrial school, Wortham 142, *210*
Hartismere, Hoxne and Thredling Incorporation (Suff) 22
Hartlepool (Dur), workhouse *203*
Hartley (Kent), Cranbrook Union Workhouse 56, *205*
Hartley Wintney (Hants)
    Union Workhouse, Winchfield *205*
    see also Farnham and Hartley Wintney School District

247

THE WORKHOUSE

Hartlib, Samuel 7
Harvey, Thomas Hill 47, *203*
Haslingden (Lancs), workhouse *206*
Hastings (Suss)
  infirmary (1868) 168–9
  infirmary (1898–1903) *211*
  workhouse (1836) 60, 61, **61**, 119, 136, *211*
Hatfield (Herts)
  children's home 191
  workhouse 191, *205*
Havant (Hants), workhouse *205*
Hay, William 18
Haycock, ___ *209*
Haycock, John Hiram 25, *209*
Hayfield (Derb), Union Workhouse, Low Leighton *203*
Hayley, William, Son & Leigh Hall *206*
Haywood, Charles S *206*
Head, Sir Francis Bond 22, 27–8, 45
  courtyard plan 46–7, 53, 54–7, **55**, 58–9, 90, **221**
  workhouses in Kent 54–7, *205*, *206*
Headington (Oxon), workhouse *209*
Headley (Hants), Gilbert Union 27
  workhouse *205*
Hearne Common (Kent), Blean Union Workhouse 53, 54, **56**, 57, *205*
Heathcote, Sir Gilbert 31
heating 61, 83, 107
Heckingham (Norf), Hales, workhouse 22–3, **23**, 31, 156, *208*
Helmsley (Yorks N R), workhouse *212*
Helston (Cornw), workhouse *202*
Hemel Hempstead (Herts)
  workhouse (18th century) 13
  workhouse (1835–6) 67, 191, *205*
Hemsworth (Yorks W R), workhouse *213*
Hendon (Mdx)
  Central London Sick Asylum (later Colindale Hospital) 176, **176**, *218*, *219*
  Union
    infirmary, Burnt Oak *207*
    workhouse, Burnt Oak *207*
Henley (Oxon), workhouse *209*
Henman, *see also* Brown & Henman
Henman, C & W 149, *220*
Henman, W **64**, 65, *204*, *205*
Henstead (Suff), Union Workhouse, Swainsthorpe (Norf) 65, *208*
Hereford
  Incorporation 11
  Vagrant House, Quakers Lane 180
  workhouse (1836) 177, *205*
Herefordshire, poor-law institutions, post-1834 *205*
Herkomer, Hubert von **117**
Herne Bay (Kent), Pier Hotel, branch school (later St Anne's Home) 149, *218*, *220*
Hertford, workhouse (later Kingsmead Special School) 191, *205*
Hertfordshire, poor-law institutions, post-1834 191, *205*
Hessle (Yorks E R), cottage homes *212*
Heswall (Ches), sanatorium 176, *206*
Hewitt, Arthur S *208*
'hexagon' plan 46–7, 53–4, **224–6**, **228**
  criticism of **51**
  workhouses built 1835–40 60, 74–7
Hexham (Northumb), workhouse 124, 125, *208*
Highgate (Lond)
  Highgate Hill, infirmary (Islington, Parish of St Mary) *215*
  St Pancras Union Infirmary 166, *216*
Highworth and Swindon Union (Wilts), workhouse, Stratton St Margaret 90, *211*
Hill, *see also* Cancellor & Hill; Fowler & Hill
Hill, Sir Rowland 163
Hill, W **168**, *213*

Hillingdon (Mdx), Uxbridge Union Workhouse 177, *207*
Hillsborough, Earl of 18
Hinckley (Leics), workhouse *207*
Hitchin (Herts), workhouse 191, *205*
Hither Green (Lond) *see* Lewisham
Hobday *see* Paine & Hobday
Hobson, ___ 6
Hodges, Henry 78
Holbeach (Lincs), workhouse 75, 76, *207*
Holbeck (Yorks W R), workhouse 160, 168, **168**, 169, *213*
Holborn (Lond), Union 107–8, *215*
  branch school, Eagle House, Mitcham *215*, *217*
  infirmary, Archway, Upper Holloway 108, 166, **166**, 167, *215*
  workhouse, Mitcham **108**, 109, *215*
  workhouse/casual ward, Greys Inn *215*
Holland, Frederick 176, *212*
Hollingbourne (Kent), workhouse *205*
Holloway (Lond) *see* Upper Holloway; West London Union
Holman & Goodman 153, *216*
Holmes, Edward *211*, *212*
Holmes & Watson 152, *212*
Holsworthy (Devon), workhouse 92, *203*
Home Office 123
Homerton (Lond)
  East London Union Workhouse 98, *215*
  Eastern (Fever and Smallpox) Hospital 163, *218*
  Hackney Union Workhouse/Infirmary, High St **128**, 166, *215*
Honiton (Devon), workhouse 65, *203*
Hoo (Kent), workhouse 54, *205*
Hopgood, ___ *205*
Hornby (Lancs), workhouse *206*
Horncastle (Lincs)
  Horncastle Cottage Homes 154, **154**
  workhouse (1734) 17
  workhouse (1837–8) 72, *207*
Hornchurch (Essex), cottage homes 145, *217*
Horndean (Hants), workhouse *204*
Hornsey (Lond), industrial school *215*
Horsfall, Richard 170, *213*
Horsham (Suss), workhouse *211*
Horsham St Faith (Norf), workhouse *208*
hospitals
  16th–17th centuries 3–10
  children 149, 176–7
  Emergency Medical Service 178, 191
  Metropolitan Asylums Board *219*
    hospital schools 149, *220*
    hospital ships 163–4, *219*
  plan types 46, 158–9, 167, 169
    pavilion planning 98, 103–4, 159
  workhouse infirmaries become hospitals, 1930s and later 190, 191
  see also infirmaries; sanatoria
Hothfield Common (Kent), West Ashford Union Workhouse 54, *206*
Houghton-le-Spring (Dur), workhouse 173, *203*
'houseless poor' 179–88
houses of correction 3, 4, 5, 6, 9, 18, 179
houses of industry x, 21–5, 28, 29, 34–6, 192
Howden (Yorks E R), workhouse *212*
Howell, W Roland 119
Hoxne (Suff), Union 142, *210*
  workhouse, Stradbroke *210*
  see also Hartismere
Hubert, S 47–8
Huddersfield (Yorks W R)
  Anti-Poor-Law riots 49
  Union Workhouse, Crosland Moor **92**, 93, 98–9, *213*
  Union Workhouse, Deanhouse 93, *213*
Hull (Yorks E R) *see* Kingston-upon-Hull
Humphries, James 61
Hundleby (Lincs), Spilsby Union Workhouse 72, *207*

Hundred, as unit for workhouses 17, 18, 20, 21, 22, 36–40
Hungerford (Berks), Hungerford (later Hungerford and Ramsbury) Union Workhouse 89, **89**, 92, 98, *201*
Hunslet (Yorks W R)
  cottage homes, Rothwell Haigh *213*
  workhouse (1760–1) *213*
  workhouse (1900–3), Rothwell Haigh 115, 170, **172**, 186, *213*
Hunt, Edward 62, *204*, *211*
Hunt, H A *217*
Huntingdon, workhouse 60, 157, *205*
Huntingdonshire, poor-law institutions, post-1834 *205*
Hursley (Hants)
  Union Workhouse (1899–1900), Chandler's Ford **116**, 117, *205*
  workhouse (1828) *205*
Hutton, William 32
Hutton (Essex), Poplar Union Training School 122, 153, **153**, *216*
Hyde, H *203*

I

idiots *see* mentally handicapped
Illustrated London News, attack on Poor Law Commission (1846) 90–1, **91**
imbeciles *see* mentally handicapped
incorporations, Old Poor Law
  rural 21–5, 30
  see also Gilbert Unions
  urban 10–13, 28, 30, 31
  workhouses taken over by New Poor Law Unions 44
industrial schools 131, 138–42, 153, **229**
  Industrial Schools Act (1866) 149
infectious diseases
  hospitals, Metropolitan Asylums Board 163–4, *219*
  in schools 140, 147–51
  vagrants carrying 180
  in workhouses 32, 51, 156, 168, 169
  see also receiving (probationary) wards/houses; smallpox
infirm *see* aged and infirm
infirmaries 71, 98, 157–61, 165–71, 175–8, 190, 191
  Old Poor Law workhouses 155
Ingleman, Richard 40
ins and outs x
'intermediate' workhouses *see* 'branch' ('intermediate') workhouses
International Modern style 177
Ipswich (Suff) 65, 156
  Christ's Hospital 4
  compulsory poor rate (1557) 4
  county gaol 34, **34**
  St Clement's Workhouse (pre-1836) 49
  Union
    St John's School 142, *210*
    workhouse (1836–7) *210*
    workhouse (1898–9) *210*
Ireland
  dispensary system 160
  immigrants from 130, 181
  workhouses 65–6, **66**
Irish Poor Law Act (1838) 65
Irthlingborough (Northants), casual wards 188
Isle of Sheppey (Kent), Union Workhouse, Minster in Sheppey *206*
Isle of Thanet (Kent), Union
  cottage homes, Manston *205*
  workhouse, Minster in Thanet 54, *205*
Isle of Wight Corporation 25, 36
  workhouse, Newport 25, 31, *205*
Isleworth (Mdx), Brentford Union Workhouse 62, *207*

Islington (Lond)
  London Fever Hospital 163
  Parish of St Mary
    industrial school, Hornsey *215*
    infirmary, Highgate Hill *215*
    workhouse, John St (now Barnsby St) 106, *215*
    workhouse, Upper Holloway **105**, 106, *215*
  St Luke's, Middlesex Parish Workhouse, City Rd **106**, 107–8, 109, *216*
Italianate style 58, 73, 76, 85, 96, 100, 133, 140, 159
itch (scabies) 155, 156, 168, 169, 170
Izard, J Grafton 148, *216*

J

Jackman, J T *212*
Jackson, George *203*
Jacobean style 53, 73, 89
Jarvis, H *217*
Jarvis, Henry *217*
Jeffery, Alfred W *211*
Jennings tip-up closets 98, **98**
Jericho (Lancs), workhouse *206*
Jervis *see* Pennington & Jervis
Johnson, ___ *203*
Jones, Dr Henry Bence 163
Jones & Parker *215*
Journal of the Workhouse Visiting Society 99–100, 160, 162, 181

K

Kay, Dr James (later Kay-Shuttleworth) 23, 138, 140
  'Report on the Training of Pauper Children' (1837–8) 138
Kedington (Suff), Risbridge Union Workhouse 94, 133, *210*
Keighley (Yorks W R)
  infirmary, Fell Lane 170–1, *213*
  workhouse, Oakworth Rd 182, *213*
Kempthorne, Sampson 46, 47–8
  model plans 46–7, 53, 90–1
    'hexagon' plan 46, 47, 60, 74–7, **224–6**, **228**
    provision for children 133, 138, **229**
    provision for sick and infirm 157
    'square' plan 46, 47, 53, 58, 60–70, **222–3**, **228**
    '200-pauper' plans 46, 47, 60, 77–8, **224**, **226–7**
    views on cross-ventilation and back-to-back wards 46, 67, 105, 107
  workhouses by 60, 61–2, 74, 76, 77–8, 201–12 *passim*
    Abingdon 74, **74**, 83
    Andover **52**, 62, 74, 78
    Bath 74, **75**
    Crediton 61, 74, **75**
    Hastings 61, **61**
    Newhaven 78, **78**
Kendal (Westmld)
  workhouse, Kendal *211*
  workhouse, Milnthorpe *211*
Kendall, H E 94–5, **94**, *211*, *215*
Kendrick, John 6, 8
Kenninghall (Norf), Guiltcross Union Workhouse 63, 124, 133, *208*
Kennington (Lond), Renfrew Rd *see* Lambeth
Kensington (Lond)
  St Margaret and St John, Westminster, Joint Parishes, workhouse, Marloes Rd 89, 160, *217*
  St Marylebone Infirmary 166, **167**, *216*

248

INDEX

Union (later Parish of St Mary Abbots)
   workhouse, Butt's Field *215*
   workhouse, Marloes Rd 89, **89,** 106, 166, 169, 191, *215*
Kensington & Chelsea School District
   Banstead Cottage Homes 144, **144,** 145, 148, **150,** *218*
   branch school, Marlesford Lodge, Hammersmith 148, *218*
Kensington School District 142
Kent
   Gilbert Unions/Parishes 27
   poor-law institutions, post-1834 205–6
   see also London
   Sir Francis Head's workhouses 53, 54–7, **55**
Kettering (Northants), workhouse 62, 72, 176, *208*
Keynsham (Som), workhouse *209*
Kidderminster (Worcs), workhouse *212*
King's Lynn (Norf)
   Incorporation 11
   workhouse *208*
King's Norton (Worcs), Union
   cottage homes, Shenley Fields *212*
   workhouse, Selly Oak 170, **171,** *212*
   see also Birmingham, King's Norton and Aston (Joint Committee)
Kingsbridge (Devon), workhouse 73, *203*
Kingsclere (Hants), workhouse *205*
Kingston-upon-Hull (Yorks E R) 47
   Incorporation, Charity Hall 11, **11**
   workhouse *212*
Kingston-upon-Thames (Surr), Union Workhouse, Norbiton 65, **168–9,** 169, *210*
Kington (Herefs), workhouse *205*
Kirby, Edmund *206*
Kirby, John Joshua *210*
Kirk, John **92,** 93, *213*
Kirkby Lonsdale (Westmld), Gilbert Union 27
Kirkby Moorside (Yorks N R), workhouse 95, **95,** 185, *212*
Kirkby Stephen (Westmld)
   East Ward Union Workhouse *211*
   Gilbert Union 27
Kirkdale (Lancs), industrial school 138, **138,** 142, *206*
Kirkham (Lancs), workhouse *206*
Knaresborough (Yorks W R), workhouse 94, 186, **186,** *213*
Knatchbull, Sir Edward 14
Knatchbull's Act (Workhouse Test Act) (1723) 3, 14, 19, 28, 193
   amendment (1795) 32
Knight, William *212*
Knightley, ____ *207*
Knightley, T E 145, **146,** *207*
Knowles, W H 115, *203*
Knutsford (Ches), workhouse *202*

L

labour colonies 123, 179, 188
labour exchanges 123
labour rate 32
Labour Test Orders 49
labour yards 103, 120, 122, 195
Ladds, John 57, 151
Ladywell (Lond) *see* Lewisham
Laindon (Essex), farm colony 122–3, *216*
Lambert, John 160
Lambeth (Lond), Parish of St Mary
   infirmary, Renfrew Rd *215*
   Norwood House of Industry (later Lambeth School) 124, 132, 145, *215*
   workhouse (1726) 15
   workhouse, Price's Candle Factory 106
   workhouse, Renfrew Rd **107,** 108, 109, **109,** 113, 122, 181, *215*
   workhouse (later test workhouse), Princes Rd 119, 122, *215*

Lampard, F J 147
Lancashire
   Gilbert Unions 27
   poor-law institutions, post-1834 *206–7*
   resistance to workhouse provision 49
Lancaster, Charles H *206, 207*
Lancaster
   workhouse (18th century) 30
   workhouse (1841) *206*
Lancefield, George *205, 206*
Lancet, Commission on metropolitan infirmaries (1865) 160
Lanchester (Dur), workhouse *203*
Lang, Charles *202*
Langho (Lancs), mental colony 174, *206*
Langport (Som), Union Workhouse, Picts Hill 76, *209*
Lansbury, George 122, 123
Lansdown, J C & G *210*
Latham, George *202*
Launceston (Cornw), workhouse *202*
Lawkland (Yorks W R), Gilbert Union 27
Lawson, Thomas 13
Lawson, V A *204*
Layland, Thomas *202*
Leavesden (Herts)
   Metropolitan Asylum for Imbeciles 165, *220*
   St Pancras industrial school 142, *216*
Ledbury (Herefs), workhouse 65, *205*
Lee, Charles 217, *218*
Lee & Smith *216*
Leeds (Yorks W R)
   industrial school, Sheepscar 96, 139, **139,** *213*
   workhouse (1738) 17
   workhouse (1858–60) **frontispiece,** 96, **96,** 100, **101,** *213*
Leek (Staffs), workhouse 95, *209*
Leeson, Richard J *208*
legislation
   before 1834 3, 4, 5–6, 8, 21, 32, 36
   on children 132, 139
   on vagrancy 179
   see also Gilbert's Act; Knatchbull's Act
   1834 onwards
      on children 134, 139, 149, 164
      on sick, mentally ill and mentally handicapped 163, 164, 174, 176, 191
      Lunacy Acts 155, 157, 161–2, 173
      on vagrancy 179, 181, 182, 185
      see also Board of Guardians (Default) Act; Irish Poor Law Act; Local Government Act; Metropolitan Poor Law Amendment Act; Old Age Pensions Act; Poor Law Amendment Act; Unemployed Workmen Act; Union Chargeability Act
Leicester 30
   St Martin's Workhouse (1714) 14
   Union 45, 47
      cottage homes, Countesthorpe 145, *207*
      infirmary, North Evington *207*
      workhouse 45, 48, 76, *207*
Leicestershire
   Gilbert Unions/Parishes 27
   poor-law institutions, post-1834 *207*
Leigh, William 34, *210*
Leigh (Lancs), workhouse *206*
Leighton Buzzard (Beds), workhouse 58, **59,** **64,** *201*
Leominster (Herefs), workhouse 44, 65, 80, **80,** *205*
less-eligibility x, 43, 194
Lewes (Suss), workhouse *211*
Lewis, Thomas Frankland 44
Lewisham (Lond)
   Park (Fever) Hospital, Hither Green 164, **164,** *218*
   St Olave's Union Workhouse for the Aged, Ladywell 118, **118,** 119, 130, *216*
   Union Workhouse, Lewisham Rd *215*

Lexden and Winstree Union (Essex), workhouse, Stanway, Colchester 47, 63–5, **64–5,** *204*
Leyburn (Yorks N R)
   Gilbert Union/Parish 27
   workhouse *212*
Leyton (Essex), West Ham Union Workhouse 100, **101,** 143, *204*
Leytonstone (Essex), Bethnal Green industrial school 142, 145–6, **146,** *214*
Liberal welfare reforms 123
Lichfield (Staffs), workhouse 46, 72, *209*
Lincoln, workhouse 73, *207*
Lincolnshire
   Gilbert Unions/Parishes 27
   poor-law institutions, post-1834 *207*
linear (in-line) plan, hospitals/workhouse infirmaries **158,** 159, 160, 166, 168
linear layout (Scott & Moffatt) 71–3
Lingfield (Surr), workhouse 17
Lingwood (Norf), Blofield Union Workhouse 65, *207*
Linton (Cambs)
   parish workshop (1577) 5
   workhouse *202*
Liskeard (Cornw), workhouse 72, *202*
Little Holland (Lincs), workhouses 6–7
Littledean (Glos), bridewell 34
Littlewood, John *206*
Liverpool (Lancs)
   Borough Gaol 34
   Parish
      cottage homes, Olive Mount, Wavertree **144,** 145, *206*
      industrial school, Kirkdale 138, **138,** 142, *206*
      infirmary, Highfield *206*
      workhouse (1732) 16
      workhouse (1769–72, enlarged 1842–3) 28, 30, **30,** 31, 89, 96, **124,** 154, *206*
      see also Toxteth; West Derby
Liverpool, West Derby and Toxteth Park Joint Committee, sanatorium, Heswall 176, *206*
Livesay, Augustus *205*
Lloyd, Sir Richard 18
Local Government Act (1929) 190
Local Government Board
   and aged and infirm 118, 119
   ban on outdoor relief 120
   and children 137, 143, 148
   and farm colonies 122, 123
   and vagrancy 185, 186–7, 188
Locke, John 10
Lockington (Yorks E R), Gilbert Union 27
Locks Bottom (Kent), Bromley Union Workhouse 90, *205*
Lockwood, Henry F 94, 96, *212*
   and Thomas Allom 89, 96, *206*
   and William Mawson 96, **96,** 99, *202, 206, 212, 213*
Loddon (Norf), Holy Trinity Church, poor box **4**
Loddon and Clavering Incorporation (Norf), workhouse, Heckingham 22–3, **23,** 31, 156, *208*
Loes and Wilford Incorporation (Suff), workhouse, Melton 22
London
   Aldersgate, workhouse (17th century) 9
   Bethlehem Hospital ('Bedlam') 4, 156
   Bishopsgate Workhouse 132
   Bridewell 4, **5,** 6, **7,** 131, 132, 179
   Central (Unemployed) Body, farm colony 123
   children, provision for
      under Old Poor Law 7, 8, 12, 16, 131–2
      under New Poor Law
         cottage homes 143, 144, 145, 152, 153
         provision for ex-workhouse children 154

   provision for illness 147–9
   scattered homes 151, 152
   separate schools 138, 140–2, 145–7, 151
Christ's Hospital 4, 7, 131, 132
Common Poor Fund for London 105, 166
compulsory poor rate (1547) 4
Corporation 7, 8, 9, 11, 12, 13
Foundling Hospital 132
   regional branches 28
Half-Moon Alley, Corporation Workhouse (1699) 12, 13
Heydon House, Minories (17th century) 7
New Ormond St, home for ex-workhouse girls (1861) 154
Playhouse Yard, Refuge for the Destitute and Houseless Poor (1840s) **180**
poor-law institutions
   Old Poor Law
      16th–17th centuries 4, 6, 7, 8, 9–10, 131
      1696–*c* 1750 11, 12, 13, 15–16, 131–2
      c 1750–1834 132
   New Poor Law *214–20*
      1834–40 45, 96–7
      1840–70 96–8
      1870–1914 105–10
   see also children; sick, mentally ill and mentally handicapped; vagrants and 'houseless poor'
St Andrew, Saffron Hill, workhouse (1730) 15
St Andrew's, Holborn, workhouse (18th century) 16
St Anne's Soho, parish poorhouses (17th–18th centuries) 9–10
St Bartholomew's Hospital 4
St Botolph, without Bishopsgate, workhouse (1730) 15
St Giles, Cripplegate, workhouse (1724) 15
St Thomas's Hospital 4
sick, mentally ill and mentally handicapped, provision for
   under Old Poor Law 155, 156
   under New Poor Law 160, 161, 162–3, 165–7, 176
   see also Metropolitan Asylums Board
vagrants and 'houseless poor', provision for 181, 182–5, 186, 188
Wardrobe workhouse, Vintry (17th century) 7
see also Bermondsey; Bethnal Green; Blackwall; Bow; Bromley-by-Bow; Camberwell; Camden Town; Central London School District; Central London Sick Asylum District; Chelsea; City of London Union; Clerkenwell; Dulwich; East London Union; Finsbury; Fulham; Greenwich; Hackney; Hammersmith; Hampstead; Highgate; Holborn; Homerton; Hornsey; Islington; Kensington; Lambeth; Lewisham; Metropolitan Asylums Board; Mile End; Newington; Norwood; Paddington; Peckham; Plumstead; Poplar; Rotherhithe; St George-in-the-East; St George's, Hanover Square; St George's Union; St Giles-in-the-Fields and St George, Bloomsbury; St Luke's, Middlesex, St Martin-in-the-Fields; St Marylebone; St Olave's Union; St Pancras; St Saviour's Union; St Sepulchre; Shoreditch; Southwark; Stepney; Stockwell; Strand; Tooting; Tooting Bec; Tottenham; Upper Holloway; Walworth; Wandsworth; Wapping; West London School District; West London Union; Westminster; Whitechapel; Woolwich

249

Long Ashton (Som) *see* Bedminster
Longley, ___ 103
Longtown (Cumb), Union Workhouse, Netherby *202*
Loudon's *Architectural Magazine* 46
Loughborough (Leics), workhouse 72, *207*
Louth (Lincs) 30
　workhouse 72, 155, *207*
Lovatt, ___ *209*
'Love-Poor, Christian' 17
Low Leighton (Derb), workhouse *203*
Lowe, Revd Robert 36, 40
Lowestoft (Suff), St Luke's Hospital 176, *219*
Lowry, ___ 189
Luck, C L **168**
Ludby, J **217**
Ludlow (Salop), workhouse *209*
Lunacy Acts (19th century) 155, 157, 162, 173
Lunacy Commissioners 162, 173
lunatic asylums
　county and borough 155, 156, 161–2
　Metropolitan Asylums Board 165
lunatics *see* mentally ill
Lunesdale Union (Lancs), workhouse, Hornby *206*
Luton (Beds)
　workhouse (18th century) 13, 16
　workhouse (1836) 58–9, **59**, *201*
Lutterworth (Leics)
　Gilbert Union 27
　workhouse 72, *207*
lying-in wards, in workhouse infirmaries, 1867–1900 169
Lymington (Hants), workhouse 60, 77–8, **77**, *205*
Lynam, Charles 134, **135**

M

Maberley, Alfred W 181, *204*, *208*
Macalpine's steam-powered washing-machine **128**
McBeath, Robert J *202*
Macclesfield (Ches), workhouse 72, 73, 83, 100, 161, 190, *202*
McIntosh, J Y **112**, **114**, *206*
Mackworth, Sir Humphrey 12
Madeley (Salop), workhouse **112**, 113, *209*
Madron (Cornw), Penzance Union Workhouse 72, *202*
magistrates, on boards of guardians 44
Maidenhead (Berks), workhouse 136, *201*
Maidstone (Kent) 56
　Union Workhouse, Coxheath 54, 127–9, **129**, *206*
Maldon (Essex), workhouse 133, *204*
Malling Union (Kent), workhouse, West Malling 56, *206*
Malmesbury (Wilts), workhouse 65, *211*
Malthus, Revd T R, *Essay on the Principles of Population* (1803) 32
Malton (Yorks N R), workhouse *212*
Manchester (Lancs) 161
　farm colony 123
　Parish *206*
　　casual wards and test workhouse, Tame St, Ancoates 122, *206*
　　industrial school, Swinton 130, 138, 142, *206*
　　workhouse, Crumpsall (1855–6) 98, 125, **125**, *206*
　　workhouse, New Bridge St (1793; rebuilt *c* 1880) 30, 122, *206*
　see also Chorlton and Manchester Joint (Asylum) Committee; Chorlton and Manchester Joint (Casual Ward and Test House) Committee
Mangnall, *see also* Travis & Mangnall
Mangnall, William *206*, *207*
Manlove's dash-wheel and hydro-extractor **128**

Manningtree (Essex), workhouse 47
Mansfield (Notts), workhouse 60, *208*
Manston (Kent), cottage homes *205*
maps *see* distribution maps
Margate (Kent), Princess Mary Hospital *219*
Market Bosworth (Leics), workhouse *207*
Market Drayton (Salop), Drayton Union Workhouse *209*
Market Harborough (Leics), Union Workhouse, Great Bowden 60, *207*
Markham, Dr William O 160
Marland (Lancs), workhouse *206*
Marlborough (Wilts), workhouse *211*
Marrable, F *219*
married couples, aged, accommodation for 117, 119, **119**
Marriott, Matthew 13–14, **14**, 15, 17
Marshall, Arthur 169, *208*, *210*, *212*
Marshall, H *205*
Marston Green (Warws), cottage homes **144**, 145, 152, *211*
Martin (Kent), Gilbert Union 27
Martley (Worcs), workhouse 60, *212*
Marylebone (Lond) *see* St Marylebone
Mason, ___ *206*
Mason, Alfred Richardson *204*
Mason, John *203*
Mason, William 65, *204*, *210*
masters' houses 115, 125
maternity blocks 169
Mawson, William 96, **96**, 99, *202*, *206*, *212*, *213*
Maynard, George *210*
measles 180
medical officers, in New Poor Law workhouses 81, 157, 158
Medland, James 181, *204*, *208*
Medway Union (Kent)
　cottage homes, Rochester *206*
　workhouse, Chatham 98, *206*
Meldreth (Cambs), workhouse 14
Melton (Suff), workhouse 22
Melton Constable (Norf), Brinton and Melton Constable Gilbert Union Workhouse 27, **27**, *207*
Melton Mowbray (Leics)
　Gilbert Union 27
　workhouse 73, *207*
Mental Deficiency Act (1913) 174
mental-deficiency colonies 174–5
mentally handicapped ('idiots'/'imbeciles') 155–78
mentally ill ('lunatics') 155–78
Mercantile Marine, workhouse boys trained for 154
Mere (Wilts), workhouse 72, 73, *211*
Meriden (Warws), Gilbert Union 27
　workhouse *211*
Metropolitan Association for Befriending Young Servants 154
Metropolitan Asylums Board 105, 161, 177, *219*–20
　asylums for imbeciles and harmless lunatics 110, 165, 219–20
　casual wards 188
　fever and smallpox hospitals 163–4, *219*
　schools/hospital schools 149, *220*
　tuberculosis sanatoria 149, 176, *219*
Metropolitan Board of Works 182
Metropolitan Houseless Poor Act (1864) 182
Metropolitan Poor Law Amendment Act (1867) 105, 120, 155, 161, 165–6
Mettrai (Switzerland), cottage-home system 143
Middlesbrough (Yorks N R), workhouse **112**, 113, 152, *212*
Middlesex
　corporation (1664), Middlesex County Workhouse 8
　Middlesex County Asylums 165
　poor-law institutions, post-1834 *207*
　　see also London
　scheme for County Workhouse and House of Correction (1753) 18, **19**

Middleton, Sir Thomas 6
Midhurst (Suss), Union Workhouse, Easebourne 26–7, **27**, *211*
Mildenhall (Suff)
　workhouse (pre-1834) *210*
　workhouse (1895–6) *210*
Mile End Old Town (Lond), Hamlet *215*
　workhouse, Bancroft Rd *215*
Mills, Alexander W *206*
Milne, ___ *208*
Milnthorpe (Westmld)
　Gilbert Union 27
　Kendal Union Workhouse *211*
Milton Regis (Kent), Union Workhouse, Sittingbourne 54, *206*
Ministry of Health
　Emergency Medical Service hospitals 178
　takes over poor-law affairs (1919) 189
Minster in Sheppey (Kent), workhouse *206*
Minster in Thanet (Kent), Isle of Thanet Union Workhouse 54, *205*
Mitcham (Surr)
　Eagle House, branch school *215*, *217*
　Holborn Union Workhouse **108**, 109, *215*
Mitchell, Ralph 11, **11**, 23, *203*
Mitford and Launditch Incorporation (Norf), workhouse, Gressenhall 22, 23, **24**, 127, *208*
model plans
　for local-authority infectious diseases hospitals 169
　for workhouses, issued by Central Poor Law Authority 46–7, 53–4, 161, 180, **221–9**
　　courtyard plan (Sir Francis Head) 46–7, 54–5, **221**
　　'hexagon' plan (Kempthorne) 46, 47, 60, 74–7, **224–6**, **228**
　　'square' plan (Kempthorne) 46, 47, 53, 58, 60–70, **222–3**, **228**
　　'200-pauper' plans (Kempthorne) 46, 47, 60, 77–8, **224**, **226–7**
Moffatt, ___ *208*
Moffatt, William Bonython 71, *211*
　partnership with Scott *see* Scott, Sir George Gilbert
Moffatt, William L 94
Monday *see* Berney & Monday
Monnington, W 147
Montgomery and Pool (Mont), house of industry 25, **25**
Moorgarth (Lancs), workhouse *206*
Morda (Salop), workhouse *see* Oswestry
Morpeth (Northumb), workhouse *208*
Morris, John, & Son 120–1, **120**, *216*
Morton, J H 114–15, 123–4, *203*, *207*, *208*, *209*, *212*, *213*
　infirmaries 170, **172**
　mental-deficiency colonies 174
　schools 136, **137**
　South Shields Union Workhouse **112**, 114–15, **114**
Mouat, Dr 113
Mountsorrel (Leics), workhouse *207*
Munday, ___ *203*
Murgatroyd, A J **125**
Murgatroyd, James *206*
Mutford and Lothingland Incorporation (Suff), workhouse, Oulton 22, *210*
Myers, George 47

N

Nacton (Suff), Carlford and Colneis Incorporation Workhouse (later Woodbridge Union Workhouse) 18, 21–2, 31, *210*
Nantwich (Ches), workhouse *202*
Nash, Edwin *218*
Nash, William T 57–8, 75, 76, **76**, 83, 157, *202*, *204*, *205*
　Buntingford Union Workhouse 48, 57, **57**, *205*
　St Ives Union Workhouse 57–8, **58**, *205*

National Health Service Act (1946) 191
National Insurance 123, 189
National Schools 134
navy *see* Royal Navy
Nelson, Charles S & Alline J **98**, 99, *202*, *212*, *213*
Netherby (Cumb), workhouse *202*
Netley (Hants), Royal Victoria Hospital 98
Nettleship, Edward 149
Nettleship, J *212*
New Cross (Kent), South-Eastern (Fever) Hospital 163, *219*
New Forest Union (Hants), workhouse, Ashurst 60, 74, 76, *205*
New Poor Law (1834) 43–52, 193–6
　life in the workhouse, 1830s 81–4
　opposition to *see* Anti-Poor-Law movement
　vagrancy 180–8
　workhouses, 1835–1840 53–84, 194
　　distribution map **54**
New Romney (Kent), workhouse *206*
New Winchester Union (Hants) *see* Winchester
New Windsor (Berks) *see* Windsor
Newark (Notts), Union
　infirmary, Bowbridge Lane *208*
　workhouse, Claypole (Lincs) *208*
Newbury (Berks) 6
　workhouse 60, 62, *201*
Newcastle-under-Lyme (Staffs), workhouse 72, 124, *209*
Newcastle-upon-Tyne (Northumb)
　cottage homes, Ponteland *208*
　workhouse *208*
Newcombe, ___ *203*
Newcombe, W L 115, *203*
Newcome, William L *210*
Newent (Glos), workhouse *204*
Newhaven (Suss), workhouse 60, 78, **78**, *211*
Newington (Lond), Parish of St Mary *216*
　industrial school, Westmorland Rd, Walworth (used as workhouse) 140, *216*
　workhouse (pre-1834) *216*
Newman, *see also* Hallett & Newman
Newman & Newman 118, *216*, *220*
Newmarket (Cambs), workhouse 58, *202*
Newport (I W), Isle of Wight Corporation Workhouse 25, 31, *205*
Newport (Salop), workhouse *209*
Newport Pagnell (Bucks), workhouse 58, *202*
Newton Abbot (Devon), workhouse 71, 72, *203*
Nicholls, ___ *211*
Nicholls, Captain George 36, 40
　as Poor Law Commissioner 32, 36, 42, 44, 46, 52
Nicholls, George B 136, **137**, *210*, *211*, *212*
Nicholson, William Adams **38**, 39, 73, *207*, *208*
Nightingale, Florence **159**, 160, 161
'Nightingale' wards 104
Nonconformists 99, 130
Norbiton (Surr), Kingston-upon-Thames Union Workhouse 65, **168–9**, 169, *210*
Norfolk
　Gilbert Unions/Parishes 27
　poor-law institutions, post-1834 *207*–8
Norman, Alfred *203*
North Aylesford Union (Kent), workhouse, Strood (later Strood Union Workhouse) *206*
North Bierley (Yorks W R), Union Workhouse, Clayton, Bradford 96, **96**, 125, **126**, *213*
North Evington (Leics), infirmary *207*
North Stifford (Essex), Stepney Union Cottage Homes 152, **152**, *217*
North Surrey School District *218*
　branch school, Bow 148–9
　industrial school, Anerley, Upper Norwood 140, 151, *218*
　Wainwright Home, Broadstairs *218*

INDEX

North Witchford Union (Cambs), workhouse, Doddington 185, *202*
Northallerton (Yorks N R), workhouse *212*
Northampton, workhouse 62, 72, *208*
Northamptonshire, poor-law institutions, post-1834 *208*
Northern Counties Joint Poor-Law Committee, Prudhoe Hall Colony 174, *208*
Northleach (Glos), workhouse 65, *204*
Northumberland, poor-law institutions, post 1834 *208*
Northwich (Ches), workhouse *202*
Norton, John **102**
Norwich (Norf)
  compulsory poor rate (1549) 4
  'hospital' (late 16th century) 4
  Incorporation (later Union) 11, 151
  workhouse 181, *208*
  wool industry 25
Norwood (Lond)
  Norwood House of Industry (later Lambeth School) (Parish of St Mary, Lambeth) 124, 132, 145, *215*
  Weston Hill, Mr Aubin's school (later Central London School District industrial school) 132, 138, 140, *218*
Nottingham 36
  Union 49
    school (formerly Radford Union Workhouse), Hartley Rd 145, *208*
    workhouse (1840–1) **128**, *208*
    workhouse (1898–1903) 137, *208*
  see also Basford; Radford
Nottinghamshire
  experiments in deterrent poor-law policy 36–42
  Gilbert Unions/Parishes 27
  poor-law institutions, post-1834 *208*
Nuneaton (Warws), workhouse, Chilvers Coton *211*
nurseries, in workhouses 137
nurses' homes 171, 177, 178

O

Oakham (Rut), workhouse 66, *209*
oakum-picking 9, 16, 61, 83, 120, 121, 122
  vagrants 179, 183, 184, 188
Oates, J *212*
Oates, J D *206*
Oates, J E *203*, *206*, *213*
Okehampton (Devon), workhouse 60, *203*
old-age pensions 117
Old Age Pensions Act (1908) 123
Old Poor Law
  children 131–2
  institutions
    1550–*c* 1750 3–20
    c 1750–1834 21–42
  lunatics and imbeciles 156–7
  sick 155–6
  vagrants 179–80
Old Windsor (Berks), Windsor Union Workhouse, Crimp Hill 53, 72, **72**, 73, *202*
Oldham (Lancs), Union 49
  scattered homes, Royton 152, **152**, *206*
  workhouse *206*
Oliver, Thomas *208*
Olney (Bucks), workhouse 13–14
Onehouse (Suff), Stow Hundred House of Industry 22, 23, **24**, 191, *210*
Ongar Hundred Incorporation (Essex) 27
  workhouse, Stanford Rivers (later Ongar Union Workhouse) 41, **41**, 80, *204*
ophthalmia 148–9, 164, 176
Ormskirk (Lancs), workhouse *206*
Orsett (Essex), workhouse 60, *204*

Oswestry (Salop), Morda, workhouse 25, *209*
Otley (Yorks W R), Wharfedale Union Workhouse 99, *213*
Ottershaw (Surr), Chertsey Union Workhouse 60, 74, 76, *210*
Oulton (Norf), Gilbert Union 27
Oulton (Suff), workhouse 22, *210*
Oundle (Northants), workhouse 62, 72, 130, **130**, *208*
outdoor relief
  1550–*c* 1750 3, 8, 14
  c 1750–1834 21, 29, 31, 32, 36
  1834–70 43, 66, 103
    General Order for the Prohibition of Outdoor Relief (1841) 44, 45, 49, 194
    under Poor Law Amendment Act (1834) 49, 53, 194, 195
  1870–1914 120, 123
  after 1914 189
overseers of the poor, duties and responsibilities x, 3, 4, 31
Owen, Thomas Ellis 62, 75, *204*, *205*
Oxford 63, 65
  Incorporation 28
  industrial school, Cowley Fields 142, *209*
  workhouse (1772–5) 25, 28, **29**, 31, 34, *209*
  workhouse (1865) *209*
Oxfordshire, poor-law institutions, post-1834 *209*

P

Paddington (Lond), Union Workhouse, Harrow Rd 163, *216*
Padgate (Lancs), cottage homes **144**, 145, *207*
Paghill/Paul Gilbert Union (Yorks) 27
Paine & Hobday *207*
Pall Mall Gazette 181
Palmer, *see also* Boulton & Palmer
Palmer, Robert *216*
Panopticon House of Industry 33–4, **33–4**, 36
Paris Exhibition (1900) 110
parish workhouses, early 18th century 13–17
parish workshops, 16th century 5
Parker, *see also* Jones & Parker
Parker, Henry W (Assistant Commissioner) 52, 90–2, **91**, *202*, *210*, *211*
Parris, R **107**
Parsons, W *207*
Parsons, William 47, *207*
Pateley Bridge (Yorks W R), workhouse *213*
Patricroft (Lancs), Barton-upon-Irwell Union Workhouse *206*
Patrington (Yorks E R), workhouse *212*
Pauper Inmates Discharge and Regulation Act (1871) 185
paupers' cottages, 17th–18th centuries 5
pavilion plan
  1840–70 98–9, 155, **158**, 159, 160
  1870–1914 103–17, 148, 165
  after 1914 177
  see also separate-block system
Peck, F 133, *204*
Peck, Frederick *205*, *206*, *210*
Peckham (Lond), scattered homes 151
Pembury (Kent), Tonbridge Union Workhouse 56, 78, **78**, 100–2, **101**, *206*
Penistone (Yorks W R), workhouse 213
Penkhull (Staffs), cottage homes *210*
Penkridge (Staffs), Penkridge (later Cannock) Union
  workhouse, Brewood *209*
  workhouse, Cannock *209*
Pennington & Bridgen 164, *219*
Pennington & Jervis *206*
Penny Satirist, The **52**
Penrith (Cumb), workhouse 78, *202*
Penzance (Cornw)
  workhouse (pre-1834) 41
  workhouse (1838) 72, *202*

Percy, Edward *203*
Perkin, W, & Son *202*
Perkin, William 96, **96**, 100, **101**, 139, **139**, *213*
Perkin & Son **112**, 113, *212*
Perpendicular style 67, 94, 100, 139
Pershore (Worcs), workhouse 60, *212*
pest-houses 156
Peterborough (Northants)
  workhouse (18th century) 13
  workhouse (1836) 59, *208*
Petersfield (Hants), workhouse *205*
Petham (Kent), Gilbert Union/Parish 27
Petworth (Suss)
  Sussex County Bridewell 34
  Union
    workhouse, Petworth *211*
    workhouse, Wisborough Green *211*
Pewsey (Wilts), workhouse 100, **100**, 174, *211*
Phillips, Thomas 15, *216*
phthisis (pulmonary tuberculosis) 119, 175–6
Pickering (Yorks N R), workhouse *212*
Picts Hill (Som), Langport Union Workhouse 76, *209*
plan types *see* block plan; circular ward blocks; corridor-plan workhouses; courtyard plan; half-butterfly plan; 'hexagon' plan; linear (in-line) plan; linear layout; pavilion plan; radial workhouses; separate-block system; 'square' plan; '200–pauper' plans
plans for workhouses *see* model plans
Plashet (Essex), St George-in-the-East Industrial School 140, **140**, *216*
Plass, John 100, **100**
Plomesgate Union (Suff), workhouse, Wickham Market 65, 133, *210*
Plowman, John 46, *204*, *205*, *208*, *209*, *211*, *212*
Plumstead (Lond), Woolwich Union Workhouse 106, *217*
Plymouth (Devon)
  Incorporation 11
  workhouse (1852–8) *203*
  workhouse (1640) 6
  see also East Stonehouse; Plympton St Mary; Stoke Damerell
Plympton St Mary (Devon), Union Workhouse (later Underwood House Public Assistance Institution) 190, *203*
Pocklington (Yorks E R), workhouse *212*
police, and vagrancy 179, 180, 188
Ponsford, Thomas 73, *203*
Pontefract (Yorks E R), workhouse *212*
Ponteland (Northumb)
  cottage homes *208*
  workhouse *208*
Poole (Dors), workhouse *203*
poor, changing attitudes to 192
poor boxes 4, **4**
Poor Law Amendment Act (1834) 32, 42, 43–52, 99, 103, 193
  and children 132
  and lunatics and imbeciles 161
  and vagrancy 180
  see also New Poor Law
Poor Law Board
  establishment 52, 85
  Points to be Attended to in the Construction of Workhouses 105, 124, 126, 161
  and school districts 140
  and workhouse infirmaries 160, 161
Poor Law Commission
  attack on (1846) 90–1
  demise of (1847) 52
  and implementing of Poor Law Amendment Act 43–52
  'Orders and Regulations to be Observed in the Workhouse' (1835) 161
  Poor Law Commissioners 30, 43, 44
  Report (1834) 40, 45
  and vagrancy 180, 181
Poor Law Committee (1831) 40
poor rates
  16th–17th centuries 3, 4, 5, 9, 15
  18th–19th centuries 25, 31, 32, 40–1, 48

poorhouse, meaning of term x, 10
Poplar (Lond), Union 120–1, 122–3, *216*
  farm colony near Laindon (Essex) 122–3, *216*
  industrial school, Forest Gate *216*
  training school, Hutton 122, 153, **153**, *216*
  workhouse, High St 120–1, **120**, 163, *216*
'Poplar experiment' 121, 123
Poplar and Stepney Sick Asylum District (Lond), Poplar and Stepney Sick Asylum, Bow 120–1, 166, *218*
'Poplarism' 123, 153, 189
Porden, William *216*
Porter, ___ *202*
Porter, Fred William *202*
Portsmouth (Hants) 36
  Portsea Island Union Workhouse 134, 159, 161, 173, **173**, 176, *205*
Potemkin, Prince 33
Pottersbury (Northants), workhouse *208*
Potts, Edward **136**, *206*
Prescot (Lancs), workhouse *206*
Preston (Lancs), Union
  workhouse, Fulwood *206*
  workhouse, Ribchester *206*
Preston (Yorks W R) *see* Great Preston
Prestwich (Lancs)
  infirmary, Booth Hall *206*
  workhouse (1819) *206*
  workhouse, Delauney Rd (1866–70) 106, *206*
prisons
  Central Inspection Principle 33–4, 46
  workhouses resembling 53, 91, 181, 194
Pritchard, Thomas Farnolls *209*
probationary wards/houses *see* receiving (probationary) wards/houses
Prudhoe (Northumb), Prudhoe Hall Colony 174, *208*
Public Assistance Committees 123, 188, 190
Public Assistance Institutions 190, 191, 196
public health committees 190
Public Health (Prevention and Treatment of Disease) Act (1913) 176
Pugin, Augustus Charles 14
Pugin, Augustus Welby Northmore, *Contrasts* **50**, 51
Pulham Market (Norf), Depwade Union Workhouse 63, **64**, *207*
Purton (Wilts), workhouse *211*

Q

Quakers, and poor relief 9, 12, 13, 18
Quatt (Salop), industrial school 138, **138**, 142, *209*
Queen Anne style 110, 171

R

Radford (Notts), Union Workhouse, Hartley Rd, Nottingham (later Nottingham Union school) 145, *208*
radial workhouses 39, **64**, 194, 195
  see also 'hexagon' plan; 'square' plan
Ramsbury (Wilts) *see* Hungerford
Ratby (Leics), Gilbert Union 27
Reading (Berks) 92
  Greyfriars Hospital 4, 5
  Oracle, The 6, **6**, 8
  Reading Union Workhouse 119, **119**, *201*
Reading and Wokingham School District (Berks), industrial school, Wargrave 142, *201*
receiving (probationary) wards/houses 61, 81, 147–8, 151–2
Redruth (Cornw), workhouse 41, 72, *202*
Reepham-cum-Kerdistone (Norf), Gilbert Union 27

251

Reeth (Yorks N R), workhouse *212*
refractory wards 61, 84
register offices 66, **66**
Reigate (Surr)
  Gilbert Union 27
  workhouse 56, *210*
relapsing fever 163, 168
religion
  religious inscriptions, in casual wards and shelters for vagrants 183–4
  see also Catholics; chapels; Nonconformists
Ribchester (Lancs), workhouse *206*
Richmond (Surr), workhouse *210*
Richmond (Yorks N R), workhouse 80, *212*
Rickwood *see* Church & Rickwood
Ringwood (Hants), workhouse *205*
ringworm 176
Ripon (Yorks W R), workhouse 96, 186, **186**, *213*
Risbridge Union (Suff), workhouse, Kedington 94, 133, *210*
River (Kent)
  Gilbert Union 27
  workhouse 27–8
  River (later Dover) Union Workhouse 54, *206*
River Ambulance Service 163, *219*
Riverdale (Herefs), Dore Union Workhouse 49, *205*
Rochdale (Lancs)
  opposition to New Poor Law 49, **49**
  Union 49
  cottage homes, Wardle *206*
  workhouse, Dearnley 87, 136, **136**, *206*
  workhouse, Marland *206*
Rochester (Kent), cottage homes *206*
Rochford (Essex), Union Workhouse (later Rochford Hospital) 177–8, **177–8**, *190*, *191*, *204*
Rockland All Saints (Norf), Wayland Union Workhouse 63, *208*
Rollesby (Norf), East and West Flegg Incorporation Workhouse 21, **21**, 22, *207*
Roman Catholics *see* Catholics
Romford (Essex)
  workhouse (1785) 34
  workhouse (1838) *204*
Romney Marsh Union (Kent), workhouse, New Romney *206*
Romsey (Hants), workhouse *205*
Roote, William P 58, **59, 64**, *201*, *202*
Roscoe, Professor ___ 161
Rosliston (Derb), Gilbert Union 27
Ross-on-Wye (Herefs), Ross Union Workhouse *205*
Rothbury (Northumb), workhouse **116**, 117, *208*
Rotherham (Yorks W R)
  Badsley Moor Sanatorium 176, *213*
  workhouse *213*
Rotherhithe (Lond)
  Parish of St Mary *216*
    workhouse, Deptford Lower Rd (later St Olave's Union Workhouse) 184, **184**, *216*
  South Wharf, River Ambulance Service *219*
Rothwell Haigh (Yorks W R)
  cottage homes *213*
  Hunslet Union Workhouse 115, 170, **172**, 186, *213*
roundsman system x, 32
Rowe, Thomas 8
Rowland, Stephen *211*
Rowntree, Joseph 154, 195
Royal Commission on Education (1861) 140
Royal Commission on the Poor Laws (1832) 43
  Poor Law Report (1834) 3, 30, 43, 44, 45, 117, 132, 180
Royal Commission on the Poor Laws (1905–9) 103, 123, 137, 153, 173–4, 188
Royal Commission on Smallpox and Fever Hospitals (1881–2) 163

Royal Navy, workhouse boys trained for 151, 154
Royston (Herts) 48, 57
  workhouse 57–8, 157, 191, *205*
Royton (Lancs), scattered homes 152, **152**, *206*
Ruddington (Notts), Gilbert Union/Parish 27
Rugby (Warws)
  Gilbert Union 27
  workhouse *211*
Ruggles, Thomas 23–5
Runcorn (Ches), Union Workhouse, Dutton *202*
rural incorporation workhouses 21–6, 29
  see also Gilbert Unions
Rushforth, T H 168
Russia 33, 115
Rustington (Suss), Millfield Hospital 149, 164, *219*
Rutland, poor-law institutions, post-1834 *209*
Rye (Suss), workhouse 90, *211*

S

sack-making 61, 83
Saddleworth (Yorks W R), Parish Workhouse, Dobcross *213*
Saffron Walden (Essex), workhouse 47, 49, 58, 83, 133, *204*
St Albans (Herts), workhouse 67, 191, *205*
St Austell (Cornw), workhouse 72, *202*
St Columb Major (Cornw), St Columb Union Workhouse 72, *202*
St Faiths Gilbert Union (Norf) 27, *208*
St George-in-the-East Parish (Lond) *216*
  industrial school, Plashet, East Ham 140, **140**, *216*
  workhouse, Prusom St, Wapping *216*
St George's, Hanover Square, Parish (Lond) *216*
  workhouse, Mount St, Westminster (1725–6) 15–16, **15**, 155, *216*
  workhouse and infirmary (later St George's Union Workhouse), Fulham Rd/Little Chelsea 125, **125**, 166, 181, 184, *216*
St George's Union (Lond) *216*
  infirmary, St Ermin's Hill, Westminster *216*
  receiving homes, Millman St, Chelsea *216*
  workhouse, Palace St/Wallis Yard *216*
St Germans (Cornw), Union Workhouse, Torpoint *202*
St Giles-in-the-Fields and St George, Bloomsbury, Parishes (Lond) 142, *216*
  receiving home for children, Lascelles Place **147**, 148, *216*
  workhouse, Endell St, St Giles 15, 17, **18**, 156
St Ives (Hunts), workhouse 57–8, **58**, *205*
St Luke's, Middlesex, Parish (Lond) *216*
  workhouse, City Rd **106**, 107–8, 109, *216*
St Martin-in-the-Fields Parish (Lond) *216*
  workhouse (1665) 8
  workhouse (early 18th century) 15
  workhouse, Hemmings Row/St Martin's (1770–7) *216*
St Mary Cray and Orpington Gilbert Union (Kent) 27
St Marylebone Parish (Lond)
  dispensaries 166
  industrial school, Southall *216*
  infirmary, Kensington 166, **167**, *216*
  workhouse, Baker St **106**, 107, 108, 109–10, **111**, 119, *216*
  infirmary 155
  vagrant wards 181, 183–4, **183–4**
St Neots (Hunts), workhouse *205*
St Olave's Union (Lond) *216*
  cottage homes, Shirley, Croydon *216*
  infirmary, Deptford Lower Rd *216*
  workhouse, Deptford Lower Rd 184, **184**, *216*
  workhouse, Parish St/Fair St, Bermondsey *216*
  workhouse for the aged, Ladywell, Lewisham 118, **118**, 119, 130, *216*

St Pancras Parish (Lond)
  industrial school, Leavesden 142, *216*
  infirmary, Highgate 166, *216*
  workhouse, Kings Rd, Camden 99, 108, **128**, 130, 163, *216*
  Cook's Terrace block 110, **110**
St Saviour's Union (Lond) *217*
  infirmary, Champion Hill, Dulwich *217*
  workhouse, Marlborough St *217*
St Sepulchre Parish (Lond) *217*
St Thomas (Devon)
  workhouse, Exeter (1638) 6
  workhouse, Exeter (1836) 60, 74, 76, *203*
Salford (Lancs)
  New Bailey Prison 34
  Union
    cottage homes, Culcheth 152–3, **153**, *206*
    infirmary, Hope *206*
    workhouse, Eccles *206*
Salisbury (Wilts)
  Alderbury (later Salisbury) Union Workhouse 136, **137**, *211*
  Salisbury Incorporation Workhouse, Crane St 133, *211*
  workhouse (1638) 6
Salt, Sir Titus 96
Saltaire (Yorks W R) **96**
Salter, Stephen *210*
Salvation Army 182, 183–4
Samford Incorporation (Suff), workhouse, Tattingstone 22, *210*
sanatoria 149, 164, 175–6, *219*
sanitation 55, 60, 83, 98, 125
  detached toilet blocks 117
  sanitary towers 98, 104, 105, 118, 125, 169
  workhouse infirmaries 160, 168, 169, 170, 175
Sapcote (Leics), Gilbert Union 27
Saunderton (Bucks), Wycombe Union Workhouse 72, *202*
Savage, James 205, 206
scabies *see* itch
Scamp, W 159
Scaping, H *208*
Scaping, H C *207*
Scarborough (Yorks N R), workhouse 93–4, 176, 179, *212*
scarlet fever 164
scattered homes 131, 151–4, 195–6
school districts, setting up 138, 140–2
schools
  Catholic 99
  district schools 140–2, 145, 148–9
  hospital schools, Metropolitan Asylums Board 149, *220*
  for imbecile children 165
  industrial schools 131, 138–42, 153, **229**
  out-of-town schools 132
  separate schools 138–42, 145–7
  in workhouses 131, 133–8
Scott, Sir George Gilbert 46, 47, 48
  workhouses by 62, **62**, *202*, *207*, *208*
  with W Bonython Moffatt 47, 53, **70–2**, 71–3, 85, *202*, *203*, *204*, *207*, *209*, *210*, *211*; chapels 71, 73, 84; infirmaries 157; provision for children 133; provision for lunatics and imbeciles 161; provision for vagrants 180; receiving wards 81
Scott, John 18–20, 46
Sculcoates (Yorks E R), Union
  cottage homes, Hessle *212*
  workhouse 96, *212*
Searle, Son & Yelf **97**, 183, *217*
Second World War, Emergency Medical Service hospitals 178, 191
Sedbergh (Yorks W R), workhouse *213*
Sedgefield (Dur), workhouse *203*
segregation
  by age and sex 30, 43, 45, 47
  by character and conduct 103, 118
Seisdon (Staffs), Union Workhouse, Trysull *209*

Selby (Yorks W R), workhouse *213*
Select Vestry Act (Sturges Bourne's Act) (1819) 32
Selling (Kent), Gilbert Union 27
Selly Oak (Worcs), King's Norton Union Workhouse 170, **171**, *212*
Semer (Suff), workhouse 22, 44, *210*
Semington (Wilts), Trowbridge and Melksham Union Workhouse 94, 181, **185**, *211*
Senior, Nassau 43, 132
Senior, Mrs Nassau 143
separate schools 138–42, 145–7
separate-block system
  asylums 165
  hospitals 159, 164
  infirmaries **158**, 166, 169–70
  workhouse schools 136, 145, 147
  workhouses 1870–1914 103–30, **104**, 195
  see also pavilion plan
Settle (Yorks W R), Union Workhouse, Giggleswick *213*
settlement, parish of 8, 179
Sevenoaks (Kent), Union Workhouse, Sundridge *206*
sewage disposal *see* sanitation
Shaftesbury (Dors)
  Incorporation 11
  workhouse *203*
Shap (Westmld), workhouse *211*
Shardlow (Derb)
  Gilbert Union/Parish 27
  workhouse *203*
Sharp, C A **127**
Shaw Heath (Ches), workhouse *202*
Shaw-Lefevre, John George 44
Shearburn, W *210*
Sheffield (Yorks W R)
  Union
    industrial school, Pitsmoor 138–9, *213*
    scattered homes 151, 152
    workhouse (1876–80) **112–13**, 113, 119, *213*
  workhouse (1628) 6
  workhouse (pre-1834) 81
  see also Ecclesall Bierlow
'Sheffield system' 151
Sheppey (Kent) *see* Isle of Sheppey
Shepton Mallet (Som), workhouse 66, *209*
Sherborne (Dors), workhouse *203*
Shifnal (Salop), workhouse *209*
Shiner, Christopher M *217*
Shipmeadow (Suff), Wangford Incorporation House of Industry 22, 100, 156, **156**, *210*
Shipston-on-Stour (Worcs), workhouse *212*
Shirley (Surr), St Olave's Union cottage homes *216*
Shooters Hill (Lond), Brook (Fever) Hospital 164, *219*
Shoreditch (Lond), Parish of St Leonard
  cottage homes, Hornchurch 145, *217*
  industrial school, Brentwood 142, *217*
  workhouse, Kingsland Rd 97, **97**, 181, *217*
  infirmary 166, **167**
Shoreham-by-Sea (Suss), Steyning Union Workhouse 115–17, **115–16**, 119, **119**, 125, **172**, *211*
Shotley Bridge (Dur)
  cottage homes *203*
  sanatorium *203*
Shrewsbury (Salop)
  Incorporation 28, 36
  workhouse 28, **28**, *209*
Shropshire, poor-law institutions, post-1834 *209*
Shutt, ___ *213*
sick, accommodation for 155–78
  see also hospitals; infirmaries; sanatoria
Sidcup (Kent), Greenwich Union Cottage Homes Village **150**, *215*
Sir William Young's Act (1795) 21, 36
Sittingbourne (Kent), Milton Regis Union Workhouse 54, *206*

INDEX

Skelton, Thomas A 205
Skiller, William 211
Skipton (Yorks W R), workhouse 213
Skirlaugh (Yorks E R), workhouse 78, 133, 212
Sleaford (Lincs), workhouse 66, 207
Slough (Bucks), Eton Union Workhouse 60, 61–2, 202
Smallburgh (Norf), workhouse 22, 23, 208
smallpox 25, 156, 160, 163–4, 168, 219
Smith, *see also* Lee & Smith
Smith, ___ (Poor-Law Inspector) 113
Smith, Dr Angus 161
Smith, E Blakeway 209
Smith, Dr Edward (Poor-Law Inspector) 86, 98, 100, 160, 161, 163
Smith, F W 177, 204
Smith, Francis J 217
Smith, John 63, 67, 202
Smith, Thomas 205
Smith, W 215
Smith & Coggan 215
Smith & Turnbull 159
Snell, Alfred Saxon 110, 111, 207, 216
Snell, Henry Saxon 106, 107–10, 108, 125, 215, 216
    casual wards 183, 184–5, 184
    infirmaries 166, 167
    schools 142
Society for the Promotion of Christian Knowledge (SPCK) 16
    An Account of the Workhouses in Great Britain (1725, 1732, 1786) 15, 17, 31, 32, 155
Solihull (Warws), workhouse 186, 187, 211
Somerset, poor-law institutions, post-1834 209
South Chailey (Suss), workhouse 210
South-East Shropshire School District, Quatt School 138, 142, 209
South Metropolitan School District 140, 145, 218
    schools
        Banstead Rd, Sutton 145, 145, 218
        Brighton Rd, Sutton 140, 145, 147, 218
        Herne Bay 149, 218
        Witham 218
South Molton (Devon), workhouse 60, 124, 203
South Shields (Dur)
    workhouse, Ocean Rd 203
    workhouse, West Harton 112, 114, 114, 203
South Stoneham (Hants), Union Workhouse, West End 205
Southall (Mdx), industrial school 216
Southam (Warws), workhouse 211
Southampton (Hants), Incorporation 28, 205
    infirmary, Shirley Warren 205
    workhouse (1776) 133, 205
    workhouse (1866–7) 160, 168, 205
Southend-on-Sea (Essex) 190
Southmead (Glos), workhouse 204
Southsea (Hants) 62
Southwark (Lond), Parish of St George the Martyr 217
    branch school, Eagle House, Mitcham 148, 217
    workhouse, Mint St 217
Southwell (Notts)
    House of Correction (1808) 36–40, 37, 132
    Union Workhouse *see* Upton
Spalding (Lincs), workhouse 59, 207
Spanton, William 205
SPCK *see* Society for the Promotion of Christian Knowledge
Speenhamland system (Berkshire Bread Scale) 32
'Spike, The' (nickname for workhouse) 186
Spilsby (Lincs) 30
    Union Workhouse, Hundleby 72, 207
'square' plan 46–7, 53–4, 58, 222–3, 228
    workhouses built 1835–40 60–70
staff, in New Poor Law workhouses, accommodation for 46
    see also masters' houses

Stafford 133
    gaol 34
    workhouse 47, 49, 209
Staffordshire
    Gilbert Unions/Parishes 27
    poor-law institutions, post-1834 209–10
Staines (Mdx), Union 81
    workhouse, Ashford 207
staircases 82, 83
Stamford (Lincs)
    workhouse (1836–7) 59, 207
    workhouse (1899–1902) 207
Stanford Rivers (Essex), Ongar Hundred Incorporation (later Ongar Union) Workhouse 41, 41, 80, 204
Stanhope (Dur), workhouse 204
Stapleton (Glos), workhouse *see* Bristol
Stathern (Leics), Gilbert Union/Parish 27
Stead, Matthew 209
Stephens, Edward W 206
Stephenson, Sydney 149
Stepney (Lond), Union 217
    branch school 148
    cottage homes, North Stifford 152, 152, 217
    workhouse, Bromley-by-Bow 98, 217
    workhouse for children (old Limehouse House of Industry) 138
Stepping Hill (Ches), infirmary 202
Stevens, Henry J 203, 208
Stevenson, J, & Son 208
Steyning (Suss), Union
    workhouse, Kingston-by-Sea 211
    workhouse, Shoreham-by-Sea 115–17, 115–16, 119, 119, 125, 172, 211
Stifford (Essex) *see* North Stifford
Stockbridge (Hants), workhouse 205
Stockport (Ches)
    infirmary, Stepping Hill 202
    workhouse, Shaw Heath 202
Stockton-on-Tees (Dur), workhouse 136, 136, 203
Stockwell (Lond), South-Western (Fever and Smallpox) Hospital 163, 219
Stoke Damerell (Devon), Stoke Damerell (later Devonport) Parish Workhouse, Devonport, Plymouth 156–7, 159, 203
Stoke-upon-Trent (Staffs)
    cottage homes, Penkull 210
    workhouse 41, 127, 133–4, 134–5, 137, 158, 159, 209
Stokesley (Yorks N R), workhouse 212
Stone (Staffs), workhouse 34, 210
stone-breaking 103, 120, 120, 121, 122, 160
    vagrants 179, 183, 184, 186–8
Stourbridge (Worcs)
    workhouse (pre-1834) 212
    workhouse (1903–7) 212
Stow Incorporation (Suff), workhouse, Onehouse 22, 23, 24, 191, 210
Stow-on-the-Wold (Glos), workhouse 65, 83, 204
Stradbroke (Suff), workhouse 210
Strand (Lond), Union 217
    industrial school, Silver St (later Edmonton Colony for Sane Epileptics) 217
    workhouses 160, 217
Stranger, G H 210
Stratford-upon-Avon (Warws), workhouse 95, 211
Stratton (Cornw), workhouse 202
Stratton St Margaret (Wilts), Highworth and Swindon Union Workhouse 90, 211
Street, G E 100
Stretton (Leics), Gilbert Union 27
Strood (Kent)
    workhouse (18th century) 16
    workhouse (1837) 206
Stroud (Glos), workhouse 65, 204
Sturdy, Francis J 204
Sturminster Newton (Dors), workhouse 62, 76–7, 77, 127, 203
Styal (Lancs), cottage homes 145, 206
Styan, George 94, 212

Sudbury, H Tatham 208
Sudbury (Suff)
    Incorporation 11, 13
    Union 142
    workhouse 65, 210
Suffolk
    discontent about New Poor Law (1830s) 49
    poor-law institutions, post-1834 210
Sunderland (Dur), workhouse 169, 175, 203
Sundridge (Kent), workhouse 206
Surrey
    Gilbert Unions/Parishes 27
    poor-law institutions, post-1834 210
    see also London
Sussex
    Gilbert Unions/Parishes 27
    poor-law institutions, post-1834 210–11
Sutcliffe *see* Elcock & Sutcliffe
Sutton (Surr)
    industrial school, Banstead Rd (later Downs Hospital) 145, 145, 218, 219, 220
    industrial school, Brighton Rd (later Belmont Asylum/Belmont Institution) 140, 145, 215, 218, 219
Sutton (Suss), Gilbert Union 27
    workhouse, Sutton End 211
Sutton Coldfield (Warws), workhouse 31
Swaffham (Norf), workhouse 66, 76, 189, 208
Swainsthorpe (Norf), Henstead Union Workhouse 65, 208
Swanley (Kent), White Oak School 149, 220
swimming-baths 151
Swindon (Wilts) *see* Highworth and Swindon
Swinton (Lancs), industrial school 130, 138, 142, 206
Switzerland, cottage-home system 143

T

Tacon, H L 213
Tadcaster (Yorks W R), workhouse 213
Talbot, Lord 48–9
Tamworth (Staffs), workhouse 210
Tarvin (Ches) *see* Great Boughton
task-masters 83
taskwork 61, 83, 103, 120, 195
    for vagrants 179, 181–2, 184, 185, 186–8
    see also bone-crushing; corn-grinding; labour yards; oakum-picking; stone-breaking
Tattersall, Richard 206
Tattingstone (Suff), workhouse 22, 22, 210
Taunton (Som)
    workhouse (1631) 6
    workhouse (1836–8) 60, 74, 76, 209
Taverham (Norf), Gilbert Union 27
Tavistock (Devon), workhouse 72, 203
Taylor, George Ledwell 217
Teesdale Union (Dur), workhouse, Barnard Castle 204
Telford, Thomas 36
Temple Cloud (Som), Clutton Union Workhouse 77, 209
Tenbury Wells (Worcs), Tenbury Union Workhouse 65, 212
Tendring (Essex), Union Workhouse, Tendring Heath 72, 204
Tenterden (Kent), workhouse 89, 206
test workhouses *see* able-bodied test workhouses
Tetbury (Glos)
    workhouse (1790) 204
    workhouse (1905–6) 204
Tewkesbury (Glos), workhouse 45, 204
textile manufacture, in workhouses
    17th century 6, 9, 12
    18th century 25, 27, 31
Teyham and Linstead Gilbert Union/Parish (Kent) 27

Thakeham (Suss), Gilbert Union (later Union) 27
    workhouse, Heath Common 56, 211
Thame (Oxon), workhouse 65, 209
Thanet, Isle of *see* Isle of Thanet
Thatcher, Frederick 210
Thaxted (Essex), workhouse 14
Thetford (Norf), workhouse 208
Theydon Garnon (Essex), workhouse 14
Thingoe (Suff) *see* Bury St Edmunds
Thirsk (Yorks N R), workhouse 180, 212
Thomason, ___ 211
Thompson, Matthew 203, 204
Thornbury (Glos)
    register office 66, 66
    workhouse 60, 77, 204
Thorne (Yorks W R), workhouse 213
Thorold, W 207
Thorold, William 63, 64, 204, 207, 208
Thorpe, T H 203
Thorpe, W H 204
Thrapston (Northants), workhouse 67, 208
Throckmorton, Charles 48, 48
Thurgarton Hundred Incorporation (Notts) 27, 36–41, 42
    workhouse, Upton 37–40, 39–41, 46, 132, 191, 208
Ticehurst (Suss), workhouse, Union St 60, 74, 76, 211
Tiltman, A Hessell 219
Timbrell, Benjamin 15, 216
Times, The, and Anti-Poor-Law movement 51, 52, 57
timetables 83
Tisbury (Wilts), workhouse 211
Tiverton (Devon)
    Incorporation Workhouse (18th century) 11, 31, 156
    Union Workhouse (1836–7) 72, 203
Todd, Dr ___ 161
Todmorden (Yorks W R)
    opposition to New Poor Law 49, 80
    workhouse, Mankinholes 124, 124, 213
Tonbridge (Kent), Union Workhouse, Pembury 56, 78, 78, 100–2, 101, 206
Tooting (Lond)
    Fountain (Fever) Hospital 164, 218
    Grove (Fever) Hospital 164, 218
    Mount House, Mr Drouet's school 132, 138, 140
Tooting Bec (Lond), Tooting Bec Asylum 165, 165, 220
Torpoint (Cornw), workhouse 202
Torrington (Devon), workhouse 60, 203
Totnes (Devon)
    workhouse (1632) 6
    workhouse (1837–9) 73, 203
Tottenham (Lond), North-Eastern (Fever) Hospital 163, 164, 218
Towcester (Northants), workhouse 72, 208
Toxteth (Lancs)
    Toxteth Park Parish Workhouse 206
    see also Liverpool, West Derby and Toxteth Park Joint Committee
training ships 151, 218
tramps *see* vagrants
Travis & Mangnall 206
Trendall, Edward William 207
Tress, R 89, 214
Tress & Chambers 141, 218
Tring (Herts), workhouse 13
Trollope, *see also* Giles, Gough & Trollope
Trollope, Mrs Frances, *Jessie Phillips* 161
Trowbridge and Melksham Union (Wilts), workhouse, Semington 94, 181, 185, 211
Trubshaw, Thomas 47, 209
Truro (Cornw), workhouse 202
Trysull (Staffs), workhouse 209
tuberculosis 119, 175–6, 177–8
    sanatoria 149, 164, 176, 219
Tudeley and Capel Gilbert Union/Parish (Kent) 27
Tudor style 53, 65, 67, 85

253

Tunstead and Happing Incorporation (Norf), workhouse, Smallburgh 22, 23, *208*
Turnbull *see* Smith & Turnbull
Turner, ___ *208*
Tutbury (Staffs), Gilbert Union 27
Twining, Louisa 154, 160, 181
'200-pauper' plans 46, 47, **224, 226–7**
workhouses, 1835–40 60, 77–8
Tynemouth (Northumb), workhouse *208*

U

Uckfield (Suss), workhouse 49, 94, *211*
Uley (Glos), workhouse 41
Ullesthorpe (Leics), Gilbert Union 27
Ulverston (Lancs), workhouse *207*
Unemployed Workmen Act (1905) 123
Union Chargeability Act (1865) 44
union offices 126, 196
Unions
 disbanded under Local Government Act (1929) 190
 set up under Poor Law Amendment Act (1834) 44
unmarried mothers *see* lying-in wards
Upper Holloway (Lond)
 Archway, Holborn Union Infirmary 108, 166, **166**, 167, *215*
 Islington Workhouse **105**, 106, *215*
Upper Norwood (Surr), industrial school, Anerley 140, 151, *218*
Uppingham (Rut), workhouse 67, *209*
Upton (Notts), Thurgarton Hundred workhouse (later Southwell Union Workhouse) **37–40**, 39–41, 46, 132, 191, *208*
Upton-on-Severn (Worcs), workhouse 60, *212*
urban corporation workhouses, 1696–1722 10–13, 192–3
urban poor-law incorporations, 1750–1800 28, 29, 31
urban workhouses, 1750–1800 28
Uttoxeter (Staffs), workhouse 72, *210*
Uxbridge (Mdx), Union Workhouse, Hillingdon 177, *207*

V

vagrants 179–88, 190, 191, 195
venereal disease 155, 156, 168, 169, 170
ventilation
 corridor-plan workhouses 85–6, 98
 Head's workhouses 55
 ideas on, 18th century 19, 20
 see also cross-ventilation
verandas 175, 176, 177
Vernon, Admiral Edward 21
Vickers, firm of 151
villa system *see* cottage-home system
Villiers, Charles 160
Voysey, Annesley 46, 61, **61**, *211*
Vulliamy, Lewis 62, **62**, 76–7, **77**, *203*, *207*
 Epping Union Workhouse 48, 62–3, **62**, 71, *204*

W

Waddington, William *206*
Wakefield, Revd Russell 123
Wakefield (Yorks W R), workhouse *213*
Wales, unions 44
Walker, J *219*

Walker, James *216*
Walker, William *203*
Wallen, William *218*
Wallingford (Berks), Gilbert Union 27
 workhouse *202*
Wallis, Charles 78, *203*
Walsall (Staffs), workhouse 65, *210*
Walsall and West Bromwich School District (Staffs), industrial school, Wigmore 142, *210*
Walsham, ___ (Assistant Commissioner) 86, 133
Walsingham (Norf), Union Workhouse, Great Snoring 63, **64**, *208*
Walters, John 51
Walthamstow (Essex), workhouse 17
Walton-on-the-Hill (Lancs), workhouse *207*
Walworth (Lond), Westmorland Rd, industrial school, used as workhouse 140, *216*
Wandsworth (Lond)
 St James' Parish, Westminster, industrial school *217*
 Wandsworth & Clapham Union *217*
  infirmary *217*
  offices, East Hill **127**
  workhouse, Church Lane *217*
  workhouse, Garratt Lane 108, 121, **121–2**, *217*
  workhouse, St John's Hill *217*
Wangford (Suff), Incorporation (later Union) 142
 Shipmeadow House of Industry 22, 100, 156, **156**, *210*
Wantage (Berks), workhouse 60, 61, *202*
Wapping (Lond), Prusom St, workhouse *216*
Ward, Henry 133, **134**, *158*, *209*
Ward, W H 122, **187**, *202*, *207*
Wardle (Lancs), cottage homes *206*
Ware (Herts), workhouse 191, *205*
Wareham (Dors), Wareham and Purbeck Union Workhouse *203*
Wargrave (Berks), Wokingham Union Workhouse (later industrial school) 142, *201*
Warminster (Wilts), workhouse 60, 74, 76, *211*
Warrington (Lancs)
 Padgate Cottage Homes **144**, 145, *207*
 workhouse *207*
Warwick, workhouse 65, *211*
Warwickshire
 Gilbert Unions/Parishes 27
 poor-law institutions, post-1834 *211*
water supply 83, 125
Waterhouse, Nathaniel 6
Watford (Herts), workhouse 47, 191, *205*
Watson, *see also* Holmes & Watson
Watson, Dr Thomas 160–1
Watson, W 65, *210*, *211*
Wavertree (Lancs), cottage homes, Olive Mount **144**, 145, *206*
Way, Mrs 142
Wayland Union (Norf)
 infirmary, Attleborough *208*
 workhouse, Rockland All Saints 63, *208*
Weardale Union (Dur), workhouse, Stanhope *204*
Webb, Beatrice 3, 121, 123, 177
Webb, Sidney 3, 121, 177
Webster, Francis *211*
Wednesfield (Staffs), cottage homes 145, *210*
Weedon, ___ 47
Weeks's 'Hot Water Apparatus' 83
Welch, Samuel T 46, 53, 67, **68–9**, 89, *204*, *209*
Wellingborough (Northants), workhouse *208*
Wellington (Salop), workhouse *209*
Wellington (Som), workhouse *209*
Wells (Som), workhouse 67, **68–9**, 89, 91, 157–8, *209*
Welwyn (Herts), workhouse 191, *205*
Wem (Salop), workhouse *209*
Weobley (Herefs), workhouse 65, *205*
Wesham (Lancs), workhouse *206*
West Ashford Union (Kent), workhouse, Hothfield Common 54, *206*

West Beckham (Norf), Erpingham Union Workhouse 88, 94, 124, 133, *207*
West Bromwich (Staffs), workhouse 169, *210*
West Derby (Lancs), Union
 cottage homes, Fazakerley 145, *207*
 test workhouse, Belmont Rd, Liverpool 122, *207*
 workhouse, Walton-on-the-Hill 143, *207*
 workhouse for chronic infirm, Alder Hey (used as children's hospital) 119, 176–7, *207*
 workhouse/infirmary, Mill Rd, Liverpool *207*
 see also Liverpool, West Derby and Toxteth Park Joint Committee
West End (Hants), workhouse *205*
West Firle (Suss), workhouse *211*
West Ham (Essex)
 farm colony 123
 Union
  infirmary, Whipps Cross *204*
  receiving homes, Aldersbrook *204*
  workhouse, Leyton 100, **101**, 143, *204*
West London School District, West London District School, Ashford 142, **142**, *218*
West London Union Workhouse, Holloway 97, **97**, 98, 119, 183, *217*
 casual wards 182, **182**
 infirmary 160
 lunatic block 163
West Malling (Kent), Malling Union Workhouse 56, *206*
Westbourne (Suss), workhouse *211*
Westbury (Wilts), Westbury and Whorwellsdown Union Workhouse *211*
Westbury-on-Severn (Glos), workhouse *204*
Westhampnett (Suss), Gilbert Union (later Union) 27, 45
 workhouse, Westhampnett Place *211*
Westminster (Lond)
 City of Westminster Union *215*
 corporation workhouse (1666) 8
 house of correction (1622), Tothill Fields 5
 Joint Parishes of St Margaret and St John 106, *217*
 workhouse, Dean St/Gt Smith St *217*
 workhouse, Marloes Rd, Kensington 89, 160, *217*
 workhouse, St Ermin's Hill/Petty France *217*
 Parish of St James 9–10, *217*
 industrial school, Wandsworth (1852) *217*
 school (1781) 132
 workhouse, Poland St, Soho (later Westminster Union Workhouse) **14**, 15, 32, **117**, *217*
 Parish of St Margaret, workhouses (17th–18th centuries) 8, 15, 156
 St George's, Hanover Square Parish Workhouse, Mount St 15–16, **15**, 155, *216*
 St George's Union infirmary, St Ermin's Hill *216*
 workhouses managed by Marriott (18th century) 13
Westmorland
 East Ward Union, workhouse, Kirkby Stephen *211*
 Gilbert Unions/Parishes 27
 poor-law institutions, post-1834 *211*
 West Ward Union, workhouse, Shap *211*
 workhouses, 18th century 20
Wetherby (Yorks W R), workhouse 95, *213*
Weymouth (Dors), workhouse 47, *203*
Wharfedale Union (Yorks W R), workhouse, Otley 99, *213*
Wheatenhurst (Glos), Union *204*
Whichcord, John 56, 78, *205*, *206*, *210*
Whipps Cross (Essex), infirmary *204*
Whitby (Yorks N R), workhouse *212*
Whitchurch (Hants), workhouse 92, *205*
Whitchurch (Salop), workhouse **129**, 130, *209*

Whitechapel (Lond)
 Salvation Army shelter 184
 Union *217*
  industrial school, Forest Gate 140, *217*
  scattered homes, Grays 151, **151**, 152, *217*
  workhouse, South Grove, Bow 108, *217*
  workhouse, Vallance Rd/Spitalfields *217*
Whitehaven (Cumb)
 Gilbert Parish 27
 workhouse (1854–6) *202*
 workhouse, Workington (1792) *202*
Whitling, H J 76, 77, *203*, *205*, *208*, *209*
Whitmore, Wolrych 138
Whitstable (Kent), Gilbert Union/Parish 27
Whittlesey (Cambs), workhouse *202*
Wickham Market (Suff), Plomesgate Union Workhouse 65, 133, *210*
Wicklewood (Norf), workhouse 22, 23, *208*
Wigan (Lancs), workhouse *207*
Wight, Isle of *see* Isle of Wight
Wigmore (Staffs), industrial school 142, *210*
Wigton (Cumb), workhouse *202*
Wild, Collins & Wild 152, *206*
Wilkinson, George 63, 65, **66**, 83, *203*, *204*, *205*, *207*, *209*, *210*, *211*, *212*
 Chipping Norton Union Workhouse **64**, 65, *209*
 Leominster Union Workhouse 65, 80, **80**, *205*
Willesden (Mdx), Union Workhouse, Harlesden 110, 113, *207*
Williams, John 58, **59**, *201*
Williams, W Clement 170, *213*
Willink, W E *206*
Williton (Som), workhouse **70**, 72, **82**, 161, *209*
Wilson, Andrew 140, *216*
Wilson, Frederick R *208*
Wilson, Richard 47
Wilton (Wilts), workhouse 62, *211*
Wiltshire, poor-law institutions, post-1834 *211*
Wimborne Minster (Dors), Wimborne and Cranborne Union Workhouse *203*
Wincanton (Som), workhouse 65, *209*
Winchcomb (Glos), workhouse 60, 77, *204*
Winchester (Hants)
 Gilbert Union/Parish 27
 New Winchester Union Workhouse 76, *205*
Winchfield (Hants), workhouse *205*
Winchmore Hill (Mdx), Northern (Convalescent) Hospital 164, *218*
Windsor (Berks)
 castle 61
 Windsor Public Assistance Institution **178**
 workhouse (18th century) 31
 workhouse (1839), Crimp Hill, Old Windsor 53, 72, **72**, 73, *202*
Wing, John 34, *201*
Winslow (Bucks), workhouse 62, **62**, 72, *202*
Winterton (Lincs), Gilbert Union/Parish 27
Wirral (Ches), Union Workhouse (later Clatterbridge (County) General Hospital) 78, 190, *202*
Wisbech (Cambs)
 workhouse (1720) **13**, 14
 workhouse (1837–8) 67, *202*
Wisborough Green (Suss), workhouse *211*
Witham (Essex)
 industrial school (later Bridge School) *218*, *219*
 workhouse (1714) **12**, 14, 15
 workhouse (1837–9) 49, 72, *204*
Withington (Lancs), Chorlton Union Workhouse 98, 106, 143, 159, **159**, *206*
Witney (Oxon), workhouse 65, *209*
Woburn (Beds)
 Woburn estate surveyor 58
 workhouse *201*
Wokingham (Berks)
 Pinewood Sanatorium *219*
 workhouse (pre-1834), Wargrave (later industrial school) 142, *201*
 workhouse (1848–50) 92, *202*
 see also Reading and Wokingham School District

254

Index

Wolstanton and Burslem Union (Staffs), workhouse, Chell 42, 73, *210*
Wolverhampton (Staffs), Union
    cottage homes, Wednesfield 145, *210*
    workhouse (1836–8) 65, *210*
    workhouse (1901–3) 169, *210*
women
    discriminated against for tuberculosis treatment 176
    fate of former workhouse girls 154
    lying-in wards and maternity blocks 169
    role in the workhouse 83, 195
Wood, William H *208*
wood-chopping 120, 122
    vagrants 179, 187–8
Woodbridge (Suff), Union Workhouse *see* Nacton
Woodhouse, *see also* Hall & Woodhouse
Woodhouse, George **136**, *206*
Woodingdean (Suss), Warren Farm Industrial Schools 142, *210*
Woodman, ___ *201*
Woodstock (Oxon), workhouse 65, 100, *209*

Woodthorpe, Edmund *205*
Wooler (Northumb), Glendale Union Workhouse 78, *208*
Woolwich (Lond)
    branch school 148
    Brook (Fever) Hospital, Shooters Hill 164, *219*
    naval and military hospitals 159
    Union *217*
        cottage homes, Bostall Heath (later Goldie Leigh Homes) *217*, *220*
        workhouse, Plumstead 106, *217*
Worcester
    Corporation 11, 12
    cottage homes *212*
    gaol 34
    hospital 25
    workhouse 34, *212*
Worcestershire, poor-law institutions, post-1834 *212*
work
    in Old Poor Law workhouses 31
    see also taskwork; textile manufacture; working-houses

Workhouse Papers (1860) 99
workhouse test x, 21, 103, 193, 195, 196
    able-bodied test workhouses x, 120–2
Workhouse Test Act (1723) *see* Knatchbull's Act
working-houses (16th–17th centuries) 3–10
Workington (Cumb), workhouse *202*
Worksop (Notts)
    infirmary, Kilton Hill *208*
    workhouse *208*
Worth, ___ *203*
Wortham (Suff), industrial school 142, *210*
Worthington, Thomas 106, 159, **159**
Worthington, Thomas, & Son *206*
Wortley (Yorks W R), Union Workhouse, Grenoside *213*
Wyatt, James 34
Wyatt, T H *219*
Wyattville, Sir Jeffry 61, 66
Wycombe Union (Bucks)
    industrial school, Bledlow *202*
    workhouse, Saunderton 72, *202*
Wylde, ___ 36, 40

Y

Yapton (Suss), Gilbert Union 27
Yarmouth (Norf), Parish
    cottage homes, Gorleston *208*
    workhouse, Great Yarmouth *208*
Yelf *see* Searle, Son & Yelf
Yeovil (Som), workhouse 60, 76, *209*
York 94, 95
    'hospital' (16th century) 4
    vagrant house 180
    workhouse 95, 133, 159, 181, *212*
Yorkshire
    Gilbert Unions/Parishes 27
    poor-law institutions, post-1834 *212–13*
    resistance to workhouse provision 49
Young, William *204*
Young, Sir William 21, 36